THE

THE
MIDDLE
PLATONISTS

80 B.C. to A.D. 220

Revised edition with a new afterword

JOHN DILLON

Cornell University Press

Ithaca, New York

First published 1977 by Cornell University Press
Cornell Paperbacks edition, with revisions
and a new afterword, published 1996.

Library of Congress Cataloging-in-Publication Data

Dillon, John M.
   The middle platonists, 80 B.C. to A.D. 220 / John Dillon. – Rev.
ed. with a new afterword.
      p.   cm.
   Includes bibliographical references and index.
   ISBN 0-8014-8316-6
   1. Platonists.   I. Title.
B517.D54   1996
184–dc20   96-13942

Printed in Great Britain

Contents

TO MY FATHER
Myles Dillon
(1900–1972)

Preface

THE period in the history of Platonism which is the subject of this book has received hitherto comparatively little attention. It seems fated to remain in the position of those tedious tracts of the Mid-Western United States through which one passes with all possible haste, in order to reach the excitements of one coast or the other. In Platonism, likewise, one tends to move all too hastily from Plato to Plotinus, with, at most, a perfunctory glance at those vast tracts of Academic scholasticism that lie between the two, and which were of such basic importance in the intellectual formation of the latter.

It is the purpose of this book to fill, to some extent, that gap. I will try to deal with the figures of the period as far as possible on their own terms, not as dimly seen milestones on the way to Neoplatonism. It has not been an easy task, however, to present a survey that will be coherent and yet stay reasonably close to the frequently exiguous evidence. There really is no body of received opinion on which one can base oneself in what is after all intended to be a relatively 'popular' book. In such a book one cannot be forever building up hypotheses step by laborious step; one must try to present conclusions. Inevitably, I have had to dwell upon details, since in many instances these details have not been dwelt upon before. I hope that the reader, appreciating the problems, will be patient.

Not, of course, that nothing has been done. We have at least one comprehensive survey, in Volume III: 2 of Eduard Zeller's vast *Philosophie der Griechen*, and a shorter, but very useful, account by Karl Praechter in Überweg's general history of philosophy. The survey of Philip Merlan (who has elsewhere contributed much to the study of the period) in the *Cambridge History of Late Greek and Early Mediaeval Philosophy* (Part I) is, however, vitiated by precisely the fault of which I am complaining, a spotty and partial treatment of the figures of the period as precursors of Plotinus.

Apart from this, scholars such as Praechter, Willy Theiler, Heinrich Dörrie, Émile Bréhier, A.-J. Festugière, Pierre Boyancé, and most Recently H.-J. Krämer, have done excellent work on particular questions, but no study of the period as a whole has yet resulted. On various important questions, such as the true state of Platonism in the second century A.D., we are still dependent on such documents as the 1906 article of Tadeusz Sinko, which advanced the hypothesis of the 'School of Gaius', adopted in all subsequent discussions of the period, and the 1936 monograph of R. E. Witt, which tried to establish a direct connexion between Albinus and Antiochus of Ascalon, via Arius Didymus. Neither of these works should have acquired the fundamental importance which they have repeatedly been accorded, for reasons which I hope to make plain. Again, Philo of Alexandria and Plutarch have been given much attention over the years, but never, it seems to me, with an adequate appreciation of their philosophical surroundings. That service I hope to perform for them here.

I have striven to write the history of the period with hardly a glance forward to Plotinus. This, as I have suggested above, has been a deliberate move, to prevent him from dominating the scene. This does not alter the fact that Middle Platonism must always be of interest chiefly as a prologue to Plotinus. Nevertheless, it seemed best to look at these men and their beliefs *in themselves*. I have also made every effort to eliminate from the scene another figure which has long dominated it, that of the Stoic philosopher Posidonius. I have accorded him a section at the end of Chapter Two, which is no less than his due, but it has been for so long such an easy option to attribute otherwise unattributable doctrines and formulations to this source that it seemed salutary now to go to the other extreme and try to write a history of Middle Platonism largely without him.

One key word employed very freely by casual surveyors of this period I have also striven to exclude—'eclecticism'. The word has a use, but it surely implies the assembling of doctrines from various schools on the basis of the personal preferences of the thinker concerned, rather than on the basis of any coherent theory as to the historical development of philosophy, and it is thus not, I think, a fair word to use for what the Middle Platonists, from Antiochus on, were doing. Antiochus, as I shall try to show, thought he had a coherent view of how philosophy had developed, and that view may not have been quite as perverse as it now appears to us. He and his successors felt justified in appropriating from the Peripatetics and the Stoics such doctrines and formulations as seemed to them to express better what Plato had really meant to say. At most, they were 'modernizing' Plato. The rationale of their procedure was clear and consistent, and it does not seem to me profitable to characterize it as eclectic. Indeed, our enthusiasm for ferreting out 'Aristotelianisms' and 'Stoicisms' in their works, and in those of Plotinus later, tends rather to lead to a false view of the situation. In fact a wide range of terms and concepts had already by the beginning of the first century B.C. become virtually common currency, and in later times there was really no sense of their ultimate provenance. Such basic terms as *'logos'* or *'koinai ennoiai'*, as used by the men to be studied in this book, are to all intents and purposes Platonic. Similarly, what is for us Aristotelian logic is for them merely logic, Aristotle's formalization of what was assumed to be the normal practice of the Academy. This view of philosophical development may seem to us unhistorical, but we must recognize in our turn that we do not command the range of documents which were available to Antiochus and his successors, on which they based their interpretation.

On the general question of the influence of earlier authorities on later ones, there is one fact of life that is liable to be overlooked by modern scholars. That is that, in this period—as indeed in most periods of intellectual development until quite modern times—one is influenced primarily by the doctrine of one's own teacher, and one sees the development of philosophy up to one's own time through his eyes. One may indeed read the original texts, but one reads them initially under the guidance of one's teacher, who read them under *his* teacher, and so on. Only if this process is borne in mind does the curious distortion of Platonic doctrine which we find in our surviving authorities become comprehensible. To talk of Plotinus, then, being influenced by the Stoics or by Posidonius, or Albinus being influenced by Antiochus, or Plutarch by Xenocrates is, I feel, grossly to oversimplify the situation. Plutarch is principally influenced by Ammonius, Albinus by Gaius, Plotinus by Ammonius Saccas and secondarily by Numenius, Severus and Albinus.

I have been much concerned in this book with the exact words and formulations of these Platonists, and have thus been compelled to quote a good deal from what survives of their works. In most cases a mere summary of what they believed would be uninformative, giving no insight into the workings of their minds. It is the way in which they arrived at their positions, and the precise terms in which they formulated them, that are of primary interest to me here. In the passages quoted, I have made free use of existing translations (usually from those of the Loeb Classical Library, where these are available, as they are for Cicero, Philo, Plutarch and Aulus Gellius). I have done this partly from a disinclination to repeat a job adequately done, but partly also in order to allow a different 'voice' to appear in the quotations. I have, of course, carefully checked the accuracy of all translations not my own and have ventured to alter them when they were not sufficiently literal or accurate for my purposes. I have also made much use of Greek terms in transliterated form. The result often appears barbarous, but the reader must become familiar with the main terms of philosophic discourse in this period if he is to follow the course of its development. I have tried to limit footnotes to a minimum, and in that spirit I have included references in the text.

I am most grateful to various friends for reading parts of this book and making many useful criticisms: Frederic Amory, Peter Brown, Gerard Caspary, Albrecht Dihle, A. A. Long, J. M. Rist, R. T. Wallis, John Whittaker, David Winston. They are not, of course, responsible for its shortcomings. I wish to thank the University of California at Berkeley for the grant of a Humanities Research Fellowship in 1971/2, which enabled me to start on the book. Finally, my eternal gratitude to my wife for her enormous patience and expertise in typing the whole manuscript, much of it more than once, and for directing numerous acute criticisms at both style and content. I dedicate the book to the memory of my father, who set me originally upon the path of scholarship, and kept me on it both by exhortation and by example until his death.

Berkeley, 1975

Abbreviations

ABBREVIATIONS of the works of individual ancient authors will be given in the survey of their works at the beginning of the chapter concerning them. I have adopted longer or shorter abbreviations of works at different points in the book according to the frequency with which the work is being quoted, e.g. Plutarch, *Isis and Osiris*, *Is. et Os.*, *De Is.* or *Is.*; Cicero, *Tusculan Disputations*, *Tusc. Disp.* or *TD.* I hope that this procedure averts more confusion than it creates. That certainly was my intention.

I give here some abbreviations used throughout the work:

Adv. Math. or *AM*	Sextus Empiricus, *Adversus Mathematicos*
CH	*Corpus Hermeticum*
DL	Diogenes Laertius, *Lives of the Philosophers*
Dox. Gr.	H. Diels (ed.), *Doxographi Graeci*
EN	Aristotle, *Ethica Nicomachea*
Met.	Aristotle, *Metaphysica*
NA	Aulus Gellius, *Noctes Atticae*
PT	H. Thesleff (ed.), *The Pythagorean Texts of the Hellenistic Period*
RE	Pauly-Wissowa, *Real-Enzyklopädie der klassischen Altertumswissenschaft*
SVF	H. von Arnim (ed.), *Stoicorum Veterum Fragmenta*
Tim.	Plato, *Timaeus*

CHAPTER ONE

The Old Academy and the Themes of Middle Platonism

PLATO, on his death in 347 B.C., left behind him a philosophical heritage that has not yet lost its vigour. This book concerns one period of intellectual history, approximately three hundred years (c. 80 B.C.–c. A.D. 220), during which the implications of that heritage were meditated upon by thinkers of varied intellectual capacity, and certain conclusions were hammered out which were not without significance for later generations. It was during this period, in fact, that much of what passed for Platonism in later ages—until a determined effort was made at the beginning of the nineteenth century in Germany to return to the actual writings of Plato, unvarnished by interpretation—was laid down.

What I propose to do in this introductory chapter is, first, to survey briefly the doctrines of the immediate successors of Plato, commonly known as the Old Academy (prefaced by a discussion of the controversial subject of the 'unwritten doctrines' of Plato), since it is with these figures—in particular Xenocrates—that a good deal of Middle Platonic scholasticism has its roots; and secondly, to outline the main philosophical problems which exercised the philosophers of the period under review. Since I propose in the main body of the book to proceed chronologically, giving each philosopher separate consideration, it will be as well at the outset to establish, according to subject matter, the main lines of philosophic activity with which we will be concerned.

A. PLATO: THE UNWRITTEN DOCTRINES

It is no part of the purpose of this book to present a survey of Plato's philosophy. A knowledge of what generally passes for Plato's philosophy, the doctrines derivable from his dialogues, is presupposed in the reader. But in order to understand the directions taken by Plato's immediate successors, it is necessary here to say a few words about what are commonly known as Plato's 'unwritten doctrines', since it is to those at least as much as to the dialogues that his immediate successors are reacting. It is often the problems left by Plato in his oral teaching that they are trying to solve.

The battle about the nature of the oral teaching of Plato has been raging back and forth now for over a hundred and fifty years, ever since an effort was made in the early nineteenth century (initially by Friedrich Schleiermacher) firmly to distinguish Plato from the Platonic tradition. This involved taking the dialogues as the sole basis for knowledge of Plato's teachings, and setting aside the reports of later writers, including such handbooks as those of Albinus (then known as Alcinous) and Apuleius, and the writings of the Neoplatonists. This was a salutary exercise at the time, but it produced distortions of its own. It is plain, after all, that the dialogues do not present by themselves a coherent body of doctrine, and it is by no means obvious to us (since no ancient writer ever tells us) what relation they bear to the serious business of the Academy. The reasons for writing the dialogues, and the conditions of their publication, are equally mysterious. It is reasonable to assume that the later, more substantial ones, at least, air certain problems—about Knowledge, the Ideas, Ethics, Cosmogony—that were exercising Plato and his colleagues at the time of composition, but they are not Plato's final word on any subject. They are used by Aristotle, for instance, as evidence, along with his other sources of knowledge, of what Plato thought, but they are not for him the sole nor even the primary evidence.

But if not the dialogues, then what? There is, in fact, considerable secondary evidence as to the views entertained by Plato on certain basic questions. A good deal of this is preserved only in late authorities, such as the commentators on Aristotle, but the greatest single source is Aristotle himself, and Aristotle had been an associate of Plato's for twenty years. We must always remember with Aristotle, however, that, although he knew what he was talking about in each instance (to assume otherwise is absurd), yet he is nearly always giving a polemical, and furthermore an allusive, rather than a scholarly and systematic account of what he knows. It is rather like trying to piece together Conservative Party policy during an election campaign solely on the basis of scattered criticisms from Labour spokesmen. Nevertheless, by looking at his evidence with a properly critical eye, one can deduce a body of doctrine which is, in its main lines at least, coherent and reasonable, and fits in well with the developments attributed to Speusippus and Xenocrates.

The details of these doctrines are necessarily disputed. I will confine myself to an outline of the main features, since they are pretty generally agreed upon, and thus suitable to a work of the scope of the present one.

To begin with first principles, it seems clear that Plato, in his later years at least, had become more and more attracted by the philosophical possibilities of Pythagoreanism, that is to say, the postulation of a mathematical model for the universe. Mathematics seems to have been a discipline much worked on in the Academy, and the insights derived from this (amplified by the researches of such colleagues as Eudoxus, Menaechmus and Theaetetus) drove Plato progressively to certain general conclusions. He arrived at a system which involved a pair of opposed first principles, and a triple division of levels of Being, which latter doctrine gave a vital central and mediating role to the Soul, both World Soul and individual soul. Reflections of these basic doctrines can be seen in such mature dialogues as the *Republic*, *Philebus*, *Timaeus* and *Laws*, but they could not be deduced from the dialogues alone.

As First Principles he established The One and the Indefinite Dyad (Ar. *Met.* 1 6, 987a29ff.), in this, as in many other respects, developing the doctrine of the Pythagoreans. The One is an active principle, imposing 'limit' (*peras*) on the formlessness (*apeiron*) of the opposite principle. The Dyad is regarded as a duality (also termed by him 'the great-and-small') as being infinitely extensible or divisible, being simultaneously infinitely large and infinitely small. The influence of the Dyad is to be seen all through Nature in the phenomena of continuous magnitudes, excess and defect in which has continually to be checked by the imposition of the correct measure. This process has an ethical aspect as well, since the virtues are to be seen as correct measures ('means') between extremes of excess and deficiency on a continuum. That such a theory of virtue was not distinctive to Aristotle is shown by such a passage as *Politicus* 284E–285B, where the all-pervasiveness of measure is asserted, with a probable reference to the Pythagoreans as originators of this concept.[1]

The Unlimited Dyad is primarily the basic unlimitedness or

---

[1] That this doctrine is Platonic as well as Aristotelian has been well demonstrated by H. J. Krämer in his work *Aretê bei Platon und Aristoteles*, Heidelberg 1959, esp. ch. 3.

otherness' on which The One acts, but it is also the irrational aspect of the Soul, and again the substrate of the physical world, the Receptacle of the *Timaeus*.

By acting upon the Dyad, 'limiting' it, The One generates the Idea-Numbers. At this point, however, the evidence becomes confused, mainly because Aristotle, in his always tendentious testimony, assumes that his readers, or hearers, know what he is referring to. We unfortunately do not have this knowledge. It seems that Plato came finally to view the Ideas as numbers, or mathematical entities of some sort. A special importance is attached by him, as it was by the Pythagoreans, to the 'primal numbers', one, two, three, and four, and their sum-total, ten (the Decad). The first four numbers seem to be in some way inherent in The One, and come to actuality in the process of the initial limitation of the Dyad. In *Met.* XIII 7, Aristotle seems to describe a process whereby the primal numbers are generated by, first, the Dyad producing the number Two, by doubling the One, and then producing the other numbers by adding to Two and to each successive number either the One or itself. But the whole process remains obscure, as perhaps it was in Plato's own mind.

From this action of the primal numbers upon the Dyad, and its reaction on them, all other Idea-Numbers are generated. This seems the most reasonable explanation, apart from emendation, that can be derived from the important passage of Ar. *Met.* I 6, which has been mentioned above:

Plato made the other principle a Dyad, because [of the fact that] the numbers, *apart from the primal ones*, are generated from it by a natural process (*euphuôs*), as from a mould (*ekmageion*, the word used for the Receptacle by *Plato* at *Tim.* 50C).

These numbers, then, are what the Platonic Ideas have become. How many of them are there? The numbers up to ten certainly hold some sort of distinctively basic position, but the multiplicity of physical phenomena requires that the basic numbers combine with each other in some way to produce compound numbers which can stand as the formulae for physical phenomena. We must not neglect, however, a bothersome passage, *Met.* XIII 8, where Aristotle seems to be saying that Plato took only the numbers up to ten as constituting the Ideas. He is probably here being deliberately obtuse, for polemical reasons, and combining Plato's view that the Decad comprised the sum of Number with his doctrine that the Ideas were Numbers. Obviously the numbers of the Decad must generate all other numbers, and there is certainly a hierarchy among the Ideas, but Aristotle's account is not likely to do justice to the full complexity of Plato's position. That he is being less than fair here is indicated by the contradictory nature of his other references to the same issue, *Met.* xii 8 (1073a14ff.), where it is admitted to be uncertain whether the number of the Ideas is ten or more than ten, and xii 3 (1070a18) where we find the statement that 'Plato said that there are as many Ideas as there are natural beings'. Theophrastus indeed, in his *Metaphysics* (6b 11ff.) seems to envisage a hierarchical arrangement when he speaks of Plato 'making all other things dependent on the Ideas, and these on Numbers, and proceeding from Numbers to the first principles'. Here a distinction is actually made between Ideas and Numbers, but I think we may take the Numbers in question here as the Decad, the Ideas being those secondary combinations dependent on them.

Within the Decad, the first four numbers (the *Tetraktys*) came to play a major part in Plato's cosmology, as they did in those of his successors. They are the principles providing the link between the absolute unity of the One and the three-dimensional physical multiplicity around us. These four also have a geometrical aspect, though how that is linked to their essential nature is not clear in Plato (in Speusippus, we shall see, the geometricals are a separate level of Being). At any rate, One is also the point, Two the line, Three the plane, and Four the solid (the last two being triangle and pyramid respectively). We have Aristotle's testimony (*Met.* 1 9, 992a20ff.) that Plato refused to analyse the Line into points, but postulated rather 'indivisible lines'. There has been much dispute as to where these fit into his metaphysical scheme, but it would seem reasonable, if Plato is going to have indivisible lines, for him to have indivisible triangles and pyramids as well, though we have no evidence of these. It may be only in the Soul that the four basic numbers assume their geometrical aspect; at any rate the composition of the Soul in the *Timaeus* is intimately bound up with the doctrine of the Four Dimensions, and the relations of proportion between them. From the Soul the four dimensions are projected upon Matter, in the form of combinations of basic triangles, to form the four elements, Fire, Air, Water and Earth. Thus an uncompromisingly mathematical model of the universe is laid down, which drew powerful criticism from Aristotle, e.g. in *De Caelo* iii 1.

The doctrine of Soul is a central, but very difficult feature of Plato's system. Once again, the dialogues, particularly the *Timaeus*, only help us when taken along with what we can unravel from secondary sources. Aristotle, for instance, is quite emphatic (*Met.* I 6 and XIII 6) that Plato, besides the Ideas, postulated the existence of what he called 'Mathematicals', or 'objects of mathematics'. These are distinguished from the Ideas by having 'many the same' and being combinable with each other (the Ideas being each one of a kind and 'non-combinable' (*asymblêtoi*)), and from physical objects by being eternal and immaterial. From other evidence it becomes clear that these mathematicals are connected with the Soul. The most natural conclusion is that the Soul, which Plato is alleged by Aristotle (*De An.* III 4, 429a27) to have described as the 'place' (*topos*) of the Ideas, receives the Ideas into itself and somehow transforms them into mathematicals, then projecting them upon Matter to form the physical world.

When we speak of the Soul here, the reference is to the cosmic entity, the World Soul, the construction of which is described in *Timaeus* 35Aff., but which otherwise only appears in Book X of *The Laws*. Of this entity the human soul is a microcosm. In its role as mediator between the intelligible and physical realms, it is composed of aspects which reflect both what is 'above' and what is 'below' it. It is properly at the level of soul that the four primal numbers take on the aspect of Point, Line, Plane and Solid. Aristotle tells us (*De An.* I 2, 404b16ff.) that Plato constructed the Soul out of these four entities, and made the equation between them and the four modes of cognition, Intuitive Knowledge (*nous*), Discursive Knowledge (*epistêmê*), Opinion (*doxa*) and Sense-Perception (*aisthêsis*). This fourfold division seems to be alluded to at *Laws* X (894A), and something like it is being used in the Line Simile of *Republic* VI, where what may be taken as Mathematicals appear at the second level (there termed *dianoia*), so that this scheme may have been already in Plato's mind at that stage.[1] Plainly the Soul is designed as the supreme mediating entity, receiving influences from the intelligible realm and passing them on, in modified form—that is to say, 'extended' and 'diversified' to bring about the creation of the sensible realm. This is the process described, with many mythological flourishes (of which the Demiurge is the chief one), in the *Timaeus*.

The principal problems left by the *Timaeus*, problems which Plato himself must have declined to solve, seem to be the following: (1)

---

[1] For a judicious discussion of this difficult question, see now J. A. Brentlinger, 'The Divided Line and Plato's Theory of Intermediates', *Phronesis* VIII (1963), pp. 146–66.

Whether the cosmogonic process described is to be thought of as taking place at any point in Time; (2) the identity of the Demiurge; (3) the identity of the Young Gods to whom the Demiurge delegates the creation of the lower part of the human soul; (4) the nature of the activity that may properly be assigned to the Receptacle; (5) the manner in which any combination of immaterial triangles can create solid substance; (6) what relation these basic triangles can have to the Ideas in their traditional form. On these questions controversy continued throughout later Platonism, beginning with Plato's immediate successors.

Speusippus and Xenocrates maintained that the process described in the *Timaeus* was timeless and eternal, and that Plato had only employed an apparent temporal succession 'for the purpose of instruction'. Aristotle, however, who may here be simply tendentious, accuses Plato of postulating a temporal beginning for the world (*De Caelo* i 12; ii 2). Plato himself cannot have made his position clear; otherwise this controversy could not have arisen. Later Platonists, however, with the exceptions of Plutarch and Atticus, whose dualistic tendencies demanded a creation out of previously existing disorderly matter, followed the lead of Speusippus and Xenocrates.

As to the identity of the Demiurge and of the Young Gods, there was some confusion in later times. Initially, the Demiurge seems to have been taken as the supreme principle, active in the world, but when under Neopythagorean influence the One, as a totally transcendent first principle, was placed above the active principle, the Demiurge came to be seen as a second God, Intellect (*nous*), the agent or *logos* of the Supreme God, and this is the view that prevails during the period under review in this book. This *nous* was always liable to conflation with the World Soul in its rational aspect, as we shall see. There is not really room in a coherent metaphysics for an Active Intellect *and* a Rational World Soul, so the World Soul of later Platonism tends to be seen as irrational, or at least sub-rational, merely receptive of reason-principles and requiring 'awakening' by God (see below, p. 205). As for the Young Gods, they could either be taken as the sub-rational World Soul, or as the class of Daemons, subservient to the World Soul. One can discern vacillation on this point in such men as Albinus and Apuleius.

The process by which the Soul acts on Matter, the activity proper to Matter, and the identity of the triangles are not problems to which one finds any satisfactory answer, or of which there is even much discussion, in surviving Middle Platonist documents, although Xenocrates, as we shall see, wrestles with them to some extent. Aristotle's criticisms of the whole scheme in the *Physics* and in the *De Caelo* were powerful, and could not really be answered.

The *Timaeus* remained the most important single dialogue during the Middle Platonic period, supported by chosen texts from the *Republic, Phaedrus, Theaetetus, Phaedo, Philebus* and *Laws* (for details check the index of passages quoted in this volume). Particularly close is the interweaving of the myth of the *Phaedrus*, and its account of the celestial ride and subsequent fall of the soul, with the *Timaeus*. In Neopythagorean circles, as we shall see, the *Parmenides*, taken as an account of metaphysical reality, comes also to be of major importance. The doctrine of the One present in such Neopythagoreans as Eudorus, Moderatus of Gades and Numenius has been brilliantly shown by E. R. Dodds[1] to be influenced by the First Hypothesis of the *Parmenides*, though the Sun Simile of *Rep.* VI, and the Three Kings of the *Second Letter* also contributed something to the mixture.

In Logic, the evidence points to Plato's maintaining the system of Division (*diairesis*), as first outlined in *Phaedrus* 265Dff., and even elevating it into a cosmogonic principle. It is the soul's business to bring order out of chaos by making the right 'divisions', hitting the right means and harmonies. There is no evidence that Plato himself developed anything as elaborate as the Aristotelian syllogistic and categories (although Aristotle's ten Categories are only a somewhat scholastic elaboration of the two basic categories of Absolute (Substance) and Relative). Plato seems to have operated with the basic categories of Absolute (*kath' hauto*) and Alio-relative (*pros hetera*), which latter was subdivided into Opposite (*pros enantia*) and Relative proper (*pros ti*), which in its turn was divided into Definite and Indefinite. So much we are told by Hermodorus (*ap.* Simpl. *In Phys.* p. 247, 30ff. Diels). Hermodorus was a pupil of Plato, and was personally acquainted with the practice of the Academy; he is not basing himself on the evidence of the dialogues, although traces of such a division can be discerned in them (e.g. *Soph.* 255C; *Parm.* 133CD; *Phil.* 51CD).

It is absurd to throw doubt on such reports as this, simply because they are not confirmed by the evidence of the dialogues. Nor should we imagine, as some do, that the only source of information on Plato's teaching apart from the dialogues comes from reports of his famous

[1] E. R. Dodds, 'The *Parmenides* of Plato and the Origin of the Neoplatonic "One"', *CQ* 22 (1928).

lecture *On the Good*. This was undoubtedly a notorious affair, at which many of those present took notes (Aristoxenus, *Harm. Elem.* II p. 30–1 Meibom; Simpl. *In Phys.* p. 151, 6ff. Diels), and it may indeed have been the only time that Plato attempted to share his philosophy with a general audience, but it is not to be imagined that his immediate successors were confined to this one lecture for their information. The lecture was not a success, as Aristotle used to recall with amusement (Aristoxenus, *loc. cit.*). The audience had come expecting, from the title, to hear something practical, such as how to become rich, healthy or strong, and when Plato began to discourse on mathematics, geometry and astronomy, and finally stated that the Good was the One, they incontinently left.

In the sphere of Ethics, as I have said, there are sufficient indications that for Plato as well as Aristotle the virtues are to be regarded as means between two extremes of 'too much' and 'too little', with Justice (symbolized by the Pythagorean *Tetraktys*) as the force holding the universe together, a metaphysical concept as well as an ethical one. Important also is Plato's distinction, in *Laws* I 631BC, between higher, or 'divine' Goods—that is, goods of the soul, the Virtues—and lower, or 'human' Goods—goods of the body (such as health or beauty) and external goods (such as good fame or wealth). This was a favourite passage for later Platonists, and constituted an important basis for mediating between the positions of Stoic and Peripatetic ethics, as these Platonists were continually having to do. A subject of active debate in later Platonism was the question whether the lower goods were or were not an essential component of Happiness (*eudaimonia*). The Stoics denied that they could be; the Aristotelians denied that they could be excluded. The Platonists were left in the middle, with texts to support either position, and, as we shall see, the battle raged back and forth throughout our period, such men as Antiochus and Plutarch siding with Peripateticism, others, such as Eudorus and Atticus, adopting a Stoic line.

On the topic that became a basic one in later times, that of the overall purpose of life, Plato is certainly on record, in two passages especially (*Theaetetus* 176AB, *Phaedo* 64E), as asserting that it consists in the withdrawal of the soul from the things of the body. The whole simile of the Cave in *Republic* VII expresses the same attitude. This became the general definition among Middle Platonists, in the form 'Likeness to God', taken from *Theaetetus* 176B. Antiochus, however, as we shall see, preferred the formula 'Concordance with Nature'. This is not properly a doctrine of Plato, but was developed in the Old Academy, particularly by its last head, Polemon, and then taken up by Zeno, the founder of Stoicism.

On the question of the self-sufficiency of the wise man, and his freedom from passions, a subject of lively debate in later times, Plato's position is ambiguous. A passage such as *Republic* III 387DE asserts the good man's self-sufficiency, but seems to envisage him as moderating his passions rather than extirpating them. The problem of when a moderated passion ceases to be a passion at all tends later to become a fruitful source of semantic confusion between Aristotelians and Stoics.

The inner-academic tradition, then, preserving as it did both accounts of the Unwritten Doctrines and the interpretations of such authorities as Speusippus and Xenocrates, continued to have a profound influence all through antiquity, an influence that we can only dimly comprehend. In the sphere of Logic, for instance, it seems to us that the later Platonists are shamelessly appropriating and fathering on Plato the distinctive discoveries and formulations of Aristotle. Now this they may indeed have done, but what is not obvious to us is how much of Aristotle's innovations grew out of work already being done, by himself and others, while he was still in the Academy, and how soon mature Aristotelian logic was accepted into the Old Academy as non-controversial. Speusippus and Xenocrates, as far as we can see, maintained the properly Platonic system of Division, and the Platonic categories described above, but what of Polemon, Crates or Crantor? Aristotelian logic was accepted as a useful tool by the Sceptical 'New' Academy after Polemon, and Polemon, as we shall see, found himself very much in agreement with Aristotle on ethical matters, so that it is not unlikely that he accepted Aristotelian (and Theophrastean) logic as well. When we come to consider a man like Albinus, we will find him assuming Plato to be well aware of Aristotelian logic and to be using it in the dialogues in a non-formal way. We may regard this assumption as absurd, but it is not one which originates with Albinus, and for all we know it may go back all the way to the Old Academy.

The purpose of this brief sketch of Plato's philosophy is to show that when later Platonists, whether Antiochus, Albinus or Plotinus, claim to derive their philosophical positions from Plato himself, they are not necessarily being quite as unhistorical as is commonly imagined. Part of the difficulty in adequately assessing the doctrines of Plato is that, on a wide range of topics, he probably did not come to any final conclusions, and declined to make an authoritative judgment, preferring to leave his disciples to worry things out for themselves. This is certainly what one would expect from what we can discern about his view as to how philosophy should be conducted. Even the dialogues are a way of putting forward theories, and working out their consequences, without having to stand over the results. Significantly, Plato never appears in any of his own dialogues. If his procedure was as devious as I imagine it to have been, it is easy to see how even his immediate followers might have given quite different accounts of what he actually believed, and much of the work of Speusippus and Xenocrates can indeed be seen as efforts to unravel the implications which they thought they discerned in the Master's various suggestions.

That said, I wish now to examine the attested doctrines of each of these men, with a view to seeing what they may have contributed to later Platonism. We must remember, after all, that when we come in the next chapter to assess the legitimacy of Antiochus' interpretation of Platonism, we must take into account not only what he may have known of Plato's oral teachings, but also what he had undoubtedly read of Speusippus, Xenocrates, and, last but not least, Polemon, for Antiochus the last legitimate head of the Platonic Academy before himself.

B. SPEUSIPPUS (*c.* 407–339 B.C.)

I. LIFE AND WORKS

Speusippus, the son of Plato's sister Potônê, succeeded him as head of the Academy, and presided over it until his death in 339. We know miserably little about his life, Diogenes Laertius (IV 1–4) being even less helpful than usual. Diogenes gives a list of 30 works of his, to which may be added the work *On Pythagorean Numbers* of which more will be said later. Most important, perhaps, were those *On Pleasure, On Philosophy, On the Gods, On the Soul*, a *Treatise On Congeners* (homoia), (10 books), *Divisions and Hypotheses relating to Congeners*, and the *Ecnomium of Plato*, in which many remarkable facts about the Master were apparently revealed, including the information that he was the son of Apollo. None of these works survives. A number of them appear to have been dialogues.

2. PHILOSOPHY

(a) *First principles*

Speusippus developed Platonism in a direction which was legitimate, perhaps, but which was to find no other partisans, so far as we can see, until Plotinus, unless we may trace certain Neopythagorean and Gnostic speculations to his ultimate inspiration. Speusippus accepted the doctrine of two opposite principles, but he altered it in an interesting direction, by laying particular emphasis on their status as 'seeds' or 'potencies' of all things. He argued that what is itself the cause of some quality in other things cannot have that quality itself in the same way, so that if The One is the cause of goodness and being for all other things, then it cannot itself be properly termed good or even existent (Fr. 34 Lang), any more than an acorn is itself an oak tree. This led him to an interpretation of Plato's One which placed it at an extreme of transcendence. In an important passage preserved in Proclus' *Commentary on the Parmenides*, only recently brought to light by Klibansky,[1] Speusippus makes his position clear (although he affects to attribute it to certain 'ancients', presumably Pythagoreans, of whom he was an even greater partisan than Plato):

Holding the One to be superior to Being and the source from which Being springs, they freed it even from the status of a principle. And so, considering that if one took the One in itself, thought of as separate and alone, adding no other element to it, nothing else at all would come into being, they introduced the Indefinite Dyad as first principle of beings.

The Indefinite Dyad is thus brought in as the cause of all differentiation and individuation, which is what is involved in being the cause of the existence of things. But the Dyad is not an evil principle, any more than the One is a good one (Fr. 35 Lang). Speusippus, reasonably, denied that 'good' or 'evil' in an ethical sense could have any meaning at this level. Good and evil only arise at the level of actualized Being, perhaps only at the level of Soul. In a way this is a question of semantics. Plato only termed his supreme principle The Good as being (a) the object of all striving, and (b) the source of goodness and existence to all things, but Speusippus is plainly trying to remove from the notion of the One (and simultaneously from that of the Dyad) any ethical colouring at all.

[1] *Procli Commentarius In Parmenidem*, ed. Klibansky, Labowsky, Anscombe, London, 1953, pp. 38, 31–41, 10.

Aristotle denounced this thesis of Speusippus' at *Met.* XII 7 (1072b30ff.):

Those then have a wrong opinion who suppose, as the Pythagoreans and Speusippus do, that supreme beauty and goodness are not at the beginning, because the beginnings of both plants and animals are causes, whereas beauty and completeness are in what proceeds from those beginnings. For the seed comes from other individuals which are prior and complete, and the first is not a seed but a complete being; for example, we must admit that a man is prior to his seed, not the man generated from the seed, but he by whom the seed was generated.

Aristotle thus puts the chicken before the egg, and his objections to Speusippus' position seem to have prevailed in the Academy, beginning with Speusippus' immediate successor Xenocrates. Aristotle's Prime Mover, an actualization rather than a potentiality, a mind thinking itself, became the concept of God dominant in our period. All the more essential, therefore, to be sure that Speusippus' position is given a fair hearing. It is, after all, no more illogical than Aristotle's. In either case one is faced with the problem of the nature of the activity of the first principle, and of why it should be moved to produce anything further. Of the two alternatives, it would seem that a first principle that is pure potentiality, that must produce in order even to exist properly, might have more reason for action than a perfectly actualized, perfectly content, self-contemplating Mind. Aristotle's position that actuality must precede potentiality is no more satisfactory logically than the reverse position maintained by Speusippus; yet it triumphed both in his own school and in the Academy for many centuries.

Aristotle levels trenchant criticisms also at other aspects of Speusippus' metaphysics. At *Met.* VII 2 (1028b18ff.) we find the following:

Thus Plato posited the Forms and the Mathematicals as two separate kinds of substance, and as a third the substance of sensible bodies; while Speusippus assumes still more kinds of substance, starting with the One, and positing principles for each substance, one for numbers, another for magnitudes, and yet another for the Soul. In this way he multiplies the kinds of substance (= Fr. 33 Lang).

Now all this, as Aristotle sets it out, does not sound very sensible. At another place (*Met.* XII 10) he becomes quite satirical on the subject:

Those who say that mathematical number is first and that hence there must always be one thing after another and different principles for each, present the being of the universe as a series of disjointed episodes (for none of the levels of being contributes anything to another) and a multiplicity of first principles. But things do not like being misgoverned in this way:

'It is not good for there to be many captains; let there be one only.' (*Iliad* II 204)

What he is accusing Speusippus of is postulating many layers of reality unconnected with each other. He enumerates, below the One and the Indefinite Dyad, numbers, magnitudes and Soul, each of which has its own first principles, presumably corresponding to the One and the Dyad on the highest level. But one asks oneself whether any intelligent man could have propounded exactly such a doctrine.

Fortunately we do not have to conjecture what Speusippus really maintained, since the researches of Philip Merlan have unearthed a piece of Speusippean doctrine embedded in ch. 4 of Iamblichus' work *On the General Principles of Mathematics* (*Comm. Math.* p. 15, 5–18, 12, Festa). In view of Iamblichus' observable habits in this work and others in the same series (his 'Pythagorean Sequence'), we may take it as very likely that we have Speusippus here more or less *verbatim*— possibly an earlier part of the work *On Pythagorean Numbers* of which we have a long extract on the Decad in Iamblichus' *Theology of Arithmetic* (p. 61, 8ff. Ast). I will give a translation of the most significant parts of the *Comm. Math.* passage:

Of mathematical numbers one must postulate two primary and highest principles, the One (which one should not even call Being (*on*), by reason of its simplicity and its position as principle of everything else, a principle being properly not yet that which those are of which it is the principle); and another principle, that of Multiplicity (*plēthos*), which is able of itself to initiate division (*diairesis*), and which, if we are able to describe its nature most suitably, we would liken to a completely fluid and pliable Matter (*hylē*).

Out of these two—coming together, Speusippus says vaguely 'by reason of a certain persuasive necessity' (a phrase recalling *Timaeus* 48A)—is generated Number, Matter providing the principle of infinite divisibility and, simultaneously, of multiplicity, the One imposing limit and quality, to produce definite numbers. It is not suitable, he says, to attribute evil or ugliness to the principle of Matter simply because it causes multiplicity. That is a value-free activity. The One, again, is neither beautiful nor good, since it is superior to and is the cause of both these attributes. It is only at a later stage than the One that Beauty appears, and only at a later stage again Goodness. He thus represses the tendency in Plato's own thinking to give ethical values to the two first principles.

A second argument is more dialectical, but yet valid enough. Although the One is not good in the normal sense, yet we praise it for its self-sufficiency and as being the cause of beauty in numbers; it is illogical, then, to describe as ugly or evil something that is naturally receptive of the One. Since Multiplicity receives the One, it is praiseworthy also, and so not the ultimate evil. Aristotle seems to recognize the validity of this argument at *Met.* XIV 4 (1092a1–5), where he points out that, if the material principle is evil and is yet receptive of the Good, then it is partaking in and desirous of what destroys it; but his conclusion is that this principle should be eliminated altogether.

Matter, or the Receptacle (*hypodoché*), thus fashions the class of numbers, by interaction with the One. Now, however, Speusippus addresses himself to the problem which seems to have led him to the position criticized by Aristotle (p. 16, 18ff.):

If one postulates one single Matter and Receptacle, it would be unreasonable not to expect that, since the form of the One that imposes itself upon it is totally uniform, we should get a uniform class of thing resulting. The consequence of that would be that all classes of thing would be numbers, for we would not be able to postulate any differentiating cause why at one stage numbers were generated, and then lines, and planes, and solid figures, and not always the same class, since they would be springing from the same principles uniting in the same way.

Speusippus here puts his finger on the problem. If we are to have gradations of Being springing from first principles, there must be some principle of differentiation either within the One or within Matter to account for these gradations. But the One is by definition totally uniform, so there must be in some way different levels or aspects of Matter.

Speusippus' solution to the problem, if solution is the word, remains obscure. He does seem to postulate separate principles for each level of Being, thus justifying at least in part Aristotle's criticism. It seemed to him necessary to postulate as principles, in the realm of numbers, the Monad in place of the One, in that of lines the Point, while the material principle in the realm of geometricals generally (line, plane and solid) is described as 'position, spatial separation, and place' (p. 17, 13–19). He makes a distinction, then, between the first principles of numbers and those of geometricals, talking of different 'Matters' for each realm (*ibid.* 1, 25ff.).

Here, then, we have the much-criticized 'episodic' nature of Speusippus' universe. But there was a unifying progression of some sort from the One to all later levels of Being. At p. 16, 12 he talks of 'Nature proceeding further away from the first principles' and thus generating first Beauty and then Goodness, and at the end of the whole extract (p. 18, 1–12), in this same connexion, he makes it clear that the 'lower' sets of principles do in fact somehow derive from the supreme antithesis of One and Multiplicity:

The elements from which numbers derive are themselves not yet either beautiful or good; but out of the union of the One and the Cause of Multiplicity, Matter, there arises Number, and it is in this realm that there first appears Being and Beauty; and next in order there has arisen out of the elements of lines the geometrical realm, in which likewise there is Being and Beauty. In neither of these, however, is there anything ugly or evil. It is at the lowest level, in the fourth and fifth realms, which are put together from the lowest elements, that Evil arises, and even then not positively (*proêgoumenôs*), but rather as a result of a failure to master some aspect of the substratum.

There is much of interest here. First, we note again that the One and Multiplicity (here described ambiguously as 'the cause of multiplicity', the genitive being either subjective or objective) are 'beyond Being', and thus strictly non-existent. Not until Plotinus is this again clearly claimed for the supreme principle (at least in official Platonism; in the Gnostic and even Neopythagorean writings the position is different, as we shall see), and even Plotinus grants the One the attributes of beauty and goodness, though he would agree with Speusippus that these words cannot be used in this connexion in their normal sense.

Then there is plainly a process of derivation going on here. *The product of one realm is somehow the first principle of the next.* This, however, does not seem to have been the more conspicuous aspect of Speusippus' system. What chiefly attracts our attention in the *Comm. Math.* passage, and what obviously caught Aristotle's attention, is Speusippus' insistence on the logical necessity of different sets of first principles for the various levels of Being. In this passage we are suddenly confronted with five of these. The first three we have met already, the One, Number, and the Geometricals, each with its proper material principle. We realize, however, that we have heard nothing yet of Soul, nor yet of any Ideas, in the traditional Platonic sense.

From other sources we know that Speusippus rejected the Ideas in

favour of numbers, or 'mathematicals' (Ar. *Met.* XII 1, 1069a33ff. =
Fr. 42 Lang), and that he separated the Soul from both mathematicals
and geometricals (*ibid.* VII 2, 1028b18ff. = Fr. 33 Lang)—this latter
move, presumably, on the ground that the Soul experiences motion,
which the higher realms do not. What it means to say that Speusippus
abandoned the Theory of Ideas depends, of course, on what we conceive that theory to have become before it left Plato's hands. What
Speusippus may very well have had no use for were the Ideal Numbers.
He revered the Tetraktys and the Decad as much as did Plato, but he
put them to different uses.

At any rate, the Soul becomes the fourth level of Being, and it is
only at this stage (and at the one lower again—that of the physical
world) that Evil first raises its head. Even then it arises not as a positive
force, but as a by-product of an inevitable failure to master completely
the substratum. We are closer here to the metaphysics of the *Timaeus*
than to what we know of Plato's unwritten views, or even to *Laws* X.
But how does this view of the soul square with Speusippus' definition
of it, as attested by Iamblichus in his *De Anima* (*ap.* Stob. 1 363, 26
Wachs. = Fr. 40 Lang): 'the Form of the omnidimensionally extended'? The testimonies do not seem necessarily to conflict. The soul
receives both number and geometrical extension from above, and
these, synthesized, become its formal principle, which then, presumably, combines with the Matter proper to soul to produce the psychic
realm. This in turn is projected onto the fifth level, and combines with
Matter again to constitute the physical world. This type of progression,
rather differently expressed, turns up in the metaphysical system of the
Neopythagorean Moderatus of Gades in the first century A.D. (below
p. 347).[1]

Speusippus' One is not to be thought of as an Intellect. We have
testimony for this from a doxographic notice (Fr. 38): 'Speusippus
declared that God was Intellect (*nous*), but this is not the same as the
One nor the Good, but of a separate and particular nature.' Garbled
and compressed as this testimony is (the Good should not be linked to
the One in this way), it gives evidence of a distinction made by Speusippus between the One and Intellect. The doxographer manages to
give the impression, by conveying this as a definition of God, that

[1] On the question of the immortality of the soul, we have a bothersome late
doxographic report (Fr. 55 Lang) to the effect that both Speusippus and Xenocrates accorded immortality to both the rational and irrational soul. If true, this
would be a significant departure from Plato's doctrine, but on the basis of such
evidence it seems unprofitable to speculate further as to what their position was.

Speusippus is describing his supreme principle, which would thus be different from, and necessarily superior to, the One. Since this is impossible, it seems as if Speusippus may have characterized as God some lower stage of Being, presumably Number, which will also be *nous*. We have a report (Cicero, *ND* I 32 = Fr. 39) that Speusippus declares that all things are administered by a *vis animalis*, an 'intelligent force', which would have to be something more active than his conception of the One. But it is dangerous to deduce too much from doxographic reports, especially such a wildly polemical one as this is, coming as it does from an Epicurean survey of opposing schools.

In placing the One above Intellect, Speusippus is at variance not only with Aristotle, but with all official Platonism up to Plotinus, beginning with his own immediate successor Xenocrates who, as we shall see, seems to have agreed with Aristotle in characterizing his supreme principle as an Intellect.

(b) Ethics

In the sphere of Ethics we have various reports of Speusippus' views. Clement of Alexandria (depending upon some doxography) tells us (Fr. 57 Lang) that Speusippus defined Happiness as 'the state of perfection in things natural'. This definition, if faithfully represented, anticipates largely the Stoic definition 'living in accordance with Nature'. Clement also reports him as declaring that good men aim at 'freedom from disturbance' (*aochlêsia*), which, again if truly reported, anticipates Epicurus' ideal of *ataraxia*. Finally, Clement reports his view that Happiness results from the exercise of the Virtues. This last remark is uninteresting as it stands; the interesting question is whether Virtue *alone* is sufficient for Happiness, as was later the Stoic claim. It emerges from the testimony of Cicero, in the *Tusculan Disputations* and elsewhere (= Fr. 58 Lang), that the Old Academy in general, Speusippus, Xenocrates, and Polemon, were united with Aristotle and Theophrastus in allowing that a modicum of physical and external goods were essential to complete happiness. They emphasized the prominent role of Virtue, but they still regarded material misfortunes as evils which would mar the perfect happiness even of the wise, and for that they were attacked by the Stoics.

Speusippus is reported by Aristotle (*EN* VII 14, 1153b1ff. = Fr. 60a Lang) as trying to disprove the argument that Pleasure, being the opposite of Pain, which is an evil, must itself be a good, in the following way (presumably in his work *On Pleasure*):

It is true that Speusippus used to employ an argument designed to defeat this reasoning, as follows: the greater is opposed not only to the less but also to the equal. (In the same way pleasure is opposed not only to pain, but also to the neutral feeling which lies between pleasure and pain.)[1] But his argument doesn't work, because he would not claim that pleasure is an evil in itself.

Again, perhaps, Aristotle is being polemical. We have the (admittedly late) evidence of Aulus Gellius (*NA* IX 5, 4) that Speusippus declared both pleasure and pain to be evils, and only the state median between them to be good. The Aristotelian commentators on the *Ethics* state that Speusippus named 'freedom from pain' (*alypia*) as the good to which these two extremes were opposed, which agrees with Clement's evidence. Aristotle's point can only be that Speusippus did not condemn pleasure strongly enough as *essentially* evil. At any rate, we can see Speusippus here utilizing as uncontroversial the doctrine of the Mean, which is popularly supposed to be distinctive of Aristotle. It is plain that it is a common Academic inheritance.

(c) *Logic and theory of knowledge*

In the sphere of Logic, Speusippus was in general an adherent of Platonic *diairesis*, but he developed certain distinctive theories. One general principle of his was that in order to define anything adequately, one must know all the differentiae (*diaphorai*) of that thing in respect to everything with which it is not identical. If pressed to its logical conclusion, this would involve knowledge of all the relations of the thing in question, however remote, with everything else in the world (Fr. 31 Lang). This did not lead him to scepticism, however, but rather to an industrious effort to classify, by means of *diairesis*, as much of reality as he could. How far he got in this ambitious project we do not know. All we have reports of is his work on Congeners or 'similar things' (*Homoia*), which is apparently a bald listing of, at least, plants and animals, by genera and species, in ten books. All our fragments, which are preserved by Athenaeus, are from Book II, which seems to have been concerned exclusively with fish. At any rate, as Lang has shown (pp. 9–15), the classificatory activities of Speusippus and other members of the Old Academy—amusingly satirized by the comic playwright Epicratês (Fr. 11, p. 287 Kock)—provided Aristotle, to a

---

[1] This sentence is not in Aristotle, but is added here to make the nature of the argument clear.

large extent, with the basis for his own comprehensive classification of the animal world.

A word must be said next on another question of classification, in which Speusippus may have provided a basis for Aristotle's theory. This is the matter of the initial classification of 'things' in the *Categories*. Aristotle makes a division, we recall, into *homonyms*, 'things which have only a name in common, and the definition of being which corresponds to the name is different' (such as 'animal' to describe both a man and a picture), and *synonyms*, 'things which have the name in common, and the definition of being which corresponds to the name is the same' (such as 'animal', the generic name to describe both man and ox). It has been frequently pointed out how crude in fact such a distinction is. In Aristotle's philosophy, it seems later to be superseded by a theory of 'focal meaning' (e.g. *Met.* IV 2). But, crude or not, it seems to spring from, and to be a refinement of, Speusippus' division of classes of name (*onoma*). This is reported by Simplicius (from Boethus) as follows (*In Cat.* p. 38, 19ff. Kalbfleisch = Fr. 32a Lang):

> Boethus reports that Speusippus employed the following division (*diairesis*), which takes in all names: of names, he says, some are tautonymous, others heteronymous; of the tautonymous, some are homonymous, others synonymous [we must understand 'synonymous' here in its old sense]; of heteronymous, some are heteronymous proper, others polyonymous, others paronymous. The meanings of the former class have been discussed previously, but *polyonyma* are different names for one thing, when the description of all of them would be one and the same, as *aor, xiphos, machaira, phasganon* [all meaning 'sword']; *heteronyma* are those names which refer to different things with different descriptions, such as 'grammar', 'man', 'wood'.

We wish that Simplicius had preserved a clear account of Boethus' discussion of Speusippus' meaning of 'synonym'. According to Simplicius in a previous passage (p. 29, 5ff.), Speusippus was not precise enough in his definition of the difference between homonyms and synonyms, being content with the distinction 'same name; same definition' and 'same name, different definition', which would allow synonyms to be homonyms and vice versa. Aristotle changed the formula to 'the *definition of being which corresponds* to the name', to make the distinction exclusive. As so often, we do not have Speusippus' own account of his distinction, so that we are not in a position to do more than note that Aristotle here seems to be reacting to Speusippus' previous classification.

As regards the theory of knowledge, Speusippus, like Aristotle

(*Post. An.* 11 19), held that first principles must be apprehended immediately if there is to be any knowledge at all. Proclus (*Comm. in Eucl.* p. 179, 8ff. Fried. = Fr. 30) records his view as follows:

> In general, says Speusippus, in the hunt for knowledge in which our understanding is engaged, we put forward some things and hold them ready for use in later enquiry, without conducting any complex sequence of thought, and our mind has a clearer contact with them than sight has with visible objects; but others it is unable to grasp immediately, and therefore advances on them step by step and endeavours to capture them by following a chain of conclusions.

These primary principles are doubtless, as with Aristotle, such axioms as the Law of Contradiction, or that equals are equal to equals. These must be apprehended immediately by the mind, as being the conditions of all other knowledge, and being themselves insusceptible of any proof. This doctrine does not, of course, conflict with that mentioned above as to the practical unknowability of any particular thing, since these principles are not particular things.

It seems likely that if we had any considerable fragment of Speusippus' logical writings, we would find both much that was sensible and acute, and also much that, although in an imperfect way, anticipates the logic of Aristotle. As I have said before, when the later Platonists appropriated Aristotelian logic, the debt did not seem to them as clear as it does to us, for the good reason that they were acquainted, as we are not, with the logic of the Old Academy. This may indeed owe more to Xenocrates than it does to Speusippus, but the contribution of Speusippus was not inconsiderable.

(d) Theory of number

It seems worth according special mention in closing to one work of Speusippus', that *On Pythagorean Numbers*, of which a report of the contents and a longish extract (on the Decad) is preserved in the (partially Iamblichean) *Theology of Arithmetic* (= Fr. 4 Lang). Speusippus, in the first half of this work, which, we are told, was heavily dependent on the writings of the Pythagorean Philolaus, discussed the 'linear, polygonal, plane and solid numbers', and also the five cosmic figures (of the *Timaeus*), their peculiarities and similarities, and the ratios between them; the second half of the work he devoted entirely to the Decad, declaring it to be the most 'natural' and perfect of numbers, and a model for the creator god (*poiêtês theos*) in his creation of the world. If this is a true account, then Speusippus identified the Paradigm of the *Timaeus* with the Decad. This is indeed a logical thing for him to do, given his proclivities, but it is good to have this confirmation of it. It would also be good to know whether this 'creator god' of his, the Demiurge of the *Timaeus*, is to be equated with the One, or, as is more reasonable and probable, with a secondary god, an Intellect which would also be the first principle of Number.

Speusippus' praise of the Decad consists in showing how it contains within itself all the ratios and harmonies that exist. It would be tedious to go through the details, but the passage preserved is invaluable as evidence of how thoroughly Pythagorean number-theory had penetrated the thought of at least this member of the Old Academy. That this work of Speusippus was still available in some form in Neopythagorean circles in the fourth century A.D. is a strong indication of its influence at earlier stages of Neopythagoreanism.

3. CONCLUSION

Speusippus, then, is responsible for interesting developments in Platonism, but not ones that appear to have had much effect on the thought of his immediate successors. His position on the One, in particular, was reversed by Xenocrates, probably under the influence of Aristotle's criticisms, and his many-tiered universe was at least considerably toned down, under pressure, no doubt, from the same source. Only in the 'underworld' of Neopythagoreanism, if anywhere, does Speusippus seem in our period to have made any impression. Nevertheless, it seemed proper to accord him some attention, if only because he is a thinker to whom something less than justice is generally done. We must now turn, however, to one whose influence on Middle Platonism is not in doubt, a man who may indeed be termed the second founder of Platonism.

C. XENOCRATES (396–314 B.C.)

1. LIFE AND WORKS

Xenocrates, a native of Chalcedon, succeeded to the headship of the Academy in 339 B.C., on the death of Speusippus. He had been a member of the Academy, we are told by Diogenes Laertius (IV 6) since early youth, and had accompanied Plato to Sicily, presumably on his second or third visit. Aristotle was abroad when Xenocrates took over the headship, only returning to Athens in 335 B.C. to set up his school in the Lyceum. Whether there really was any kind of contested election between these two for the headship is not clear, but certainly Aristotle in his surviving works adopts an almost universally polemical tone when dealing with Plato and the Academics, which would support the conclusion that relations were not good. On the other hand, it is not necessary to suppose that Aristotle, because of his views on the Theory of Ideas and the mathematicization of the universe, could not have succeeded to the headship. Plato did not impose any set of doctrines on his pupils, as did, for instance, Epicurus later, and Aristotle, had circumstances been slightly different, could have functioned comfortably enough as the successor of Speusippus. Those later Platonists, beginning with Antiochus, who persisted in viewing the Academy and the Peripatos as essentially one movement were not by any means so far off the mark as they are normally considered to be.

However, by whatever method of choice, the headship went to Xenocrates. He appears to have set himself to systematize as far as possible what he understood to be the philosophical system of Plato, partly, no doubt, in response to the shrewdly aimed criticisms levelled from the Lyceum. In the process he inevitably formulated much that was new, since, as I have suggested, Plato, as is the habit of great philosophers, left many loose ends behind him.

Xenocrates is credited with being the first to distinguish formally between the three branches of philosophy, Physics, Ethics and Logic (Fr. 1 Heinze)—although Aristotle does seem to make the distinction in *Topics* I 14. Seventy-six works of his are listed (albeit in garbled form) by Diogenes Laertius (IV 11–14), covering all of these fields. Of these perhaps the most important are those *On Nature* (in six books); *On Wisdom* (in six books); *On Being*; *On Fate*; *On Virtue*; *On Ideas*; *On the Gods*; *On the Soul*; *On the Good*; *Solution of Logical Problems* (in ten books); and *On Genera and Species*. He also wrote on the Pythagoreans and on Numbers, which indicates a continuation of Speusippus' interests in this area. All his works without exception have perished. We do not even have of him, as we do of Speusippus, a verbatim extract, to give us some indication of his style or of his methods of argument. All we are left with are essentially doxographic reports, sympathetic, hostile or neutral.

2. PHILOSOPHY

(a) Physics

Under this heading the ancients generally included the discussion of first principles, what we would term now Metaphysics. I shall preserve the ancient terminology throughout this work, as all of the philosophers with whom we shall be dealing adopt this threefold division of philosophy, even though their order of topics may vary, as we shall see.

(*i*) *First principles.* Xenocrates, like Plato and Speusippus, postulated a pair of supreme principles, which he seems to have termed the Monad and the Dyad (Fr. 15 Heinze), the latter being a principle of multiplicity and unlimitedness (*apeiria*). This latter term is attested to by Plutarch in the first chapter of his work *On the Creation of the Soul in the Timaeus* (= Fr. 68), where he is discussing Xenocrates' doctrine of the soul, to which we shall come later. Plutarch, as we shall see, is, apart from Aristotle, our chief source for the doctrine of Xenocrates, and seems to have been much influenced by him. Like his predecessors, Xenocrates does, as I have said, describe his second principle as a Dyad, but we also find preserved, in a doxographic source (Fr. 28), a distinctive term which he used, 'the Everflowing' (*to aenaon*), by which, says the source, he intended to designate Matter. *Aenaos* is a poetical word, but it is also a Pythagorean one, figuring notably in the Pythagorean Oath, where the Tetraktys is described as 'the fount containing the roots of ever-flowing Nature'. Admittedly in this context it is being attached, not to primordial Matter, but rather to the physical universe, product of the harmonies contained in the Tetraktys, but the term is at least attested as Pythagorean, and may very well have been used by them in other contexts as well.

As regards the Monad, Xenocrates differs significantly from Speusippus in declaring it to be an Intellect (*nous*) (Fr. 16). Unfortunately, we do not have more than the bare information that he did this, but he is possibly reacting to Aristotle's criticisms of Speusippus. At any rate, the essentially Aristotelian concept of a self-contemplating divine mind is that which is dominant in all subsequent official Platonism up to Plotinus.

Another point of difference between Xenocrates and his predecessors is the comprehensiveness of his attempt to derive the totality of existence from his first principles. This is attested by his contemporary,

Aristotle's pupil Theophrastus, in the following extract from his *Metaphysics* (6a23ff.):

> But now most people go to a certain point (*sc.* in explaining the Universe) and then stop, as do those who set up the One and the Indefinite Dyad; for after generating numbers and planes and solids they leave out almost everything else, except to the extent of just touching on them and making this much, and only this much, plain, that some things proceed from the Indefinite Dyad, e.g. Place, the Void and the Infinite, and others from the numbers and the One, e.g. Soul and certain other things; but of the heavens and the remaining things in the universe they make no further mention; and similarly Speusippus and his followers do not do so, nor does any of the other philosophers except Xenocrates, for he does somehow assign everything its place in the universe, alike objects of sense, objects of reason, mathematical objects, and divine things as well.

Xenocrates is here praised by Theophrastus for continuing his derivation of the universe from his first principles all the way down to the realm of sense-objects. What this involved we learn, to some extent, from other sources. First let us consider in more detail the report of the doxographer Aetius, referred to earlier (Fr. 15):

> Xenocrates son of Agathenor of Chalcedon held as Gods the Monad and the Dyad. The former, as the male principle, has the role of Father, ruling in the heavens. This he terms Zeus and Odd (*perittos*) and Intellect, and it is for him the supreme God. The second is as it were the female principle ... in the role of the Mother of the Gods[1] ruling over the realm beneath the heavens. This he makes the Soul of the Universe. He regards the Heaven also as a God, and the stars as fiery Olympian gods, and he believes also in other beings, invisible sublunary daemons. He also holds the view that material elements, too, are animated by certain divine powers. Of these, that which occupies the air he terms Hades, as being formless (*aeides*), that which occupies the water Poseidon, and that which occupies the earth Demeter the Seed-Sower. All these identifications he adapted (*metapephrakē*) from Plato, and passed on to the Stoics.

This comprehensive survey poses some awkward questions. First, is the Monad to be seen as transcending the universe, or merely as residing in the noblest part of it, perhaps in the sphere of the fixed stars? It certainly sounds from this report as though the Monad is immanent

[1] Pierre Boyancé, 'Xenocrate et les Orphiques', *REA* 36 (1948), pp. 218ff., wishes to take *dikēn* here (which would otherwise be the rather poetical preposition 'in the role, or manner, of') as meaning Justice personified (*Dikē*). This is tempting, but not absolutely convincing. I prefer to postulate a corruption in the text here.

within the cosmos, and this impression is confirmed by our other evidence (Frr. 16–18). There would be, then, for Xenocrates nothing higher than the outer rim of the cosmos, the *hyperouranios topos* of the *Phaedrus* Myth. Zeus is for him what he was subsequently to become for the Stoics, the force presiding over the cosmos, inherent particularly in the noblest part of it—with the important difference that Xenocrates maintained that his supreme principle was immaterial (a principle of Number) rather than a material entity (pure fire), for which position he was condemned by Zeno (Fr. 67). Altogether the image of the *Phaedrus* Myth, with its talk of Zeus and the other gods, seems to lie at the back of this passage, and Aetius is probably oversimplifying grievously. His reference to Xenocrates' 'adapting' or 'paraphrasing' Plato may refer to Xenocrates' use of this myth, and also of the passage of *Timaeus*, 39E–41A, where certain suggestions for allegorizing the Olympian Gods are adumbrated. In fact, as we shall see presently, Xenocrates' triadic division of reality provides for a purely intellectual realm which seems to correspond to the 'supercelestial place' described in the *Phaedrus* (247C).

As for the Dyad, which is elsewhere, as we have seen, identified with Matter, it seems here to be made the World Soul, taken as an irrational entity requiring informing and intelligizing at the hands of the Monad. There is a great difficulty here, however. The Indefinite Dyad is, for Xenocrates, an evil and disorderly principle. This the World Soul is not. If we turn to Plutarch's *Isis and Osiris*, which is certainly influenced by Xenocrates, we find two distinct entities, represented by Isis and Seth-Typhon, the former of which is the World Soul, the latter an evil principle of disorder. Certainly the World Soul requires ordering by God, but it receives this gladly. It is not an evil principle. I suggest that either the doxographer Aetius is conflating entities here, or else there is a lacuna in the text (such as there certainly is in two later places) between 'female principle' and 'mother of the Gods'. The World Soul is, as we learn from Plutarch (*Proc. An.* 1012 DE) formed from the Monad and Dyad, and so is not itself the Dyad. The World Soul may be taken to have its (or her) seat in the Moon, or at least at the boundary between the superlunary and sublunary spheres. The Monad is not, however, to be connected with the Sun, although the Sun is for Xenocrates a god, as are all the other planets.

Below the Moon, there are both daemons, of whom more will be said later, and divinities presiding over the three sublunary elements (Fire being taken as the element of the celestial realm). Whatever about

Xenocrates' borrowing from Plato in this regard, there is no question but that the Stoics took up these suggestions of his with enthusiasm, and made them their own. It is interesting here, in view of later developments, to see the realm of Hades being made the Air. The identification of the sublunary realm with Hades is common, as we shall see, in Middle Platonism. We may also note in this connexion Plutarch's testimony (*Quaest. Plat.* IX 1, p. 1007F = Fr. 18) that Xenocrates distinguished two Zeuses, an upper (*hypatos*), who presides over the intelligible realm, and a lower (*neatos*), who rules the sublunary realm. This lower Zeus must be identical with Hades. This theory imparts an almost Gnostic flavour to Xenocrates' thought. More remarkable still is his division of the gods into Olympians and Titans, sprung from Heaven and Earth respectively. That this is not just mythologizing, but expresses a basic belief of Xenocrates, is indicated by a notice of Porphyry's, *à propos* our 'guard-duty' (*phroura*) at *Phaedo* 62B (Fr. 20). Xenocrates, it seems, identified this 'guard-duty' of ours, that is, our being confined upon the earth, as a result of our 'Titanic' nature. As such we are under the command of Dionysus. Since the connexion of Dionysus with Hades goes back at least to Heraclitus, we may reasonably postulate the identification here. Besides the dualistic attitude revealed here, the use of Orphic mythology is noteworthy.

As Theophrastus says, Xenocrates went further than Plato or Speusippus in attempting to derive the universe of existing things from his first principles. His first problem was that bequeathed to him by his predecessors, the derivation of Number from the One and the Dyad, and then the derivation of Point, Line, Plane and Solid from Number, or perhaps from the first four numbers, the Tetraktys.

There is an interesting passage of Aristotle's *Metaphysics* (XIII 9, 1085a7ff.) which seems to refer to Xenocrates. Some followers of Plato, it seems, try to derive lines, planes and solids from numbers by postulating species (*eidē*) of the Great and the Small, which will be responsible for producing these geometrical entities. Lines come to be from the Long and the Short; planes from the Broad and the Narrow; solids from the Deep and the Shallow. Speusippus is never attested as having thought of this formulation, though the *Comm. Math.* passage indicates that he was working towards something of this sort with his suggestion of different types of Matter. It is more probable that this rather scholastic suggestion is the contribution of Xenocrates.

Aristotle is not, of course, concerned to give it a sympathetic interpretation, and is thus of little help. What I would suggest is that Xenocrates postulated that each successive geometrical principle combined with Matter, which, being infinitely pliable, modified itself to receive it, to generate the principle of the next level. The Point would thus combine with Matter *qua* Long and Short, to produce the Line. The Line, which for Xenocrates was an irreducible entity not dissoluble into points (cf. Frr. 41–9), on the one hand generated all geometrical lines, but on the other combined again with Matter, now appearing as the Broad and Narrow, to generate the Plane, and so on. This explanation, I fully recognize, goes beyond the evidence, and leaves the basic mystery of the activity of Matter untouched. I put it forward simply as a contribution to the understanding of the problem that Xenocrates was grappling with. If his solution was something on these lines, we can see in what respect it could have been viewed as less 'episodic' than that of Speusippus.

We must next consider what Xenocrates did with the Platonic Ideas. We have a passage in Aristotle (*Met.* VII 2, 1028b24ff. = Fr. 34H), which the commentator Asclepius tells us refers to Xenocrates (Aristotle has just mentioned Plato and Speusippus):

Others, however, say that Ideas and Numbers have the same nature, and that everything else is derived therefrom, including lines and planes as well as the substance of the heavens and the sensible realm.

Speusippus had found no use for Plato's Ideal Numbers; Xenocrates, it seems, found no use for the mathematicals. Here and at various other points in the *Metaphysics* Aristotle asserts that he postulated only Ideas, which he identified with numbers. Without having in any detail the arguments propounded by either Speusippus or Xenocrates, we can do no more than conjecture the reasons behind their respective simplifications of Plato. However, since Xenocrates defined the soul as 'self-moving number', it is reasonable to suppose that he fixed the phenomenon of mathematical numbers and geometrical entities, the existence of which had caused Plato to propound his thesis of mathematicals, at the level of Soul. Mathematical entities the Ideas may be, but they are still the causes of sensible particulars. Xenocrates is on record (Fr. 30) as defining an Idea as 'the paradigmatic cause of regular natural phenomena', a definition intended to rule out Ideas of artificial things (such as beds or shuttles) and unnatural perversions (*ta para physin*), such as fever or ugliness. This became the standard definition in Middle Platonism (e.g. Albinus, *Didaskalikos* p. 163, 21).

The next question is where we are to place the Ideas. We recall that Xenocrates' supreme principle is an Intellect, and an Intellect necessarily thinks. One may suppose that he is engaged in self-contemplation, but even so, what are the contents of this self? It seems inevitable that what Xenocrates' Monad contemplates is the sum-total of the Idea-Numbers, which form the contents of his mind. The doctrine that the Ideas are in the mind of God may thus with great probability be attributed to Xenocrates. By the time of Antiochus, at any rate, it is established doctrine, and it was certainly not devised by the New Academy.

It is to Soul that we may now turn. We learn from Plutarch (*Proc. An.* 1012DE) that Xenocrates gave a description of the formation of the Soul which was simply a development of the creation of Number. Basing himself upon Plato's account in *Tim.* 35A, he identified the 'undivided essence' with the One, and the 'divided' with Multiplicity, or the Dyad. The One imposes limit on the unlimited multiplicity, and Number is the result. This, however, is not yet Soul. It lacks motion, and Soul is 'Number moving itself'. We must add the elements of Sameness and Otherness, the former representing stability, the latter motion and change, and it is by the mixture of these two further elements that the soul is produced. How far this is an explanation the reader may decide for himself, but what we can at least observe is an attempt by Xenocrates to fit the various parts of Plato's system together into a coherent whole.[1]

For Xenocrates, as for his predecessors, the soul was the mediating entity *par excellence* in the universe, and it is thus necessary that it contain within itself elements which can relate both to the intelligible and to the sensible realm, as well as all the ratios out of which the harmony of the cosmos is constituted. We have seen Plato already projecting the four primal numbers onto the soul, and equating each of them with a different cognitive faculty. It is very likely that his followers subscribed to this formulation. The soul is, then, for Xenocrates a numerical entity, non-material, though having elements within it which relate to the sense-world. It is immortal, and Xenocrates, like Speusippus, is credited by Olympiodorus (*In Phaed.* p. 98 Finckh = Fr. 75) with according immortality to the irrational part of the soul as

---

[1] Also credited to Pythagoras (e.g. in Cicero, *ND* I 27) is the view that 'the entire substance of the universe is penetrated and pervaded by a soul, of which our souls are fragments', a doctrine, derivable from Plato's *Timaeus*, which may very well also have been fathered upon Pythagoras by Xenocrates.

well as the rational. What either of them had in mind for it we cannot say.

It is noteworthy that Xenocrates makes a point of declaring a man's soul to be his daemon (Fr. 81), etymologizing *eudaimōn*, 'happy', as 'with one's daemon in a good state'. Plato does, at *Tim.* 90A, describe as 'a daemon given by God to each man' the highest part of the soul, that is, the rational soul, and Xenocrates need not be doing more than echoing this, but it is possible that this piece of etymologizing is to be connected with his belief in our 'Titanic' nature, as described above.

(*ii*) *Triadic division of the universe.* A feature which seems to be peculiar to Xenocrates' philosophy is his preoccupation with triadic distinctions. In Sextus Empiricus, *Adv. Math.* VII 147ff., we find the following account of his views:

Xenocrates says that there are three forms of existence (*ousia*), the sensible, the intelligible, and that which is composite [of these two], the opinable (*doxastē*); and of these the sensible is that which exists below the heaven, the intelligible is that which belongs to all things outside the heaven, and the opinable and composite is that of the heaven itself; for it is visible by sense-perception, but intelligible by means of astronomy.

This, then, being the situation, he declared that the criterion of the existence which is outside the heaven and intelligible is knowledge (*epistēmē*), that of what is below the heaven and sensible is sense-perception (*aisthēsis*), and the criterion of the mixed existence is opinion (*doxa*).

He links to each of these realms one of the three Fates, Atropos to the intelligible realm, Clotho to the realm of sense, and Lachesis to the intermediate, heavenly realm—a curious adaptation of Plato's use of the Fates at *Rep.* x 617C, which we shall see exerting its influence upon Plutarch and others (below, p. 215).

This establishing of the heavens as median between the intelligible and sensible realms is only, perhaps, a development of Aristotle's view of them as expounded in the *De Caelo*, but the strong suggestion of ratio involved seems peculiar to Xenocrates.

A rather different, and more peculiar, triadic division is recorded by Plutarch (*De Fac.* 943F = Fr. 56). The question arises *à propos* the median role of the Moon in the universe, and the principle of proportionality by which the universe is held together. Xenocrates, says Plutarch, taking his start from Plato's description in *Timaeus* 31Bff. and 40A of the means and proportions by which the universe is held together, propounded a scheme involving the four elements and a pair of opposites, 'the tenuous' (*to manon*) and 'the dense' (*to pyknon*), which latter is also a musical term. These opposites go back originally to Anaximenes, but Xenocrates is here trying to fit them into the framework of Platonic cosmogony. He postulates three *pykna*, which combine with the three elements, fire, air and water, to produce a three-layered universe:

Xenocrates says that the stars and the sun are composed of fire and the first *pyknon*, the moon of the second *pyknon* and the air that is proper to her, and the earth of water and the third of the *pykna*.

Pyknon must be regarded as a physical principle of density, since Xenocrates is reported next as declaring that neither *to pyknon* by itself, nor its opposite *to manon* (the principle of rarefaction), is receptive of soul (and so capable of creating the universe, which is imbued with soul). If Xenocrates means by *to manon* in effect the elements themselves, viewed as non-material geometric compositions (pyramid, octahedron and icosahedron), as Plato presents them at *Tim.* 53cff., then *to pyknon* may be viewed as the material element without which these geometrical shapes could not form a physical world. This, then, would be Xenocrates' attempted solution (drawing creatively on concepts of Milesian cosmogony) to the baffling problem which Plato bequeathed to posterity, how one gets from combinations of non-material triangles to the solidity of the material world. Obviously the Receptacle of *Tim.* 51A must have something to do with this, and Xenocrates is simply making more explicit the process of combination as he sees it.

This theory of Xenocrates' appears as an extension of that of Speusippus on various types or levels of Matter. It implies three different 'densities' of Matter, combining with three different elements to form a three-layered universe, in which the moon, and the air surrounding it, forms the middle and mediating element. Xenocrates makes no distinction between the sphere of the fixed stars and that of the planets, as Plato (and others) tended to do, but prefers to draw his line between the Sun and the Moon.

(*iii*) *Daemons.* This triadic division of the cosmos, with the Moon occupying the median position, is reflected in Xenocrates' theory of daemons, for which, once again, Plutarch is our source. In his essay *On the Obsolescence of Oracles* (416CD), we have the following testimony (Fr. 23):

In the confines, as it were, between gods and men there exist certain natures susceptible to human emotions and involuntary changes, whom it is right that we, like our fathers before us, should regard as daemons, and, calling them by that name, should reverence. As an illustration of this subject, Xenocrates, the companion of Plato, employed the order of the triangles; the equilateral he compared to the nature of the gods, the scalene to that of man, and the isosceles to that of the daemons; for the first is equal in all its lines, the second unequal in all, and the third is partly equal and partly unequal, like the nature of the daemons, which possesses human emotion and divine power.

This may be only an illustration, but it is a significant one. Xenocrates is giving mathematical expression to the doctrine of Plato's *Symposium* (202E), which describes daemons as 'of an intermediate nature, bridging the gap between man and god, and preventing the universe from falling into two separate halves'. Daemons share characteristics with both men and gods—with gods immortality, with men subjection to passions—and may therefore be seen as the mean between the two. Plutarch goes on to connect their position with that of the Moon and of the World Soul, and it seems almost inevitable that the connexion was made already by Xenocrates.

The equation cannot, however, be complete. For one thing, the daemons would seem to be inferior to the moon, both in rank and station (they are described, after all, in Fr. 15 as 'sublunar' (*hyposelē-noi*)); for another, there are, according to Xenocrates, two types of daemon, good and evil. In the essay *On Isis and Osiris* (360E), Plutarch quotes him for the opinion that 'among daemons as among men, there are different degrees of virtue and vice' (Fr. 25; cf. *Def. Or.* 417B). For Xenocrates such phenomena as days of ill omen, and festivals which involve self-laceration, lamentation, obscenity, or such atrocities as human sacrifice can only be explained by postulating the existence of evil spirits that take delight in such things, and who must be placated (*Is. et Os.* 316B; *Def. Or.* 417C = Fr. 25). It would almost seem as if two proportions would be required between gods and men, good and evil daemons representing different ratios, such as, perhaps, 4 and 6 between 2 and 8. Xenocrates' demonology does not, in fact, seem to fit with entire neatness the logical-mathematical frame created for it. However, such as it is, it gives further testimony to his desire to formalize all levels of the universe, and work out their mutual relations.

(*iv*) *Creation and structure of the world*. We have already seen that Xenocrates was inclined to allegorize certain of the Olympian gods as spirits of the elements. We learn from Simplicius (= Fr. 53) that he attributed to Plato a theory of five elements, interpreting thus the five cosmic figures of *Timaeus* 53cff., making the dodecahedron the aether. This interpretation was to introduce an element of confusion into Middle Platonic doctrine on this question. The more Stoic among the Platonists maintained a theory of four elements, taking the celestial element as the purest kind of fire, while the Peripateticisers were prepared to recognize Aristotle's fifth element.

On another important point of interpretation he is at one with Speusippus, as has been mentioned earlier, in denying that Plato meant the description of the creation of the world to be taken literally. The world was not created at any point in time. Plato is simply employing the same licence as that employed by geometers when they construct a figure out of points and lines, for instructional purposes (Fr. 54). This, as I have said, was to become the standard explanation of the *Timaeus* in later times, disputed only by Plutarch and Atticus.

(*b*) *Ethics*

This was an area of philosophy to which Xenocrates devoted a good deal of attention, as we can see from the list of his writings in Diogenes Laertius. Here, as elsewhere, he seems concerned rather to formalize what he takes to be Plato's teaching than to develop theories of his own. He declared the purpose of philosophy to be 'the elimination of all causes of disturbance in life' (Fr. 4). He is thus in agreement with Speusippus that the ideal state is one of 'freedom from disturbance'.

His definition of Happiness is conveyed to us, as was Speusippus', by Clement of Alexandria (*Strom.* II 22 = Fr. 77): 'the possession (*ktêsis*) of the excellence (*aretê*) proper to us and of the power (*dynamis*) subservient to it'. The seat of happiness is the soul, it is brought about by the virtues, and is made up of noble actions and good habits and attitudes. It requires as indispensable accompaniments both bodily and external goods. This is not very informative, though showing signs, in Clement's summary, of scholastic schematization. Like Speusippus, and the Old Academy in general, he insists on the necessity of bodily and external goods, although in a subsidiary role. That is perhaps what is referred to by the *dynamis* of the basic definition.

With the question of Happiness is bound up also that of the *archai*, 'first principles', and of the *telos*, the 'end' or purpose, of existence. Antiochus of Ascalon, as we shall see in the next chapter, was insistent in attributing his own formulae for both of these, which seem from our perspective to be purely Stoic, to the Old Academy, and specifically to Xenocrates and Polemon. According to his evidence (Fr. 79) and to that of Plutarch (Fr. 78), Xenocrates declared the first principles of existence to be 'the primary natural instincts' (*ta prôta kata physin*), the basic instincts of self-preservation granted to every creature at birth. Basing oneself on the observation of these, one could derive a preliminary ethical (or pre-ethical) code. Man then acquires full use of his reason, and with it the opportunity, and duty, to exercise the virtues. The 'end' of human existence is, then, 'life according to Nature', which implies 'life according to Virtue'. The only difference with later Stoic doctrine arose from the question as to whether or not, when one had gained virtue, one should abandon the primary natural instincts, or at least exclude them from any part in the *telos*. Xenocrates saw no need to abandon them, but simply subordinated them to the exercise of Virtue, thus taking up a position of basic agreement with Aristotle. We will hear more of this question at various points in the book.

Xenocrates does, however, seem to have held a theory of 'things of neutral value' (*adiaphora*), intermediate between the good and the evil. This would accord superficially with Stoic doctrine, except that we do not know what sort of things Xenocrates would have labelled 'indifferent'. Perhaps nothing more important than trimming one's fingernails or blowing one's nose. Certainly the things which the Stoics considered 'indifferent', such as wealth or poverty, health or sickness, he considered as goods or evils respectively (Frr. 87–92). At any rate, Sextus Empiricus, at the beginning of his treatise *Against the Ethicists* (=*Adv. Dogm.* v), gives us a brief insight into Xenocrates' methods of argumentation (which may also help to explain why his works did not survive). Sextus is saying that all the dogmatic philosophers make a threefold distinction between things good, bad and indifferent, and Xenocrates is no exception (*Adv. Dogm.* v 4–6 = Fr. 76):

. . . but Xenocrates, in phrases peculiar to himself and using the singular case, declared that 'Everything which exists either is good or is evil or neither is good nor evil.' And whereas the rest of the philosophers adopted this division without a proof, he thought it right to introduce a proof as well. 'If,' he argued, 'anything exists which is apart from things good and evil and things neither good nor evil, that thing either is good or is not good. And if it is good, it will be one of the three; but if it is not good, it is either evil or neither evil nor good; and if it is evil, it will be one of the three, and if it is neither evil nor good, again it will be one of the three. Therefore everything which exists either is good or is evil or neither is good nor is evil.'

As Sextus remarks, this 'proof' proves no more than what was stated in the initial threefold division. The important question is not whether there is some fourth category, but rather whether there is a class of things that are 'indifferent', and this he has set out to argue for. Sextus makes something of the fact that Xenocrates uses the singular where his predecessors used the plural, but the significance of this change is not obvious, unless he was countering some such sophistic argument as Sextus goes on to describe (*ibid.* 8–14). But this has in any case no bearing on his ethical theory.

That is all the information we have as to Xenocrates' ethical position. That he was an effective lecturer on the subject we must believe as it was Polemon's accidental bursting in upon a lecture of Xenocrates on Moderation that, in popular tradition, led to his taking up the philosophic life.

On the practical level, there is some evidence that Xenocrates, no doubt on Pythagorean principles, favoured abstention from meat. Porphyry, in his *De Abstinentia* (IV 22 = Fr. 98), gives us an account by Xenocrates of why the hero Triptolemus forbade the Athenians to harm animals. It may have been, he suggests, because it is wrong to kill things kindred to us, or perhaps because he saw that men were killing what was most useful to them. At any rate, it sounds from the passage as if Xenocrates thought that Triptolemus was right. His sympathy for animals was evidently well known, since we have an anecdote in Aelian (*Var. Hist.* XIII 31 = Fr. 101) about his saving a sparrow, which had taken refuge in his bosom from a pursuing hawk. Here he appears almost in the light of a St. Francis. All this may well be a result of his Pythagorean sympathies.

(c) Logic and theory of knowledge

We have observed earlier Xenocrates' triadic division of the universe, and that answering to each division there is a distinct faculty of cognition, *epistêmê* for the intelligible realm, *aisthêsis* for the realm of sense-objects, below the Moon, and for the celestial realm, which is cognizable partly by the senses and partly by the intellect, a mixed faculty which he terms *doxa*. That this is a significant alteration of the Platonic concept of *doxa* will be obvious immediately. *Doxa* is for Plato certainly an intermediate state of cognition (*Rep.* v 476Dff.), but it is intermediate between 'knowledge' (*epistêmê*), which is of 'that which is', and 'ignorance' (*agnôsia*), which is of 'that which is not', not between *epistêmê* and *aisthêsis*. It becomes plain, after much discussion, that *doxa* in fact concerns the realm of popular opinion and customary belief. It has nothing to do with the cognizing of a region of the universe. When we come to the famous simile of the Divided Line in *Republic* vi (509cff.), *doxa* is definitely the faculty which relates to the world of appearance, the physical world. In the *Theaetetus* also (187A–210B) and in the *Timaeus* (51Dff.), *doxa* relates to the sense-world, as opposed to reason (*nous*), which apprehends the Ideas. In the dialogues at least, then, *doxa* is not distinguished, as regards its objects, from *aisthêsis*.

It is, however, possible to see how Xenocrates' systematizing mind could put together the Platonic doctrine of the intermediate nature of *doxa* with the Aristotelian doctrine (of *De Anima*, Book II) that *aisthêsis* is the faculty proper to the sense-world, and the further Aristotelian doctrine (from *De Caelo*, Book I) of the intermediate nature of the celestial realm, that is, of the essential difference between the 'fifth element' of which it is composed and the four which comprise the sublunar world. We cannot be sure, of course, that it is precisely these doctrines which Xenocrates is drawing on; all we can do is point to them as possible sources.

But what, one asks, epistemologically speaking, is the point of this theory? It does certainly satisfy Xenocrates' liking for bridging gaps between extremes in his universe, in this case between the non-material intellectual and the material sensible realms. How far Sextus Empiricus' formulations in *Adv. Math.* vii 147ff. are to be trusted is not clear, but he describes *doxa* as 'partly true, partly false (or illusory)'. One might conjecture as follows: the physical appearance of the heavenly bodies is illusory—the Sun seems only a foot or so across, some of the planets seem to stop and go in their courses, and so on—but by the application of reason we can arrive at true and unshakeable conclusions about their substance, sizes, motions and speeds, such as is not possible in the case of sublunar phenomena, which are constantly changing, even as we try to describe them. The intelligible realities, the Monad, the Dyad, the Ideas, the Soul, are absolutely knowable, but present no appearance to the senses. Celestial phenomena may thus reasonably be seen as intermediate between these two extremes.

Xenocrates does seem also, however, to have operated with a dichotomy between the intelligible and the sensible. We have a rather confused report from Clement of Alexandria (*Strom.* II 5 = Fr. 6) that Xenocrates distinguished, in an Aristotelian manner (*EN* VI 7), between *sophia* as the knowledge of first causes and intelligible essence, and *phronêsis*, which for Aristotle denotes practical knowledge. Xenocrates, however, makes a division of *phronêsis* into practical and theoretical, and denominates theoretical *phronêsis* as 'human *sophia*', thus implying, presumably, that true *sophia* is a form of knowledge not attainable by humans. Xenocrates will then be making the point that the knowledge that God or the heavenly beings have of themselves or of the truths around them is qualitatively different from our theoretical wisdom, and this in turn is different from our practical wisdom; and that is the sort of (distinctively Pythagorean) position that one would expect Xenocrates to hold (cf. the report of Pythagoras' view of *sophia*, that it is unattainable by man, in Diodorus Siculus x 10).

One may note here the use of the method of *diairesis*. We distinguish between divine and human knowledge, and then within human knowledge we distinguish between theoretical and the practical (cf. the different, but analogous, division of knowledge in Plato, *Politicus* 259Dff.). It seems that Xenocrates, like Speusippus, remained faithful to Platonic logic. He recognizes the two main categories of Absolute and Relative (Fr. 12) seeing no point in Aristotle's ten, and instead of syllogistic, he seems to have practised Division. He wrote books *On Dialectic*, *On Opposites*, and *On Genera and Species*, but we have no information as to their contents. As we shall see, later Platonists— beginning perhaps with Antiochus, perhaps already with the New Academy—turned for their logical theory, not to Speusippus or Xenocrates, but to Aristotle and the Stoics (combining the two logical systems without a qualm), thus recognizing the real advances that had been made since Plato.

(d) Pythagorism and allegorizing

I bring these two topics together at the end of the discussion of Xenocrates as they are at least partly interlocking, and both are of considerable significance for later philosophy. By 'Pythagorism' here I mean a more than objective interest in the thought and personality of

Pythagoras, and a tendency to try to reconstruct his teachings, father-ing the theories of later men, including even one's own, on him in the process. This tendency begins in Platonism with Speusippus, if not with Plato himself, and is observable in most later Platonists to a greater or lesser degree, the extremists in this regard being those who would term themselves 'Pythagoreans' rather than Platonists—such men as Moderatus, Nicomachus and Numenius, and perhaps also be-fore them, Eudorus. We know that Xenocrates was much interested in Pythagoras. We have one work of his attested, of unknown contents, entitled *Pythagoreia*, and a good deal of his work on mathematics was probably Pythagorean in outlook. We have an extended, though second-hand, report by Porphyry (*In Ptol. Harm.* p. 213ff. Wallis = Fr. 9) of Xenocrates' account of Pythagoras' discovery of musical harmony, and his regulation of the disorder of the sense of hearing by the application of *logos*. We have seen evidence also of Xenocrates' aversion to meat-eating.

Again and again in the doxographic tradition we have a Xenocra-tean doctrine or formulation attributed also to Pythagoras (Monad and Indefinite Dyad as first principles, Stob. *Ecl.* 1 10, 2 (from Aetius); theory of daemons, Fr. 24; ideas and numbers, Frr. 28, 35; definition of the soul, Frr. 60, 63; immortality of the soul, Fr. 67). It is very possible, as I have said, that a certain impulse to such attribution was given by Xenocrates himself. In this case, he, along with Speusippus, becomes in effect the father of Neopythagoreanism.

Another interesting tendency is that towards allegorization of the Olympian Gods as forces of nature, such as we have seen in Fr. 15. This was picked up eagerly by the Stoics and greatly developed by such men as Chrysippus. His use of the Orphic myth of Dionysus and the Titans (Fr. 20, mentioned above, p. 27) to explain our 'guard-duty' here on earth is evidence to the same effect.[1]

3. CONCLUSION

Unlike Speusippus, Xenocrates does seem to have had a dominant effect on later Platonism. The teachings of Plato seem to descend to the later Academy largely in the form in which Xenocrates presented

---

[1] An interesting snippet of allegorical interpretation of Homer (*Iliad* xi 38–40) preserved in the scholia, should almost certainly be attributed not to Xenocrates (as Heinze does, Fr. 55), but (emending the scholion, with Rein-hardt) to Crates of Mallos.

them, although reference back to the dialogues never ceased to be made. Significantly, of all his many works, only two sound from their titles like dialogues, *Arkas*, or *On the Unlimited*, and *Archedemus*, or *On Justice*. The dialogue form was not suited to his formalizing, scholastic temperament. No doubt it was to this that Plato was referring when he used to exhort Xenocrates to 'sacrifice to the Graces' (DL IV 6).

In many respects he seems to have conceded points to Aristotle, specifically on the nature of the supreme principle and on ethics, but there is much also that remains distinctive.[1] Some of his triadic formulations find a later echo only in Plutarch, but his definition of an Idea, and of what things there are Ideas, had great influence, and became the standard school definition, appearing in Albinus' *Didaskalikos*. Part of the difficulty in assessing the full extent of his influence on Middle Platonism is the fact that very little serious philosophy survives from that period, and it is from the sort of detailed technical treatises and commentaries which we do not have that we would be able to judge the extent of his influence. Even in the case of Plutarch we are lacking a good many technical treatises, on such questions as the Ideas, Matter, the theory of Knowledge, which would give us a far better idea both of what Plutarch was capable, and of how great Xenocrates' influence on him and others really was.

D. POLEMON (*c.* 350–267 B.C.)

Xenocrates was succeeded on his death in 314 by Polemon, son of Philostratus. In contrast to Xenocrates, Polemon was a native of Athens, and of very good family. Tradition has it that he lived a loose and riotous life until converted to philosophy by Xenocrates, after which time he developed exemplary decorum and self-control, to such an extent that his self-control and impassiveness in the face of danger is what later ages remembered most about him. Since he would hardly have been eligible to take over the Academy at an age of less than about thirty-five, it seems reasonable to place his birth at around 350 B.C. Since he lived to 267 B.C., we cannot place his birth much earlier than this. He will not, then, have known Plato or even Speusippus, though

[1] We may note that after Aristotle's death relations between Academy and Peripatos seem to have improved somewhat. Theophrastus, as we have seen, speaks with respect of Xenocrates in his *Metaphysics*, and took the trouble to make a *Summary* of Xenocrates' doctrines, in two books, which was not necessarily polemical.

he could perhaps have heard Aristotle, had he not still been living the life of a rake. He administered the Academy for over fifty years, and certainly left a mark on it, though of the nature of that mark we are miserably ill-informed. Two other Platonists are closely associated with him during his long tenure, namely Crantor and Crates. Arcesilaus, the founder of the Sceptical Academy, joined the Academy under Polemon, though he seems to have attached himself rather to Crantor (DL IV 22). Crantor predeceased Polemon, dying about 290, but Crates survived him, and presided over the Academy for a few years before dying in his turn, whereat the headship passed to Arcesilaus.

Polemon was remembered only for his ethical theory (and practice). His views on logic and metaphysics are probably fairly expressed in a dictum of his preserved by Diogenes Laertius (IV 18) to the effect that 'we should exercise ourselves with practical matters, and not with logical speculations, which leave us, like a man who has got by heart some paltry handbook on harmony but never practised music, able, indeed, to win admiration for skill in propounding theoretical questions, but utterly at variance with ourselves in the ordering of our lives'.

This last phrase reflects a basic principle of Polemon's ethics, one which he seems to have bequeathed to his pupil, the Stoic Zeno, namely the principle of coherence of life. We know from Clement of Alexandria (*Strom.* VII 32) that Polemon wrote a book entitled *On the Life According to Nature*, which indicates that his ideal was not only a life consistent with itself—without internal contradictions—but also one that was in accord with the laws of Nature, though as to what he meant by that we do not have very clear indications (except that it involved abstention from meat (*loc. cit.*)). Clement also (*Strom.* II 133) preserves for us Polemon's definition of Happiness, 'a self-sufficiency (*autarkeia*) in respect of all, or at least of the most and greatest, goods'. This definition, as it stands, is hardly satisfactory. If, however, the 'most and greatest goods' are to be taken as being the goods of the soul, or the virtues, then we have a modification of the Peripatetic and Old Academic ideal in the direction of what was to become the Stoic, and this seems to be confirmed by the fact that he also asserted (*loc. cit.*) that, while there could be no happiness without virtue, yet virtue alone, even without bodily and external goods, was essentially sufficient for happiness.

Our main source of information on Polemon is in fact Antiochus of Ascalon, whom we shall meet in the next chapter, his views being relayed to us by Cicero. In Cicero's works, Polemon is normally mentioned at the end of a litany of Old Academic and Peripatetic authorities (Speusippus, Xenocrates, Aristotle, Theophrastus), in whom, for Antiochus, all truth and wisdom resided. From such passages as *TD* v 39, *Fin.* IV 14, and *Acad.* II 131, we learn that Polemon, following Xenocrates, defined the purpose of life (the *summum bonum*, or *telos*) as 'living a virtuous life while enjoying those primary things which Nature recommends to Man' or simply 'to live in accordance with Nature' (cf. also *Fin.* II 34, and Plutarch *Comm. Not.* 1069E). Antiochus lays stress in these passages on Polemon's agreement with Aristotle, which would seem to indicate a tendency towards reconciliation with the Peripatetics on the part of Polemon himself. In his latter years, in any case, Aristotle's school under Straton had turned almost exclusively to physical investigations, and was hardly in contention in the field of ethics.

The question might be raised as to whether Polemon did not also to some extent prefigure the Stoic doctrine of 'self-conciliation' (*oikeiôsis*). Antiochus, at *Fin.* v 24, is quite firm about ascribing to the 'ancients' (*veteres*)—his normal term for the Old Academy—the doctrine that 'every living creature loves itself, and from the moment of birth strives to secure its own preservation'. This basic principle is then pursued in all its ramifications, up to the rational purpose of human life, 'concordance with Nature' (*ibid.* 27). The Stoics are described as simply 'adopting' this theory. This, together with Antiochus' claim (*ap.* Cic. *Acad.* I 43) that 'Stoic theory should be considered a correction of the Old Academy rather than actually a new system', may be taken, I think, as *prima facie* evidence that Polemon had uttered sentiments that could be construed as equivalent to Zeno's later formulation of the *oikeiôsis* doctrine.[1]

The chief contribution of Polemon, then, seems to be an increase in austerity of ethical theory which anticipates the doctrine of Zeno and his successors. It is doubtful, on the other hand, whether Polemon in any way anticipated Stoic materialism or the theory of the Logos. Even his ideal of conformity with Nature does not necessarily involve the Stoic doctrine of Fate in its strong form. Yet Polemon is important in the history of Platonism in that it is he above all who gives Antiochus, two hundred years after him, the stimulus for his synthesis of

---

[1] Theophrastus' doctrine of *oikeiotês* probably had some part to play also in the development of the doctrine. See C. O. Brink, 'Theophrastus and Zeno on Nature in Moral Theory', *Phronesis* I (1956), pp. 123–45.

Platonism, Peripateticism and Stoicism which was to prove so fruitful in the succeeding centuries.

I have confined myself in this survey to heads of the Academy, as they were the men who exercised most influence over what came later. There were, of course, many other pupils of Plato and of his successors, and a full history of the Old Academy, such as still requires to be written, should take account of all of them. Here I will simply mention them.

Other pupils of Plato were the mathematician and astronomer Philippus of Opus, who is generally credited with writing the *Epinomis*, which had considerable influence on later demonology; Hestiaeus of Perinthus, praised by Theophrastus along with Xenocrates (*Met.* 6b10) for extending his metaphysical theory beyond the first principles into the universe (he is credited also with a version of Plato's notorious lecture on The Good); Heraclides of Pontus, a copious writer on many subjects, including Pythagoras, who went over to Aristotle after being passed over for the headship of the Academy on the death of Speusippus; and Hermodorus, who preserved an account of Plato's unwritten doctrine made use of later by Simplicius. There are no pupils of Speusippus or Xenocrates who made any contribution to Platonism, but with Polemon, as we have seen, are associated Crantor and Crates. Crates did indeed become head of the Academy for a short time, but he is not reckoned by Antiochus among the founding fathers, so that he is of no importance for our present purpose. Crantor was famous in later times for an essay *On Grief*, which seems to have embodied the essence of Academic theory on not only the passion of grief, but passions in general, that they are to be controlled rather than eradicated. He is also accorded the distinction of being the first to comment on Plato's *Timaeus* (Procl. *In Tim.* 1 76, 2), whatever that may be held to involve. He did at any rate have an opinion on what Plato meant by depicting the world as 'created'. He took this to mean simply 'dependent on a cause other than itself' (*ibid.* 277, 8). Plutarch, in *Proc. An.* 1012D, reports that he understood the soul in the *Timaeus* to be compounded of the 'intelligible nature and that which exercises opinion (*doxa*) about sense-objects', these being the circles of the Same and the Other respectively. The task of the soul, he said, was to exercise judgment about both intelligible and sensible objects, and to discern their differences and similarities. Since it must be able to cognize all things, it must be made up of them all (on the principle of like being known by like). He is also on record as preferring to depict the numbers composing the soul by a lambda-shaped figure rather than a straight line (*ibid.* 1027D), and as proposing to take 384 (rather than 1) as a base figure, in order the better to calculate the various subdivisions between each of the seven primary numbers without resorting to fractions (1020B). In this he is followed, as we shall see, by Eudorus of Alexandria in his commentary. It seems, then, very much as if to Crantor must be awarded the distinction of writing the first formal commentary by a Platonist on a work of Plato's (the comments of Speusippus and Xenocrates do not seem to have been embodied in formal commentaries on a particular dialogue). His activity shows that, despite Polemon's apparent lack of interest in such things, work on metaphysics was undertaken in the Academy during Polemon's reign.

E. THE DOMINANT THEMES OF MIDDLE PLATONISM

We have now given some account of the Academy up to the time of its reconstitution at the hands of Arcesilaus. He and his successors, the greatest of whom was Carneades (*c.* 213–129 B.C.), introduced the sceptical method into the Academy, a development for which they could, and did, claim the authority of Socrates. Much excellent philosophizing resulted, but it is not our business to survey it here,[1] since the sceptical tradition has no place in Middle Platonism. Our interest begins again only with Antiochus of Ascalon in the first century B.C.

It remains now to survey briefly the main themes which will recur in the following chapters, the philosophical issues that exercised the Platonists of the three hundred years covered by our survey. I shall deal with them under the three main subdivisions of philosophy distinguished by Xenocrates, Ethics, Physics and Logic, beginning with Ethics.

1. ETHICS

All the main concerns of ethics have appeared already in the Old Academy, but they acquire new ramifications as our period goes on. The first issue is, naturally, the purpose of life, or as it was termed 'the end of goods' (*telos agathôn*). This can also be taken as the definition

[1] The subject is well dealt with in ch. 3 of A. A. Long's *Hellenistic Philosophy* (1974).

of happiness, and we have seen definitions of happiness produced by Speusippus, Xenocrates and Polemon. Polemon's formula of 'life in accordance with nature' is that which commended itself to Antiochus of Ascalon, powerfully influenced as he was by the Stoics, who had adopted it before him. When we turn to later Alexandrian Platonism, however, in the person of Eudorus, we find that the Stoic-Antiochian definition has been abandoned in favour of a more spiritual, and perhaps more truly Platonic, ideal of 'Likeness to God' (*homoiôsis theôi*), derived from the famous passage of the *Theaetetus* (176B), and this formula remained the distinctive Platonic definition of the *telos* ever afterward. In this, as in so much else, Antiochus' lead was not followed.

A second key issue was whether Virtue is sufficient to Happiness. By Antiochus' time the battle lines on this issue had been clearly drawn between the Peripatetics and the Stoics, and the Platonists had to take their pick. Antiochus, although Stoic in all else, sided here with the Peripatetics (and the Old Academy, of course) declaring that for complete happiness all three classes of good were required in some measure, goods of the body and external goods as well as the virtues. Once again, in this he was opposed by Eudorus, who declared that the two inferior classes of good could not be accounted an integral part of happiness, or the *telos*, thus siding with the Stoics. This time, however, the argument was not over. All through the period the two alternatives secured adherents, Plutarch and Taurus, for instance, agreeing with Antiochus and the Peripatetics, Albinus and Atticus with the Stoics. Along with this taking of sides went a certain amount of polemic, anti-Stoic or anti-Aristotelian, as the case may be.

A question with considerable consequences for ethics, though it also had physical dimensions, was that of Free Will and Necessity. Before the Stoics, and Chrysippus in particular, had stated the problem of determinism in its starkest form, the question had not been one of great urgency. Plato treats of it really only in mythical form, in the myths of the *Republic* and the *Phaedrus*, and raises more problems than he solves, but he does, as does Aristotle, maintain a belief in personal freedom of choice. Aristotle, in the *Nicomachean Ethics* (III), treats the suggestion that there is no such thing as freedom of choice as a mere sophistic paradox. Xenocrates did write an essay on Fate (*heimarmenê*), but we do not know what he said in it. For the Middle Platonists, however, the problem of free will and necessity, with which is intertwined God's Providence (*pronoia*), could not be dismissed so easily, and they did not find much help in Plato or Aristotle, though they did make appeal to key passages of both, as we shall see. We cannot be quite sure what Antiochus' stance was, as the attribution of Cicero's *De Fato* is uncertain, nor can we say anything about Eudorus' position. Philo gives us the first defence of the Platonist position, which asserts both freedom of the will and the existence of Providence against Stoic *heimarmenê* with more vigour than logical force. Plutarch also touches on the theme repeatedly, though his most serious discussions of the subject have not survived. The document *On Fate* surviving under his name is certainly not by him, but it is of great interest, and I will deal with it in connexion with Apuleius. All in all the Middle Platonists, though producing many scholastic formulae on the subject, failed to solve the problem, and bequeathed it in all its complexity to Plotinus, who writes a magnificent, if inconclusive, treatise on the topic in *Enneads* III 2–3.

2. PHYSICS

Throughout our period, the question of the nature and activity of the supreme principle, or God, is dominant. Later Platonists preserved the Old Academic opposition of Monad, or One, and Dyad, though they varied in the relationship that they postulated between the two. Antiochus, indeed, seems simply to accept the Stoic pair of an active and a passive principle, but Eudorus of Alexandria, while re-establishing the Academic and Pythagorean Monad and Dyad, places above them both a supreme One, possibly drawing some inspiration here from the metaphysical scheme of the *Philebus*. With Plutarch we are back to the basic duality, but he, and his follower Atticus, grant the Dyad rather more independence than orthodox Platonism would allow. For Albinus, by contrast, God is dominant and Matter simply passive, not even attaining to actuality. In the Neopythagoreanism of Numenius, on the other hand, a radical dualism seems to be asserting itself, though partially held in check by the influence of orthodox Platonism. Since it is from Numenius rather than from more orthodox Platonism that Plotinus derives his inspiration, this tendency to dualism persists as a tension within his thought.

Besides the first principles, there is, as an intermediate and mediating entity, the World Soul. This is basically the entity whose creation is described in the *Timaeus*, but traces appear, in such men as Philo and Plutarch, of a rather more august figure, which almost seems to reflect a Speusippean Dyad, a figure not evil but simply responsible for multiplicity, and thus for all creation. In Philo, as we shall see, the figure of Sophia appears, who is interchangeable with the Dyad, and Plutarch, in the preface of his essay *On Isis and Osiris*, seems to describe such a figure, whom he identifies with Isis. Elsewhere, as in Albinus, the World Soul is depicted as an irrational entity, requiring 'awakening' by the Demiurge, and even in the latter part of the *Isis and Osiris* (369ff.) Plutarch makes Isis rejoice at 'impregnation' by the Logos of God, thus producing somewhat of a discrepancy with the portrayal in the preface.

The reason for the vacillation as regards the status of this figure seems to lie in another development characteristic of Middle Platonism, deriving not from the Old Academy but rather arising as a development from Stoicism, that is, the distinguishing of a first and second God. The distinction is between a completely transcendent, self-intelligizing figure, and an active demiurgic one. The later Platonists adopted the Stoic Logos into their system as the active force of God in the world, and when they reinstated a transcendent immaterial First Principle, as did Alexandrian Platonism after Antiochus, they arrived at two entities, one basically the Demiurge of the *Timaeus*, the other the Good of the *Republic* and the One of the first hypothesis of the *Parmenides*. In Philo, partly, no doubt, because of his strongly monotheistic inclinations, we have a contrast rather between God and his Logos than between a first and second God, but later Platonists such as Albinus, Apuleius or Numenius postulate two distinct Gods, both Intellects certainly, but one in repose and turned in upon itself, the other in motion and directed outwards, both above and below itself. Some Pythagoreans, such as Moderatus of Gades and Numenius, go further and postulate a trio of Ones or Gods in descending order, deriving the inspiration for this, perhaps, from a curious passage of the Second Platonic Letter (312E). In either case, however, the third member of the trio turns out to be the World Soul, so that the basic metaphysical scheme is unchanged.

Besides these major figures, the Platonic cosmos was filled with subordinate, intermediate beings, the race of daemons. There are broadly two theories on the nature of daemons, one static, so to speak, the other dynamic, and both are represented within our period. Xenocrates already, as we have seen, had elaborated on Plato's doctrine of the intermediate nature of daemons, expressing it in geometrical terms. Such daemons sound like permanent fixtures in the universe, though the question of their relationship with disembodied souls is unclear in the evidence available to us. The alternative theory, represented by Plutarch and by Apuleius, is one according to which daemons are in fact souls, either on their way up or on their way down the scale of being, either heading for complete purification (and thus divinization) in the Sun, or for embodiment on the Earth. For this theory Plutarch could appeal back to the authority of Empedocles (*Is. et Os.* 361c). The theory is not presented by Plutarch with complete coherence, however; the static theory also appears. In particular, evil daemons are recognized, as they were by Xenocrates. Are these daemons permanent elements in the universe, or are they souls in the process of being punished for misdeeds during incarnation? Both possibilities seem to be entertained by Plutarch, as we shall see. Truly evil daemons, as opposed to avenging agencies of God, are not a properly Platonic conception, but rather a concession to popular belief, or perhaps an influence from Persian dualism. 'Avenging' daemons, on the other hand, are a more acceptable concept, since they are subordinate to God and their activity is ultimately beneficent. Even Philo finds such entities compatible with his monotheism. Besides daemons proper, there is also mention made of heroes and angels, the latter possibly in origin non-Hellenic but certainly accepted in Neoplatonism into the Platonic universe. Heroes are more respectable, but the distinction between them and daemons in the Platonic period is not quite clear. Posidonius wrote a treatise on the subject, but it is lost. One distinction can be that heroes are souls formerly embodied, but this distinction assumes a permanent class of unembodied souls, which is only acceptable on the 'static' theory. Whatever the differences in detail, however, it is common ground for all Platonists that between God and Man there must be a host of intermediaries, that God may not be contaminated or disturbed by a too close involvement with Matter.

The Platonic Ideas or Forms suffered various transformations during our period. We are hampered, as I have suggested earlier in this chapter, by not really knowing what stage the theory of Ideas had reached in Plato's maturest thought. It is very probable, however, that for Plato already the Ideas were numbers, though explicitly differentiated from mathematical numbers by being unique in their kinds. Neither Speusippus nor Xenocrates liked the distinction between Ideas and Mathematicals, and, as we have seen, each abolished it in different directions. What Polemon thought about the Ideas is unknown to us.

When the theory surfaces again with Antiochus, it looks very much as if they have become assimilated in his mind to the Stoic 'common notions', which would dispose of their transcendental aspect. For the source behind *Tusculan Disputations* I they still seem to be transcendent entities; there is *anamnēsis* of them, which involves their existence outside the human mind. But it is not certain that the source of *TD* I is Antiochus, and even there it is by no means clear that we are dealing with the Platonic Ideas in their pristine form; it is much more probable that they are to be seen as thoughts in the mind of God.

With the assimilation of the Platonic Demiurge to the Stoic Logos, the situating of the Ideas in the mind of God becomes more or less inevitable—if, indeed, they had not already been established there by Xenocrates. When the distinction is later made between a First and a Second God, the Ideas gravitate towards the mind of the second, demiurgic God. It seems also as if they were thought to exist in the World Soul in a secondary, 'extended' form; at least we find in Plutarch and the later Pythagoreans the equation of the soul with the Platonic 'mathematicals' which in the context of Middle Platonism correspond to something intermediate between Ideas proper and sensible objects.[1]

But if there was significant theorizing in the Middle Platonic period on the theory of Ideas, not much sign of it has survived. Albinus summarizes the accepted Middle Platonic formulae as to what there are Ideas of, and what relationship they have to other entities, such as God and the physical cosmos, but he gives no hint of serious thought as to their nature or their relevance to a theory of knowledge. Plutarch wrote a work (now lost) entitled 'Where are the Ideas situated?' (*Cat. Lampr.* 67), but it probably did not raise any basic questions. The complacency of the later Platonists about the theory of Ideas is, as it stands, extraordinary, considering the powerful arguments that Aristotle had directed against it.

Another issue that surely merited serious questioning, but does not seem to have received it, is that of the relationship of the Ideas to Matter, and the related question of the creation of the physical world out of the basic atomic triangles. I can discern no sign of philosophic questioning behind Albinus' summary of Platonic physical theory in chh. 12–22 of the *Didaskalikos*, which may be taken to represent the established position (up to the mid-second century A.D.) on these questions. For Antiochus, who accepted Stoic materialism, the problem

---

[1] See Philip Merlan, *From Platonism to Neoplatonism*, ch. 1.

of the relation of the immaterial to the material did not arise, but for all subsequent Platonists it was, one would think, a very serious issue. Yet we do not find them worrying about it. Albinus, for instance, simply summarizes the *Timaeus*, and leaves it at that.

The only issue on which we find much dispute in this area (and even this disagreement is partly vacillation) is as to whether we are to accept a four-element or a five-element universe, rejecting or accepting Aristotle's theory of aether as the element proper to the heavenly realm. Even this tends to dissolve into a dispute about formulations. Many Platonists assimilated Aristotle's aether to the Stoic pure fire, and the Stoics recognized that the fire of the heavenly realm was of a superior type to that of our experience, though they were not specific as to its innate circular motion. We shall see men like Philo and Plutarch apparently veering back and forth on this question within one and the same treatise, which seems to indicate that they found the two theories compatible. On the basic issue all were agreed, that the heavenly realm was qualitatively different from our own, intermediate, indeed, between the sublunar and the intelligible realms, a place of unchanging, divine forms pursuing perfectly regular courses. Once this is agreed, the issue of four or five elements becomes secondary.

If the Middle Platonists seem uninterested in questions of what we would term Physics, they are after all only reflecting the remarkably non-scientific bias of the age in which they lived. After the active period of Alexandrian scientific speculation, the civilized world relapsed into an attitude so anti-experimental that a man like Plutarch, if he wished to find out the answer to some practical question, turns instinctively to some 'authority', such as Aristotle's *Problems*, rather than conduct an experiment himself. His *Quaestiones Conviviales* are full of futile discussions on matters of this sort, with the learned disputants quoting ancient authorities at each other on practical questions which could only be solved by experiment. Only in the field of medicine, in the person of Galen, does one find a refreshing reliance on experiment and first-hand observation.

3. LOGIC

In the field of Logic, the primary 'achievement' of the Middle Platonists was to appropriate Aristotelian logic, together with the developments attributable to Theophrastus and Eudemus, for Plato. Theophrastus and Eudemus had developed the system of hypothetical syllogisms which had been more or less ignored by Aristotle (Alex. *In An. Pr.* 326, 20ff.; 389, 32ff.), distinguishing 'pure' and 'mixed' hypotheticals, the latter being those adopted later by the Stoics. Insofar, then, as the Middle Platonists borrowed from Stoic logic, they felt justified in this by finding it prefigured in Theophrastus. We find this synthesis exhibited in Albinus' *Didaskalikos*, ch. 6, where both categorical and hypothetical syllogisms are discerned in the dialogues, particularly the *Parmenides*. Plato is also credited there with knowledge of the Ten Categories, which Albinus discerns in the *Parmenides*, while Plutarch (*Proc. An.* 1023E) sees them operating in *Timaeus* 37AB.

The process of synthesis, though with explicit dependence on Stoic logic, can be seen already established in Cicero's *Topica* (see below, pp. 103–4), so that the origin of it may be attributed with some probability to Antiochus of Ascalon—although Aristotelian-Theophrastean Logic may have been accepted already into the New Academy. At any rate, the Old Academic loyalty to diairesis and the two basic categories of Absolute and Relative has been abandoned in our period. In an important article,[1] Michael Frede has shown that the distinction which we make between the logic of terms (Aristotelian) and propositional logic (Stoic) was not obvious to the ancients, and that their mutual exclusivity was based on other and more trivial grounds. Certainly the Middle Platonists saw no incompatibility between the two logics, and were happy to view Plato as the father of both.

Along with this tendency to synthesis, however, there existed a tradition, among the anti-Aristotelian wing of Platonists, men such as Eudorus, Nicostratus and Atticus, of criticizing Aristotle's *Categories*.[2] This hostile tradition takes a polemical and often foolish form, but it uncovers in the process a few interesting points, showing traces of later logical refinements. The anti-Aristotelians challenged Aristotle's originality (he was accused of filching the ten categories from Archytas), his completeness, and the validity of some of his distinctions. Also taking him to be making a division of reality rather than a

[1] 'Stoic vs. Aristotelian Syllogistic', *Archiv f. Gesch. d. Phil.* 56 (1974), pp. 1–32. He pays no attention to Theophrastus, however. See A. Graeser, *Die logischen Fragmente des Theophrast.* 1973.

[2] The criticism is confined to the *Categories*. Aristotle's syllogistic was not attacked, presumably because it had long since been claimed for Plato. Even the Categories are attacked only in detail, not as an overall theory. See on this subject the useful article of A. C. Lloyd, 'Neoplatonic Logic and Stoic Logic', *Phronesis* 1 (1956).

division of language, they asserted that his distinctions were suitable only to the sensible realm, not to the intelligible one, and this left the way open for Plotinus later (in *Enneads* VI 1–3) to establish the five 'greatest genera' of the *Sophist* as categories of the intelligible world. Despite all this activity, however, it cannot be said that the Middle Platonists added much that is valuable to the science of Logic. There are a few lost works of Plutarch, such as *A Reply to Chrysippus on the First Consequent*, a *Lecture on the Ten Categories*, *A Discourse on Hypothesis*, and *On Tautology*, which sound interesting, but there is no reason to suppose, on the basis of Plutarch's attested performance, that they contributed anything of basic importance.

4. CONCLUSION

We shall see throughout our period the philosophers of Middle Platonism oscillating between the two poles of attraction constituted by Peripateticism and Stoicism, but adding to the mixture of these influences a strong commitment (after Antiochus, at least) to a transcendent supreme principle, and a non-material, intelligible world above and beyond this one, which stands as a paradigm for it. The influence of Pythagoras and what was believed to be his doctrine was also dominant throughout our period. The view that Plato is essentially a pupil, creative or otherwise, of Pythagoras grows in strength and elaboration among all classes of Platonist, attaining its extreme form among those who unequivocally declared themselves to be Pythagoreans. Nevertheless, despite all the variations in doctrine that emerge, we can observe in this period the growth of a consistent body of thought, constituting a Platonic heritage that could be handed on, first to Plotinus and his followers, and thence to later ages.

CHAPTER TWO

Antiochus of Ascalon: The Turn to Dogmatism

A. LIFE AND WORKS: SKETCH OF PHILOSOPHICAL DEVELOPMENT

ANTIOCHUS, with whom our survey proper begins, was born in the town of Ascalon in Palestine in approximately 130 B.C. This part of the world had been contributing intellectuals to the Hellenistic literary scene for some time, though not from Ascalon in particular. The great Stoic philosopher, Posidonius, Antiochus' contemporary, came from Apamea in northern Syria, and Gadara, nearer by, had produced Meleager, the writer of epigrams and collector of the *Garland*, Menippus the satirist, and Antiochus' younger contemporary, the Epicurean philosopher and epigrammatist Philodemus. The only literary figure known from Ascalon before Antiochus' time is a Stoic philosopher named Sosus, who may have exercised some influence on Antiochus' choice of career. At any rate, Antiochus dedicated to him a dialogue the writing of which marks a significant point in his development, as we shall see presently, and which is one of the few works of his of which we know the title.

Apart from being, presumably, the scene of his childhood and youth, Ascalon has no place in Antiochus' philosophical development that is observable to us. We have Cicero's word for it (*Tusc. Disp.* v 107) that once Antiochus had left Ascalon he never returned. Whether this statement excludes the possibility of a brief visit late in life when Antiochus was back in the area on campaign with Lucullus is uncertain, but plainly he never returned there to live. For his higher studies, at least, he came to Athens, still the world centre for philosophy. Once in Athens, he attached himself to the Platonic Academy, and to its head at that time, Philo of Larisa. It has been accepted in some quarters, following a statement of Numenius' (Fr. 28 Des Places), that Antiochus attended first the lectures of the head of the Stoic school, Mnesarchus, a pupil of Panaetius. The evidence of Cicero,[1] however, does not seem to support this, and it is probably a fabrication of later times designed to show that Antiochus was a vacillator, or a crypto-Stoic from the beginning, or both.[2] It is not unlikely that he attended the lectures of Mnesarchus at some stage of his career, but probably later rather than sooner.

There is no question, however, about the fact that Antiochus was the pupil of Philo of Larisa. We have the evidence of Cicero (*loc. cit.*) that Antiochus 'studied under Philo . . . for such a long time that it was agreed that nobody had studied longer'. If this be pressed, it would imply that Antiochus attached himself to Philo not long after Philo became head of the Academy in 110 B.C., and that we may regard as the approximate date of his arrival in Athens.

For about twenty years, then, Antiochus remained a more or less orthodox member of the New Academy of Arcesilaus and Carneades, as modified by Philo. He is reported, in the passage of Cicero referred to above, to have written in this period well-argued works vigorously defending positions which he was later, in old age, to attack with equal vigour. We need not assume, however, as hostile contemporaries implied, that Antiochus' conversion to dogmatism was in the nature of a brainstorm, any more than that it was prompted by personal rivalry with Philo.[3] It is far more likely that it was the result of a gradually growing dissatisfaction with the barrenness of Academic scepticism, which, without Carneades' brilliance to sustain it, must have become increasingly unsatisfying to anyone of positive and dogmatic tendencies. There is also the circumstance that Philo's tentative steps towards recognizing the possibility of 'evidence' (*enargeia*) made the whole sceptical position less consistent.

The open break with Philo, however, does not seem to have occurred until after the flight of the philosophers to Rome in face of Mithridates' advance on Athens in 88 B.C. Philo and Antiochus stayed in Rome for some time, and Philo at least gained wide fame in Roman society for his lectures, which were heard by, among others, Q.

---

[1] *Acad. Pr.* 69, quoted below.

[2] What Numenius actually says is: 'At any rate, having attended the lectures of Mnesarchus the Stoic, he developed doctrines contrary to his master Philo, and attached innumerable alien features to the Academy.' Numenius may equally well be referring to a later period, just before Antiochus' open break with Philo. The evidence of Augustine (*Contra Acad.* 3, 41), '*auditis Philone Academico et Mnesarcho Stoico*', points in this direction, wherever he derived it.

[3] Cic. *loc. cit.*, cf. Aug. *Contra Acad.* 2, 15. Plut. *Cic.* 4.

Lutatius Catulus and Cicero. In Rome Antiochus was noticed, as Philo's most distinguished pupil, by the aristocrat L. Lucullus, with whom ever afterwards he remained on the closest terms. When Lucullus left Rome to be quaestor under Sulla in Asia in 87 B.C., Antiochus went with him on his staff, and it is in Alexandria in the winter of 87/6, while Lucullus was in Egypt trying to raise a fleet, that an incident is described as taking place which brought to a head the break with Philo.

As we have the story in Cicero's *Academica Priora* (11ff.), Lucullus himself is relating the circumstances, but it is not unlikely that Cicero is in fact using here Antiochus' own dialogue *Sôsus*, which was the outcome of the dispute dramatized in the story. Antiochus may have described the circumstances in a prologue, such as Cicero is in the habit of prefixing to his own dialogues. However, here is Lucullus:

When I was in Alexandria during my proquaestorship, Antiochus was with me, and there was already at Alexandria a friend of Antiochus', Heraclitus of Tyre, who had been for many years a pupil of Clitomachus and of Philo, a proved and notable champion of that philosophy which is now being revived from near extinction (*sc.* that of the New Academy). I often heard Antiochus arguing with him, but amicably on each side. Then, however, those two books of Philo's which Catulus was discussing yesterday were brought to Alexandria, and came into Antiochus' hands for the first time. Now Antiochus was a very mild fellow—none milder—but when he read these he got quite angry. I was astonished, as I had never seen him like that before. He begged Heraclitus to stir his memory, and asked him if this sounded like Philo, or if he had ever heard such views as these expressed by Philo or by any other Academic. Heraclitus said that he had not, but acknowledged the work as written by Philo. Nor indeed could this be doubted, as there were present some learned friends of mine, Publius and Gaius Selius and Tetrilius Rogus, who said that they had heard these views stated in Rome by Philo and asserted that they had copied down the two works in question from Philo's own manuscript.

Then Antiochus said to Heraclitus what Catulus recalled yesterday as having been said by his father to Philo, and a lot besides; nor was he satisfied until he had actually written a book against his teacher, to wit, the *Sôsus*. At that time, then, while I was earnestly listening to Heraclitus holding forth against Antiochus and Antiochus, similarly, against the Academics, I paid special attention to Antiochus, in order to get his whole position quite clear. And so, with the participation of Heraclitus and a number of other scholars, among them Antiochus' brother Aristus, and also Ariston and Dion, who were his chief supporters, after his brother, we spent a considerable space of time in discussing that single subject.

I quote this at length, since it serves to dramatize a decisive point in Antiochus' philosophical development.[1] We need not doubt the historicity of this episode, though we may well doubt that Cicero is dependent for his information on the oral testimony of Lucullus. We can learn from this passage a certain amount about the time and nature of the break. We note that Antiochus and Heraclitus knew nothing of this work of Philo's, and were astonished by its contents. On the other hand, these Roman friends of Lucullus', whom we must presume to have joined the entourage later, perhaps just at Alexandria to spend the winter, knew the books and had made copies of them. It would seem to follow from this, then, that after Antiochus' departure from Rome, Philo composed a work which made explicit some position or positions which he had not made clear before; otherwise Antiochus' astonishment, no matter how exaggerated for rhetorical purposes, would have no meaning at all.

What, then, was there in this work of Philo's which excited Antiochus to such unwonted wrath? Apparently its main theme was the essential unity of the Academic tradition—an explosive subject, as between these two men. This involved on the one hand the emphasizing of the aporetic and sceptical nature of Socrates' teaching, and even of many of Plato's dialogues, and on the other some modification of the extreme sceptical position of Arcesilaus. Clitomachus had already gone quite far in establishing a positive philosophy, with a theory of probability and of 'things to be preferred and rejected', and Philo, either now or earlier, went so far as to admit that there were things that were clear (*enargê*) in the Stoic sense, but he denied the possibility of subjective certainty (*katalêpsis*) (*Acad. Pr.* 32, Sextus Emp. *PH* 1 235). It was probably the attempt to prove the unity of the tradition that Antiochus found astonishing. It must have been a point on which the New Academy in general had not laid any emphasis, and Philo's stand on the subject may actually have been provoked by enquiries made by Roman hearers of his lectures as to how far his teaching in fact accorded with the doctrine of Plato. Philo's bold reply was that there was no discrepancy.

Antiochus' view was diametrically opposed to this. He saw a clear break between what he terms 'the ancients' (a title of honour which comprised, as a solid group, Plato, Speusippus, Xenocrates, and Polemon, with the Peripatetics Aristotle and Theophrastus), and the

---

[1] It also introduces us to a number of minor characters, who will be adverted to later.

sceptical tradition, begun by Arcesilaus and continuing down to Philo himself. It was perhaps in the *Sôsus* that Antiochus first explicitly stated his position on this. Certainly in later years he never tired of restating it; it appears as a kind of litany at the head of every essay of his which Cicero has relayed to us. An example of this would not be amiss, as it is a very characteristic feature. Let us take, for instance, *Acad. Post.* 15ff. (Varro is speaking, as Antiochus' mouthpiece):

Socrates was the first person who summoned philosophy away from mysteries veiled in concealment by nature herself, upon which all philosophers before him had been engaged, and led it to the subject of ordinary life, in order to investigate the virtues and vices, and good and evil generally, and to realise that heavenly matters are either remote from our knowledge or else, however fully known, have nothing to do with the good life.[1]

Varro goes on to describe Socrates' method of philosophizing, admitting his irony and apparent destructive argumentation. He then continues:

But originating with Plato, a thinker of manifold variety and fertility, there was established a philosophy which, though it has two appellations, was really a single uniform system, that of the Academic and Peripatetic Schools, which, while agreeing in doctrine, differed in name; for Plato left his sister's son Speusippus as heir, so to speak, to his system, but two pupils of outstanding zeal and learning, Xenocrates, a native of Chalcedon, and Aristotle, a native of Stagira; and accordingly the associates of Aristotle were called Peripatetics, because they used to debate while walking in the Lyceum, while the others, because they carried on Plato's practice of assembling and conversing in the Academy, got their appellation from the name of the place. But both schools drew plentiful supplies from Plato's abundance, and both framed a definitely formulated rule of doctrine, and this fully and copiously set forth, whereas they abandoned the famous Socratic custom of discussing everything in a doubting manner and without the admission of any positive statement. Thus was produced something that Socrates had been in the habit of reprobating entirely, a definite science of philosophy, with a regular arrangement of subjects and a formulated system of doctrine. At the outset, indeed, this was a single system with two names, as I have said, for there was no difference between the Peripatetics and the Old Academy of those days. Aristotle excelled, as I at all events think, in a certain copiousness of intellect, but both schools drew from the same source, and both made the same classification of things to be desired and avoided.

---

[1] This account of Socrates' attitude goes back to Xenophon's *Memorabilia* I 1, 11ff.

We cannot be quite certain whether this rather frank admission of the deviation of the Platonists from the practice of Socrates is Antiochus' own, or rather added in maliciously by Cicero. At *Fin.* v 7, we get a simpler roll-call:

> . . . the Old [Academy], which includes, as you heard Antiochus declare, not only those who bear the name of Academics, Speusippus, Xenocrates, Polemon, Crantor and the rest, but also the early Peripatetics, headed by their chief, Aristotle, who, if Plato be excepted, I almost think deserves to be called the prince of philosophers. (cf. also *De Orat.* iii 67)

The speaker here, and expounder of the Antiochian doctrine in Book V of the *De Finibus*, is M. Pupius Piso Calpurnianus, a student of Antiochus', who had been a pupil also of the Peripatetic philosopher Staseas of Naples, and who sets out Antiochus' doctrine, rather curiously, as Peripatetic teaching (e.g. v 9; 14), though identified with the Academic. It simply shows how little the distinction mattered to Antiochus.

The first principle of Antiochus' history of the Academic school was, then, the essential identity between early Academics and Peripatetics. We may well wonder, from our perspective, how he could possibly have maintained this, in face of Aristotle's own sharp criticisms of Plato and the Academy, as well as the many radical developments which Aristotle seems to us to have made. Before dismissing Antiochus' view out of hand, however, we should look more closely. We must realize that he was looking at the Old Academy from a different perspective, at once closer and more distorted. Closer, because Antiochus had available to him, as we do not, the works of Speusippus and Xenocrates, the exoteric works of Aristotle, the writings of Theophrastus, and, last but not least, the works of Polemon, for Antiochus the last orthodox head of the Academy before himself; distorted, because in face of all these later interpretations, the actual dialogues of Plato and the exoteric works of Aristotle, which are all that remain to us, seem to have receded somewhat into the background—not forgotten or unread (Cicero quotes Plato often enough), but simply overlaid and even distorted by the work of their immediate successors. We have discussed in the previous chapter the various changes that befell the Theory of Ideas (pp. 47–8). In metaphysics, the notion of a transcendent, immaterial divinity seems to have been dropped; in ethics, and ultimately in logic also, the system and formulations of Aristotle seem to have won acceptance from the Academy. The key to

all this unanimity is surely Polemon, as I have suggested. It was to Polemon that Antiochus primarily looked back, and repeatedly he links Polemon's name with that of Aristotle. At *Fin.* v 14 we find: 'Our master Antiochus seems to me to adhere most scrupulously to the doctrine of the ancients, which according to his teaching was common to Aristotle and to Polemon.'[1] We are in no position to doubt the accuracy of Antiochus' view of Polemon's position; indeed the little we know about Polemon's views tends to support it (see above, pp. 39ff.).[2]

Polemon was also, as we have seen, the key factor in Antiochus' second principle: the substantial identity of the teaching of the Old Academy with that of the Stoa. Consider *Fin.* iv 3 (Cicero himself is expounding the Antiochian position against the Stoics, represented by Cato):

My view then, Cato, is this, that those old disciples of Plato, Speusippus, Aristotle and Xenocrates, and afterwards their pupils Polemon and Theophrastus, had developed a body of doctrine that left nothing to be desired either in fullness or finish, so that Zeno, on becoming a pupil of Polemon, had no reason for differing either from his master himself or from his master's predecessors.

De Finibus Book IV is a polemical work, however; Antiochus was not always so harsh to Zeno.[3] He did maintain, though, that such of Stoic doctrine as was correct was merely a verbal development of Academic doctrine, while inasmuch as Zeno was original he was in fact distorting the teaching of 'the ancients'. In the sphere of ethics, for instance, Zeno accepts the 'correct' Academic principle that 'the earliest impulse bestowed upon us by nature is a desire for self-preservation' (*Fin.* iv 25), but he deviates from this incorrectly when he denies that bodily excellences are 'goods'. This Academic principle, the doctrine of *oikeiôsis* (which most scholars, indeed, regard as a Stoic formulation), was plainly for Antiochus primarily a doctrine of Polemon's, so that once again Polemon must be seen as the pivot upon which Antiochus' history of philosophy swings. In our evaluation of Antiochus' posi-

---

[1] cf. *Fin.* ii 34, 'Polemon, and also before him Aristotle'.

[2] The notion of substantial identity between the Schools was not original to Antiochus. Panaetius, and after him Posidonius, wished to read Stoic teaching into Plato, and in fact took a good deal from Plato into their versions of Stoicism. As for Carneades, it was one of his favourite contentions that there was no substantive difference between Peripatetic and Stoic ethics (*Tusc. Disp.* v 120).

[3] cf. *Acad. Post.* 35–42, a survey of Zeno's doctrines without polemical heat. In expounding positive doctrine, in *Fin.* v and in the *Academica*, Antiochus

tion, then, we must bear in mind that we are almost entirely ignorant of the works of the chief figure in his reconstruction, and that the little we do know of Polemon does tend to suggest that Antiochus knew what he was talking about, though his assumption that Polemon's teaching was identical with that of Plato is plainly erroneous.

The above has been a digression arising from a discussion of the content of Antiochus' dialogue *Sôsus*. It remains to mention the other works of Antiochus whose names are known to us. First, the *Kanonika*. We find Book II of this work quoted by Sextus Empiricus (*Adv. Log.* I 201). From another casual reference, *ibid.* 162, if it be from the same work, we might conclude that the subject was the Theory of Knowledge. It is not clear precisely what the title means. *Kanonikon* was the Epicurean term for 'principles of methodology' (their substitute for Logic, which they rejected), but it is unlikely that Antiochus would borrow a distinctively Epicurean term. Otherwise, *kanonika* should mean, in general, rules of conduct. Since Sextus is discussing throughout Book One of his work *Against the Logicians* the *kritêrion*, the criterion of certainty, it seems likely that Antiochus' work was an exposition of his Theory of Knowledge and of Certainty, preceded by an elaborate historical survey, of which Sextus may well preserve traces. We know a good deal about Antiochus' Theory of Knowledge from Cicero, although no source-work is mentioned. The *Kanonika* sounds like a fundamental exposition of Antiochus' philosophy, or at least of his epistemology, but one cannot be certain.

Another work the title of which has come down to us is a book *On the Gods*. Antiochus seems to have written this while on campaign with Lucullus at some time after October 69 B.C., since he found occasion to mention the battle of Tigranocerta in it, saying, rather hyperbolically, that 'the sun had not seen such another' (Plut. *Luc.* 28, 8). We do not know whether this remark comes from some dedicatory preface or from the body of the work. It certainly does not tell us much about Antiochus' views on the gods. What these may have been we shall consider later.

There is also recorded (Cic. *De Nat. Deor.* II 16) an essay of Antiochus' dedicated to Q. Lucilius Balbus, the Stoic and pupil of Panaetius, which seems to have been devoted to one of Antiochus' favourite

adopts Stoic formulations and doctrines wholesale—without acknowledgement, since he persuaded himself that he was merely taking back for the Academy what belonged to it. cf. Sext. Emp. *PH* I 235: 'Antiochus . . . tried to demonstrate that the doctrines of the Stoics were present already in Plato.'

points, the essential agreement between the Stoics and the Peripatetics. Since the dramatic date of this dialogue can be fixed in 77 or 76 B.C., and Antiochus is described as writing his treatise 'recently' (*loc. cit.*), we may date it to *c.* 78 B.C.

From which, if any, of the works above-mentioned the doctrines recorded by Cicero are taken is not clear, though the *Kanonika* is plainly the most likely candidate, followed by the *Sôsus*. The possibility that Cicero also made copious notes of the lectures he heard in 79–78 cannot be entirely discounted. However, his borrowings from Antiochus in *De Finibus* IV and V and in the *Academica* do seem to be adaptations of continuous treatises, basic expositions of ethics or epistemology. We must rest content with the circumstance that in the case of Antiochus we have on the one hand the titles of some works and on the other a good deal of basic doctrine, and the one does not explicitly correspond to the other. We would like to hear of treatises *On Ends* or *On the Criterion*, as we find recorded of other philosophers, but we do not. There is no doubt, however, that Antiochus lectured on these subjects, as what we have is at least a literary version of these lectures.

Whether Antiochus can properly be described as having been 'head of the Platonic Academy' depends on what one takes that title to mean. He gave his lectures, not in the Academy itself, which was deserted (Cic. *Fin.* V 1ff.), but in the Ptolemaion gymnasium (*ibid.*), in the city. He may be described as head of the Academy as being the (self-appointed) heir to Plato's doctrines, but that he inherited any physical plant as well seems unlikely. If Philo had had anything to hand over, he would hardly have bequeathed it to Antiochus, and it is doubtful whether after 88 B.C. there was anything much to hand over. The latest opinion on the matter[1] is that Plato's Academy, as a physical institution, collapsed in 88 with the fall of Athens, and that it was not revived *as an institution* until the late fourth century A.D. We shall have more to say on this question in later chapters, in connexion with Plutarch and the 'Athenian School'.

At any rate we find Antiochus lecturing in Athens in 79 B.C. as the sole available authority on Platonism.[2] Cicero attended his lectures for six months in the winter of 79–78, and formed a devotion to him which lasted the whole of his life. Since, however, Cicero persisted in cling-

---

[1] See on this question the interesting study of John Lynch, *Aristotle's School*, Berkeley 1972, esp. pp. 177–89.
[2] Cic. *Fin.* V 6: 'and there is no other lecturer to go to.'

ing to the scepticism of the New Academy, at least in the moderate form put out by Philo, it was rather Antiochus' ethical doctrine, and his eloquence,[1] which attracted him. Antiochus also approved of participation by the Wise Man in public affairs, and indeed encouraged Cicero to return to Rome and politics after the death of Sulla (Plut. *Cic*.4, 3).

Antiochus died not long after 68 B.C., still, apparently, on campaign with Lucullus in Syria. We have seen that he managed to bring Lucullus' victory at Tigranocerta into a philosophical work he was writing, and Lucullus is made to say (*Acad. Pr.* 61) that Antiochus advanced the doctrines which he had heard him state at Alexandria 'much more dogmatically still when he was staying with me in Syria shortly before his death'. Lucullus returned to Rome at the end of 67, so the date of Antiochus' death is thus fairly closely circumscribed.

There remains to be discussed the question of Antiochus' successors, and of the survival of his 'School'. While Antiochus was in Syria, the school, if there was a school, was presumably being run back in Athens by his brother Aristus. Aristus continued to preside after Antiochus' death, at least until 50 B.C., when Cicero looked in on him on his way back from his command in Cilicia. Indeed, from the way in which Cicero refers to him in the *Brutus* ('my friend and guest Aristus', 332), with no suggestion that he is now dead, we may assume him to be still alive in the spring of 46 B.C., the date of the dialogue. M. Junius Brutus was a close friend of Aristus, who, on Plutarch's evidence (*Brutus* 2, 2), though a most pleasant fellow, was not really much of a philosopher. Hardly the stuff, it seems, of which great philosophical movements are made.

Aristus was in turn succeeded by one Theomnestus, of Naucratis in Egypt. He was reigning in 44 B.C., when Brutus attended his lectures (Plut. *Brutus* 44). If we may credit Philostratus (*Lives of the Sophists* 1 6), he was more of a sophist than a philosopher, and thus probably even more lightweight than Aristus. What happened to Antiochus' school after the death of Theomnestus we have no idea. Possibly nothing. The centre of Platonic philosophy seems now to move to Alexandria, where Heraclitus of Tyre was well established, as we have seen, by 76 B.C. Heraclitus was a New Academic, but Antiochus' chief pupils Ariston and Dion also operated in Alexandria. Ariston set up

---

[1] Plut. *Cic.* 4, 1: 'On coming to Athens, he (Cicero) attended the lectures of Antiochus of Ascalon, and was charmed by his fluency and the grace of his diction, although he disapproved of his innovations in doctrine.' cf. Cicero, *Brutus* 315.

as a Peripatetic (though what dispute this entailed with Antiochus' synthesis is hard to see), but Dion remained a Platonist, and was still prominent in 57 B.C., when he was sent to Rome as leader of an embassy of one hundred citizens to oppose the reinstatement of Ptolemy Auletes. While in Rome, he was murdered at the house of his host, L. Lucceius (Cic. *Pro. Cael.* 23–4 and 51–5). A possible pupil of his was Eudorus of Alexandria, whose *floruit* is put at 25 B.C. Of Eudorus more will be said in the next chapter.

Of Antiochus' Roman pupils the only one of significance to the history of philosophy, apart from Cicero, is M. Terentius Varro (116–28 B.C.), the most learned Roman scholar of his age. Varro's interests were very wide, but in philosophy he was an Antiochian Platonist. It is to Varro that Cicero allots the exposition of Antiochus' philosophy in the second edition of his *Academica*. Partly through Varro, perhaps, a certain amount of influence from Antiochus seems to have descended to Seneca, and, much later, to St. Augustine.

B. PHILOSOPHY

This survey of Antiochus' philosophy must be prefaced with a warning. Of Antiochus' own writings, as we have seen, nothing substantive remains. What we know of his philosophy must be gleaned primarily from a group of works of Cicero which are stated by Cicero himself to be accounts of Antiochus' philosophy, to wit, *De Finibus* v, a review of ethics and of the End of Goods, or *summum bonum* (with which the critiques of Stoicism in IV and of Epicureanism in II are closely connected in outlook), the *Academica Priora* (*Lucullus*) and *Academica Posteriora*, two versions of a general summary of Antiochus' philosophy, and in particular, in *Acad. Pr.* 11–60, of his Theory of Knowledge. Other works of Cicero which have been seen as Antiochian, and of which I have made more or less cautious use, are *De Legibus* I and II, *De Fato*, *Tusc. Disp.* I, *Topica*, and parts of the *De Oratore*. Such works as *De Natura Deorum* II and *De Divinatione* are certainly Stoic treatises, but in the case at least of *De Nat. Deor.* II, we are given a strong hint by Cicero that Antiochus' views did not differ significantly from the views therein contained.

To avoid laborious circumlocutions, I have normally treated the basic texts above-mentioned as if they were works of Antiochus. This is reasonable, I think, if the reader bears always in mind that the stylistic form of these works is due to Cicero's adaptation, as he says himself (*Fin.* 1 6, *Ep. ad Att.* XII 52), and so only the technical terms (with, probably, the basic similes and other images), can be claimed for Antiochus. I have included in brackets, sometimes the original Greek equivalent of Cicero's Latin, where this is certain, sometimes the Latin, where the original is not certain, in order to familiarize the reader with the technical terms involved.

Antiochus is reported in *Acad. Pr.* 29 as declaring that 'the two greatest things in philosophy are the Criterion of Truth (*kritêrion tês alêtheias*) and the End of Goods (*telos agathôn*), and no man can be a Sage (*sophos*) who is ignorant of the existence of either a beginning of the process of knowledge or an end of appetition, and who consequently does not know from what point he is starting or at what he ought to arrive'.

This, with its polemic against Antiochus' predecessors in the New Academy, is a useful statement of his position with which to begin. We will examine first these two topics, the Criterion and the Supreme Good or 'End of Goods', before turning to his views on other matters. But first we must say a word about the scholastic divisions of philosophy.

Antiochus himself divided philosophy, as was customary in the Schools of his time, into three parts, Physics, Ethics and Logic. This was the order followed by the Stoics, and attributed to Xenocrates, and thus to the Old Academy,[1] but from Cic. *Acad. Pr.* 19 one might conclude that Antiochus preferred the order Ethics—Physics—Logic. He will then have favoured the Stoic analogy of the Egg, whereby Ethics is the yolk, Physics the white, and Logic the shell (Sextus, *loc. cit.*). Argument as to the order of topics may seem futile to the reader, but small points like this must be noted none the less. Having duly noted the division, however, I think it preferable to take Antiochus' philosophy under heads which will have more meaning to us, beginning with the topic which, as we have seen, he regarded as of prime importance.

1. THE CRITERION OF CERTAINTY

The question of the criterion of certainty is plainly at the centre of Antiochus' philosophical position. It was the cause of his break with

---

[1] Sextus Empiricus, *Adv. Math.* 7 16–19, where the whole list of possibilities is set out. We find the threefold division, in the order Ethics-Physics-Logic, used rather casually by Aristotle in *Topics* I 14, 105b19ff., as if it were normal.

Philo and the New Academic tradition, and is the foundation of his metaphysics.[1] Dogmatism revived in the Platonic tradition when Antiochus accepted the Stoic doctrine of certainty, the doctrine of the *kataleptike phantasia*,[2] or, as we may term it, 'cognitive impression'. The Stoic definition of a cognitive impression is as follows: 'A cognitive impression is an impression derived from an object which really exists, and which is imprinted and stamped (on the subject) *in accordance with* such object, *of such a kind as could not be derived from a nonexistent object*' (italics mine). It was to this last clause in particular that exception was taken by the sceptical tradition, including the New Academy. Even if one accepted, as Carneades did, that there were impressions which were 'probable', that is, not contradicted by subsequent impressions, and thus adequate to be acted upon, it did not seem philosophically respectable to assert that there was a class of senseperceptions that came to the mind with a stamp of infallibility upon it. The sceptical array of arguments was impressive, though much use was made, in a manner which seems curious to us but is in fact not an unreasonable convention, of situations and characters from Homer and Greek Tragedy. A reading of Sextus Empiricus, or indeed of A. J. Ayer's *The Problem of Knowledge*, will give an adequate survey of these objections.

The position of the Stoics and of Antiochus was one of what may be termed Scientific Realism. They rejected the naive realism of the Epicureans (who maintained the perhaps true, but trivially true, position that *all* sense-impressions were infallible, and that only our interpretation of them could err), but held that where there was present a subjective feeling of certainty, accompanied by normal subjective and objective conditions, that is normal vision and mental state, normal visibility, reasonable proximity, and so on, a true perception took place. What they claimed, and what Carneades disputed, was that there was an unmistakable distinction, immediately apparent to the mind, between *certain* perceptions and any degree of doubtful perception. Any degree of doubt, such as, for example, whether that is a real or a stuffed horse standing in the field, the mind strives to dispel by conducting further tests, e.g. coming closer, touching,

[1] In the ancient classification, this topic would actually come under the heading of Logic.
[2] *Kataleptike* means literally, 'susceptible of being grasped', or, 'able to grasp' (the adjective may be active or passive, and is probably deliberately ambiguous), from *katalambano*, 'I grasp firmly'. The noun *katalepsis*, 'firm grasp', is also much used by the Stoics in this connexion.

tasting, until certainty is reached. Antiochus dismissed arguments from dreams and hallucinations, as he did those from deceptive appearances (e.g. 'the oar in the water'), by denying that the mind was here operating in normal circumstances. This involves assuming that the mind in a normal waking state *is* operating 'in normal circumstances', that we are not *now* dreaming. Antiochus would have dismissed this suggestion as meaningless; *this* is the world for which our language is designed, and this is the world within which our concept of certainty operates, not the world of dreams, nor yet some other, 'higher' world.

A more serious objection is the common one that no amount of *subjective* certainty can guarantee objective truth. This is the issue that revolves round the verb 'to know'. What does 'to know something' signify more than to believe with absolute conviction that something is the case? We recognize the verb 'know', like the verb 'remember', as having the distinctive property, as distinct from 'believe' or 'imagine', of making a statement about the state of the objective world. If we 'know' something, we mean that we believe it to be the case, *and it is the case*. The Stoics expressed this feeling by saying that certain percepts strike our senses accompanied by a certain distinctive mark, a mark of 'clarity' (*enargeia*), which makes it impossible for us to disbelieve them, and *which guarantees their truth*. This is obviously a dangerous assertion to make, but it might not have provoked such controversy had its application been confined to the description of simple perceptions that do not cause the mind to hesitate, such as the observation, under normal conditions, of one's immediate surroundings; however, the Stoics really wanted this principle to guarantee the truth of certain dogmas (such as that the world is ruled by Providence), which they claimed to be as clear as the normal 'clear' perception. It was this position that the New Academy countered with able arguments, but which Antiochus finally found himself driven to accept.

We must consider Antiochus' defence of his position, as found in *Acad. Pr.* 19ff.

> Let us begin therefore from the senses, whose verdicts are so clear and certain that if human nature were given the choice, and were interrogated by some god as to whether it was content with its own senses in a sound and undamaged state or demanded something better, I cannot see what more it could ask for.

A brave flourish to begin with! Antiochus then asserts that since he is not in the position of defending *every* sense-perception, like the

Epicureans, the well-known cruxes of the Oar in the Water and so on are not relevant. He recognizes the existence of deceptive impressions, but asserts that they do not in fact deceive us; rather they provoke the mind to investigate further, until it has worked out the true situation, that is, until it has received a truly 'cognitive impression'. This is not an adequate answer to the Academic objections, but it is the best we are going to get.

He continues:

... in my judgment the senses contain the highest truth, given that they are sound and healthy and also that all obstacles and hindrances are removed. That is why we often desire a change of the light and of the position of the objects that we are observing, and diminish or enlarge their distances from us, and take various measures, until the power of sight itself makes us trust the judgment that it forms. The same is done in the case of sounds and smell and taste, so that among us there is nobody who feels the need for keener powers of judgment in the senses, each in its class.

So much for the criterion of clarity in simple perceptions. The theory becomes more controversial a little lower down (21):

But then whatever character belongs to these objects which we say are grasped by the senses must belong to that following set of objects which are said to be grasped not by actual sensation *but by a sort of sensation*, as for example: 'Yonder object is a horse, yonder a dog.' Next follows the rest of the series linking on a chain of larger percepts, for instance the following, which embrace as it were a fully completed grasp of the objects: 'If it is a human being, it is a rational mortal animal.' From this class of percept are imprinted upon us our *notions of things*, without which all understanding and all investigation and discussion are impossible. (italics mine)

Thus Antiochus leads us from simple sense-perceptions through complex ones, where the mind makes a judgment, linking its present perception to a system of past ones, finally to hypothetical *propositions*, the establishment of the validity of which is the point of the exercise.

It will be noted that the big jump which Antiochus makes is between basic sense-data and what we might term 'simple percepts', which, in Cicero's words, are perceived *non sensibus ipsis . . . sed quodam modo sensibus*, ('*quodam modo*' perhaps translating a Greek '*hoion*'). Sextus Empiricus (*AM* VII 343ff.) criticizes this move well enough:

For that which is to perceive what is true in the real objects must not only be moved by a 'white' or a 'sweet' feeling, but must be brought to have an impression (*phantasia*) regarding such an object, that 'This thing is white', and 'This thing is sweet'. . . . But to perceive an object of that kind is no longer the task of sense (*aisthēsis*).

The senses themselves cannot make judgments, Sextus claims, nor can they combine or order sense-data so as to form concepts. But this is to take a 'low' view of the senses, setting them in exclusive opposition to the intellect, and this, Platonist though he was, Antiochus refused to do. For him, the mind, that is, the Stoic 'leading part' or *hēgemonikon*, was also a sense, though of a superior nature to the other five (*Acad. Pr.* 30):

For the mind itself (*nous*), which is the source of the senses, and even itself a sense, has a natural force which it directs to the things by which it is moved. Accordingly, some sense-presentations (*phantasiai*) it seizes on so as to make use of them at once, others it as it were stores away, these being the source of Memory, while all the rest it builds into systems by reason of their mutual resemblances (Latin: *similitudinibus construit*), and from these are formed the concepts of objects which the Greeks term *ennoiai* and sometimes *prolēpseis*.[1] When thereto there has been added Reason (*logos*) and syllogistic argumentation and an innumerable multitude of facts, there comes cognitive perception (*katalēpsis*) of all these things, and thus this same Reason, having been by these stages made complete (*teleios*), finally attains to Wisdom (*sophia*).

In order to clarify Antiochus' conception of the relation between the mind and the senses, we may utilize the distinction which W. Theiler (*Die Vorbereitung des Neuplatonismus*, Part I) has given good reason for tracing back to Antiochus. Within the Criterion, then, we must distinguish (1) the 'agent' (Greek: *to hyph' hou*)—lit. 'the by which'), which is man himself, or rather his rational part; (2) the instrument (*to di' hou*, 'the through which'), which is the senses; and (3) what Sextus calls 'the onset and relationship' (*prosbolē kai schesis*), by which he means the occurrence of the *phantasia*, its impinging upon the senses. This may also be termed in Greek *to en hō*, 'the in which', or the material conditions of perception. We are concerned at this point only with the first two. The mind is the 'source of the senses', that is, it is the agent which sets them working. It has a 'force', which it directs outwards at the physical world *through the instrumentality* of the senses.

---

[1] Antiochus seems to make no distinction between these two terms, but *prolēpsis*, 'pre-conception', should signify a more basic type of concept than *ennoia*. The same equation of these terms occurs in Cicero's *Topica* 31. See on this the discussion by F. H. Sandbach, 'Ennoia and Prolepsis in the Stoic Theory of Knowledge', in A. A. Long, *Problems in Stoicism*, pp. 22ff.

From a purely Platonic standpoint (and indeed even from the standpoint taken in *Acad. Post.* 30ff., as we shall see below), there is a clear distinction between the activities of the senses and those of the mind. For a Stoic, however, and for Antiochus, the mind is not an immaterial entity (there being no such thing), and it can have no source of information except the senses. The distinction between the two is that only the mind, by employing its faculties of memory (*mnēmē*) and analogical inference (*analogistikē metabasis*) can construct concepts. Sextus' distinction between sense-data and mental constructs is not one that Antiochus would accept, as it presupposes a chasm between the senses and the mind such as he denied. Only if one admits this chasm can there be any question of fallibility as between a 'cognitive' sense-datum and any concept based upon it. The mind, then, as agent, cannot be mistaken with regard to any sensation received by it through its instrument. Only thus can the position of Antiochus and the Stoics be defended. But if any distinction at all is made between the *hēgemonikon* and its fivefold instrument, there is room for a Sceptic to drive a wedge. Antiochus actually inveighed against any theory which would eliminate the *hēgemonikon*; Sextus (*AM* VII 201), reports him as criticizing, in Book II of the *Kanonika*, the physician Asclepiades of Cos for holding 'the sensations are really and truly perceptions, and that we apprehend nothing at all by the reason'; but he would not, on the other hand, allow the *hēgemonikon* to differ generically from the other senses.

However, we are not concerned with evaluating Antiochus' philosophical position, but simply with understanding it. It is a common enough philosophical activity to try to fix what, if anything, we can be sure of, and then build a system on that. Antiochus accepts the Stoic *kataleptikē phantasia* as his basis, and on these 'cognitive impressions' he seeks to found the basic principles of his physics and ethics—largely, of course, Stoic principles. These basic principles are the 'notions' or 'preconceptions' (*ennoiai* or *prolēpseis*) referred to in the quotation above. Since these *ennoiai* or *prolēpseis* are necessarily as perspicuous as simple sense-impressions, it follows that they must be common to the whole human race, that is to say, to the general consensus of the human race, excluding the few madmen and eccentric intellectuals who inevitably arise from time to time. These notions are thus termed by the Stoics 'common notions' (*koinai ennoiai*), and their validity is based on the fact that their truth is irresistibly impressed upon the human mind, in every period of history and in every part of the world. Such a proposition would be the thesis 'that gods exist'. The Stoics, particularly Chrysippus, consulted historical records, and gathered all available information about distant peoples, and established that there was no record of a nation or group of people (untainted, that is, by philosophical aberrations) that did not, for instance, believe in gods of some sort. The fact that such people as Diagoras of Melos ('the Atheist') or Theodorus of Cyrene[1] should have existed does not affect the validity of the principle, though if a whole tribe were to be discovered which had no notion of the existence of gods the principle would be in serious jeopardy, and if on examination no corrupting philosophical influence could be uncovered, this particular principle would presumably collapse.

This, then, is Antiochus' Theory of Knowledge, taken over wholesale from the Stoics—although some of his *ennoiai*, as we shall see, differed significantly from theirs. This might have been thought to throw some doubt on the whole theory (such disagreements, indeed, provided one of the chief weapons in the arsenal of the Sceptics), but it does not seem to have bothered Antiochus. As he implies in his accounts of Zeno,[2] Zeno started from correct notions, but simply did not read the signs correctly. Antiochus is putting him back on the right path, in accord with the precepts of Nature herself.

Although confident of the agreement of Nature, Antiochus seems to have had some difficulty in reconciling his principles with the teaching of the Old Academy, as we see from Varro's speech in the *Academica Posteriora*. There we have an exposition of the teaching of Antiochus under the guise of 'the ancients', followed by an account of the innovations introduced by Zeno. However, in the matter of the Theory of Knowledge, Antiochus gives a rather blurred account of the doctrine of Plato (30–2), which does not accord with the doctrine of the *Academica Priora*, and later (40–2) Zeno's 'innovation', which accords with it exactly.[3]

2. ETHICS

(a) *The basic principle*

Antiochus himself seems to have been primarily interested, as indeed does Polemon before him (see above p. 40), in the ethical branch of

---

[1] cf. Cic. *De Nat. Deor.* I 2 and 63.   [2] e.g. *Acad. Post.* 35ff., *Fin.* IV 14ff.
[3] On this see below, p. 83.

philosophy. It has been necessary, however, to discuss first the criterion of certainty, since Antiochus employs this dogma in the establishment of all his other principles. Before dealing with the Supreme Good, or 'End of Goods', however, we must record a basic principle of Antiochus' ethics—the doctrine of *oikeiôsis* or 'self-conciliation'. This is expounded most fully in Cicero's *De Finibus* Book V, 24ff. The principle is as follows:

Every living creature loves itself, and from the moment of birth strives to secure its own preservation; because the earliest impulse bestowed on it by nature for its life-long protection is the instinct for self-preservation and for the maintenance of itself in the best conditions possible to it in accordance with its nature. (My italics)

In this, its most general form, the principle embraces all living things—even plants (*ibid.* 33)—but is not clearly articulated, being simply an instinctive striving (*prôtê hormê*). In man, however, this 'earliest impulse' naturally develops into a conscious striving towards those things which are in accordance with his nature. Unfortunately, however, Nature, having provided the initial impulse, is not capable of carrying man's desire for self-preservation unerringly to a correct conclusion. If it did, there would be no problem of evil in the world, or at any rate of evil caused by man to man. For the understanding and attainment of the supreme good, or final purpose of life (*telos*) man requires the aid of Philosophy—Antiochus would specify, Platonic Philosophy. It is this which reveals to him the Supreme Good.[1]

(b) The 'End of Goods', or Supreme Good

The definition of the Supreme Good, or End of Goods, was a favourite preoccupation of Hellenistic philosophy, and it was, as I have said, a matter of vital interest to Antiochus. It was also his main point of controversy with the Stoics.

On the basic principle quoted above, Antiochus was in complete agreement with Zeno, or as he would put it, Zeno was in perfect agreement with Polemon and the 'ancients'. It was only in the later conclusions that he came to that Zeno went astray. Zeno declared that the supreme good resided in virtue alone, which was a condition of the intellect, and that no bodily or external attribute, such as health,

---

[1] For an exposition by Cicero of the relation between the first natural strivings, the 'sparks' (*igniculi*) of Virtue, and its completion through Philosophy, cf. his preface to Book III of the *Tusculan Disputations*.

beauty, or wealth, could be considered part of the supreme good, or, therefore, to be good at all. Antiochus objects. Man is composed of both body and soul, and he is situated in the external world. Polemon intended his basic principle to apply to man in his entirety, not to some imaginary disembodied entity. 'Chrysippus', says Antiochus, 'so classified Man as to make the mind the principal part of him; and yet he so defined man's End as to make it appear, not that he is principally mind, but that he consists of nothing else!' (*Fin.* v 28).

In this connexion the testimony of Varro is of great importance (*ap.* Aug. *Civ. Dei* xix 3). In his *De Philosophia* Varro is, on his own assertion (*ibid. ad fin.*) relaying the opinions of Antiochus:

Since Philosophy seeks the supreme good not of a tree, nor of a beast, nor of God, but of man, we must put the question what man himself is. In man's nature there are two things, body and soul; and of these two certainly the soul is the better and by far the more excellent. But is the soul alone the man, and is the body to him as the horse to the horseman? For the horseman is not a man and a horse, but is only a man, because he bears a certain relation in respect to a horse. Or is the body alone the man, bearing some relation to the soul, like that of a cup to the drink? For it is not the cup and the drink that it contains which are together called the cup, but the cup alone; yet it is so called because it is designed to hold the drink. Or again is it neither the soul alone nor the body alone but both together that constitute the man, of whom the body and soul are each a part, while the whole man consists of both, as we call two horses yoked together a pair, though we do not call either the near or the off horse, however related to the other, a pair, but only call both together a pair?

Varro naturally chooses the third possibility, and concludes therefore that the *summum bonum* must comprise both the *prima naturae* and virtue, 'which instruction implants in us as an art of living' (cf. *Fin.* v 16). Virtue does not supplant the primary wants of nature, but takes them over and seeks to fulfil them in accordance with herself:

Here, then, is the sort of human life that is termed happy, a life that enjoys (*fruitur*) virtue and the other goods of soul and body *without which virtue cannot exist*; a life is called happier, if it enjoys one or more of the goods that virtue can lack and still exist; and *happiest*, if it enjoys absolutely all goods, so that it lacks not one of the goods either of soul or of body.

Virtue must certainly be assigned the dominant position in the definition of the supreme good, but it seemed to Antiochus illogical to deny the contribution of bodily or external goods—especially since

Zeno (and all the Stoics, except the extremist Ariston) in fact recognized a scale of 'things preferred' and 'things rejected' within the genus of things classed as 'indifferent' (*adiaphora*). If you want to be a Cynic, says Antiochus, well and good, but if in fact you prefer comfort to misery, health to sickness, peace to war, and so on, then let us admit the fact without resorting to new classifications and coinages.[1]

This is rather the voice of robust common sense, however, than the voice of strict philosophical analysis. The Stoics had their arguments, and Antiochus must resort to mockery to counter them. 'I think sometimes that the Stoics must be joking when they say that, as between a life of virtue and a life of virtue plus an oil-flask and scraper, the Wise Man will prefer the life with those additions, but yet will not be any happier because of them' (*ibid.* 30).

Antiochus' main line of argument against the Stoics, however, was an appeal to the Ancients, to what Polemon *meant*. From the Ancients Antiochus conceived that he had inherited the following theory of human development: Nature provides the 'primary natural objects of desire' (*ta prôta kata physin*) and the 'seeds' or 'sparks' of the virtues; Reason (*logos*) enables man to develop these beginnings into a coherent philosophy of life.

And this is the fountain-head from which one's whole theory of Goods and Evils must necessarily flow. Polemon, and also before him Aristotle, held that the primary objects were the ones I have just mentioned [i.e. good health, sound mind, comfortable surroundings]. Thus arose the doctrine of the Old Academy and of the Peripatetics, maintaining that the End of Goods (*telos agathôn*) is *to live in accordance with Nature*, that is, to enjoy the primary gifts of Nature's bestowal with the accompaniment of virtue. (*Fin.* II 34)

The phrase which I have italicized is, of course, the basic Stoic definition (Zeno as extended by Cleanthes), but into this Antiochus slips certain non-Stoic qualifications. 'To enjoy the primary gifts of Nature's bestowal' (*frui primis a natura datis*, in Cicero's Latin) is here a phrase to note carefully, as it is used to make a bridge between Stoic and Peripatetic ethics. Certain notions, after all, 'life according to Nature' and 'perfection' (*teleiotês*) could be traced back securely to the Old Academy. We have in Clement of Alexandria (*Strom.* 2, 133) Speusippus' definition of Happiness (*eudaimonia*): 'a state of perfection in respect of things according to Nature, or, the settled possession of

[1] cf. Cicero, *De Legibus* I 55.

Goods, a state for which all men have a striving'. The latter part of this definition is a little muddled as it comes down to us, but the main definition, if only we can trust Clement's accuracy, is very useful. Another definition of the *telos*, given at *Fin.* v 26–7, is even more explicit in making the connexion with Aristotelian ethics:

This leads to the inference that the ultimate Good of man is life in accordance with Nature, which we may interpret as meaning life in accordance with human nature, *developed to its full perfection and supplied with all its needs.*

(The italics are mine.) 'Perfection' here must, I think, be taken in the Aristotelian sense of the 'perfect mean', as defined by Aristotle at *Met.* v, 16, 1021b12ff., or *Eth. Nic.* II 5, 1106b8ff. In Cicero's Latin, '*undique perfecta*' lays stress on Antiochus' view that bodily as well as psychic advantages must be included in the *telos*.

But what of the famous Stoic claim that, since the happiness produced by wisdom is not a quality that can be lost, or affected by external accidents at all, the Wise Man will remain perfectly happy even, for example, in the Bull of Phalaris? Against this Antiochus produces the remarkable formulation which we have seen above in the quotation from Varro's *De Philosophia*, again much more a product of robust common sense than of strict philosophical analysis. He makes a distinction between the Happy Life and the Happiest Life, or the Perfectly Happy Life (*bios eudaimōn* and *bios eudaimonestatos*). He was entirely willing to concede the overwhelming superiority of the goods of the soul, or Virtue, to the goods of the body, but he made the distinction that, if these goods of the body (including external goods) were absent (as they would be to a superlative degree in the infamous Bull, but also to a lesser extent in the case of a Stoic philosopher with a toothache), then the life of the Wise Man, though still 'happy', would not by Antiochus be accounted supremely happy:

The things we reckon as bodily goods do, it is true, form a factor in supreme happiness, but yet happiness is possible without them. For those supplementary goods are so small and slight that in the full radiance of the virtues they are as invisible as the stars in sunlight. (*Fin.* v 71, cf. *Tusc. Disp.* v 22)

But, asserts Antiochus, the stars are none the less there. The most concise and comprehensive statement of his views comes in *Acad. Post.* 22–3 (he has just distinguished the three kinds of goods):

And this corresponds with the three classes of goods which most people think to be intended by the Peripatetics. This is indeed correct, for this classification is theirs, but it is a mistake if people suppose that the Academics quoted above and the Peripatetics were different schools. This theory was common to both, and both held that the End of Goods was to acquire *either all or the greatest* of the things which are by nature primary,[1] and are intrinsically worthy of desire; and the greatest of these are the ones which have their being in the mind itself and in virtue itself. Accordingly the whole of the great philosophy of antiquity held that happiness lies in virtue alone, yet that *happiness is not supreme* without the addition of the goods of the body and all the other goods *suitable for the employment of virtue* that were specified above. (cf. also Varro, in *CD* xix 3 quoted above.) (My italics.)

The first and last of the phrases italicized above contain matter which requires comment. The doctrine of the 'things primary by nature' (*ta prôta kata physin*), mentioned above, is a key concept in Antiochus' attempt at synthesis. It seems to have been in fact Carneades who first put forward 'the enjoyment of the things primary by nature' as the *telos*, even if he did it not dogmatically but merely for the sake of argument (*Fin.* v 20). These may be defined as 'the earliest objects which nature prompts a new-born animal to seek', and thus can be seen to include goods of all categories, particularly, at first, bodily and external. The Stoics, of course, accepted this concept, but held that these 'first things' were only the basis laid down by Nature for the human being by which he should ascend to a comprehension of Virtue, which for an adult then becomes the *telos*. Antiochus agreed, but with the proviso that Nature does not intend the lower 'first things' to be then rejected. Against this background, the 'greatest' (*megista*) things, as Antiochus specifies, are the Goods of the Intellect, but a life adorned with these *alone* can only be 'happy', not supremely happy.

In this connexion Antiochus is reported, at *TD* v 22, as using an argument which was popular in later Platonism: 'Most things get their name from that which forms, even if a fraction be missing, the greater part of them, such things for instance as strength, health, riches or honour, which are reckoned broadly rather than with mathematical accuracy (*genere non numero*); in the same way, the Happy Life, even though it should in some respect be deficient, yet gets its name from that which forms the greater part of it.' The distinction between 'all' and 'most' is thus deprived of much significance.

In all this, Antiochus is behaving rather more like an arbitrator in an industrial dispute than a true philosopher. It is almost as if he had

---

[1] This formula also occurs at *Fin.* iv 15, where it is attributed explicitly to Xenocrates and Aristotle.

taken seriously the exhortation jokingly made by L. Gellius Poplicola in 69 B.C. during his proconsulship in Athens, when 'he called together the philosophers of the time and urgently advised them to come at length to some settlement of their controversies' (Cic. *De Leg.* I 53). Antiochus' formula is eminently sensible, but it can have satisfied no serious Stoic.

The second phrase worthy of note concerns the notion of 'use' or 'employment' (*chrêsis*) of the virtues. Antiochus, as one might expect of a man who had urged Cicero to return to public affairs, favoured the so-called 'mixed life', a blend of the contemplative life (*bios theorêtikos*) and the practical life (*bios praktikos*) (Aug. *CD* XIX 3). Admittedly, Aristotle distinguished the two, giving the supreme place to the former, but he also stressed that virtue could only exhibit itself in action, that it was a way of *acting*. For Antiochus, then, everything is activity (*praxis*), even what would be normally regarded as *theôria*, such as the contemplation of the heavens:

It is therefore at all events manifest that we are designed by Nature for activity. Activities vary in kind, so much so that the more important actually eclipse the less; but the most important are, first, the contemplation and the study of the heavenly bodies and of those secrets and mysteries of nature which reason has the capacity to penetrate; secondly, the *practice and theory* of politics; thirdly, the principles of Prudence, Temperance, Courage and Justice, with the remaining virtues and the activities consonant therewith, all of which we may sum up under the single term of morality; towards the *knowledge and practice* of which, when we have grown to maturity, we are led onward by Nature's own guidance. (*Fin.* V 58)

Here Physics, Politics and Ethics are mentioned, in that order, with a subtle blend of *praxis* and *theôria* woven throughout. The phrases italicized above, '*administratio aut administrandi scientia*' and '*cognitionem et usum*' in Cicero's Latin, seem deliberately to combine the two traditional sides of human activity. Cicero himself, indeed, might be considered a type of the Antiochian Wise Man, though the tension between the life of action and the life of contemplation in his case, to which he bears frequent testimony, would cause him to fall short of the ideal.

(c) *The virtues*

Antiochus frequently mentions, as in the last passage quoted, the four basic virtues adopted by Plato and Aristotle, Prudence (*phronêsis*),

Temperance (*sôphrosynê*), Courage (*andreia*), and Justice (*dikaiosynê*), though he also hints at more (e.g. 'the remaining virtues', mentioned above). Under the general head of Justice at *Fin.* v 65 are listed 'family loyalty, kindness, liberality, goodwill, courtesy and other graces of the same kind'. He also frequently talks of Virtue (*aretê*) in the singular, as the sum total of these four (e.g. *Fin.* IV 37).

To this Platonic-Peripatetic base, however, Antiochus added some distinctively Stoic formulations. First, there is the question of the mutual entailment (*antakolouthia*) or indivisibility of the virtues. The Stoics held that one could not possess one virtue without possessing them all. From this it would follow that Courage, for instance, present in a man unaccompanied by say, Moderation, was not the true virtue of that name, but a bestial imitation, and the same would hold in the case of each virtue. Such a view is attributed already to Xenocrates (Heinze, p. 23), and indeed adumbrated by Plato in the *Gorgias* (507C), but the Stoics seem to have been the first to state the doctrine formally. That Antiochus held this is shown by his words in *Fin.* v 65–6, where he is discussing Justice. After a list of minor virtues mentioned above, Antiochus adds: 'And while these belong peculiarly to Justice, they are also common to the other virtues.' In 66 he speaks of 'this general union and combination of the virtues', a reference to the doctrine of *antakolouthia*.

In the Stoic manner, again (cf. *SVF* I 200–1), Antiochus apportions spheres of activity among the four chief virtues (*Fin.* v 67). Courage is virtue 'in labours and dangers' (the Stoic *en hypomeneteois*); Temperance is virtue 'in the forgoing of pleasures' (this represents indirectly the Stoic *en energeteois*); Prudence is virtue 'in the choice of goods and evils' (*en haireteois*); Justice is virtue 'in giving to each his due' (*en aponemeteois*). We see here both the doctrine of the unity of Virtue, and the dominant influence of Stoic formulations.

In the case of Prudence, we can observe some vacillation in Cicero's versions between *prudentia* (*phronêsis*) and *sapientia* (*sophia*), but we cannot be sure on the evidence whether Antiochus made any distinction between these terms, i.e. between *practical* and *theoretical* wisdom. *Scientia* or *cognitio* (*epistêmê*), too, is highly praised at *Fin.* v 48–9, in the sense of 'the desire to know', but it is not specifically denominated a virtue, as it had been, for instance, by the Stoic heretic Herillus, who saw it as the only virtue.

In the realm of Ethics generally, Antiochus seems to have adopted some of the Stoic 'paradoxes', while he rejected others. If we may accept the hostile evidence of Cicero at *Acad. Pr.* 136f., it seems that he supported the Stoic position that only the *sophos* (the Stoic sage) is a king, is wealthy, is handsome, is free, and so on. One is the more ready to believe that he did from the fact that we have from the pen of Philo of Alexandria a very Stoic tract on this topic, *That Every Good Man is Free*, which indicates that this was by his time a proper position for a Platonist to take. Again, he agreed that the Sage never holds an opinion (*ouden doxazein*), that is, that anything he knows, he knows with certainty (*Acad. Pr.* 113). On the other hand, he rejected strongly the Stoic doctrine that all sins are equal (*ibid.* 133), here exhibiting that streak of realism which we have observed before.

I mention these rather minor points simply to show how the remarkable amalgam of Stoicism and Platonism in Antiochus' doctrine goes down to the smallest details.

(d) The passions

There were, in Stoic theory, four passions (*pathê*): Desire (*epithymia*), Fear (*phobos*), Pleasure (*hêdonê*), and Distress (*lypê*). These are contrary to Nature, being irrational motions of the soul, based on false opinions (*doxai*), and the Sage should have nothing to do with them.

On this topic, we may begin with yet another Stoic axiom adopted by Antiochus (*Acad. Pr.* 135), 'that the Sage is never moved by desire nor elated by pleasure'. Here Cicero convicts him triumphantly both of inconsistency with himself and of deserting the Platonists:

I want to know when the Old Academy adopted 'dogmas' of that sort. . . . That school were upholders of the mean in things, and held that in all emotion there was a certain measure that was natural. . . . How indeed that ferocity of yours forced an entrance into the Old Academy I do not know. . . . Where did Xenocrates hint at those views, or Aristotle (for you maintain that Xenocrates and Aristotle are almost identical)?

Antiochus, then, accepted the Stoic ideal of *apatheia* (freedom from passion) as opposed to the Academic-Peripatetic *metriopatheia* (moderation in the passions). It is not impossible, however, that Antiochus took the Stoic term and gave it a meaning consonant with Peripateticism. After all, he could argue, a passion is defined as an 'immoderate impulse' (*hormê pleonazousa*); if an impulse is under the control of moderation, it is not *pleonazousa*, and therefore not a passion 'within the meaning of the Act'. There were, after all, in Stoic theory, so-called 'equable states' (*eupatheiai*) corresponding to all of the *pathê* (except Distress, of which there could be no reasonable form), and it would not have been beyond the wit of Antiochus to equate these with the Peripatetic 'means'. The difference, he might well say, is more verbal than real.

In general, however, Antiochus in his Ethics stayed closer to the Stoics than to the Old Academy and Peripatos, although his doctrine constitutes a real, if precariously balanced, compromise, which, naturally, attracted the wrath of both schools equally.

(e) Political principles

(i) The ideal state. The basic principle of Antiochus' Ethics, as we have seen above (p. 70), is the so-called Doctrine of *Oikeiôsis*, that 'every living creature loves itself, and from the moment of birth strives to secure its own preservation'. The ultimate origin of this principle is not clear, as we have seen in discussing Polemon in Chapter One; it may go back no further than Zeno, if that far—perhaps no further in its full form than Diogenes of Seleucia; Antiochus, of course, would claim it for the Old Academy, and he may have known what he was talking about. Since we are not in command of the collected works of Xenocrates, Theophrastus or Polemon, as I have said before, we are not in a strong position to pass judgment, and it is of small importance for our present purpose. What is important is that this basic principle can be used equally well to found a theory of politics.

Antiochus' theory of politics and natural law did not differ from that of contemporary Stoicism. Later Stoicism had retreated from the stance of political quietism which the Cynic-influenced doctrine of 'world-citizenship' (the *kosmopolitês*) involved, in favour of a defence of national patriotism. To be at all acceptable to the Roman aristocracy, after all, Stoicism had to find a place for loyalty to the nation state and for the duty of public service, and Panaetius certainly supplied this. It could in fact be done without much effort, and without abandoning the great overall vision of the 'cosmopolis', by tracing a hierarchy of loyalties upwards and outwards from the individual's basic sympathy with himself (*oikeiôsis*), through family loyalties, friendships, and then national patriotism, to the sympathy of all human beings with one another. The best passage in this connexion is Varro *ap.* Aug. *CD* XIX 3:

The happy life is also social, and loves the good of friends itself for its own sake as being its own good, and wishes for them for their own sakes what it wishes for itself, whether by friends we mean those who are in one's house, such as wife or children and other members of the household, or neighbours with houses in the same locality, such as fellow-citizens of a city, or men anywhere in the whole world, such as nations with whom we are joined through the fellowship of men (*societas humana*), or inhabitants even of the universe, which is designated by the term heaven and earth, that is, the gods and daemons.

We may note here both the absolute assertion of the possibility of friendship for its own sake, strongly maintained by Cicero in the *De Amicitia*, and as a result of this passage shown to be Antiochian, and the lack of any recognition of a transcendent god. Antiochus' universe is essentially a Stoic one. The assertion of fellowship between men, daemons and gods here shows that such doctrines cannot be claimed exclusively for Posidonius. They find expression, indeed, in the Ninth Platonic Letter (358A), which is, however, of uncertain authenticity.

There is no evidence that Antiochus took any active interest in Plato's type of utopia-building, but it is very probable that he had a theory of politics. The doctrine that man is a social animal he necessarily accepted (*Fin.* v 65); it was plainly the doctrine of 'the ancients', laid down explicitly by none other than Aristotle. The institutions of the family and the State are thus in accordance with the workings of Nature. As regards details of political organization, we cannot be sure of his views, since we cannot claim that Cicero's *De Re Publica* owes anything to Antiochus' teaching. Indeed the doctrine therein enunciated by Scipio is more or less explicitly referred to Panaetius and Polybius (*Rep.* 1 34). On the other hand, the fact that a doctrine is proposed by Panaetius certainly does not exclude the possibility of its being adopted by Antiochus.

The type of state favoured by Scipio in the *De Republica* is the Mixed Constitution, seen and celebrated by Polybius in Book VI of the *Histories* as being best exemplified in the Roman State. Apart from this, however, Scipio confesses a preference for a monarchical regime, if only a perfect Wise Man could be found to run it. This thoroughly dangerous speculation may have been entertained by Panaetius, but it may also have been championed by Antiochus. The doctrine of the Wise Man as King, after all, is respectable Stoic, as well as Platonic, teaching. It is also not incompatible with a preference for the Mixed Constitution; indeed Cicero in the 50s does seem to have hankered after a combination of his *concordia ordinum* with the presence of some *rector*, some *pater patriae*, to exercise an overall guiding influence such as Scipio is made to talk about in Book I of the dialogue, this *rector* being Pompey, or, in his wilder moments, himself. But, as I say, what Antiochus' position was on all this, it is impossible for us to discern. We may take it as unlikely, however, that he was a democrat.

(*ii*) *The natural law.* On the other hand, it is very likely that the discussion of the Natural Law in Cicero *De Legibus* I is basically Antiochian. It contains the characteristic mark of Antiochus' presence, a survey of the doctrines of the Old Academy and of Zeno's agreement with it (an extended passage beginning at I 38), and the doctrine is precisely what we should expect Antiochus to hold. Reverence is continually paid to Plato, but the hands, so to speak, are the hands of Zeno.

It is worth while, I think, to dwell briefly on this exposition of the Natural Law, since, througn Cicero, it has had a considerable influence on European thought. Of course, the doctrine is not original to Antiochus either, but he may be given credit, I think, for passing it on to Cicero. The principles laid down are as follows:

(1) The whole universe is governed by the Providence of God (I 22). This providence is the activity of his Reason, his *Logos*, which is expressed in the world as the Law of Nature.

(2) Man is the only creature in the world which has been endowed by God with Reason, and this is a bond between God and Man:

Therefore, since there is nothing better than Reason, and since it exists in both Man and God, the primary common possession of Man and God is Reason. But those who have reason in common must also have right reason (*orthos logos*) in common. And since right reason is Law (*nomos*), we must believe that men have Law also in common with the gods. Further, those who share Law must also share Justice; and those who share these are to be regarded as members of the same commonwealth. (I 23)

The Natural Law, then, not only binds man to man, but man to God.

(3) The definition of Natural Law is as follows. It is simply the Stoic definition (cf. Chrysippus, *SVF* III 314):

Law is the highest reason, implanted in Nature, which commands what ought to be done and forbids the opposite. This reason, when firmly fixed and fully developed in the human mind, is Law.

This 'highest reason' is simply the Logos working in nature; but there is the necessary implication that the Logos is a moral force, at least in its subjective aspect, in the minds of men. It commands patriotism, for instance, and forbids rape (*Leg.* II 10).

The confusion with laws of physics, which is the basic flaw in the theory of natural law, comes out clearly in another passage, where this rule of Law is said to be based on the essential similarity of all men with one another:

This fact will immediately become plain, if you once get a clear conception of man's fellowship and union with his fellow men. For no single thing is so like another, so exactly its counterpart, as all of us are to one another. Indeed, if bad habits and false beliefs did not twist the weaker minds and turn them in whatever direction they are inclined,[1] no one would be so like his own self as all men would be like all others. (1 29)

So then—the laws of nature would be like laws of physics, that is, invariable patterns of behaviour, if all men were uncorrupted or, rather, unconscious creatures of habit. But alas, they are not, and so the Natural Law survives only as a pricking of the consciences of the best members of the human race, which tells them what they and all others must do.

As has been said before, none of this is original to Antiochus, and indeed the influence behind *De Legibus* I has been much disputed, as between Panaetius, Posidonius and Antiochus. But what the champions of the various views do not seem to recognize is that the theories of these three men on this question are almost bound to be identical. All that is distinctively Antiochian is the strenuous desire to trace this doctrine back to the Old Academy, although admittedly neither of the other two would be concerned to deny the connexion.

3. PHYSICS

(a) *The composition of the world*

Antiochus does not seem to have been much interested in physical speculations, though this may only seem so to us because these questions did not happen to interest Cicero. However, 'Varro', in *Acad. Post.* 26ff., does set out succinctly the physical system which Antiochus accepted. It was, not surprisingly, a blend of Platonic and Stoic

---

[1] This is the Stoic doctrine of *katēchēsis*, which for Zeno meant the corruption of the young human being through evil influences. It owes something, probably, to Plato's description in the *Timaeus* of the confusion that assails the human soul at birth.

doctrine, and it is important as being the first extant development of what will henceforth become Middle Platonic physical theory.

Varro begins with a division of 'qualities' (*poiotêtes*) into primary and secondary. The primary qualities are simple, and are the traditional four elements, Fire, Air, Water and Earth; the first two of these are active elements, the latter two passive. Antiochus is uncomfortable about Aristotle's 'fifth essence'; he does not condemn it, nor yet does he adopt it. He preferred, as the substance of the stars and of minds, the Stoic Pure Fire. In *Fin.* iv 12 he speaks of this as a 'very difficult question'.

As a substratum for these elements, there is Matter (*hylê*). Antiochus' account of Matter is based on Plato's account in the *Timaeus*, but I feel that it is worth repeating in detail, simply because of its importance in connexion with later Middle Platonic formulations (*Acad. Post.* 27ff.):

> But they [the Platonists] hold that underlying all things is a substance called 'Matter', entirely formless and devoid of all quality, and that out of it all things have been formed and produced, so that this Matter can in its totality receive all things and undergo every sort of transformation throughout every part of it, and in fact even suffer dissolution, not into nothingness but into its own parts, which are capable of infinite section and division, since there exists nothing whatever in the nature of things that is an absolute least, incapable of division.

In other words, no atoms. Note also that the fact that Plato himself does not use the term *hylê* in the *Timaeus* is ignored by Antiochus, as it was by all subsequent Platonists. He goes on, about Space, the Universe, and the Logos, or Soul of the World:

> all things that are in motion move by means of interspaces (*diakena*), these likewise being infinitely divisible.

Antiochus uses the Stoic term *poiotês* to describe the Platonic Forms or Ideas in their descent into Matter:

> And since the force that we have called 'quality' moves in this manner and since it thus vibrates to and fro, they think that the whole of Matter also is itself in a state of complete change throughout, and is made into the things which they term 'qualified' (*poia*), out of which in the concrete whole of substance, a continuum united with all its parts, has been produced one world, outside of which there is no portion of Matter and no body, while all the things that are in the world are parts of it, held together by a sentient being, in which perfect Reason is immanent, and which is immutable and

eternal since nothing stronger exists to cause it to perish; and this force they say is the Soul of the World, and is also perfect intelligence (*nous teleios*), and wisdom, which they entitled God, and is a sort of 'Providence' (*pronoia*), knowing the things that fall within its province, governing especially the heavenly bodies, and then those things on earth that concern mankind.

This is still an exposition of the *Timaeus*, but with a number of Stoic concepts introduced, to wit, *poia* for material things, and the Logos equated with the World Soul. There is no mention here, we may note, of *ekpyrôsis*, the Stoic theory of periodic destruction of the world by fire; the world here is eternal and indestructible, as there is nothing outside it which can affect it. This is interesting, since the theory of periodic conflagration received support from the myth of Plato's *Politicus*, and was adopted by a number of later Platonists.

There are a number of curious aspects of this text, however, that require discussion. First, Plato's Demiurge and World Soul have here been merged, and become one positive force immanent in the world, the Logos. Secondly, the passage begins with the mention of '*illa vis quam qualitatem esse diximus*'. Now nowhere in Cicero's text has there been any mention of a singular *qualitas*; what we have just had mentioned were the four basic elements and their derivatives, and these were termed *qualitates* (*poiotêtes*). What we have here suddenly is the Stoic concept of *to poioun*, the active creative principle in the Universe, which can be equated with the elements Fire and Air, but which is properly the *logos* again, in its role of organizer of Matter. Something has been slipped over on us, either by Antiochus himself, or by Cicero's inaccuracy.

The last and most awkward question concerns immateriality. There is no mention in this text of either this 'quality', or the World Soul being immaterial, and our suspicion must be that Antiochus in fact agreed with Zeno's well-known position (one of Zeno's chief quarrels with the Platonists), that nothing incorporeal was capable of acting or being acted upon (*Acad. Post.* 39). This principle is mentioned in the passage just quoted as a point on which Zeno disagreed with Xenocrates specifically, not with Platonists in general (he could, after all, appeal to *Sophist* 248c if he cared to), and there is no indication that Antiochus disagrees with Zeno. A passage of *De Finibus* IV is very interesting in the connexion. Antiochus is criticizing those (the Stoics) who behave as if man was nothing but mind:

while others on the contrary ignore everything but mind, just as if man had no body; and that though even the mind is not an empty, impalpable something (a conception to me unintelligible), *but belongs to a certain kind of material substance* . . . (IV 36)

An extraordinary remark for a Platonist to make, surely. Talk of immaterial substance is to Antiochus 'unintelligible'. How he managed to ignore Plato's doctrine on immaterial substance is mysterious. He seems to make it a particular aberration of Xenocrates. For Antiochus, the most subtle substance, that from which souls and stars and even God was made up, was the Stoic Fire in its most refined form, the true home of which was in the highest, or furthest, reaches of the Universe. This must be borne in mind when considering his views on immortality, or the soul in general, as well as his views on the gods. There is no possibility for Antiochus of anything immaterial, transcendent or external to the material universe. Since transcendence and immateriality were unquestioned doctrines of Middle Platonists at a later stage, however, it is plain from this that Antiochus cannot be regarded as the sole father of the movement. But this is a matter to be raised in more detail later.

(b) Fate and free will

The basic text continues with a brief reference to Fate. Here again the point of view seems entirely Stoic, and this gives rise to a problem:

This force (*sc.* the action of the *logos*) they also sometimes call Necessity, because nothing can happen otherwise than has been ordained by it under a 'fated and unchangeable concatenation of everlasting order'; although they sometimes also term it Fortune (*tyché*), because many of its operations are unforeseen and unexpected by us on account of their obscurity and our ignorance of causes.

This is a straight exposition of Chrysippus' views on Fate. The definition given is Stoic (cf. *SVF* II 912ff.), and the explanation of the illusion of chance (and of free will) is Chrysippan. Free will is a purely subjective phenomenon; we feel free, and appear to ourselves to make decisions, because we do not possess full knowledge of the whole chain of causes—we do not have a God's eye view of the world. Things seem to us to happen by chance for the same reason. These words, therefore, 'free will' and 'chance', have meaning for us, but there is no objective reality underlying them.

Platonists and Aristotelians found Chrysippus' arguments very difficult to deal with. The treatise of the Peripatetic Alexander of Aphrodisias *On Fate* is a good example of the kind of arguments to which they had to resort. The problem was that neither Plato nor

Aristotle had dealt thoroughly with the problem of Fate and Free Will,
since it was not recognized as a problem—in its acute form—before
the Stoics. All the elements were there, but strangely the dilemma had
never been presented in its full starkness. It had been more of a subject
for the tragic poets to brood on. Aristotle in the *Ethics* and in the
Physics[1] defines in his characteristic manner all the terms involved,
but robustly refuses to recognize that there is any problem.

Antiochus here seems 'to budge not a step from Chrysippus' (cf.
Acad. Pr. 143), but this is a very summary account. There remains to
be discussed the problem of the sources behind Cicero's *De Fato*, a
text of which only a section has come down to us, but which provides
none the less a coherent theory of Fate and Free Will.

In this work the Stoic position is certainly attacked, but the question
requiring examination is from precisely what angle this is done. In the
first surviving section of the body of the work (sect. 3), some examples
of remarkable prophecies quoted by Posidonius are being refuted;
then, in sect. 4, we turn to Chrysippus. What is chiefly being discussed
and criticized is Chrysippus' theory of the truth of statements about
the future, and his difficulties on this point with the strict position of
Diodorus Cronus, that future statements, if true at all, are *necessarily*
true. Chrysippus wished to preserve the concept of possibility (*to
dynaton*), which for him covers actions which will certainly happen one
way or the other, but which *could* still, from the perspective of our
limited knowledge, happen otherwise; and this seemed to him to be
the position with future actions. He wished to alter the form of statements about the future from hypothetical statements to negations of
conjunctions (p. 2), and some fun is had at his expense on this account.
The arguments against Chrysippus here seem to be taken directly
from Carneades, who is mentioned repeatedly, but the most significant
part of the work, I feel, is the penultimate section (19), where, after
Chrysippus' place in the history of the controversy about Fate has
been analysed (17–18), it is asserted that the difference between
Chrysippus' position and that of the author 'is a matter of terminology,
rather than substance (*verbis . . . non re dissidere*)'. This seems to me a
position much more appropriate to Antiochus than to Carneades
himself.

The positive doctrine advanced in the *De Fato* is as follows, and it
is a significant development on the voluntarism of Carneades. We
agree that 'nothing happens without a cause', as Chrysippus maintains.

---

[1] *Eth. Nic.* III 1–6; *Phys.* B 4–9.

But one must distinguish between external and internal causes (18). By an internal cause is meant an impulse arising within the subject himself, as opposed to an influence or push arising from some outside force. The object of this argument is to establish that the human soul is capable of originating its own impulses, that it is itself an autonomous cause of action. This is not perhaps an unassailable line of argument, but is of importance as being that which all later Platonists were going to follow. Chrysippus himself made the distinction between 'perfect and principal causes' and 'auxiliary and proximate' ones. A perfect and principal cause is one which, in our terminology, is necessary and sufficient for action, whereas the auxiliary and proximate cause is necessary but not sufficient. An example which Chrysippus used was that of the cylinder being rolled down a slope. To start rolling it needs an initial push; that is the auxiliary and proximate cause. To keep rolling, however, or indeed to roll at all, it is indebted to its own 'volubility'. This is the perfect and principal cause of its rolling; without its 'volubility'—if it were square, for example—the push would not suffice to set it rolling. Let us take now the instance of assent to perceptions. If the perception did not take place, there could certainly be no action on the basis of it, but on the other hand, without the decision of the human mind to assent, or perhaps its general inclination to do this, the perception alone would not result in action. And that is all that is meant by free will, simply that our assent does not follow necessarily on our perceptions, that we are not automatons.

The author behind the *De Fato*, as I have said, wishes to show that the dispute between Chrysippus and those who are unwilling to accept that 'nothing happens without an antecedent cause' because they hold that the human will is autonomous, is simply a question of terminology. One must simply define more accurately the concept of 'antecedent cause'. These opponents of Chrysippus are certainly the New Academy, and Carneades himself in particular, but it was by no means the desire of Carneades to show that there was no substantive quarrel between himself and Chrysippus. This significant passage, together with the criticism of Posidonius back in sect. 3, seems to me to point strongly to Antiochus as the authority behind this work. The possibility that Cicero himself, at this stage of his grand literary design (spring 44 B.C.), had either the time or the inclination to compose original works of philosophy, as opposed to adapting suitable sources, is surely very remote.[1]

[1] My conclusions here follow the analysis of Albert Yon, in the introduction to his Budé edition of the *De Fato* (pp. xl–xlvi).

That Antiochus should lean heavily on Carneades for his arguments should occasion no surprise. Antiochus had not rejected the teaching of Carneades *in toto*; he simply disagreed on the question of *katalêpsis*, and basic though that disagreement was, he retained great respect for Carneades' command of logic, and freely used his arguments and formulations.[1]

It is interesting to compare with the theory of the *De Fato* the account of causality given in Cicero's *Topica*, a short work hastily composed a few months later than the *De Fato* in circumstances which are described below, under *Logic* (pp. 102–4), and which is generally held to be Antiochian in inspiration. There, in sects. 58–66, we find an essentially Stoic theory of causality, which does not, however, exclude free will.

In sect. 58 we have a distinction between two types of cause, the efficient and the material, a use of Aristotelian terms for Stoic concepts. The material cause is that which is 'necessary but not sufficient', the *sine qua non*, called by Chrysippus the 'procatarctic cause'. It is made clear that the Stoic concept of Fate is concerned only with this latter type of cause (59):

Among the causes without which an effect cannot be produced, some are passive, inactive, one might say without initiative, such as Time, Matter, building materials and other things of the same sort; others, however, contribute some impulse to the effect, and provide from themselves some elements of assistance, though nòt such as to necessitate the effect, as for instance 'Meeting was the cause of love, love of the crime'. It is out of this class of causes, depending one upon the other from all eternity, that the Stoics weave their concept of Fate.

The Stoic *heimarmenê* is thus confined to the class of material causes, and the human will is left free to operate as an efficient cause (63). Nor is Chance excluded from the list of causes (64), but an effort is made to subsume it beneath the general rule 'nothing without cause', by describing things which happen by chance as happening from a cause which is hidden. This formula would satisfy Chrysippus, but it does not preserve Chance as an independent type of cause.

[1] e.g. *Fin.* v 16: 'Let us therefore adopt the classification of Carneades (of possible supreme goods), which our teacher Antiochus is very fond of employing'; also *TD* III 59, *Acad. Pr.* 97–8; and even when he disagreed with him, *ibid.*, 28. It is possible also, from the form in which mention of Antiochus is made by Sextus Empiricus, e.g. *Adv. Log.* I 162, that Sextus is here using him as a source for his survey of the New Academy, and particularly for Carneades. In that case, it is a very fair-minded account on Antiochus' part.

In both the *De Fato* and the *Topica*, then, Cicero is basing himself on a theory of causality which, while utilizing Stoic formulations, is not prepared to face up to the full consequences of Chrysippus' argumentation by admitting the illusory nature of free will, and instead finds a formula to preserve its reality. If this is not Cicero's own contribution, then it may most credibly be assigned to Antiochus.

The contradiction between the doctrines of the *De Fato* and the *Topica* on the one hand, and the bald Stoic statement in the *Acad. Post.* on the other, is, I think, only apparent. There, Antiochus is discussing Physics. In the realm of physics, that is, of inanimate objects, even Carneades would have agreed that there is 'a fated and unchangeable concatenation of everlasting order'. It was only in the sphere of psychology that he wished to assert freedom, or rather an *internal* cause.

Even if doubt remains whether the doctrine of the *De Fato* and the *Topica* is in fact that of Antiochus, the texts cannot be ignored, as they exhibit the main lines of the position on Fate and Freewill taken by all later Platonists, as we shall see in due course.

(c) *The gods*

Theology, in the ancient arrangement, was reckoned under Physics, so we may discuss it at this point. There is no evidence that Antiochus in his views on God or 'the gods' deviated in any way from the Stoic line, and some evidence to suggest that he did not.

In Cicero's treatise *On the Nature of the Gods*, representatives of all the other current schools of philosophy are assembled together, Epicurean, Stoic, and the New Academic, but there is no representative of Antiochus' 'Old Academy'. Cicero draws attention to this (*ND* 1 16):

'Well, I too,' he replied, 'think I have come at the right moment, as you say. For here are you, three leaders of three schools of philosophy, met in congress. In fact we only want Marcus Piso[1] to have every considerable school represented.'

'Oh,' rejoined Cotta, 'if what is said in the book which our master Antiochus lately dedicated to our good Balbus here is true, you have no need to regret the absence of your friend Piso. Antiochus holds the view that the doctrines of the Stoics, though differing in form of expression, agree in substance with those of the Peripatetics (*re concinere videntur, verbis discrepare*).'

Q. Lucilius Balbus, the Stoic spokesman, vigorously denies this, as befits a loyal Stoic, but his denial refers to the sphere of Ethics, not to

[1] The expounder of Antiochus' doctrine in *De Finibus* v.

the nature of the gods. What Cicero in fact seems to be telling us here is that there is no point in giving both the Stoic doctrine and that of Antiochus, since they differ in no significant respect. We can see, in fact, from what has been quoted above from the *Acad. Post.* about the Universe, how Antiochus managed to transfer Stoic doctrine on this topic bodily to the 'Old Academy'. Balbus' speech in *ND* II, then, although it is a Stoic discourse, perhaps taken from a treatise of Panaetius (possibly that *On Providence* which Cicero begs from Atticus in *Ad Att.* XIII 8), or of Posidonius, may be taken as good evidence for Antiochus' views.

(d) Divination

As in the case of Theology in general, so in that of Divination, Cicero provides us (in *De Divinatione* I) with a Stoic treatise to represent the dogmatic point of view—all signs point to Posidonius as the source—but again seems to drop a hint that the views of Antiochus were not much different, though the hint is not as explicit as in *ND* II. In *Div.* I, 5 he notes that virtually all philosophers, except Xenophanes and Epicurus, have believed in divination:

For example Socrates and all of the Socratics, and Zeno and his followers, continued in the faith of the ancient philosophers, *in which the Old Academy and the Peripatetics also agreed.*

Cicero's Latin for the last phrase, '*vetere Academia et Peripateticis consentientibus*', conveys what should by now be a familiar thought. The roll-call of philosophers in this case, however, continues with a mention of Pythagoras, which is not a normal feature of an Antiochian doxography, but is due rather to Posidonius' influence.

Without, then, claiming any of the details of *De Div.* I for Antiochus, we may perhaps venture to assert that he believed in divination, both artificial and natural (sect. 12ff.), and that it was the result of the working of the divine *logos* in the world (cf. sect. 110). It comes to us in dreams, when our souls are most free from bodily influences, and it, occupies to a special degree certain parts of the earth, such as Delphi and certain privileged individuals, such as sibyls. It also works through irrational beasts and even inanimate objects. It is possible for men by careful study to learn and understand the signs with which these agents provide us.

This is the basic doctrine of *De Div.* I, and it was certainly accepted by all later Middle Platonists. In the battle over Fate and Freewill, the fact of divination was never at issue between Stoics and Platonists or Peripatetics. All the Platonists wished to do was to limit the sway of Fate to the events of the physical world, and to allow the human mind its power of decision-making, even though the events leading up to and out from its decision were bound to each other by the 'inevitable concatenation of cause and effect'.

(e) Daemons and other intermediate beings

There is no mention in *ND* II of such beings as daemons or heroes, but that Antiochus recognized them is more or less guaranteed by the evidence of his pupil Varro. In the preface to Book Sixteen of his *Civil Theology* (quoted by Augustine, *Civ. Dei* VII 6), Varro discusses the topic of Natural Theology (Greek: *physikê theologia*):

God is the soul of the universe, and this universe is God. But just as a wise man, though consisting of body and mind, is called wise because of his mind, so the universe is called God because of its mind, though it likewise consists of mind and body.

All this, Stoic as it is, we may reasonably take as Antiochian doctrine. Varro, although the most learned Roman of his day (as has been noted above, p. 62), and yielding to no man on such subjects as grammar, agriculture, or Roman antiquities, did not claim to be an original philosopher, but rather a faithful pupil of Antiochus. His only original contribution in the area of philosophic discourse would have been the introduction of Roman illustrations and analogies, as indeed we see him doing here (and as we see Cicero doing generally). Varro continues:

The universe is divided into two parts, heaven and earth; the heaven is twofold, divided into aether and air, and the earth in turn is divided into water and land. Of these the highest is the aether, the second air, and third water and the fourth earth. All these four parts are full of souls, immortal souls in the aether and the air, mortal souls in the water and on land. From the highest circle of heaven to the circle of the Moon are aetherial souls, the stars and the planets, and these are not only known by our intelligence to exist, but are also visible to our eyes as heavenly gods. Then between the circle of the Moon and the highest region of clouds are aerial souls, perceived as such by the mind, not by the eyes. They are called heroes and *lares* and *genii*.

The terms *lares* and *genii* are plainly attempts to find native Roman equivalents for the Greek term *daimones*. This passage as a whole is of great importance, as presenting Antiochus' version of the basic Middle Platonic doctrine on daemons, such as is found later in Philo, Plutarch and Apuleius, for instance. The argument that each of the elements must have its proper inhabitants, and that the true inhabitants of the air are not birds, as might be thought, but rather invisible pure souls or daemons, is later the standard argument. We may observe also in Varro a distinction made between daemons and heroes. This distinction was made also by Posidonius in his work *On Heroes and Daemons*, but we do not know the details of his doctrine on the subject, any more than we can perceive Varro's here. It is not clear whether any distinction is being made between good and evil daemons, such as was certainly already made in the Old Academy by Xenocrates, but it is very probable that such a distinction was made.

The details of demonology are being dealt with in a later chapter. All we need note now is that Antiochus may be credited with great probability with reintroducing the doctrine of daemons into Platonism. It is very doubtful, after all, that the New Academy took much account of them.

4. PSYCHOLOGY

(a) *Antiochus and the theory of ideas*

The topic of the Gods belongs, as noted above, to 'Physics'; we now pass to a topic included by the Ancients under Logic, but which we may more conveniently group with the questions of the nature, and immortality, of the soul, and regard as a part of Psychology, namely the question of the Platonic Ideas.

We do not have from Antiochus himself a description of the nature of the Soul, but Lactantius (*Op. Dei.* 17) tells us that Varro's view was that 'soul is air conceived in the mouth, warmed in the lungs, heated in the heart, and diffused about the body'. Now Varro is not likely to have diverged from his master's views on this subject, and doubly unlikely to have diverged in the direction of Stoicism, so that there is a high probability that this is Antiochus' doctrine. This being so, what room do we have for transcendent Ideas and Recollection?

We need not here go over the vexed question of the final status of the Ideas in the Old Academy. The question before us now is what Antiochus did with them. The answer to this question, as in the case of many others in this chapter, is not entirely clear. We may start from the summary presented in *Acad. Post.* 30ff.:

> The criterion of truth arose, indeed, from the senses, yet was not in the senses: the judge of things was, they held, the mind—they thought that it alone deserves credence, because it alone perceives that which is eternally simple and uniform and self-identical. This thing they call the *idea*, a name already given to it by Plato.

This statement, except for the use of the term 'criterion of truth', perhaps, is purely Platonic, and seems to envisage the Ideas as independent, transcendent objects of knowledge. The Latin *id quod semper (est) simplex et unius modi et tale quale (est)* is very reminiscent of the language of *Phaedo* 78CD, for instance, as well as of *Timaeus* 27D. But did Antiochus envisage the Ideas in their pristine Platonic form? As we read on, this becomes increasingly doubtful. He first makes a perfectly Platonic distinction between the senses and the intellect, the former being the sphere of opinion (*doxa*), where nothing is certain or clearly perceived because of its constant flux, the latter the sphere of knowledge (*epistêmê*), where the objects of perception should be the eternal, immutable Ideas. What in fact he says is, however: 'Knowledge on the other hand they deemed to exist nowhere except in the notions and reasonings of the mind.' He then goes straight on to discuss logic. The Latin *notiones* and *rationes* should correspond to the Greek *ennoiai* and *logismoi*, both Stoic terms. Here the objects of the mind's contemplation are the mind's own contents; but, one may ask, are the transcendent Ideas necessarily excluded by this? The real question is, though, were they ever there for Antiochus? In the passage quoted above, Antiochus uses the characteristically Platonic description of the Ideas, but it is not necessary, nor even likely, that he thought of them as objective entities at all. We must also bear in mind that this passage is not a straight statement of doctrine, but an historical summary, which may colour the language somewhat. To get a clearer notion of his real views, we may take into evidence the passage *Acad. Pr.* 30 (quoted above, p. 67), where Lucullus is expounding Antiochus' theory of knowledge.[1]

This exposition is plainly Stoic in the first instance, but if it is to be related to Plato's teaching, as Antiochus would wish to do, it is rather

---

[1] We may also note the curious tone of *Acad. Post.* 33, where Varro-Antiochus is beginning a description of deviations from the original Platonic doctrine: 'Aristotle was the first to undermine the Forms of which I spoke a little while

to the *Theaetetus* than to the *Phaedo* or the *Republic* that it looks back. We note here that memory has nothing to do with Platonic *anamnêsis*, but is simply a mental process which stores away certain sense-perceptions; most significant, however, is the description of the process by which concepts are formed. The mind perceives *similitudines* (which translates the Greek *analogiai*), and constructs from them general concepts; no role is left for any transcendent Ideas. They are not recalled by *anamnêsis*, and they have no influence on the formation of general concepts.

If Antiochus is then prepared to talk about Ideas, as, indeed, being a professed Platonist, he could hardly help doing, the conclusion seems unavoidable that he identified them with 'cognitive perceptions', the objects of knowledge in the Stoic system. That he can use to describe these entities terminology reminiscent of the *Phaedo* may seem astonishing, but we must remind ourselves again that we are quite ignorant of the intermediate steps, among both the Old Academicians and Antiochus' more immediate predecessors, by which the notion of Ideas came down to him. If Antiochus read the *Phaedo*, as he presumably did, he will have read it through curiously distorted spectacles.

A further useful insight into Antiochus' use of the Theory of Ideas may perhaps be gleaned from a passage in Cicero's *Orator* (8ff.). The *Orator* is much more original in composition than Cicero's philosophical works, but at the outset Cicero describes the search for the perfect orator in terms which may very well be Antiochian.[1] Certainly somebody's Theory of Ideas is here represented, and it accords with Antiochus much more closely than with Plato himself:

> But I am firmly of the opinion that nothing of any kind is so beautiful as not to be excelled in beauty by that of which it is a copy, as a mask is a copy of a face. This ideal cannot be perceived by the eye or ear, nor by any of the senses, but we can nevertheless grasp it by the mind and the imagination. For example, in the case of the statues of Phidias, the most perfect of their kind that we have ever seen . . . we can, in spite of their beauty, imagine something still more beautiful. Surely that great sculptor, while making the image of Zeus or Athena, did not look at any person whom he was using as a model,

---

before, which Plato had adopted with such great enthusiasm that he spoke of them as possessing a sort of divinity.' I detect a note of irreverence in this passage. Particularly *mirifice* seems to me to represent the Greek *thaumastôs hôs*, with its mildly ironic overtones. Can Antiochus be suggesting that Plato made somewhat too much of the Ideas?

[1] For the connexion with Antiochus, see Theiler, *Vorbereitung*, p. 40.

but in his own mind there dwelt a surpassing vision of beauty; at this he gazed and all intent on this he guided his artist's hand to produce the likeness of a god.

Accordingly, as there is something perfect and surpassing in the case of sculpture and painting—an intellectual ideal (*cogitata species*) by reference to which the artist represents those objects which do not themselves appear to the eye, so with our minds we conceive the ideal of perfect eloquence, but with our ears we catch only the copy.

These patterns of things are called *ideai* by Plato, that eminent master and teacher both of style and thought; these, he says, do not come to be (*gigni*, Greek *gignesthai*); they exist for ever, and are the possession of intellect and reason (*ratione et intellegentia contineri*); other things come to be and pass away, are in flux and do not remain in the same state.

This required extended quotation in order to see precisely what Cicero envisaged the Ideas as being. First of all, we may note that 'rhetoric' is not an entity of which Plato would have seriously postulated a transcendent idea. Then there is no mention, in spite of the talk of their eternity and immutability, of the Ideas being anywhere but in the mind of the beholder. The phrase *ratione et intellegentia contineri* is particularly significant. There is no mention of the Reason beholding anything *outside* itself; the ideas are simply its contents. Their 'eternity' consists in the fact that in every human mind they are the same. 'White' for instance, meant the same thing to Aristotle or Cicero as it does to you or me. Of course, it may be said that Justice or indeed Rhetoric does *not* mean the same thing to different people, but this objection may be directed even more powerfully against the transcendent Ideas of Plato. The point to be made is that Antiochus' 'ideas', like the Stoic 'common notions' (*koinai ennoiai*), derive their eternity and immutability not from their existence in a transcendent realm, but rather from the essential uniformity of the human intellect.

We may note also, in passing, the very different status accorded to artistic creation in this passage from that allotted it by Plato in Book X of the *Republic*. Since Plotinus, in his view of the artist, agrees with this passage (*Enn.* v 8, 1), and since Phidias and his statues (in particular that of Olympian Zeus) henceforth become an *exemplum* in this connexion, we may perhaps credit Antiochus with at least an intermediary role in establishing this higher view of artistic creation in contrast to Plato's low estimate. Here the artist is not making a copy of a copy, but is rather in direct contact with the archetype, and in a way which is, it is suggested, uniquely open to him as an artist.

Whether this is a conscious contradiction of Plato is not quite clear, but it is hard to believe that it is not.

Despite what we may glean from the *Orator* passage, however, the problem of the eternity and unchangeability of the Ideas is not quite settled. These attributes would seem to give them *some* objective existence. Relevant here, in fact, is the question of the means used by the Demiurge to create the world in the *Timaeus*. If, as we have seen, the Demiurge—and the World Soul—are identified by Antiochus with the Stoic Pneuma-Logos, there is nothing left for the Paradigm of the *Timaeus* to be but the content of the intellect of the Logos, the sum-total of his *logoi spermatikoi*, on the pattern of which the physical world is constructed. Now by agreement among all later Platonists, the Paradigm of the *Timaeus* was nothing but the sum total of the Ideas, which are given no place as such in the *Timaeus*. The *logoi spermatikoi* of the Logos thus inevitably become for Antiochus the Ideas in their 'transcendent' or 'objective' aspect. A suitable home has been found for them; they may now be termed 'the thoughts of God'. Unfortunately, Antiochus (as filtered down to us through Cicero) never makes this identification in so many words, and so certain scholars have persisted in regarding the origin of this concept as a mystery, but since it appears as non-controversial in the writings of both Philo Judaeus and Seneca, as we shall see, and as it is the natural conclusion of Antiochus' general theory of knowledge, the matter seems hardly to admit of much doubt.[1] We cannot be sure, on the other hand, that Antiochus was the *first* to regard the Ideas as thoughts of God; such a notion may well go back to the Old Academy. Certainly the criticisms of Aristotle against the transcendent Ideas had to be recognized, and Polemon, in ethics at least, as we have seen, was an admirer of Aristotle. But this question has been discussed already in Chapter One.

In fact, then, Antiochus' theory of knowledge is the Stoic theory, as we observed earlier in the case of his doctrine of the criterion. He was able to convince himself, however, by the judicious use of Old Academic authorities, that Zeno was simply formalizing the true doctrine of the Academy. In this connexion his critique of Zeno in *Acad. Post.* 40ff. is interesting. In spite of his declared intention, 'Varro' finds very

---

[1] The fact that Varro (*ap.* Aug. *CD* vii 28) went so far as to allegorize Jupiter, Minerva and Juno as God, Ideas and Matter, the Ideas springing from the mind of God, is a further indication that this doctrine was familiar to Antiochus. Varro may have concocted the Roman allegory, but not the basic philosophic doctrine.

little to criticize in Zeno, apart from his views on the sufficiency of Virtue for Happiness (35-6). In the sphere of Logic, the only thing that sounds like a criticism is the declaration in 42 that Zeno 'deemed the senses also trustworthy', whereas in the Platonic survey in 31 they were spoken of as 'dull and sluggish, and entirely incapable of getting a clear grasp of anything which came within their ken'. When examined, however, this difference is seen to have little substance. For both Antiochus and Zeno, the senses were the sole means of knowledge, though for neither did cognition take place until the mind applied itself to the sense-data. What we must note is that there is no mention of Zeno having demolished, or even having criticized, the Theory of Ideas, though Aristotle was earlier mentioned as having 'undermined' it, in sect. 33 (see above, p. 92, n. 1). We may, I think, conclude that the Theory of Ideas was not a subject on which Antiochus was inclined to dispute with Zeno and the Stoics. He thought that he could fit it in coherently with their theory of knowledge.

(b) *The immortality of the soul*

Antiochus' views on the immortality of the soul are difficult to ascertain with any certainty. There is nothing on this subject in the approved texts, the *Academica* and the *De Finibus*. If any conjecture were to be made solely on the basis of these, together with Lactantius' report of Varro's doctrine, it would be that Antiochus followed the Old Stoic doctrine that the pure fire of which the soul was composed simply rejoined the aether, even as the other elements of the body rejoined their kindred elements, and that there was no personal immortality.

But this will not quite do. First of all, the later Stoics, from Chrysippus on, did in fact recognize the possibility of survival for all or some individual souls for a greater or lesser time after death. Secondly, we may ask what Antiochus did about the extensive Platonic treatment of the immortality of the soul, its pre-existence to the body, and its afterlife. He is quite capable of reinterpreting Plato, as we know, but he could not surely ignore or reject a whole aspect of his teaching. In fact, we are faced with two Ciceronian texts in particular in which quite an elaborate theory of immortality and the afterlife is presented on distinctly Platonic lines, though with Stoic characteristics, namely the *Somnium Scipionis* in Book VI of the *De Re Publica*, and the treatise *On Death* which comprises most of Book I of the *Tusculan Disputations*. There is no evidence to connect either of these treatises with Antiochus, although Georg Luck has made a plea for Antiochian authorship in the case of the former.[1] It has also been suggested that the authority behind them is Posidonius, who was strongly influenced by Platonism, and this has been forcefully argued against by Karl Reinhardt in his article on Posidonius in Paully-Wissowa (pp. 575–86). To whichever side one inclines there are difficulties, as we shall see.

One might ask, even if these two works did depend on Posidonius rather than Antiochus, are we to suppose that Antiochus was *more* Stoic in this matter than Posidonius? If Posidonius was prepared to accept the immortality of the soul, why should Antiochus reject it? It seems to me that either one must postulate that Cicero, finding no teaching on the immortality of the soul in any recent author, reached back to the Old Academy on his own account, perhaps to Heraclides of Pontus, for guidance[2]—in which case we should expect to find some mention of this remarkable fact somewhere in his writings—or we may conclude that these two works may at least be taken as evidence for contemporary Platonic doctrine, even as was Book II of the *De Natura Deorum*, even if the authority actually used in these works was officially a Stoic rather than a Platonist.

TD 1 begins as a disputation, in the New-Academic spirit, on the question whether Death is an Evil, and this continues until sect. 17, where the interlocutor begs Cicero to give a continuous oration. Cicero demurs, makes a New-Academic disclaimer of dogmatism, and then launches into a distinctly dogmatic discourse. It is at this point that we may assume an essay *On Death*, by whomsoever it was composed, to be introduced into the work.

We begin (18) by defining our terms, to wit, Death and Soul. This effort at definition becomes a doxographic survey of views on the nature of the Soul. In this survey it is notable that the Stoics are dismissed in a line ('Zeno the Stoic holds that the soul is fire'—which is something of an over-simplification in any case, especially as it is then argued that this fire will burn itself out), while Plato and Aristotle are treated with great respect ('Aristotle who, if one excepts Plato, far surpasses all others in both genius and industry . . .'), and Aristotle's

---

[1] *Der Akademiker Antiochos*, pp. 30–42.

[2] The possibility of Cicero here having turned to the Old Academy for inspiration is not eliminated by the fact that in *TD* 1 the soul is seen, not as an immaterial entity, rising above the material universe, but rather as the purest type of fire, which rises until it finds its natural place in the sphere of the fixed stars. This view is attested for Heraclides of Pontus (Tert. *De An.* 9) and he also believed that they resided in the Milky Way (Iambl. *De An.* p. 378 Wachsmuth), so that a work of his may be at least the remote source behind this text.

'fifth essence' goes uncriticized; all of which seems a little extreme even for such a Plato-lover as Posidonius—but the tone of this doxography may well be influenced by Cicero's desire to appear 'sceptical'. The treatise then moves on to the first subject: 'That the Soul survives' (26ff.). We begin with an appeal to the instinctive belief both of the earliest men of whom we have record, and of the most remote and uncultivated peoples of the present day, in the survival of the soul after death. (This is a distinctly Stoic method of procedure (*koinai ennoiai*), and strongly reminiscent of the beginning of *ND* II). Next, Nature herself implants in us a desire to be remembered after death, and also inspires men to deeds of heroism, even though death be involved; all of which implies an instinctive belief in survival.

If Nature tells us that souls survive, it is by Reason that we must settle the second question: 'In what region do they dwell?' (36). The underworld must be a myth. If souls survive, being composed either of hot air (*anima inflammata*) or of fire, they must rise upwards. The earth is at the centre of the universe; they must then proceed towards the periphery. The mind is the swiftest thing known; this makes it all the more likely that, freed from the body, it will penetrate the thicker, cooler air which immediately surrounds the earth (43ff.). When it finds surroundings of similar material to itself, there it will stop, as having found its natural position. This will be the region of the stars. The chief desire of the mind is for knowledge. This it can only achieve to a small extent while in the body; freed from the body, on the other hand, and among the stars, it will acquire a much more comprehensive view of the truth. (This is the belief which inspires the *Dream of Scipio*.)

Let us not be disturbed by the fact that we cannot imagine in what form the soul exists apart from the body (50ff.). Are we so sure that we can imagine in what form it exists *in* the body? Learn to know the mind through the mind: this is the meaning of Apollo's precept 'Know Thyself'. We *are* our minds, not our bodies.[1] To further our enquiry

---

[1] It could be maintained that this statement is diametrically opposed to Antiochus' known view, which is a basic principle of his ethics in *Fin.* v and Aug. *CD* XIX 3, that we are both mind and body, but one might argue in reply that Antiochus could in fact consistently hold both views. In this life we are certainly a combination of mind and body, and it is foolish for the Stoics to ignore the fact, but it is equally obvious that after death, if we survive at all, we are purely mind. In a treatise on Death or Immortality, it is that that one would naturally emphasize; in a treatise on Ethics, the other fact. A second-rate philosopher with a good rhetorical training is liable to modify his doctrines according to his theme. Philo of Alexandria is an example of this.

into the nature of mind, we have a quotation from Plato (*Phaedrus* 245cff.).

The human soul has within it certain faculties over and above what it shares with animals and plants. First, it has Memory. Here there is a reference to the doctrine of *anamnêsis* (recollection of pre-natal truth) in Plato's *Meno* and *Phaedo*, which concludes with the following remark:

And indeed there is no other way in which we could from boyhood on hold fixed in, and as it were stamped upon, our minds the notions—the so-called *ennoiai*—, were it not that the mind, before it entered the body, had been active in acquiring knowledge (*in rerum cognitione viguisset*) (57).

Immediately following on this, we have a reference to the eternity of the Ideas.

Even if this text were to be credited to Posidonius, we may ask ourselves whether acceptance of the doctrine of *anamnêsis* would be inconsistent for Antiochus. Somewhat inconsistent, one must admit, with what we have observed from the *Acad. Pr.*, but not impossibly so. The process of concept-formation is still, after all, a gathering and sorting of impressions, even though the doctrine of *anamnêsis* implies that the reason that these impressions fall into place is that there is a memory of an archetype in the mind already which these impressions stimulate to activity, whereas the pure Stoic view must be that the mind perceives resemblances and systems entirely on its own. Antiochus' ability to gloss over differences, however, must not be underestimated. Similarly, the eternal ideas here may perfectly well be situated in the mind of God. It does, however, seen unavoidable that they are the *res* which we contemplate before birth.

We turn next to a panegyric of man's normal memory (59ff.), and especially of his powers of invention, designed to prove that this is a divine gift, and indeed that the mind is a god—the thesis boldly stated at *Somn.* 26. It is stressed that, of whatever substance it is composed (and Cicero, or his source, hesitates between *anima*, fire and Aristotle's 'fifth substance'), we must admit that it is none of those substances near the earth, not even the air or fire that we know, as none of these possesses intelligence.

Now we come to an important passage (72ff.), based on the *Phaedo*, which distinguishes the fates of pure and impure souls. The impure 'go a road apart, separated from the company of the Gods'; the pure have an easy ascent to the stars. There is emphasis in this connexion on the *Phaedo*'s view of philosophy as a 'practising of death', as the separation, as far as is possible in this life, of the soul from the body. The matter of the different destinies of pure and impure souls is not discussed further here, but in *Somn.* 13 we find the view that only the souls of the great attain a definite place among the stars:

For all those who have saved, or helped, or enlarged their fatherland, there is a definite place allotted in the heavens, where they may enjoy in happiness everlasting life. For nothing of all that happens on earth is more pleasing to that supreme God who rules this whole universe than the councils and unions of men, linked together by the rule of law, which are called States, and the rulers and preservers of these, who, having descended from this realm, ascend again hither.

This is a remarkable adaptation of the old, heroic view, according to which the good man in a *moral* sense had no part in the Isles of the Blessed, but rather the famous warrior. It is hardly credible that Cicero would in fact exclude the good man from heaven, even if he were of private station, but the passage does suggest a distinction in the after-life between the 'good' (including the famous, or 'good' in the Homeric sense), and the bad (or simply undistinguished), with *personal* immortality being enjoyed only by the former—if we can conclude this from the 'definite place' (*certus locus*) assigned to them. In *De Leg.* II 28, again, we find a distinction made between the general run of souls, which are all immortal, and those of the 'brave and good', which are *divine*. This is not a contrast between personal and merely generic immortality, but it is at least a contrast of some sort, and thus interesting.

All this is not really a throwback to Homer. Rather it reflects a dispute within the Stoic school. Cleanthes believed that the souls of all men survived until the *ecpyrôsis*, while Chrysippus held that only the souls of the wise did so. Those of the 'foolish' (i.e. all others) lasted 'for some certain time', while the souls of irrational animals perished immediately (*SVF* II 809, 811). Zeno himself seems to have thought that the soul held together for some time after death, but finally dispersed (*SVF* I 146). In contrast to this, the normal Platonic belief would be in a process of purgation which brought in even the worst—or perhaps all but the very worst, if we follow the *Phaedo* myth—ultimately to a place among the stars.

But where, one might ask, does reincarnation enter into all this?

This is not made clear in either *TD* I or *SS*. If a distinction is to be made between 'the good' and the others, it may be that the former are exempt from reincarnation, while the others are subject to being ploughed back, either a specific number of times or indefinitely. There is some warrant for such a distinction to be derived from Plato, specifically from the Myth of the *Phaedrus*, which is, indeed, referred to at the end of *SS* (29)

The question of immortality and the nature of the afterlife is of considerable interest to later Platonists, as we shall see particularly in the case of Plutarch, so that whether they looked back for their doctrines to Antiochus or elsewhere, the matter merits discussion at this stage. Whoever is in fact the mediator, we may perhaps look, for the ultimate authorship of these speculations, to Xenocrates or Heraclides of Pontus.

At sect. 78 the discourse turns from the question of immortality to that of death itself, and so we may leave it, noting merely that the whole tone of the treatise is considerably more Platonic than that of the central group of Antiochian documents. The Stoics, and in particular Panaetius, are roundly condemned for denying immortality. The treatise even seems to accept the tripartite, or at least bipartite, division of the soul. In 20 the tripartite division is mentioned, rather irrelevantly, as Plato's doctrine of the soul (though Reason is termed *principatus*, the Stoic *hêgemonikon*), and in 80 a bipartite division is used to refute Panaetius' claim that the soul is subject to passion, and so mortal. Even this, however, is not orthodox Stoic, though it is Posidonian.[1]

There are, then, three possibilities: either Posidonius is a more faithful Platonist than Antiochus, or Antiochus is rather more of a Platonist than one supposed, or Cicero himself is here constructing a Platonism of his own, looking back himself to Xenocrates or Heraclides of Pontus—for the tone, for all its superficial Scepticism, is not Carneadic. The last possibility must be accounted unlikely, in view of Cicero's known methods of composition. Of the first two, each is plausible; both may very well be true (Antiochus may be borrowing from Posidonius). All that need be said here is, that, whoever is the authority behind *TD* I, it remains an important document in the history of Middle Platonism.

---

[1] The bipartite division of the soul is taken as the basis for exposition in *TD* IV, a treatise on the passions which is probably Posidonian (IV 10–11), and accepted also in *TD* II 47.

(c) *The structure of the soul*

As has been pointed out above in connexion with *TD* 1 80, the bipartite division of the soul is contrary to strict Stoic doctrine. This was that the soul was unitary, but might be divided into seven faculties, presided over by an eighth, the *hêgemonikon*, or 'leading element'. The seven faculties consisted of the five senses, together with the power of speech and the power of procreation. The *hêgemonikon* receives and co-ordinates the data of the five senses (as we have seen described in *Acad. Pr.* 30), and issues commands to all seven faculties. The *hêgemonikon* is often equated with the more traditional term *nous* ('mind'), and this makes it possible for Antiochus to take it as the rational part of the soul in Plato's system.

For practical purposes, Antiochus seems to have accepted the Stoic view of the structure of the soul, although in his 'doxographic' account of Platonic philosophy in *Acad. Post.* he makes a contrast between the nous and the *aisthêseis* (senses), which could be taken to imply a bipartite soul, but can in fact be reconciled with the Stoic theory. Nowhere is any use made of the tripartite scheme of the *Republic* (though it is mentioned as Plato's dogma in *TD* 1 20, as we have seen). As for a bipartite scheme, there is better evidence for attributing this to Posidonius than to Antiochus. Certainly the authority behind *TD* II and *TD* IV accepted it (cf. above, p. 101, n. 1). For a Stoic such as Chrysippus, for instance, there was no such thing as an irrational (*alogon*) part of the soul, or an irrational soul; the various passions were simply 'the soul in a certain state' (*pôs echousa*), the result of false opinions (*doxai*) wrongly assented to.

Antiochus probably took Plato's divisions of the soul, particularly the tripartite one, as 'poetical' expressions of the truth which a thinker like Chrysippus finally formalized scientifically, but we lack evidence as to precisely how he faced the problem.

5. LOGIC

On this question too, we may start from the summary in the *Acad. Post.* (32):

They approved the method of defining things (*definitiones rerum*, Greek *horismoi*) and applied these 'definitions' to all the subjects they discussed. They also gave approval to the derivation of words, that is the statement of the reason why each class of things bears the name that it does—the subject termed by them *etymologia*; and then they used derivations as 'tokens' or, so to speak, marks (*symbola*) of things, as guides for arriving at proofs or conclusions as to anything of which they desired an explanation; and under this head was imparted their whole doctrine of Dialectic, that is, speech cast in the form of logical argument.

This tells us a certain amount, but not everything. Definition and Etymology are mentioned, though what is meant by the latter is not clear—presumably the activity exemplified in Plato's *Cratylus*—and Proof (*apodeixis*) and Syllogistic are alluded to, but no details are given. Antiochus was proud of the dialectic of the Academy (*Acad. Post.* 5; *Fin.* v 10), which includes the methods of argument used by Carneades, but it seems as if for technical logic he turned to Chrysippus. We have, at any rate, the (admittedly hostile) testimony of *Acad. Pr.* 143:

Surely our friend Antiochus does not approve any doctrine of these teachers? On the contrary, he does not even accept anything from his own ancestors; for where does he follow either Xenocrates, who has many volumes on Logic (*de ratione loquendi*) that are highly thought of, or Aristotle himself, who is assuredly unsurpassed for acumen and finish? He never diverges a foot's length from Chrysippus (*a Chrysippo pedem nusquam*).

Now even a hostile witness, as Cicero is in this case, could not make such a remark without some basis in fact. To be sure, he is here primarily discussing the criterion, but the remark refers to Logic in general.

Cicero's comment here receives confirmation if we take into evidence the short treatise *Topica*, a description of the chief headings of argument which Cicero compiled for his young friend Trebatius Testa. This essay bears every mark of having been composed under more or less the conditions under which Cicero claims to have composed it—on board ship between Velia and Rhegium in July 44, in the course of his abortive flight from Italy, when he was separated from his library and thus unable to make direct use of a source work. The work is brief, summary and informal, but it employs a logical scheme which accords very well with what we should expect of Antiochus.

Cicero is applying this general framework to the technical requirements of jurisprudence, inserting his own examples, but the framework can be easily isolated. The logical doctrine is essentially Stoic. It is not written from a Stoic viewpoint, however, but from an Academic one, as the Stoics are mentioned from an outsider's point of view (sect. 6) as having greatly developed the science of judging the truth-value of arguments, whereas Aristotle pointed the way both in the matter of discovering and of judging modes of argument. The work is remotely based on Aristotle's own *Topics*, but only remotely. The best explanation seems to be that the source behind Cicero was encouraged by Theophrastus' adoption of hypothetical syllogisms to go a step further and take Chrysippus' logic as essentially a development of Academic-Peripatetic logic, as indeed to a large extent it was. This, of course, is a proceeding entirely characteristic of Antiochus.

Points of particular interest are the following:

(1) In sect. 26, on the subject of Definitions, we find a distinction made between two classes of entity, 'things existing' and 'things thought'. The first are physical objects, the second are abstract concepts, which have no material substratum. This division is proper only for someone who, like Antiochus, agreed with the Stoics in rejecting non-material substance. What for a true Platonist would be Ideas, are for him simply *notiones* (Greek *ennoiai, prolêpseis*) impressed upon the mind (27). This is confirmed in sect. 31.

(2) In sects. 53–7, on the subject of Consequence, Antecedence and Contradiction, Stoic hypothetical syllogisms are used without hesitation as the normal type of syllogism (53), and then the whole system of Stoic syllogistic is described as the normal subject-matter of Dialectic—though Cicero gives not five, but seven modes of indemonstrable argument, which is a later development on the Chrysippan scheme.

These passages, together with the section on Causation dealt with previously (p. 87), lend credence to the hypothesis that the logical theory assumed by Cicero in the *Topica* is essentially that professed by Antiochus. Certainly it accords with any other evidence we have as to his position. We may conclude, then, that Antiochus freely used the Chrysippan syllogistic to elucidate 'Platonic' doctrine, and thus contributed the Stoic strand to the amalgam of Stoic and Aristotelian logic which we find prevalent in later Platonism. We may note, however, that when Albinus, in ch. 6 of the *Didaskalikos*, gives his exposition of Platonic Logic, he confines himself to Theophrastean formulations, adopting nothing distinctively Stoic in his account of syllogistic.

6. RHETORIC

We should take note of Rhetoric, as Antiochus, like Philo before him, seems to have been an advocate of a reconciliation between philosophy and oratory. This was a development from the attitude of his immediate predecessors, both Stoic and Academic. We find in Cicero's *De Oratore* 1 83–93 a record of a dispute between Mnesarchus the Stoic and Charmadas, the pupil of Carneades, on the question of the orator, Mnesarchus asserting, with Stoic paradoxicality, that only the wise man could be an orator, and Charmadas denying that there was any science of Rhetoric at all.

Antiochus himself, like the Stoics, seems to have ranked Rhetoric with Logic proper (Dialectic) as the second chief division of *Logikē*, cf. for instance, the continuation of the passage *Acad. Pr.* 32, quoted above:

> To this as a counterpart (*quasi ex altera parte*, representing the Greek *antistrophon*) was added the faculty of Rhetoric, which sets out a continuous speech adapted to the purpose of persuasion.

Cicero was much attracted by the excellence of Antiochus' speaking style, as we have seen (above, p. 61, n. 1) though for rhetorical studies he actually went elsewhere, first to Demetrius the Syrian at Athens, then to Apollonius Molon in Rhodes (*Brutus* 315–16). Nevertheless, we may, I think, credit Antiochus with once more accepting Rhetoric as a province of philosophy, and with insisting that the good orator must also be a philosopher.

C. CONCLUSION

This has been a comparatively extended survey of a man who was not really a first-rate philosopher. Nor can he be said to be the immediate founder of Middle Platonism. He was too firmly wedded to Stoic physics for that. Another important element was required, as we shall see, before the movement truly emerges. Nevertheless, Antiochus is a significant figure, inasmuch as he turned the Platonic Academy away—for ever, as it turned out—from the Scepticism that had taken its inspiration from Socrates, and which had produced so much excellent philosophizing (by modern standards) under Arcesilaus and Carneades in the New Academy.

Certainly the acceptance of the great wealth of new terminology which the Stoics (especially Chrysippus) had contributed to philosophy was not a process in the Academy which began with Antiochus. When Carneades said, 'Without Chrysippus, there would have been no

Carneades', he might have acknowledged not only a rich source of arguments, but of terminology as well. But Antiochus must have cemented the union. His only quarrel with the Stoics seems to have been on the question of the self-sufficiency of virtue, and there the substance of their difference was actually small; Antiochus is superior in humanity and common sense (qualities which appealed to Cicero), though deficient in logical rigour. On the question of free will we cannot be quite certain. In matters of physics and theology he seems to have differed from them not at all. God had yet to be put back in his heaven, and freed from all taint of Matter. This was a task for other hands.

D. THE PROBLEM OF POSIDONIUS

Although the philosopher Posidonius was not a Platonist but a Stoic, his position in the intellectual history of the first century B.C. is such that he cannot be ignored in a survey of Middle Platonism. Fifty years ago, it is fair to say, it was a matter of near unanimity that Posidonius was the dominant intellectual influence on later school Platonism, as well as upon more popular levels of thought. Such books as those of Werner Jaeger, *Nemesios von Emesa* (1914), and Karl Reinhardt, *Poseidonius* (1921) and *Kosmos und Sympathie* (1926), had great influence in spreading this belief in ever-widening circles.

Some counter-attack was inevitable, as hard evidence, in the form of explicitly attested references to Posidonius,was from the outset very thin on the ground. The chief figure in this counter-attack was Ludwig Edelstein. In an article, 'The Philosophical System of Posidonius', published in 1936 in the *American Journal of Philology* vol. 57, he declared it to be his principle to proceed solely on the basis of attested fragments, and in that connexion promised a collection of the fragments, which he worked on until his death in 1965, and which has only recently been brought to completion by I. G. Kidd.[1] Posidonius is at the moment recognized, certainly, as the dominant intellectual figure of his age, whose researches in the areas of history, geography, mathematics and the sciences formed the basis of many later works, and who, in philosophy, was at least the vehicle if not the propounder of certain ideas, such as Cosmic Sympathy, which were most influential

[1] *Posidonius, Volume I: The Fragments,* by L. Edelstein and I. G. Kidd. Cambridge, 1972. (Vol. 2, the Commentary, has not appeared at time of writing.)

in later times, but the tendency to refer later developments back to him wholesale has now been brought under control. It is not that his holding of many of these beliefs is denied; it is simply that he is seen as more of a representative of certain developments than as an originator of them. Other factors in the situation, particularly the Neopythagorean writings, have been justly accorded greater weight than before, and the doctrine of the Old Academy has been more adequately evaluated. The Old Academy we have dealt with; the *Pythagorica* will be treated briefly in the next chapter, in connexion with Eudorus.

However, if only because of the role he has played in past scholarship, a brief survey of Posidonius' contribution to philosophy, so far as it can be discerned, would seem to be in order here.

1. LIFE AND WORKS

Posidonius was a native of Apamea in Northern Syria, born in 135 B.C. He travelled widely in the Mediterranean area, even visiting Cadiz to observe the Atlantic tides, and the Celts of Southern France, to acquaint himself with their curious customs. At some stage of his career he studied with the Stoic Panaetius at Athens, but made his permanent home on the island of Rhodes, which he made, by virtue of his presence, a notable centre of intellectual activity, and by which he was duly honoured in return, by the bestowal of citizenship, a magistracy, and in 87/6 by being sent as ambassador to Rome, to treat with Marius. He died in 51 or 50 B.C., at the age of 84, numbering among his active admirers such notable figures as Pompey and Cicero.

None of his large body of works survives, except in fragments or second-hand reports. The nearest thing we have to a continuous work of his is Book I of Cicero's *De Divinatione*, which is based on his work *On Divination*; we also have in Galen's work *On the Doctrines of Hippocrates and Plato* an extended account of his theory of the passions. I will list here only those of his works which are most relevant to our present enquiry, omitting those of an historical or purely scientific nature: (1) a *Protreptic to Philosophy*; (2) a *Physikos Logos*, in at least 8 books; (3) *On the Cosmos* (more than one book); (4) *On the Gods* (at least 5 books); (5) *On Heroes and Daemons* (more than one book); (6) *On Fate* (at least 2 books); (7) *On Divination* (5 books); (8) *On the Soul* (at least 3 books); (9) an *Ethikos Logos* (more than one book); (10) *On the Passions* (more than one book); (11) *On Duty*;

(12) *On the Criterion*; (13) *On Conjunctions*; and (14) last but not least, a commentary of some sort on Plato's *Timaeus*, which has generally been taken to be the source of much of his influence on Middle Platonism.

The friendly interest in Plato that such a commentary implies Posidonius inherited to some extent from Panaetius, who was himself much devoted to Plato, but with Posidonius we have on the Stoic side the counterpart to the move made from the Platonist side by Antiochus, which led to a large measure of assimilation between the two schools. This assimilation was considerably lessened in later generations as, beginning with Eudorus, Platonism reinstated transcendence, and the later Stoics returned to Chrysippus, but as between Antiochus and Posidonius themselves there was very little room left for disagreement, except perhaps in the sphere of ethics. What the personal relationship, if any, of these two contemporaries was we have no idea. Cicero never speaks of them meeting or commenting upon each other. The possibility of mutual influence, however, cannot be excluded, though Antiochus' attested instructor in Stoicism was not Posidonius, but Mnesarchus, another pupil of Panaetius.

2. PHILOSOPHY

About Posidonius' scientific and historical work I will say nothing here, but will simply review briefly his attested beliefs in the sphere of philosophy proper, following the order which he himself followed, Physics, Ethics and Logic (*Fr.* 87 Edelstein-Kidd). He is on record as comparing Philosophy to a living being, Physics being the flesh and blood, Logic the bones and sinews, and Ethics the soul (Fr. 88). The older Stoics, like Zeno and Chrysippus, began their instruction with Logic; Posidonius, following Panaetius, began with Physics (Fr. 91).

(a) *Physics*

He accepted the two First Principles of the Stoics, the Active (*poioun*) and the Passive (*paschon*) (Fr. 5), as indeed did Antiochus, as we have seen (above, p. 82). The latter took some trouble to align them with the doctrine of the *Timaeus*, and it is not improbable that Posidonius did also. There is no indication in his thought of any transcendent principle. God is for him 'a fiery and intelligent *pneuma*, having no definite shape, but changing into whatever it wishes and assimilating itself to all things' (Fr. 101), or 'penetrating all *ousia*' (Fr. 100). (In his penetrating capacity, he is termed *logos*, Fr. 5.) Although God's *ousia* is the whole cosmos (Fr. 20), yet he is present to different parts of it in different ways. His *nous* or *hêgemonikon* is the heavens, whereas in the earth he is present only as *hexis*, the principle of cohesion (Frr. 21, 23). We may note in this connexion that Posidonius does *not* declare the Sun to be the *nous* of the cosmos, but the heavenly realm as a whole, which makes him less of a champion of 'Solar Theology' than Cleanthes, for instance, who did regard the Sun as the cosmic *nous*.

God is, therefore, the active principle in the cosmos; the passive is Matter. Matter (which, following Stoic terminology, he also terms *ousia*) is without qualities or form, inasmuch as it has no shape or quality proper to itself, but is always in some particular shape or quality (Fr. 92). This doctrine does not differ essentially from Plato's doctrine of the Receptacle in the *Timaeus*.

Posidonius accepts a four-element universe, taking Fire and Air as aspects of the active or eidetic principle, Water and Earth as aspects of the passive or hylic principle (Fr. 93). This, again, is the scheme which we find Antiochus following (above, p. 82). He differed from Plato and Aristotle, however, in asserting the existence of void (*kenon*) outside the cosmos—not infinite void, however, but just enough for the cosmos to dissolve itself into. Posidonius therefore accepted the doctrine of periodic cosmic destruction (*ekpyrôsis*) which had been abandoned by his immediate predecessors Panaetius and Boethus of Sidon (Fr. 99b), and his curious position on Space is presumably prompted by a feeling that the substance of the cosmos would expand somewhat in the process of *ekpyrôsis*.

So far there is not much to differentiate Posidonius from the main stream of Stoic thought. In his doctrine of Fate and Providence, however, he takes an independent line. The general Stoic doctrine was that Fate (*heimarmenê*) ruled all things, and indeed Posidonius is on record, along with Zeno and Chrysippus, as holding that all things are 'according to Fate'. We have a doxographic notice (Fr. 103), however, that Posidonius held Fate to be 'third from Zeus': 'For Zeus is first, Nature (*physis*) is second, and Fate is third.' What are we to make of this? It is the sort of triadic division that one would expect from Xenocrates, and which one sees operating later in one strand of the Middle Platonic doctrine on Fate (below, p. 324), but it is hard to see what use Posidonius made of this theory, unless it has something to do with a distinction between the heavenly realm, which is administered by God's *nous*, the inanimate, earthly sphere, where he operated as *hexis*, and in between, presumably, the animate sphere, where he rules as *psyché* or *physis*—taking *physis*, as is often the case in later philosophy, as equivalent to the irrational level of *psyché*. But this is mere conjecture. In practice, as far as we can gather from Cicero's *De Fate* (= Fr. 104) and *De Divinatione* (= Frr. 106–10), Posidonius regarded human affairs as being subject to the ineluctable chain of causation, and he based his theory of divination on this theory of the regularity of the universe. We learn from *Div.* I 125 (Fr. 107) that he derived different arguments for divination from each of these three sources, God, Fate and Nature, but here we have not to do with three sources of inspiration, but only two, God (or the gods), who works through dreams and visions (Div. I 64), and Fate or Nature, which provides signs for 'artificial divination' to interpret.

It is in connexion with divination that we find a statement of Posidonius' doctrine of cosmic *sympatheia* (*Div.* II 33–5 = Fr. 106). He adduces the results of his vast geographical and biological researches —considerations of the behaviour of animals, seeds, tides—to prove that all parts of the cosmos are linked together by a natural affinity, which he terms *sympatheia*. This makes it possible, for instance, for the shape of a sacrificial animal's liver to have a bearing on the outcome of a battle. This is not necessarily an original notion. Posidonius himself refers to Xenophanes and the atomist Democritus, as well as to Pythagoras and Socrates, for this general conception (*Div.* I 6; 131), and it is a natural corollary of the basic Stoic theory of *heimarmené*. Posidonius, however, was much interested in astrology (Frr. 111, 112), and this will have lent new force to the doctrine in his hands.

(b) The soul

Posidonius is on record as defining the soul as hot '*pneuma*', but also, perhaps in his comments on the *Timaeus*, as 'the Idea of the omnidimensionally extended, constructed according to number which comprises harmony' (Fr. 141), which is simply a development of Speusippus' definition. Most interestingly, he makes here an explicit equation between the soul, which is in the mid-place between the intelligible and sensible realms, and the Platonic mathematicals, which hold a like position.

The question next arises as to whether the soul for Posidonius survives the body, and if so, what sort of survival this could be. By stitching together an explicit reference to Posidonius in Achilles (*Isag. in Arat.* 13, p. 41, 1ff. Maass = Fr. 149) with a parallel argument in Sextus Empiricus (*Adv. Phys.* I 72) we can, I think, reclaim for Posidonius a belief in the soul's survival and existence independent of the body. His view comes up in the context of a criticism of the Epicureans:

> The Epicureans say that the planets are not living things, since they are held together by bodily substance, but the Stoics say quite the opposite. Posidonius in fact says that the Epicureans do not realise that it is not bodies which hold together souls, but rather souls which hold together bodies, as in the case of glue, which controls both itself and the things which it holds together.

Posidonius here refers to the doctrine of *Timaeus* 36E, which has the soul of the world holding the body of the world together. Sextus does not mention Posidonius in the passage above-mentioned, but from other places where he does so (*ibid.* I 363; *Adv. Log.* I 19 and 93), it is plain that he is using him as a source, and indeed from *Adv. Log.* I 93 that that source was a commentary by Posidonius on the *Timaeus*, or at least a work in which Posidonius discussed doctrines of the *Timaeus*. Here is the relevant passage (*Adv. Phys.* I 72):

> Also they (*sc.* souls) survive on their own, and are not, as Epicurus said, scattered abroad like smoke when released from their bodies. For before that it was not the body that was in control of them, but it was they that were the causes of the continued coherence of bodies, and much more, of their own [a reference, I think, to the glue simile]. For having quitted the sphere of the sun they inhabit the region below the moon, and there, because of the purity of the air, they continue for a considerable time, and for their sustenance they use the exhalation (*anathymiasis*) which arises from the earth, as do the stars as well, and in those regions they have nothing to dissolve them.
>
> If, then, souls survive, they are the same as daemons; and if daemons exist, one must declare also that gods exist, their existence being in no wise hindered by the preconception (*prolêpsis*) about the legendary doings in Hades.

In this passage we have an argument for the survival of the soul, which itself is designed to lead to a proof of the existence of daemons and gods. The doctrine is Stoic, and the argument against the Epicureans parallels closely that in the passage from Achilles, although the types of soul being discussed in the two passages are different. I suggest in the next chapter (p. 116) that Achilles is quoting Posidonius through the mediation of Eudorus, but Sextus seems to have direct access to a work of Posidonius. Kidd follows the salutary principles of Edelstein in including only the Achilles passage, since Sextus does not name Posidonius. One must await his commentary, however, to see whether he thinks that this passage implies a belief by Posidonius in the soul's survival. The doctrine of the Sextus passage is essentially that of Plutarch in the myth of the *De Genio Socratis* (below, p. 222). Although the ultimate source of Plutarch's doctrine is probably Xenocrates, yet the fact that Plutarch uses in his account such Stoic terms as *tonos* and *anathymiasis* does point to Posidonius as an intermediary.

(c) *Ethics*

It is in his ethics, and particularly in his theory of the passions, that Posidonius becomes significantly heretical, moving substantially in the direction of Platonism. Our chief authority for his views in this area is Galen, in his large work *On the Doctrines of Hippocrates and Plato*, where he is using Posidonius (with considerable glee) as a stick with which to beat Chrysippus.

Galen declares that all of Posidonius' ethical theory is dependent upon Plato, since he accepted the Platonic theory of the passions and of the different faculties of the soul (Fr. 150a E–K).[1] This is a direct rejection of the doctrine of Zeno and Chrysippus, who postulated a unitary soul and held the passions to be simply mistaken judgments which could be eradicated by the application of reasoned argument (Fr. 151). Posidonius accepted Plato's tripartite division of the soul, and regarded the passions as springing from the irrational part of the soul (Fr. 157). They cannot therefore be utterly eradicated, and their cure must rely on careful training as well as purely rational exhortation, which leads to their control rather than their rooting out (Frr. 31; 165, ll. 86ff.; 167). This Platonic theory, we may note, Posidonius makes a point of referring back to Pythagoras (Fr. 165, ll. 168ff.).

3. CONCLUSION

This brief survey of the chief philosophical doctrines of Posidonius

---

[1] For a good account of Posidonius' ethical position, see I. G. Kidd, 'Posidonius on Emotions', in A. A. Long, *Problems in Stoicism*, pp. 200–15.

should suffice to make it clear that, like Antiochus, he cannot be claimed as the necessary and sufficient condition of the emergence of Middle Platonism. Like Antiochus, Posidonius was in physics a Stoic materialist, and it is in the realm of physics, with a new belief in immaterial substance and divine transcendence, that Middle Platonism is most clearly to be distinguished from what immediately preceded it. In ethics and logic there was much room for diversity, and the Platonists oscillated between the poles of Stoicism and Aristotelianism, but in their metaphysics they were quite distinctive. Posidonius was certainly an influential figure, both in his own day and in later times, but his influence on Platonic doctrine was peripheral, and much less than his influence in such areas as history or geography. For the true origins of Middle Platonism we must, I think, look elsewhere.

CHAPTER THREE

Platonism at Alexandria: Eudorus and Philo

ANTIOCHUS undeniably turned Platonism in a new direction, but he cannot, as we have seen, be regarded as the direct ancestor of the whole constellation of doctrines which we think of as Middle Platonism. Such characteristics as belief in the transcendence and immateriality of God and the existence of immaterial substance in general, as well as a vivid interest in mathematics, and particularly in mystical numerology, are not to be found in Antiochus as we know him. The *summum bonum*, too, in later Platonism is generally not the Stoic 'life according to Nature', which Antiochus adopted, but the more theological formula 'becoming like unto God', taken from Plato's *Theaetetus*. As for such doctrines as personal immortality and the autonomy of the human soul, or 'free will', whether Antiochus can be said to have accepted them depends on whether we feel able to reconcile *Tusculan Disputations* I and the *De Fato* with the rest of the Antiochian corpus, and both of these, as we have seen, present difficulties.

The same objections that can be made against Antiochus as the key figure are more forcible still in the case of Posidonius. He may well have influenced the early Middle Platonists, in that they read his works and adopted some of his concepts, such as the famous *sympatheia*, but on such matters as transcendence, immateriality and free will—and perhaps also personal immortality—Posidonius remained a Stoic, and could thus not stimulate the movement that was about to arise. Indeed one has the distinct impression that Posidonius in particular is in Philo's mind in his repeated attacks on the 'Chaldaean mentality' (e.g. *Migr. Abr.* 178), which sees no further than this universe and recognizes no higher authority. Philo's pretext for attack is derived from the Old Testament, but the sentiments he expresses would be perfectly proper to any Platonist who believed in a transcendent God. Certainly Posidonius was used by such later Platonists as Plutarch and Galen, but he cannot be said to be the driving force behind their philosophies.

A. EUDORUS OF ALEXANDRIA

1. LIFE AND WORKS

However, even as the fortunes of Antiochus and Posidonius as founding fathers have begun to wane, another star has risen above the horizon, in the person of Eudorus of Alexandria. Eudorus is to us a rather shadowy figure, to an even greater degree than either of his two predecessors, but there are nevertheless in the scanty evidence sufficient clues to suggest that he may be rather more what we are looking for.

All we know of Eudorus chronologically is that he was earlier than Strabo (64 B.C.–A.D. 19), and than Arius Didymus, Augustus' court philosopher and the friend of Maecenas, since Arius uses him as his source for Platonic doctrine in his general survey of philosophic doctrines, of which extracts have been preserved in the *Anthology* of Stobaeus. From Strabo's evidence (Book 17, 790) we may gather that Eudorus was a contemporary of Antiochus' pupil Ariston, whom we met briefly in the last chapter as having gone over to Peripateticism. It seems that both Ariston and Eudorus had written works on the source of the Nile flood, and each accused the other of plagiarism. Strabo professes himself unable to decide between them, so the works must have appeared at more or less the same time, since Strabo is writing almost as a contemporary himself. On the other hand, Eudorus receives no mention from Cicero, which one might have expected, had he been in Antiochus' immediate circle. One may, I think, conclude from this evidence that Eudorus learned his Platonism in Alexandria rather than from Antiochus directly, and only began to be conspicuous after Cicero's death (although Cicero did not keep in touch with the latest philosophical developments in Alexandria in his last years). This points to some teacher of Antiochian Platonism in Alexandria in the 60s of the first century B.C., and for this position we have in fact a plausible candidate in Ariston's fellow-pupil Dion, who, as we have seen (above, p. 62), was a considerable public figure in Alexandria in this period.

However, even if Dion is accepted as a plausible transmitter of dogmatic Platonism to Eudorus, this is not a complete explanation of the phenomenon. For with Eudorus there enters into Platonism a new influence, an influence which completes the amalgam of doctrine to which we give the name of Middle Platonism, that of Neopythagoreanism.

Of Eudorus' works we know only one by title, but we have evidence of a number of others. First we have what we may entitle *A Concise Survey of Philosophy* (*Diairesis tou kata philosophian logou*), of which a portion of the part devoted to Ethics (and probably also some of the Physics) is preserved for us in summary form by Arius Didymus (*ap.* Stob. *Ecl.* II 42, 7ff. Wachs). Arius tells us that this work, which he described as a 'book well worth buying', went through the whole field of philosophy *problêmatikôs*, that is, arranged according to *problêmata* or topics. After his summary of the whole subject-matter of ethics, Arius, it seems, goes on to give us a number of these *problêmata*.

We also find Eudorus commenting on Plato's *Timaeus*. Plutarch refers to him in a number of places in his essay *On the Generation of the Soul in the Timaeus* (see below, p. 207), and it is even possible that Plutarch was using Eudorus as his primary authority for the views of the older Academics (Xenocrates and Crantor) and the 'Pythagoreans'. Thirdly, Eudorus is reported as making a series of criticisms of Aristotle's *Categories*, presumably in a formal commentary on the work. Our authority for this work is Simplicius in his *Commentary on the Categories.*[1] We also know from Simplicius (*In Physica*) that Eudorus wrote on the first principles of the Pythagoreans, though what form this work took is not clear. It does seem, however, to have been a basic statement of Eudorus' own philosophy.

He may also have commented on Aristotle's *Metaphysics*. We have a curious notice, in Alexander of Aphrodisias' commentary on the *Metaphysics* (p. 59, 1 ff.), of an emendation which Eudorus made to the text of *Metaph.* I 6, 988a7, in the interest of 'proving' the assertion that Plato believed that Matter is a creation of the One (see below, p. 128, n. 1).

Then, we have, in the *Introduction to Aratus' Phaenomena*[2] of Achilles, a number of references to Eudorus, of a type which suggest that a work of Eudorus was a major source for Achilles. Whether this work was itself a commentary on Aratus or a more general work

---

[1] The fact that Ariston also wrote a *Commentary on the Categories* is not, I think, irrelevant in this connexion. I would suggest that Eudorus' work is a reaction to that of Ariston.

[2] I give this work its more usual title, although in fact the best ms. seems to specify that the title of Achilles' work was actually *On the Universe*, and that it is only being used by an excerptor as an introduction to Aratus. This has some bearing on the question as to what the subiect of Eudorus' work is likely to have been.

on astronomy is not clear. At any rate, Eudorus seems to have been himself using as a source the Stoic Diodorus, a pupil of Posidonius.

Lastly, we have the afore-mentioned work on the source of the Nile flood, which involved him in controversy with Ariston, and was perhaps ultimately inspired also by Posidonian scientific studies.

2. EUDORUS AND NEOPYTHAGOREANISM

The revival of interest in Pythagoreanism in philosophical circles is one of the more noticeable intellectual developments of the first century B.C. Cicero provides good evidence for this in the introduction to his translation of Plato's *Timaeus*, of which, unfortunately, only the beginning has come down to us. Here there is no sign of Antiochus; instead a new figure appears, Publius Nigidius Figulus (98–45 B.C.), the most learned Roman of his day, after Varro. One is unwilling to credit that a Roman should ever have initiated any intellectual movement in the ancient world, but Cicero's testimony is quite categorical:

He was not only versed in all the other arts which are proper to a gentleman, but was also a keen and diligent investigator of those things which lie hid in Nature. Last but not least, it was he, in my judgment, who, following on those noble Pythagoreans, whose system of philosophy, after flourishing for a number of centuries in Italy and Sicily, was somehow extinguished, arose to revive it.

Cicero does not explicitly say that Figulus was the *first* to revive it, but his words (*'hunc exstitisse qui renovaret'*) seem to imply as much. I would suggest that Figulus may have learned his Pythagoreanism from the Greek scholar Alexander Polyhistor, who was brought to Rome as a slave in 82 B.C. at the end of the Mithridatic War, and was given citizenship by Sulla. Alexander wrote a book on Pythagorean symbols and a *History of Philosophy*, which certainly included a survey of Pythagoreanism (see Diogenes Laertius VIII 25–35). Alexander taught in Rome in the 70s. Cicero never mentions him, though he should have known of him. He may not have got on with him, and perhaps ignored him for that reason, or Alexander may have died before Cicero could make his acquaintance. At least, however, we can conclude from Cicero's evidence that neither Antiochus nor Posidonius, great as their respect for Pythagoras may have been, can be considered to have revived Pythagoreanism in the special sense which Cicero has in mind.[1] It is also interesting that Figulus is brought in here by Cicero in the place of the Pythagorean Timaeus of Locri, to expound a Latin version of the *Timaeus*. It is plain that this dialogue is the key, not only to the rapprochement between Platonism and Stoicism which took place in the persons of Panaetius, Antiochus and Posidonius, but also to the re-introduction of Pythagoreanism into serious philosophical circles. But to get to the roots of this movement one must go back a little way, murky though the path is. There had, it seems, grown up in the early Hellenistic era (third and second centuries B.C.), after the dying out of the old Pythagorean tradition (lamented in the quotation above by Cicero) in the last half of the fourth century B.C., a remarkable series of texts, purporting to be the work of various old Pythagoreans, some famous, some quite obscure, on various subjects of philosophic interest. They were composed, for the most part, in a 'literary' Doric dialect, to accord with that presumed to have been used by the Pythagoreans of Italy and Sicily, and they incorporate much Platonic and Aristotelian doctrine, apparently with a view to substantiating the claim that both these philosophers owed much to Pythagoreanism.

The best known of these works are two cosmological treatises, *On the Soul of the Universe and On Nature*, by 'Timaeus of Locri' (purporting to be the original of Plato's *Timaeus*, straight from the horse's mouth, so to speak), and *On the Nature of the Universe*, by 'Ocellus the Lucanian', but there were a host of others, on a wide variety of subjects, mostly ethical, of which we have many fragments preserved, particularly in Stobaeus' *Anthology*. Of these only some works attributed to the fourth-century Pythagoreans Philolaus and Archytas have any chance of being genuine, and, if they are, they may have provided a stimulus to the creation of the rest.

In spite of the excellent work in recent years of such scholars as Holger Thesleff and Walter Burkert,[2] much remains obscure about

---

[1] We do find Varro, the follower of Antiochus, bringing out, at some time after his 84th birthday (that is, later than 32 B.C.), a work entitled *Hebdomades*, a very Pythagorean and rather senile encomium on the number Seven (Aulus Gellius *NA* III 10). Such interests cannot safely be attributed to Antiochus, however. Varro was a man of enormous and varied erudition, and in this work seems actually to be influenced by Nigidius Figulus (*ibid.* 3).

[2] Thesleff, *An Introduction to the Pythagorean Writings of the Hellenistic Period*, 1961; *The Pythagorean Texts of the Hellenistic Period*, 1965; Burkert, 'Hellenistische Pseudopythagorica', *Philologus* 105 (1961); *Weisheit und Wissenschaft*, 1962 (Eng. trans. 1972). Both Thesleff and Burkert made useful contribu-

these writings. We do not know who wrote them, or when, or why. On the basis of the appearance of some of them first in Philo (of surviving writers), and from the fact of the revival of Pythagoreanism in Cicero's time, we may conjecture that there was a corpus of these works in existence some time before the middle of the first century B.C., and long enough before that time for these works to be accepted by then as genuine.

We may guess from the contents of the works that their purpose was to reveal Pythagoras, or at least some Pythagorean, as the originator of various Platonic and Aristotelian doctrines, and perhaps to satisfy the demand in Hellenistic libraries for 'genuine' Pythagorean works. (King Juba of Mauretania, for instance, was a great enthusiast for *Pythagorica*). The fact of their having been composed at all does testify to a continuing interest in some quarters in the Pythagorean tradition. It is in this period also, presumably, that the myth of Pythagoras' life took the shape which we find reflected later in the Lives of Pythagoras by Diogenes Laertius, Porphyry and Iamblichus, since this image of Pythagoras serves as an inspiration to Apollonius of Tyana in the first part of the first century A.D., and indeed as a stimulus to Philo in composing his portrait of Moses.

All this Pythagorean activity, however, seems to have occurred on the non-philosophical, or at least sub-philosophical, level. The treatises are bald and didactic, stating their doctrine without attempt at proof, and aimed at an audience which, it would seem, was prepared to substitute faith for reason. The new development which appears to take place in Cicero's day, and by which Eudorus is obviously affected, is the introduction of all this Pythagoreanism into a serious philosophical milieu.

In Eudorus' case, what we seem to see is a desire to return to at least relatively genuine Pythagoreanism, that is to say, to the writings of Archytas and Philolaus, together with the accounts of Pythagoreanism given by fourth-century Platonists and Peripatetics, such as Speusippus, Xenocrates, Heraclides of Pontus, Aristotle and Aristoxenus. Eudorus seems to have presented his doctrines as those of the Pythagoreans,[1]

tions to the 1972 *Entretiens* of the Fondation Hardt, *Pseudopythagorica* I, modifying their previous views.

[1] It is perverse, I think, of scholars to take such a passage as Eudorus' account of 'Pythagorean doctrine' in Simplicius *In Phys.* 181, 10ff. (see below) as a mere historical report. By that reckoning, Antiochus must be taken simply as a faithful reporter of Old Academic doctrine, and indeed Philo as an accurate interpreter of the philosophy of Moses.

even as Antiochus had presented his as those of the Old Academy; indeed one may even see this as a move on Eudorus' part to outdo Antiochus and his followers in 'genuineness'. There was a good deal of simple 'one-upmanship' involved in the Neopythagorean movement (Plato can now be viewed as a mere pupil of Pythagoras), and it is a game in which, as we shall see, Philo joined with a will, putting forward Moses as the greatest authority of all, as being the teacher of Pythagoras, and indeed of all Greek philosophers and lawgivers, Hesiod, Heraclitus and Lycurgus, for example. Like Antiochus, Eudorus foisted certain innovations of his own onto his authorities, notably, as we shall see, the doctrine of a supreme first principle above a pair of opposite principles.

Apart from Ocellus Lucanus and Timaeus Locrus, the most interesting *Pythagorica* in connexion with Eudorus are 'Archytas' *On the Ten Categories* and the fragment *On First Principles*, together with references to the doctrine of Archytas, Brotinus, and Archaenetus (who may be just a variant of Archytas) made by Syrianus in his *Commentary on the Metaphysics*. The difficulty with all these works is, of course, the impossibility of dating them accurately, and thus the impossibility of estimating whether Eudorus is following them, or perhaps, both are following a lost common source. Nevertheless, their evidence must be noted.

The question of the relations between 'Archytas' *On the Categories* and Eudorus' critique of Aristotle's *Categories* I will leave to the section on Eudorus' Logic. The other references, concerning as they do first principles, must be considered now.

'Archytas' *On First Principles* (Stob. 1 278–9 Wachs. = p. 19 Thesleff *PT*) recognizes, above the two principles of Form (*morphē*) and Matter (*ousia*), corresponding to the Monad and the Dyad, a third, superior to both, that brings them together. This he described as 'that which moves itself and is primary in power. Such an entity must be not merely *nous*, but something superior to *nous*; and it is clear that what is superior to *nous* is what we call God.'

On this interesting text, Philip Merlan has this to say (*Camb. Hist.* p. 85):

It is difficult to imagine a more syncretistic passage in so small a compass. The two principles of form and matter are Aristotelian; to call the latter *ousia* is Stoic; to teach that form and matter must be brought together by another principle is Aristotelian again; to call this third principle self-moved is Platonic; to call it above intelligence is Platonic—unless we say that it is also Aristotelian, because in *On Prayer* (Fr. 49 Rose) Aristotle says that God is either intelligence or something above intelligence, and because, in the *Eudemian Ethics* (VII 2, 1248a27–9), he says that there is only one thing which is superior to knowledge and intelligence, viz. God.

Whether it is syncretism we see here, or simply a development of Speusippean doctrine, is debatable. The main point of interest for our purposes, however, is the postulation of a principle above the pair of Monad and Dyad. This doctrine is also found in Syrianus' report (p. 166, 3ff. Kroll *CAG*): Archaenetus, Philolaus and Brotinus postulate a 'unitary causal principle (*heniaia aitia*) above the two causes'. Archaenetus calls it a 'cause above a cause'; Philolaus 'the first principle of all things'; while Brotinus says that it is superior to all *nous* and *ousia* in power and seniority. There were, then, available, at least to Syrianus in the fifth century A.D., Pythagorean documents containing this doctrine, but how far back we can date their composition is unfortunately quite uncertain.

I am inclined to believe that Eudorus had some pseudepigraphon on which to base his doctrine, but whether it was any of those above-mentioned is obscure. The same uncertainty, as we chall see in Chapter 7, prevails in the case of Moderatus and the later Pythagoreans.

3. EUDORUS' PHILOSOPHICAL POSITION

Eudorus seems to have taken the three divisions of philosophy, as did Antiochus, in the order Ethics-Physics-Logic,[1] as opposed to the Stoic order Physics-Ethics-Logic (or occasionally Logic-Physics-Ethics). The basic question here seems to be whether one decides that one must begin philosophy by training the mind to conduct logical argument, as did Aristotle, the Stoics and the New Academy, or whether, with Antiochus, one held that first of all one must determine 'whither one is aiming and whence one is starting out', which implies beginning with ethics. Eudorus seems to have started his general survey with the question of the *telos*, which would imply agreement with Antiochus on this point, but his definition of the *telos* was significantly different, as we shall see.

[1] This is the order presented in Seneca's *Ep.* 89, a letter which in other respects is dependent on Arius Didymus' *Epitomê*. Since Seneca always elsewhere adopts the Stoic order of subjects, this may be taken as Arius', and thus Eudorus', arrangement.

(a) Ethics

Eudorus divided the subject of ethics into Theory (*theôria*), Impulse (*hormê*), and Practice (*praxis*). This threefold division, which is found also in Seneca's *Letter 89*, seems to be peculiar to Eudorus. The concept of *hormê* was a basic component of ethical theory in Eudorus' time (Diog. Laert. VII 84), but nowhere else is it raised to the rank of a generic division of ethics, along with Theory and Practice. Under *hormê* Eudorus lists the topics of Impulse in general and of the passions. The topic of the passions would normally be treated under Theory, though of course the passions are material for a treatise by themselves, and were often accorded this honour, notably, in the previous generation, by Posidonius.

An impressive list of divisions and subdivisions is set out before us in Arius' summary, most of them not original to Eudorus, but rather taken over from existing Stoic-Platonic scholasticism. The formal side of ethical theory did not develop very much after Stoics like Chrysippus laid down the main themes in exhaustive detail. Eudorus' terminology is as fully Stoic as that of Antiochus, although, like Antiochus, he would not have admitted that it was distinctively Stoic, but would claim it as the normal current language of philosophic discourse. We, from our perspective, attach too much importance to ferreting out Stoic, and even Epicurean, terms, in Platonic writers. By Eudorus' time, the technical language of philosophy was very largely uniform. Only the meanings given to certain terms by the various schools might differ.

Now let us consider a few key topics. First, the *telos*. With Eudorus we find a most significant change in the formulation of the purpose of life, and one which was subsequently adopted by Platonists over the more Stoic *telos* of Antiochus. Antiochus had defined the *telos* as 'living in accordance with man's nature, it being complete in every way and lacking in nothing' (Cic. *Fin.* v 26). Eudorus, on the other hand, speaks of it as follows:

Socrates and Plato agree with Pythagoras that the *telos* is assimilation to God (*homoiôsis theôi*). Plato defined this more clearly by adding: 'according as is possible (*kata to dynaton*)', and it is only possible by wisdom (*phronêsis*), that is to say, as a result of Virtue.

This is a most important passage, both in its form and in its content. First we note how Pythagoras is brought in as the originator of the definition, with Plato portrayed as agreeing with and amplifying him.

The reference is in fact to a famous passage of Plato's *Theaetetus* (176B), though Eudorus has here given it a subtle twist in meaning. For Plato, '*kata to dynaton*' meant 'as far as possible (for a mere mortal)'; Eudorus takes it to mean rather 'according to that part of us which is capable of this', that is to say, the intellect, and its particular virtue, Wisdom. Of course, Plato also believed this, but what is in fact in the text a modest disclaimer of human capabilities becomes to the more dogmatic mind of Eudorus a specification of precisely the faculty by which we become like God. He goes on to elaborate on a parallel between the wise man's establishment and maintenance of a virtuous life and establishment and maintenance of the cosmos.

This definition, which Eudorus sees as a development of Pythagoras' exhortation 'Follow God', gained universal currency in later Platonism, as we shall see. With this change of definitions of the *telos* we may reasonably see a growth in religiosity in philosophical speculation, even as Pythagoreanism is more of a religion, in our sense, than Stoicism.

The *telos*, then, is 'to live in accordance with Virtue, and that in turn means both the acquiring (*ktēsis*) and the exercising (*chrēsis*) of perfect virtue'. When stated in this way, the *telos* of Eudorus does not differ so very greatly in practice from that of Antiochus; it is in the formulation, as well as in the emphasis on virtue alone, that the difference consists.

Eudorus also gives some attention to what he calls the *hypotelis*, or preliminary *telos*. This concept seems to have been first propounded by a Stoic, Herillus, who intended it, however, to mean the *telos* of the ordinary man as opposed to the Sage (*SVF* I 411), whereas Eudorus uses it for 'the initial instinctive striving of the living thing', which is simply what we saw Antiochus in the last chapter describing as the 'primary impulse' (*prôtê hormê*). Eudorus maintains that 'the Ancients' recognized this concept, though he has to admit that they were not familiar with the term itself.

The next great philosophic issue to be discussed is the question whether Happiness depends on Virtue alone, or on a combination of Virtue with bodily and external Goods. We have seen in the last chapter that Antiochus held to the Peripatetic view that all three levels of 'good' were required for the perfectly happy life. Philo, as we shall see, condemns this view vigorously. The question is, what was the attitude of Eudorus on this topic?

In fact it seems that Eudorus took a more strictly Stoic view than

Antiochus. He speaks of such things as friendship, pleasure, fame and good natural endowments (*euphyia*) not as Goods but as 'things preferred' (*proëgoumena*), using the distinctively Stoic term (e.g. *SVF* I 192). Later, in discussing the *telos*, he criticizes the 'more recent Peripatetics' for defining it as 'the sum-total of all goods'. 'That would imply', he says, 'that which is made up of the three types of "good".' This is not correct; it is not the case that all the "goods" are *parts* of the *telos*, for neither bodily nor external goods are parts of it, but only the activities springing from virtues of the soul. It would have been better, then, to say instead of "made up of", "produced from", in order to bring out the fact that Virtue consists in use (*chrêsis*)' (rather than in the simple possession of 'goods', that is). The bodily and external goods, then, are not to be given a place, as they were by Antiochus, in the composition of the *telos* (or of the Happy Life) but allowed only a preliminary role in contributing to it.[1]

This downgrading of the bodily and external goods signifies in Eudorus an anti-Peripatetic tendency which is also apparent in his attack on Aristotle's *Categories* (see below, pp. 133–4). One may be forgiven, perhaps, for seeing in this tendency a certain element of personal rivalry. We recall the mention earlier of a dispute which Strabo records between Eudorus and Ariston as to who was borrowing from whom on the question of the Nile flood. Now Ariston, we recall, had for some reason gone over to Peripateticism, and it is possible that Eudorus' hostility to Aristotelian ethics and logic may be at least partly motivated by inter-school rivalry.[2] Such rivalry, the constant campaigning for disciples, is certainly attested at Athens in later times, and seems to me to explain a good deal of the polemical in-fighting between the schools on matters that must strike us as trivial.

Such a situation, besides explaining Eudorus' own attitudes, would

[1] If indeed, as I would maintain, Arius Didymus' account of Peripatetic ethics, which he gives after his accounts of Platonic and Stoic ethics (*ap.* Stob. II 116–52 Wachs.), is taken from Ariston (it shows strong syncretistic, 'Antiochian' traits), we may have here some trace of school controversy. The view of the composition of the *telos* which Eudorus criticizes as that of 'the younger Peripatetics after Critolaus' is explicitly repudiated in this text (p. 126, 12ff.), which might indicate that it is an answer to his criticisms. But we cannot be sure that Arius himself is not taking a hand in all this.

[2] The alternative possibility, that Ariston turned Peripatetic in reaction against the increasing Pythagorean tendencies of Alexandrian Platonism, is put by W. Theiler in his article 'Philon von Alexandria . . .' (see Bibl.), p. 204, and is equally plausible. The sequence of cause and effect in these manoeuvres is quite obscure. It is probable that the revival of Aristotle's esoteric works by Andronicus of Rhodes in the 70s constituted an attraction to Aristotelianism.

account for the curious mixture of asceticism and attachment to the good life exhibited by Philo, who combines attacks on the three grades of Good with a distinctly un-Stoical appreciation of the comforts of civilized existence (below, pp. 147, 153). Such a combination of attitudes would most naturally spring from a Platonism engaged in factional strife with Aristotelianism (though we must not neglect the possibility of an inconsistency of attitude quite personal to Philo).

The other topics preserved for us by Arius are entitled 'On Goods and Evils' and 'Whether Everything Noble is to be Chosen for its own Sake'. We may consider each of these briefly.

On the question of Goods and Evils, Eudorus bases himself on the Platonic text *Laws* I (631BC), where Goods are divided into 'divine' and 'human', the divine being in fact the virtues, the human bodily attributes such as health, beauty and speed of foot. The latter are not goods without the accompaniment of the former. This Platonic text is thus most useful for supporting Eudorus' Stoic position.[1]

Expanding on this quotation, Eudorus goes on to list various divisions which Plato makes in Goods. First, he divides them in two according to class (*genos*), the divine and the human mentioned above (to the human Eudorus now adds external Goods). Then there is a threefold division according to 'position' (*topos*), into goods of the soul, goods of the body, and external goods. This is simply a restating of the previous division under a different rubric, and is a distinctly scholastic move. The third division is a fivefold one, according to form (*eidos*). This is more interesting. First, we have the Idea of Good; secondly, we have the mixture of Wisdom and Pleasure; thirdly, Wisdom by itself; fourthly, the combination of knowledge and crafts (*technai*); fifthly, Pleasure by itself.

All these divisions he claims to derive from Book I of *The Laws* and the *Philebus*. Certainly the fivefold division by *eidos* owes much to the *Philebus*. Whatever about the details, we clearly have here a recognized place for the 'human' goods, however inferior they may be to the divine ones, and this is not in substance much different from the doctrine of Antiochus, though the difference in emphasis is of great significance.

There follows, in Arius' summary, another, 'severer' account of Plato's doctrine, to the effect that only what is noble (*to kalon*) is good, the Stoic position. But this is immediately modified in fact by the explanation 'inasmuch as nothing that exists is good, if it does not

[1] It is a favourite text also of Philo's, e.g. *Vit. Cont.* 39, *Heres* 69.

partake of virtue'. This is reinforced by the similes of the torch or the iron being hot only through the agency of fire, and the Moon having light only from the Sun. Nevertheless, some place is left for the lower 'goods'. In combination with Virtue, they also are good; and this is, after all, all that Antiochus had wished to maintain.[1]

The final *problêma* dealt with by Arius is 'Whether everything noble is to be chosen for its own sake', and the answer is, in Plato's case, unequivocally yes. This is supported by a typically Greek etymology—the noble (*kalon*) is so called because it has an innate power of summoning things to itself (*klêtikon*).[2] Aristotle is said to differ from this position slightly in holding that the states (*hexeis*) of Virtue are not to be chosen for themselves, but only the activities based on Virtue, and we have a reminder that Plato places happiness in both the possession and the use of Virtue, whereas Aristotle places it in use alone.

There is, it must be said, no direct criticism of Aristotle in the extracts preserved by Arius, though this may be the consequence of censorship by Arius, who was not concerned in his work with relaying inter-school polemics. However, there is an important criticism (mentioned above, p. 124) of the 'younger Peripatetics after Critolaus' as to what may be included in the *telos*, which could be seen as aimed at Ariston.

(b) Physics

(i) *Pythagorean first principles.* The Neoplatonist commentator Simplicius (*In Phys.* 181, 10ff., Diels) gives us an account by Eudorus of the 'Pythagorean' doctrine of first principles. The Pythagoreans, says Eudorus, postulated first a Supreme Principle which they called The One, and below that a pair of opposites, a Monad and a Dyad, the Monad representing Form, the Dyad Matter.

It must be said that the Pythagoreans postulated on the highest level the One as a First Principle, and then on a secondary level two principles of existent things, the One and the nature opposed to this. And there are ranked below these all those things that are thought of as opposites, the good under the One, the bad under the nature opposed to it. For this reason these two

---

[1] It is not quite clear what relation this latter passage bears to what precedes it. Arius introduces it with the excerptor's rubric '*allôs*' ('otherwise', 'elsewhere'), but it is at any rate not in contradiction with the preceding doctrine. Arius is, one trusts, summarizing a source document more coherent than himself.

[2] Also found in Arius' summary of Peripatetic ethics (Stob. II 123, 9 Wachs.) and in Philo *Aet. Mundi* 76.

are not regarded as absolute first principles by this School; for if the one is the first principle of one set of opposites and the other of the other, then they cannot be common principles of both, as is the (supreme) One.

Eudorus goes on to make this supreme One the causal principle of Matter as well as of all created things, and to call it the Supreme God (*ho hyperanô theos*). Further on again, he gives the name of 'Unlimited Dyad' to the principle opposed to the second One, and finally calls this second One the Monad.[1]

Now Eudorus here is merely combining elements which were readily available to him from Plato, if not from Old Pythagoreanism (though we are in no position to judge this, so much having been lost). From the *Philebus* (26E–30E) he could have gleaned the elements of this theory, since the monad and the dyad are inevitably also Limit and Limitlessness, and the Cause above them, though not called there The One, has a unifying purpose, and is identified with Mind and God (or at least with Zeus).[2] The Old Pythagoreans, on the other hand, do not seem to have postulated a single supreme principle, but rather a pair, Limit and the Unlimited, which for Eudorus is only secondary.

The possibility of Eudorus' originality here is increased by the fact that the *Pythagorean Memoirs* used as a source by Alexander Polyhistor (see above, p. 117) present a system involving simply a Monad, from which arises an Unlimited Dyad, with no sign of any supreme One above both monad and dyad, and we may take it that this was the only authoritative statement of Pythagorean doctrine known to Alexander in about 70 B.C. If 'Archytas', 'Brotinus' and 'Archaenetus' precede Eudorus, they will have to be fitted in, I think, in the period between Alexander and Eudorus, a pretty tight fit.

The postulation of a supreme, utterly transcendent First Principle,

---

[1] It is possible that it is ultimately to Eudorus that Syrianus is referring in his *Commentary on the Metaphysics* (p. 112, 14ff., Kroll), on *Met.* XIII 1079a15ff.: 'Those men (*sc.* those who believe in the Ideas) used to say that, after the one principle (*archê*) of all things, which they liked to call the Good or the One above Being, there were two causal principles (*aitiai*) in the universe, the Monad and the Indefinite Dyad, and they used to assign these *aitiai* conformably to every level of being.' 'Archytas', however (cf. *ibid.* p. 151), or 'Brotinus' (p. 166) is a more likely immediate source.

[2] Eudorus could also have taken up Aristotle's criticism in *Met.* XII 1075b18: 'Moreover, those who posit two principles must admit another superior principle, and so must the exponents of the Forms; for what made or makes the particulars participate in the Forms?' But this is surely the problem which Plato in fact addresses in the *Philebus*, 26Eff.

It is possible also that Eudorus is influenced by the First Hypothesis of the *Parmenides*, cf. Dodds *CQ* 1928, 135ff.

which is also termed God, is a most fruitful development for later Platonism. If we may take Philo into evidence, Eudorus saw his supreme God as transcending all attributes whatever. Since the monad and the dyad were respectively Limit and Limitlessness, the One necessarily transcends both. It is not unlikely that the substance of Albinus' account of the supreme God in the *Didaskalikos* (ch. 10), with its developed negative theology, reflects that of Eudorus.

The One is the ground of all existence; it is also the causal principle of Matter.[1] This doctrine of Eudorus', which contradicts not only Old Pythagoreanism but also strict Platonism, leads to a monism more extreme than that favoured by later Middle Platonism. It appealed to Philo, however, as it fits in with the absolute power accorded to Jahveh, and it is the doctrine, later, of the *Chaldaean Oracles* (e.g. Fr. 34 Des Places, and Psellus *Hypot.* 27).

Eudorus' doctrine of the Ideas is not recorded,[2] but one may reasonably conjecture, on the evidence of Philo, that he saw them as 'thoughts of God', taking 'God' in this case as the Monad. If we may connect what we find in Philo with the evidence presented above as to the Monad and the Dyad, we arrive at the following picture. The Monad will be the archetype of Form, the Dyad the archetype of Matter. The working of the monad on the dyad produces the world of Forms, or Ideas, which, as reason-principles or *logoi* (or, collectively, as the *Logos*), create the material universe. Philo, as we shall see, consistently postulates two supreme principles, or powers, as primal manifestations of God, with the Logos as the principle of their combined activity. His evidence is complicated by the fact that he finds various identifications for these principles in the Septuagint, but the basic notion is not, I think, something which he invented *ad hoc*. This pair is something which would only be found in the Old Testament by someone having already a philosophical reason for wanting to find it there.

It seems reasonable, again, to assume, both from Philo's evidence

---

[1] Apart from the reference above, this is also shown by Eudorus' remarkable 'emendation' to Aristotle, *Met.* 988a10–11, where he makes the One the cause of Matter as well as of the Ideas (*ap.* Alex. Aphrod. *In Met. ad loc.*).

[2] Unless we may take the banal exposition of Plato's Theory of Ideas by Arius Didymus (*ap.* Eusebius *PE* xi 23 = Diels, *Doxogr.* p. 447) as essentially the view of Eudorus. Arius defines an Idea as 'an eternal substance, cause and first principle of each thing being such as it is', 'thing' being taken to denote only natural entities, not artificial creations. They are at least transcendent, which for Antiochus they were not. Albinus adopts Arius' exposition almost word for word (*Did.* ch. 12, see below, p. 269), and it is basic for later Platonism.

and from Eudorus' own known Pythagoreanism, that Eudorus saw the Ideas as numbers. Elaborate number-mysticism is one characteristic element in Philo's Platonism which points to a Pythagorean source, and Eudorus' interest in the numerical composition of the Soul in *Timaeus* 35BC (*ap*. Plutarch, *Proc. An.* 1019Eff.) is thoroughly Pythagorean.

(*ii*) *The physical world: heaven and earth.* We must not neglect to mention what we can recover of Eudorus' views on astronomical questions, since a number of connexions become apparent in this area which help to establish his philosophical position.

We have seen above that Eudorus is used by the writer on astronomy Achilles (? third century A.D.) as a source in compiling his *Introduction to Aratus' Phaenomena*. The first reference (p. 30, 20 Maass) serves to connect Eudorus, in matters of practical science at least, with the school of Posidonius. Diodorus of Alexandria, whom Eudorus in turn is using as a source, was a pupil of Posidonius, and a contemporary of Eudorus himself:

The philosopher Eudorus says that the astronomer Diodorus of Alexandria said that Astronomy differs from Physics in this respect, that Astronomy is concerned with the attendant circumstances (*parhepomena*) of Substance [e.g. 'From what cause and how do eclipses come about?'], whereas Physics concerns Substance itself [e.g. 'What is the *nature* of the Sun?' . . .]. But although these sciences are different in the questions they ask, they are interconnected, since one needs the other.

This sounds like an introductory statement by Eudorus to a work on Astronomy, perhaps an exegesis of Aratus' *Phaenomena*, perhaps not. The fact that he is using the Stoic Diodorus as an authority would naturally lead us to assume that he accepted the Stoic, or at least the Posidonian, account of the heavens, and there is nothing to contradict this assumption. This need not have conflicted with his belief in a transcendent Supreme God, any more than it did later for Philo, who also accepts an essentially Stoic view of the heavens.

Since Achilles is not a man of great original scholarship, so far as we can observe, it is not unreasonable to take Eudorus as being responsible for all references in this work to Diodorus and Posidonius and also, I feel, for general references to Stoic doctrine. We can thus derive a fairly clear idea of Eudorus' doctrine in this area. The heavens are composed, not of aether, but of pure fire, as the Stoics teach (p. 40, 15). There are thus only four elements; the Aristotelian fifth is definitely excluded. The stars are divine heavenly bodies, composed of the same substance as is the place in which they are situated, i.e. pure fire[1] (p. 39, 6). As regards the existence of a void, Achilles at any rate seems to come down against the Stoics in favour of there not being one (p. 38, 11ff.), so that one cannot be quite sure of Eudorus' opinion. Philo, however, propounds the Platonist argument against a void (*Plant.* 7), which may be a pointer to the attitude of Eudorus.

It would be beyond the scope of the present book to go through all the details of astronomical doctrine that might be recovered for Eudorus from Achilles. More significant for our purpose is another set of references which one is much tempted to claim for Eudorus also, those to Plato and the Pythagoreans. The references to the Pythagoreans, especially, would entirely fit in with his known tendencies. The references follow passages where the influence of Eudorus is attested, and they are not taken from the other doxographical work that Achilles was using. Pythagoras or the Pythagoreans are referred to seven times in all, and Plato is quoted or referred to twelve times (mainly from the *Timaeus*).

To the Pythagoreans, for instance, is attributed (pp. 37–8) Plato's apportioning of the five basic geometrical figures to the four elements and the universe as a whole (*Tim.* 55BC), an attribution which might, but need not, imply an acquaintance with *Timaeus Locrus* (98D). At. p 39, 28ff. and 45, 31ff., they are credited with the doctrine that not only the planets, but also the fixed stars, have their proper motion (*Tim.* 39A = *Tim. Locr.* 97C). Perhaps the most interesting reference to the Pythagoreans, however, since it provides a point of contact between Achilles and Plutarch *De Proc. An.*, another work for which Eudorus is plainly a source, is an account of the Pythagorean system of harmonic intervals between the heavenly spheres.[2] The musical details are too abstruse to go into here, but in both cases (Plut. 1028F, Achilles p. 43, 29ff.) the Sun is placed in the central, 'Chaldaean', position among the planets (although Achilles becomes confused on this point at p. 44, 7). It is interesting in this connexion that Philo too adopts this non-Platonic order of the planets (e.g. *Heres* 222–5). No

---

That Eudorus regarded the visible world as a god, though not the supreme god, appears from Stob. II 49, 16–17 Wachs: '[By "following God", Pythagoras means] not the visible and most obvious god, but rather he who is intelligible only, and the cause of harmonious order for this cosmos.'

[2] See on this the discussion of Burkert, 'Hellenistische Pseudopythagorica', *Philologus* 105 (1961), pp. 28–43, which does not, however, bring Eudorus into the picture.

doubt Posidonius is somewhere at the back of this, but Philo's more immediate source will much more probably have been Eudorus. The question of the relation of Eudorus to 'Timaeus Locrus' has recently been dealt with by M. Baltes in a monograph on the latter,[1] in pp. 22–6 of his Introduction. He does not take Achilles into account, but confines himself to the evidence of Eudorus' doctrine in Plutarch, *Proc. An.*, where there are a number of points of coincidence, the most remarkable (1020c) being the choice of the number 384 as the basic number for working out the division of the Soul in *Tim.* 35B (cf. *TL* 96B). Eudorus is actually in this detail following Crantor, as Plutarch (and perhaps Eudorus himself) tells us, not the Pythagoreans, which suggests that such a work as *TL* was not available to him. Baltes cannot, I think, show that *TL* was actually using Eudorus, since the details which he exhibits in common with him can all be traced back to the Old Academy, but his evidence does seem to demonstrate that *TL* is the later of the two. All one can reasonably do, at this stage of scholarship on the subject, is to note the parallels and leave it at that. One is even driven to consider the wild possibility that Eudorus forged some of these *Pseudo-pythagorica* himself; but this solution will not work quite so well for Pseudo-Archytas, as we shall see shortly.

(iii) The composition and nature of the soul. In Plutarch, *Proc. An.* 1013B, Eudorus is stated to consider that both Xenocrates and Crantor, in their theories of the composition of the soul, 'have some portion of probability'. Now Xenocrates declared the soul to be 'a number set in motion by itself', while his pupil Crantor described it as a mixture of the intelligible nature (*noêtê ousia*) and 'that which forms impressions of perceptible objects by means of opinion'. Xenocrates saw the description of the creation of the soul in *Timaeus* 35Aff. as describing the generation of numbers from the One and the Unlimited Dyad, while Crantor laid stress on the necessity of the soul's being able to relate both to the intelligible and to the physical worlds, a circumstance which required it to be compounded of elements of both, symbolized by the natures of Sameness and Otherness.

It is easy to see that Eudorus was anxious to accommodate both views, and indeed they are not necessarily mutually exclusive. The creation of the soul is also the generation of Number, and this generation moves from One, the first principle of all things, to Four, the

[1] *Timaios Lokros: Über die Natur des Kosmos und der Seele, Ein Kommentar*, M. Baltes. *Philosophia Antiqua* XXI. Brill, Leiden, 1972.

number proper to solid bodies. From the abrupt way in which Eudorus is brought in, without introduction, as agreeing with both of these opinions, one might be excused for concluding that he is in fact Plutarch's primary source for the whole treatise.[1] This would accord with the normal method of work of essayists like Plutarch. They quote from various remoter sources without acknowledging any intermediary, and then one casually lets drop the true source by mentioning his views on some minor point, or his 'agreement' with his predecessors. There was no strict rule about accurate attribution of sources in the ancient world.

When Eudorus is brought in again, at 1019E–1020E, it is stated that he is following Crantor in his treatment of the numbers of the soul in *Tim.* 36A, a good indication that here Plutarch is deriving Crantor's views from Eudorus. The exposition of the number-theory behind Plato's description is presented as Pythagorean doctrine.

Another question on which Eudorus is stated (also at 1013B) to be in agreement with both Xenocrates and Crantor is on the question of the eternity of the soul and of the world, that is, that neither was created by God at any point in time. This was a matter of controversy in later Platonism, as we shall see. The orthodox view, which derived already from Speusippus and Xenocrates, was that the world and the soul were not created at a point in time, and that Plato's apparent description of this process in the *Timaeus* was simply presented by him 'for purposes of instruction', as one would, for instance, depict a point growing into a line in geometry. Crantor maintained that the world might be termed 'created' as having been produced from a cause outside itself, and not being self-generated, or self-substantial.

What we must imagine Eudorus' position as being, I think, is that he agreed with Xenocrates that Plato's account of the creation must not be taken literally, but that the world might be said to be created (*genêtos*), though not 'in Time', since Time is a product of the motion of the world itself. The world must thus be taken to have been created extra-temporally, in the sense that it is dependent on an external cause, to wit, God. This is in fact Philo's position in his work *On the Creation of the World*. Absolute eternity would deprive the world of any dependence on an outside cause. There would then be no place for God's

---

[1] It is possible that Plutarch is using also at first hand Posidonius, the only other authority quoted (although Eudorus could very well be reporting Posidonius), but for Old Academic doctrine it is probable that he has contented himself with Eudorus.

Providence (*pronoia*), nor could God have any feeling of attraction (*oikeiôsis*) for something which he had not created (*Opif.* 8–10). Of course, Philo might be considered to be committed to a created world by the text of *Genesis.* That the issue was a very lively one in his time is shown by his curious 'school essay' *On the Eternity of the World*, in which the Peripatetic arguments for the eternity of the world are set out, apparently for subsequent refutation.

Since we have no other explicit evidence for Eudorus' views on Physics, I will give what details we have for Philo when we come to him, with the proviso that it is most improbable that Philo differed from his immediate philosophic source or sources in basic doctrine, and that his source is someone not far distant in doctrine from Eudorus.

(c) Logic

As has been said above, Eudorus exhibits a certain animus against Aristotelianism. This animus is exhibited most clearly in his attack on Aristotle's *Categories.* We have, preserved by Simplicius, nine passages in which he takes issue with Aristotle. His criticisms are certainly in most cases trivial and sophistic, but they are of some importance for identifying his philosophical position, as well as for illustrating the level at which interschool polemic was carried on.

At Simpl. *In Cat.* 174, 14ff., for example, Eudorus shows by the form of his criticism that he is himself adopting the so-called Old Academic categories of Absolute (*kath' hauto*) and Relative (*pros ti*):

Eudorus complains (*ad Cat.* 6a36) that Aristotle, having made the contrast between the absolute and relative categories, discusses the relative, but makes no further mention of the absolute.

These two Platonic 'categories' can be traced back to Xenocrates (Fr. 12 Heinze) and, if we can believe the pupil of Plato, Hermodorus (*ap.* Simpl. *In Phys.* 248, 2 ff. Diels), to the oral teaching of Plato himself, except that Plato is recorded as making a distinction within a category of 'alio-relative' (*pros hetera*) between 'contrary' and simple 'relative'.[1] We may note that Sextus Empiricus, in his exposition of Pythagorean doctrines, at *Adv. Math.* 11 263ff., reports that the Pythagoreans make

---

[1] See Heinze's discussion, p. 37f. of his *Xenokrates.* In fact Plato *Soph.* 255c can be taken as assuming some such division: 'But I suppose you will admit that of existing things some are always said to be absolute (*auta kath' hauta*), others relative (*pros alla*).' We may note also the use of the Platonic categories in Neopythagorean circles, in 'Callicratidas' *De Dom. Fel.* p. 103, 12–13 Thesleff, where the Even is 'of the nature of the Absolute' and the Odd 'of the nature of the Relative'.

a distinction between Absolutes, Contraries, and Relatives, though for 'absolu⁺e' he here uses the term *kata diaphoran*. It is certainly tempting to see Eudorus as an intermediary here. At any rate, he does appear to be using this Academic system of categories to criticize Aristotle.

Another significant move is his rearrangement of the order of Categories (*op. cit.* 206, 10ff.).[1] He wishes to put Quality second after Substance, then Quantity, and then, it seems, Where and When, which he identifies with Space and Time. It is not clear where he ranked Relation:

Eudorus declares that the account of Quality is to be subjoined to that of Substance, and after that should come the discussion of Quantity. For Substance exists only in conjunction with quality and quantity, and after these should be taken the categories of Time and Space. For every substance is 'somewhere' and 'at some time'.

Eudorus' explanations here show that he is taking Substance to refer only to material substance, and thus he is assuming Aristotle's *Categories* to be concerned only with the physical world. This is an important development in the Platonist criticism of the *Categories*, as it leads to the consequence that Aristotle's categories have no relevance to the intelligible world, wherein true being resides. This consequence is developed most fully later by Plotinus in his attack on the *Categories*, in *Ennead* VI 1–3, but also before him by the second-century Platonist Nicostratus (see below, pp. 233–6).

In connexion with these innovations of Eudorus an interesting question arises. What is the relation between Eudorus and the surviving work of Pseudo-Archytas *On the Structure of Discourse*, which purports to be the Pythagorean original from which Aristotle borrowed his *Categories?* Eudorus was, as we have seen, a great champion of Pythagoreanism. Nothing would have pleased him more than to be able to use a Pythagorean original in order to confute Aristotle. But there are difficulties. In his recent edition of this work,[2] Szlezak argues convincingly that 'Archytas' is in fact himself reacting at various points to the formal developments made by the first generation of commentators on the *Categories*, beginning with Andronicus, and thus could be,

---

[1] This order of the Categories was plainly taken less seriously by Aristotle than it was by the commentators. At the beginning of *Met.* XII (1069a20), for instance, he places Quality before Quantity, and we find the same order at 1069b10, with 'Where' subjoined. Further, at *EN* I 6, 1096a25, we have the order Substance—Quality—Quantity—Relation—Time—Place, the latter two being identified with 'When' and 'Where'.

[2] *Pseudo-Archytas Über die Kategorien*, herausg., übers. u. komm., T. A. Szlezak. De Gruyter, Berlin, 1972.

at the earliest, no earlier than the time of Eudorus himself. 'Archytas' takes it for granted that the categories concern only the sensible world, not the intelligible (e.g. pp. 22, 31 and 31, 5 Thesleff). Like Andronicus, 'Archytas' separates the *Postpraedicamenta* from the *Categories* proper. He agrees with Andronicus and Ariston in improving on Aristotle's definition of Relation (*ap.* Simpl. 202, 2ff.), Szlezak is thus justified in seeing 'Archytas', not as a source for, but as a result of, the critical activity of such men as Eudorus. 'Archytas' in fact differs from Eudorus on a number of details, specifically the ranking of Relation, Space and Time. He puts Relation fourth, after Quality and Quantity, and Space and Time at the end of the list—a move in which he is followed by Philo, as we shall see. So if there is to be a Pythagorean source for Eudorus' innovations, it cannot, I fear, be the surviving work of Pseudo-Archytas.

As for Eudorus' own logical system, it will have been Old Academic, rather than simply Stoic, although he might well, like Philo after him, have felt free to use Stoic formulations when it suited him, as being essentially, as Antiochus had 'established', Platonic.

Eudorus' reordering of the categories must also be seen, however, in connexion with his metaphysics. If The One be taken to represent Substance, then the Monad and the Dyad may be seen as answering to Quality and Quantity respectively, Quality being equivalent to Form, or the Logos, which imposes itself on indeterminate Quantity to create the rest of the idea-numbers, and thus the world. Relation might then be taken to correspond to the *logos* immanent in the world. Certainly Moderatus, later, regards the indefinite element in the intelligible world as Quantity (*poson* or *posotês, ap.* Simpl. *In Phys.* 230, 41ff.), and it would be natural for Eudorus to regard it in the same way.

That Eudorus in fact made these equivalences is not, unfortunately, provable, but Philo dwells repeatedly on the links between logic and metaphysics, especially in connexion with the Logos (e.g. *Fug.* 12–13). With the Stoics themselves, after all, logic was closely linked to metaphysics, so why not with Stoic-influenced Pythagoreanism?

B. SOME MIDDLE PLATONIC SCHOLASTIC FORMULATIONS

W. Theiler, in his important work *Die Vorbereitung des Neuplatonismus*, drew attention to, among other things, two of Seneca's *Letters*,

58 and *65*, in which Seneca is plainly borrowing from a Platonic source.[1] In *Letter 58*, Seneca sets out what he refers to as Plato's Six Modes of Being; in *65* he is discussing the Four Causes of Aristotle, 'to which Plato adds a fifth' (*65*, 7)—a perverse way of putting it. Now the formulae which he produces are nowhere to be found in Plato, although with ingenuity and perseverance their germs may be discovered here and there throughout the dialogues. On the other hand, for a man like Albinus, such systematizations are to be accepted unquestioningly as Platonic. Theiler wishes to trace these formulae back to Antiochus, but since the doctrine of the Five Causes, at least, with its accompanying 'metaphysic of prepositions', is to be found in Philo, while on the other hand Cicero shows no knowledge of such scholastic complexities, Eudorus seems a better candidate. Since Seneca wrote these letters probably not much more than ten days apart, he is probably poking around in the same handbook on both occasions.

However, without deciding the question absolutely, we must list and discuss this evidence, as it is unquestionably important for the history of Middle Platonic scholasticism.

To turn first to *Letter 58*, we find here (*ss.* 16–22) a sixfold division of 'the things that are' (*ta onta*), a curious jumble which took its start, perhaps, from Plato's *Sophist*, but is not to be found as such in the Platonic corpus. It goes on as follows:

(1) *The Intelligible* (*cogitabile*, Greek *noēton*), 'that which is perceived neither by sight nor touch nor any sense'. Mentioned as examples of this are: the genus Man, the genus Animal.

(2) Being '*par excellence*' (*per eminentiam*, Greek *kat' exochēn*), 'that which stands out above and surpasses everything', as for instance when the term 'the Poet' stands *kat' exochēn* for Homer. 'Being' in this sense is the term for God. God, then, is not here reckoned as 'beyond Being'; he is simply Being *par excellence*, 'that which is (*to on*)'.

(3) *The Truly Existent* (*ea quae proprie sunt*). These are the Platonic Ideas, and are infinite in number. There follows the definition of an Idea; 'the eternal exemplar of things which are brought into being in accordance with nature', which is essentially Xenocrates' definition (Fr. 30 Heinze), given also by Albinus (*Didasc.* ch. 9, p. 163, 23 Herm.) and in Diogenes Laertius' summary of Platonic philosophy

---

[1] See on this question the discussion of Ernst Bickel, 'Senecas Briefe 58 and 65', *Rheinisches Museum* 103 (1069), pp. 1–20.

(III 77). The Ideas envisaged here are in effect the Stoic *logoi spermatikoi*, seminal reason-principles, which are the only Ideas which Antiochus, as we have seen, would have recognized as objectively existent entities. Seneca uses as an illustration the example of the artist using your face as an exemplar for a portrait of you. As examples of Ideas he gives 'man', 'fish', 'tree'—all natural objects.

(4) The *eidos*, or *immanent Idea*. This is a noteworthy distinction, with the Greek word *idea* confined to transcendent ideas, and *eidos*, 'form', 'shape', being used for their counterparts in Matter. Whether immanent ideas are in fact envisaged at the end of the *Phaedo* is disputable, but they were certainly seen there by later Platonists, who also discerned immanent ideas in *Timaeus* 51A, where the term *eidos* is in fact used.[1]

(5) *Ordinary existents (ea quae communiter sunt)*[2] such as individual men, cattle, or pieces of property—physical individuals, in fact.

(6) Quasi-existents (Greek: *ta onta pôs*), such as Space and Time. These the Stoics would term immaterial entities (*asômata*), while 'quasi-existents' was the term which they gave to the Platonic ideas. Some Platonist here, then, is turning their terminology around. However, it is hard to believe that it is not in fact Matter that is being referred to here. The reference seems to me to be ultimately to *Tim.* 52C, where Space, as the Receptacle, is said to 'cling to existence in some way or other' (*hamôs ge pôs*), and this by all later Platonists was taken as Matter.

We have here a remarkable list of grades of Being—Being itself, the Demiurge, the Ideas, the immanent Forms, physical individuals, and (I think) Matter—constituting a regular Middle Platonic metaphysical scheme. Only the first category does not seem to fit into the hierarchy. It seems rather to be a term common to the second and third categories. Nevertheless, the whole scheme is coherent, and, together with its surrounding material, seems to be taken from a basic handbook of Platonic doctrine. One thinks, inevitably, of Arius Didymus.

In *Letter 65* (sects. 4ff.) we have first, a statement of the Stoics' two causes, then a description of Aristotle's four causes, and then the

---

[1] The distinction between *idea* and *eidos* is made also by Albinus in the *Didaskalikos* (chs. 4 and 10). See below, p. 274.

[2] The distinction between *proprie* and *communiter* seems at first to be a translation of the (primarily) Stoic terms *idiôs* and *koinôs*, but, if so, they are being used in a completely topsy-turvy way, since the Stoics used *idiôs (poia)* to denote individual qualities, *koinôs* to denote general qualities. But perhaps *proprie* is intended to translate *kyriôs*.

curiously phrased statement (7), 'to these Plato adds a fifth, the para-digmatic cause (*exemplar*), which he himself calls the idea'. These 'ideas', Seneca tells us, God contains within himself, and he embraces within his mind the numbers and modes of all the things which must be created. 'He is full of these geometrical shapes (*figurae*), which Plato calls "ideas", immortal, unchanging, and never wearing out.' Here the Ideas are clearly thoughts of God, and also numerical, or geometrical entities, a concept which goes back, certainly, to Xenocrates, but is also distinctly Pythagorean. The analogy with the human craftsman is also used here, as it was by Cicero at *Orator* (7ff.), and will be by Philo (*Opif.* 20).

Seneca now lists the five 'Platonic' causes (8), giving them in the form of *prepositional* phrases:

There are, then, five Causes, as Plato says: (i) that from which (Greek: *to ex hou*), (ii) that by which (*to hyph' hou*), (iii) that in which (*to en hôi*), (iv) that towards which (*to eph' ho*), (v) that for the sake of which (*to hou heneka*).

These are equivalent, respectively, to Matter, Agent (Demiurge or Logos), Immanent Form, Paradigm, Final Cause. This 'metaphysic of prepositions', as Theiler terms it, turns up in later authors in a number of forms. The mysterious 'eclectic', Potamon of Alexandria, probably to be dated in the generation after Eudorus, in defining the Criterion (Diog. Laert. *Proem.* 17), distinguished between *to hyph' hou*, which he takes as the *hêgemonikon*, or intellect, and *to di' hou*, which he sees as 'the most accurate impression' (*akribestatê phantasia*), which is only a non-technical equivalent of the Stoic *katalêptikê phantasia*. As first principles, Potamon took the Stoic active and passive principles, the creative force (*to poioun*) and Matter (*hylê*), Quality (*poiotês*), and Place (*topos*). These he designated respectively as *hyph' hou, ex hou, di' hou*,[1] and *en hôi*. Plainly the metaphysic of prepositions was already popular before Seneca's time. Potamon is placed by Suidas 'shortly before and contemporary with Augustus'.

Since Philo is also acquainted with these formulations (e.g. *Prov.* 1 23; *Cher.* 125ff.), I am inclined to credit them to Alexandrian Platon-ism and to Eudorus, but the claims of Antiochus, pressed by Theiler, cannot be excluded either. Varro, after all, in connexion with his

---

[1] Where one expects *di hou*, the mss. in fact have an anomalous *poiôi*. I take this as a gloss on *poiotêta* which has crowded out the true reading.

allegorization of God, Matter and the Ideas mentioned in the last chapter (p. 95, n. 1), identifies Jupiter with the *hyph' hou* (*a quo*), Juno (Matter) with the *ex hou* (*de qua*), and Minerva (the Logos, or the Ideas, with the *kath' ho* (*secundum quod*)—a variation on the *eph'ho* or *di hou*—which would certainly argue in favour of Antiochus.

In the fragmentary state of our knowledge, we cannot be sure that the system does not go back even further, to the New Academy. We have seen that Carneades was not averse to such scholastic formulations, which Antiochus in turn gladly borrowed from him. But at any rate we can see here the visible origins of what was to become a most popular formula in later Platonism.[1]

C. PHILO

1. LIFE AND WORKS

Philo of Alexandria is one of the most remarkable literary phenomena of the Hellenistic world. He was a member of what was probably the richest and most prominent Jewish family in Alexandria. His brother Alexander was Alabarch (a high imperial tax official), and was declared by Josephus (*Ant.* xx 100) to have been the richest man of his time in Alexandria (Herod Agrippa once borrowed 200,000 drachmas from him). Alexander's son, Philo's nephew, was Tiberius Julius Alexander, who became Procurator of Judaea in A.D. 46, and later, under Nero, Prefect of Egypt. Tiberius Julius became completely Romanized, and, as Josephus says (*loc. cit.*), 'did not remain true to the customs of his ancestors', a circumstance which caused his uncle much pain. Two treatises of Philo's, *On Providence* II and *Whether Animals Have Intelligence*, are addressed to this irreverent nephew. Tiberius seems to have taken a generally Sceptical, New Academic line when arguing with his uncle.

The only secure date we have from Philo's own life is the winter of A.D. 39, when he led an unsuccessful embassy on behalf of the Jews of Alexandria to Caligula (Jos. *Ant.* XVIII 257–60), of which Philo tells the story in his own work *The Embassy to Gaius*. Since he speaks of himself at the beginning of this work as an old man, we may assume

[1] On all this see Theiler, *Vorbereitung*, pp. 18ff. The doxographer Aetius, we may note (Diels, *Doxogr.* p. 288), of the first century A.D., knows the formula well; he gives the three Platonic principles, God, Matter and Idea, as *hyph' hou*, *ex hou*, and *pros ho* respectively.

him to have been approaching sixty at this time. The date of his birth is thus generally assumed to fall between 20 and 15 B.C.

The evidence of his own writings indicates that the atmosphere in his family circle was cosmopolitan and luxurious, but also intellectual. Philo obviously acquired an excellent education. It was not a traditional Jewish education, however, but an Hellenic one. His knowledge of Greek literature, Homer and the poets (particularly Euripides), Demosthenes, and finally and most overwhelmingly, Plato and the Stoics, is evident on every page of his work. His prose, though florid and repetitious, after the custom of his time, is in irreproachable Greek, and redolent of Herodotus, Thucydides, Xenophon and Isocrates, as well as of the chief influences mentioned above.

Above all, however, he is steeped in Plato. His particular favourites are the *Timaeus* and the *Phaedrus*, though he employs also the *Phaedo*, and key portions of the *Theaetetus, Symposium, Republic* and *Laws*.[1] Of course, this selection and order of preference is in no way peculiar to Philo, and merely shows him to be fully in tune with the preferences of contemporary Platonism, but he does not, on the other hand, seem to be dependent on handbooks, as one often suspects to be the case with, for instance, the Church Fathers. Certainly, in the Academy, there was a generally agreed selection of important passages on definite subjects extracted from the dialogues, since the same passages are always quoted in the same connexions by later Platonists, but a man of the stature of Philo will have read the dialogues himself, and the form of his allusions certainly suggests that he had committed a good deal of Plato to memory.

Philo went through the full Greek basic education, or *enkyklios paideia*, as any young Greek of good family would have done, and he speaks of the process repeatedly, and with great respect, even when he is officially inveighing against pagan learning (an attitude which he took up in later years). In the treatise *On Consorting with the Preliminary Studies (De Congressu)*, which, as a symbolic exegesis of *Gen.* 16:1–6, is concerned with the meaning of Abraham's relations with Sarah (Virtue or Philosophy) and her handmaid Hagar (the Preliminary Studies, or *propaideumata*), Philo tells us something of his own experience:

For instance, when first I was incited by the goads of Philosophy to desire her, I consorted in early youth with one of her handmaids, Grammar, and all that I begat by her, writing, reading, and study of the writings of the

[1] See index in Cohn-Wendland ed., under 'Plato'.

poets, I dedicated to her mistress. And again I kept company with another, namely Geometry, and I was charmed with her beauty, for she showed symmetry and proportion in every part. Yet I took none of her children for my own use, but brought them as a gift to my lawful wife.

Music, too, he pursued in the same way, always in the service of philosophy. Philosophy in its turn, he adds, is only the handmaid of Wisdom (*sophia*), which for Philo means Theology:[1]

And indeed just as the school subjects (*ta enkyklia*) contribute to the acquiring of philosophy, so does philosophy to the getting of wisdom. For philosophy is the practice and study of wisdom, and wisdom is *the knowledge of things divine and human and their causes.*

(Note here, by the way, the Posidonian version of the Stoic definition of Philosophy; cf. Cic. *Off.* ii 5, and Seneca, *Ep.* 89, 4.)

Philo's view of his own development is, we may suspect, somewhat idealized (it reminds one somewhat of Augustine's protestations in the *Confessions*). It is unlikely that Philo had in his mind from his earliest years exactly what his philosophy of life was; it is much more probable that at a certain stage of his education he experienced a kind of conversion, a rediscovery of his own culture and traditions. This took a curious form. It was not a rejection of Greek culture and in particular of Greek philosophy, but rather an application of it to the Jews' sacred books, particularly the Pentateuch, the books of Moses.

Such an application was made easier precisely by the gaps in Philo's own knowledge. He knew no Hebrew (or certainly not enough to read a text),[2] and did not even understand the conventions of Hebrew poetry. He was dependent on the Septuagint version of the Bible, and the uncultured Greek of that work is even on occasion too much for his perfectly educated sensibility, so that he frequently misunderstands Hebraisms or colloquialisms.

But the great revelation for Philo was that this apparently primitive collection of works, Genesis, Exodus, Leviticus, Numbers and Deuteronomy, when looked at with a properly trained eye, contained the highest and most profound philosophy. He had learned from the Stoic

[1] Philo's attitude to the *enkyklia* is closely paralleled in Seneca *Ep.* 88, esp. ss. 2off., which are explicitly taken from Posidonius, indicating a dependence, either direct or indirect, of Philo upon Posidonius. Note, too, how Philo manages to blend the Bible story with the Cynic-Stoic allegory of the Suitors consorting with Penelope's handmaids in the *Odyssey* (Bion, *ap.* Plut *Lib. Educ.* 73). For another parallel to Seneca, *Ep.* 88, cf. *Cher.* 114.

[2] For his etymologies of Hebrew proper names, he seems to be dependent on a glossary of some kind (cf. below, p. 182).

(and perhaps Pythagorean) exegesis of Homer what philosophic truths could be concealed behind battles and fornications, shipwrecks and homecomings, and it must have suddenly struck him that this was just what was going on in the Pentateuch.

Once he had decided on this, his life's work was determined. He embarked upon a vast scheme of exegesis; first, a sequence beginning with the essay *On the Creation of the World*, and continuing with Lives of the Patriarchs—seen as 'living laws'—including a life of Moses; which seems modelled on the existing life-myth of Pythagoras; followed in turn by a series of works on the Ten Commandments and the particular laws which fall under each of these. This sequence ends with the treatise *On Rewards and Punishments*. Then we have an even more heroic conception, a virtual line-by-line exegesis of Genesis, beginning with the three books of *Allegories of the Laws*, and continuing, with sundry gaps, to the treatise *On the Change of Names*, which is an exegesis of *Gen.* 17:1–22. To this sequence he appended three books *On Dreams*, of which the latter two are extant, dealing with the dreams of Jacob (*Somn.* I) and of Joseph, Pharaoh, and the chief baker and chief butler (*Somn.* II). Then there is a third sequence, surviving as a whole only in Armenian, covering Genesis and Exodus in the form of Problems and Solutions.

In what order these three great sequences were composed is not clear, but at least that which I have listed first seems to show both more complete Hellenic influence and a less-developed system of allegory than the latter two. In his line-by-line exegesis, Philo is making very creative use of the Stoic method of allegorical exegesis of Homer which was given its final development by Crates of Mallos in the second century B.C., and which seems to have involved the discussion of the literal, ethical and metaphysical meanings of a chosen passage, in that order, with copious use of parallel passages, and of wild etymologies of words, particularly proper names. Since the work of Crates himself, and of his immediate successors, is lost, and we are otherwise dependent for our view of Stoic exegesis upon scattered references and such a later compilation as Heraclitus' *Allegories of Homer*, Philo's evidence is very valuable for reconstructing the form of this type of commentary. The same form is to be seen again much later in the type of allegorical exegesis of Plato practised by the Neoplatonists from Porphyry onwards.

There does, admittedly, seem to have been some native Jewish tradition of allegorical exegesis of scripture. Philo makes reference from time to time to predecessors in this work with whom he agrees or, more often, disagrees (although one sometimes has the uncomfortable feeling that he is inventing these figures, in order to have something to correspond to the periodic criticism of previous commentators, and solving of 'problems', which he found in his Stoic models), but their work cannot in any case have been of the scale and particular form of his.

The work of Philo, tedious though it undoubtedly is in parts, deserves to be ranked as one of the more considerable *tours de force* in the history of thought. His guiding principle was that Moses was a great philosopher (in fact, as it turns out in practice, a great Middle Platonist), that all parts of his work are replete with philosophic content, and are coherent and consistent with each other. As the Stoics claimed for Homer, so Philo claims that any apparent inconsistencies or infelicities are simply signs by Moses to the intelligent reader that the passage is to be taken allegorically. The true meaning lies beneath.

How, one may ask, does Moses come to be, not just a Greek philosopher, but a fully-fledged Middle Platonist? One half of the answer lies in Philo's view of the history of philosophy, which I have alluded to earlier. According to this view, Plato was a follower of Pythagoras (this we have seen already emphasized by Eudorus, and indeed by Posidonius), and Pythagoras was a follower of Moses. Philo may well have been acquainted with that part of the Pythagoras legend that we find evidence of much later in Iamblichus' *Life of Pythagoras* (14), according to which Pythagoras spends a while in Palestine 'consorting with the descendants of *Mochos* the prophet and philosopher'. Now this Mochos takes on something of a life of his own in Hellenized tradition, but he does sound suspiciously like a garbled form of Moses himself. Be that as it may, for Philo Moses was not only a philosopher, but the very father of philosophy, from whom all Greek thinkers take their best ideas.[1]

The philosophy which we find Moses expounding, however, bears an extraordinary resemblance to the type of Stoicized Platonism which Antiochus professed, and is particularly closely related to everything that we learn of the doctrine of Eudorus. All that Philo brings to the mix is a distinctive streak of Jewish piety, a greater personal reverence for God than one would expect to find in a Greek philosopher, even a

---

[1] e.g. *Leg. All.* 1 108, *QG* IV 152, *Heres* 214 (Heraclitus); *Prob.* 57 (Zeno); *Aet.* 18–19 (Plato and Hesiod). Note also Parmenides, Empedocles, Zeno and Cleanthes spoken of as 'divine men' and 'a holy choir', *De Prov.* II 48.

Pythagorean. This piety also leads on occasion to a downgrading of the ability of the human intellect (unaided by God's grace) to comprehend truth, which comes out curiously, at times, as Scepticism. Indeed Philo at one point is able to make use, more or less unaltered, of Aenesidemus' Ten Points against Dogmatism, a most unexpected development (*Ebr.* 162–205).[1]

Our concern in this work is not with Philo as a whole, fascinating a subject though that is, but simply with the evidence which he provides for contemporary Platonism. We cannot, therefore, go into the Jewish side of his thought, such as that was, or into any aspect of his philosophizing which may possibly be original to himself. The reason for this is that there is no evidence that Philo himself had any influence on the course of Middle Platonism, though he certainly influenced the Christian Platonists of Alexandria, Clement and Origen. Apart, however, from the slight possibility that Numenius may have been acquainted with him (which would be an important fact, could it be proved), there seems to be no acquaintance with Philo on the part of any later Platonist. The reader will thus be given a somewhat incomplete view of Philo, but this cannot be helped.

Philo's work is not in general an organized exposition of doctrine. It is a commentary on a source-work, and he may thus be involved in stating his views on any subject at any time. He is also guilty of inconsistencies on various points, but these are a product of his different reactions to different passages, as well as to an acceptance on his part of various equally valid formulations (as it seemed to him) of certain philosophical truths, and they need not disturb us excessively. It does not, for instance, much matter to Philo whether the soul has two 'parts' or three, or whether the division should be between the *hēgemonikon* and the seven faculties. The broad division between a higher and a lower soul is the main thing. Such variations should not be seized upon as evidence of 'eclecticism'; they were permissible variations within contemporary Platonism, at least when some polemical school controversy was not being conducted. I propose to take the divisions of philosophy in turn, and dwell upon the main points on which Philo provides useful evidence.

---

[1] This use of Aenesidemus, who actually professed himself to be a follower of the New Academy of Arcesilaus and Carneades, demonstrates, as in the case of Antiochus' use of Carneadic arguments, how the dogmatic Platonists were prepared to use sceptical arguments for their own purposes. cf. *Jos.* 140–2, where the connexion of these arguments with the Platonic doctrine of e.g. *Tim.* 43Aff. is much clearer.

2. PHILOSOPHY

In general, Philo favours the order of the divisions of Philosophy Logic-Ethics-Physics (e.g. *Leg. All.* 1 57, *Spec. Leg.* 1 336), and the analogy of the Garden (which for Philo is the Garden of Eden). In *Agr.* 14–15, we find the order Physics-Ethics-Logic, still with the analogy of the Garden. One would like to find the order Ethics-Physics-Logic exemplified in Philo, but one does not. It is an argument against his slavish following of any one master, such as Eudorus. Philo was a man who read the basic texts, such as Plato, Aristotle or Chrysippus, for himself.

(a) *The criterion and the telos*

On the question of the criterion of knowledge, Philo accepted the Stoic definition, the *kataleptikê phantasia*. In *Congr.* 141, for instance, he gives the definition of knowledge (*epistêmê*) as 'a sure and certain conception (*katalêpsis*) which cannot be shaken by argument'. This is the Stoic definition (*SVF* 1 68), and presupposes the whole Stoic theory of knowledge. Just above, indeed, Philo gives the definition of an art (*technê*) as 'a system of conceptions co-ordinated to work for some useful end' (Zeno's definition, *SVF* 1 73). All this should not surprise us, but it is welcome confirmation of our previous impression, gained from Eudorus, that Alexandrian Platonism was, if anything, more Stoic in its formulations than that of Antiochus (cf. also *Immut.* 41–4 and *QG* III 3, where the Stoic theory of sense-perception is given).

In the sphere of Ethics proper this becomes even clearer (see below). However, on the question of the *telos*, or purpose of life, Philo follows Eudorus' adoption of 'likeness to God' (*homoiôsis theôi*) for example at *Fug.* 63, where he actually quotes Plato, *Theaet.* 176AB—though he also holds fast to the concept of concordance with Nature (e.g. *Dec.* 81). When speaking of the Patriarchs, for instance (*Abr.* 4ff.), he sees them as being themselves, like the hypothetical Stoic sage, 'laws endowed with life and reason'. Each of them followed instinctively the Natural Law (6):

They gladly accepted conformity with Nature (*akolouthia physeôs*), holding that Nature itself was, as indeed it is, the most venerable of statutes (*thesmos*), and thus their whole life was one of happy obedience to the Law.

What the Patriarchs did is plainly what all of us *should* do. Philo is, then, able to embrace both the Stoic definition of the *telos* and the more

Pythagorean one, without experiencing any discomfort. Since for him 'Nature' is the *logos* of God in action in the world, 'living in conformity with Nature' is simply 'following God'. He relates the Stoic ideal to his own very clearly at *Praem.* 11–13, where he asserts that the ideal of acting in accordance with Nature is quite inadequate unless it also means 'setting one's hopes on God':

> The hope of happiness incites also the devotees of virtue to pursue philo-sophy, believing that thus they will be able to discern the nature of all that exists and 'act in accordance with Nature', and so bring to their fullness the best types of life, the contemplative and the practical, which necessarily make their possessor a happy man.

If they stop there, however, they are to be condemned.

> He alone is worthy of approval who sets his hope on God both as the source to which his coming into existence itself is due and as the sole power which can keep him free from harm and destruction.

There may be in this a note of specifically Jewish piety, but we may assume, I think, a certain increase in piety also, as I have said, in Pythagoreanizing Platonism.

(b) Ethics

(*i*) *General principles.* The mention above of theoretical and practical lives may serve to bring us to the difficult question as to whether Philo felt that Virtue alone was sufficient to Happiness—the strict Stoic view. If put thus baldly, he would doubtless have answered that it was. At *QG* IV 167, for instance, he traces back to Moses the view of 'some of the more recent philosophers', that 'the Good alone is desirable and pleasing for its own sake, but that which is not of this nature is loved for its usefulness'—that is, for its contribution to the virtuous life. This is very much the view of Eudorus, which is itself essentially Stoic.

Certainly Philo opposes vigorously the threefold good of the Peripatetics. He chooses as a representative of this position the figure of Joseph (initially because of his coat of many colours), and he at-tacks him on this ground repeatedly. Let us take a passage from the treatise *That the Worse is Liable to Attack the Better (Det.)* 7:

> (Joseph) is one who moulds his theories with an eye to political advantage rather than to truth. This appears in his treatment of the three kinds of Goods, the external, the bodily, and the intellectual. These, though separated from

each other by complete diversity of nature, he brings together and combines into one, claiming to show that each is in need of each and all of all, and that the aggregate resulting from taking them all together is a perfect and really complete Good; but that the constituents out of which this is compacted, though indeed parts or elements of good things, are not good things in perfection.

He points out that neither fire nor earth nor any of the four elements out of which the universe is formed is a world (*kosmos*), but the coming together and blending of these elements into one; and he argues that in precisely the same way Happiness (*to eudaimon*) is found to be neither a peculiar property of external things, nor of things of the body, nor of things of the soul, taken by themselves. Each of the three classes mentioned has the character of a part or element, and it is only when they are taken all together in the aggregate that they produce happiness.

Joseph must be sent off to his brothers in Sechem (Gen. 37:13), who believe the correct doctrine, that only the Noble is Good (*monon to kalon agathon*), the Stoic dogma (*SVF* III 30 = Diog. Laert. VII 101). The attitude of Joseph described here is precisely that criticized by Eudorus as that of 'the more recent Peripatetics after Critolaus' (above, p. 124). Their doctrine was, we recall, that the *telos* was made up of the three types of good *as essential components*, not even Virtue, that is, being sufficient to produce any happiness by itself. This doctrine was also adopted by the 'eclectic' Potamon (DL *Proem.* 21; cf. above, p. 138). With Philo, as with Eudorus, we may see here an element of polemic against contemporary Peripatetics.

Philo does not always, however, stick to this high line. Here is a passage from the treatise *Who is the Heir of Divine Things?* (*Heres*) 285–6, where he shows that the Antiochian view of Happiness would suit him equally well:

So then, if a man be 'nourished with peace' (Gen. 15:15), he will depart, having gained a calm, unclouded life, a life of true bliss and happiness. When will this be found? When there is welfare outside us, welfare in the body, and welfare in the soul, the first bringing ease of circumstance and good repute, the second health and strength, the third delight in the virtues. For each part needs its own proper guards. The body is guarded by good repute and unstinted abundance of wealth, the soul by the complete health and soundness of the body, the mind by the acquired love of the various forms of knowledge.

There is not necessarily gross inconsistency here. Philo would still maintain—as would Antiochus—that true happiness lay in virtue, and that virtue alone could provide a happy life—but not a supremely happy life. And what Philo is here describing is the supremely happy life. The 'younger Peripatetics', as portrayed by Eudorus, took the two lower kinds of good as *essential* components of happiness, and it is on the question of their essential participation that a polemical dispute could flourish.

There is another passage, however, which goes even further to-wards compromise, *QG* III 16, where Philo is speaking of 'the perfec-tion (*teleiotês*) arising from three goods, spiritual, corporeal and ex-ternal'. 'This doctrine', he continues, 'was praised by some of the philosophers who came afterwards [i.e. after Moses], such as Aristotle and the Peripatetics. Moreover, this is said to have been the legislation of Pythagoras.'

To link Aristotle with Pythagoras and Moses is to confer great distinction upon him, and the doctrine approved seems to involve happiness being a combination deriving its perfection from all three components. The truth may after all be that Philo, who was not a naturally ascetic man,[1] was prepared to accept now the Stoic, now the Antiochian (or even Peripatetic) formulation, according as he was stimulated one way or the other by his text. Such a text as *Deut.* 28:1–14, for example, where Jahveh dwells in some detail on the material benefits he will bestow on the Jewish race if they behave themselves, seemed to necessitate a recognition of the three classes of Good, and Philo certainly does so in commenting on this text at *Virt.* 78–126.[2]

But Philo's ethics is predominantly Stoic, at least in formulation. A perusal of Von Arnim's *Stoicorum Veterum Fragmenta* will reveal how much, in the absence of the primary authorities, Philo has contributed to our knowledge of Stoic doctrine and terminology. However, superimposed upon this Stoic base are certain characteristics which might be considered Jewish, but might also be claimed as Pythagorean.

As has been pointed out already, the ideal of likeness to God takes on a different meaning from the Stoic ideal of conformity to Nature, if one believes in a transcendent God and holds that escape from the toils of this world and from the prison of the body to a better life is both desirable and possible. A passage at the end of Book I of the *Allegories of the Laws* is worth quoting in this connexion:

---

[1] cf. his denunciation of ostentatious Cynic-Style asceticism at *Fug.* 33.

[2] He also pays eloquent tribute to the Aristotelian 'mean' (*mesotês*) in his exegesis of the 'Royal Road' of Num. 20:17 (*Deus* 162ff.; *Spec. Leg.* IV 168).

That is an excellent saying of Heraclitus, who on this point was following Moses' teaching. 'We live', he says, 'their death, and are dead to their life.' He means that now, when we are living, the soul is dead, and has been entombed in the body (*sôma*) as in a sepulchre (*sêma*); whereas should we die, the soul lives forthwith its own proper life, and is released from the body, the baneful corpse to which it was tied.

We find in this short extract, beside testimony to a more than Stoic asceticism, a reference to Heraclitus learning from Moses, the use of the famous *sôma-sêma* formula (probably taken from Plato, *Gorgias* 493A, but generally attributed to the Pythagoreans, and to Philolaus in particular), and finally a veiled reference to that unpleasant story about the Etruscans, that they tied live men to corpses as a punishment (cf. Arist. *Protr.* Fr. 10b Ross—an *exemplum* which had plainly by this time become a sophistic commonplace).

(*ii*) *The virtues.* A distinctly Pythagorean element emerges, again, in the praise of Justice which occurs at the end of *Special Laws* IV, where Philo sets out to discuss, as an appendix to his treatment of the individual laws, the activities falling under each of the virtues in turn, beginning with Justice. The virtues actually discussed are not the basic four (Wisdom, Justice, Courage and Moderation), although Philo normally quotes these as a group, and accepts their Stoic definitions (e.g. *Leg. All.* I 63–5). Here, however, he discusses Justice, Courage, Philanthropy, Repentance and Good Breeding, a rather mixed bag. But let us consider now a significant extract from his praise of Justice, which he sees as a product of the Pythagorean concept of Equality (*isotês*), the force which keeps the world in equilibrium:

> But as for Justice itself, what writer in verse or prose could worthily sing its praise, standing as it does superior to all that eulogy or panegyric can say? Indeed one, and that the most august, of its glories, its high lineage, would be a self-sufficient matter for praise if all the rest were left untold. For the mother of Justice is Equality, as the masters of natural philosophy (*sc.* the Pythagoreans) have handed down to us, and Equality is light unclouded, an intelligible sun, if the truth be told, just as its opposite, Inequality in which one thing exceeds or is exceeded by another, is the source and fount of darkness. (*Spec. Leg.* IV 230–1)

This is a most satisfactory passage, linking as it does Equality and Inequality with the equally Pythagorean principles of Light and Darkness, and introducing as well the idea of Equality as the intelligible archetype of the Sun, thus borrowing something from the Sun simile of the *Republic*. The number Four is also brought in here, as elsewhere, as the symbol of Justice.

It is by such touches as this that Philo superimposes Pythagoreanism upon the Stoic basis of his ethics[1]—though it is more probable, indeed, that such a superimposition was already fully executed by Eudorus. Philo, however, makes Piety (*eusebeia*) or Holiness (*hosiotês*), the queen of the virtues (*Spec. Leg.* 135), rather supplanting Wisdom, which he only ranks second to this. When talking of Philanthropy, however, in his essay *On the Virtues* (95), he ranks it as the twin of Piety—*philanthrôpia* being that goodwill towards men, and indeed towards creation in general, that is the counterpart to the honouring of God, defined by the Stoics as 'the science of the service of the Gods' (*SVF* II 1017). *Philanthrôpia* does not seem to have been listed as a virtue by the Stoics, but Philo could refer back for this notion of its twinness with *eusebeia* to Plato's *Euthyphro*, 12cff., where holiness is made one division of justice. The other division is not given a name by Plato, though it is referred to in 12E as 'that part (of Justice) which has to do with the service (*therapeia*) of men'. That Philo had the *Euthyphro* well in mind is shown by the echoes of *Euth.* 13Aff. in *Det.* 55–6.[2]

Philo is also prepared to accept the Aristotelian concept of virtue as a mean between extremes (*Eth. Nic.* II 6–7). His exegesis of the 'Royal Road' down which the Israelites promise to travel, 'turning aside neither to the right hand nor to the left' (Num. 20:17) leads him to propound this doctrine. *Deus* 162–5 is a good passage to illustrate this. All the four virtues (with Piety taking the place of Justice) are depicted as means between excesses. In this connexion, at *Migr. Abr.* 147, we have the following:

Hence it is that some of those who follow the mild and social form of philosophy have said that the virtues are means, fixing them in a borderland, feeling that the overweening boastfulness of a braggart is bad, and that to adopt a humble and obscure position is to expose yourself to attack and oppression, whereas a fair and reasonable mixture of the two is beneficial.

---

[1] We may note, however, that Philo's Pythagoreanism does not extend to sympathy with animals. In the treatise *On Whether Animals have Reason* he maintains, against his nephew Alexander, the Stoic position that they do not.

[2] For a good discussion of what may be termed 'the Canon of the Two Virtues' here adopted by Philo and probably brought back into philosophy by Posidonius, see A. Dihle, 'Der Kanon der Zwei Tugenden', *Arbeitsgemeinschaft fur Forschung des Landes Nordrhein-Westfalen*, Heft 144 (1968).

The 'mild and social form of philosophy' is plainly Aristotelianism, to which Philo is being polite here, while not entirely identifying himself with it.

(*iii*) *The passions*. Philo is normally an advocate of the extirpation of the passions (*apatheia*), as opposed to their mere control (*metriopatheia*)[1] (e.g. *Leg. All.* iii 129, *Agr.* 10), but we find him, for instance, praising pity as 'that most necessary passion and most akin to the rational soul' (*Virt.* 144). This could be taken as a mere lapse from philosophical consistency (he should say '*eupatheia*' rather than '*pathos*'), but the sympathy shown to animals and plants in this whole section of the treatise *On the Virtues* (125–59) is not consistent with Stoicism, and much more proper to Pythagoreanism, although it is also provoked, of course, by the relevant texts from the Pentateuch.

At *QG* ii 57, on Gen. 9:3 ('Every reptile that lives shall be to you for food'), Philo takes the opportunity to contrast in a Stoic manner the passions with their corresponding *eupatheiai* or 'equable states' (cf. above, Chapter 2, p. 77):[2]

> The passions resemble unclean reptiles, equability (*eupatheia*) the clean. And answering to the passion of Pleasure (*hêdonê*), there is Joy (*chara*) and Happiness; answering to Desire (*epithymia*), there is Will (*boulêsis*) and counsel; answering to Grief (*lypê*), there is a pricking of conscience (*dêgmos*) and vexation; and answering to Fear (*phobos*), there is Caution (*eulabeia*).

A comparison with the basic text for Stoic doctrine, *DL* vii 116 (*SVF* iii 431) will reveal an interesting addition by Philo, to wit, a rational equivalent to Grief. The Stoics allowed only three *eupatheiai*, declaring that Grief had no rational equivalent (Cic. *Tusc. Disp.* iv 12 = *SVF* iii 438). Philo, as we have seen above, produces such an equivalent in *dêgmos*, and we find the same term attested later by Plutarch

---

[1] *Metriopatheia* is, however, a state proper to the *prokoptôn*, the man still making progress (which means in fact most of us, since the Sage is hardly, if at all, to be found). The *prokoptôn* is symbolized by the figure of Aaron (*Leg. All.* iii 132). But *metriopatheia* seems to be accepted at *Virt.* 195 as the natural opposite to 'lack of control of the passions'.

[2] The text survives only in Armenian translation, and the best information I can obtain indicates that the translator largely missed the point of Philo's exegesis. Marcus' *Loeb* translation is quite inadequate. The Arm. tr. gives the same word, *berkruthiwn*, to translate *eupatheia* and *chara*, showing that he misunderstood the passage. Again, instead of 'fear' (*phobos*), he seems to be translating 'desire' (*pothos*, Arm. *p'ap'akumn*), which makes nonsense in the context, and indicates either a misreading of, or a mistake in, his Greek original.

(*Virt. Mor.* 9, 449A). Philo is thus the earliest evidence for a modification of Stoic doctrine, which may most reasonably be credited to the Stoicizing Platonists of Alexandria.[1]

At *Heres* 245, Philo employs the Stoic definition of Passion, 'immoderate impulse' (*hormê pleonazousa*) in the course of an attack on the vices, in which he also connects them, as he likes to do, with the Unruly Horse of the *Phaedrus* myth. A strict Stoic position cannot be assumed in this passage, however, as Philo has been attacking excessive manifestations of the passions which every Platonist and Aristotelian would agree with him in wishing to repress. Nevertheless, Philo in his ethical theory reflects the 'swing to the right' that had taken place in Alexandrian Platonism vis-à-vis Antiochus' more 'broadminded' position.

(*iv*) *The path to virtue: nature, instruction, practice.* In the *Life of Abraham* (52–4), Philo avails himself of a scholastic formulation, going back to Aristotle (*EN* x 9 1179b20ff.; *EE* 1 1, 1214a16ff.; cf. *DL* v 18), but doubtless received by Antiochus' time into the bosom of Platonism,[2] which distinguished three elements necessary to the acquisition of perfect virtue, nature, instruction and practice (*physis—mathêsis—askêsis*). The pupil must be of a nature apt to ethical instruction, he must fall in with a suitable instructor, and he must practise assiduously the instructions received. If any of these conditions be lacking, perfect virtue will not be achieved. Philo identifies each of these three conditions with one of the three Patriarchs, Abraham representing *mathêsis*, Isaac *physis*, and Jacob *askêsis*, basing his identification on his customary fanciful etymologies. The passage deserves quotation:

The holy text (*hieros logos*—actually *Ex.* 3:15) seems to be searching into types of soul, all of them of high worth, one which pursues the Good (*to kalon*) by means of instruction, one by natural aptitude, one through practice.

He then identifies Abraham, Isaac and Jacob with these three in order, noting that of course they all possess all three qualities, but that each gets his name from that which chiefly predominates in him. Here,

---

[1] Note also *Leg. All.* II 8, where Philo declares that the passions can be a help to man, if properly employed. Here *lypê* and *phobos* are praised for 'biting' (*daknonta*) the soul and warning it never to relax its guard.

[2] It also turns up in the *Pythagorica* ('Archytas', *De Educ.* 3, p. 41, 20ff., Thesleff), the triad there being *physis*, *askêsis*, and *eidêsis* (knowledge).

we may note, he uses another scholastic formulation, that we have seen also used by Antiochus (*ap.* Cic. *TD* v 22). A hint of previous allegorizing is given by his report that 'another name is given to them by men, who call them the Graces, also three in number; either because these values are a gift of God's grace to our kind for perfecting its life, or because they have given themselves to the rational soul as a perfect and most excellent gift.'

(*v*) *Politics*. Philo's political practice and theory has been excellently set forth by E. R. Goodenough in his monograph *The Politics of Philo Judaeus* (Yale, 1938), and I will be relying heavily upon it in this section.

Like Antiochus, Philo was in favour of the wise man's entering politics. He does not approve of excessive asceticism, or of a monastic retirement from society, except for short periods of recuperation, such as were, perhaps, his own visits to the Therapeutae. His essay *On Flight and Finding* provides a good passage on this subject (*Fug.* 33ff.):

Truth would properly blame those who without examination abandon the transactions and business activity of civic life and profess to despise fame and pleasure. For they are pretending, and do not really despise these things; they are only putting forward their filthiness, their gloominess, and their austere and squalid way of life as a bait, on the pretext that they are lovers of propriety and self-control and patient endurance.

He goes on for some time on this theme. The challenge of Cynic asceticism plainly bothered him somewhat, and he goes to considerable lengths to denounce it. As an individual, then, Philo was not prepared to renounce his inherited position of prominence within the Alexandrian Jewish community, much though he might complain about its burdens from time to time.

This does not, of course, as we have seen, prevent him from attacking the concept of the politician in the person of Joseph (*Det.* 7), and the Peripatetic ethical theory which he sees behind it. All this is a sign of inner tensions. Goodenough acutely discerns in Philo a lively hatred of the Roman regime under which the Jews had to exist, a hatred, however, which he never, for reasons of prudence, allowed to come to the surface.

But this has little to do with Philosophy. What philosophical principles did Philo bring to the subject of Politics? His principles are ultimately Stoic, though filtered through contemporary Platonism, and also, perhaps, through that of certain Neopythagorean writings, such as the treatises of 'Diotogenes', 'Ecphantus' and 'Sthenidas' *On Kingship*. In spite of interesting resemblances, though, the dating of these documents is so uncertain that the nature of their relationship to Philo's doctrine is impossible to decide.

Perhaps the central principle of Philo's political theory is, not surprisingly, the Logos as God's agent in the world, conveying to men, and to Nature in general, the Natural Law (*nomos tês physeôs*), by which all men are bound. Individual forms of government and empires rise and fall, but the Logos works on harmoniously towards the establishment of a cosmic order, which Philo curiously terms a 'democracy'. A good passage is *Immut.* 176 (he has just been listing, with some satisfaction, the successive fall of certain well-known empires):

> For the divine Logos moves in a cyclic dance, which the majority of men call Fortune (*tychê*); in its constant flux it makes distribution city by city, nation by nation, country by country. What these had once, those have now. What all had, all have. Only on a temporary basis does it change the ownership from each to each, so that the whole of the inhabited world (*oikoumenê*) should be as a single state (*polis*), enjoying that best of constitutions, Democracy.

Whence Philo derived this remarkable concept of Democracy it is hard to see. Surely not from the Platonic, Aristotelian or Stoic traditions, where democracy is never an ideal constitution, rarely even a tolerable one. It may possibly have figured in more popular Cynic tradition, but there is no evidence on this point. From the contexts in which Philo uses the term (*Agr.* 45; *Confus.* 108; *Abr.* 242; *Spec. Leg.* IV 237; *Virt.* 180), we gather that it means to him a constitution in which each is given his due—what Plato and Aristotle would call 'geometrical equality', implying a proper weighting of power in favour of the well-to-do. It is probable that for him Augustus' settlement was an establishment of 'democracy' in this sense. So much at least one might gather from the unfavourable comparison that Philo makes between Caligula's rule and that of Augustus in the *In Flaccum* and the *Embassy*.

On the cosmic level, a world 'democracy' will be an order, ruled by the Logos itself, in which each nation, large and small, has its due, and no more nor less than its due. Thus both within the state and on a world scale Philo stands for what Plato and Aristotle would simply term *politeia,* or the constitution *par excellence.* How he arrived at this rather controversial term for it, however, is something of a mystery.

(c) Physics

(i) *God and the world.* Philo follows a system in which the supreme principle is the One, though for him it is also, of course, the personal God of Judaism. He calls it frequently the One, the Monad, or the Really Existent (*to ontôs on*), for example at *Deus* 11 and *Heres* 187[1] At *Spec. Leg.* II 176, the Monad is said to be 'the incorporeal image of God', whom it resembles because it also stands alone. Among other normal epithets of God, such as 'eternal', 'unchanging' and 'imperishable', Philo produces others for which he is our earliest authority. At *Somn.* I 67, for example, God is described as 'unnamable' (*akatonomastos*) and 'unutterable' (*arrhêtos*) and incomprehensible under any form (*kata pasas ideas akataléptos*), none of which terms are applied to God before his time by any surviving source. The question thus arises as to whether Philo is responsible for introducing the notion of an 'unknowable' God into Greek thought. I find it difficult to credit, however, that a man like Albinus (in ch. 10 of his *Didaskalikos*) is influenced by Philo. There is no indication that any of the school Platonists ever read Philo. The alternative is that the influence of the First Hypothesis of the *Parmenides,* which is behind Albinus' negative theology, was already at work in Alexandrian Platonism before Philo's time. I have suggested above (p. 128) that Eudorus' highest God is a suitable recipient of such epithets as these, being as he is above Limit and Limitlessness, but the nature of the evidence does not permit of certainty.

There is a remarkable passage, *Opif.* 100, where Philo is praising the number Seven, which is worth quoting at length for the Pythagorean lore which it contains:

It is in the nature of Seven alone, as I have said, neither to beget nor to be begotten. For this reason other philosophers liken this number to the motherless and virgin Victory [i.e. Athena], who is said to have appeared out of the head of Zeus, while the Pythagoreans liken it to the ruler of all things, as that which neither begets not is begotten remains motionless; for creation takes place in movement, since there is movement both in that which begets and that which is begotten. There is only one thing that neither causes motion

---

[1] Philo does often vary the Platonic title 'That Which Is' (*to on*) with a more personal form derived from the Septuagint, 'He Who Is' (*ho ón*). This may be taken as influence from Judaism, and so is of no concern to us.

nor experiences it, the supreme Ruler and Sovereign. Of him Seven may be fitly said to be the image (*eikôn*). Evidence of what I say is supplied by Philolaus in these words: 'There is a Ruler and Sovereign of all things, God, ever One, abiding, unmoved, like only to himself, different from all else.'

The Hebdomad itself is the symbol, properly, of the Logos in its transcendent aspect, as is plain from other passages (e.g. *Heres* 216; *Spec. Leg.* ii 58ff.), but the Supreme God is also being discussed here. In Philo's text this comes up in connexion with the Sabbath, but in a *Commentary on the Timaeus*, for example, it would be appropriate in connexion with *Tim.* 36D, where Plato describes the seven circles into which the Circle of the Other is split. The quotation from Philolaus is most interesting (even though other sources quote this passage as from Onatas, cf. Thesleff *PT* p. 140), as being evidence of the influence of Neopythagorean texts on the Platonism on which Philo is drawing.[1]

Philo is not always content to refer to God as The One, however. On occasion he goes further, indulging in flights of negative theology. In the essay *On the Contemplative Life* (2), he speaks of the Therapeutae as worshipping 'the Existent (*to on*), which is better than the Good, purer than the One, and more primordial than the Monad' (cf. also *Praem.* 40, and *QE* ii 68, where he describes him as 'superior to One and Monad and Origin (*archê*)'. This goes further than Eudorus, who would make the Good and the One epithets of the Supreme Principle, both being more primordial than the Monad. But then one must not treat an essentially rhetorical flourish as if it were a strictly philosophical statement. Philo is quite content on many other occasions to use any of these terms to designate God. He is obviously acquainted, however, with the formulae of negative theology. A good passage in this connexion is the following, from the beginning of the *Embassy to Gaius* (*Leg.* 6):

For reason (*logos*) cannot attain to God, who is totally untouchable and unattainable, but it subsides and ebbs away, unable to find the proper words (*kyria onomata*) to use as a basis to reveal, I do not say Him Who Is (*ho ôn*), for if the whole heaven should become an articulate voice, it would lack the apt and appropriate terms needed for this, but even God's attendant powers (*doryphoroi dynameis*).

---

[1] Philo explicitly names a Pythagorean text on only one occasion—*Aet.* 12, where he says that he has read the work of Ocellus Lucanus *On the Nature of the Universe*, which, he says, is thought by some to be the source of the doctrine propounded by Aristotle of the eternity of the world. This effort to rob Aristotle of the credit for originality in this matter smacks of Eudorus.

In this situation, as he explained just previously, a kind of mystical vision is the only thing that can connect us to any extent with God, or even with his Powers.

When one has established a totally transcendent God, there straightway arises in an acute form the problem of his relations with the universe. Philo's doctrine in this regard requires close attention; while there is much here which he derived from contemporary Platonism, there are certain aspects of his doctrine which are peculiar, and may be non-Hellenic or even original.·

These we will turn to presently, but first we must consider certain basic doctrines of his which are certainly Platonic. In an important passage near the beginning of his treatise *On the Creation of the World* (7–9), he sets out his doctrine on the relation between God and the world. As will be seen, he attacks Aristotle and adopts a Stoicized version of Plato's account in the *Timaeus*. It is accepted that the world was created. This is not a creation in Time, however, since Time comes into being only *with* the world cf. sects. 26–7, but it is creation in the sense of dependence for its existence on an external cause. This, as we shall see, was the general Platonic view in later times, given its greatest elaboration by Calvenus Taurus (below, pp. 242–3). The text is as follows:

There are some people (*sc.* the Peripatetics), who, having the world in admiration rather than the Maker of the world, pronounce it to be without beginning and everlasting, while with impious falsehood they postulate in God complete inactivity; whereas we ought on the contrary to be struck with wonder at the powers (*dynameis*) of God as Maker and Father (cf. *Tim.* 28C), and not to assign to the world a disproportionate majesty. Moses, both because he had attained the very summit of philosophy, and because he had been divinely instructed in the greater and most essential part of Nature's lore, could not fail to recognise that in the realm of existence (*ta onta*) there are two elements, an *active* causal principle and a *passive* element (basic Stoic doctrine, *SVF* 1 85), and that the active cause is the perfectly pure and unsullied Mind of the universe, transcending virtue, transcending knowledge, *transcending the Good Itself and the Beautiful Itself*, while the passive part is in itself incapable of life or motion, but, when set in motion and shaped and enlivened by Mind, changes into the most perfect masterpiece, namely this world.

The equation of the active principle with Mind goes back to Plato *Philebus* 30A–E, a most fruitful passage for later Platonism. Placing God 'above' the Good and 'above' the Beautiful does seem to be a conscious 'improvement' on *Rep.* VI 508–9 and *Symp.* 211D, where these entities are respectively made the supreme principle, but it also agrees with the doctrine of Speusippus, filtered, perhaps, through Pythagorean sources.

As Philo goes on to argue, denial of creation involves also the denial of Providence, as the interest which God takes in the world is that of a father in his offspring or a craftsman (*dēmiourgos*) in his handiwork; there can be no common bond of interest (*oikeiōsis*) between a non-creator and what he has not created.[1]

As to whether God also creates Matter—a non-Platonic view already propounded by Eudorus (above, p. 128)—there are passages in Philo which would seem to point either way. On the one hand, the account given above certainly envisages a basic, passive *stuff* out of which the active principle fashions the world, and there are other passages in which Matter is treated as preceding the creation of the world. At *Heres* 160, for example, he speaks of a pre-existent Matter in a thoroughly Platonic manner. In *Leg. All.* II 2, on the other hand, it is said that 'neither before creation was there anything with God, nor, when the universe had come into being, is anything to be ranked with him', and in the *De Providentia* (I 8) he argues that there can never have been a time when Matter was not organized by God, from which it follows that he sees it as dependent on God in the same way as the universe.

The doctrine of Book I of the *De Providentia* is much more definite about the creation and destruction of the world than the rest of Philo's writings, and Plato is quoted in support of this position (sects. 21–2), against the more normal Platonist doctrine; yet not even this work, contaminated as it may be by Armenian Christian elements, can be adduced to prove a concept of creation *ex nihilo* in Philo.

(*ii*) *The ideas and the logos.* Philo believed that he saw in *Genesis* the description of a double creation, first that of the intelligible world (*noētos kosmos*), then that of the sensible world (*aisthētos kosmos*):

---

[1] Though created, the world will never be destroyed, by special decree of the Demiurge. This doctrine of the *Timaeus* (41B) finds expression at *Heres* 246, in a formula, 'destructible, but never to be destroyed', which does not occur in the *Timaeus* itself, but echoes, or is echoed by, *Timaeus Locrus* (94D). The non-eternity of the world is also the Platonic doctrine presented in Seneca *Ep.* 58, 27–9: 'For the universe abides, not because it is eternal, but because it is protected by the care of Him who governs it; that which was imperishable would need no guardian'—precisely Philo's argument. We may perhaps see Eudorus at the back of this consensus.

Having resolved to create this visible world of ours, he fashioned first the intelligible world, in order that in fashioning the physical world he might be able to use an immaterial and most godlike model, producing from this elder model a younger imitation which would contain within itself as many sensible classes of being as there were intelligible ones in the original. (*Opif.* 16)

Here the model or *paradeigma* of Plato's *Timaeus*, which was there something independent of the Demiurge, becomes his creation. This development, or rather 'tidying-up', of Plato's thought is doubtless not original with Philo; we find no explicit statement of it in Antiochus, but the intelligible cosmos is simply the Ideas taken as a whole, and once the Ideas are agreed to be the thoughts of God the dependence of the Paradigm on God would seem to follow.

That the Ideas are to be viewed as numbers becomes clear from a number of passages, e.g. *Opif.* 102, where the numerical nature of the primal forms according to which material things are fashioned is alluded to, or *Heres* 156, where God is described as employing all numbers and all forms in the bringing to completion of the world. The numbers primarily involved are the primal numbers comprised in the Decad, each of which has its particular virtues. I do not propose to go through these here, but it is important to note that Philo is fully acquainted with Pythagorean numerology in the form in which we find it in later sources such as Plutarch, Theon of Smyrna or Nicomachus of Gerasa. Philo's special treatise *On Numbers* has not survived, but there is quite enough evidence scattered through his existing writings to make clear what its contents were, and they were thoroughly Pythagorean.

The Logos, the divine reason-principle, is the active element of God's creative thought, and is often spoken of as the 'place' of the Ideas. Through the influence of the Logos, the Ideas become seminal reason-principles (*logoi spermatikoi*), a concept borrowed from the Stoics. They actually are called this only at *Legatio* 55; more often it is the Logos itself in the singular that is referred to as *spermatikos* (e.g. *Leg. All.* III 150; *Heres* 119), but the Logos is only the sum-total of the Ideas in activity, as the intelligible cosmos was only their sum-total viewed as being at rest.[1] As *logoi spermatikoi*, the Ideas serve as the models and creative principles of the physical world. What Philo has in mind comes out clearly enough at *Opif.* 20:

[1] The *logos*, or *nous*, is equated on occasion also with the Stoic *pneuma*, e.g *Fug.* 133, where it is described as 'a hot and fiery *pneuma*'.

As, then, the city which was fashioned beforehand within the mind of the architect held no place in the outer world, but had been imprinted on the soul of the craftsman as by a seal, even so the world (*kosmos*) that consists of the Ideas would have no other location than the divine Reason (*theios logos*), which was the author of this physical world.

A concept that deserves special notice is that of the Logos as Divider (*tomeus*). It is not clear where, if anywhere, Philo found this image, but it dramatizes, on both the logical and the cosmological level, the role of the Logos as articulator (by a process of division) of the undifferentiated material substance of the world. This image is developed at enormous length in the latter part of the treatise *Who is the Heir of Divine Things?* (*Heres* 133–236), arising out of the exegesis of *Genesis* 15:10 ('And he brought Him all these, *cut them in two*, and laid each half over against the other'). The Logos here practises not Aristotelian analysis but rather Old Academic diaeresis, dividing in two in the manner of the *Sophist* and of Speusippus, but perhaps also of the Neopythagoreans (a work such as 'Archytas' *On Opposites* is a possible source). The Logos is responsible not only for arithmetical equality, but (152ff.) for proportional equality as well. It itself is symbolized by the number Seven, and occupies a central position in the cosmos, analogous to the Sun (221–3). This whole passage is of great interest for Philo's doctrine of the Logos, and the antecedents of it, as I say, are by no means clear.

Another dominant concept is that of the Logos as the instrument (*organon*) of God in the creation of the world. We have come across this in connexion with the 'metaphysic of prepositions' earlier (p. 138), where the Logos is given the appellation 'through which' (*di' hou*), but Philo provides some useful evidence for the further elaboration of this notion. Consider *Leg. All.* III 96 (arising out of the etymologizing of Bezalel as 'in the shadow of God'):

Bezalel means, then, 'in the shadow of God'; but God's 'shadow' is his *logos*, which he made use of like an instrument, and so made the world.

Philo goes on to develop the idea of the Logos being an image (*eikôn*) of God as archetype (*paradeigma*), whereas it itself is an archetype to all other things, which are its images. The verb translated above 'made use of' (*proschrêsthai*) is significant as being the basis of the technical term which Numenius later employs to describe the 'use' made of a lower divine being by a higher (see below pp. 371–2).

At *Cher.* 125ff. again, in giving a comprehensive account of the metaphysic of prepositions, Philo describes the Logos as the *di' hou,* the *organon* of God.

All this is orthodox Middle Platonic doctrine. There are some more idiosyncratic features, however, of the provenance of which we cannot be so sure.

(*iii*) *The powers.* The description of the divine *logoi* as 'powers' (*dynameis*) of God is not necessarily un-Platonic. In Plato's *Cratylus* (405A), indeed, there is mention of the *dynameis* of a god, in this case Apollo. If *dynamis* be taken in the sense of 'potentiality', which can proceed to *energeia* or 'actuality' in the physical world, then the notion is Aristotelian in origin, but easily adopted by Middle Platonism. We find the Ideas called *dynameis*, indeed, in the Pseudo-Aristotelian work *On the World*, the dominant influence in which seems to be Pythagorean.[1] At 398A we find mention of the Power of God, which goes through all the Universe, where it is not fitting that God himself should go, any more than it is consistent with the dignity of a ruler to pay attention to all the minor details of his kingdom.[2] There follows then an elaborate comparison with the Great King of Persia, his servants (*doryphoroi*) and his spies, which is of importance as being a favourite image of Philo's.[3]

However, this *dynamis* of the *De Mundo* is a single entity, closely analogous to the Logos. In Philo we find a more elaborate system. I will confine myself to a discussion of the two chief Powers, as they are of most importance, and it is in their connexion that Pythagorean influence is clearest.

As supreme and immediate manifestations of God, Philo discerns two entities, which he terms Goodness (*agathotês*) and Sovereignty (*exousia*). By virtue of the former God creates the world; this is therefore termed his creative power (*poiêtikê dynamis*). By virtue of the latter God rules his creation; that is therefore termed his regal power (*basilikê dynamis*).

In the exegesis of the two cherubim with the flaming sword guarding

---

[1] Ocellus Lucanus, who is in turn influenced by Peripateticism, talks of the *dynameis* of material things as immaterial *logoi*, II 7—where the word means 'potentiality' rather than 'power'. But in Pythagorean circles the mathematical sense of *dynamis* must always have been present.

[2] At *Migr.* 182 Philo says the same thing, that God himself (*to on*) should not be spoken of as being *in* the Universe, but only his *dynamis* (here described as his 'goodness', *agathotês*).

[3] cf. *Legatio* 6, *Leg. All.* III 115, *Spec. Leg.* I 45, etc.

Paradise (*Cher.* 27ff.), the cherubim are the two powers, and the sword between them is the Logos. The relation of the Logos to the two Powers is not quite clear in this passage, but from *QE* II 68 we gather that it is superior to them. They are divided off from it, 'as from a fountainhead'. The passage I wish to quote, however, is from the *De Abrahamo* (120ff.), where the subject of discussion is the three Strangers who visit Abraham in his tent in Gen. 18. Philo has just been explaining that the Supreme Being may sometimes, in the clear light of revelation, be seen as One, but sometimes he casts a sort of shadow, which leads to his being viewed as Three:

No one, however, should think that the shadows can be properly spoken of as God. To call them so is a calculated misuse of language (*katachrêsis*), indulged in merely to give a clear view of the fact which we are explaining, since the real truth is otherwise. Rather, as anyone who has approached nearest to the truth would say, the central place is held by the Father of the Universe, who in the sacred scriptures is called He that Is (*ho ôn*) as his proper name, while on either side of him are the most senior powers (*presbytatai dynameis*), the nearest to him, the creative and the regal. The title of the former is 'God' (*theos*), since it made and ordered the universe; the title of the latter is 'Lord' (*kyrios*), since it is the fundamental right of the maker to rule and control what he has brought into being.

We may note here the concept of a Being superior even to the title of 'God' (although Philo is normally content to call him by this title). The identification of 'God' with the creative function depends on one of the current Greek etymologies of *theos*, as being from the root *the-*, in the sense of 'lay down', 'set in order'. *Kyrios*, the other title of Jahveh in the Septuagint, fills its role more obviously.

We seem to see here a tendency towards the extreme transcendentalizing of God, placing him above all attributes or functions. That this is a Neopythagorean trait acquires confirmation, not only from the tendencies which appear in Numenius a century later, but from what follows in the same passage:

So the central Being, attended (*doryphoroumenos*) by each of his Powers, presents to the mind which has vision the appearance sometimes of One, sometimes of Three; of One, when that mind is highly purified and, passing beyond not merely the multiplicity (*plêthê*) of other numbers, but even the Dyad which is next to the Monad, presses on to the ideal form which is free from mixture and complexity, and being self-contained needs nothing more; of Three, when, as yet uninitiated into the highest Mysteries, it is still a votary only of the minor rites and unable to apprehend the Existent alone by itself and apart from all else, but only through its actions, as either 'creative', or 'ruling'. This, as they say, is a 'second-best voyage' (*deuteros plous, Phaedo* 99D, etc.).

Besides Pythagoreanism, there is also, however, a probable Stoic influence here, though whether mediated through Platonism or not is not clear. Certainly the Stoics used the term *dynamis* to describe an aspect or attribute of the Supreme God. Diogenes Laertius (VII 147) reports as follows:

He (*sc.* the Supreme God) is, however, the artificer of the universe and, as it were, the father of all, both in general and in that particular part of him which is all-pervading (i.e. the Logos), and which is called by many names according to its various powers (*dynameis*).

Diogenes then goes on to list etymologies of the Olympian Gods which show them as aspects of the all-pervading Logos. These are not relevant to the present enquiry, but there is other evidence that is. The Stoic mythographer Cornutus (ch. 9) allegorizes two mythological figures, Justice (*Dikē*) and the Graces (*Charites*), explaining that Justice is that *power* of God which brings concord into the affairs of men and forbids them to act unjustly to one another, while the Graces are his sources of grace and beneficence to men. Philo was familiar with this Stoic allegorizing, which goes back to Chrysippus, and he makes use of it repeatedly in his doctrine of God's Powers. The Graces are equated with the 'merciful' power of God at *Post. Caini* 32, and *QE* II 61, and Dike is frequently represented as his 'assessor' (*paredros*), e.g. *Spec. Leg.* IV 201, or 'attendant' (*opados*), e.g. *Conf. Ling.* 118.

All this explains a certain amount, but it does not, I think, account entirely for the very prominent role which the two chief Powers play in Philo's metaphysics. That may, after all, be his own contribution. But I will return to this problem, after first dealing with *Sophia*.

(*iv*) *A female creative principle: Sophia.* The quotation from the *De Abrahamo* above ended, fittingly, with a well-worn Platonic tag. We see in it essentially the same system as that outlined by Alexander Polyhistor (above, p. 127) as Pythagorean: a Monad accompanied by, but superior to, a Dyad. Presumably the Dyad is to be identified in this context with the two chief Powers, but the Indefinite Dyad as such does find a place in Philo's system, sometimes identified with Matter

(*Spec. Leg.* III 180, *Somn.* II 70), but often, and more significantly, disguised as either Justice (*Dikē*) or Wisdom (*Sophia*).

The Greek figure of Dike sitting beside Zeus as his assessor (*paredros*) and the Jewish figure of Wisdom at the right hand of Jahveh blend in Philo's thought into a female life-principle such as was to surface later in Plutarch, and again in Neoplatonism. This principle is, admittedly, normally equated with the Logos, but there are some passages in which it acquires an independent existence. In *Fug.* 109, for example, we find the Logos described as the son of God and Sophia, 'through whom the universe came into existence'. The use of the preposition 'through' here shows that Sophia is envisaged as an organic and not as a material cause, but her presence at all is nevertheless interesting. At *Det.* 115–16, however, she acquires the Platonic epithets of Matter in the *Timaeus*, 'foster-mother' and 'nurse', and is described as 'the Mother of all things in the Universe, affording to her offspring, as soon as they are born, the nourishment which they require from her own breasts.' Sophia is here almost an Earth Mother, except that she still seems to be a transcendent entity. Philo is always liable to be led into confusion by his own rhetoric. Her offspring is even here the Logos, now seen as the Manna, which Philo in turn, drawing on the alleged meaning of the Hebrew, identifies with the highest Stoic category, 'something' (*ti*).

On the whole, it seems true to say that in Philo's thought there is present the recognition of a female life-principle assisting the supreme God in his work of creation and administration, but also somehow fulfilling the role of mother to all creation (cf. also *Ebr.* 30). If this concept reveals contradictions, that is perhaps because Philo himself was not quite sure what to do with it.[1] From our point of view, this rather enhances its value, as indicating that Philo found the concept already established, presumably in contemporary Platonized Pythagoreanism. When we turn to Plutarch, we will observe the significance of this. Especially in such a passage as *Ebr.* 30–1 we can see Sophia coming very close to Plutarch's concept of Isis in the *Is. et Os.*

(*v*) *Other powers.* The Logos, then, proceeds from God and Sophia

---

[1] Sarah, for instance, who normally represents Virtue, appears at *Leg. All.* II 82 as 'the ruling Sophia', and at *Ebr.* 61 takes on the characteristic epithet of Athena, 'motherless' (*amētōr*), and is said to 'rise above the whole material cosmos, illumined by the joy residing in God'. Yet this same epithet, 'motherless', is attached to the number Seven at *Opif.* 100, where it is equated with the Logos. Plainly we are in a marshy area of Philo's thought.

(*Fug.* 109), and produces in turn the two chief Powers (*Cher.* 27ff., *QE* II 68), now revealed as the Dyad. At *Agr.* 51, Philo refers to the Logos as the 'first-born son' of God, who has been put in command of the cosmos as his deputy (*hyparchos*). The Great King image seems to obtrude itself here, as so often elsewhere. Besides the two chief Powers, however, Philo makes mention of the other powers of God, generally in such a way as to make them indistinguishable from the Ideas. Thus the Logos is spoken of as being filled by God completely with his immaterial powers (*Somn.* 1 62) and as being the 'charioteer' of the powers (*Fug.* 101)—the imagery of the *Phaedrus* myth, creatively applied. At *Fug.* 94ff., prompted by the necessity of allegorizing the Cities of Refuge of Deut. 19, Philo comes up with five Powers of God, ruled over by the Logos, the Creative, the Regal, the Merciful, the Legislative and the Forbidding, but one cannot be sure that this is not an *ad hoc* fabrication. The last two Powers, for example, are nothing else but the positive and negative sides of the Law of Nature in the Stoic formulation, 'ordering what must be done, and forbidding what must not be done' (*SVF* III 314).

There is, however, the curious circumstance that Ahriman, the supreme deity of Zoroastrian religion, is attended by five Powers, and this may conceivably be an influence on Philo's thought, the five cities merely providing an occasion. At *QE* II 68, after all, there is a remarkable passage in which the relationships of the Powers are worked out rather differently, without reference to the Cities of Refuge (the subject is the fixtures on the Ark of the Covenant, at *Ex.* 25:10ff.), but wherein they still amount to five. This passage has been mentioned above, but it is worth quoting in full here, as it contains a comprehensive survey of Philo's theology:

In the first place there is He who is elder than the One and the Monad and the Beginning. Then comes the Logos of the Existent (*to on*, or *ho ôn*), the seminal substance of existing things. And from the divine Logos, as from a spring, there divide and break forth two Powers. One is the creative, through which the Artificer (*technitês*) established (*ethêke*) and ordered all things; this is named 'God'. And the other is the royal, since through it the Creator (*dêmiourgos*) rules over created things; this is named 'Lord'. And from these two Powers have grown the others. For by the side of the creative there grows the merciful, of which the name is 'beneficent', while beside the royal there grows the legislative, of which the apt name is 'punitive'. And below these and beside them is the Ark; and the Ark is a symbol of the intelligible world.

The Ark, we are told, contains all the Powers above it, including the Logos. Though not itself properly a power, it constitutes a fifth entity in the intelligible realm below the Logos, and it is this creation of a group of five that I wish to stress here. The apparently superfluous generation of entities, which became such a mania in Gnostic circles in the century or so after Philo's death, does seem to show itself in this matter of the Powers. At *Fug.* 94, the legislative (*nomothetikē*) is divided in two, simply to produce a total of five; here the fifth place is taken up by the *kosmos noētos* as a whole. I do not wish to claim that Philo is consciously following a Persian model, but one must ask: What is the purpose of these two latter powers? What do they really add to the two from which they have sprung?

In fact, it must be admitted, the number Philo stresses in this passage is *seven*, as he adds to the total the Logos itself and the supreme deity, whom he terms here 'the Speaker' (*ho legōn*)—a logical counterpart to the term Logos, certainly, but not a term for God that I find used anywhere else in the Greek tradition. The only entity omitted from this survey is Sophia, but then she cannot be fitted suitably into the present exegesis. Since the Speaker is described at the outset as being 'elder than the Monad', however, we may perhaps identify the Monad with the Logos; Sophia, as Dyad, would thus be his consort in producing the Powers. This would be somewhat at variance with what we find at *Fug.* 109, unless in fact 'God' in that passage is to be taken as simply the Logos in its transcendent aspect, the offspring of it and Sophia being the Logos immanent in the world, as seems, indeed, to be the case.

(*vi*) *Free will and providence.* Philo's views on this vexed subject fall within the spectrum of Middle Platonic theory, but nevertheless deserve study.[1] Like any Platonist, he must resist Stoic determinism, and yet reconcile the doctrine of the freedom of the will with that of the Providence of God. If he does not quite succeed in this, he is no worse off in that respect than any of the other Platonists with whom we shall be dealing.

A passage such as *Deus* 47–8, for instance, is a strong statement of the doctrine of Free Will:

For it is the mind alone which the Father who begat it judged worthy of freedom, and loosening the fetters of necessity (*anankē*), allowed it to range

[1] I am much indebted, on this topic, to the article of David Winston, 'Freedom and Determinism in Philo of Alexandria', *Studia Philonica* 4 (1976).

free, and of that free will (*hekousion*) which is his most peculiar possession and most worthy of his majesty endowed with such portion as it was capable of receiving. For the other living creatures in whose souls the mind, the element set apart for liberty, has no place, have been committed under yoke and bridle to the service of man, as slaves to a master. But man, possessed of a spontaneous and self-determined judgement, and whose activities rest for the most part on deliberate choice, is with reason blamed for what he does wrong with premeditation (*pronoia*), praised when he acts rightly of his own will. In the others, the plants and animals, no praise is due if they bear well, nor blame if they fare ill: for their movements and changes in either direction come to them from no deliberate choice or volition of their own. But the soul of man alone has received from God the faculty of voluntary movement, and in this way especially is made like to Him, and thus being liberated, as far as might be, from that hard and ruthless mistress, Necessity, may justly be charged with guilt, in that it does not honour its liberator.

This, one would think, is as absolute an assertion of free will as one could hope to find, but in fact it must be seen against the background of Philo's equally uncompromising assertion of the rule of God's providence. Philo operates, as we have seen, with the concept of the Logos as the agent of God in the world, this Logos both being immanent in each one of us and pervading the cosmos as a whole. It is the presence of God's Logos in us that produces the sense of conscience, that makes us capable of right and wrong action (e.g. *Deus* 127-39, a most instructive passage).

Such a passage as *Cher.* 128 well expresses Philo's view of us as instruments of God's providence:

For we are the instruments (*organa*) through the tension and slackening of which each particular form of action is produced; and it is the Craftsman (*technitês*), by whom all things are moved, who contrives this striking (*plêxis*) of our bodily or psychic powers.

Here the subject of discussion is actually Joseph's dreams, but the application extends to all human activity. We may note the musical imagery. God, through his Logos, plays upon us as upon a stringed instrument. This doctrine explains our higher impulses, but it does not explain our tendency to evil. There Philo is left with his assertion of free will.

The most extended account of the working of God's Providence occurs in the treatise *On Providence* I (preserved only in Armenian translation), where we find Philo essentially appropriating a standard Stoic treatise on providence (the analogies with Cicero, *De Natura*

Deorum 11 are very close), and fitting it into his Platonic metaphysical scheme. A reading of this treatise by itself would lead one to the conclusion that Philo was a determinist.

But in truth Philo is neither a determinist nor a believer in absolute free will. He is caught between these two poles of opposition. Nor is his dilemma peculiar to himself. It is shared, as we shall see, by all the Platonists of our period. The Platonist position maintained the autonomy of the will, in order to preserve the basis of ethical judgments. In his assertion of our free will, Philo is really concerned above all to assert our liability to praise and blame. But yet every Platonist wished to maintain the doctrine of God's Providence. Without that, one would fall into Epicurean atheism, and once again there would be no objective basis for ethical judgments. We shall find Atticus later abusing the Peripatetics for nullifying Providence in fact while asserting it in theory, and being thus worse than the Epicureans. The Platonists are thus caught in what is, if not a contradiction, at least a profound tension between free will and determinism. If Philo's various stances appear contradictory, therefore, the contradiction is at least not peculiar to himself, but one common to all Platonists.

(*vii*) *Cosmology:* (α) *A triadic division of the universe.* At *QG* IV 8 (which, like *Abr.* 120ff., is an exegesis of Gen. 18), we have a disquisition on the significance of the three measures of wheat flour, out of which Abraham told Sarah to make scones for the three strangers. This results in a portrayal of the Universe as divided into three parts, which can be taken as Pythagorean in general inspiration, but also as deriving, perhaps, ultimately from Xenocrates (Fr. 5 Heinze). It is he who is responsible for the triadic scheme appearing, later, in the myth of Plutarch's essay *On the Face in the Moon* (see below, p. 214). (The scheme there, however, concerns only the physical cosmos, not the intelligible, whereas in Fr. 5 Xenocrates takes in the supercelestial, intelligible realm as well):

And most in accord with reality (*physikôtatos*) is the passage concerning the three measures (Gen. 18:6), for in reality all things are measured by three, having a beginning, middle and end. . . . Hence Homer's statement is apt (*Iliad* 15, 189): 'All things are divided into three.' And the Pythagoreans assume that the triad among numbers, and the right-angled triangle among figures, are the foundations of the knowledge (*gnôsis*) [or 'coming into being'—*genesis*] of all things. And so, one measure is that by which the incorporeal and intelligible world was constituted. And the second measure is that by which the perceptible heaven was established in the fifth element (*sc.* aether), attaining to a more wonderful and divine essence, unaltered and unchanged in comparison with these things below, and remaining the same. And the third measure is the way in which sublunary things were made out of the four powers (*dynameis*), earth, water, air and fire, admitting generation and corruption.

Each of these divisions, Philo goes on to say, has a causal principle proper to it. The cause of the intelligible world is 'the eldest of causes', that is, God himself; of the heavenly, or aetherial world, God's Creative Power (*poiêtikê dynamis*); and of the sublunary world of growth and decay, his Regal Power (*basilikê dynamis*).

This assigning of the two chief powers each to a division of the cosmos is a remarkable development, and this passage stands alone in Philo's work. There are, certainly, suggestions elsewhere that the Regal Power is somewhat lower on the scale of perfection than the Creative Power—although normally only their functions are distinguished, not their essential status. At *Fug.* 97ff., for instance, three levels of ascent to God by the individual are distinguished. The most gifted will ascend all the way to a vision of God himself; others, however, will only attain to a knowledge of the Creative Power, being inspired by love for God as creator of the world; others again will rise no further than knowledge of the Regal Power, and are held to their duties simply by fear of punishment. There is here a clear hierarchy of grades of piety in the individual. What we have in *QG* iv 8, however, is the projection of this hierarchy onto the cosmic plane, with the Regal Power presiding over the lowest level, the sublunary realm.

That our world is ruled directly by a being other than the supreme God is, in its starkest form, a doctrine which one would tend to characterize as Persian or Gnostic. Indeed, Philo's concept of the 'regal power' here is not unlike, in particular, the Demiurge of the Valentinians (see below, Chapter 8, p. 387). Certainly Plato, in the *Timaeus*, envisaged the handing over of the formation of the lower soul by the Demiurge to the 'young gods', and we have seen that Philo takes up this doctrine in the *Opif.* The intermediary role of angels or daemons is also a recognized part of Platonism. But the role here accorded to the Regal Power is something else again. We find a remarkable echo of what seems to be the doctrine here in the belief which Plutarch puts into the mouth of his teacher Ammonius in the essay *On the E at Delphi* (see below, p. 191). There Ammonius speaks of the sublunary realm as being ruled over by a 'god, or rather daemon, whose office is concerned with Nature in dissolution and generation', who may be termed Hades or Pluto, in distinction from the god who presides over the heavenly realm, who may be termed Apollo.

This doctrine of a sublunar demiurge had a long and lively history in later Platonism. He was not, in Platonism proper, an evil or malevolent figure (though somewhat rough in his methods, perhaps), and indeed Philo here, in keeping with his strict monotheism, identifies him with an aspect of God himself, but it is hard to resist the conclusion that we have here a reflection, at least, of a contemporary doctrine about a distinct god or daemon who rules the world below the Moon, whether as an agent or as a rival of the Supreme Deity.

(β) *The elements.* A passage of the *De Plantatione* (1–8) is interesting in connection with Philo's theory of the elements, the harmony of the Universe, and the non-existence of void. The awkward thing here is that at one moment Philo seems to envisage a five-element universe on the Aristotelian model, and the next moment we are back with four elements. Perhaps in fact Philo is reconciling the two views, by taking aether not so much as a fifth substance as rather the purest form of fire.[1] This is the view of Apuleius, for example, later (*De Deo Socratis*, ch. 8). It is not entirely satisfactory, of course, but it preserves both the four-element universe of the *Timaeus* and the notion of a substance which moves naturally in a circle, and is not subject to growth and decay. It also reconciles Aristotle and the Stoics on this question. At any rate this is what he says, presenting God to us as the Supreme Planter (2–3):

It is the lord of all things that is the greatest of planters and most perfect in his art; and it is this world that is a plant containing in itself the particular plants all at once in their myriads [note creative adaptation of *Tim.* 31A], like shoots springing from a single root. For when the moulder of the world (*kosmoplastēs*), finding all that existed confused and disordered of itself, began to give it form, out of confusion into distinction of parts (*Tim.* 30A), he caused earth and water to occupy the position of roots at its centre; the trees, that is air and fire, he drew up from the centre to the midspace (*metar-*

---

[1] But the fifth element is apparently accepted as a distinct entity, at *QG* IV 8, though elsewhere (*Heres* 283; *QE* II 73) it is attributed to others, presumably Aristotelians. At *QG* III 3 he presents the five animals of Gen. 15:9 as the five elements, but then the highest two turn out to be simply the substance of the planets and of the fixed stars respectively. At *Heres* 152–3 we have a four-element system accepted without question, though on the authority of 'those who have most carefully examined the facts of Nature'.

sios, used in a technical sense); and the encircling region of *aether* he firmly established and set it to be a boundary (*horos*) and guard of all that is within.

He then proceeds to etymologize *ouranos* (heaven) as deriving from *horos*.

What we seem to have here in fact is a three-tiered Universe, such as we have just been considering, which is more Xenocratean than Aristotelian. The three levels distinguished are the earth, the heavens, and the *metarsia*, defined by Achilles (*Comm. in Arat.* 32) as 'the area between the aether and the earth' (Achilles' dependence upon Eudorus we have already observed).

Philo goes on, however, to combat the notion of a void (*kenon*), in the process employing only four elements, in much closer accord with the *Timaeus*:

It is unlikely that any material body has been left over and is moving about at random outside, seeing that God had wrought up and placed in orderly position all matter wherever found. For it was fitting to the greatest artificer to fashion to full perfection the greatest of constructions, and it would have fallen short of full perfection, had it not had a complement of perfect parts (cf. *Tim.* 32CD). Accordingly this world of ours was formed out of all there is of earth, and all there is of water, and air and fire, not even the smallest particle being left outside.

No mention of aether here, nor at a similar passage, *Det.* 154, where the influence of *Timaeus* 32C is equally strong. Either, then, Philo is guilty of mindless vacillation within the space of one page, or else he thought that the aether could be fitted in to a four-element universe. Later Platonists, such as Albinus and Apuleius, for example, did believe this, taking aether in a Stoic sense, as the purest form of fire, though in fact also taking it in the Aristotelian sense, as having naturally circular motion and being the stuff of which the stars are formed. Philo makes the distinction, indeed, at *Vit. Mos.* II 148, between the heavenly fire and our everyday fire. A certain sleight of hand is required to reconcile the Platonic and Aristotelian universes, but that is what these Platonists thought that they were doing.

(*viii*) *Daemons and angels.* Between God and Man, and subordinate to the Logos—who receives at some points the title *archangelos*, in the sense of 'leader of the angels' (*Heres* 205, *Somn.* I 157)—are battalions of intermediate entities. Philo can appeal for authority in this matter to Scripture, but in fact his exposition is thoroughly Platonic.

First of all, we find, to our surprise, some recognition of the role of the 'young gods' of *Timaeus* 41Aff., identified firmly by Philo's time with the planetary gods. The 'young gods' are introduced by way of a 'problem' (*aporia*), a common exegetical device, raised in connexion with *Gen.* 1:26: 'Let us make man after our image and likeness.' Why, asks Philo, is a plural word used by God here? Does God need helpers, whom he is here addressing? (*Opif.* 72). 'Can it be that He to whom all things are subject is in need of anyone whatsoever?' God alone knows for certain, says Philo, but he himself proposes the cause which by probable conjecture seems plausible and reasonable (cf. *Tim.* 29CD). This in fact turns out to be an adaptation of the reason given by Plato at *Tim.* 41Dff. God does not wish to be personally involved in creating a being which is capable of both virtue and vice, as is Man, since he does not want to be responsible for creating evil.

So we see why it is only in the instance of Man's creation that we are told by Moses that God said 'Let *us* make', an expression which plainly shows the taking with Him of others as fellow-workers. It is to the end that, when Man orders his course aright, when his thoughts and deeds are blameless, God the universal ruler may be owned as their source; while others from the number of his subordinates are held responsible for thoughts and deeds of a contrary sort. (*Opif.* 75)

The identification of these helpers with the planetary gods is not made here, but at *Opif.* 46 Philo speaks of God's 'offspring in the heavens, on whom he bestowed powers, but not independence', and this seems to settle the matter.[1] Philo does not approve of the worship of the heavenly bodies, which he attacks repeatedly as 'Chaldaean' idolatry (e.g. *Migr.* 178–9), they are mere servants and creatures of the true God, after all—but he does recognize them as 'living creatures endowed with mind, or rather each of them a mind in itself, excellent through and through and unsusceptible of any evil' (*Opif.* 73).

Besides the planetary gods, however, there are a host of pure souls in the air, which may be termed daemons or angels. He deals with these most fully in his essay *On the Giants*. At *Gig.* 6–9, he uses a common Platonic argument for the existence of daemons. They (and not birds)[2] are the proper inhabitants of air, even as there are proper

[1] At *Fug.* 69 God is said to address this to his Powers. This is not necessarily a contradiction, however, but rather an indication of where Philo was inclined to rank the planets.

[2] Birds do seem to be recognized as the proper inhabitants of air, however, at *Plant.* 12. Philo is presumably there reverting to the more original form of this *topos*, which was not a proof of the existence of daemons, but rather of the animate nature of the heavenly bodies.

denizens of all the other elements, even fire—the so-called *pyrigona*, or fire-born creatures (cf. Arist. *HA* v 19, and Apuleius below, p. 318).

And so the remaining element, the air, must be filled with living beings, though indeed they are invisible to us, since even the air itself is not visible to our senses. Yet the fact that our powers of vision are incapable of any perception of the forms of these souls is no reason why we should doubt that there are souls in the air, but they must be apprehended by the mind, that like may be discerned by like (8–9). . . . Now some of the souls have descended into bodies, but others have never deigned to be brought into union with any of the parts of earth. They are consecrated and devoted to the service of the Father and Creator, whose custom it is to employ them as ministers and helpers, to have charge and care of mortal man. (12)

Daemons, angels and souls, says Philo, are only different terms for the same class of being (*ibid.* 16). With a reference to *Symposium* 202E, he designates the angels as 'ambassadors backwards and forwards between men and God'.

The doctrine is set out again at *Somn.* 1 134–5 and 141–2.

Philo also recognizes evil angels or daemons (*ibid.* 17–18). From *Qu. in Ex.* 1 23, it would appear that these are created by God to do his work of punishment, and also, like the 'helpers' of *Opif.*, to insulate him from the imputation of being the cause of Evil. But it is not entirely clear how they fit in to the overall metaphysical scheme, and later in the same passage we find a remarkably dualist, almost Gnostic doctrine (cf. e.g. *CH* IX 3), which can, however, be connected, at least remotely, with that of Plato in *Laws* x, 896Eff.

Into every soul at its very birth there enter two powers, a salutary and a destructive. If the salutary one is victorious and prevails, the opposite one is too weak to be visible. But if the latter prevails, no profit at all or little is obtained by the salutary one. Through these powers the world too was created. People call them by various names; the salutary one they call powerful and beneficent, and the opposite one unbounded and destructive.

The two 'powers' cannot easily be identified with the Powers of God in Philo's normal doctrine, although they do seem to relate to the doctrine of *QG* IV 8, described above, p. 169). The epithet 'unbounded' (*apeiros*) attached to the destructive power would seem to connect it with the Pythagorean Unlimited Dyad. But it has here become an evil principle, akin to the Persian Ahriman and to the Evil Soul of *Laws* x. Altogether this passage of the *Questions on Exodus*, together with the passage from *Questions on Genesis* dealt with earlier, reveals a streak of dualism in Philo such as is not evident elsewhere in his writings, but which agrees well with the doctrine of Plutarch, as we shall see (below, pp. 202f.).[1] If only we could be certain as to what chronological relation *QG* and *QE* have to the main sequence of commentaries, we could draw some conclusions for the growth or decline of dualistic influences in Philo.

Philo's angelology (or demonology) is, then, essentially Middle Platonic. On occasion the angels seem to be identified with the *logoi* (*Leg. All.* III 177), but more usually they are described as pure souls, e.g. *Sacr.* 5: 'the angels are the army (*stratos*) of God, bodiless and happy souls', with, as so often in Philo, a reference to the *Phaedrus* Myth (247A). For angels as messengers or intermediaries, the image of Jacob's Ladder is subtly interwoven with *Symposium* 202E in a way that is typical of Philo (*Somn.* I 133ff.). (For further exposition of Middle Platonic demonology the reader is referred to pp. 216ff. and 317ff.)

(*ix*) *Psychology:* (α) *The parts of the soul.* Philo observes the normal bipartite division of the soul, into rational (*logikon*) and irrational (*alogon*) parts (e.g. *Leg. All.* II 6; *Spec. Leg.* I 333). This rational part is identified with the *nous* (intellect) or the *hêgemonikon*, the Stoic 'ruling part', the irrational with the senses. Although this is the basic division, Philo, like Antiochus, sees no contradiction in talking also of a division into the rational, spirited, and passionate parts, the tripartite division of Plato's *Republic* (e.g. *Spec. Leg.* IV 92, where the influence of *Rep.* IV is strong, and reinforced by the *Phaedrus* Myth and *Timaeus* 69C; also *Heres* 225). He also feels free, if it suits him, to utilize the Stoic division into the *hêgemonikon* and the seven physical faculties, i.e. the five senses along with the faculties of speech and reproduction, e.g. *Opif.* 117, where he is in the process of extolling the hebdomad, and a group of seven dependent on a monad is what he wants. Again, at *QG* II 59, he makes a tripartite division which is more Aristotelian than Platonic, distinguishing as the three parts the nutritive (*threptikon*), the sense-perceptive (*aisthêtikon*) and the rational (*logikon*).[2] This is not chaotic eclecticism, however, as I have pointed out already

---

[1] In fact, Philo's concept of two opposed powers in the soul of man seems to have its closest parallels in post-Biblical Jewish literature, e.g. *Test.* XII *Patr. Ass.* 1; 6; *Jud.* 20. Also in Qumran texts, 1 *QS* 3, 13ff.; 4, 15f. I am indebted for these references to Prof. A. Dihle.

[2] In this connexion there is a passage in *QG* IV 117 which is worthy of note. Here we have a comparison between the elements of speech, vowels, semi-vowels and consonants, and the three parts of a man, mind, sense-perception and

in the case of Antiochus (above, p. 102); for Philo each of these divisions expresses some aspect of the truth, but the most basic truth remains the division into rational and irrational. When the crunch comes, the spirit (*thymos*) and the passions (*epithymia*) are to be linked together in opposition to the Reason. One of Philo's basic allegories, indeed, is that of Adam as the *nous* and Eve as *aisthêsis*, sense-perception, or the irrational soul (e.g. *Leg. All.* II 24, *Cher.* 58–60), the union of which two is required for the human mind in the body to function. This is a distinctly Pythagoreanizing piece of imagery, and it finds an interesting parallel in a passage of 'Callicratidas', *On Happiness in the Home*, preserved in Stobaeus (p. 103 Thesleff *PT*). Here the *logismos* is compared to the master of the house, *epithymia* to the wife, and *thymos* to the young son, who obeys now one and now the other. 'Callicratidas' is here operating with a tripartite soul, admittedly, and he is in any case quite undatable, but he serves as evidence of the use of this sort of imagery in Neopythagorean circles.

A more substantial inconsistency would be a distinguishing of two souls, though this contradiction also is more apparent than real. Philo becomes involved in this distinction, apparently, in response to certain Biblical passages, notably Gen. 9:4, Lev. 17:11 and 14, and Deut. 12:23, where we have the statement that 'the blood is the life'. As a Platonist, Philo could not accept this at face value. The rational soul is an immaterial entity, so Moses must be referring to a lower soul, the irrational. The essence of this may be agreed to be blood, even as the essence of the rational soul is immaterial *pneuma*. At *QG* II 59 (on Gen. 9:4) we have a strong distinction between the rational part (*meros*) of the soul, whose substance is divine *pneuma*, and the nutritive and sense-perceptive parts, whose substance is blood; and a distinction is made between the veins and the arteries, the latter of which contain a

---

body—an application of the Stoic analogy between logic (which includes grammar) and physics.

The mind is analogous to the vowels, sense-perception to the semi-vowels, and the body to the consonants. The body can make no sound (take no action) without mind and the senses, but also the sense without the mind can only 'make lame and imperfect sounds', that is, they cannot make judgments on the basis of their perceptions alone. Only when mind 'extends itself, and is fused with and engraved upon' the senses, do rational perception and speech result. Unlike the other two, the mind can operate by itself (even as the vowels can produce adequate sounds by themselves, whereas the other elements cannot), and it can also act as chorus-leader (*chorêgos*) to the senses, giving them their cue as to when to act. We have here a strong distinction made between *nous* and *aisthêsis* which is both Platonic and Aristotelian, as well as a creative use of Stoic formulations.

preponderance of *pneuma*, and only a small amount of blood, and are thus the proper seat of the rational soul, whereas the veins, having more blood than *pneuma*, are the seat of the lower parts.[1] At *Det.* 82-3 we find what are initially called two *dynameis* or faculties of the soul, the vital (*zôtikê*), or life-principle, and the rational, but they quickly begin to sound like separate entities. The life-principle is mortal. At *Fug.* 67 it is seen as that part of the soul which God handed over to his 'helpers' to create, which, in imitation of *Timaeus* 41E, is termed the 'mortal part'. The true Man is to be identified with his mind in its purest state, of which God by himself is the creator (*ibid.* 71).

This notion of a double creation of man, which Philo extracted from the double description in Genesis (1:26 and 2:7), was to prove most fruitful in the 'underworld' of Middle Platonism. In the Hermetic *Poemandres* (12–15), for instance, there is an elaborate account of the creation first of the Essential Man, an intelligible being, and then of ordinary men. Philo expounds the difference in *Opif.* 134, commenting on Gen. 2:7:

> He shows here that there is a vast difference between the Man being fashioned now and the one that was created before 'in the image of God'. The one moulded now is perceptible by the senses, participates in quality, is a compound of body and soul, either male or female, by nature mortal. The one created 'in the image' is a sort of Idea or genus or seal (*sphragis*), intelligible, immaterial, neither male nor female, by nature imperishable.

As we have seen, this 'true' Man may be identified with the intellect, but it is also a transcendent archetype in the intelligible world. In the Hermetic writings this archetypal Man (*Anthrôpos*) tends to become a personalized figure, around whom a mythology forms.

As for the notion of two souls, this turns up later in Numenius, as we shall see (pp. 376f.). Porphyry (*ap.* Stob. 1 350, 25 = Num. Fr. 44 Des Places) definitely attributes to Numenius the doctrine that we have not a bipartite soul, but two souls, a rational and an irrational. We will investigate the ancestry of this concept more fully later, but we must not ignore here the distinct suggestion of it in Philo, and the Old Testament passages which provoked this notion in him.

(β) *The immortality of the soul.* We have just seen that the irrational soul—or the irrational *part* of the soul, as I think Philo would in

---

[1] This was an accepted medical distinction, cf. Gellius *NA* XVII 10, where Taurus puts an ignorant country doctor straight on this subject.

general prefer to say—is mortal. It disperses on the death of the animal. What of the rational? Philo certainly believes in its immortality, and explicitly opposes the Stoics in this. Consider, for instance, *QG* III 11, which is an exegesis of Gen. 15:15 ('But thou shalt go to thy fathers with peace, nourished in a good old age'):

Clearly this indicates the incorruptibility (*aphtharsia*) of the Soul, which removes its habitation from the mortal body and returns as if to the mother-city (*mêtropolis*) from which it originally removed its habitation to this place. For when it is said to a dying person, 'Thou shalt go to thy fathers', what else is this than to represent another life without the body, which only the soul of the wise man ought to live?

There are two points here already to notice. One is that the pre-existence of the Soul is also recognized, as in correct Platonic-Pythagorean doctrine; the second, that there is a suggestion here, in the specification 'the soul of the wise man', that only the souls of the Wise enjoy immortality, a notion which we have seen traces of elsewhere (above, p. 96), and which seems to go back to Chrysippus. Chrysippus, however, would only preserve the souls of the Wise within the universe until the *ekpyrôsis*, and there are no such limitations made here.

Philo goes on to oppose those who interpret the 'fathers' of this passage as 'the elements of the universe'. Who put forward this Stoic interpretation is hard to see. Either one must suppose a group of Stoicizing Jewish allegorists, or one must accuse Philo of making up this interpretation in order to refute it. In either case, he firmly refutes the Stoic view.

While the Stoics are rejected, it is nevertheless not quite clear what Philo had in mind for the soul of the average man, who would come under the Stoic heading of *phaulos* ('of no account'). From *QG* I 16, for instance, one might reasonably conclude that he denied such a one immortality:

The death of worthy men (*spoudaioi*) is the beginning of another life. For life is twofold; one is with corruptible body; the other is without body and incorruptible. So that the evil man 'dies by death' (Gen. 2:17) even while he breathes, before he is buried, as though he preserved for himself no spark at all of the true life, which is excellence of character. The decent and worthy man, however, does not 'die by death', but, after living long, passes away to eternity, that is, he is borne to eternal life.

One might conclude from this *a fortiori* that the evil man perishes after death, and has no personal immortality, a view which would after all accord with contemporary Platonist thinking.

Lastly, we may note in Philo traces of a notion popular in later Platonism that this world is really the Hades of the poets. At *Heres* 45, for example, he refers to ordinary humans as 'skulking in the caverns of Hades', and *ibid.* 78 as 'partaking in things earthly and nurtured on the things in Hades'. Cf. also *Somn.* I 151, II 133. Presumably this conception stems ultimately from Stoic allegorizing of Homer, or of Greek mythology in general. It is, according to Numenius (Frr. 32, 34, 35 Des Places), a secret doctrine of Pythagoras that Hades is the whole area between the earth and the Milky Way, which is the abode of souls.

(*d*) *Logic:* (*i*) *Theory of categories.* When we turn to examine Philo's use of logical terminology, we should expect to find a mixture of Stoic and Aristotelian characteristics, and so indeed we do. As regards the Categories, we have seen that Philo, like Eudorus, gives us the tell-tale order 'Substance-Quality-Quantity', which Eudorus may have presented as the more correct 'Pythagorean' order. The whole passage in which this occurs (*Dec.* 30f.) is worth considering in some detail. First of all, the Categories are spoken of as being 'in Nature', making explicit an uncertainty left by Aristotle as to whether they were categories of speech or of reality, and also denying their applicability to the intelligible realm.

Then we have the following statement:

There is nothing which does not participate in these categories. I have Substance (*ousia*), for I have borrowed what is all-sufficient to make me what I am from each of the elements out of which this world was formed, earth, water, air and fire.

What has happened here is that the Aristotelian concept of *ousia* has been overlaid, if not supplanted, by the Stoic sense (e.g. *SVF* I 87), where *ousia* is the equivalent of Matter (*hylē*). Philo does not seem to notice this discrepancy. He continues:

I have Quality in so far as I am a man, and Quantity as being of a certain size. I become 'relative' when anyone is on my right hand or my left, I am active when I rub or shave anything, or passive when I am rubbed or shaved. I am 'in a particular state' (*echein*) when I wear clothing or arms, and 'in a particular position' (*keisthai*) when I sit quietly or am lying down, and I am necessarily both in place (*topos*) and time (*chronos*), since none of the above conditions can exist without these two.

There is much of interest here. First, Philo uses Aristotle's example for substance, 'Man', as his example for Quality, again thinking of a Stoic entity, 'qualified substance' (e.g. *SVF* II 38off.). Then he chooses to use 'shave' and 'be shaved' (*keirein/keiresthai*), for Aristotle's example 'burn' 'and be burned' (*kaiein/kaiesthai*). There might appear to be no sense in this, until one takes into consideration another passage (*Cher.* 79) where the peculiar property of the verb *keirô*, and its usefulness in logical discussions, becomes apparent. *Keirô* can be used (as can a number of other verbs, of course) in both the middle and the passive voices, so that a scholastic logician can make a distinction between a passive use of the verb (as when a sheep *is shorn*), and a middle or reflexive use (as when a man *has his hair cut*). This distinction seems to be of Middle Stoic provenance, attributed by Diogenes Laertius (VII 63 = *SVF* II 183) to Apollodorus of Athens (fl. *c.* 140 B.C.), and is reported as follows:

Reflexive predicates are those among the passive which, although in form passive, are yet active operations, as 'he gets his hair cut' (*keiretai*), for here the agent includes himself in the sphere of the action.

Philo uses the distinction in a way which may be original to himself, but which has obvious Stoic implications, to illustrate what should be one's attitude to adversity. One may submit to it willingly, like a man going to have his hair cut, or unwillingly, like a sheep going to the shearing. This is itself only an alternative image to Zeno's famous one of the little dog behind the cart (*SVF* II 975).

This digression may seem excessive, but only in this way can we hope to unravel the tangle of influences on Philo's thought. Even such a small matter as substituting *keirein* for Aristotle's *kaiein* is not casual or accidental.

More significant than this, however, is the positioning of the categories of 'when' and 'where', and their transformation into Time and Place. Aristotle, we must recall, does not make the identification in the *Categories*, in fact ranking Time and Place at *Cat.* 4b24 under the head of Quality, while he makes 'when' and 'where' separate categories in the *Categories* and in *Topics* I 9. These categories, now identified with Time and Place, Philo puts at the end of the list, though emphasizing that they are the *sine qua non* of all the others. Their final position is emphatic, therefore, rather than a sign of demotion.

Here, as with Eudorus, Pseudo-Archytas is relevant. Philo is in fact in agreement with Pseudo-Archytas, whereas Eudorus, as we recall, put Time and Place immediately after Quantity. The fact that Philo does not follow Eudorus here in this detail (though he agrees with him in asserting the logical priority of Time and Space) shows us once again that any too close linking of Philo with Eudorus would be rash. Here, as in the case of Eudorus' triple division of Ethics, Philo is not found to adopt the distinctive innovations of the earlier Platonist.

Philo's view of the *Categories* is conditioned, then, more by Platonist-Pythagorean criticism in general than by Eudorus in particular. That none of this is his original contribution is suggested both by his way of introducing the passage (it is the doctrine of 'those who involve themselves with the doctrines of philosophy'), and by the agreement of 'Archytas'. The commentary of Boethus of Sidon may be his source, but it is perhaps foolish to try to be too specific about this.

Philo's employment of the Aristotelian categories here does not, however, prevent him from utilizing the Stoic categories also, when it suits him. When discussing Manna, for instance, at *Leg. All.* III 175, he comes out with the following: 'We have a proof of this in his feeding us with his own most generic (*genikôtatos*) *logos*; for "manna" means "something" (*ti*), and this is the most generic of all terms.' '*Ti*' is the highest or most general category of the Stoics (*SVF* II 333), being more general than the Aristotelian Substance. There are two points of interest here. One is that Philo makes no bones at all about adopting this Stoic term, whereas he is somewhat devious above, in the matter of the Aristotelian categories. Secondly, we may note how the Stoic logical category has also a physical aspect. It is the Logos of God, the basic formative principle of the world. One might continue the parallel, as I have ventured to do earlier (p. 135), identifying Quality with the Logos immanent in the world, and Quantity with Matter.

That Philo was inclined to accept Stoic logic in general might be concluded from such a passage as *Agr.* 141, where he gives the whole Stoic theory of *lekta*. He is there condemning the scholastic quibbling of dialecticians, but it is notable that it is to Stoic logic that he turns for his example, which may be taken as a backhanded compliment.

(*ii*) *The origins of language: etymology.* Something should be said, finally, of Philo's theory of the origin of language, as it reflects contemporary Platonist speculations, and also help to explain his curious efforts at bilingual etymologizing.

Platonist speculations on language take their start from the *Cratylus*, particularly from such a passage as 430A–431E, where the idea is put forth that on the one hand names for things were ordained by a lawgiver, but that the names that he gave to things were 'correct', that is, true representations of their natures. The Stoics simply developed this theory further, Chrysippus, for instance, contributing the famous account of the naturalness of the first person pronoun, *egô*—one is pointing with one's lower jaw towards the heart, the true seat of the personality (*SVF* II 895).

In Cicero's *Tusculan Disputations* I 62, Pythagoras is given as the authority for attributing to a primordial sage the naming of things and the organizing of language, and that notable Pythagorean P. Nigidius Figulus is recorded by Aulus Gellius (*NA* X 4) as using the personal pronouns just as Chrysippus had done to 'prove' the naturalness of language, in his *Commentaria Grammatica*. There is thus a consensus among Platonists, Stoics and Pythagoreans by Philo's time that words are attached to things by nature, not by convention.

Philo congratulates Moses at *Leg. All.* II 14–15 for correctly identifying the originator of natural names:

Greek philosophers said that those who first assigned names to things were wise men. Moses did better than they, first of all in ascribing it not to some of the men of old but to the first man created. His purpose was that, as Adam was formed to be the beginning from which all others drew their birth, so too no other than he should be regarded as the beginning of the use of speech: for even language would not have existed, if there had not been names. Again, had many persons bestowed names on things, they would inevitably have been incongruous and ill-matched, different persons imposing them on different principles, whereas the naming by one man was bound to bring about harmony between name and thing, and the name given was sure to be a symbol, the same for all men, of an object to which the name was attached or of the meaning attaching to the name.

Nature and human initiative are thus united in the person of Adam. He is the primordial 'lawgiver' of whom the Greeks have preserved a confused recollection (cf. also *QG* I 20).

Fortified by this theory, Philo apparently sees no difficulty in giving Greek as well as Hebrew etymologies for certain proper names in the Pentateuch. For instance, Pheison, one of the four rivers of Eden, means in Hebrew 'alteration of mouth' (*Leg. All.* I 74ff.), while in Greek it means 'sparing' (from *pheidesthai*, ibid. 63ff.), and thus represents the virtue of Prudence. Again, Leah, the elder daughter of

Laban, whom he married to Jacob instead of Rachel, is made to mean
in Hebrew 'rejected and weary' (*Cher.* 41), but is also connected with
the Greek *leia*, 'smooth'. In either case she represents Virtue in general.
Normally Philo gives simply what he takes to be the Hebrew etymology (derived, necessarily, from some Alexandrian handbook of
etymologies, since he clearly does not know Hebrew himself), and
derives his conclusions from that, but his occasional excursions into
double etymologies reveal clearly his bizarre view of language, which
was not, however, necessarily different from that of contemporary
Stoicism or Platonism. (Cf. also his etymology of *septem*, the Latin
for seven, which he derives from the Greek root *seb-*, 'worship', *Opif.*
127.)

3. CONCLUSION

As I made clear at the outset, this has been a deliberately partial study
of Philo, attempting to isolate in his thought those elements which may
derive from contemporary Platonism. My chief thesis (as against
such an authority as H. A. Wolfson, for example) is that Philo was not
so much constructing for himself an eclectic synthesis of all Greek
philosophy, from the Presocratics to Posidonius, as essentially adapting contemporary Alexandrian Platonism, which was itself heavily
influenced by Stoicism and Pythagoreanism, to his own exegetical
purposes. If this is the case, then, used with proper caution, he is
plainly good evidence for the state of Platonism at Alexandria in the
first decades of the Christian Era.

Of course, the distinction between what is Greek in Philo, and what
is Jewish or even original, is not in practice always easy to make. Such
questions as the origin of his doctrine of Powers, or his sense of man's
nothingness in relation to God, must, I think, remain obscure. There
is also the very real possibility, particularly in the latter case, of a mixture of influences. As for his relationship with the other extant representative of Alexandrian Platonism at this time, Eudorus, it is not, as
we have seen, particularly close, although they are certainly in the
same tradition, but Eudorus was active about fifty years before Philo,
and he is only one representative of what was doubtless a fairly popu-
lous tradition. It is also undeniable that Philo, despite the generally
coherent tradition on which he is drawing, vacillates on occasion in the
direction of Peripateticism, if that seems to suit his text or his mood.
Taken all in all, however, Eudorus and Philo seem to constitute ade-

quate evidence of a type of Platonism, heavily influenced by Pythagorean transcendentalism and number mysticism, which, rather than the Stoicizing materialism of Antiochus, is the true foundation of Middle Platonism, in the sense in which that term is understood in this book.

CHAPTER FOUR

Plutarch of Chaeroneia and the Origins of Second-Century Platonism

A. INTRODUCTORY

In this chapter our attention turns to the figure of Plutarch, and through him to the state of Platonism in the century after Philo, that is, from about A.D. 50 to about A.D. 150. The centre of interest now returns to Athens. We have no information as to what was going on in philosophic circles in Athens during the period covered by the last chapter. Our first firm date now becomes A.D. 66–7, when we find Plutarch's teacher Ammonius in charge of the Platonic Academy (or, perhaps we should say, a Platonic Academy), giving a philosophical education to Plutarch and his friends. We will consider Ammonius in more detail below, but we may note straight away that his Platonism is in the direct line of the dogmatic synthesis that has been by this time a century and a half established, in Athens and in Alexandria. Ammonius himself was an Egyptian (Eunapius, *Lives of the Philosophers*, p. 454, Boissonade), so that for all we know he may have brought back serious Platonism in his own person from Alexandria to Athens.

We do know of at least one Platonist in this blank period who was elsewhere than in Alexandria (although he too came from Alexandria), and that is Thrasyllus, the court philosopher of Tiberius. He produced a new edition of Plato's dialogues, ordering them in tetralogies,[1] and according to subject-matter, and giving each a descriptive subtitle in addition to its traditional name (DL III 49–62). As to his philosophical position we have very few hints, but those that we have are useful. First of all, he was an accomplished astrologer, and it was in that

---

[1] Thrasyllus did not invent the division into tetralogies. It can be traced back at least to before him, and is known to Varro (*De Lingua Latina* VII 37).

capacity, rather than as a philosopher, that he attracted the notice of Tiberius, when Tiberius was in exile on Rhodes (Suet. *Tib.* 14; Tac. *Ann.* VI 20f.). Again, he professed Pythagoreanism. We hear from an essay of Longinus preserved by Porphyry in his *Life of Plotinus* (20), that Thrasyllus wrote on 'the first principles of Pythagoreanism and Platonism'.[1] Porphyry (*ad.* Ptol. *Harmon.* p. 266) also mentions a work 'On the Seven (Musical) Tones', which is a subject lending itself to Pythagorean elaboration. He also composed a work on the heavenly bodies, referred to twice by Achilles *In Arat.* (pp. 43, 9; 46, 30 Maass), and utilized a century later by Theon of Smyrna in his *Expositio* (see below, Chapter 8, p. 397).

Thrasyllus, then, like the shadowy figure of Dercyllides, who seems to precede him, constitutes further evidence for the Pythagoreanizing and astrological tendencies of Alexandrian Platonism of this time, a milieu out of which Plutarch's teacher Ammonius seems also to have come.

Before discussing him, however, we should review briefly Plutarch's life and works. I must make at the outset the same reservation in dealing with Plutarch that it was necessary to make in the case of Philo. We are concerned in this work only with Plutarch as a representative of contemporary Platonism, not with the whole man, essayist, historian, teacher, conversationalist, statesman. (Such a study of Plutarch as a whole has been admirably done already by D. A. Russell.)[2] Plutarch was by no means a great original philosopher, but he is an important link in the chain of evidence for the development of Middle Platonism, and he is also, as we shall see, not quite devoid of originality in his doctrines.

B. LIFE AND WORKS

Since Plutarch represents himself as being a beginning student of Ammonius in A.D. 66–7 (*De E.* 387f.), it has been reasonably conjectured that he was not much more than twenty years old at this time, which would place his birth in about A.D. 45. There is nothing to contradict this estimate. He is mentioned by Eusebius in his *Chronicle* as

---

[1] It is possible that we have the substance of this work in the account of Pythagorean doctrine given by Sextus Empiricus, *Adv. Phys.* II 248–83. I will discuss this passage at the beginning of Chapter 7 (see below, pp. 342–4).

[2] *Plutarch*, London 1972.

being still alive, as an old man, in A.D. 119, and indeed as being appointed Procurator (*epitropos*) of Achaea by Hadrian in that year.[1] On the other hand, it is reasonably pointed out that if he had lived much longer than this, he would have rated a mention in later times as one of those who had lived to a *very* great age (e.g. in Lucian's work *On Octogenarians*). It is therefore suggested that he did not quite reach the age of 80, dying, perhaps, about A.D. 125.

Plutarch's family was an old and respectable one in the small town of Chaeroneia in Boeotia, and although Plutarch studied in Athens and travelled widely, having many good friends, for instance, in Rome, he always remained faithful to Chaeroneia, and lived there to the end of his life, gathering round him a circle of friends and disciples (who constituted a kind of mini-Academy), and conscientiously holding various local offices.

His other great loyalty was to the temple of Apollo at Delphi, of which he became a priest, and on whose antiquities and ceremonies he became a great authority. A considerable proportion of his essays relate to Delphi in one way or another.

A vast body of work by Plutarch has been preserved to us, with much of which we are not now concerned. An evaluation of his biographies of famous men, and of his non-philosophical essays, cannot be entered upon here. We must confine ourselves to those works in which philosophical issues preponderate. These may be divided into those which are expository and those which are polemical.

Plutarch was a Platonist, according to the understanding he had of that term, which grew out of the development in Platonism in the century before his birth, such as I have outlined above in Chapters 2 and 3. He was, of course, indebted (indirectly) for many formulations to both Peripateticism and Stoicism, which does not, however, prevent him from attacking the latter, at least, in a series of polemical treatises.[2] We shall see also at various points evidence of Pythagorean influence. Plutarch's early interest in number-symbolism (*De E* 387F), as well as his youthful objection to meat-eating, as evidenced in the early double

---

[1] This post involved supervising the management of the imperial estates in the province, and it is probable that for a man of Plutarch's age it was purely honorary. Trajan had earlier granted him the *ornamenta consularia*, the privileges of a consul, which was a high honour also.

[2] The Peripatetics are not attacked in this formal way, but a sharp distinction is made between Aristotelian and Platonic teaching on such subjects as the Ideas and the immortality of the soul, *Adv. Col.* 1115Aff., and there is implicit criticism of the Peripatetic position in such an essay as that *On the Control of Anger*.

essay *On The Eating of Flesh*, and his sympathy with animals and championing of their rationality, in the essay on *The Cleverness of Animals* and the dialogue *That Irrational Animals Use Reason* (a question on which he is at odds with Philo, and presumably with all Stoicizing Platonists), are evidence of his Pythagorean background.

The serious philosophical treatises with which we shall be concerned are the following (in the order of their usual appearance in the *Moralia*): *On Isis and Osiris* (*De Is.*); *On the E at Delphi* (*De E*); *On the Oracles at Delphi* (*De Pyth.*); *On the Obsolescence of Oracles* (*Def. Or.*); *Is Virtue Teachable?* (*An Virt.*); *On Moral Virtue* (*De Virt.*); *On Delays in Divine Punishment* (*De Sera*); *On the Daemon of Socrates* (*De Gen.*); *On the Face in the Moon* (*De Fac.*); *Problems in Plato* (*Plat. Quaest.*); *On the Creation of the Soul in the Timaeus* (*Proc. An.*). Interesting things are said elsewhere, scattered, for example, through the biographies, in the nine books of *Table Talk* (*Quaest. Conv.*), or in the many other essays which, though Plutarch would have considered them 'philosophical', we would have to term merely 'literary', and I will not neglect such as are relevant to our purpose.

We have also a number of treatises of a polemical nature, directed against other schools, notably the Stoics and the Epicureans. Against the Stoics: (1) *On the Contradictions of the Stoics* (*Stoic. Rep.*); (2) *On 'koinai ennoiai', against the Stoics* (*Comm. Not.*); and against the Epicureans: (1) *That One Cannot Live Happily by Following Epicurus* (*Non posse*); (2) *Against Colotes* (*Adv. Col.*); (3) *On the Correctness of the Doctrine 'Lathe biôsas'* (*Lat. viv.*).

It may not be amiss to list here also some titles of Plutarch's lost works, from the Catalogue of Lamprias, in order to show the full range of his philosophical interests. These works are a sad loss, as they would throw much light on the development of Middle Platonism. In some cases we can guess from the title the philosophical position taken up in the work, but often this remains a tantalizing enigma.

No. 44 is *On the Fifth Substance*. Does Plutarch accept or reject it? The evidence of his surviving works is conflicting, as we shall see. No. 48 is an *Introduction to Psychology*. No. 49 is *On the Senses*. No. 58, *On Fate*, in two books, is not the work that we have, and it, together with No. 154, *On What Lies in our Power: Against the Stoics*, would give us Plutarch's views on Fate and Free Will, which probably differed little in their main lines from basic Middle Platonic doctrine. The existing pseudo-Plutarchan *De Fato* is not in fact doctrinally incompatible with what we know of Plutarch.

No. 66 is *On the Fact that in Plato's View the Universe had a Beginning*, which would maintain the same line which we find set out in the *Proc. An.* Nos. 67, *Where are the Forms?*, 68, *The Manner of the Participation of Matter in the Forms*, namely that it constitutes the *Primary Bodies*, and 185, *On Matter*, would be of great interest for his metaphysics. Nos. 144, *What is Understanding?* and 146, *That Understanding is Impossible*, would concern the theory of knowledge, the latter having a curiously sceptical ring—as, indeed, does No. 210, *Whether He Who Reserves Judgment (ho epechôn) on Everything is Involved in Inaction*, which sounds like a defence of the Sceptical Academy. No. 158, *On Pyrrho's Ten 'Methods of Procedure' (tropoi)*, may also have been sympathetic to scepticism. There are also essays *On the Unity of the Academy since Plato* (no. 63), and *On the Difference between the Pyrrhonians and the Academics* (no. 64), which indicate Plutarch's willingness to welcome the New Academy into the company of Platonism, and to distinguish their brand of scepticism from that of Pyrrho, presumably as being less absolute and negative. Plutarch is thus at odds with Antiochus (and, as we shall see, with Numenius) on this important question.

No. 177, *On the Saying 'Know Thyself'*, and *That the Soul is Immortal*, seems to echo the contents of a treatise such as Cicero's *Tusculan Disputations* I, and presumably took a similar line. A work *On the Soul* (No. 209) of which we have some fragments, would presumably be Plutarch's definitive statement on Psychology. No. 226, *That the Soul is Imperishable*, would cover the same ground as No. 177.

No. 192 is a *Lecture on the Ten Categories*, which would have given us Plutarch's position on this very popular subject. He does not seem to be among those who would attack Aristotle on this question. He took an interest also in various other philosophical questions. There is an essay *On Tautology* (No. 162), and a *Reply to Chrysippus on the 'First Consequent'* (No. 152)—a way of referring to the First Indemonstrable?—which indicates a disposition to attack Stoic logic.

Finally, we may note No. 221, *What is the* telos *according to Plato?*, which presumably identifies the *telos* as 'likeness to God', but would be most useful to have, none the less, for any discussion of the alternative possibilities that it might have contained.

This survey is not exhaustive, but picks out only those lost works which sound as if they were of particular philosophical interest. Presumably they perished, when so much that is more light-weight remained, because they were comparatively technical, inner-school treatises, and were thought to be rendered obsolete in later times by more 'advanced' Neoplatonic treatments of the same topics, but from our point of view their disappearance is a great misfortune.

As we have seen already, ancient traditions of literary and philosophical polemic did not make for accurate criticism of one's opponents, nor did they necessarily reflect one's true views on the subjects discussed. The Epicureans were truly excluded from Plutarch's synthesis, as they were from that of all Middle Platonists, but the Stoics were not, and the true extent of Plutarch's opposition to them needs careful evaluation.[1]

A word should be said at this point about the nature of Plutarch's more rhetorical compositions on ethical subjects. He habitually takes up in these an austere, 'Stoic' attitude, and this has led commentators astray on occasion. What must be realized, however, is that he is writing, in such works, within a well-defined tradition, that of the Cynic-Stoic diatribe, on the basic themes, or *topoi*, of which he is only playing a series of variations. An essay such as that *On Freedom from Anger*, for example, advocates the extirpation of anger (*aorgêsia*) rather than its mere control, and attacks those (the Peripatetics) who would dignify this passion with the name of 'greatness of soul' or 'righteous indignation' (456F); whereas in his essay *On Anger*, of which a fragment is preserved in Stobaeus (Fr. 148 Sandbach), he adopts the (Platonic and Peripatetic) view that anger, *thymos*, should be made 'the ally of virtue' and thus subject to Reason, and that only its excess should be expelled from the soul. As we shall see, it is this latter position that accords with his philosophic stance on ethics. In the former essay he is following the tradition, and so it is with many other diatribes of a similar nature (e.g. *On Tranquillity of Mind, On Exile*). Before deducing Plutarch's true views from a given passage, the literary form of the writing in which it is found must always be considered.

C. PLUTARCH'S TEACHER, AMMONIUS

Before, however, we turn to a consideration of Plutarch's own philosophical position, we must attempt to evaluate that of his teacher Ammonius. We have, unfortunately, nothing to go on here except

---

[1] See on this subject especially D. Babut, *Plutarque et le Stoicisme*, Paris 1969.

Plutarch's own evidence, which, as it comes in the form of putting sentiments into the mouth of Ammonius as a character in dialogues, must be treated with caution. Nevertheless, from an examination, particularly, of Ammonius' speech in *The E at Delphi* (391E–394C), a distinct type of Platonism emerges, which Plutarch, one concludes, would have had no reason for attributing to Ammonius had he not been an adherent of it. In fact, since Ammonius seems to be a product of Alexandrian Platonism, the views with which he is credited should not occasion much surprise.

The dialogue is set in 66–7 A.D., during Nero's visit to Greece, when Plutarch was only beginning his studies under Ammonius. The date is useful to have, although we do not, of course, have to believe in the historicity of the actual conversation. Plutarch prefaces Ammonius' speech with the remark that 'he plainly held that in mathematics was contained not the least important part of philosophy', which, in the context, means Pythagorean number-theory. Plutarch earlier (387F) has confessed that he himself at that time 'was devoting myself to mathematics with the greatest enthusiasm, although I was destined soon to pay all honour to the maxim "Avoid extremes", when once I had joined the Academy'. We may gather from this testimony, as well as from other remarks attributed to Ammonius on numerology (*Quaest. Conv.* 744B), that Ammonius, at this stage of his life, was inclined not to take this part of philosophy as seriously as it was taken in some quarters (as we have seen from Philo), although he still respected it (*De E* 391E). We may at least conclude that it was an important element of his philosophic background which he was now tending to transcend, and which he taught his pupils also not to take too seriously. In this conversation, he in fact rejects the notion that the E denotes the number Five, arguing that Seven is really the number proper to Apollo. He then proceeds to take it as an assertion of the god's Being (*Ei* signifying 'Thou art'). This, we may note, Philo would accept as an entirely appropriate salutation of God.

There follows a sharp contrasting of the realms of Being and Becoming, in the former of which we are asserted to have no part, nor can our intellects by straining towards it grasp it. Heraclitus' dictum 'It is impossible to step into the same river twice' (Fr. 91 DK) is then quoted, and he is quoted again just below (392C).[1] All this is perfectly

---

[1] The same description of the physical world, with the same reference to Heraclitus, is found in Seneca *Ep.* 58, 22–3, a letter which we have seen above (p. 136) to contain a compendium of Middle Platonic doctrine.

Platonic, if rather gloomy, but as the speech proceeds the dualism develops remarkably.

After a resounding affirmation of the oneness and unchangingness of the Supreme Deity (393Aff.), for whom 'Apollo' (etymologized as 'Not-Many') is the perfect epithet, and a correction of those who would identify Apollo with the Sun rather than with the Sun's intelligible archetype, Ammonius is made to declare that all those 'acts and experiences' conventionally attributed to this supreme god are really to be referred 'to some other god, or rather daemon, whose office is concerned with Nature in dissolution and generation'—that is, to the sublunar realm. This god or daemon may properly be termed 'Hades' or 'Pluto'.

Now this is a most interesting development, anticipating the Neoplatonic identification of Hades with the 'sublunary demiurge', and recalling the doctrine which we discerned in Philo *QG* IV 8 (above, p. 169). The fixing of the realm of Hades in the air between the Moon and the earth is accepted by Plutarch in, for instance, the Myth of *De Genio* (591AB), and seems to go back to Xenocrates (Fr. 15 Heinze) and even, perhaps, to Plato (*Laws* x 904D), but the notion that the earth has been given over to the care of this being, who, even if he is not to be thought of as positively evil, is at least contrasted with a perfectly good supreme god, is a development which seems more Persian than Greek, Pluto coming rather close to Ahriman (cf. *De Is.* 369E, *Proc. An.* 1026B).[1]

Whether this belief can be linked securely with Ammonius on the basis of his speech in this dialogue is doubtful, but for the history of Middle Platonism that is not of primary importance. There the belief stands, whether it belongs to Ammonius or to Plutarch. However, as I have said, there is no reason for Plutarch to father on Ammonius views which would be entirely alien to him. I suggest, then, that such Persian influence and knowledge about Persian religion as we find in Plutarch (particularly in the essay *On Isis and Osiris*) came to him primarily from his teacher.

Ammonius was probably dead by about A.D. 80, since he is not represented as ever visiting Plutarch's circle in Chaeroneia, as Plutarch would surely have been glad to have him do. He was a distinguished citizen of Athens, being three times (at least) elected *stratêgos* (*Quaest.*

---

[1] The curious formulation of Xenocrates (Fr. 18 Heinze, quoted at *Plat. Quaest.* 9, 1007F), distinguishing between an 'upper' and a 'lower' Zeus, ruling respectively the realms above and below the Moon, may provide a model for this.

Conv. VIII 3, 1), and his descendants continued to be prominent in Athenian society for many generations.[1]

D. PHILOSOPHICAL POSITION

It seems to me useful to conduct the survey of Plutarch's philosophy in the same general order which I have established for his predecessors. Discussion of Plutarch's philosophy generally centres on those doctrines of his which appear most remarkable at first sight, his dualism, his demonology, his belief that the world had a temporal beginning. These characteristics, particularly his demonology, are liable to be emphasized disproportionately, simply through an inadequate appreciation of the overall framework of Middle Platonism into which they fit.

I. ETHICS

(a) The telos

For Plutarch, as for all Middle Platonists of whom we have knowledge subsequent to Eudorus, the supreme object of human life is Likeness to God, not Conformity with Nature. We find this expressed well in a passage of the dialogue *On the Divine Vengeance (De Sera* 550Dff.), where Plutarch himself is speaking:

Consider that God, as Plato says (*Theaet.* 176E), offers himself to all as a pattern of every excellence, thus rendering human virtue, which is in some sort an assimilation to himself (*exhomoiôsin . . . pros hauton*), accessible to all who can 'follow God'. Indeed this was the origin of the change whereby universal nature, disordered before, became a 'cosmos': it came to resemble after a fashion and participate in the form and excellence of God. The same philosopher says further that Nature kindled vision in us so that the soul, beholding the heavenly motions and wondering at the sight, should grow to accept and cherish all that moves in stateliness and order, and thus come to hate discordant and errant passions and to shun the aimless and haphazard as the source of all vice and jarring error; for man is fitted to derive from God no greater blessing than to become settled in virtue through copying and aspiring to the beauty and the goodness that are his.

---

[1] See on this C. P. Jones, 'The Teacher of Plutarch', *Harvard Studies in Classical Philology* 71, 1966, pp. 205–13, a full survey of the literary and epigraphic evidence.

The latter part of this passage is a summary and interpretation of Plato's encomium of sight in *Timaeus* 47A–C.[1] It is thus through our eyes, rather than by means of our intellect, that Plutarch says that assimilation is to be achieved. The eyes, however, are obviously only the agents of the intellect in this matter, as we can see by comparing with this his remarks at the beginning of the *Isis and Osiris*.

The *telos* is brought up again clearly in a passage of the essay *On Quietude*, of which we have a fragment preserved by Stobaeus (Fr. 143, Sandbach):

How wise a thing, it would seem, is quietude (*hêsychia*)! In particular it serves for studying to acquire knowledge and wisdom (*phronêsis*), by which I do not mean the wisdom of shop and market-place, but that mighty wisdom which makes him that acquires it like to God.

Here we have a clear contrast between practical and theoretical wisdom. The only word that Plutarch uses here is *phronêsis*, but *sophia*, the more correct term for theoretical wisdom, is used just below, and the true object of *sophia* is here recognized as *homoiôsis theôi*.

(b) The virtues

On the subject of virtue and happiness, Plutarch inclines on the whole to the more 'broadminded' ethical position of Antiochus, as against the Stoic-Pythagorean asceticism observable in Eudorus and Philo. Significantly, his terminology in this area is Aristotelian rather than Stoic. In his essay *On Moral Virtue* we have a useful statement of his ethical theory. The work, from its tone, seems early, even perhaps an essay written while Plutarch was still attending Ammonius' Academy. It takes the form of an attack on the Stoic, and in particular Chrysippan, position that the soul is unitary, and that there is no such thing as a distinct irrational part. Moral virtue (*êthikê aretê*), says Plutarch at the outset, is to be distinguished from theoretical virtue, in that it is concerned with emotion (*pathos*) as its subject-matter and reason as its form—whereas theoretical virtue is concerned solely with the rational part of the soul.

Having stated the subject of the essay, Plutarch then gives us a doxography, in the best school manner. First the views of the Stoics

---

[1] A detail worth noting is that Plutarch here says that Nature 'kindled' (*anhapsai*) vision in us. This verb is not used in fact by Plato in this passage, but is by Timaeus Locrus in the corresponding passage of the *Peri Physios* (100C). This does not mean necessarily that Plutarch read TL, but it may be a result of his use of Eudorus, whose points of agreement with TL we have noted (p. 131).

are surveyed (440E–441D), and then we hear of the views of Pythagoras, Plato and Aristotle, all of whom saw that our soul is twofold rather than unitary. The way in which these three are presented is interesting (441Eff.):

... this, it is likely, was not unknown to Pythagoras, if we may judge by the man's enthusiasm for music, which he introduced to enchant and assuage the soul, perceiving that the soul has not every part of itself in subjection to discipline and study, and that not every part can be changed from vice by reason.

It is obviously important for Plutarch to bring in Pythagoras as the father of the theory (as we saw Eudorus doing with the doctrine of the Likeness to God, above p. 122), but the full development of the theory is left to Plato:

Plato, however, comprehended clearly, firmly and without reservation both that the soul of this universe of ours is not simple nor uncompounded nor uniform, but that, being compounded of the potentialities (*dynameis*) of Sameness and Otherness, in one part it is ever governed in uniformity and revolves in but one and the same order, which maintains control, yet in another part is split into movements and circles which go in contrariety to one another and wander about, thus giving rise to the beginnings of differentiation and change and dissimilarity in those things which come into being and pass away on earth.

This is a straight exegesis of *Timaeus* 35Aff., with which Plutarch will deal more thoroughly in *Proc. An.* Here he goes on to say that the human soul, being a part or copy of the World Soul, has the same twofold division, into rational and irrational. Plutarch, like all later Platonists, deals with Plato's tripartite division of the soul in the *Republic* by taking the two lower divisions there described as two parts of the irrational soul (442A), assuming Plato's basic division (surely correctly), to be bipartite.[1]

Following on Plato, we have Aristotle:

Aristotle at first made use of these principles to a very great extent, as is obvious from his writings [these will be his earlier writings, the lost *Dialogues*]. But later he assigned the spirited to the appetitive part, on the ground that anger is a sort of appetite and desire to cause pain in requital (cf. *De*

---

[1] We find an interesting passage in this connexion in *Plat. Quaest.* 9 (1007Eff.), where the division of the soul into three parts situated in different parts of the body is rejected (1008E) in favour of a non-spatial distinction of 'powers' of the soul. Here Plutarch is discussing a tripartite soul, but it is clear that for him the basic division is into rational and irrational.

An. 403a30); to the end, however, he continued to treat the passionate and irrational part as distinct from the rational. . . .

Aristotle's deviation from Plato was thus not substantive.[1] That allows Plutarch, in fact, to use Aristotelian ethics, without hesitation or apology, to combat the Stoics. His doctrine is taken from the *Nicomachean Ethics*, particularly from Book II, chs. 5–7. We have the doctrine of the 'mean' expounded at 444C–445A, with much elaboration. Only intellectual virtue, or *sophia*, should not be described as a mean (444C):

> For we must not declare that every virtue comes into being by the observance of a mean, but, on the one hand, Wisdom, being without any need of the irrational and arising in the activity of the mind, pure and uncontaminated by passion, is, as it were, a self-sufficing perfection and power of reason, by which the most divine and blessed element of knowledge becomes possible for us; on the other hand, that virtue which is necessary to us because of our physical limitations, and needs, by Zeus, for its practical ends the service of the passions as its instrument, so to speak, and is not a destruction nor abolition of the irrational in the soul, but an ordering and regulation thereof, is an extreme (*akrotēs*) as regards its power and quality, but as regards its quantity it is a mean (*mesotēs*), since it does away with what is excessive and deficient.

It is interesting that Plutarch, although in other respects dependent on Alexandrian Platonism, takes in ethics an Aristotelian tack. Admittedly, all Platonists accepted the duality of the soul, which is what Plutarch is here defending, but this could be combined with a Stoic position in ethics.

We may note, however, in Plutarch's account of Virtue as a Mean an element not present in Aristotle's exposition of the doctrine at *EN* II 5–6, and which is even in contradiction with it. Aristotle speaks of Virtue simply as a 'state' (*hexis*) in the mean between two extremes (1106b36); he expressly denies that it is an activity or a faculty (1106a-5ff.). Plutarch describes Virtue at *Virt. Mor.* 444F, on the other hand, as 'an activity (*kinēsis*) and faculty (*dynamis*) concerned with the irrational, which does away with the remissions and overstrainings of impulse (*hormē*) and reduces each passion to moderation and faultlessness.'

---

[1] Plutarch is in fact ready to adopt the Aristotelian fivefold division of the soul, as set out in the *De Anima*, into nutritive, sense-perceptive, and then the three Platonic parts, appetitive, spirited and rational, *De E* 390F, *De Def.* 429E.

He has just emphasized the senses in which Virtue is *not* a mean:
(a) it is not a compound of uncompounded substances, such as black
and white; (b) it is not a mean in the sense that that which 'contains'
and 'is contained' is a mean between what it contains and what it is
contained by, as eight is a mean between twelve and four; (c) it is not a
mean in the sense of partaking of neither of two extremes, as the 'indifferent' (*adiaphoron*) is a mean between good and evil:

But it is a mean, and is said to be so, in a sense very like that which obtains
in musical sounds and harmonies. For there the mean, or *mesê*, a properly-
pitched note like the *nêtê* and the *hypatê*, escapes the sharpness of the one and
the deepness of the other.

This scholastic enumeration of three incorrect senses of 'mean'
leading up to the 'correct' one, that of a musical harmony, is a notable
development upon Aristotle. The introduction of the musical analogy
suggests Pythagorean influence. Certainly in the *Pythagorica* we find
Virtue described as a 'harmonizing' (*harmonia, synharmoga*) of the
irrational by the rational soul ('Archytas', *On Law and Justice*, p. 33,
17 Thesleff; 'Metopos', *On Virtue*, p. 119, 27; 'Theages', *On Virtue*, p.
190, 1ff.; 'Damippus', *On Wisdom and Good Fortune*, p. 68, 26; (of
Justice) 'Eccelus', *On Justice*, p. 78, 3), and Philo also approves of the
concept (e.g. *Immut.* 24, *Sacr.* 37). Arius Didymus, on the other hand,
in his summary of Aristotelian ethics, sticks closely to Aristotle in his
account of the Mean (*ap.* Stob. II 137–142 Wachs). Plutarch does seem
here to be involved in 'correcting' and amplifying Aristotelian ethical
theory in a Pythagorean direction. (He would not, of course, admit
that he was involved with Aristotelian theory at all, except in so far as
Aristotle agreed with Plato.)

What we do not hear about in this essay is the status of the three
types of Good, the psychical, the bodily and the external, and their
relation to the *telos*. Plutarch does, however, as a 'Peripateticizer',
favour *metriopatheia* (moderation of the passions) over *apatheia*, their
extirpation (451Bff.). It is interesting to note how in the process of
stating this position he makes use of what we would regard as a piece
of Stoic terminology, but which he feels no difficulty about using
against them, the fourfold distinction of principles of combination (a
formulation also freely used by Philo, e.g. *Leg. All.* II 22; *Immut.*
33–50):

And in general, as they themselves (the Stoics) assert and as is manifestly
so, some things are ruled by cohesion (*hexis*), others by natural growth

(*physis*), others by irrational soul, others again by rational soul, in all of which principles man participates to some extent or other, and owes his existence to all the above-mentioned modes. For he is held together by co-hesion, nurtured by the principles of natural growth, and he makes use of reason and intellect; therefore he also partakes of irrational soul, and has innate within him the causal principle of passion, not introduced from out-side but as a necessary part of his being, and not to be done away with entirely, but requiring care and training.

The force of this argument depends upon the assumption that any-thing which has a higher form of unifying principle, such as rational soul, necessarily possesses all the lower ones as well, though not *vice versa*. Man thus, by the Stoics' own argument, if he possesses rational soul, must also possess irrational soul as well as natural growth and basic cohesion.

Plutarch did in fact also hold that all three types of Good contri-bute to the *telos*, or to happiness. We find him in another polemical anti-Stoic treatise (*Comm. Not.* 1060cff.) attacking Chrysippus—rather as Antiochus had done—for not admitting bodily and external goods as forming an essential part (*symplêrotika*) of Happiness, al-though Nature commends them to us. Plutarch's position is thus that criticized by Eudorus as the view of 'the more recent Peripatetics' (see above, p. 124), and so, despite his access of Pythagoreanism, in ethics Plutarch is back with Antiochus as against the more austere Alexan-drians.

It seems worthwhile to quote here a passage from a fragment of Plutarch's lost essay *In Defence of Beauty* (Fr. 144 Sandbach); rhetori-cal though it is, as it expresses the same attitude about the body being an essential component of man as we saw earlier in Antiochus (pp. 70ff.):

What? Is not man's nature a thing compounded of body and soul? Or is one enough for us without the other? How can it be enough? The former could not exist without the aid of a soul, and the soul could not exist if it had nothing to bind it together. Well, then, they are both equally, so to speak, adorned by their cognate virtues, the soul by justice, moderation and wisdom, the body by strength, beauty and health. Surely it would be a strange thing to record the beauties of the soul but to overlook those of the body.

Of course the sphere of ethics comprised much more than the analysis of the *telos*, and Plutarch has views on a very wide range of practical ethical questions, but I am concerned here only with basic questions of theory, with a view to placing him as accurately as possible within the general stream of Middle Platonism. Further, as has been said above, his true views on ethical questions are frequently obscured in the more rhetorical treatises by the tradition which he is following, which is normally Cynic-Stoic.

(c) *Politics*

A word should, however, be said about Plutarch's politics. He was a strong supporter both of the political life and of the principle of monarchy. He condemns both the Epicureans (*Adv. Col.* 1125cff.) and the Stoics (*Stoic. Rep.* 1033EF) for disdaining politics, and declares the position of the statesman to be the noblest and most generally beneficial of occupations (*An Seni* 786B). Not unnaturally he was no admirer of democracy. He adopted, as had Philo, the theory of kingship propounded by the Stoics, that the Ruler is the image (*eikôn*) of God who rules the universe (*Ad Princ. Inerud.* 780E), and that he is God's agent in the administration of men (*ibid.* 780D). In his essay *On Monarchy, Democracy and Oligarchy*, again, he appeals to the authority of Plato for the thesis that monarchy is the most excellent of constitutions (827B).

He wrote a number of works on political subjects,[1] though without ever going deeply into questions of basic importance. In his attitude to the contemporary political scene, Plutarch is typical of Middle Platonist philosophers. We hear of no 'Platonist Opposition' to the Principate to match the Stoic Opposition. The dissent of a Platonic philosopher in this period would be limited to details of misconduct by individual emperors (such as Nero or Domitian), not to the principle of monarchy itself.

As to the virtue of an active life, however, there might well be differing views. On this question Plutarch, like Antiochus, and obviously like his own master Ammonius, is firmly on the side of political activity, though always in the interest of the *status quo*. He was plainly, towards the end of his life, a figure of considerable influence throughout the province of Achaea. This satisfactory relationship with power was also characteristic of his follower Calvenus Taurus, as we shall see in the next chapter.

---

[1] *That Philosophers should Discourse especially with Rulers* (776Aff.); *To an Uneducated Leader (Ad Princ. Inerud.)* (779cff.); *On Monarchy, Democracy and Oligarchy* (826Aff.); *Whether an Old Man should take part in Politics (An Seni)* (783Aff.).

2. PHYSICS

(a) First principles: God; the One and the Indefinite Dyad

Plutarch's view of God—that is, of the Supreme Being—is just what one expects of a Platonist: God is Real Being (*to ontôs on*), eternal, unchanging, non-composite, uncontaminated by Matter (all these attributes derived from Ammonius' speech in *De E*, 392Eff., which may, I think, reasonably be taken also to represent Plutarch's views). The fact that in this passage the subject of discussion is Apollo simply shows how, for philosophers like Plutarch, the various traditional Gods had become aspects of the godhead. We have seen Philo also using attributes of Apollo and of Athena, as well as of Zeus himself, to describe the supreme God, or the *logos*. God also knows all things (*De Is.* 351D) and directs (*kosmei*) all things (*ibid.* 382B). He thus exercises *pronoia*, which will be discussed below. He is also presented as 'the object of striving for all Nature', for instance at *De Fac.* 944E, which reflects the Aristotelian doctrine of the Prime Mover (*Met.* XII, 7; *Phys.* I, 9).

Besides being 'really existent', God also for Plutarch possesses the two other basic Platonic epithets: he is the Good (*Def. Or.* 423D), and he is One (*De E.* 393BC). Being One, the Deity can be accommodated to the Pythagorean system of first principles (*Def. Or.* 428F). Here the essential dualism of Plutarch's world view emerges, as he talks of the Old Pythagorean pair of principles, with no hint of Eudorus' supreme principle above these:

Of the supreme (*anôtatô*) Principles, by which I mean the One and the Indefinite Dyad, the latter, being the element underlying all formlessness and disorder, has been called Limitlessness (*apeiria*); but the nature of the One limits and contains what is void and irrational and indeterminate in Limitlessness, gives it shape, and renders it in some way tolerant and receptive of definition. . . .

Admittedly this pair of principles is produced here in connexion with the origin of Number, but they are plainly also to be understood as basic principles of creation. How precisely the Indefinite Dyad is to be understood will be discussed below. It is not simply Matter, as will be seen, although in this passage there is no hint that it is anything more.

(b) The Logos and the Ideas

God, thus established, must relate to the world through suitable inter-mediaries, of whom the first is, not surprisingly, the Logos. The Logos has, of course, two aspects, the transcendent and the immanent. In a passage of the *De Is.* (373AB), the two aspects, or moments, of Osiris are distinguished as his soul and his body. His soul is 'eternal and in-destructible', whereas his body is repeatedly torn asunder by Typhon and is constantly being reassembled by Isis. The body of Osiris is the Logos, or the Ideas, immanent in Matter:

For what [truly] exists and is intelligible and is good prevails over des-truction and change; but the images (*eikones*) which that which is perceptible and corporeal fashions from it, and the *logoi*, forms and likenesses which it assumes, are like *figures stamped on wax* in that they do not endure for ever. They are seized by the element of disorder and confusion which is driven here from the regions above and fights against Horus, whom Isis brings forth as an image of the intelligible, he being the perceptible world (*kosmos aisthêtos*).

The image used here for the imprinting of forms on matter is one borrowed from the *Theaetetus* (191cff.), not one used in the *Timaeus*. This image of the seal on wax, however, was generally current in Middle Platonism, as is evident from its use by Arius Didymus in his *Compendium of Platonic Doctrine* (*ap.* Eusebius, *Pr. Ev.* XI 23, 3–6), and by Philo (e.g. *Ebr.* 133; *Migr.* 102ff.; *Mut.* 134ff.).

The Logos appears again, in an interesting way, in the *Dialogue on Love.* This work is in other respects modelled loosely on the *Symposium* (as regards the preliminary encomia of the God Eros), with much influence from the *Phaedrus*, but when it comes to the culmina-ting speech, delivered by Plutarch himself, we find that Eros, instead of being portrayed as a daemon, as in the *Symposium*, is unequivocally a God. Now Plutarch can claim authority for this from Greek belief in general, going back to Hesiod, but his specific purpose here seems to be to identify Eros with the intelligible archetype of the Sun, and thus in fact The Good of *Republic* VI.

His exposition begins with the remark (764B) that the Egyptians regard Eros as the Sun, and Aphrodite as the Moon. We may agree at least, he says, to a similarity, if not to an identity (764D):

It is, then, likely that the resemblances of the Moon to Aphrodite and of the Sun to Eros are much stronger than those which these stars have to the other gods; yet they are by no means identical, for body is not the same as soul, but different, just as the Sun is visible while Eros is intelligible.

Plutarch goes on, then, to suggest that the activities of Sun and Eros might be seen as antithetical, the Sun drawing our attention down from intelligibles to sensibles,[1] while Eros leads us up by stages from sensibles to intelligibles, and finally to the vision of Beauty itself (765A, where Diotima's speech in the *Symposium* asserts its influence). Eros is thus the Middle Platonic Logos in its anagogic aspect, presiding over the noetic cosmos, the realm of Ideas, but also exerting its influence upon our souls to lead us up to that realm. As for Aphrodite, she becomes a figure analogous to Isis in the allegorization of the myth of Isis and Osiris (to be discussed below). At 770A Plutarch alludes to the doctrine of the early physicists to the effect that the Sun loves the Moon, and that they unite and propagate. Through the intermediacy of the Moon, the Sun continually fertilizes the earth. We have hints here of the triadic scheme which emerges in a number of other passages (below, pp. 214f.).

As for the Ideas, we see them in the *De Is.* passage in their immanent aspect, as the content of the immanent Logos. In their transcendent aspect, 'in themselves', Plutarch plainly takes them as the thoughts of God, as did his Middle Platonic predecessors. There is an interesting passage in the essay *On the Divine Vengeance* (*De Sera* 550D, quoted above, p. 192), where this comes out clearly, God himself, as the totality of the Ideas, being the model (*paradeigma*) for the physical world, and particularly for Man. The *paradeigma* in the *Timaeus* is to be taken as the totality of the Ideas, and God here is his own *paradeigma*. Note also how the ideal of 'likeness to God' and 'following God' is connected here with God containing within himself all the archetypes according to which the world is fashioned. In *Problems in Plato* 3 (1001Eff.), he gives a more or less orthodox account of the Ideas, arising out of a discussion of the Simile of the Divided Line in *Rep.* VI.

Besides the theory of Ideas in general, Plutarch produces, at *Def. Or.* 428Cff., a remarkable doctrine connecting the five 'greatest genera' (*megista genê*) of Plato's *Sophist* (256cff.), Being, Identity, Difference, Motion and Rest, with the basic constituents of the physical world, the four elements earth, fire, air, water, together with the physical world as

---

[1] He is even described as 'bewitching' (*goêteuôn*) us, making his activity analogous to that of the Sophist of Plato's *Sophist*, whom the Neoplatonists saw as a symbol of the sublunary Demiurge.

a whole. He is taking here the five basic molecules described by Plato in the *Timaeus* (53C–56C), the cube representing earth, the pyramid fire, the octahedron air, and the eikosahedron water, and relating these respectively to Rest, Motion, Identity and Difference. 'The dodeca-hedron', he says, 'which is comprehensive enough to include the other figures, may well seem to be an image of Being, with reference to the whole corporeal realm.' This is suitable, since Being is the most com-prehensive of the *megista genê*, but one half-expected to find the Aris-totelian aether brought in here, since Plutarch accepts it as a fifth element on other occasions (e.g. *De E.* 390A, and just previously at *Def. Or.* 427A). Here, however, he is staying close to the *Timaeus*, and is content with four elements. This connecting of the *megista genê* with the basic elements of the physical world is perhaps a natural scholastic development for later Platonism to make, but I can find no trace of it earlier than Plutarch.[1] The genera of the *Sophist* were, how-ever, later produced as truly Platonic Categories, to rival both the Aristotelian and Stoic systems of Categories, and Plotinus bases him-self upon them, for instance, in his critique of Aristotle's *Categories* in *Enn.* VI 1–3. It is therefore most interesting to see them being used in this way here. Eudorus and Philo, as we saw, in their attack on Aris-totle, turned to the Stoic categories, ignoring the possibilities of the *Sophist*.

(c) The irrational soul: Plutarch's dualism

The dualism of Plutarch comes out in the description of the Ideas being 'seized by the element of disorder and confusion which comes down from the region Above'. This seems to imply not just the rather negative unruly principle of the *Timaeus*, but a positive force, a 'Maleficent Soul', which has at some stage itself broken away from the intelligible realm. We seem thus to be brought close to Gnostic beliefs, but Plutarch can claim the authority of Plato in this matter, as indeed he does earlier in the essay (370E). In Book Ten of the *Laws*, his last work, Plato had postulated (896Dff.), in opposition to the beneficent World Soul, another 'of the opposite capacity', which is responsible for all irrational motion in the universe (898B), or to be specific, in the sublunar world to which irrational motion is confined. (In Plato, however, this soul does not 'come down from the region Above'—that

---

[1] We may note also his equation of the five *megista genê* (or *kyriotatai archai*, 'most basic principles', as he calls them) with the five 'causes' of the *Philebus* (*De E.* 391BC). These are still metaphysical principles, however, not logical ones.

sounds like a Gnostic concept.) Anything which is Soul is also alive and self-moving, so that a considerable step has been taken beyond the inanimate principle of Otherness or 'Necessity' postulated in the *Timaeus*. Plato, as so often, leaves this disquieting development in philosophy hanging in the air, but what he let slip in this passage is enough for a man like Plutarch to build on.

Plutarch, as in all probability Ammonius before him, seems to have been stimulated in his interpretation of Plato (as perhaps was Plato himself in making the suggestion) by a study of Persian religion. At *De Is.* 369E, he bestows high praise on the Zoroastrian theology, referring to it as the 'opinion of the majority of the wisest men'. Just before this, however, he sets out his own view as follows, employing, as was so popular in his time and later, an appeal to immemorial antiquity:

There has, therefore, come down from the theologians and lawgivers to both poets and philosophers [he has quoted Heraclitus and Euripides] this ancient belief, which is of anonymous origin, but is given strong and tenacious evidence—that the universe is not kept on high of itself without mind and reason and guidance, nor is it only one principle that rules and directs it as it were by rudders and curbing reins, but that many powers do so who are a mixture of evil and good. Rather since Nature, to be plain, contains nothing that is unmixed, it is not one steward that dispenses our affairs for us, as though mixing drinks from two jars in an hotel.[1] Life and the cosmos, on the contrary—if not the whole of the cosmos, at least the earthly one below the moon, which is heterogeneous, variegated and subject to all manner of changes—are compounded of two opposite principles (*archai*) and of two antithetic powers (*dynameis*), one of which leads by a straight path and to the right, while the other reverses and bends back. For if nothing comes into being without a cause, and if good could not provide the cause of evil, then Nature must contain in itself the creation and origin of evil as well as of good.

This has merited extended quotation as being a definitive statement of Plutarch's dualism, a doctrine which commended itself to his follower Atticus, and to Numenius (who attributes it to Pythagoras, Fr. 52D, below pp. 373f.), but which was firmly rejected later by Plotinus and all subsequent Neoplatonists. Plutarch held that this Maleficent Soul had, before God created the cosmos proper (which thus had a temporal beginning), itself created a dim prefiguration of the cosmos,

---

[1] An irreverent allusion to the Homeric image of the two jars standing in the hall of Zeus, out of which he dispenses evil and good to men (*Iliad* 24, 527-8).

such as seems to be described in *Timaeus* 52Eff., and in the *De Is.* is represented by the elder Horus. At 373C we have the statement: 'Before this world became manifest and was brought to completion by Logos, Matter, being shown by its nature to be incomplete of itself, brought forth the first creation.' This first creation, says Plutarch, was only a 'wraith and phantasm' of the world that was to come into being. And yet this creation seems to be a token of Isis' desire for order, not a malicious fabrication of Seth-Typhon, the principle of disorder and unreason (the Indefinite Dyad).

On the Indefinite Dyad we have already quoted *Def.* 428E, in connexion with the One, but more might be said of it here. It is 'the element underlying all formlessness and disorder'. Number, and the cosmos, is created by the One 'slicing off' greater or smaller sections of multiplicity (429A). 'If the One be done away with,' says Plutarch, 'once more the Indefinite Dyad throws all into confusion, and makes it to be without rhythm, bound or measure.' Since Plutarch does not seem to believe in periodic *ekpyrôseis*, this can presumably only happen on a minor scale, but the tension is always there. This whole passage, 428E–429D, is thoroughly Pythagorean in inspiration, as will become plain from a comparison with what we know of Moderatus' and Nicomachus' doctrine (below, Chapter 7). The Dyad in the form of the maleficent World Soul will be discussed further below, in connexion with the creation of the world, since it figures largely in the essay *On the Creation of the Soul in the Timaeus* (e.g. 1014DE, 1015D, 1024C).

(d) *The irrational soul and matter*

Isis herself, being equated with the Receptacle of the *Timaeus* and with Matter (372E) as well as with Wisdom (351Eff.—though *eidêsis* and *phronêsis* are the words used, not *sophia*), takes on very much the same character as Sophia in Philo's system, suggesting a tendency in Alexandrian Platonism to identify at least the positive aspect of Matter with the World Soul, and to connect both of them with the Pythagorean-Old Academic Dyad, and with such mythological figures as Dike and Rhea, as well as, in Philo's case at least, with the Sophia of Jewish Hellenistic theology. This amalgam produces an entity which is on the one hand fallen and imperfect, though filled with longing for completion by the *logos* of God, while on the other being the cause of our creation and the vehicle by which we can come to know God. Inevitably, personification and myth spring up around such a being, resulting in Gnostic entities, such as Sophia and her offspring the Demiurge in Valentinian theology (below, Chapter 8), who are the equivalent of Isis and her offspring Horus (the younger) in the present myth. Plutarch interprets Isis as follows (372E):

Thus Isis is the female principle in nature and that which receives all procreation, and so she is called by Plato (i.e. *Tim.* 49A, 51A) the Nurse and the All-receiving (*pandechês*). . . . Imbued in her she has a love of the first and most sovereign principle of all, which is the same as the Good, and this she longs for and pursues. The lot which lies with evil she shuns and rejects; she is, indeed, a sphere of activity (*chôra*) and subject-matter (*hylê*) for both of them, but she inclines always of herself to what is better, offering herself to it for reproduction, and for the sowing in herself of effluxes and likenesses. In these she rejoices and she is glad when she is pregnant with them and teems with procreations. For procreation in Matter is an image of Being (*eikôn ousias*) and an imitation of That which Is.

In connexion with this picture of the irrational World Soul, we should note the remarkable image of the 'slumbering soul' in Plutarch, as it turns up also in Albinus (*Didasc.* ch. 14, 169, 30ff. Hermann). There is a striking passage in this connexion in the *Proc. An.* (1026EF):

Nor is the Nature which presides over the heavens (*sc.* the rational or Demiurgic World Soul) free of this participation in two principles, but, as in a kind of balance, at the moment it is kept on the right path thanks to the dominance of the movement of the Same, and it can direct the world; but there will come a portion of time, as there often has in the past, during which its intelligence becomes dulled and goes to sleep, filled with forgetfulness of its proper role, and that element which ever since the beginning has been in communion and sympathy with Body drags it down and makes it heavy and unwinds the progress of the universe towards the right; it cannot, however, altogether disrupt it, but the better element rouses itself again and looks towards the Model, with God aiding it to turn again and straighten itself out.

This is obviously inspired by the Myth of Plato's *Politicus* (269cff.), but it is rather disturbing that Plutarch should introduce it here, as it implies a cyclic sequence of order and disorder in the universe which he does not seem to hold elsewhere. However, from the conclusion he himself draws just subsequently, it appears that he is not after all taking this cyclic theory literally. He merely wants to emphasize the continued presence of the Disorderly Soul in the world (1027A):

Thus it is proved to us in various ways that the Soul is not entirely the work of God, but that it bears within it innately a share of evil; God can only organise it, limiting Unlimitedness by means of the One, in order that it may become a substance which participates in Limit, and mixing together by the power of Sameness and Otherness order and change and difference and likeness, and contriving for all these, as far as is practicable, community and friendship with each other by means of numbers and harmony.

So Plutarch, having raised the issue of cyclic world phases by introducing the *Politicus* myth, appears now to make nothing of it. This image of the sleeping World Soul (the 'Sleeping Beauty' myth, one might call it) is rather mysterious in origin. It is not a Platonic image in this form, though the image of our life as a sleep or dream is an old and respectable one. It may simply be an imaginative development of the *Politicus* myth, but the fact that it is found in both Plutarch and Albinus suggests that it is older than both—although it is chronologically quite possible for Albinus to have read Plutarch. At any rate, it shows an irrational World Soul, an Isis-figure, which is completely interwoven with the Rational Soul, maintaining a constant cosmic tension.

In Plutarch's metaphysics, in place of the more traditional Platonic triad of principles—God, Matter, and the Ideas or the Logos—we seem to have as many as five entities: a pair of opposites, God (Monadic Intellect) and an evil principle (Indefinite Dyad), represented for Plutarch by the Persian pair Ahuramazda and Ahriman (*De Is.* 369E), as well as by the Soul of Osiris and Seth-Typhon; then the immanent Logos, represented by the Body of Osiris, and the World Soul-cum-Matter, Isis; and, finally, their offspring, the sensible cosmos, Horus. Plutarch does indeed speak of three Platonic entities (*ibid.* 373E), the Intelligible (*noêton*), Matter, and the product of these two, but he speaks of these as being elements of 'the better and more divine nature', which as we have seen is not a complete description of reality. Also, Plutarch is here obscuring a distinction he has just made between the two aspects of the Active Principle, the transcendent and the immanent.

(e) The World Soul and the individual soul: creation of the world

The acceptance of the doctrine of an eternal, independent Irrational Soul naturally has consequences for Plutarch's views on the composition of both the soul of the world and the individual soul, as described, in particular, in the *Timaeus*. Indeed, Plutarch writes a whole treatise, *On the Creation of the Soul in the Timaeus* (*Proc. An.*) which constitutes a detailed exposition of his views, in the form of an extended commentary on *Tim.* 35AB.

The specific problem concerns what we are to understand by 'the substance which is divisible about bodies' in the description of the elements of the soul at *Tim.* 35A. Plutarch distinguishes two views among his predecessors (1012Dff.) (which he indicates were combined by Eudorus (1013B), who appears, as I have said (p. 116), to be his immediate source for the doxographic portion of the treatise), that of Xenocrates and that of Crantor. Xenocrates sees the soul as composed of One and Multiplicity (*plēthos*), which he calls also the Indefinite Dyad; Crantor takes it as being composed of 'intelligible substance' and 'that which is opinable in the sensible realm'. For Crantor, these two elements are the intellect and the senses, both parts of one soul. No second soul is involved. Plutarch, in his critique of this latter position (1013C), points out that a mixture of intelligible and sensible substance could be said to lead to the creation of any aspect of the cosmos, not specifically to that of Soul. Soul, he implies, cannot come to be out of parts that are themselves soulless. As for Xenocrates, although the dyad might seem to be akin to what Plutarch wants here, he in fact condemns the identifying of the soul, which is essentially kinetic, with numbers, which are essentially static. Further, both these schools of thought deny that the creation of the ordered soul, or of the world, took place at a point in time, whereas, for Plutarch, Plato's statements in the *Timaeus* clearly indicate such a creation.

As Plutarch sees it, the troubles of previous commentators arise from the fact that they are not prepared to recognize the existence of a disorderly soul pre-existing the demiurgic creation. If, however, one applies the doctrine of *Laws* x to the *Timaeus*, such an entity clearly emerges:

For creation does not take place out of what does not exist at all but rather out of what is in an improper or unfulfilled state, as in the case of a house or a garment or a statue. For the state that things were in before the creation of the ordered world (*kosmos*) may be characterised as 'lack of order' (*akosmia*); and this 'lack of order' was not something incorporeal or immobile or soulless, but rather it possessed a corporeal nature which was formless and inconstant, and a power of motion which was frantic and irrational. This was the disorderly state of a soul which did not yet possess reason (*logos*). (1014B)

So then, this disorderly element which Plato in the *Timaeus* (48A, 56C, 68E) calls Necessity (*anankē*), cannot be taken as something negative and characterless, such as Matter, but must be a positive force, the disorderly or 'maleficent' soul. We must distinguish between Matter, as described at *Tim.* 50E, which is bereft of all quality and power of its own, and this refractory element in the universe, which has distinct qualities and powers. Plutarch adduces *Philebus*, 24Aff. and *Politicus* 273B to fortify his position, and, all in all, puts forth a well-argued and coherent case, though it depends, of course, on the premise of the unity of Plato's thought.

At any rate, we have in Plutarch's thought an entity, represented by the 'divisible substance' of *Timaeus* 35A and by Isis in the *De Is.*, that is a positively disorderly element in the universe, but which nevertheless, as shown by his description of Isis (and of Poverty in his exegesis of the *Symposium* Myth, *De Is.* 374cf.), desires order, and welcomes 'impregnation' by the divine Logos. This element, the irrational soul, can be described as 'cause of evil' (*kakopoios*), but not strictly as evil itself. The positively evil element in the Universe is something else again, the Indefinite Dyad (Typhon or Ahriman), and that is a more distinctively non-Platonic element in Plutarch's thought than is the irrational soul, although not, perhaps, alien to Xenocrates.

(f) Fate, providence and free will

As we have seen, one matter of controversy between the Stoa and all Platonists and Peripatetics was the Stoic doctrine of Fate and Necessity. The inescapable chain of causality which Chrysippus, in particular, propounded was repugnant to any thinker who wished to maintain the autonomy of the human soul, not to mention the transcendence and providence of God. Opponents of Chrysippus, however, found it remarkably difficult to refute him. We have seen efforts made in this direction already, in Cicero's *De Fato*. By Plutarch's time the main lines of the controversy had been more or less laid down, and we find Plutarch in fact rather inserting himself into the on-going debate than contributing any new insights. The existence in the Lamprias Catalogue of works *On Fate* and *On What Lies in Our Power: Against the Stoics* show his interest in the problem, and, in the case of the second title at least, give evidence of his philosophical position.

Unfortunately, the treatise that has come down to us *On Fate* among Plutarch's works cannot, on stylistic grounds, be credited to him, and is in fact to be assigned, for reasons to be discussed below in Chapter 6 (pp. 320ff.), to the Athenian School of a later period. However, it seems, from what other evidence we can gather, that he would not have disagreed with its doctrine.

For a glimpse of his own views, however, we must turn to such a passage as *Quaest. Conv.* IX 5 (740C), where Plutarch's brother Lamprias (who is frequently his spokesman in dialogues) expounds what he conceives to be Plato's doctrine on Fate and Free Will (in connexion with the Myth of Er in *Republic* X):

> Plato constantly touches on the three Causes, as is natural enough for a man who first or most particularly observed how in the course of nature the operation of Fate (*to kath' heimarmenên*) mingles and interweaves with that of Chance (*tychê*), while our free will (*to eph' hêmin*) in its turn combines with one or other of them or with both simultaneously. So in this passage (*Rep.* 614Bff.) he has admirably suggested the influence that each cause exerts in our affairs, assigning the choice of lives to our free will [for 'virtue obeys no master' (*Rep.* 617E)—nor does wickedness], while associating with the compulsion of Fate the good life of those who choose correctly, and the contrary condition of those whose choice is bad; then, the fall of the lots as they are scattered haphazard introduces Chance, which predetermines many things in our lives, by reason of the various forms of upbringing and society which different groups happen to enjoy.

He ends by affirming stoutly that it is absurd to look for a cause for what happens by chance.

It is not quite clear to what text Lamprias is referring in his attribution to Plato of the doctrine of the Three Causes, but *Laws* IV 709B could give a scholastic mind occasion for such a formula.[1] There the Athenian says:

> God controls all that is, and Chance and Opportunity (*kairos*) co-operate with God in the control of all human affairs.

God can conveniently be taken as either Fate or Providence, and *kairos* as 'that which is in our power'. From our perspective, however, the obvious passage is not from Plato, but Aristotle's *Nicomachean Ethics* III 3, 1112a32, where three Causes, Nature, Necessity and Chance, are listed, followed by Mind, and Free Will (*to eph' hêmin*). Here we have, on the face of it, five, but Nature could be assimilated

---

[1] Plutarch uses this passage elsewhere only at *Comm. in Hesiod*, Fr. 63, in connexion with a praise of *kairos*, but it is used by Maximus of Tyre in his discussion of Providence and Freewill (*Or.* XI 7).

to Mind, and both raised to a level above the other three. The Old Academy may have produced further formulations of this sort.

All this is really no answer to the Stoic challenge, but it constitutes interesting evidence for the Platonist line on this question. The treatise *De Fato* presents Platonic doctrine in a more organized form. Here it is only brought in by the way, in the course of a dinner-party conversation on a more trivial subject.

In a more serious context, the discussion of the composition of the Moon in the *De Fac.*, we find Lamprias (again) making a strong distinction, in opposition to the Stoics, between Fate, or the order of Nature, and Providence (*pronoia*) (927Aff.). God, through his Providence, brings it about frequently that the elements of the universe are not in their 'natural' position. Thus the Moon, which should according to Nature be fiery, is according to Providence earthy. What use is there, asks Lamprias, in having a master-craftsman, if the product creates itself perfectly without his intervention? Thus the Stoics are confused in their equating of Zeus and Providence with Fate and Necessity.

Again it must be said that Plutarch is not really addressing himself to the problem. Only by postulating that such movements as the circular motions of the heavenly bodies are not 'natural'—the Stoic fire should simply move upwards—can he give Providence a distinct role. Again, the fact that the Moon, though earthy, does not fall towards the centre of the cosmos, is precisely what is requiring to be proved. It is not admitted by the Stoics. Even if it were, the phenomenon could be accommodated without bringing a force superior to the laws of Nature into the Universe. One simply propounds a new law. Nevertheless, as a sample of Platonist argumentation, this is all historically valuable.

The question comes up again in connexion with the causes of prophetic power, in the *Def. Or.*, and once more Lamprias is the spokesman. In this case he is defending himself against the complaint of Ammonius that, by his exposition of the physical causes of prophetic power (i.e. exhalations from the earth), he is eliminating the influence of divine providence. Lamprias is most embarrassed, and denies that such was his intention. He then sets out a doctrine of double causality, which he attributes to Plato (435F). This does not quite square with the doctrine of the Three Causes described above. There we had God, Chance and Free Will; here we have simply God and Necessity. The discrepancy may be explained by the fact that the Three Causes refer only to the sublunar world in which we operate, whereas this two-fold distinction embraces the whole universe. The three causes are thus really only subdivisions of the material cause.

Lamprias starts from Plato's criticism of Anaxagoras' account of causality, as given at *Phaedo* 97BC. He then continues:

Plato himself was the first of the philosophers . . . to assign to God, on the one hand, the origin of all things that are in keeping with reason (*kata logon*), and on the other hand, not to divest Matter of the causes necessary for whatever comes into being, but to realise that the perceptible universe, even when arranged in some such orderly way as this, is not pure and un-alloyed, but that it takes its origin from Matter when Matter comes into conjunction with the *logos*.

This passage bases itself on the *Timaeus* (48Eff.) in its investing of Necessity with the properties of Matter. In the process, however, the nature of the problem of determinism seems to be lost sight of. That the world is the product of matter and *logos* is not in dispute. The problem is what place the workings of this combination leave for individual freedom of choice. This problem is not addressed at all in the present passage, and is countered in the previous passage only by dogmatic assertions.

This, I fear, we will find to be the case generally with Middle Platonic efforts to deal with Fate and Free Will. Only Plotinus, in *Enneads* III 2–3, comes seriously to grips with the problem, and he only suc-ceeds ultimately in demonstrating its insolubility.

(g) *Soul and mind*

Plutarch makes a clear distinction between the human soul and the human mind (*nous*). Of course, such a distinction had always been present in some form in philosophic speculation, but never before had such an unequivocal distinction of them as separate entities been made. The passage to be considered first comes from the Myth at the end of the essay *On the Face on the Moon*, and is not spoken by Plutarch, but there is no reason to doubt that he regarded it as philosophically correct (*De Fac.* 943Aff.):

Most people rightly hold a man to be composite, but wrongly hold him to be composed of only two parts. The reason is that they suppose mind to be somehow part of soul, thus erring no less than those who believe soul to be part of body, for in the same degree as soul is superior to body, so is mind better and more divine than soul. The result of soul and body commingled is the irrational or the affective factor, whereas of mind and soul the conjunction produces reason; and of these the former is the source of pleasure and pain, the latter of virtue and vice.

We may note here, so far, besides the unequivocal tripartition of the human being, the notion of three terms and two conjunctions (*synodoi*), that of body and soul producing the irrational soul (*to alogon*), that of soul and mind producing the reason (*logos*). The rational soul, then, is not to be seen as being mind in its pure state. That is something higher again. This tripartition is alluded to dimly in the treatise *On Moral Virtue* (441Dff.), but in such a way as to suggest that Plutarch had not then fully worked it out:

But it seems to have eluded all these philosophers (*sc.* the Stoics) in what way each of us is truly twofold and composite. For that other twofold nature of ours they have not discerned, but merely the more obvious one, the blend of soul and body.

Here we might seem to be about to hear the same account as in the *De Fac.* but in fact what Plutarch goes on to expound is simply Plato's theory of the tripartite soul, which Plutarch (as I have said above, p. 194) sees as essentially a bipartite division between rational and irrational elements.

In another myth, however, that of the essay *On the Daemon of Socrates*, we do get a clear statement of the theory (591Dff.):

Every soul partakes of mind; none is irrational or unintelligent (*anous*). But the portion of the soul that mingles with flesh and passions suffers alteration and becomes in the pleasures and pains it undergoes irrational. Not every soul mingles to the same extent; some sink entirely into the body, and becoming disordered throughout are during their whole life distracted by passions; others mingle in part, but leave outside what is purest in them. This is not dragged in with the rest, but is like a buoy attached to the top, floating on the surface in contact with the man's head, while he is as it were submerged in the depths; and it supports as much of the soul, which is held upright about it, as is obedient and not overpowered by the passions.

Now the part carried submerged in the body is called the soul, whereas the part left free from corruption is called by the multitude the mind, who take it to be within themselves, as they take reflected objects to be in the mirrors that reflect them; but those who conceive this matter rightly call it a daemon, as being external.

This presents a slightly different picture from the *De Fac.* The mind is seen here as 'external' (*ektos*) to the body, presiding over it as its daemon. For this latter formulation we can turn to *Timaeus* 90A, where Plato refers to 'the most authoritative element of our soul' as a daemon, which God has given to each one of us, and which raises us up from earth towards our kindred (*syngeneia*) in the heavens. Here a certain externality is implied, though not stated.

The *Timaeus* can also be seen as providing at least a starting-point for the doctrine of the distinctness of mind and soul. At *Tim.* 30B we find the Demiurge 'carpentering together the universe by setting mind in soul and soul in body'. This, admittedly, is described as being done on the cosmic, not the individual, level, but the construction of the individual may be taken as mirroring that of the cosmos. Further, at 41Dff., a sharp distinction is made between the rational element in soul, which is fashioned by the Demiurge himself, and the irrational, the making of which he delegates to the 'young gods'. W. Hamilton, in an article in the *Classical Quarterly* 28 (1934, pp. 24–30), rightly points to these passages as sources for Plutarch's scheme here, but it must be admitted that at least a process of formalization has taken place in the interval between Plato and Plutarch. Aristotle's remarks on the separateness and immortality of the *nous* in *De An.* III 5 have obviously exerted their influence, for a start.

There may be other influences at work also, however. In the *Corpus Hermeticum* (Tractates I and X in particular) we find a doctrine of the distinctness of *nous* and *psychê*. This may itself have roots in Platonism, but in the Hermetic concept of *nous* there is another element which is not properly Platonic. *Nous* appears in *CH* x not simply as the intellectual faculty in man, but rather as a daemon sent by God to reward or chastise man according to his deserts. Even this concept can find some support in *Tim.* 90A, but there is no denying that the whole thought-world of the Hermetic Corpus is alien to that of Plato. The Hermetic and Gnostic concepts of *nous* will be discussed in a later chapter (p. 391), but it seemed necessary at least to mention them here, as being influences to which Plutarch was not, perhaps, immune.

It is noticeable in the Myth that not every soul appears to have a *nous*-daemon attached to it, and that even in the case of those which do the relation of the soul to its *nous*-daemon seems to vary. We have seen that 'some souls sink entirely into body', while others 'only mingle in part, but leave outside what is purest in them' (591D). Only these latter, it seems, have separate *nous*-daemons. But then we find (592AB) that some of these *nous*-daemons (seen as stars) ride quietly above their souls, 'like the corks we observe riding on the sea to mark nets', while others 'describe a confused and uneven spiral, like spindles as they twist the thread, and are unable to reduce their movement to a straight and steady course'. These latter are having trouble in controlling the refractory tendencies of the souls over which they preside, and only bring them to obedience by firm chastisement. We seem to have here three classes of person, one without any higher element in their souls at all, another with a higher element to which they are obedient, and a third with a higher element against which they struggle, but by which they are finally subdued. This rather curious division seems to take part, at least, of its inspiration from the myth of Plato's *Phaedrus* (248A), as the language which Plutarch uses indicates. He seems to be thinking of the three classes of human charioteers and pairs described there. On the other hand, the suggestion that not all souls have *nous*, and that, for some of those who have, *nous* is a punishing agent, finds a definite echo in Tractate X of the *Corpus Hermeticum* (cf. especially sections 19–21, and Appendix B, pp. 138ff. of the Budé edition). In short, there seems to appear in this myth an 'elitist' theory of *nous* which has distinct Gnostic overtones, but which is after all not too dissimilar from the selective immortality described in Cicero's *Somnium Scipionis* (see above, p. 100), whatever may be the source of that.

(h) Divisions of the universe and hierarchies of being

The threefold division of the individual has its equivalent on the cosmic level, in the form of a threefold division of the universe. This we find in the *De Facie* (943F). Here Plutarch bases himself upon the peculiar theory of Xenocrates (above, p. 31) of the three *pykna*, or 'densities', of Matter. It is an interesting instance of Plutarch's dependence on Xenocrates. Whether the latter was also responsible for the separation of *nous* from *psyché* is not clear.

More interesting still from a philosophic point of view is a feature of the myth of the *De Genio Socratis*, namely an elaborate four-level hierarchy of Being, expanding on the threefold distinction made in the *De Facie* by the addition of a further term at the top, the Monad. The scheme curiously prefigures the Plotinian system of hypostases, and its exact interpretation is a matter of some uncertainty. There is no reason to doubt, however, that it is a theory of which Plutarch approved. Here is the relevant passage:

Four principles (*archai*) there are of all things: the first is of Life (*zoé*), the second is of Motion, the third of Generation (*genesis*), and the last is of Decay (*phthora*). The first is linked to the second by the Monad, at the Invisible (*to aoraton*), the second to the third by Mind at the Sun, the third to the fourth by Nature (*physis*) at the Moon. A Fate, daughter of Necessity, holds the keys and presides over each link: over the first, Atropos, over the second Clotho, and over the link at the Moon Lachesis. The turning-point of birth is at the Moon (591B).

The 'Invisible' we may perhaps take as the outer rim of heaven, to preserve the analogy, but it is a—perhaps intentionally—obscure term. 'Nature' can be taken as synonymous with Soul, in its sub-rational aspect. In its firm separation of Mind and Soul, which are connected with the Sun and Moon respectively, this scheme is in accord with that of the *De Facie*. The three Fates also play analogous roles in both myths (cf. *De Fac.* 945C). What is new is the level of 'Life', and the Monad which links it (*syndei*) to the level of Motion.

H. J. Krämer has a good discussion of this passage (*Ursprung* p. 98, n. 250). The fact that the supreme principle is called the Monad does not mean that it is not also a mind; but a distinction is made between it and *nous*. This *nous* must be the Demiurgic Mind, combining the Demiurge of the *Timaeus* with the rational part of the World Soul. The Monad is therefore a transcendent, self-contemplating Mind, the ultimate principle of all Being, including that of the Demiurge. The scheme is analogous to those of Moderatus and Numenius (pp. 347, 366–8). The denomination of the highest term as *Zoé*, a life-principle, is somewhat unexpected. A life-principle is thus placed above the Demiurgic Mind, even as it is in the Chaldaean Oracles, and in later Neoplatonism. An eccentricity, it seems to me, is the apparent distinguishing of the spheres of *genesis* and *phthora*, which are usually linked closely together as joint characteristics of the sublunary world. They may not, in fact, be sharply distinguished here. It is simply that the Moon has been assigned the role of generator, and the Earth that of corrupter. They both co-operate, however, to produce the realm of Nature. We seem, in fact, to be back to the basic Xenocratean three-way division of reality.

In both the myths, Mind is connected with the Sun and Soul with the Moon, and a 'double death' is envisaged for the individual, the soul (with the mind) leaving the body and taking up its abode in the Moon, and the mind then leaving the soul behind and rising to the level of the Sun. The reverse process also takes place, the Sun sowing minds in the Moon, and the Moon sowing the now intelligized souls into bodies (*De Fac.* 945BC). All this talk of sowing can be referred back to the description of the activities of the Demiurge in *Timaeus*

41-2, but it is plain that a good deal has happened in the way of formalization to Plato's original description. The Demiurge is now the Sun, and the 'young gods' the Moon. An essentially solar theology has taken over, perhaps already a development of that of Xenocrates'.

(i) Daemons

The more transcendent the Supreme God becomes, the more he stands in need of other beings to mediate between him and the material world, over which, in Platonism, he always exercises a general supervision (*pronoia*). We have seen how the Logos serves this function, but Plutarch, like all Middle Platonists, also postulates a daemonic level of being, which figures prominently in his writings.

Plainly Xenocrates' theory of daemons, which was dependent in turn on his theory of proportions and intermediaries in the universe, was a fundamental influence on Plutarch here. In the essay *On the Obsolescence of Oracles* (*Def. Or.* 416cff.), the conversation turns to how long these daemons live, and Cleombrotus of Sparta makes a statement which we may take to express Plutarch's view, since it is not contradicted:

On the boundary, as it were, between gods and men there exist certain natures susceptible to human emotions and involuntary changes, whom it is right that we, like our fathers before us, should regard as daemons, and, calling them by that name, should reverence them. As an illustration of this subject, Xenocrates, the companion of Plato, employed the order of the triangles; the equilateral he compared to the nature of the gods, the scalene to that of man, and the isosceles to that of the daemons; for the first is equal in all its lines, the second unequal in all, and the third is partly equal and partly unequal, like the nature of the daemons, which possesses human emotion and divine power.

Nature has placed before us perceptible images and visible likenesses (of all three classes of being), of the gods the Sun and the stars, and of mortal men, lightning, comets and meteors . . . but there is a body with complex characteristics which actually parallels the daemons, namely the Moon; and when men see that she, by her being consistently in accord with the cycles (*periphorai*) through which those beings pass [presumably an allusion to the belief that daemons may be demoted and promoted, as Empedocles taught, cf. *Is.* 361c], is subject to apparent wanings and waxings and transformations, some call her an earthlike star, others a 'heavenly earth' (cf. *De Fac.* 935c) and others the domain of Hecate, who belongs both to the earth and to the heavens.

Now if that air that is between the earth and the moon were to be removed and withdrawn, the unity and coherence (*koinônia*) of the universe would be destroyed, since there would be an empty and unconnected space in the middle; and in just the same way those who refuse to leave us the race of daemons make the relations of gods and men remote and alien by doing away with the 'interpretative and ministering nature' as Plato (*Politicus* 260D, *Symp.* 202E) has called it, or else they force us to a disorderly confusion of all things, in which we bring God into men's emotions and activities, drawing him down to our needs, as the women of Thessaly are said to draw down the moon.

This passage deserved, I think, extended quotation as containing all the basic elements of Plutarch's theory of daemons. Both God's *pronoia* and his transcendence must be preserved, and the universe can tolerate no sharp divisions or sudden transitions. The basic inspiration for this concept of the role of daemons in linking the incompatible extremes of the universe together is the famous passage in Plato's *Symposium* referred to above, but the details were obviously worked out further by Xenocrates, whom we saw earlier providing the basis for the threefold division of the world in the Myth of the *De Fac.* (943E = Fr. 56 Heinze).[1] The Moon, which served in that myth as the place of souls, and indeed as the symbol of the World Soul, now is made to serve also as the place of daemons (who are after all themselves souls); in either case the sphere of the Moon is the essential arena of mediation and transition in the world scheme.

Daemons, then, serve as a link between men and gods, intervening in the details of human existence in a way that would be undignified for God, and inconsistent with his untroubled serenity. One of the criticisms of Christianity, indeed, made by Platonists like Celsus in the generation after Plutarch, was precisely this too intimate involving of God with the sublunar world.

In the *Def. Or.*, the chief subject of discussion is the administration by daemons of oracles, but they are to be credited in fact with all active interventions of the supernatural in human life which had vulgarly been credited (or debited) to gods. Daemons are subject to passions, and thus can on occasion go to the bad. A passage from the *De Fac.* is relevant here (944CD):

Yet not forever do the daemons tarry upon the Moon; they descend hither to take charge of oracles, they attend and participate in the highest of the

---

[1] Xenocrates could, however, point to Plato's adumbration of this in *Gorgias* 508A, where he speaks of the 'geometrical equality' which holds together heaven and earth and gods and men.

mystic rituals (*teletai*), and they flash forth as saviours manifest in war and on the sea. [A reference to the Dioscuri in particular.] For any act that they perform in these matters not fairly but inspired by wrath or for an unjust end or out of envy they are penalised, for they are cast out upon the earth again confined in human bodies.

There are, then, evil daemons, though not, I think, in Plutarch's system, *primally* evil ones, such as one finds in Zoroastrianism or in Gnostic systems. Such evil daemons as there are are fallen from a good state, and may again be promoted to that state. It must be admitted, however, that the presentation of daemons in the *De Is.*, if taken by itself, tends far more towards the postulation of inherently evil daemons, and indeed Plutarch in this essay does seem to be in a rather more Zoroastrian, dualistic frame of mind than elsewhere. In the *De Is.* (particularly 360Dff.) he is using the theory to explain the existence of such entities as Typhon and the Giants and Titans, who are, after all, primevally evil beings. These monsters, however, at least the Giants and Titans, could be regarded, despite popular views as to their origins, as 'fallen' daemons confined for punishment in bodies, and this is how they are regarded at *De Fac.* 945B, even Typhon being included in the list. For such daemons as these it is confinement in bodies that constitutes their punishment, 'and even these in time the Moon takes back to herself and reduces to order' (*loc. cit.*).

We find also, however, evil daemons in a permanently disembodied state, and that indeed is how Greeks in general would normally think of them. Xenocrates is quoted at *Is.* 361B as an authority for the view that there are 'great and strong natures (*physeis*) in the atmosphere, malevolent and morose, who rejoice in (gloomy sacrifices), and after gaining them as their lot, they turn to nothing worse'. These beings have a permanent status in the universe, and must be propitiated continually. There does appear to be a contradiction here between two views of evil daemons, but I will discuss this and other problems at the end of the section.

From evil daemons proper there must be distinguished daemons who are simply delegated by God to punish us, such as we have seen envisaged by Philo (above, p. 123). Plutarch also recognizes these. He speaks at *Def. Or.* 417B of those who 'go about as avengers (*timôroi*) of arrogant and grievous cases of injustice', a concept which goes back at least to Hesiod (WD 254–5). Such daemons will, of course, be ranked with the good, and if they exceed their commission in any way, will themselves be punished and demoted.

There is further a distinction to be made between daemons and heroes (*ibid.* 415B), again going back to Hesiod (WD 122), although the basis of differentiation is not made clear. Heroes are ranked below daemons, and may most probably be taken as those superhuman souls who have been most recently in bodies. There is in fact a scale of promotion envisaged by Plutarch which is most interesting. He does not believe in a static universe in which every level of being is fixed in place. There is continual promotion and demotion:

Others [than Homer and Hesiod] postulate a transmutation for bodies and souls alike; even as water is seen to be generated from earth, air from water, and fire from air, as their substance is borne upward, even so the better souls obtain their transmutation from men into heroes and from heroes into daemons. And from the daemons yet a few souls, in the long reach of time, because of supreme excellence, come, after being purified, to share completely in divinity (*theiotês*).

Admittedly the views here quoted are not given as that of Plutarch's spokesman (Lamprias), but as that of 'others' (presumably such thinkers as Empedocles), but they are quoted with approval and not refuted, so there can be little doubt that Plutarch accepted them. That a man may, in rare cases, become a god (as did Heracles and Dionysus in traditional mythology)—or if one thinks in monotheistic terms, partake fully in divinity—is a remarkable theory, agreeing with that of Plotinus as against later Neoplatonists such as Iamblichus, who preferred to maintain an unbridgeable gap between Man and God, although human souls might ascend to the daemonic level. As for the corresponding process of descent to a lower level, certainly daemons descend, as we have seen, but I doubt that Plutarch conceived of a god descending. He is not specific on this point, however.

(j) The guardian daemon

It remains to speak of the personal or guardian daemon, the most notable example of which, for the Middle Platonists, was the daemonic voice by which Socrates claimed to be guided. We have already seen that, in the Myth of the dialogue *On the Daemon of Socrates* (591Dff.), we have a description of the *nous* as a daemon. A little further on, however, at 593Dff., we have the doctrine that, while the Gods themselves take over the guidance of a favoured few, such as Socrates, the rest of men are presided over by a class of disembodied souls. These are certainly distinct from any part of the individual's own mind. The passage is worth quoting at length, not least for the lively imagery it contains:

For as athletes who from old age have given up training do not entirely lose their ardour and their love of bodily prowess, but look on with pleasure as others train, and call out encouragement and run along beside them, so those who are done with the contests of life, and who, from prowess of soul, have become daemons, do not hold what is said and done and striven after in this world in utter contempt, but are propitious to contenders for the same goal, join in their ardour, and encourage and help them to the attainment of virtue when they see them keeping up the struggle and all but reaching their heart's desire.

For daemons do not assist all indifferently, but as when men swim at sea, those standing on the shore merely view in silence the swimmers who are still far out and distant from land, whereas they help with hand and voice alike such as have come near, and running along and wading in beside them bring them safely in, such too, my friends, is the way of daemons: as long as we are head over ears in the welter of worldly affairs and are changing from one body to another like conveyances (*ochêmata*), they allow us to fight our way out and persevere unaided, as we endeavour by our own prowess to come through safe and reach a haven; but when in the course of countless births a soul has stoutly and resolutely sustained a long series of struggles, and as her cycles draw to a close, she approaches the upper world, bathed in sweat, in imminent peril and straining every nerve to reach the shore, God holds it no sin for her daemon to go to the rescue, but lets whoever will lend aid.

One daemon is eager to deliver by his exhortations one soul, another another, and the soul on her part, having drawn close, can hear, and is thus saved; but if she pays no heed, she is forsaken by her daemon and comes to no happy end.

There is much of interest in this passage. First, the imagery, after beginning with lively pictures, first, of retired athletes coaching the young, then of the scene at the end of a 'Channel Swim', ends with a much more exalted image of the soul struggling in the stormy sea of life, with distinct echoes of the shipwreck of Odysseus in *Odyssey* v (long since allegorized in this sense by the Stoics, and appearing already in Philo), and of the *Phaedrus* Myth.

Secondly, these guardians are, it seems, all souls who have been through it themselves and have now earned their release from the cycle of rebirth, not souls that have never suffered incarnation. Only noble souls, we are glad to hear, qualify to serve as guardians. The guardian is not able to help the soul in all the struggles of life, however, but only when it has already come through the bulk of them, or even of those of a series of lives.

This picture of the guardian daemon will be further rounded out when we come to consider Apuleius, who also wrote an essay on the daemon of Socrates, which contains much useful doctrine, though in a distinctly rhetorical form (pp. 317ff.).

Consideration of a passage in the essay *On Tranquillity of Mind*, however, reveals an elaboration of the notion of a guardian daemon which is somewhat disquieting. Here Plutarch postulates two daemons for each individual, one good and one evil (474BC):

For it is not true, as Menander says, that

'By every man at birth a spirit stands
A guide of virtue for life's mysteries;'

but rather, as Empedocles affirms (Fr. 122DK), two Fates (*moirai*), as it were, or *daimones*, receive into their care each one of us at birth and consecrate [or simply 'rule over'] us. . . . The result is that since we at our birth received the mingled seeds of each of these affections (*pathê*), and since therefore our nature possesses much unevenness, a man of sense prays for better things, but expects the contrary as well, and, avoiding excess, deals with both conditions.

It is not clear to me how far Plutarch is in fact personifying these *daimones* that he talks of here. He refers to them just below as *pathê*, which suggests to me that he is thinking only of tendencies rather than of spirits, but there the passage stands, with its distinctly dualistic overtones (cf. *Corpus Hermeticum* IX 3, where the dualism is real. The soul may take its 'seeds' either from God or from one of the daemons). We may recall in this connexion the equally disquieting doctrine that Philo produced at *QE* I 23 (above, p. 173). It does seem that somewhere in the lower reaches of Middle Platonism the notion of an evil guardian as well as a good one was floating about. As for Empedocles, what he had in mind is not clear to me.

(*k*) *Contact of the immaterial with the material*

In connexion with his theory of the Guardian Daemon, and also with the theory of divine inspiration in general, Plutarch indulges in certain speculations about the mode of contact between the daemonic and the human mind, and between mind and matter. As one would expect, he does not go into the question very deeply. He simply states his views on the subject, or rather, allows the Pythagorean Simmias to do so.

Nevertheless, the views expressed are of some interest, as the question is one that must torment any philosophy which seeks to establish a distinction, and then a connexion, between material and immaterial essence.

As regards the connexion between soul and body, he sees no real problem (*De Gen.* 588F–589B):

The soul of man, which is strung with countless impulses (*hormai*) as with resilient cords is, when rationally dealt with, by far the most sensitive of all instruments, moving at a slight impulse towards the goal conceived by the intellect [cf. the puppet image at Plato, *Laws* I 645AB]. For here it is in the intellect, to which they are made fast and taut, that the passions and impulses have their origins; and when it is struck, these are pulled and thereby exercise traction on man and give him tension.

Indeed it is most of all by this that we are enabled to comprehend the great power of what is intelligised (*to noêthen*); for insensate bones and thews and flesh saturated with humours, and the inert and prostrate mass they constitute, the instant the soul conceives a purpose in the intellect and sets its impulse going for that end, arise as a whole, tensed and co-ordinated in all its parts, and fly as if winged to carry the idea to execution [cf. *Virt. Mor.* 442C–E].

It is not, then, a hard or hopeless task to understand by what manner of impact, co-ordination (*synentasis*) and suggestion the soul receives a thought and thereby with its movements draws after it the corporeal mass.

One would have thought that this was precisely the difficult thing to understand. What Plutarch might have argued was that we see this actually happening, however inexplicable it is, and thus the influence of daemonic soul on human soul is easier to comprehend, as being at least the influence of like on like. But he seems to think that he is explaining something here by means of his Pythagoreanizing imagery. It is interesting that he uses a Stoic technical term, *synentasis*, to express the co-ordination of psychic and bodily motions. For a Stoic there is no problem; for a Platonist there is.

Of course, once one has dismissed the problem of the interaction of soul and body, the rest is easy. Spirit can communicate with spirit by the lightest touch, 'like light producing a reflection' (589B). The image of the human soul as a stringed instrument, well or badly tuned, taut or slack (589DE), is a distinctively Pythagorean one, suitable to utterance by Simmias, and, purged of the awkward aspects of the *soul-as-harmonia* theory as set out in the *Phaedo*, it is well suited to Plutarch's argument. We have here a reasonably coherent account of the mode of communication between higher beings and the embodied soul, and that, after all, is what Plutarch is primarily concerned with in this passage. On the question of the connexion between Soul and Body, it seems to me, no light is thrown.

(*l*) *Demonology: some conclusions*

As one surveys the range of Plutarch's utterances on daemons, certain problems become evident. First of all, how do we reconcile the doctrine of daemons with the doctrine of the ascent and descent of souls set out in the myths of the *De Facie* and the *De Genio?* Necessarily, daemons are souls, but are all souls now incarcerated in human bodies potential daemons? I think Plutarch would have to say that they were, but, perhaps, that only a small proportion are active in human affairs for good or ill. Then what of those evil daemons that are disembodied? Are they on their way to incarnation, or are they established permanently in the air below the moon? On Plutarch's theory of punishment for daemonic misbehaviour, they cannot be permanently disembodied; they must be on their way to birth. And yet that seems unsatisfactory. If birth is the punishment, it should surely take effect immediately.

That evil daemons are involved with birth is suggested by a passage in *Def. Or.* (417B), which actually complicates the issue further:

For as among men, so also among daemons, there are different degrees of virtue, and in some there is a weak and dim reminder of the passionate and irrational element, a kind of dregs, as it were, while in others this is extensive and hard to stifle.

Thus it would seem that some daemons bring with them a large measure of *to alogon* from a previous incarnation, though we are not told why this should be. They have plainly not been purged adequately by their exile in the body. But perhaps, rather, these are not daemons sent down for punishment, but souls who descended in the ordinary course of 'necessity', and behaved badly while in the body. These now become wicked and irrational daemons in the interval before descending again. Certainly they are credited with the same delight in gloomy and cruel sacrifices as were the Xenocratean daemons referred to at *De Is.* 361B, who sounded permanently established. It does seem as if there is an incoherence here in Plutarch's thought, resulting, perhaps, from a clash of Persian (and popular) influences with more purely Platonic ones.

Again, what of the pure minds who die the 'second death' and ascend from the moon to the sun, leaving behind their souls? Surely they are necessarily now divinized? And yet we have a description of their being sowed again into the moon (though with no suggestion of punishment for misbehaviour, *De Fac.* 945BC), and thence descending again into bodies. These, it could be said, are men who have become gods, and vice versa. All this is possible, but one would like to hear how and when, if at all, one breaks free from the cycle of rebirth. Plutarch seems to envisage a continual ascent and descent, though with the suggestion (particularly at *Def. Or.* 415B) that only a select few in fact achieve the 'second death' which raises them to godhead.

On the other hand, there is a passage in the *De Facie* myth (944DE) where the subject of discussion is these good daemons who were once on earth, such as the Idaean Dactyls and the Corybantes of Phrygia. These are described as ascending to what sounds like permanent bliss:

Their rites, honours and titles persist, but their powers (*dynameis*) have been directed to another place, as they achieved the most excellent alteration. They achieve it, some sooner and some later, once the mind has been separated from the soul. It is separated by love for the image (*eikôn*) inherent in the Sun, through which shines forth manifest the desirable and the beautiful and divine and blessed towards which all Nature, in one way or another, strives.

This is worth quoting, also, for the solar theology revealed in it (although the Sun is here no more than the image of the true godhead). As to the main point, it does sound as if these good daemons, who formerly walked the earth, have achieved permanent divinity. But one can never be quite sure.

I do not wish to force coherence on Plutarch's thought where none, perhaps, exists. It is more profitable to develop as fully as possible all the conflicting tendencies within it, bearing evidence as they do to a rich variety of theorizing in Plutarch's time about daemons and the overall relation between them and God.

(m) A multiplicity of worlds

In the *Timaeus*, after describing the five elements of the universe, Plato raises the question of the number of worlds that one should postulate (55CD). Though he himself opts for a single world, he admits the possibility of there being five, in words which seem to have misled certain later Platonists. In the *Def. Or.*, the question of the multiplicity of worlds having come up, Cleombrotus speaks as follows (421F):

You will remember that [Plato] summarily decided against an infinite number of worlds, but had doubts about a limited number; and up to five he conceded a reasonable probability to those who postulated one world to correspond to each element, but for himself, he kept to one. This seems to be peculiar to Plato, for the other philosophers conceived a fear of plurality, feeling that if they did not limit matter to one world, but went beyond one, an unlimited and embarrassing infinity would at once fasten itself upon them.

This last remark primarily refers to Aristotle, *De Caelo* I 8–9 (276a18 ff.), where he criticizes the notion of a multiplicity of worlds, but in spite of the very tentative nature of Plato's statement, it seems to have been a continuing matter of argument between Peripatetics and Platonists. Here both Cleombrotus and Demetrius (423A) deny that Plato meant to entertain the possibility of five worlds, but the grammarian Heracleon of Megara seems to accept the idea (422F) that Plato may have wished to take the domains of each of his five elements as a *kosmos*, though Heracleon here (remaining true to Plato) takes the dodecahedron as comprising the whole universe. If one took the dodecahedron as referring to the Aristotelian aether (as was also done by Platonists; cf. *De E* 390A), the theory would make better sense.

The theory that Plato postulated five worlds goes back, it seems, to one Theodorus of Soli, who wrote a work explaining the mathematical theories of Plato (*Def. Or.* 427Aff.). He gives an elaborate explanation of the need for five different *kosmoi* of matter to create the five elements, a summary of which is given by Lamprias in the dialogue. None of this can be taken as representing Plutarch's views, as it is argued against subsequently by Ammonius, but it seems worth mentioning as being, apparently, a possible line for Platonists to take.

3. LOGIC

Technical logic was not among Plutarch's more vital concerns, and there is in his extant works not much to indicate which system he followed, although there is no reason to think that it differed much from that set out somewhat later in Albinus' *Didaskalikos*, which is itself a basic account of Middle Platonic Logic. Plutarch did write a *Lecture on the Ten Categories* (*Lamprias Cat.* 192), now lost, of which one would dearly love to know the contents. Did he remain true to Aristotle, or did he, perhaps, adopt some of the Pythagorean 'corrections' brought in by Eudorus? We find two other works also the titles of which sound 'logical', *A Reply to Chrysippus on the First Consequent* (*to prôton hepomenon*) (*Cat.* No. 152), and *On Tautology* (*Cat.* No. 162), as well as some works on Rhetoric, which was accounted a part of Logic. Apart from revealing a tendency to attack the Stoics, which is what we should expect from Plutarch, these titles do not tell us very much.

That Plutarch regarded Plato as being already in full possession of the so-called Aristotelian logic is shown by a passage of *An. Proc.* (1023E), which is a commentary on *Timaeus* 37AB, a passage in which, with the eye of faith, most of the Aristotelian categories could be discerned. It is, I think, worth quoting the Timaeus passage, as it must have figured largely in Middle Platonic arguments about the origins of logic:

... whenever she (the Soul) touches anything which has its *substance* (*ousia*) dispersed or anything which has its substance undivided, she is moved throughout her whole being and announces what the object is identical with and from what it is different (Quantity and Quality), and in what *relation* (*pros ti*), *where* and how, and *when*, it comes about that each thing exists (*einai* = Action) and is acted upon by others (*paschein* = Passivity), both in the sphere of Becoming, and in that of the Ever-Uniform.

I have italicized and/or inserted the relevant categories. Sceptics might object to such efforts as the equating of the examination of identity and difference with Quantity and Quality, and the equating of a thing's *existence* in a certain state with its *activity*, but a loyal Platonist could argue that, after all, any distinguishing of a thing from other things must involve a statement of its quantity and quality, and that, on Plato's own principle as laid down in the *Sophist* (248c), existence means acting and being acted upon. Further, the categories *keisthai* and *echein* can conceivably be viewed as latent in the latter part of the sentence. The Aristotelian categories are thus 'demonstrated' to have been perfectly familiar to Plato. He was, however, the argument would go, simply not concerned to enumerate them in any place as baldly as did his pupil. So Plutarch can here state confidently: 'Having given in this passage a sketch of the ten categories, he makes himself still clearer in what follows,' referring to the continuing passage *Tim.* 37BC, in which the soul is said to produce, when operating on the level of sense-perception, opinions and beliefs which are fine and true, and when operating on the level of pure reason, intelligence and knowledge. These true opinions and beliefs, a Platonist would claim, are naturally expressed in syllogistic form.

In another passage, in the polemical treatise *Against Colotes* (1115 Dff.), Plutarch appears to identify Plato's discussion of not-being as 'otherness' in the *Sophist* (255A–258E, esp. 257B) as providing a stimulus both to Aristotelian and Stoic logic:

> But in Plato's view there is a world of difference between 'is not' and 'is not-being', for by the former is meant the denial of any kind of being, while by the latter is meant the 'otherness' (*heterôtês*) of the entity participated in from that which participates in it, an otherness which later philosophers took simply as being the difference between genus and species, or so-called common and particular qualities, not going any higher than that, as they became involved in problems more purely dialectical.

Aristotle and the Stoics, the argument seems to run, seized on the concepts of 'not-being' and 'otherness' discussed in the *Sophist*, divested them of their metaphysical implications, and founded purely logical systems upon them. We may well wonder whether in fact any metaphysical implications were intended by Plato in this part of the *Sophist*, and if so what they were, but it is plain that Plutarch thought that some were to be found, and that he thought he knew what they were. He seems to understand this passage of the *Sophist* as somehow involving the participation of particulars in Forms, whereas there is no question of this in the text. Any participation (*methexis*) involved is that of one Form in another (e.g. 255B, 259A). It seems rather as if Plutarch is viewing the passage through Xenocratean spectacles, seeing in the discussion of Not-Being and Otherness a description of the interaction of the Indefinite Dyad and the Monad, and the resulting creation of the sensible world.

In projecting Aristotle back into Plato, Plutarch is in agreement with what we find in Albinus' *Didaskalikos* (ch. 6), which itself represents the consensus of one wing, at least, of Middle Platonism. Albinus does not oblige us by making use of the above-quoted passage of the *Timaeus*, but he declares that the ten Categories are to be found in the *Parmenides* 'and in other places' (p. 159, 35 Hermann). He does not elaborate on this statement, unfortunately, since he does not discuss the Categories, but concentrates on syllogistic logic. I would suggest, then, that Plutarch probably did not see any need to adopt Eudorus' Pythagoreanizing 'improvements', his attitude to Aristotle being, like that of Albinus, non-polemical. This tolerance was not, as we shall see, shared by certain later Platonists of the Athenian school, such as Nicostratus and Atticus.

Finally, it is, I think, worth noting the speech of Plutarch's friend Theon in the essay *On the E at Delphi*, as it seems to me to be good evidence of how Stoic logical concepts had been absorbed into the body of Platonic doctrine. There is no reason to make Theon a Stoic except on the basis of this speech, which, I suggest, is poor evidence. It is more natural to assume that he is a Platonist. He is here holding forth on the virtues of the syllable *ei*, if taken as the logical connective 'if' (386–7A):

Certainly in Logic this copulative conjunction has the greatest force, inasmuch as it clearly gives us our most logical form, the syllogism. Must not the character of the hypothetical syllogism be of this sort: granted that even wild animals have apperception of the existence of things, yet to man alone has Nature given the power to observe and judge consequences (*akolouthon*). That 'It is day' and that 'It is light' assuredly wolves and dogs and birds perceive by their senses; but '*If* it is day, then it is light' no creature other than man apprehends, for he alone has a concept of antecedent and consequent, of apparent implication and connexion of these things one with another, and their relations and differences, from which our demonstrations derive their most authoritative inception.

Since, then, philosophy is concerned with truth, and the illumination of truth is demonstration (*apodeixis*), and the inception of demonstration is the hypothetical syllogism (*synêmmenon*), then with good reason the potent element that effects the connexion and produces this was consecrated by wise men to the god who is, above all, a lover of the truth.

Theon is teased mildly after this for being such a lover of logic, and his explanation of the *Ei* is only one of the preliminary ones, but, even if we take him as being a Stoic (he does, admittedly, allude to Heracles, a Stoic hero, and is teased on that account), yet his logical formulations are not rejected as such, so that it is a reasonable inference that Plutarch accepted the logical content of his contribution as non-controversial. If so, we have here evidence of the effective fusing of Aristotelian and Stoic logical concepts. Certainly later Peripatetics had developed the theory of hypothetical syllogisms, but they would not have declared 'If' to be the basic component of syllogistic reasoning. For Aristotle and his successors, hypotheticals were secondary, and reducible to categoricals. That is not the attitude taken here.

E. CONCLUSION

When one considers Plutarch in the context of Middle Platonism in general, it becomes easier to see which aspects of his doctrine are traditional, and which peculiar to himself—or at least outside the main stream of the Platonic tradition. In Ethics, as we have seen, he represents a return from what appears to be Alexandrian Stoicizing to the more 'broadminded' Peripateticizing stance of Antiochus. If, in fact, Antiochus' Academy had some dim survival in Athens over the century intervening between Plutarch and the last-known successor of Antiochus, then Plutarch might represent a survival, in ethics, of this point of view, but there is no evidence for such a continuity. We do not know Ammonius' views on ethics, but he was a man who did not shun dinner parties or public office, so that his views should not have been too ascetic. Ammonius came from Egypt, but then so did Theomnestus, the last recorded head of the 'Academy' before him, so that we can conclude nothing about his ethics from that.

As regards the *telos*, on the other hand, the ideal of Likeness to God is adopted by Plutarch as by everyone else after Eudorus.

In Physics, we see the influence of Pythagoreanism on Plutarch in the use he makes of the Indefinite Dyad, as well as in the number mysticism to which he says he was devoted in his youth. More distinctive is his insistence on the temporal creation of the world, and the pre-existence of a disorderly, 'maléficent' World Soul. In this doctrine, which he argues for well in the *Proc. An.*, he is followed by no one except Atticus, to our knowledge. Whether he owes this to Ammonius or his own devising is not clear, but the way in which he argues for it suggests that he felt he was discovering the true meaning of Plato for himself. His respect for things Persian he could have derived from Ammonius, but this tendency goes back to the Old Academy, specifically to Eudoxus.

As for the question of daemons, Plutarch is plainly less original than many commentators upon him seem to imply. He does, however, seem to have views on evil daemons, which, though attested for Xenocrates and thus Platonically respectable, do not cohere entirely with his other views on the nature of daemons as souls in the process of ascent or descent.

Plutarch's logical interests were minimal, but he does bear witness to the synthesis of Aristotelian and Stoic logic that had been adopted by the Platonic school in his day.

His relation to the contemporary Academy—if there was an Academy—is not clear. He was certainly revered among Athenian Platonists. His nephew Sextus became a Platonic philosopher, and tutor to Marcus Aurelius. A generation after his death, Calvenus Taurus speaks respectfully of 'our own Plutarch' (Aulus Gellius *NA* 1 26), Atticus obviously regarded himself as a follower, and for centuries afterwards it was a proud claim to be a descendant of Plutarch of Chaeroneia. 'In the third century the sophist Nicagoras, the holder of the rhetorical chair at Athens, proclaimed his descent from Plutarch and Sextus; his son Minucianus was also a distinguished sophist, and his grandson, again named Nicagoras, an eccentric Neoplatonist. A lesser philosopher of the same period as the elder Nicagoras rejoiced to be called "sixth in descent from Plutarch".'[1] Yet ultimately Plutarch was not accepted as an orthodox Platonist. His view on the origin of the world became a notorious heresy for the Neoplatonists, all the worse for its resemblance to the doctrine of the Christians, and his more serious philosophical works were allowed to perish, leaving only those which show him rather as a litterateur and antiquarian than as a serious philosopher.

[1] C. P. Jones, *Plutarch and Rome*, p. 11.

CHAPTER FIVE

The Athenian School in the Second Century A.D.

A. INTRODUCTORY

Plutarch stands at the beginning of a period in the history of Platonism about which we have considerably more evidence than about the period which immediately preceded him—though even that is not saying a great deal. Not that Plutarch is to be regarded as being responsible for all this philosophic activity—he had direct influence on only one aspect of it, the 'Athenian School', which was for the duration of the second century dominated by pupils or followers of his—but he does come at what is, for us at least, a beginning, and he is certainly by far the best-known figure in the philosophy of this period, though not necessarily the most substantial philosopher.

In the second century we may discern, for convenience, three main schools or tendencies, which may be termed, with suitable qualifications, the Athenian School, the School of Gaius, and the 'Pythagoreans' and I will deal with them in turn, in consecutive chapters. How far in fact such a three-way division is either comprehensive or real may reasonably be questioned, but it will suffice, I think, as a provisional framework.

When one speaks of a 'school' in this context, one means no more than what is conveyed by the Greek expression 'those about (*hoi peri*) X'. We have many references in later (Neoplatonic) authorities to *hoi peri Gaion*, *hoi peri Noumenion*, and *hoi peri Ploutarchon kai Attikon*, and we take this expression to mean at least 'a school of thought', no doubt the result of instruction in some form by the figures mentioned. We know a certain amount about Plutarch's informal circle in Chaeroneia, and also, as we shall see shortly, about the instruction given by Taurus, who ran a formal school, and we assume that such men as Gaius and Numenius had around them either informal circles or formal schools, in which their doctrines were expounded, although we have no definite evidence. It is certain, at least, that one could study under Albinus, the pupil of Gaius, because Galen did that, as we shall see. We also know of a certain Cronius, who is always referred to as the 'companion' (*hetairos*) of Numenius, never as his pupil, and we do not know quite what to make of that.

Apart from the school philosophers, there are a number of individuals (e.g. Apuleius and Galen) who, while not quite philosophers themselves, constitute good evidence for the school Platonism of the time, and they will be given due consideration in the next chapter. There are also a few figures, such as Theon of Smyrna or Celsus, who cannot readily be attached to any school, and they will have to be fitted in at the end of the survey. A popular Platonism is also being purveyed in this period by the Sophist Maximus of Tyre, and he deserves at least brief notice.

All these Platonists held many beliefs in common, but rather than enter upon a general summary at this stage, I think it preferable to begin with the detailed survey. Too much generalization has taken place in this area already.

B. THE PROBLEM OF THE 'ATHENIAN ACADEMY'

Grave doubts have recently been raised, and reasonably so, as to the very existence of anything that could be termed a Platonic Academy in our period. Certainly, Plutarch speaks of himself as entering 'the Academy' under Ammonius, but none of the figures with whom I propose now to deal, Nicostratus, Taurus and Atticus, is ever described as either head or member of the Platonic Academy. Taurus, about whom we have the fullest information, is described by his pupil Aulus Gellius, rather vaguely, as *vir memoria nostra in disciplina Platonica celebratus* (*NA* VII 10); his school is termed by the same source a *diatriba*, which is the usual term for a philosophical school, but nowhere is he called a Platonic Successor (*diadochos*) or his school an Academy. That does not, indeed, prove that he did not call his school the Platonic Academy, but even if he did, there remains the problem, ever since Antiochus of Ascalon, as to what exactly that meant. The old Academy seems to have remained deserted, and no direct inheritance of real property or books from it can be assumed. On the other hand, Taurus does seem to have been the acknowledged head of Athenian Platonism in the period around A.D. 150, as was

Atticus somewhat later, so that an assumption is created that some form of Platonic school was recognized of which one could become the head. Whether this went back beyond Ammonius all the way to Antiochus and his brother Aristus is quite uncertain. On the whole, I prefer to speak simply of an Athenian School, as the term 'Academy' summons up associations which I believe to be illegitimate.

In A.D. 176 (Dio Cassius LXXII, 31), the Emperor Marcus Aurelius established at Athens four Chairs of Philosophy, in Platonism, Aristotelianism, Stoicism and Epicureanism, endowing each with an annual salary of 10,000 drachmae. Herodes Atticus was given the task of appointing the first incumbents (Philostratus *VS* 566); after that they were appointed by 'the vote of the best citizens' (Lucian, *Eunuchus* 2), a vague phrase, perhaps denoting a special committee, perhaps the Areopagus. Lucian, in the sketch just mentioned, gives a most amusing account of the election to the Chair of Peripatetic Philosophy in about A.D. 179.[1] After 176, then, we may assume that the leading Platonist in Athens is holder of the Chair of Platonic Philosophy. We may now pass to the consideration of individual figures in Athenian Platonism.

C. NICOSTRATUS

On an honorary decree in Delphi (Ditt. *Syll.* II³, no. 868) on the same stone as, but to be dated some years earlier than, a similar decree in honour of Taurus (to which we shall come presently), we find the name of Claudius Nicostratus, Platonic philosopher. He is listed third in a group of four Platonists being granted similar honours by the Delphians. The others, Bacchius of Paphos, Zosimus, and M. Sextius Cornelianus, are unknown, except that Bacchius is described as the adopted son of one Gaius, who may conceivably be the philosopher.[2] Karl Praechter, in an article in *Hermes* (vol. 57 (1922), pp. 481–517), has identified this Claudius Nicostratus convincingly with the Nicostratus who is repeatedly quoted by Simplicius in his *Commentary on*

---

[1] Unfortunately Lucian complicates the issue (sect. 3) by talking of *two* Chairs of Peripatetic Philosophy, one of which had fallen vacant. Nowhere else is there a suggestion that there were two Chairs, either for Peripateticism alone or for each of the sects, so that Lucian's testimony is mysterious.

[2] This Bacchius, as Praechter argues, may well be the same as the tutor of Marcus Aurelius, mentioned by him in *Meditations* I 6, 6. If so, this provides Marcus with a second Platonist teacher, in addition to Sextus of Chaeroneia, and would explain, perhaps, why Bacchius actually heads this list of philosophers.

the Categories as a hostile and tendentious critic of Aristotle's *Categories*, following in the tradition started, as far as we can see, by Eudorus.

The question arises as to where in the Platonic tradition this Nicostratus can be fitted in. Now that we have him on a stone, being honoured in the same way that Taurus is honoured some years later, it is not unreasonable to conjecture that he was in more or less the same position as Taurus was later. Since yet another, earlier, honorary inscription on the same stone honours the philosopher, Gaius, son of Xenon—perhaps the Gaius who is otherwise known to us—we may see in all this a tendency on the part of the Delphians (perhaps as a result of the influence of Plutarch) to honour prominent Platonists. Now I do not wish to claim that Nicostratus was anything like the 'head of the Academy' before Taurus; I have already expressed my doubts as to the very existence of that institution; but since his attitude to Aristotle squares very well with the attitude taken up later by Taurus, and, more violently, by Atticus, and since he occurs in a context which places him somewhat before Taurus in time, it seems suitable to deal with him now.

In truth, any study of Nicostratus must remain rather one-dimensional. All we know of him is his eristic attack on the *Categories*, in which he appears to be merely building on the work of a certain Lucius. Most of his criticisms are absurd, and unworthy of serious consideration, but since he exemplifies a certain persistent attitude to Aristotelian logic, and the influence of Aristotle in general, among certain Platonists, and since his work formed the basis for the tendentious part of Plotinus' later criticism of the *Categories* in *Enn.* VI 1–3, it is worth pausing over.

We have observed already the tendency in Eudorus and Philo to attack Aristotle, or at least contemporary Peripatetics, on certain points of doctrine, and we have seen in Antiochus, and again in Plutarch, a tendency to synthesize, and play down the differences between, Plato and Aristotle. We shall see both these tendencies at work in the second century.

Simplicius (*In Cat.* 1, 19ff.) gives the following account of Nicostratus' work:

Others have chosen simply to present a series of problems arising from the text, which is what has been done by Lucius and after him by Nicostratus, who took over for himself the work of Lucius. They set themselves to produce objections to pretty nearly everything that is said in the book, and this not even with discrimination, but with shameless tendentiousness. We may be grateful to them, however, for this at least, that most of the problems they raised have some substance, thus providing those coming after them with stimuli to the solution of problems and for many worthwhile discussions in general.

To this work are to be attributed, I feel, not simply the *aporiai* credited explicitly by Simplicius to Lucius and/or Nicostratus, but all the anonymous objections as well, which altogether make a very large collection. I will simply select a few passages which go to show both Nicostratus' Platonism and his tendency to use Stoic formulations to confute Aristotle. The reasonableness or otherwise of his arguments I will leave out of consideration.

In his criticism of Aristotle's definition of a homonym, for example, right at the beginning of the *Categories*, he uses terminology developed later by the Stoics in order to make Aristotle appear confused or inexact (Simpl. p. 26, 22ff.). A 'name' (*onoma*), he says, must be significatory (*sêmantikon*) of some definite thing. A homonym is necessarily indefinite in its signification, as it refers to a plurality of things of which the definitions differ. Therefore a homonym cannot be a 'name' at all. He also attacks Aristotle's use of 'common' (*koinos*), using a fourfold distinction of the meanings of the word which sounds distinctly Stoic in origin.

Again, in commenting on *Cat.* 13a37, where Aristotle, in discussing types of contrary, makes the assertion that only those utterances of which there is the possibility of assertion or denial must be either true or false, Nicostratus objects that being true or false is not an attribute of all such utterances, and he adduces such things as questions, oaths and exclamations, as being neither true nor false. That this objection is based on an application of Stoic doctrine is made clear by the account given in Diogenes Laertius VII 65ff. (= *SVF* II 186), where the same list of non-propositional sentences is given.

Nicostratus may, of course, be using Stoic logical terms simply to refute Aristotle, without any serious philosophical commitment on his part. In the last sentence of the passage here referred to, he adds 'statements about the future' to his list, thus parting company with the Stoics, who regarded statements about the future as being necessarily either true or false (*SVF* II 198). We may reasonably suppose a favourable attitude on his part to Stoic logic, which would not, however, prevent him from attacking them on other points. The denial of the truth-value of future statements, for instance, looks like an attack on

Stoic determinism, and at *In Cat.* 388, 4ff. he is found criticizing the Stoics for adopting the Aristotelian definition of an Opposite.

Nicostratus, unlike Eudorus, seems to have accepted Aristotle's order of the categories. At *In Cat.* 156, 16ff., at any rate, he is found criticizing Aristotle for dealing with Relation before Quality, but in the process he accepts the order given by Aristotle in ch. 4. He does, however, also make use here of the Old Academic division of categories into Absolutes and Relatives, taking Substance, Quantity and Quality as Absolutes, in contrast to Relation and the 'relative' categories which follow it (*ibid.*).

We may get a dim suggestion of Nicostratus' position in ethics from a passage (*In Cat.* 402, 12ff.) in which he is disputing Aristotle's statement at *Cat.* 13a20 that contraries can change into each other. Nicostratus objects that the Good Man (*ho spoudaios*) cannot become bad (*phaulos*). This was a doctrine shared by certain philosophers outside the Stoic school proper, but the use of the traditional Stoic terms here seems to suggest—what is on all other counts extremely probable— that Nicostratus' ethical theory was Stoic rather than Peripatetic. He will thus be siding with Eudorus before him and Atticus after him against Antiochus, Plutarch and Taurus.

That he believed in transcendent Forms (which, as a Platonist, one would expect him to do) is confirmed by such passages as *In Cat.* 73, 15ff., where he is enquiring whether Aristotle's categories are to be taken as referring to the physical or to the intelligible world or to both, establishing thus a firm Platonic distinction between the two worlds, and *ibid.* 429, 13ff., where he is criticizing Aristotle for using the example of a square as something which can be increased without being altered (*Cat.* 15a30). If Aristotle means a material square, says Nicostratus, he is correct, but if he is talking about the immaterial Form of square, then he is quite mistaken.

Nicostratus, then, is of importance as being the major figure among the critics of Aristotle's *Categories*, a sport which had begun with Eudorus, and was to continue, through Atticus, to Plotinus. Only with Plotinus' pupil Porphyry was the quarrel healed, and Aristotelian logic definitively accepted as a proper introduction to the higher realms of (Platonic) philosophy.

D. CALVENUS TAURUS

I. LIFE AND WORKS

Calvenus Taurus was a native of Berytus (Beirut).[1] His *floruit*, which normally denotes one's arrival at the age of forty, but sometimes a definite high point in one's career, is placed by Eusebius (*Chron.*, Year of Abraham 2161) in A.D. 145. This would normally imply a birth-date of A.D. 105. That, however, produces a small difficulty. A passage in Aulus Gellius (*NA* 1 26) presents Taurus as telling an anecdote about Plutarch, in the course of which he refers to him as 'Plutarchus noster', an expression which in the context seems to imply personal acquaintance. Now even for the young Taurus to have been acquainted with the elderly Plutarch we would have to push Taurus' birth-date back to at least A.D. 100, even if we extend Plutarch's life-span to A.D. 125. Taurus certainly speaks and acts like a patriarch in Gellius' pages. When Gellius was studying with him, in the late 140s, he was in his twenties, and Taurus addresses him condescendingly on one occasion as '*rhetoriske!*' (i.e. approximately 'my young rhetorician!') (*NA* XVII 20). The impression conveyed is certainly of man in his fifties. At some stage in his career, after 145, Taurus was honoured by the Delphians in the same way as Nicostratus had been before him. To assume this was during his visit to the Games reported by Aulus Gellius is rash. Taurus probably never missed a Games, and if some special honour had come his way on that occasion, Gellius would hardly have failed to mention it. We simply do not know when Taurus received this honour, but it was probably in the 150s.

How long Taurus was the head of his school we also do not know, but since he is reported as being the teacher of Herodes Atticus (*c.* A.D. 101–177), it is plain that he had been teaching for some years by the time Gellius arrived. Eusebius' date of A.D. 145, if it is not Taurus'

---

[1] There has been some confusion as to the correct form of his name. In the mss. of Aulus Gellius his gentile name is given (once, at *NA* XVIII 10) as Calvisius. However, on the honorary inscription at Delphi previously mentioned the name is given as Calvenus. This latter was not a name borne by any distinguished Roman, but it was a respectable Italian provincial name, and since Berytus had been a Roman colony for a considerable time before Taurus' birth, it is very possible that some Italian merchant or veteran of that *gentilicium* had settled there. Unfortunately, there is as yet no inscriptional evidence of this.
On Taurus, see now the essay of H. Dörrie, 'L. Kalbenos Tauros', *Kairos* 1–2 (1973) pp. 24–35.

fortieth year, might be taken as the date of his accession to the head-ship of whatever it was he headed, perhaps something termed 'the Academy', and perhaps the same institution of which Ammonius had earlier been the head. He probably did not last much longer than A.D. 165. By 176–80, it would seem, Atticus was the leading Platonist in Athens, in what capacity must be discussed later.

Thanks to Aulus Gellius' reminiscences, we have a reasonably full picture of the workings of Taurus' school. There were obviously formal sessions, at which the works of Plato were read and studied, and even, it seems, works of Aristotle, though only, perhaps, the more strictly 'scientific' works, such as the *Problems* (*NA* xix 6). At *NA* xvii 20 we find the *Symposium* being read in class. On this occasion Taurus is reported as calling for a properly philosophical approach to Plato:

> One must penetrate to the utmost depths of Plato's mind and feel the weight and dignity of his subject matter, and not be diverted to the charm of his diction or the grace of his expression.

One might alternatively, it seems, take a set problem in philosophy and discuss that, adducing various authorities.

After the formal discourse, Taurus encouraged his pupils to raise questions. We see the process described at *NA* i 26:

> I once asked Taurus in the *diatriba* whether a wise man got angry. For after his daily lectures he often gave everyone the opportunity of asking whatever questions one wished. On this occasion he first discussed the disease or passion of anger seriously and at length, setting forth what is to be found in the books of the ancients and in his own commentaries.

The great man, then, quoted on occasion from his own works on various subjects. On this occasion, besides telling an anecdote about Plutarch, he makes reference to Plutarch's *On Freedom from Anger*, and the 'ancients' referred to by Gellius would perhaps be those whom Plutarch was relying on in that work, such as the Peripatetic Hierony-mus of Rhodes. But more detailed speculation would be pointless.

Taurus was in the habit of inviting certain favoured pupils to his home for dinner, and, as Gellius tells us (*NA* vii 13), one was expected on these occasions to bring (in lieu of a bottle) topics for discussion, which were raised after dinner. We have a number of examples, and they closely resemble those presented by Plutarch in his *Symposiaca*. The problem raised in vii 13, for instance, 'At what moment can a dying man be said to die?' leads Taurus into an exposition of the notion of 'instant', based on Plato's *Parmenides*, 156D. At XVII 8 the question arises as to why oil congeals, the problem being raised on this occasion by the prank of a slave boy.

Besides dinner parties, there were expeditions to the country. At XVIII 10 some of the school accompany Taurus to visit Herodes Atticus' villa at Cephisia, where Gellius is lying ill, afflicted with a bout of diarrhoea. At XII 5 occurs the account of the journey to attend the Pythian Games at Delphi, on which Taurus is accompanied, again, by a group of pupils. We also find him, in II 2, receiving distinguished visitors, namely the Governor of Crete, who had come to Athens expressly to visit the philosopher, accompanied by his father. Here Gellius portrays Taurus as sitting outside the door of his *cubiculum* (which sounds like a small room) after class. When the governor and his father arrived, there was only one spare chair (on which circumstance the anecdote turns). All this seems to denote a very simple establishment. We may also observe here the satisfactory relationship between the ranking Platonic philosopher in Athens and the Roman regime.

These glimpses of academic life are most welcome. What they reveal is, not a full-scale Academy, but rather a one-man show. There is no suggestion of any other professor besides Taurus himself, or of any property besides his (modest) personal possessions. If we talk about the Athenian Academy at this period, then, we must bear in mind that it may be no more than what we see described here.

But Taurus was not just the convivial, avuncular college tutor that we find in the pages of Gellius. We have evidence of some works from his pen. Gellius mentions his *commentaria* on the subject of Anger (1 26), and a book against the Stoics (XII 5) in which he set out both their differences from the Academy and their internal contradictions, on the latter question at least borrowing, no doubt, from Plutarch's work on the subject. We know from the *Suda* (s.v.) that he also wrote a work on the differences between Aristotle and Plato, thus defending the Academy against syncretistic tendencies in that direction. In this he is in accord with his contemporary Nicostratus and his successor Atticus, indicating a consistent attitude on the part of Platonists at Athens. Of course, this polemic must not be taken to imply that Athenian Platonism was free of either Aristotelian or Stoic terminology; it simply means that, for motives of self-assertion, the Athenian School was concerned, on certain key questions of dogma, to flay the opposition, where a man like Albinus, for instance, did not feel so compelled.

The issue of doctrinal purity *versus* eclecticism is in constant danger of being overplayed, as we shall see.

The *Suda* also reports a work *On Corporeals and Incorporeals*, which might concern logic, but more probably concerns metaphysics. Besides such works, we have evidence of commentaries by Taurus on Plato. Gellius refers at VII 14 to the first book of a *Commentary on the Gorgias*, which implies a number of books. Similarly, John Philoponus (*De Aet. Mundi* p. 520, 4 Rabe) refers to the first book of Taurus' *Commentaries on the Timaeus*, again implying a multi-volume work. Iamblichus, in his *De Anima* (*ap.* Stob. I 378, 25ff. Wachs.), refers to his views on the descent of souls into bodies, perhaps referring to his *Timaeus* Commentary, perhaps to some work on the Soul. There is enough evidence here to demonstrate serious scholastic activity, if not, perhaps, great brilliance or originality.

2. PHILOSOPHY

(a) *Ethics*

The same passage in Aulus Gellius (XII 5) which reports the journey to Delphi also gives us the basic position which Taurus took in ethics. The occasion for the discourse is a visit, on the way to Delphi, to a Stoic philosopher who is ill and suffering considerable pain, which, however, he is resisting manfully. Even if we feel that the ostensible occasion for this discourse is somewhat too convenient to be credible, that does not invalidate the genuineness of the attribution to Taurus.

What we find is most interesting, but not unsuitable to a follower of Plutarch. Taurus says (sect. 5):

You know that I am no great friend of the Stoics, or rather of the Stoa; for it is often inconsistent with itself and with us, as is shown in the book which I have written on that subject.

Taurus then complains of the Stoic love of obscurantist jargon—a favourite Platonist gibe, which we have seen indulged in long before by Antiochus. The basic principles of Taurus' ethics, also, are so reminiscent of those of Antiochus that one might almost suspect Gellius of borrowing from Cicero *De Finibus* v (cf. above, p. 70):

Nature, who produced us, implanted in us and incorporated in the very elements from which we sprang a love and affection for ourselves, to such a degree that nothing is dearer or of more importance to us than ourselves. And this, she thought, would be the underlying principle for assuring the perpetuation of the human race, if each one of us, as soon as he saw the light, should have a knowledge and understanding first of all of those things which the philosophers of old have called 'the first things according to Nature' (*ta prôta kata physin*); that is, that he might delight in all that was agreeable to his body and shrink from everything disagreeable.(7)

The doctrine of *ta prôta kata physin* is, naturally, not credited to the Stoics, but rather to what was also Antiochus' favourite class of philosopher, the *veteres*, the 'Ancients'. Next, Taurus outlines the growth of reason 'from its seeds (*semina*)', and its attendant virtues. He adopts the Stoic principle that nothing is good unless it is virtuous, and nothing evil unless it is vicious. He even adopts the Stoic doctrine of 'indifferents', though he emphasizes the distinction between 'things preferred' (*proêgmena*) and 'things rejected' (*apoproêgmena*). Where he makes his stand is, like Antiochus, on the issue of whether these lower, primal impulses can be eradicated, as opposed to being simply controlled. The ideal of eradication of passions (*apatheia*) Taurus feels to be absurd, and actually to be rejected even if it were possible, and he calls even Panaetius to witness on his behalf (10).

It is not, of course, necessary to postulate any direct influence of Antiochus upon Taurus here—Plutarch, after all, takes this same line in the *Virt. Mor.*—but it is interesting to find the ethical doctrines of the Academy so clearly formulated here in Antiochian terms. An application of this doctrine occurs at *NA* 1 26, where Gellius has raised, after class, the question 'Will the Wise Man get angry?' After telling an anecdote about Plutarch to illustrate Plutarch's view, Taurus gives his own view, which is entirely in accord with that of Plutarch. Gellius summarizes it as follows:

Now the sum and substance of Taurus' whole disquisition was this: he did not believe that *aorgêsia* (freedom from anger) and *analgêsia* (lack of feeling) were identical, but that a mind not prone to anger was one thing, a spirit *analgêtos* and *anaisthêtos*, that is callous and unfeeling, another. For as of all the rest of the emotions which the Latin philosophers call *affectus* or *affectiones*, and the Greeks *pathê*, so of the one which, when it becomes a cruel desire for vengeance, is called 'anger', he did not recommend as expedient a total lack, *sterêsis*, as the Greeks say, but a moderate amount, which they call *metriotês*.

On the question of the passions, then, as on the question of the three grades of good, Taurus is in agreement with Plutarch. He chooses the Aristotelian 'mean' over Stoic absolutism.[1]

For a Platonist, it is always open season for Epicureans, and, like Plutarch, and indeed like any Middle Platonist, Taurus is always ready to attack them. Gellius records him (*NA* IX 5) as being fond of quoting a saying of the Stoic Hierocles against the Epicurean doctrine of Pleasure as the *telos*: 'Pleasure the *telos*: a harlot's creed!'

(b) Physics

Of Taurus' views in this area of philosophy we have only fragmentary information, but what we have is important. Taurus did not accept the doctrine of Plutarch (taken up again by Atticus) that Plato taught the temporal creation of the world. He returned to the more usual Platonist view, laid down by Speusippus and Xenocrates, that Plato in the *Timaeus* describes an apparent temporal creation only for the sake of 'clarity of instruction', prefixing, however, the view that this contributed to piety (*eusebeia*), since otherwise men would imagine that the soul, being uncreated, was coeval and co-ordinate with God (Philop. *Aet. M.* VI 21, p. 187, 2ff.). This additional explanation is important, as being adopted, together with the normal one, by Calcidius in his *Commentary on the Timaeus* (ch. 26). For Taurus the problem centres on how we are to understand the word *gegonen* ('it is created') at *Tim.* 28B. We have an extended quotation from his discussion of the passage in his *Commentary on the Timaeus*, preserved to us by the sixth-century Christian philosopher John Philoponus, in his polemical work *On the Eternity of the World* (p. 145, 13ff, Rabe). Taurus' special contribution is the distinguishing of four meanings of the word *genêtos* (normally translated 'created', but here rather 'subject to coming into being'). After a short doxography, which takes in Aristotle and Theophrastus, Taurus continues:

Certain others have held that the cosmos according to Plato is created, and others again that it is uncreated. But since those who claim that it is created base themselves principally on the text 'It was created; for it is visible and tangible. . . .' (*Tim.* 28B), it is necessary to distinguish how many senses of 'created' there are; for thus we will discover that Plato does not use the word 'created' in the sense in which we say that things which derive their existence from some beginning in time are 'created'; for this is what has led the majority

---

[1] Gellius also preserves (*NA* XIX 12) a discourse of Taurus' pupil Herodes Atticus against Stoic *apatheia*.

of interpreters astray, when they hear this word 'created', into assuming that this is the meaning.

'Created', then, can have the following meanings: (1) *That is said to be 'created' which is not in fact created, but is of the same genus as things that are created.* Thus we describe something as 'visible' which has never in fact been seen, nor is now being seen, nor will ever be seen, but which is of the same genus as things that are visible, as if for instance there were a body at the centre of the earth.

(2) *That is also called 'created' which is in theory composite, even if it is has not in fact been combined.*[1] Thus the *mesê* [in music] is a 'combination' of the *nêtê* and the *hypatê*; for even if it has not been combined from these two, its value is seen to be an equal proportion between the one and the other; and the same thing goes for flowers and animals. In the cosmos, then, there is seen to be combination and mixture, so that we can by [mentally] subtracting and separating off from it the various qualities analyse it into its primary substratum.

(3) *The cosmos is said to be 'created' as being always in process of generation,* even as Proteus is always in the process of changing into different shapes. And in the case of the cosmos, the earth and everything up to the Moon is continuously changing from one form into another, whereas those things above the Moon, while remaining more or less the same, with very little change as regards their substance, yet change their relative positions, even as a dancer, while remaining the same in substance, changes into many positions by means of gesticulations. Even so the heavenly bodies change, and different configurations of them come about as a result of the movements of the planets in respect of the fixed stars and of the fixed stars in respect of the planets.

(4) *One might also call it 'created' by virtue of the fact that it is dependent for its existence on an outside source,* to wit, God, by whom it has been brought into order. Thus even according to those for whom the cosmos is eternal, the Moon possesses 'created' light from the Sun, although there was never a time when she was not illuminated by him.

My apology for quoting this text at such length is simply that it constitutes excellent evidence for Middle Platonic scholasticism, and further that it is by no means easy of access to the non-specialist reader. Taurus here sets out a solution to the embarrassing problem of Plato's real meaning in the *Timaeus* by means of a comprehensive list of

---

[1] This is reminiscent of the Neopythagorean attribution to Pythagoras of the doctrine that the world is 'theoretically (*kat' epinoian*) created' (Stob. 1 186, 14 Wachs. = Diels *Dox.* pp. 330, 15ff.).

alternative definitions, which in fact merely codify various suggestions that had already been made. We find meanings (3) and (4) adopted by Albinus (*Did.* ch. 14), meaning (4) by Calcidius (*In Tim.* ch. 23) and meaning (1) by Apuleius (*De Plat.* 1 8), none of whom would necessarily be dependent on Taurus for their definitions. Taurus himself seems to favour particularly the last definition, if one may judge both from its position on the list and from the modest way in which it is introduced. He thus returns, in effect, to the formulation also expressed by Philo at *Opif.* 7–9 (above p. 157).

It is, perhaps, strange that Taurus, such an admirer of Plutarch on ethical questions, should have turned against him on this point. We may conclude, I think, that he was not attracted by Plutarch's dualism in general. Certainly no impression of even vaguely dualistic tendencies reaches us from Gellius' reports of him, or from any other source.

From the fragments of the *Timaeus Commentary* we also derive the information that he rejected the Aristotelian fifth element, the aether, which had been accepted (though not quite consistently) by Plutarch. This rejection, which represents a hardening of attitude towards Aristotelianism, comes in the course of an effort to connect the five senses with the four elements, arising out of a combination of the exegesis of *Tim.* 31B with *Tim.* 65C–68D, where the senses are described together with their subject-matters (*ap.* Philop. p. 520, 4ff.). For those who accepted five elements, such as the Pythagoreans and Platonists represented in Stob. 1 476, 17ff. Wachs. (Diels, *Doxogr.* p. 397) and in Plutarch *De E* 390B, there was no problem; sight was matched with the aether, hearing with air, smell with fire, taste with water and touch with earth. Aristotle himself, introducing this notion in *De Sensu* 428b19ff., in fact says nothing about aether, making the essence of the eye watery, and linking taste and touch together as to do with earth, but Taurus seems to imply that Theophrastus made sight aetherial, and it seems that some Platonists accepted this. Taurus himself connects sight with fire and touch with earth, following the text of the *Timaeus*; then taste with water and hearing with air. He is thus left with smell unaccounted for. Instead of linking it with any other sense, he proposes for it a quasi-element on the borderline of air and water (derived in fact from the 'mist or smoke' of *Timaeus* 66DE), which he terms 'vapour' (*atmis*). This he sees as a 'mean' between air and water, even as air and water are 'means' between fire and earth.

The only justification for imposing these details upon the reader is, as I have said, the possibility of thereby setting up some connexions between the various individuals and schools. In this case a connexion presents itself in the person of the physician Galen, who in a number of places in his works adopts the same scheme of equivalents. Now Galen (b. A.D. 129) is approximately a generation younger than Taurus, and could thus perfectly well have read Taurus' commentary on the *Timaeus*, but in fact Galen avows himself to be a pupil rather of Albinus, and to have learnt his Platonism in Asia Minor, and this, combined with Galen's known use on other occasions of the Stoic Posidonius, creates the possibility of Posidonius' *Commentary on the Timaeus* being the ultimate source here for both Taurus and Galen. Whatever its significance, however, such a connexion as this must be noted.

As regards Taurus' theory of the Soul, we have one interesting report preserved by Iamblichus in his *De Anima* (*ap.* Stob. 1 378, 25 ff. Wachs.) which appears on the face of it to concern not Taurus himself, but rather two conflicting schools of thought among his followers. This concerns the reasons for the descent of souls into bodies. It is possible, however, that Iamblichus is simply recording two different views of Taurus himself, whom he may well not have consulted at first hand, and making somewhat eccentric use of the common periphrasis 'those about X':

The Platonists 'about' Taurus say that souls are sent by the Gods to earth, *either*, following the *Timaeus*, for the completion of the universe, in order that there may be as many living things in the cosmos as there are in the intelligible realm; *or* declaring that the purpose of the descent is to present a manifestation of the divine life. For this is the will of the gods, for the gods to reveal themselves (*ekphainesthai*) through souls; for the gods come out into the open and manifest themselves through the pure and unsullied life of souls.

I have substituted 'either—or' for Iamblichus' 'some—others', thus slanting the translation in favour of my interpretation of what we have here. Those who prefer to postulate two rival schools of Taurians may reverse the substitution. The first of these alternative explanations (which are not, however, mutually exclusive) is based on the passage of the *Timaeus* (41B) where the Demiurge is addressing the young gods on the subject of the creation of man and the lower animals: 'Three kinds of mortal beings are yet uncreated. And if these be not created, the world will be imperfect; for it will not have within it all kinds of living things; yet these it must have, if it is to be perfect.'

Possibly this explanation of Taurus' is taken from his exegesis of this passage in his commentary, but perhaps, again, from a special treatise on the Soul.

The second explanation is far more remarkable. The notion that the soul of the sage is an image of God, or that the souls of those who have lived nobly can become divine, is old and widespread by this time, and can be documented readily from Philo and Plutarch, among Taurus' more immediate predecessors, but the idea that souls are sent down 'for the honour and glory of God', so to speak (all souls or only certain ones?) is, as far as I am aware, previously unattested.[1] The use of the verb *ekphainein* for 'reveal' brings us into the realm of religion rather than philosophy. The verb, and its noun *ekphansis*, are very popular in Neoplatonism from Iamblichus on as terms for divine epiphanies.

At least we can deduce from this that Taurus did not have a dualistic or Gnostic distaste for the world or for the soul's incorporation in it, as did certain other Platonists of his time, such as Numenius. The world is good, for Taurus, and we are put into it for a noble purpose. It is for us to fulfil that purpose by striving to live 'according to the likeness of God'.

(c) *Logic*

Nothing can be said of Taurus' activities, if any, in the field of Logic, except that we see him taking an interest in the logical problem of instantaneity, basing himself on *Parmenides* 156D (Gellius *NA* VII 13). We find him also (*ibid.* XIX 6) criticizing Aristotle, *à propos* the reading of one of the *Problems* (which Taurus naturally attributed to Aristotle himself) for telling us the 'what' of a certain problem, but not the 'why', a complaint which shows at least a desire to put Aristotle in his place. There is no sign of his having taken part in the game of criticizing the *Categories*, however.

(d) *Exegetical method*

A word or two may be said on Taurus' method of commentary, as it is of some importance for the study of the development of the commentary form in this period. From the fragments of the *Timaeus Commentary* preserved by Philoponus we get the impression of a fairly detailed exegesis of consecutive sections of the text, involving

---

[1] Unless we may conclude that Albinus' brief phrase 'by the will of the Gods', in *Did.* ch. 25 (see below, p. 293) is a version of this theory.

elucidation of Plato's meaning (including some textual criticism and emendation), and then general discussion of the philosophical subject matter, preceded, when suitable, by a doxography of previous opinions. From his discussion of the lemma, *Tim.* 27C, it looks as if he took first a longish passage for the general discussion of the content, and then broke it up into phrases—the same division into *theória* and *lexis* that we find in the later Neoplatonist commentators. I will have more to say on the possible form of the Middle Platonic commentary in connexion with the Anonymous Theaetetus-Commentator in the next chapter.

Both of Taurus' recorded commentaries, as we have seen, were multi-volume works, though since he is still in Book I at *Timaeus* 31B (*ap.* Philop. p. 523, 4), his work cannot have been by any means as vast as that of Proclus, say, who begins his third Book with this lemma. The report of Taurus' *Commentary on the Gorgias* which we have from Gellius (*NA* VII 14) poses something of a problem. Gellius tells us that Taurus 'in the first book of his commentaries on the *Gorgias*' discussed the question of the reasons for punishment. Now the text which properly gives occasion for such discussion is 525B, almost at the end of the dialogue, in the course of the final myth. Taurus, in common with other theorists, discerns three reasons for punishment, reformation, the preservation of honour, and deterrence, as against Plato's two, reformation and deterrence. But it is not entirely clear from Gellius' account whether Taurus himself was discussing this text of Plato, or whether Gellius is introducing it against him. In any case, I would suggest that Taurus must be raising this question in some prefatory part of the *Commentary*. He cannot have been still in Book I in the final myth. The other possibility is that he introduced this discussion at 477Eff., another passage where a discussion of the purposes of punishment would be relevant, and which could reasonably still form part of a first book. The elaboration of the various reasons for punishment is a scholastic development analogous to the distinction of the various meanings of *genêtos* in the *Timaeus Commentary*.

E. ATTICUS

I. LIFE AND WORKS

As to whether the philosopher Atticus can be regarded as the successor of Taurus in the 'Athenian Academy', and indeed as to whether there was such an institution at all, I have expressed my doubts already. He was at any rate, as far as we can see, the next leader of Platonism at Athens after Taurus, and he certainly speaks in his surviving writings as 'Defender of the Faith'. We have for Atticus no faithful Gellius, as we had for Taurus, to relay to us pleasing anecdotes, so we are far less well informed about the details of his life and works. Eusebius in his Chronicle (*Ol.* 238) gives his *floruit* as A.D. 176–80, describing him not as 'Platonic successor' or 'head of the Academy', but simply as 'philosopher of the Platonic sect'.

'Atticus' is a rather curious name to be borne by an Athenian, if indeed, Atticus was an Athenian. It is possible that he was connected with the great house of Herodes Atticus, although the lack of any mention of this in our sources is an argument against any such connexion. The *Suda*, which is normally a source for basic biographical information ignores Atticus, while having entries for such contemporaries of his as Taurus, Numenius, Harpocration, Aristocles, and Alexander of Aphrodisias. Atticus must have known Taurus, and might be expected to have studied under him, though he attacks him, as we shall see, on various points of doctrine.

As regards his official position, the fact that his *floruit*, as given by Eusebius, coincides with the date (A.D. 176) at which Marcus Aurelius established the chairs of philosophy at Athens, creates the possibility that Atticus was in fact the first incumbent of the Chair of Platonic Philosophy—appointed to that position by Herodes Atticus (who, as I have suggested, may possibly have been a relative). If in fact he was the holder of the Chair, it would help to explain his fierce attack on the Peripatetics, as will be argued below.

Our view of Atticus' philosophical position is somewhat distorted by the fact that what we have preserved from him (by Eusebius, in Books 11 and 15 of his *Praeparatio Evangelica*) is a polemical tract against the Peripatetics, asserting the profoundest possible difference between the doctrines of Plato and Aristotle, and going through, in a most rhetorical manner, the various respects in which Aristotle is inferior. A good deal about Atticus' own views can be derived from this document, but we must consider also the circumstances in which it may have been issued, since to take it without qualification as an exposition of doctrine, as has been done by most scholars, would be grossly misleading.

The work belongs clearly to the genre of interschool polemic, such as flourished throughout our period. Apart from the straight discussion of philosophical problems, and the exegesis of the works of the founder of the School, the members of the various sects indulged from time to time in polemic against each other. The level at which these arguments are carried on is not in general edifying. We have several good examples in the dialogues of Cicero, for instance, all marked by a high degree of rhetorical unreasonableness. Antiochus attacks the Stoics and the New Academy; the New Academy attacks Antiochus and the Stoics; the Stoics attack Antiochus; everybody attacks the Epicureans and they attack everybody. Somewhat later, I venture to discern traces of a polemic conducted by Eudorus against the Peripatetics, directed primarily, I suspect, against his own contemporary Ariston. A hundred years later we find Plutarch attacking both Stoics and Epicureans with total lack of objectivity, and in this he is followed by Taurus. Plutarch, as has been noted, does not attack the Peripatetics, though Taurus wrote an essay on their differences with the Platonists which was probably polemical in tone.

And now we find Atticus launching a full-scale assault on the Peripatetics. What, one asks, is the reason for all this activity? To some extent the answer is obvious: they disagreed with each other philosophically. But one wonders still, why the great heat of polemic? The unfairness and superficiality of many of the criticisms made can be explained by the rhetorical and eristic traditions of the ancient schools, which did not take much account of fairness to one's opponent, but simply strove to state one's own case as powerfully as possible. The whole attack on Aristotle's *Categories*, although it gives rise incidentally to some good points, is animated primarily by the eristic spirit.

However, a particular attack, like this of Atticus against Aristotle, must, I think, be provoked by some definite occasion. Now the worst fate which could befall the leader of a philosophical school is to see his system of philosophy taken over or rendered obsolete by another. That is at the root of the dislike of the New Academy and of the Stoics for Antiochus, and the mutual antipathy of Eudorus and Ariston. Where the threat is less immediate, as in the case of Plutarch vis-à-vis the Stoics or Epicureans, the criticism, though trenchant, is more good-humoured. The pattern which I would discern here is the presence or absence of a specific threat to one's own school. If there exists a rival whose teachings can draw away pupils by appearing to teach the same doctrine, or worse, a more modern version of the same doctrine, then steps must be taken to assert the distinctness and the validity of one's

own doctrine. One is most likely, I suggest, to do this either in consequence of the publication of a provocative work by a rival, or simply
on attaining the headship of one's own school. I would take the
treatise of the Peripatetic Alexander of Aphrodisias *On Fate*, addressed
in or about A.D. 198 to the Emperors Septimius Severus and Caracalla,
on the occasion of his appointment to the Chair of Peripatetic Philosophy at Athens, with its polemical attack on the Stoic doctrine of
Fate, as a document of this class. It is an assertion of the right of
Aristotelianism to exist and to serve the state; the Stoics are branded as
subversives and immoralists. There is some attempt at philosophical
argument, but the general tone is 'popular' and rhetorical.

Atticus' attack on the Peripatetics is an example of the same genre.
Either he put it out on being appointed to the Chair of Platonic
Philosophy (if he *was* so appointed), or it is a response to a provocative
work by a Peripatetic. But we can identify any such work? It seems to
me that we have a possible candidate in the very work which Eusebius,
in the *Praeparatio Evangelica*, quotes immediately before that of Atticus as his authority for Pre-Socratic Philosophy, the *History of
Philosophy* of the Peripatetic Aristocles, the teacher of Alexander, and
presumably his predecessor in the Chair. This book was not an attack
on Platonism, but in fact something far more insidious. It praised
Plato as an excellent philosopher, hailed him as the fulfilment of all
previous philosophy—and then showed how his doctrine was in turn
perfected by Aristotle.[1]

This whole digression, I realize, contains a large measure of conjecture, but I have indulged in it because I believe that we have here,
in this motive of simple self-preservation, the explanation of a good
deal of interschool polemic. Not that the real opposition of Atticus to
Aristotelianism is to be disregarded; but the nature of this particular
document must be taken into account when evaluating Atticus' true
position. His Platonism is not to be considered for this reason to be
entirely free of alien influences, as opposed to the frequently alleged
eclecticism of the School of Gaius; it is simply purged of certain overt

---

[1] Atticus does, indeed, refer three times in his work to 'the Peripatetic' (794C,
799B, 804D), and once (795C) addresses him rhetorically in the vocative, but it
does not sound from the contexts as if in fact he is referring to a particular individual. He seems to have in mind, rather, a representative Peripatetic. This does
not, however, conflict with the possibility of the treatise's being provoked by a
particular work of a particular man. K. Mras ('Zu Attikos, Porphyrios und
Eusebios', *Glotta* 1936, pp. 183–8) conjectures that the Peripatetic being reacted
to by Atticus is Alexander, but chronology militates against this. It is strange that
Mras did not think of Aristocles.

Peripateticisms. As we shall discover, Atticus, as a consequence of his abhorrence of Aristotle, is drawn inevitably, like Eudorus before him, towards the Stoa.

As for his works, apart from the effusion we have just been considering, we have evidence from Proclus of commentaries on the *Timaeus* (*In Tim.* I 276, 31ff.; 381, 26ff.; 431, 14ff. etc.) and the *Phaedrus* (*In Tim.* III 247, 15). We may also gather from Simplicius (*In Cat.* 30, 16ff.; 32, 19ff.) that he built further upon Nicostratus' attack on the *Categories*, but how extensive his work on the subject was is not clear. Both Proclus and Simplicius are pretty certainly deriving their information on Atticus from Porphyry.

2. PHILOSOPHY

Atticus, in his division of philosophy (*ap. PE* 509B), adopts, as we should expect, the order of topics Ethics-Physics-Logic, stamping in the process a moralizing and religious tone upon his whole doctrine. The purpose of Ethics is 'to render each one of us noble and good, and to order our households in the best possible manner, and also to adorn the State with the most excellent constitution and the most accurate laws'—that is, we have three divisions, ethics proper, economics, and politics. The object of Physics is 'to conduct us to the knowledge of things divine, the Gods themselves and the first principles and all other (related) matters'. Logic simply serves these pious ends.

The tone of this brief survey is not very surprising, being in accordance with the primary preoccupation of later Greek philosophy, but it is interesting to compare it with the similar summary of Antiochus' views given by Cicero in *Acad. Post.* 19ff. Both are primarily ethical in emphasis, but where Antiochus turned primarily to Nature, Atticus turns primarily to God.

(a) Ethics

And yet in his ethics, Atticus sides with Eudorus as against Antiochus or Plutarch, adopting the doctrine that Virtue is sufficient for Happiness—a characteristically Stoicizing move (794Cff. = Fr. 2 Baudry). He abuses Aristotle roundly for degrading the noble ideals of Plato:

His first disagreement with Plato is in a most general, vast and essential matter: he does not preserve the condition of Happiness, nor allows that Virtue is sufficient for its attainment, but he abases the power of Virtue, and considers it to be in need of the advantages accruing from Chance, in order with their help to be able to attain happiness; left to itself, he alleges, it would be quite incapable of attaining happiness.

Atticus continues for quite some time in this vein, becoming progressively more rhetorical and abusive. All we need note is his own view, a one-sided but possible interpretation of Plato (e.g. *Rep.* VIII 544A, IX 580B), but which is in its more immediate inspiration Stoic. As to what rank he would give to the lower classes of good we receive no guidance at all. He is only concerned with making the greatest possible contrast between Plato and Aristotle.

(b) Physics

In the area of physics he gives somewhat more positive information, and here we are able to supplement his polemic with evidence from his *Timaeus* Commentary, gleaned from Proclus.

The first point on which he attacks Aristotle is the extent of God's Providence. He accuses Aristotle of banishing God from active intervention in the world (Fr. 3, 799A), presumably basing himself here on an interpretation of the doctrine of the First Mover which draws much of its inspiration from Stoicism (Fr. 8, 814A ff.). He identifies Providence, Nature and the World Soul, and, although the Logos is not directly mentioned, it is that in fact that is the unifying concept:

> Further, Plato says that the Soul organises the Universe, penetrating (*diēkousa*) throughout all of it, . . . and that Nature is nothing else but Soul—and obviously rational Soul—and he concludes from this that everything happens according to Providence, as it happens according to Nature. With none of this is Aristotle in agreement.

All that has happened here is what took place in Platonism at least as far back as Antiochus—the Demiurge and the World Soul have merged into the more 'modern' and 'scientific' conception of the Logos. The only difference from Stoicism, as has been pointed out before—and it is an important one—is that God himself is transcendent. The Logos is not just an aspect of God; it is his instrument.

For Atticus, the question of the creation of the world is closely linked to the doctrine of Providence. As Philo had argued in the *Opif.* (9–10, see above p. 158), something that has no beginning does not require the guidance of a force superior to it. On this question Atticus has this to say (Fr. 4, 801C):

> First of all, in considering the question of the creation of the world, and thinking it necessary to pursue this mighty and widely useful doctrine of

Providence in all its ramifications, and reckoning that that which never came into being has no need of any creator or any guardian to ensure its proper existence, in order that he might not deprive the world of Providence, he removed from it the epithet 'uncreated'.

I reproduce faithfully Atticus' rather ponderous sentence-structure. Whereas Philo had preferred to understand 'created' simply in the sense of 'dependent on a cause outside itself' (the meaning favoured later by Taurus, as we have seen), Atticus follows Plutarch in envisaging a stage before creation, dismissing all the subtleties of his predecessor on this subject, and chiding him, indeed, for giving in to Aristotle (802D).

The logical problems raised by Aristotle bother Atticus not at all. Here he is much more the dogmatic theologian than the philosopher. He dwells on the insult to God involved in suggesting that he could not create whatever he wanted to, and further that, having created it, he could not, if he wished, keep it in existence indefinitely. He does, admittedly, make some attempt to counter on the philosophical level Aristotle's principle (*De Caelo* I 12, 282a31ff.), that whatever is indestructible must be ungenerated, and whatever is generated must be destructible, by asking what force, external or internal, could bring about the destruction of something which by definition comprises all the material substance that there is (803D–804A); but the general tone is one of *furor theologicus.*

Atticus also deals with the question of the creation of the world in his commentary on the *Timaeus.* Commenting on *Tim.* 28B (Procl. *In Tim.* I 276, 31ff. Diehl), he asserts, like Plutarch, that the universe was in disorderly motion before the creation of the cosmos, and, since Time is the measure of Motion, even of disorderly motion, Time existed before the cosmos. The universe in its unordered state does not have a beginning (*ibid.* 283, 27ff.).

The key passage in this connexion for Atticus, as it had been for Plutarch in the *De Proc.* (e.g. 1014B, 1016D), is *Timaeus* 30A:

For God, desiring that all things should be good, and that, so far as this might be, there should be nothing evil, having received all that is visible, not in a state of rest, but moving without harmony or order (*plēmmelôs kai ataktôs*), brought it from its disorder into order, thinking that this was in all ways better than the other.

Atticus quotes this in his polemical tract (801D), and Proclus gives the substance of his comment upon it in his *Timaeus* commentary (1 381, 26ff.):

Plutarch of Chaeroneia and Atticus grasp eagerly at these words, as bearing out their claim that the cosmos has its coming-into-being in Time, and they say that unordered Matter pre-existed the creation, and that there also pre-existed the Maleficent Soul (*kakergetis psyché*) which moved this disordered mass. For whence could motion come if not from soul? And if the motion was disorderly, then it must stem from a disorderly soul.

Atticus, then, like Plutarch (*De Proc.* 1014E), appeals to *Laws* x 896Eff., where the activities of the Maleficent Soul are described. On the creation of the cosmos, this soul receives a share of *nous*, and becomes 'sensible' (*emphrôn*)—not *rational*, though—and carries on henceforth an ordered motion. This, in terms of Plutarch's *Isis and Osiris*, is an Isis-figure rather than a Typhon-figure. It is the result of the assimilation of the maleficent soul of the *Laws* to the 'receptacle' of the *Timaeus*, as it was in Plutarch's case. The maleficent soul, then, becomes in effect a lower world soul, while the World Soul proper, as we have seen above, becomes an active principle, taking over the role of the Demiurge of the *Timaeus*. What, then, becomes of the Demiurge himself?

As we learn from Porphyry's criticism of him (Procl. *In Tim.* 1 305, 6ff.), Atticus made the Demiurge his supreme God, identifying him with The Good, and calling him also Intellect (*nous*). What then, asks Proclus, does he do with the Paradigm? Is it to be superior to the Demiurge, or in him, or inferior to him? If Proclus had had Atticus' own work in front of him, instead of relying on Porphyry, he could presumably have answered this question himself. In fact the answer comes later, through Porphyry (*In Tim.* 1 431, 14ff.), and it is that the Demiurge is superior to the Paradigm. Atticus there argues that if the Paradigm (or Intelligible Living Being) embraces all things, then it must embrace the Demiurge as well, in which case he is inferior to it. Or it does not, in which case it is incomplete. His solution seems to be that the Demiurge must be superior to the Paradigm, and must thus be outside and above the totality of things. Atticus' supreme god is thus on a plane above the realm of the Ideas.

On the other hand, from Atticus' discussion of the relation of the Ideas to God in his polemical tract (Fr. 9, 815Aff.) one might be excused for concluding that the Ideas are simply the thoughts of God, in what seems to be the normal Middle Platonic formulation:

It is just in this respect that Plato surpasses all others. Discerning, in relation to the Ideas, that God is Father and Creator and lord and guardian of all things, and recognising, on the analogy of material creations, that the craftsman first forms a conception (*noêsai*) of that which he is proposing to create, and then, once he has formed his conception, applies this likeness to the material, he concludes by analogy that the thoughts (*noêmata*) of God are anterior to material objects, models of the things that come to be, immaterial and intelligible (*noêta*), always remaining identically the same.

Porphyry, however, got quite a different impression of Atticus' views. At Procl. *In Tim.* I 394, 6 he complains as follows:

Atticus, with his doctrine of the Ideas, subsisting by themselves and lying outside the (divine) intellect, presents them to us as inert objects, like the models of the statuette-makers.

Porphyry cannot be entirely mistaken in his interpretation, though we may allow for some polemical distortion. The two impressions we receive must somehow be reconciled. It seems to me that Atticus is simply falling victim, in Porphyry's criticism, to the much greater degree of sophistication which the issue as to whether the Ideas were within or outside the divine Intellect took on in the century after his death. Porphyry himself bears witness to this debate most vividly in his own case (*Life of Plotinus* 18). He himself originally held that the Ideas were outside (this being the doctrine that he had picked up in the Athenian School under Longinus). He was then, after a long debate, converted to the alternative Plotinian view (see *Enn.* v 5, perhaps the result of this very debate)—and he now turns triumphantly to refuting the unfortunate Atticus. Porphyry himself, however, reveals the true situation at the beginning of his elaborate critique (*ibid.* 391, 6ff., as emended by Festugière in his trans. *ad loc.*). There he criticizes Atticus for proposing a multiplicity of interconnected first principles (*archai*), Matter, the Demiurge, and the Ideas. All Atticus is doing, in fact, is accepting the traditional Middle Platonic triad of principles, God, Matter and Idea, as listed succinctly e.g. in Aetius' *Placita* (I 3, 21, p. 288, Diels *Doxogr.*).[1] What has presumably happened is that Atticus, wishing to maintain the transcendent simplicity of his supreme God, used language in his *Timaeus Commentary* (affected, perhaps, in particular by the *pros* ('towards') of *Tim.* 28C–29A and 39E) which made the Ideas (the *paradeigma*) external to, though necessarily subject to,

---

[1] There, however, 'Idea', though an *archê*, is defined as 'an immaterial essence in the thoughts (*noêmata*) and conceptions (*phantasiai*) of God'.

God. This distinction of the Ideas from the essence of God seems, on Porphyry's evidence, to have been the doctrine of Athenian Platonism up to Longinus.

One can see the difficulty for a Middle Platonist involved in associating the multiplicity of Ideas too intimately with the supreme God, whom he would naturally think of as One, or the Monad, as well as Intellect. Plotinus and his followers disposed of this difficulty by postulating an entity higher than the Intellect, and from this exalted vantage point they were able to criticize their predecessors.

The later Neoplatonist Syrianus, in his commentary on the *Metaphysics* (on *Book* M, 1078b12ff., p. 105, 35ff. Kroll), introduces a further complication. He has been listing the various things that the Platonic Ideas are *not*, and he criticizes Atticus (along with Plutarch and the later Platonist Democritus) for holding that the Ideas are 'general reason-principles (*logoi*) subsisting eternally in the essence of the soul'—presumably the World Soul. We cannot be sure that this is the exact formula used by Atticus, as opposed to Syrianus' interpretation, but if it is, it must mean that Atticus situated the Ideas at the level of the World Soul, not in the mind of the supreme God. If we may take 'Soul' here as denoting the demiurgic intellect-cum-World Soul, then this evidence would confirm what can be derived from our other evidence. Otherwise, it complicates the situation vastly.

On a number of smaller issues Atticus makes his position clear through his disagreement with Aristotle. He condemns utterly the Aristotelian aether as fifth substance, ridiculing it as a 'bodiless body' (Fr. 5, 804Bff.). He also asserted the immortality of the soul, as we should expect him to do (Fr. 7, 808D–811C). He denounces Aristotle for assuming only the immortality of the intellect (810D). How could one have an intellect without a soul, he asks, relying on such passages as *Tim.* 30B, *Soph.* 248E, and *Phileb.* 30C. From this it might seem as if Atticus claimed immortality for the whole soul, but in fact we learn from Proclus (*In Tim.* III 234, 17ff.) that Atticus (whom he links here with Albinus) makes the irrational soul mortal, and so interprets *Tim.* 41C: 'weaving the immortal together with the mortal'. That is to say, the soul does in fact become pure mind after its final purification from the body, and his attack on Aristotle was mere polemic.

We learn a few other details on this question from Iamblichus' work *On the Soul*. At 375, 1ff. Wachs., Iamblichus distinguishes Plutarch and Atticus from Numenius in that, unlike him, they postulate a harmony between the two elements, rational and irrational, in the soul, while he postulates a constant struggle. Now obviously, as we have seen from Plutarch, there subsists a tension, both in the individual and the world, but Iamblichus' testimony suggests a less dualistic attitude to the world in Plutarch and Atticus than is to be found in Numenius. Iamblichus also reports (379, 25 ff. Wachs.) that, in contrast to himself, Atticus and other Platonists 'unite all souls to bodies according to one method of union, postulating in the same way always and at every embodiment of souls as a substratum the irrational soul, but imposing upon it the ordering influence of communion with the rational soul'. This account is confirmed by Proclus' report of Atticus' interpretation of the composition of the soul at *Tim.* 35A (*In Tim.* II 153, 25ff.), where Atticus, following Plutarch, takes the 'undivided essence' as the divine soul, and that 'divided about bodies' as the irrational soul, both pre-existing the rational soul, which is their product; the soul is thus ungenerated as regards its substratum, but generated in its formal aspect.

3. EXEGETICAL METHOD

That is all that we know of Atticus' views on any subject of significance. His interest in logic was not great, but he does seem to have added something to Nicostratus' attack on the *Categories*, as has been mentioned earlier. A few words might be said of his work as a commentator, since we have preserved for us some details from his *Timaeus* commentary. He is revealed, on the evidence of Proclus (who is merely relaying Porphyry) as 'most industrious' (*In Tim.* III 247, 12), 'accustomed to stick closely to the text' (*ibid.*), and at I 284, 13 as 'a terrible fellow for quibbling about words'. He plainly wrote a sound, pedantic Middle Platonic commentary. Of course, it is his literal interpretation of Plato's language about the creation of the world that particularly attracts the (unfavourable) attention of Porphyry and Proclus, but we find him also contributing to the discussion on the identity of the Absent Guest (*Tim.* 17A, I 20, 21ff.)—he suggests that he was just a foreigner travelling with Timaeus; and on the question whether Sais is a colony of Athens or vice versa (*Tim.* 21E, I 97, 30ff.), where he accuses Theopompus of malice for preferring the former alternative, and offers as proof of the latter a visit paid by a delegation of Saites to Athens in his own day, presumably thus acknowledging Athens as their mother city. From these details we can see something of the range and nature of things discussed in a Middle Platonic commentary, evidence that is confirmed by what we know of Harpocration's great commentary (see below), and by what remains of the

Anonymous Commentary on the *Theaetetus* (see next chapter). All in all, what we know of Atticus gives the impression of a school philosopher for whom Platonism is a religion to be fiercely defended— though this impression may be distorted by the circumstance of our having virtually nothing of his except this impassioned anti-Aristotelian polemic. On certain important doctrines—the temporal creation of the world and the existence of a disorderly world soul, he followed Plutarch, but his stance against Peripateticism inclined him, it would seem, to a more Stoic line than Plutarch, at least in the sphere of ethics. In metaphysics, there was no question, for any Middle Platonist, of getting back to what we would regard (perhaps wrongly) as the real teaching of Plato, so that to speak of Atticus as a purist is to that extent an oversimplification. If he appears less tolerant of other schools than, say, Albinus, this is largely because we are contrasting a polemical tract with a basic handbook of Platonism. In fact, as we shall see, the points of difference between the two are confined to a restricted number of topics, the same on which argument had always been raging in the Platonic School, such as the self-sufficiency of Virtue, and the real meaning of Plato's doctrine of creation in the *Timaeus*.

F. HARPOCRATION OF ARGOS

We must turn now to examine a rather shadowy figure, Harpocration of Argos, who nevertheless exhibits certain interesting traits. Harpocration is attested by Proclus (*In Tim.* I 305, 6) as a pupil of Atticus. He complicates our picture, however, by apparently drawing much inspiration also from the Neopythagorean school of Numenius and Cronius. Not much can be established about his life. He is reported by the *Suda* as being a 'confidant (*symbiôtês*) of Caesar', a term which seems to imply a place in the imperial household. Now a Harpocration is recorded (*SHA, Verus* II 5) as a tutor of the future emperor Verus, but since Verus was born in A.D. 130, and this Harpocration is listed as a *grammaticus* rather than as a philosophy tutor, his services would presumably be required in and around A.D. 142, which causes considerable chronological difficulties. Further, it seems hardly suitable for a Platonic philosopher to be serving as a *grammaticus*, Verus' philosophic needs being seen to, in fact, by, among others, Plutarch's nephew Sextus.

For Harpocration to be a pupil of Atticus, on the chronology that has been established for the latter, a *floruit* of around A.D. 180 would be required, so that an identification with the tutor of Verus must, I think, be abandoned. All we can say is that he was in the entourage of some emperor, and presumably not Marcus Aurelius, or he would surely have been acknowledged in the introduction to the *Meditations* along with all of Marcus' other spiritual guides.

Harpocration is credited by the *Suda* with two works, a *Commentary on Plato*, in 24 books, and a *Platonic Lexicon*, in two books. Each of these works, in their own way, appears to have been a compendium of Middle Platonic doctrines and scholarship up to his own time. Of the two, it is plainly from the former that any reports of his own doctrines will have come. We have, in all, fifteen of these, of varying value, in later writers,[1] a number of them showing that he dealt in his Commentary with points of considerable detail in the text of the dialogues. What concerns us now, however, is his doctrinal position.

On the one hand, Harpocration subscribes to the doctrine of Plutarch and Atticus that the world had a temporal beginning (*Schol.* in Procl. *In Remp.* II 377, 15ff., Kroll). He is ranked with Numenius, on the other hand, and against Atticus, in his view of the nature of the Demiurge (Procl. *In Tim.* I 303, 27ff.). The text on which Proclus, at least, is commenting is *Timaeus* 28c: 'Now to discover the creator and father of this universe is a task in itself, and having discovered him, to declare him to all men is quite impossible.' It is from this famous text that Numenius takes his start. He distinguishes three gods, of whom he calls the first 'Father', the second 'Creator', and the third 'Creation', by which last he means the cosmos. He thus takes the 'creator and father' of *Tim.* 28c as referring to two different beings, and in this he is followed by Harpocration. Proclus reports Harpocration's doctrine as follows:

I would be surprised if even Harpocration himself found his account of the Demiurge satisfactory; he follows Numenius, on the one hand, in postulating a series of three gods, and in making the Demiurge double, but he calls his first God Ouranos, and Kronos, his second one Zeus and Zen, and his third 'Heaven' and 'Cosmos'; and then again he changes his ground, calling his first God Zeus and king of the intelligible world, and his second 'Ruler' (*Archôn*), and thus the same entity is for him Zeus and Kronos and Ouranos.

—that is to say, son, father and grandfather. Proclus is being somewhat

[1] See my collection of the fragments, 'Harpocration's *Commentary on Plato*: Fragments of a Middle Platonic Commentary', in *California Studies in Classical Antiquity*, vol. 4 (1971).

satirical here at Harpocration's expense, and I suspect that he is being less than fair to the complexities of his exposition. What I think we have here is a conflation made either by Proclus, or already by Porphyry, of exegeses by Harpocration of different passages of Plato. *Cratylus* 396A–C comes to mind as a basis for the first identification; *Phaedrus* 246Eff., for the second. It may indeed be that we have a garbled record of three different comments by Harpocration, if we assume that he commented on *Timaeus* 28C as well, there adopting Numenius' interpretation. There would still, thus, be inconsistencies in his exegesis, but they would not be so incomprehensibly stark as Proclus is trying to make out.

If I am right in postulating that Harpocration dealt with the *Phaedrus* passage, then he took the Zeus there as representing his first God, with the same status as the first God of Numenius (below, pp. 366–9), and a being which he denominates 'Archon' as his second, the Demiurge proper. Whence he derived this term is obscure to me (at *Phaedr.* 247a3 the Olympian gods are termed '*theoi archontes*', but this plural does not help us much). It has a Gnostic ring to it. The Gnostic Basilides (*c.* A.D. 130) called the Demiurge 'the great Archon, the head of the cosmos' (Hipp. *Ref.* x 14, 6). We may recall also that Satan is repeatedly termed the '*archôn* of this world' in St John's Gospel (12:31; 14:30; 16:11). Harpocration's view of this world tends in other respects towards Gnosticism, as we shall see, but we cannot conclude on the evidence that he considered his second God to be a malevolent force, since he is prepared to identify him with the Zeus of the *Cratylus*.

A number of Harpocration's views on the soul have been preserved, and help to fill out our picture of his position. First, the question of the immortality of the soul. Harpocration is reported by the Neoplatonic commentator Hermeias (*In Phaedr.* p. 102, 10ff. Couvreur) as regarding every sort of soul as immortal—'even those of ants and flies'. In this Harpocration seems to be in agreement with Numenius, if we can so interpret the report in the *B* commentary on the *Phaedo* (p. 124, 13ff. Norvin) that Numenius regarded everything down to the basic life-principle (*empsychos hexis*) as immortal. This is a more extreme view than either the Athenian school or that of Gaius would hold, as far as we can see, and what Numenius and Harpocration thought happened to the irrational part of the soul after death is not clear. Presumably it survived indefinitely in the sublunar realm, constantly subject to recycling in connexion with rebirth.

Another question on which Harpocration is in general agreement with Numenius is on the origin of evil in the soul. On this we have the testimony of Iamblichus, *De Anima* (*ap.* Stob. 1 375, 12ff. Wachs.). Iamblichus has been saying that there has long been a controversy in the Platonic school as to whether there are or are not irreconcilable elements in the soul. Plotinus and Numenius are singled out by him as protagonists in this debate. Certain others, such as Plutarch and Atticus, recognize a struggle of warring elements, but postulate a reconciliation of them. All these, and Albinus as well, it seems (375, 10) must assume a flaw in judgment, a 'sin', within the soul itself; the group to which Harpocration belongs imagines evil as external to the soul, and thus considers the world a totally evil place:

Of those who are at variance with these thinkers (*sc.* Plutarch and Atticus) and who would attach evil to the soul in some way from elements which have accrued to it from outside, Numenius and Cronius in many places derive it from Matter, Harpocration also on occasion from the very nature of these bodies of ours.

This is an important problem in Platonism, and Harpocration is here placed in the ranks of the world-negaters. His position might be taken as even more extreme than that of Numenius and Cronius, if he regards the body itself as a source of evil, rather than matter in general. For him, there is no coming to terms with the body.

He is linked again with Numenius and Cronius in the view that *all* incarnation is evil, in a passage where Iamblichus is dealing with the varieties of union which the soul may have with the body. Harpocration, it seems, felt that there were no significant varieties (*ibid.* 380, 14ff.):

Some of the more recent philosophers, however, do not make this division, but, without taking into consideration the differences, they mix up together the entries into body of all souls, and maintain that all such entries are evil. Notable representatives of this view are Cronius, Numenius and Harpocration.

Although, therefore, Harpocration seems to have agreed with Plutarch and Atticus on the temporal creation of the world (and presumably thus of the rational soul), he is ranked against them, and with Numenius and Cronius, in the matter of the essential evil of incarnation and of the world. Including him with the Athenian School has thus involved some anticipation of the views of the 'Pythagoreans', but there is not necessarily any harm in that. It is a reminder that the differences between the schools were by no means absolute.

Of Harpocration's views on ethics or logic we unfortunately know nothing. The remaining references to him in the sources are interesting for the evidence they give of Middle Platonic methods of commentary, but they contain no doctrine of significance.

G. SEVERUS

Another rather mysterious figure may be fitted with some plausibility into the spectrum of the 'Athenian School', and that is Severus. We have no details of his life or place of operation, and his date is quite uncertain, but Proclus mentions him at one point (*In Tim.* III 212, 8), in conjunction with Plutarch and Atticus, in what appears to be reverse chronological order (Severus-Atticus-Plutarch), which would place him near the end of the second century or the beginning of the third. He was one of those whose works were read in Plotinus' circle (Porph. *V. Plot.* 14), which makes it incumbent upon us to set forth as fully as possible whatever we know of his doctrines. We know from Proclus that he wrote a *Commentary on the Timaeus* (*In Tim.* I 204, 17, etc.), and we have in Eusebius' *Praeparatio Evangelica* (XIII 17) an extract from a work of his *On the Soul*, from which a doxographical reference in Iamblichus' *De Anima* (p. 364, 4 Wachs.) is probably taken.

All indications conspire to show Severus to be anti-Aristotelian and pro-Stoic. Like Plutarch and Atticus, he is the object of attacks from the Peripatetics (Proclus, *In Tim.* III 212, 8) for his assertion that the world had a beginning in time, and is held together only by the will of the Father (interpreting thus *Tim.* 41AB). Following Atticus and Nicostratus, he seems to have rejected Aristotelian in favour of Stoic logic. At any rate, he is reported by Proclus (*In Tim.* I 227, 13ff.) to have postulated, in his exegesis of *Tim.* 27D, the Stoic supreme category *ti* ('something') as a common element uniting intelligible and sensible substance, here providing an answer to the difficulty raised by Nicostratus (*ap.* Simpl. *In Cat.* 76, 13ff.) as to how *ousia* can be one *genos*, if the categories are to refer to the intelligible world as well as the sensible.

On the question of the criterion of knowledge, we have a report (Pr. *In Tim.* I 255, 5ff.) which again presents Severus as a Stoicizer. Instead of the two more normal faculties of *noêsis* and *aisthêsis*, acting as criteria of the intelligible and sensible worlds respectively, he postulates as a single judging faculty (*kritikê dynamis*) the *logos*, and disturbs Proclus by making *noêsis* subordinate to it, as being one of its *organa*—the other, presumably, being *aisthêsis*. Such a doctrine seems to presuppose a unitary rather than a bipartite soul, and such an impression will be confirmed presently.

Turning to Physics, we see that he agrees with Plutarch and Atticus about the non-eternity of the world. We learn elsewhere, however (*ibid.* 1 289, 7ff.), that he introduced an interesting qualification here:

[Severus] says that the cosmos is in the absolute sense eternal, but that this particular cosmos which now exists and is in motion in this way is created. For there are two cycles (*anakykleseis*), as the Eleatic Stranger revealed (*Polit.* 270B), the one on which the universe is at present turning, and the other one which is opposite to it. So the cosmos, insofar as it is turning according to this cycle, is created and had a beginning, but absolutely it is not.

This use of the myth of the *Statesman* to extricate oneself from the problem of the creation of the world is not attested unequivocally for any other Middle Platonist, though we have suggestions of it both in Plutarch (above, p. 205) and Numenius (below, pp. 370f.). In so far as the theory of world cycles agrees with the Stoic theory of *apokatastasis*, this is also a Stoicizing trait. The postulation of absolute eternity is a rather subtler attempt to meet Aristotelian criticisms than that employed by Atticus.

Severus discusses the nature of the Soul both in the course of his *Timaeus Commentary* and in a special treatise on the subject. He parts company with Plutarch and Atticus on the question of the interpretation of Plato's account of its composition in *Tim.* 35A. Plutarch and Atticus had taken the indivisible and divisible parts to refer to the rational and irrational World Souls respectively. Severus seems not to want to postulate the formation of a unitary entity like the soul out of two opposed elements, and gives what both Iamblichus (*De An.* p. 364, 4ff.) and Proclus (*In Tim.* II 153, 24) call a 'geometrical' interpretation of the soul's composition, taking the 'undivided portion' as the point, and the 'divided' as extension (*diastêma*), presumably as being the first principles of the intelligible and sensible realms.

The passage which Eusebius quotes is an argument by Severus against those who would construct the soul out of that substance which is not subject to passions and that which is, like some intermediate colour out of·black and white. Such a construct, argues

Severus, could not be immortal, but must dissolve sooner or later into its component parts:

Do we not see that that which is naturally heavy, even if it is borne upwards either by us or by some natural lightness that has been attached to it, nevertheless is forced downwards again by its own peculiar nature . . . for it is impossible for something which is constructed out of two opposites forced together to remain stable unless there is some third substance always present in them. The soul, however, is not a third thing put together from two elements contrary to one another, but simple and by its very nature impassible and immaterial. (*PE* XIII 17, 3–4)

This assumption of the soul as a unitary entity, the apparent rejection of any distinction between the rational and irrational elements within it, may also be seen as a Stoicizing trait. Certainly it sets Severus in opposition to the dualism of Plutarch and Atticus, and brings him much closer to a Chrysippan doctrine of the unity of the soul than any other Platonist of our period.

Severus is criticized by Proclus' teacher Syrianus (*In Met.* p. 84, 23 Kroll) for 'misusing mathematical concepts in the explanation of physical questions', presumably a reference to his theory of the soul. Severus seems to be returning to a position akin to that of Speusippus, whose definition of the soul as 'the idea of the omnidimensionally extended' had been adopted later, as we have seen, by Posidonius, but by no later Platonist. Severus also plainly took an interest in the harmonic division of the soul as described in *Tim.* 35BC. Proclus reports that he preferred, in opposition to the Peripatetic Adrastus, to represent the divisions of the soul by a straight line rather than by a lambda-shaped figure (*In Tim.* II 171, 9), as better resembling the division of the musical canon. He also held the view that Plato intended his division to end not with a full tone but with a semi-tone, or *leimma* (*ibid.* 191, 1ff.), and he laid out a scheme, starting from a base number of 768, which achieved that result. No doubt Severus' preference for the straight-line diagram (also adopted by modern commentators) is partly at least the result of his desire to emphasize the unity of the soul.

All in all we see, I think, in Severus evidence of a superior intellect, with the workings of which one would have desired better acquaintance.

H. CONCLUSION

The 'Athenian School', then, has revealed not one but many faces, and none of them could properly be described as 'orthodox'. I have argued before this, and shall continue to argue, that the labels 'orthodox' and 'eclectic' are not really useful in characterizing later Platonists. We must rather see things in terms of the pull of various attractions, Peripatetic, Stoic and Pythagorean, which produce various sets of attitudes within an overall Platonic framework. Of the men we have reviewed, Nicostratus, Atticus and Severus are plainly anti-Aristotelian and pro-Stoic, Taurus an instance of the opposite tendency, and Harpocration an interesting mixture, tending to Pythagoreanism. We can hardly, on our flimsy evidence, speak of a 'School'. That there was in any physical sense an Academy is, as we have seen, doubtful, and there is no real unity of doctrine between such men as Taurus and Atticus. The School of Athens must, then, be accounted an empty name. The same, as I shall now seek to prove, must be said of the School of Gaius.

CHAPTER SIX

The 'School of Gaius': Shadow and Substance

A. GAIUS

Over against the Athenian school of Platonism in the second century A.D. is commonly placed that brand of Platonism associated primarily with the names of Albinus and, to a lesser extent, Apuleius, and generally agreed to have as its founder the teacher of Albinus, one Gaius. It will be our task in this chapter to investigate the nature of this 'school' of Platonism, and its relation to that of the Athenians.

Facts are hard to come by. We have the testimony of the famous medical writer Galen that he took lectures at the age of 14 (i.e. in A.D. 143) in Pergamum, from an unnamed pupil of Gaius (*De Anim. Morb.* ch. 8, v 41 Kühn, p. 31, 24ff. Marq.),[1] and that some years later, at some time between A.D. 149 and 157, when he had transferred himself to Smyrna, he attended the lectures of Albinus (*De Propr. Libr.* ch. 2, p. 97, 6ff. Müller). Such data would seem to place the activity of Gaius himself in the early decades of the century. The multiple inscription to which I have already alluded in connexion with Nicostratus and Taurus (*SIG* ii³ 868, see above pp. 233f.) has, as its earliest part, an honorary inscription conferring the freedom of Delphi on one 'Gaius, son of Xenon, philosopher'. This is dated with probability in or around A.D. 145. The identification of this Gaius with our philosopher is not, I think, unreasonable. If it is accepted, then this honour will have been conferred on him at a fairly advanced age.

Even as we do not really know when Gaius taught, so we have no clear indication as to where he taught. It has been assumed generally

---

[1] This man was, Galen says, much occupied with public affairs at the time, since the citizens made constant demands on him, which meant that Galen got little value from him. This, besides explaining Galen's relative lack of scholastic subtlety in his Platonism, is useful evidence of the role of philosophers in public affairs at this time.

that he operated either in Alexandria or in Asia Minor, in which latter area such of his pupils as we hear of are found. On the other hand, Apuleius of Madaura, whose summary of Platonic philosophy has been taken to be a product of the same brand of Platonism as Albinus, pursued such study of Platonism as he did pursue at Athens, in the period 145–50 A.D., and only toured Asia Minor (*Flor.* 15; *De Mundo* 17). But no secure arguments can be based on Apuleius, as I shall argue later. The place of Gaius' teaching activity remains uncertain.

Of his works nothing survives. It is even possible that he wrote nothing himself. We have a record, in a manuscript in Paris (*Cod. Par. gr.* 1962, fol. 146v), of 'Notes of Gaius' Lectures', in seven books, by Albinus, now unfortunately lost. They were used, however, by the late Neoplatonist Priscian in his *Answers to King Chosroes*. Porphyry, in his *Life of Plotinus* (14), mentions 'commentaries' of Gaius as being read in Plotinus' seminar, but these may simply have been these lecture-notes of Albinus. Further, the references in Proclus' *Timaeus Commentary* to the opinions of 'Gaius and Albinus' on various points may simply reflect Albinus' tendency in his commentaries to appeal to the authority of his master. At any rate, we have no clear record of any work from the pen of Gaius.

Attempts have been made, however, on the basis of a comparison of Albinus and Apuleius, together with small contributions from other sources, to reconstruct a body of doctrine of Gaius. Since it is precisely this attempt that I wish to examine in this chapter, there seems no point in setting forth any possible doctrines of Gaius at this stage, before we have considered in some detail the content of the documents that survive. It is to these, therefore, that I will now turn, taking them in an order which, if not securely chronological, is at least in accordance with their importance.

B. ALBINUS

1. LIFE AND WORKS

There is not much to be said under this heading. As to Albinus' life and area of operation, we have only one datum. At some period between A.D. 149 and 157, as has been mentioned above, Galen took lectures from him on Platonism in Smyrna. This would make Albinus an approximate contemporary of Taurus, and a generation older than Apuleius, and this places him satisfactorily. He will be a contemporary, also, of the mathematician Theon of Smyrna, whose work *A Mathematical Introduction to Plato* will be discussed briefly in Chapter Eight.

Of Albinus' works there are preserved only two basic school handbooks, *An Introduction to Plato's Dialogues* (*Eisagôgê*) and the *Guide to the Doctrines of Plato* (*Didaskalikos*). The first of these is a very short work (only four-and-a-half pages of the modern edition), discussing the form and content of Plato's dialogues, distinguishing them according to type, and setting out a course of reading and instruction in them. I will say more of this below in discussing Albinus as a teacher and commentator.

The second text, the *Didaskalikos*, came down to us in the manuscripts under the false name of 'Alkinoos', and until a German scholar, Freudenthal, in the last century, pointed out that this was a simple corruption in a minuscule manuscript for 'Albinus', the shadowy figure of Alcinous presided over the treatise. In fact it agrees stylistically with the *Introduction*, and doctrinally with what we know otherwise about Albinus. It is a bald scholastic survey of Platonic doctrine, with various interesting innovations which will be noticed in due course. Comparing this textbook with the more florid utterances of other contemporary Platonists, scholars have been betrayed into assuming that Albinus is a very sober-sided fellow, and that the more mystical and enthusiastic elements of Platonism were not for him. We must not, however, simply compare the *Didaskalikos* with what we have of the representatives of other schools of Platonism, but rather ask ourselves to consider carefully, if we had a handbook of Platonism from the hand of Plutarch or Taurus or Atticus or Numenius, how it would differ from that of Albinus. On certain obvious questions of doctrine, such as the self-sufficiency of virtue or the temporal creation of the world, there would be differences, of course, but what of the overall tone? In fact, Albinus in ch. 10 of his work exhibits a distinctly mystical tendency, so much so that authorities have been found to declare the chapter spurious, when it may in fact be more reasonably regarded as one of the more 'genuine' or original parts of the work.

There arises in connexion with this work the interesting question, investigated in detail by the Polish scholar Tadeusz Sinko, as to its relation to the work *De Platone et eius Dogmate* (On Plato and His Doctrine) of the Roman lawyer and rhetorician Apuleius, more famous as the author of the *Golden Ass*. That there is some relation is obvious enough; precisely what it implies is not so obvious, as we shall see in due course. Sinko hoped to be able from a comparison of the two works to reconstruct something of the doctrine of Gaius, which he assumed to be the source of both. I shall discuss presently the difficulties involved in this theory.

Another question that must be considered is the extent to which the *Didaskalikos* represents doctrines or formulations original to Albinus. The very nature of the work makes it highly unlikely that it would contain much, if anything, that was original, but we happen to have a piece of evidence (over and above the general resemblance to Apuleius' work) which creates a strong presumption as to what the source of at least the main substance of the work was. Chapter 12 of the *Didaskalikos*, which concerns the Ideas, begins as verbally identical, and continues as a close paraphrase of, a section of Arius Didymus on the same subject which chances to be preserved to us both by Eusebius (*PE* XI 23, 2) and Stobaeus (*Anthol.* I 135, 19 Wachs.). If we may extrapolate from this—and there seems no reason not to—we may view Albinus' work as essentially a 'new edition' of Arius' *On the Doctrines of Plato*. How far this 'new edition' is to be seen as 'a new, *revised*, edition', however, is not quite clear. This question will be raised again later, in connexion with individual passages of the *Didaskalikos*.

Another awkward question is raised by the presence, in the same manuscript list of contents that mentions the 'nine (or ten) books of *Lectures of Gaius*', of a work by Albinus *On the Doctrines of Plato*— the same title as that borne by Arius' work. Scholars have been led by this, as well as by the form of the *Didaskalikos*, to suppose that it is itself an epitome of a longer work by Albinus. Certain manuscripts of the work, indeed, describe it as an epitome. Certainly the *Didaskalikos* is summary in places to the point of being cryptic, and if this report in the above-mentioned list of contents is accurate there is no difficulty in supposing it to be a short form of a longer work. To postulate that it is a later, Byzantine epitome of a work by Albinus, however, as some scholars have done, is unnecessary.

Whether Albinus in addition to these works wrote commentaries on inidvidual dialogues of Plato is not quite clear. Proclus certainly talks of him as commenting on the Myth of Er in the *Republic* (*In Remp.* II 96, 12 Kroll), but this need not imply a full commentary. Since Gaius is mentioned in the same passage as commenting also, this may simply be a reference, to Albinus' reports of Gaius' lectures. In his *Timaeus*

Commentary, again, Proclus mentions Albinus on three occasions, on one of which, at least, Albinus is commenting on (in fact, emending) a specific passage of the *Timaeus* (27C, *In Tim.* I 219, 2 Diehl), but this is only minimal evidence of a commentary. In the second passage (*ibid.* 340, 24) he is linked with Gaius in such a way as to suggest that he is quoting him, so that we may be back with his lecture-notes.

There is, on the other hand, the question of the authorship of the *Anonymous Theaetetus Commentary*, a fragment of a commentary on the dialogue preserved on a papyrus discovered in Egypt in 1901 and first published in 1905. The beginning is missing; the papyrus begins towards the end of the preface, and continues to *Theaet.* 153DE, though in a very fragmentary condition in places, and there is another short passage covering 157E–158A. The commentary comprises simple elucidation of the text, answering of *aporiai*, and notes of a grammatical and antiquarian nature, and in general maintains a level of stupefying banality. Occasionally a passage prompts the author to an excursus (e.g. 143D on *oikeiôsis*, 147D on irrationals) or criticism of other schools, Stoics, Epicureans or Sceptics. The work is mainly interesting for the snippets of school doctrine which it contains, and as being the only surviving representative of a Middle Platonic commentary (apart from that of Calcidius, the Middle Platonic nature of which is disputed, as we shall see in Chapter Eight). Diels and Schubart, who edited the text, recognize its close affinity with the Platonism of Albinus as revealed in the *Didaskalikos*, but they produce a number of difficulties in the way of identification. On the one hand, it is difficult to believe that the author of this work, who also by his own account produced commentaries on the *Phaedo* (col. 48, 10), the *Symposium* (70, 12) and the *Timaeus* (35, 12), should be someone quite unknown to us, especially when we have some evidence of a commentary of Albinus on the *Timaeus*, and perhaps also on the *Phaedo* (rather vague references in Tertullian, *De Anima* 28–9). We must bear in mind, however, not only that we know of at least one other, unnamed, pupil of Gaius teaching at the same time as Albinus (above, p. 266), but that Proclus, in giving a list of Middle Platonic commentators on the *Republic* (*In Remp.* II 96, 10ff.), produces at least one man, Maximus of Nicaea, of whom we have no other record. The papyrus itself belongs to the first half of the second century, which means that it must be almost contemporary with its composition.

The first difficulty that the editors produce is that of style. This is a shaky criterion except in extreme cases, and this is not one of those.

While admitting that the type of Greek written by Albinus and the Theaetetus Commentator are essentially the same, they point to such a characteristic as the frequency of synonyms in Albinus as opposed to their non-occurrence in the commentary. This is the only specific distinction that the editors produce, and they themselves make the point that the two works are of different types, the *Didaskalikos* being directed to a more general public, and thus showing reasonably a greater polish in its language. On such more basic matters as the avoidance of hiatus, both texts are in agreement in ignoring it.

A more bothersome point arises out of an error in quotation; it is a small detail, but it is the sort of detail that is rather difficult to explain away. Both Albinus in the *Eisagôgê* (p. 150, 27 Hermann) and the Commentator (on two occasions, 3, 2–3 and 15, 21–3) quote the definition of knowledge in the *Meno* (98A), 'true opinion fastened down by reckoning of causality' (*aitias logismôi*)'. The Commentator on both occasions misquotes this as 'by the causal principle of reckoning (*aitiâi logismou*)', an easy error to make, since it involves a more natural word-order. Albinus, however, quotes it correctly. This, as I say, is bothersome, but any reader who has ever had the experience of re-reading a well-known text to discover that he has been misquoting for years a supposedly familiar passage will agree that such a detail is not conclusive proof of difference of authorship. It might simply mean that the *Eisagôgê* is later than the *Commentary*.

Against these discrepancies must be weighed the fact that on all questions of doctrine or terminology Albinus and the Commentator are in agreement, though admittedly we are dealing in all instances with relative commonplaces. Like Albinus, the Commentator holds that the *telos* is 'likeness to God' (7, 14), condemning *oikeiôsis* as a basis for Justice (and thus for the good life in general). Like Albinus, he uses the Stoic term *physikai ennoiai* to describe the innate Ideas (46, 43; 47, 44, cf. *Did.* 155, 23; 156; 17, and *Isag.* 150, 22). The Commentator also distinguishes the 'natural virtues' (*euphyiai*) from the perfected virtues (4, 12; 11, 12ff.), as does Albinus (see below, p. 301). Again, both Albinus and the Commentator define the first task of noble love as the distinguishing of a worthy object of Love (*ho axierastos*) (*Did.* 187, 35; *Comm.* 8, 23ff.). As I say, these are all doubtless commonplaces, but they add up. There is at least no doctrinal divergence between Albinus and the Theaetetus Commentator, though an assertion of their identity would be rash, perhaps, owing to the unsatisfactory nature of the evidence.

2. PHILOSOPHY

(*a*) *General principles*

What follows here will, perforce, be simply an exposition, with comments, of the content of the *Didaskalikos*. As I have said, there is not likely to be much in this work that is original to Albinus, so that it must be borne in mind that, in expounding it, we are in fact giving more an account of Middle Platonic doctrine in general, as first formalized, perhaps, by Arius Didymus, than of Albinus' doctrine in particular. Where I feel that Albinus is being original, I shall say so.

The work begins with some basic definitions. Philosophy is 'a striving after wisdom', *or* 'the release and turning away (*periagôgê*) of the soul from the body', this latter definition, drawing its inspiration from the *Republic* (cf. esp. VII 521cff.), being that more favoured by Albinus. The definition of wisdom as 'knowledge of things divine and human' is ultimately Stoic in formulation, but had long since been adopted by school Platonism and become a commonplace. A Platonist could, after all, refer back to *Rep.* VI 486A. It is worth noting that Albinus does not append to this definition the distinctively Posidonian addition '. . . and their causes', which is adopted, for instance, by Philo (*Congr.* 79, above, p. 141).

In the matter of the ordering of the topics of philosophy, we have, in the *Didaskalikos*, a distinctive development. Not only does Albinus give (ch. 3) the order Physics-Ethics-Logic, but he equates Physics with *theôria* and Ethics with *praxis*, thus connecting the divisions of philosophy with the distinction of the two Lives, the theoretic and the practical, which he has made in the previous chapter. This order appears to rank the three subjects rather in descending order of nobility, since for purposes of practical instruction Albinus takes them in the order Logic-Physics-Ethics—the normal Stoic order, as opposed to that followed by most Platonists, to our knowledge, since Antiochus. He does not use the traditional terms for these divisions, but employs rather the terms *dialektikê*, *theôrêtikê*, *praktikê*. This renaming of the divisions, which owes much to Aristotle, actually betokens an increase in comprehensiveness. Physics proper is now only a subdivision of *theôria*. That part which concerns the first causes and things divine is Theology (cf. Ar. *Metaph.* E. 1026a18–19); that which concerns the movements of the heavenly bodies and the cosmos in general is Physics; and as a third subdivision we have Mathematics, which performs the same role in *theôria* as Dialectic does in the whole of philosophy, that of providing a *method*. Ethics, again, is only one of three subdivisions of *praxis*, the others being economics and politics. Dialectic, finally, has various subdivisions that need not concern us at present. The whole of the *Didaskalikos* is permeated by these scholastic distinctions, as befits, after all, an elementary textbook.

(b) Theory of knowledge: the kritêrion

Albinus, in fact, takes this as his first topic (ch. 4), since it constitutes the first subject of Dialectic. His doctrine is basically, as one would expect, a formalization of Plato, but there are certain details which merit attention.

He begins (154, 8ff. Hermann) by distinguishing three elements, the faculty making the judgment (*to krinon*), the object of the judgment (*to krinomenon*), and the judgment itself (*krisis*), which last may most properly be termed the *kritêrion*, or standard of judgment. This term may also be applied, however, to the judging faculty, which in turn may be analysed into two elements, the mind itself, which constitutes the agent (*to hyph'hou*) of judgment, and what he calls the *logos physikos*, which constitutes the instrument (*to di'hou*).

There are various points here to be noted. First, the *krisis* is the result of the mind's assenting to an impression, and is thus in fact a 'cognitive impression' (*kataleptikê phantasia*), a phrase not in fact used by Albinus, though it is found in the *Theaetetus Commentary* (61, 19). Then the distinction between agent and instrument of judgment, using the characteristic prepositional phrases, goes back to the beginnings of Middle Platonism (see above, ch. 2, p. 67 and ch. 3, p. 138; also utilized by the Theaetetus Commentator, 2, 23).

Finally, we have the term *logos physikos*, which almost defies translation. Here Albinus is being subtle, though we cannot be sure that he is being original. If we return to Antiochus, however, we find that for him (*Acad. Pr.* 30), the instrument of judgment is sense-perception (*aisthêsis*), which he would regard as the only source of impressions. He speaks also, however, of a 'natural force' of the mind —presumably a *dynamis physikê*—'which it directs to the things by which it is moved'. This corresponds to Albinus' *logos physikos*, which one might render 'an activity of the mind working through nature'. It is in fact the mind *in act*, engaged in receiving impressions from the outside world. Albinus does not wish to bring the senses in at this point, because he recognizes another source of knowledge superior to sense-perception, the direct apprehension of intelligible reality, which in its pure form is the mode of perception proper to God, but which is also possible for us. Such a faculty had no meaning for a thinker as Stoicized as Antiochus, as we have seen, but it was essential for all later Platonists from Eudorus on. The type of *logos* which apprehends the intelligibles (*ta noêta*) Albinus terms *epistê-monikos logos* (hereinafter termed *EL*), and its product is scientific knowledge, *epistêmê*. That which concerns itself with the sense-world (*ta aisthêta*) is *doxastikos logos* (*DL*), and its product is opinion, *doxa*. This distinction is, of course, perfectly Platonic (*Rep.* v 476cff.), though the formalization of two types of *logos* is a subsequent scholastic development.

This distinction of a category of knowledge independent of sense-perception, then, is a radical departure from Antiochus, but basic to Middle Platonism in its developed form. The name for this activity of the mind is *noêsis*, 'intellection'. Albinus defines it (155, 17f.) as 'the activity of the mind in contemplating the primary intelligibles (*ta prôta noêta*)'.

This in turn leads us to an interesting distinction, that between 'primary' and 'secondary' objects of intellection. The 'primary intelligibles' are the ideas in their transcendent aspect, 'secondary intelligibles' are the forms-in-matter (*eidê*), a distinction we have already seen being made by the Platonic source behind Seneca's *Letter* 58 (above, p. 137).

Sense-perception, in turn (defined by Albinus (154, 29f.) as 'an affection (*pathos*) produced in the soul by the body which presents the report, primarily, of the faculty affected'), has two types of object, 'primary perceptibles', corresponding to qualities (*poiotêtes*), and 'secondary perceptibles', corresponding to accidents of bodies, or embodied individual qualities; and arising from these there is the composite body (*athroisma*), such as fire or honey. This double division allows Albinus finally to present an elaborate schema of modes of perception, utilizing the scholastic term 'with the necessary accompaniment of' (*ouk aneu*, abbrev. o.a.), as follows:

The primary intelligibles are judged by intellection o.a. the *EL*, by immediate and non-discursive apprehension;

the secondary intelligibles are judged by the *EL* o.a. intellection;

the primary and secondary sensibles are judged by sense-perception o.a. the *DL*:

the composite body is judged by the *DL* o.a. sense-perception.

What is the point of such a scheme? We have here, at least, a useful distinction between 'immediate' and 'discursive' thought. The objects of both *noésis* and *aisthésis* are unanalysed, primary impressions; their respective *logoi* are then brought to bear on them, and there result from this process the proper objects of these *logoi*, that is to say, secondary constructions arrived at by discursive reasoning. Both mind and sense-perception, then, have powers both of receiving immediate impressions and of forming constructions out of these.

We have here what is certainly a well-developed epistemology, but the neatness of the scholastic scheme crumbles somewhat on closer examination. For one thing, the objects of the respective *logoi* differ in type. The object of the *DL* is, very properly, the composite body, which is an aggregate of sense-data; but the object of the *EL* would surely be, on this analogy, mental constructs—ethical and political laws, mathematical and scientific systems. Instead we have the forms-in-matter, which are a type of construction, certainly, but analogous rather to the qualities in bodies, one would think, than to the bodies themselves.

Then we have, in the realm of sense-perception, the distinction between qualities (*poiotêtes*), such as colour or whiteness, and what Albinus calls 'accidents' (*ta kata symbebêkos*), but which are elsewhere termed *poia*, which may be rendered 'embodied qualities'. Albinus is deriving his formulations here ultimately from the *Theaetetus*, 156cff. There we have a distinction made between the sensation 'whiteness', which is what is produced by the conjunction of the stream of light from the eye and the stream of colour from the object, and on the other hand the state of the object itself after the conjunction has taken place, which is termed 'a white thing'. Albinus is not making a contrast here, then, between general and particular qualities, but simply between two aspects of the same phenomenon, as described in the *Theaetetus*.[1]

In contrast with these primary percepts, we have the construction which *aisthêsis* makes out of regularly conjoined sense-data, that is, material objects, *athroismata*. (Albinus uses here the term found in *Theaet.* 157c. It may be noted that this passage of the *Theaetetus* is actually presented by Plato simply as a speculative theory which Socrates is 'feeding' to Theaetetus; for Albinus it has become dogma.)

Another thing to be considered is the status of the *DL*. This cannot have the same relation to *aisthêsis* as the *EL* has to *nous*. *Aisthêsis* by

---

[1] The distinction between *poiotêtes* and *poia* is also made by Aristotle in ch. 8 of the *Categories* (10a27ff.), and Albinus doubtless has this passage in mind also.

itself cannot, on Platonist theory, make judgments of any sort; for this there is required a mental act. The *DL* must in fact be an agent of *nous* even as is the *EL*, but an agent which uses the senses to interpret the sense-world. This difference in logical status is obscured by Albinus' rigid schematization, but he himself shows no consciousness of any difficulty.

In spite of these problems, however—inevitable, perhaps, in a summary handbook such as Albinus is writing—the epistemology revealed in the *Didaskalikos* is impressively coherent. The *ouk aneu* formulation is a useful way of distinguishing the primary from the auxiliary agents involved in each type of cognition or perception. The distinction of primary and secondary objects of intellection and sense-perception, while somewhat confused in its application to intelligibles, is at least philosophically respectable.

Chapter 4 ends with a distinction between *theôria* and *praxis* which is Aristotelian in general formulation, but which uses also the Stoic term *physikê ennoia* ('natural, or innate, concept') (156, 13ff.):

Right reason (*orthos logos*) does not judge in the same way those things which fall in the sphere of *theôria* and those which involve action, but in the sphere of *theôria* it considers what is true and what is not, whereas in the sphere of *praxis* it considers what is proper and what is alien, and what is to be done. For it is by having a natural concept of the noble and the good, employing our reason, and referring to the natural concepts as to definite yardsticks, that we make judgements as to whether such and such is so or otherwise.

This is Aristotle's distinction between theoretical and practical wisdom, set out in *EN* vi, but the *physikai ennoiai* to which one refers as to *metra* are innate ideas such as were introduced into Platonism from Stoicism by Antiochus. We must bear in mind always, however, that Albinus himself is not conscious of these as alien influences; only from our distorted and fragmentary perspective can he be regarded here as 'eclectic'.

(c) Logic or dialectic

Albinus' approach to the problem of expounding Plato's logic is to attribute to him without reservation the whole system of Peripatetic Logic as worked out by Aristotle, and further elaborated by Theophrastus and Eudemus, finding in the dialogues examples illustrative not only of categorical syllogisms, but also of both 'pure' and 'mixed' hypotheticals. Once again, this is not eclecticism. There is a great difference between using what one recognizes as Peripatetic logic to elucidate the arguments in Plato's dialogues (as a commentator today might use modern symbolic logic for the same purpose) and on the other hand assuming the explicit formulations of Aristotle and Theophrastus to be already present in the dialogues. What Albinus is doing is reclaiming formal logic for Plato. In this he is being neither 'eclectic' nor original. Any Middle Platonist, as far as we can see, would hold that formal logic was not an invention of Aristotle, but rather of the Platonic School in general, and that Aristotle simply wrote the handbook for it. Even if one attacked the Categories, this did not mean that one denied either their usefulness or that Plato had known them; the point was that Aristotle had got the doctrine confused in some way or other.

This caution having been issued, let us proceed. Albinus' chapters 5 and 6 are a most useful exposition of later Peripatetic logic, but presented in such a way as to make it seem essential Platonism. He begins (ch. 5) with a number of definitions and general principles, all of which are, indeed, reasonably Platonic. The basic principle of Dialectic is to examine the substance of each thing and then its accidents. Substance may be examined either by 'descending' (a priori), by the processes of division and definition, or by 'ascending' (a posteriori), by analysis. Accidents may be examined either 'from the aspect of the things contained' (i.e. the accidents themselves), by induction (*epagôgê*); or 'from that of the containers' (i.e. the objects in which the accidents inhere), by syllogistic (*syllogismos*). (This pair, however, is taken from Aristotle, *Topics* I 12). We thus get, in all, five types of dialectic reasoning, three concerned with substances, two with accidents. This is simply a formalization of various processes discussed and practised by Plato, and there is nothing original to Albinus about it; nor is there about the subdivisions of these types that follow for the rest of the chapter.

A good example of the scholastic method which Albinus is following is his description of the three types of analysis. The first is the ascent from sensible objects to the 'primary intelligibles'. An example given of this is Diotima's discourse to Socrates in *Symposium* 210Aff. The second is the ascent through those propositions that can be proved and demonstrated to propositions which are indemonstrable and immediate. The illustration for this process is the enquiry into the immortality of the soul in *Phaedrus* 245cff. The third is that which proceeds from an hypothesis to non-hypothetical principles. This is described by Plato in *Republic* VI 510Bff. Plato never in the dialogues sets these three processes side by side; that is the work of the school-men. At what stage this, and other formulations, were first made is a very doubtful question. The tendency to attribute much of this scholastic activity already to the Old Academy under Xenocrates and his immediate successors is gaining ground, and I must say that I see little reason to dispute it. Nevertheless, we must proceed from the evidence available to us, and that is Albinus' handbook.

He ends this chapter with a comment on Induction which manages to combine wonderfully in one short sentence three terms, one of which we would take as characteristically Aristotelian, the next Platonic, and the third Stoic. It may be quoted as a neat example of the mixed tradition within which Albinus is working: 'Induction is extremely useful for stirring up the innate concepts.' The overall inspiration here is certainly Platonic, in particular *Meno* 85cff., from which comes the term 'stir up' (*anakinein*), but the name given to the process is Aristotle's (*epagōgē*), while the term used for the Ideas is ultimately Stoic, as I have said above (*physikai ennoiai*). In all this, of course, Albinus will not be conscious of any mixture of terminology.

In Chapter 6 we turn to the syllogism, the whole theory of which, as I have said, is claimed for Plato. First, an account of the types of propositions (*protaseis*)—affirmation, negation, and, within either of these, general and particular. Then, a division of propositions into categorical and hypothetical. After this Albinus gives what is in fact Aristotle's definition of the syllogism: 'A syllogism is a form of words in which, when certain assumptions are made, something other than what has been assumed necessarily follows from the things assumed.' (*Anal. Pr.* 24b18–20). But now a development on Aristotle:

Of syllogisms, some are categorical, others hypothetical, and others are mixed. Those are categorical of which both the premisses and the conclusions are simple propositions; those are hypothetical which are formed from hypothetical propositions; and those are mixed which combine the two. (158, 12)

These latter two types were first devised by Theophrastus,[1] and adopted from him by the Stoics, and perhaps even by such Old Academics as Polemon. Certainly by Antiochus' time (if we may take

---

[1] See the useful collection of fragments and commentary of Andreas Graeser, *Die Logische Fragmente des Theophrast*, Berlin 1973, esp. Frr. 29–30, and the commentary thereon. Graeser, however, pays no attention to Albinus.

the *Topics* of Cicero as being essentially inspired by him) all these types of syllogism were regarded as the common currency of philosophic discourse. The only problem for Platonists was to find good examples of each in the dialogues.

Of the categorical syllogisms, Albinus gives examples of all three figures, the first from the *Alcibiades* (115Aff.), the second and third from the *Parmenides*. Of pure hypothetical syllogisms, he finds the first two figures in the *Parmenides* (137Dff.), and the third in the *Phaedo* (72E, 75C).[1] He then goes on to give examples of each of the three Theophrastean hypotheticals, all from the *Parmenides*, although he changes Theophrastus' order of these in favour of that of later authorities (probably Boethus) who switched his second and third to bring them more closely into line with order of categorical figures.

Of the 'mixed' syllogism, which is also the characteristic Stoic type, Albinus gives one example from the *Parmenides* (145A) of what he calls the 'constructive' (*kataskeuastikos*) type (corresponding to Chrysippus' first indemonstrable), but—unless there is a lacuna in the mss. —none of the second, 'destructive' (*anaskeuastikos*), type, that is to say, where the conclusion is negated (as is the case with Chrysippus' second, third and fourth indemonstrables).

He also claims the Categories for Plato (159, 34f.), giving a rather vague reference to 'the *Parmenides* and elsewhere'.[2] We have seen Plutarch already finding them in *Timaeus* 37AB. In the *Parmenides* a diligent investigator might uncover the following 'categories', some in the First Hypothesis (137D–142A), being denied of The One, others in the Second (142A–155E) being asserted of it; Quantity (150B), Quality (137D, 144B), Relation (146B), Place (138A, 145E), Time (141A), Position (149A), State (139B), Activity and Passivity (139B). I give them here in the normal Aristotelian order, but we may note that in fact Quantity is dealt with last of all.

What actually appears to us rather more clearly in the *Parmenides* are the five 'greatest genera' of the *Sophist*, but no one before Plotinus seems to have thought of adopting these as alternative, Platonic categories.

Albinus, then, adopts the Aristotelian categories as Platonic, but he also subordinates them to the more general Old Academic categories of Absolute and Relative. We can see him employing these basic

[1] *Anon. Theaet. Comm.* sees the third figure exemplified at *Theaet.* 152BC (66, 11ff.).
[2] *Anon. Theaet. Comm.* finds categories employed at *Theaet.* 152D (68, 1ff.).

categories both earlier, at the beginning of ch. 5, in the definition of Substance and Accident, and later in ch. 9, where the Ideas and the Cosmos are distinguished as Absolute and Relative (163, 37).

The *Cratylus* is claimed, of course, as the basic text on etymology (159, 35ff.), having as its doctrine that words are formed by convention (*thesis*), but a convention which is in accordance with Nature (*physis*). Since the Stoics substantially adopted Plato's theory of language, there is no occasion to postulate 'eclecticism' here. We may note, however, that the very term *etymologia*, with its adjective *etymologikos*, is post-Platonic, and occurs first, to our knowledge, in Stoic sources.

(d) Physics or Theoretic

As we have seen, Albinus divides the subject of Theoretic into three, Theology, Physics and Mathematics. We will take each in turn, in the order which he observes, which happens to be the reverse one.

(*i*) *Mathematics.* Mathematics is presented in ch. 7 in terms borrowed from *Rep.* VII (525Bff.) as an activity which trains and sharpens the mental faculties for the perception of intelligible reality. Its divisions, as laid down in the *Republic*, are arithmetic, geometry, stereometry and astronomy. Music does the same for the faculty of hearing as astronomy, properly pursued, does for the faculty of sight, that is, it leads the mind through the exercise of that faculty to a knowledge of the intelligible. There is in all this no element that is faintly original to Albinus or even to Middle Platonism.

(*ii*) *First principles.* From this we pass to the consideration of first principles (*archai*), beginning in ch. 8 with Matter. Albinus simply gives a summary of the doctrine of *Timaeus* 49Aff., in which there is nothing non-Platonic except the actual word *hylê*, which Plato notoriously never uses to mean 'matter' in the dialogues, though his immediate successors certainly did. Only one formulation occurs which is Aristotelian rather than Platonic: Matter is described as 'not body, . . . but potential (*dynamei*) body' (cf. below, p. 314).

In the next chapter we pass to the 'paradeigmatic' first principle, the Ideas. Here Albinus' evidence is important, although once again in no way original. His definition of an Idea runs as follows:

The Idea is, considered in relation to God, his thought (*noêsis*); in relation to us, the prime object of intellection (*prôton noêton*); in relation to

Matter, measure; in relation to the sensible cosmos, the model; in relation to itself, substance.

We may note the unhesitating description of the Ideas as thoughts of God, who is himself, of course, a mind. The Ideas are therefore presumably not 'outside' this mind.

Albinus continues with the definition of an Idea: 'an eternal paradigm of things natural (*ta kata physin*)'. This is simply the definition of Xenocrates (Fr. 30 Heinze), and is basic Middle Platonic doctrine. By this formula are definitely excluded such entities as artificial objects, perversions of natural states (such as diseases), individuals (Socrates, Plato), relational concepts (largeness, smallness), and even 'things of no account', such as dirt and straw—many of which, as we know, occur as candidates for the status of Idea in the Dialogues. There has been a rigorous cleaning up and clarification of the concept, a process which fairly certainly began in the Academy under Plato himself, and resulted in the various solutions put forth by Speusippus and Xenocrates (above, pp. 17, 28–9). It is on the subject of the Ideas, which comes up again in ch. 12, as I have pointed out, that we have the clearest evidence of the essential unoriginality of Albinus' handbook, and of his dependence upon Arius Didymus.

Following on his definition of the Ideas, Albinus gives a series of syllogistic proofs of the necessity for their existence (163, 28ff.). There are four of these, and they are all couched in the form of Stoic hypotheticals. It seems to me worth while to give them in full as examples of Middle Platonic argumentation:

(1) Whether God is Mind, or a being with mind (*noeron*), in either case he must have thoughts (*noēmata*), and these must be eternal and unchanging; if this is so, the Ideas exist.

(2) If Matter is essentially unmeasured (*ametros*) according to its own nature, it must receive measure from something superior to it, something immaterial; but the former, therefore the latter.

(3) If the cosmos did not come to be what it is by chance, it has come to be not only out of something, but also by the agency of something, and not only this, but also on the model of something; and that on the model of which it has come to be can be none other than the Idea; thence it would follow that the Ideas exist.

(4) If Knowledge is different from True Opinion (*doxa*), then the object of knowledge must also be different from the object of opinion; if this is the case, then there are intelligible entities distinct from the opinable; from that

it would follow that there are also primary intelligibles, even as there are primary sense-objects; if this is the case, then Ideas exist. But in fact Knowledge does differ from Opinion; so that Ideas exist.

These four arguments we may term respectively (1) the argument from the nature of God, (2) the argument from the nature of Matter, (3) the argument from the nature of the Cosmos, (4) the argument from the difference between Knowledge and Opinion. Among other interesting features, we may note, in Argument (3), the use of the prepositional terms 'that from which', 'that by which', and 'that in reference to which', which we saw to be established in Alexandrian Platonism before Philo's time.

In ch. 10, perhaps the best-known section of the whole work,[1] we come to the third *arché*, namely God himself. Here we have three entities set out in ascending order of importance, Soul, Mind, and the Primal God, in a way which suggests a hierarchy of Being.

The chapter begins with yet another hypothetical syllogism to prove that intelligibles are distinct from sensibles, which seems only to be a proof of the existence of primary intelligibles, and may in fact have come adrift from the end of the previous chapter. It is followed by the statement that man, being laden with sense-organs, cannot behold the intelligible purely even if he wants to, but tends inevitably to attach material attributes to it, whereas the gods have no such problem. This again more properly concerns the discussion of the Ideas.

The text then continues:

Since Mind is better than Soul, and Mind in activity (*kat' energeian*), intelligising all things simultaneously and eternally, is better than mind in potentiality (*dynamei*), and nobler than this is the cause of this and whatever might exist superior to these, this would be the Primal God, which is the cause of the eternal activity of the mind of the whole heaven (i.e. of the cosmos). The former, being motionless itself, directs its activity towards this latter, even as the sun towards vision, when someone looks at it, and as an object of desire sets desire in motion, while remaining itself motionless; even thus will this Mind move the mind of the whole heaven.

But since the first Mind is the noblest of things, the object of its thought must also be noblest, and nothing is nobler than it is itself; so therefore it would have to contemplate eternally itself and its own thoughts, and this activity it has is Idea.

---

[1] The chapter is translated, with useful comments, by A. J. Festugière, *Rév. d'H.T.* IV, pp. 95–102.

It is clear from this that, although Albinus postulates an entity, the Primal God, above the (demiurgic) mind of the world, this Primal God is nevertheless a mind, although a mind at rest as opposed to a mind in activity. It is in fact the Aristotelian Prime Mover of *Metaphysics* XII. This description of God is to be seen neither as original to Albinus nor as, properly speaking, eclectic. As far as Albinus is concerned, Aristotle is simply in this case giving a true account of Platonic doctrine. As to the relationship between the Mind and the Soul of the world, that will be discussed below.

Albinus goes on, in a way befitting a basic handbook, to give a bald list of epithets applicable to the Supreme God (164, 28ff.). Most of them are obvious enough, but there are some interesting ones. First of all, God is eternal and indescribable (*arrhêtos*); then we find three epithets ending in *-telês*—*autotelês, aeitelês, pantelês*—to each of which Albinus appends an explanatory gloss, 'wanting nothing', 'eternally perfect', 'entirely perfect'. Such a string of rhyming epithets is more than scholastic, it is positively hymnal—the sort of litany one would expect to find at the end of an Hermetic tractate. From the way in which Albinus presents these terms, it is plain that he has not invented them himself. They are part of the tradition on which he is drawing. Unfortunately we do not find these three terms united in any surviving text, and indeed one, *aeitelês*, is found nowhere else at all. I can only testify that to me they have, if anything, a Neopythagorean ring. *Autotelês*, at least, is a Neopythagorean epithet of the Monad (Nicomachus, *ap. Theol. Ar.* p. 3, 18 De Falco).

These adjectival epithets are followed by five substantival ones: Divinity (*theiotês*), Substantiality (*ousiotês*), Truth, Symmetry, Good. The first two go together, and are thoroughly peculiar. It is not possible to parallel the use of either of these abstract nouns, as used in this sense (which I take to be 'form' or 'principle' of God and Substance), in normal Greek usage. *Theiotês* is used in the Septuagint and by St. Paul, but a text which presents particularly interesting analogies is the twelfth tractate of the Hermetic Corpus, in sect. 1 of which, which concerns Nous, both of these terms are used.

Albinus next gives explanations of a series of four terms, only two of which (Good and Truth) in fact occur in his initial list. Of particular interest is his explanation of the term 'Father':

[God] is Father by reason of the fact that he is cause of all things and orders the heavenly Mind and the Soul of the World in accordance with himself and with his thoughts; for by his own will (*boulêsis*) he has filled al things with himself, rousing up the Soul of the World and turning it towards himself, *as being the cause of its Mind*. And this latter, being set in order by the Father [or, 'its father'] itself sets in order the whole of Nature within this world.

It will be observed here that the cosmic Mind is referred to in this passage as the mind of the World Soul. Now J. H. Loenen, in an article in *Mnemosyne*,[1] has maintained strongly that Albinus does not envisage a cosmic Mind as an entity distinct from the World Soul. Loenen says much that is useful in this article, but I think that here he is obscuring the situation. There are, surely, two distinct entities, but they are not to be distinguished simply as Mind and Soul. What I think we have here is what we saw distinctly in Atticus' metaphysical scheme, on the one hand an entity which combines the Demiurge of the *Timaeus*, the Logos (a term not used by Albinus, in fact), and the rational World Soul, or rather the World Soul in its rational aspect; and on the other hand the irrational World Soul or the World Soul in its irrational or unorganized aspect. This latter is the entity which requires awakening and ordering. That these two entities are not truly distinct in Albinus' metaphysics I would grant. They are not Plotinian hypostases so much as two aspects of what is essentially one entity, the World Soul, but Albinus does treat them for most purposes as distinct, and only this phrase 'the cause of its mind' alerts us to the true situation.[2]

Albinus has said earlier in the chapter (164, 31ff.) that all these epithets of God are not to be thought of as *defining* him, but simply as ways of naming him. He now (165, 5ff.) launches into a sequence of three methods of 'describing' God, all of which were obviously long established in the school tradition. The first is that of Negation, or 'removal of attributes' (*kat' aphairesin*). This he illustrates from the First Hypothesis of the *Parmenides*, and the passage is a classic example

[1] 'Albinus' Metaphysics: An Attempt at Rehabilitation', *Mnemosyne* ser. IV, vol. 9 (1956), pp. 296–319, and vol. 10 (1957), pp. 35–56.
[2] We may note also in the present passage the mention of God's will. This was to become an important concept in later Christian Platonism (Clement, Fr. 7, p. 214, 11ff. Koetschau; Origen, *Princ.* II, 9, 1), so it is interesting to get at least a suggestion of it here. We get a similar suggestion at Pseudo-Plutarch *De Fato* 573B ('the will or intellection (*noêsis*) or both' (*sc.* of the Father of All)), where *boulêsis* and *noêsis* are taken as more or less equivalent. The Will of God is a more definite entity in Calcidius *In Tim.* c. 176, but it is still equated with his *nous* and with *pronoia*. God's *boulêsis* is actually mentioned by Plato at *Laws* XII 967A, so the concept is not entirely unPlatonic.

of what was later termed the *via negationis*. The second is that of Analogy (*kat' analogian*, or *via analogiae*), for which he takes as an example the Sun Simile in *Republic* VI. The third is that of *Anagôgê* ('leading upwards', *via eminentiae*); the example given of this is Diotima's famous speech in the *Symposium*.

Having given these three methods, Albinus returns to his syllogistic proofs of God's attributes, or lack of them. He is shown to be partless, changeless, and then bodiless, and on this topic the chapter ends. It is certainly a jumble, but not an entirely incoherent one, and it contains within it various pieces of doctrine which afford us most useful glimpses of Middle Platonic scholastic theology, though to whom precisely the various formulae should be credited is quite uncertain.[1] We can see, at least, that Albinus is not as innocent of mystical theology as he is often portrayed as being. His apparent dryness and sobriety stem simply from the fact that he is engaged in writing a basic handbook.

The section on first principles ends with a short chapter (11) proving, by a series of syllogisms, that qualities (*poiotêtes*) are immaterial. Since no Platonist after Antiochus would have disputed this, this might seem superfluous to establish, but it serves as a sort of bridge-passage to the discussion of the material world in the succeeding chapters. A strong contrast is made between the characteristics of the immaterial and the material, in the process of which it becomes clear that *poiotês* (quality) is being connected with *poiein*, 'to make, to create' (166, 25ff.): 'If the qualities are incorporeal, then that which creates them must be incorporeal. Further, the creative elements (*ta poiounta*) would be none other than the incorporeal'. This is an etymological connexion which we have observed already operating in Antiochus (*ap.* Cic. *Acad. Post.* 27ff.; above, p. 83), who had in turn picked it up from the Stoics. The *poiotêtes* are thus *logoi spermatikoi*, or forms immanent in matter.

(*iii*) *The physical world*. We turn now, from chapters 12 to 22, to the subject-matter of physics proper, for which Albinus' source is the *Timaeus*, or rather, perhaps, a previous epitome based on the *Timaeus*. As we have seen, at least the beginning of ch. 12 is lifted, with minimal changes, from Arius Didymus, and a reasonable presumption is thereby

[1] The doctrine of God's changelessness, at least, is laid down in *Rep.* II 381BC but the particular form of the argument used here seems to go back rather to Aristotle's lost essay *On Philosophy* (Fr. 16 Walzer-Ross).

created that Arius' handbook is the basis for this whole section, if not for the whole work.

I will merely select points of interest or possible originality from what is in general a bald survey of Plato's doctrine. First, we have in ch. 13 (p. 168, 33ff.), in connexion with the description of the basic geometrical figures in *Tim.* 54Bff., a detailed treatment of the fifth figure, the dodecahedron, which is merely alluded to by Plato ('And seeing that there still remained one other compound figure, the fifth, God used it up for the Universe in his decoration thereof', 55C). Albinus connects the dodecahedron with the twelve signs of the zodiac, the 360 subdivisions of the zodiacal circle corresponding to the 360 triangles in the dodecahedron. We cannot say who first propounded this scholastic elaboration on Plato, but a likely candidate is that same Theodorus of Soli who was reported by Plutarch as discussing the number of worlds (above, p. 225).

In connexion with the dodecahedron arises the question as to whether Albinus accepted the aether as a fifth element. In ch. 13 he is following the *Timaeus* closely, and makes explicit mention of only the Platonic four elements, but since he interprets Plato's vague phrase 'the universe' in *Tim.* 55C as meaning 'the heavens', it seems likely that he did in fact postulate a fifth element. This impression is confirmed by ch. 15, where, in his discussion of daemons, he mentions them as inhabiting all the elements except earth—*aithêr*, fire, air and water. At the end of the chapter, admittedly, he confuses things somewhat by referring to aether as the outermost element, 'divided into the sphere of the fixed stars and that of the planets', to which he adds: 'After which (*sc.* two spheres) comes that of Air, and in the middle (of the universe) Earth with its own wet element.' In a thoroughgoing five-element universe there should be a sphere of Fire between Aether and Air, in and around the Moon. Perhaps after all Albinus only means by 'aether' pure fire, in the Stoic manner. Certainly this is what Apuleius meant by the word, as we shall see presently (below, p. 315).

Another question on which Albinus might seem to vacillate, but in fact does not, is as to whether the world was created in Time. When he is following the *Timaeus* closely, in chs. 12 and 13, he gives the impression—as does Plato, after all—that the Demiurge fashioned the world out of chaos, but in ch. 14 he is careful to set matters straight (169, 26ff.):

When he [Plato] says the world is 'created', we must not understand this to mean that there was ever a time when there was no world; what it means is that it is constantly in a state of coming-to-be, and reveals a cause of its existence more sovereign than itself.

In fact, meanings (3) and (4) of *genêtos* as set out by Taurus (above, p. 243). He follows this, however, with a description of God's ordering of the World Soul which seems to imply a period when the World Soul was dormant. I have alluded to this passage previously, in connexion with Plutarch's doctrine of the periodically slumbering World Soul (above, p. 206).

The Soul of the World, which exists eternally, God does not create, but merely brings into order (*katakosmei*); he could be said to create it only in this sense, that he rouses and turns towards himself its Mind and itself from, as it were, a sort of trancelike sleep (*karos*), that it may look upon the objects of his intellection and so receive to itself the Forms and shapes, in its striving towards his thoughts.

He has said essentially this already in ch. 10, but the sleep of the soul is more explicitly stated here, and the interesting word *karos* is used, which suggests a mythic dimension to this doctrine, dredged up from somewhere in the underworld of Middle Platonism.[1]

The rest of ch. 14 is taken up with the heavens, and here there is little that is not present in *Timaeus* 36E–40A. We find, however, the formal definition of Time as 'the extension (*diastêma*) of the motion of the cosmos' (170, 21), and a parallel definition of Eternity as 'the measure of the stability of the eternal (i.e. intelligible) cosmos', which latter definition hardly makes much sense. The names of the last three planets, Saturn, Jupiter and Mars, which are passed over in the *Timaeus*, are added here for the sake of completeness. All these Albinus declares to be 'intelligent beings and gods and spherical in shape', entirely in accordance with the doctrine of the *Timaeus*.

(*iv*) *Daemons*. Following on his exposition of the planetary gods, Albinus turns to deal with daemons. His account seems to be the result of a misunderstanding of *Timaeus* 40A in the light of *Epinomis* 984Dff. In the *Timaeus* Plato only talks of the heavenly beings as gods; by those of the air and water he simply means birds and fish. But the *Epinomis* postulates daemons in all these elements. Since, however, the *Epinomis* is not by Plato, but rather emanates from the Old Academy, it follows that a systematic doctrine of daemons was only

[1] The word is used also by Maximus of Tyre (*Or.* x 1), with reference to the 'slumber' of the soul in the body.

worked out in the Old Academy from Xenocrates on. Here, at any rate, was an area in which later Platonic scholasticism could develop on its own, though building on the *Epinomis*, and such passages as *Phaedo* 107Dff., *Politicus* 271D, *Rep.* 617E, *Cratylus* 397Dff., and, last but not least, *Symp.* 202E. Albinus' account is as follows:

There are also other *daimones* (*sc.* than the planetary gods just mentioned) whom one might also call 'created' (*gennētoi, Tim.* 40D) gods, throughout each of the elements, in aether and fire and air and water, in order that no part of the cosmos should be devoid of soul nor of a living being superior to mortal nature; and to these are made subject all things beneath the Moon and upon the earth.

There now follows a sentence which has been taken as mindless vacillation on the part of Albinus as to whether or not the world had a beginning in Time, but which is in fact simply a summary of the Demiurge's speech to the Young Gods at *Tim.* 41Aff.: 'God is the creator of the Universe and of the gods and daemons, which Universe has no dissolution, in accordance with his will.' This need not imply temporal creation, in view of the explanation offered by Albinus in the preceding chapter.

Daemons, he says, have charge of all types of divination, both natural and 'artificial', that is, that in which human art is involved. That oracles are administered by daemons rather than by the gods themselves is normal Middle Platonic doctrine, as we have seen from Plutarch, particularly in his essay *On the Obsolescence of Oracles*. This was also the view of Posidonius (Cicero, *De Div.* 1 64), so that he could be seen as an influence here. The origins of this doctrine may be perceived in *Epinomis* 985C, where daemons are said to communicate with us in dreams, and through oracles and prophecies.

That daemons, not birds, are the proper inhabitants of air is, as we have seen (Philo *Gig.* 6–9, above, p. 173), a common Middle Platonic argument for the existence of daemons. Air, it is argued, which is the means for the preservation of life to everything else, cannot itself be devoid of living things of its own. Birds are properly earthy, so that we must postulate truly aerial beings, and these are daemons.

(*v*) *The sublunar world.* The Young Gods of the *Timaeus* are thus equated by Albinus not so much with the planetary gods as with daemons. To these is entrusted the work assigned by the Demiurge to the Young Gods in *Tim.* 41Dff., that is, the fashioning of all the lower forms of existence, and the insertion of souls into those which have souls. This is the subject of Albinus' ch. 16, which follows the above-mentioned section of the *Timaeus* closely.

The question arises as to what relation these agents of God have to the World Soul, or to its *nous*. Is there an incoherence here in Albinus' thought? In Apuleius, after all, we will see, as we saw in the case of Atticus, that the World Soul has taken over the functions of creation with respect to the physical world. Albinus' incoherence may be simply the result of his following the text of the *Timaeus* too closely. I would suggest that the active god of ch. 16 is identical with the Mind of the World or rational World Soul of ch. 10, and that the daemons are in the service of this World Soul. But the working of ch. 16 follows the *Timaeus* so faithfully that it is hard indeed to be sure how everything fits together.

In ch. 17 we may note a detail which is significant as being an example of how later Platonists systematically incorporated in their exegesis of Plato (particularly of the *Timaeus*) later developments in all branches of philosophy, including the natural sciences. It was not realized in Plato's time—not indeed, until the work of the great Alexandrian doctors Erasistratus and Herophilus—that the brain was the centre of the nervous system, or indeed that there were such things as nerves. But at 173, 6f., we find the sentence: 'They (the Young Gods) established the ruling part of the soul according to rational calculation in the head, where are situated the sources of marrow and of the nerves (*neura*). . . .' Plato mentions the marrow as having its source in the brain (*Tim.* 73D), but specifically denies the presence of *neura*, by which he means simply 'sinews' (75C, 77E). No doubt all this would have received full discussion in a commentary on these parts of the *Timaeus*, such as we know Galen, at least, to have written. Here all we have is one short phrase.

In ch. 18, which is a discussion of sight (taken from *Tim.* 45B–46C) we have, as in the *Timaeus* (46Aff.), a passage on mirrors and the theory of refraction. This does not depart from Plato's doctrine, but formalizes it with the addition of a number of technical terms. One of these is *anaklasis*, 'refraction', a word attested for Aristotle, but not for Plato. It is an obvious enough word to use, but it may nevertheless provide a small clue in the Mystery of the Anonymous Theaetetus Commentator.

There exists a small piece of papyrus (*Oxy. Pap.* XIII 1609) of the second century A.D., containing a fragment of a Platonic commentary. The text is on the subject of mirrors and refraction, uses the term *anaklasis*, and refers to the author's *Commentary on the Timaeus* for a fuller discussion. One of two other places where the text of Plato would justify a disquisition on this subject is *Theaetetus* 193C (the other is *Sophist* 266C, but it is less suitable; anyhow, we know of no ancient commentary on the *Sophist* earlier than Iamblichus). I suggest that this fragment (attributed hopefully by the editor of *Oxy. Pap.* to Eudorus) is in fact a piece of the same *Theaetetus Commentary* of which we already have a large section. The fragment is too small for useful stylistic comparison, but the author does refer to his other works with the same formula as that used by the Theaetetus Commentator, and also to Empedocles' doctrine of 'effluences' (*aporrhoai*), which are mentioned in the *Theaet. Comm.* (70, 48). All this by itself does not amount to a cogent proof of anything—we are dealing, always, with commonplaces—but in conjunction with the other pieces of evidence it is, I think, worth noting.[1]

Chapter 19 deals with the four remaining senses, hearing, smell, taste and touch, simply summarizing *Timaeus* 65C–67C, but in reverse order to Plato. It is notable that Plato actually has no explicit treatment of touch, but regards it as a sensation of the whole body (61Dff.). Later scholasticism simply added a section on touch to complete the list. Since Albinus and Apuleius (*De Plat.* I 14) have more or less identical texts at this point, it is plainly part of the tradition, going back, no doubt, at least to Arius Didymus. Apuleius does, however, as we shall see, make the connexion between the senses and the elements, as Taurus had done, but as Albinus does not do.

(*vi*) *Psychology:* (α) *The nature of the soul.* As one would expect, Albinus combines a formal acceptance of the Platonic tripartite soul with an actual division of the soul into rational and irrational, or 'passionate' (*pathêtikon*), as he terms it (ch. 24, p. 176, 36). In contrast to Plutarch (above, p. 194, n. 1), he seems to take literally the spatial distinction of the parts of the soul as described in the *Timaeus*. Chapter 23 is a description of the fashioning of the mortal parts of the soul by the Young Gods which follows closely *Timaeus* 44DE and especially 69C–72D. In ch. 24 he turns to a defence of the distinction between the rational and irrational parts. Such an argument is directed

---

[1] Apuleius discusses mirrors and refraction at *Apol.* 15–16, giving a brief doxography (Epicurus, Plato, Archytas, Stoics), but not agreeing particularly closely with Albinus. He refers, in fact, to a work of Archimedes on the subject, as if he had read it.

ultimately against the Old Stoa and in particular Chrysippus, who, as we have seen, championed the unity of the soul. In this argument the Platonists were joined by Posidonius. Albinus is simply giving a summary of what by his time must have been the standard Platonist position: contraries cannot exist simultaneously in the same place, and the parts of the soul may often be observed to be at variance with one another. As an example of the spirited element (*thymos*) fighting against the reason, he adduces Medea, giving two lines from Euripides' *Medea* (1078–9); as an example of desire (*epithymia*) fighting against reason, he adduces Laius, giving two lines from Euripides' *Chrysippus* (Fr. 841). Both these references are commonplaces. The *Medea* passage is used by Calcidius, whose commentary on the *Timaeus* is derived from Middle Platonic sources, in ch. 183, where he is discussing the same topic (he also uses *Odyssey* XX 17–18), and the *Chrysippus* passage is used by Plutarch in *Virt. Mor.* 446A, again in support of the same position. Chrysippus himself, indeed, seems to have used both quotations (*SVF* II 473), though quite how he did is not clear, since on the face of it they flatly contradict his theory of the soul.

Proofs of the immortality of the soul take up most of ch. 25. The proofs are taken from the *Phaedo*, along with the 'self-motion' argument from *Phaedrus* 245E. It is interesting to observe, in view of later disputes among the Neoplatonists, that Albinus has no doubt that all the proofs in the *Phaedo*, including the Argument from Opposites and the Argument from Recollection, are full proofs of immortality. His description of the process of recollection (*anamnêsis*) is rather fuller than one finds in Plato, and reflects the centuries of theorizing on the subject that had gone on in the interval, particularly in relation to the Stoic theory of general concepts:

There is no other way in which learning could come about than as a result of the recollection of things that one had known in a previous existence. For if we formed general concepts from a survey of individual objects, (a) how could we make a comprehensive survey of particular objects, seeing that they are infinite; or (b) how could we form such concepts on the basis of only a few? For we would be deceived, as for instance if we concluded that only what breathes is an animal. Further, how would concepts (*ennoiai*) acquire their dominant role (*to archikon*)? We form concepts, then, by means of recollection, stimulated by small sparks (*aithygmata*), on the basis of individual sense-data recollecting things we knew in a previous existence, of which we acquired forgetfulness when we entered the body.

Thus the Platonic theory is asserted over the Stoic. It will be recalled that Antiochus appeared in *De Fin.* v and *Acad. Pr.* to be adopting the Stoic theory without qualification, whereas the author of *Tusculan Disputations* I holds to Platonic *anamnêsis*, and our problem was to try to reconcile the two positions if we wished to claim *TD* I for Antiochus. Here the Stoic doctrine that one can form general concepts from an accumulation of sense-data is forcefully argued against. The use of the Stoic terms *ennoiai* and *aithygmata* in the service of Platonic doctrine is noticeable—though possibly noticeable only to us, not to Albinus.

(β) *The irrational soul and the embodied soul.* That the rational soul is immortal Albinus establishes as Platonic doctrine. But what of irrational souls? This he regards as a disputed question (178, 20–1), but he himself holds them to be mortal, since they have no share in mind. In connexion with this may be mentioned the testimony of Proclus (*In Tim.* III 234, 9ff.) that 'Atticus and Albinus and others like them' permit only the rational soul to be immortal, and consign to destruction all irrational soul and the pneumatic vehicle of the soul. By this Proclus means the irrational part of the human soul, and this is thus a development of what Albinus is saying in the *Didaskalikos*, where he is concerned with the souls of irrational animals.

Whether or not Albinus was familiar with the term 'vehicle' (*ochêma*) for this part of the soul is not certain, but we may at any rate conclude that he felt that all that part of the soul which was subject to passions, or which concerned bodily needs, dissolved at death. Something archetypal *answering to* the spirited and libidinous parts of the soul does survive, however, as we learn from an interesting account of the state of the divine and the disembodied soul, reported just below (178, 32ff.). Partly, perhaps, as a result of the *Phaedrus* myth, in which the souls of the Gods are also pictured as charioteers and pairs (each horse of the pair, however, being of noble birth and good behaviour), Platonists held the theory that in divine souls there must be archetypal equivalents of the spirited and libidinous parts of the human soul. Albinus here gives the details. The divine soul has three aspects, the critical or cognitive (*gnôstikon*), corresponding to our rational part, the appetitive or 'dispositional' (*parastatikon*), corresponding to our spirited, and the 'appropriative' (*oikeiôtikon*), corresponding to our libidinous. This is also the case, he adds, with souls before they have descended into bodies. On their embodiment, they undergo change into the parts which we possess.

The occasion and the reasons for descent into bodies have been discussed by Albinus just above this (ll. 26ff.). The soul enters the body at the moment of the formation of the embryo. This is a contradiction of the Stoic position that the soul enters the body at the moment of birth (*SVF* II 804ff.), and was obviously a matter of active school controversy. He next asserts that the soul passes through many incarnations, both in human and non-human bodies, thus committing himself to the literal interpretation of Plato's remarks about incarnation into animal bodies, an interpretation which was rejected by the Neoplatonists, from Porphyry on.

As regards the reason for the soul's descent, another point of active discussion within Platonism, as we can see from the various views put forth by Taurus and/or his followers (above, p. 245), Albinus has four suggestions to offer:

(1) *The maintaining of a constant number of souls.* This would only explain the continued descent now to fill existing gaps, not an original descent. If the world is eternal, of course, we cannot talk of an original descent, but then neither can we properly talk of the maintaining of a number, since that seems to presuppose the original establishment of a number. The fuller form of this very compressed argument is presumably the same as the first reason offered by Taurus, namely 'the completion of the cosmos, that there may be as many living things in the physical cosmos as there are in the intelligible'.

(2) *The will of the Gods.* Again, this needs amplification, and for that we may turn again to Taurus. We may recall that the second reason given by 'Taurus and his followers' is the will of the Gods 'to make themselves manifest through souls'. We cannot be sure that this is what Albinus meant. He does not tell us. But there must, surely, be a purpose behind the will of the Gods, and this is at least one contemporary explanation of what it was.

(3) *Wantonness (akolasia)*, that is, sinful wilfulness on the part of the soul—a rather Gnostic conception. Here Iamblichus' treatise *On the Soul* is of help. At Stob. I 375, 2ff. Wachs. he gives quite a doxography of reasons for the descent of the soul. As that of the Gnostics he gives 'derangement and deviation', and as that of Albinus, immediately subsequently, 'the erring judgement of a free will', which is an elaboration of the reason given here. This third reason, then, is presumably to be regarded as the one favoured by Albinus himself.

A problem arises as to what work of Albinus' Iamblichus is quoting from. Some have postulated a special treatise on the soul. This is certainly possible, but it is reasonable also to suggest that it is simply the larger work *On the Doctrines of Plato*, of which, it has been suggested above, the *Didaskalikos* is an epitomized version. In that case, Albinus must have made his own views clearer there than he does here.

(4) *Love of the body* (*philosômatia*). This final reason does not sound very different from the previous one. Presumably in this case there is no wilfulness postulated, but rather a natural affinity, or weakness— among some souls, or all?—for embodiment. The next sentence in the text would seem to confirm this: 'Body and soul have a kind of affinity (*oikeiotês*) towards each other, like fire and asphalt.' If we press this simile, it would imply that when soul in the course of its peregrinations in the universe comes into a certain degree of proximity to body, it must spring towards it and ensoul it, and this would happen without any forethought on the part of the soul in question. Embodiment is thus a necessary consequence of the arrangement of the universe, and not a fault to be imputed to soul.

To judge from Iamblichus, then, it was the third of these theories that Albinus favoured. This would give him a more austere view of the human condition than, for instance, Taurus, who adopted one or both of the first two, and brings Albinus closer to a pessimistic, 'Gnostic' view of human life. A significant distinction between philosophers of this age, Platonist and otherwise, lies in their attitude to this world and our involvement in it. Either it is a necessary result of the structure of the universe, and so essentially a good thing (though a state from which we should strive to ascend to higher realms), or it is a disaster, due to some past sin or wilfulness, which must be undone as soon as possible. In either case, freedom from the body is a good thing, but the attitude to the world differs fundamentally. Middle Platonism in general (Taurus, I think, constituting an exception) tended to a dualistic, hostile view of the world; it was left to Plotinus in the next century (when the social and political situation was in fact far worse than it had been in the previous two centuries) to reaffirm the goodness of all creation.

(*vii*) *Fate, Providence and Free Will.* This is a subject that will have to be discussed more fully later on (below, pp. 320ff.), in connexion with Apuleius. It is sufficient here to note that Albinus shows no trace of the very distinctive doctrine on Fate, Providence and Free Will which we find set out in two sister treatises, Pseudo-Plutarch *On Fate* and the essay on Fate preserved by Calcidius in his *Commentary on the Timaeus* (chs. 142–90, *ad Tim.* 41E) (and summarized by Nemesius, *Nat. Hom.* ch. 38), and of which we observe distinct indications in Apuleius. The origin of this doctrine is mysterious, and will require discussion below, but the vague notion that it may be attributed to Gaius is rendered improbable by the fact that his only attested pupil, Albinus, in an admittedly summary account, shows no trace of it. It is not, I think, possible to argue that he knew of it but compressed it out of existence in his summary. It is too distinctive for that. Apuleius, after all, in an equally summary account (*De Plat.* I 12) gives, as I have said, unmistakable signs of following it.

We do, however, have in Albinus the bare bones of a theory, which is probably to be regarded as the basic Middle Platonic theory. It is as follows:

(1) All things are within the sphere of (lit. 'in') Fate, but not all things are fated.

(2) Fate has the status of a law. It does not say, as it were, that such-and-such a person will do this, and that such-and-such another will do that, for that would result in an infinity of possibilities, since the number of people who come into being is infinite, and the things that happen to them are also infinite.

(3) [If all things are fated], then what is in our power (*to eph' hēmin*) will disappear, and therefore praise and blame and everything like this.

(4) [The chain of causality begins] because, if a soul chooses such and such in life, it will then also perform such and such actions, and such and such results will follow for it. The soul is thus autonomous, and it is in its power to act or not, and this is not forced upon it, but what follows upon its action will be brought about in accordance with Fate.

The examples of Paris' Rape of Helen and of Laius' disobedience to Apollo's oracle are then quoted.

There is nothing in this brief chapter of the distinctive doctrines of the *De Fato*, the distinguishing of Fate 'in activity' from Fate 'in substance', and the identification of the latter with 'the soul of the world in all three of its divisions', together with the triadic division of the universe that follows on this, and the bringing in of the three Moirai (Fates) to preside over these divisions. On the other hand all the general principles enunciated above are found also in the *De Fato*. (1) is discussed at 570cff.; (2) is discussed at 569Aff.; (3) the 'praise and blame' argument is not discussed but it is referred to at the end (574D). It is found in Cicero's *De Fato* (17) however and is developed by the Peripatetic Alexander of Aphrodisias in his treatise *On Fate* (ch. 34, p. 206 1ff. Bruns).

Of the four heads of doctrine given here, the second and the fourth, that Fate has the status of a law and that it operates hypothetically, seem most worthy of discussion. This was, as I have said, a basic Middle Platonic principle. Pseudo-Plutarch describes Fate (569D) as having 'the quality of the law of a state, which in the first place promulgates most, if not all, of its commands as consequents of hypotheses (*ex hypotheseôs*), and secondly, so far as it can, embraces all the concerns of the state in the form of universal statements (*katholou*)'.

This comparison is found also in Calcidius (chs. 150 and 179) and in Nemesius (*Nat. Hom.* ch. 38). The point being made is one that is vital for the preservation of the doctrine of free will. Our own powers of decision are to be taken as answering to the basic precepts of the law, or, as in Calcidius' comparison (ch. 15), the primary hypotheses of a science such as geometry. What follows from these is fixed, or 'fated', but the principles are in our power to establish and observe or not. In Nemesius' example (sect. 145), 'It is in our power whether to undertake a sea-voyage; this has the status of an hypothesis (*kath' hypothesin*). Once it is established that we make the voyage, then there follows from this hypothesis that we are either shipwrecked or not.'

The Platonists do not permit us to consider, however, the causes that might have led us to decide to take the voyage. On their argument it must have no external motivation, as if we were to take, for no conscious reason, one of two equally good roads home. But even in this latter case Chrysippus would probe further. *Something* must have induced us to take the left fork rather than the right. Unless one denies absolutely any causation here, one is caught again in the ineluctable chain. The Platonist argument is, then, only another way of declaring dogmatically that the mind is 'self-causative'.

In his summary of the doctrine, Albinus contrives to combine the Myth of the *Republic* (x 617Dff.) with the ordinance of Adrasteia in the *Phaedrus* Myth (248C). The phrase 'If a soul . . .' (*hêtis an psychê . . .*) is the beginning of Adrasteia's statement. This is quoted in full in the *De Fato* (570A). Calcidius (cc. 153–4) adduces the oracles to Laius, and adds the prophecy of Thetis to Achilles. He also quotes *Rep.* 617E. All this, then, is part of the common Platonic inheritance.

The first principle, that all things are 'within' (*en*) Fate, but not all things are 'in accordance with' (*kata*) Fate, is properly explained in the *De Fato*, and constitutes an introduction to the concepts of the possible, the voluntary and chance. Again, the comparison with Law is used (570CD):

For neither is everything included in law 'lawful' or 'in accordance with law'; for law includes treason, desertion, adultery and a good many other things of the sort, none of which one would term 'lawful'; indeed I should not even call an act of valour, the slaying of a tyrant, or the performance of any other right action (*katorthôma*), 'lawful'.

There is a certain amount of linguistic juggling going on here, but yet a valid point is, I think, being made. Treason, for instance, is dealt with by law, it comes within its sphere of activity, but it plainly cannot be described as being 'in accordance with law'. Even thus, it is argued, Chance, for instance, comes within the sphere of Fate, but is not in accordance with it. This is a pretty vacuous comparison, perhaps, but the second part of the argument is rather better. Conspicuous bravery, for example, is not 'in accordance with law', for otherwise lack of it— ordinary performance of duty—would be unlawful, and thus punishable. Yet such bravery concerns matters within the sphere of law, such as performing one's military duty. The voluntary (*to eph' hêmin*) similarly, operates within the sphere of Fate, but it is not 'in accordance with' it. Since the Stoic argument is itself based on ambiguities of language, namely the terminology of causation, it perhaps deserves to be countered with arguments of similar type, but to an impartial observer the Platonist arguments must appear basically unsatisfactory.

At any rate, following what seems to be a traditional Middle Platonic exegetical format, Albinus goes on to give brief definitions of 'the possible', the voluntary or 'what is in our power' (*to eph' hêmin*), and then a discussion of potentiality and actuality. These questions are all discussed, as being 'things contained by Fate' in the *De Fato* (570Eff.), but, again, the discussion of all these topics goes back a very long way, ultimately to Aristotle's treatment of them in the *Nicomachean Ethics* (III 1–3) and the *Physics* (II 4–6), so that there is nothing distinctive here.

Nevertheless, it is at this point of a discussion on Fate that a Platonist, or anyone who is trying to preserve free will, has to put forth his best efforts, so that it is worth considering in some detail how Albinus treats this topic, and comparing with him the rather more scholastic, but not very dissimilar version of the *De Fato*. Albinus' account is as follows:

The potential (*dynamei*) differs from what is termed the 'established' (*kath' hexin*) and the actual. For the potential signifies a capacity in one who has not yet the characteristic (*hexis*) in question; as for instance the child will be said to be potentially a grammarian, a fluteplayer or a carpenter, but will only then be in possession (*hexis*) of one or two of these when he learns or acquires some one of these characteristics (*hexeis*). He will be any of these in actuality, on the other hand, when he can act on the basis of the possession of that characteristic which he has acquired. The possible is neither of these, but, being an indefinite state, is given truth-value by the operation of the voluntary (*to eph' hēmin*) by virtue of its inclination one way or another.

My difficulties in translating *hexis* here will be noted. 'Habit' or 'disposition' will plainly not do; 'achieved state' is more the sense.

The *De Fato*, as I have said, is more scholastic. The possible is first declared to be prior to the contingent (*endechomenon*), which in its turn underlies the voluntary as substratum (*hylē*). Albinus had simply said that the voluntary 'presides over' (lit. 'is mounted upon', *epocheitai*) the possible. The *De Fato* notes that Chance intervenes accidentally in the sphere of the voluntary; Albinus does not mention Chance at all.

The *De Fato* then makes a threefold distinction between potentiality (*dynamis*), 'the potent' (*dynamenon*), i.e. that which is capable of acting, and the possible. The potent agent, as a substance, is logically prior to the potentiality, which in its turn is logically prior to the possible (571A). All this may not solve any substantial philosophical problems, but it shows a methodological advance on what we have of Albinus. It is not just a question, then, of Albinus being extremely abbreviated in his account; even where the distinctive formulations of the *De Fato* could be given in a short phrase he shows absolutely no sign of knowing them.

(e) Ethics

The last part of the work (chs. 27–34) concerns ethical questions, concluding with a chapter on politics. Chapter 27 deals with the good for man; 28, the *telos*; 29, Virtue; 30, the virtues in detail; 31, a discussion of the doctrine that no one does wrong voluntarily; 32, the Passions; 33, Friendship. I will examine these briefly in turn.

(i) *The good for man.* The good for man, says Albinus (179, 34ff.), consists in 'the knowledge and contemplation of the Primal Good, which one might term God and First Intellect'. Every other good is good by participation in this. Albinus, as would any Platonist, equates the Good of *Republic* VI with the Supreme God, who is for him, of course, an Intellect.

The question next arises as to what status is to be accorded to the two lower classes of good, the bodily and the external. Here we find Albinus in agreement, rather unexpectedly, with Alexandrian Platonism (and with Atticus) that Happiness is to be found in goods of the soul alone; that is to say, Albinus upholds the principle of the self-sufficiency of Virtue. He employs (180, 37ff.) the same passage of Plato's *Laws* (1 631BC) as did Eudorus (above, p. 125), with its contrast of 'divine' and 'human' goods. Only the divine goods, that is, the virtues, contribute to Happiness (180, 13ff.). Apart from Virtue, the human or mortal goods are simply 'matter', which may be used for good or evil. No doubt Albinus is indebted for all this to Arius Didymus' handbook, but he was surely enough of an independent mind not to choose this tack unless he wished to. In Ethics, then, Albinus is not 'Aristotelian', in contrast to Plutarch and Taurus. In the passage immediately preceding the quotation from *Laws* I, after a contrast of the souls of the wise with those of the mass of men, based on a contrast of the celestial ride in the *Phaedrus* Myth with the Allegory of the Cave in *Republic* VII, he comes out with both the slogans of the Stoics, and so of the Stoicizing wing of Platonism, 'Only the Noble is Good' and 'Virtue is sufficient for Happiness'.

(*ii*) *The telos.* In the formulation of the *telos*, also, Albinus is at one with Eudorus. The purpose of life is 'likeness to God', *Theaetetus* 176B being appealed to as the prime authority for this. Here Albinus gives the same curious twist to the phrase *kata to dynaton* as did Eudorus (p. 123), seeming to understand it as 'according to that part of us which is capable of this', which is, says Albinus, our intelligence (*phronêsis*). Doubtless again Albinus is following Arius, but again he doubtless knows what he is doing. The alternative, Antiochian *telos* of 'concordance with Nature' is implicitly rejected (it is explicitly rejected, we may note, in the *Theaetetus Commentary*, 7, 14), although Albinus does introduce a significant qualification into the formula of Eudorus. After giving a number of other Platonic references in support of it (*Phaedo* 82A, *Rep.* X 613A), he adds: 'By "God" is obviously meant the God in the heavens (*epouranios*), not, by Zeus, the God above the heavens (*hyperouranios*), who does not possess virtue, but is superior to it.' This has the appearance of a reservation entered by Albinus himself to what he must have regarded as an insufficiently exact traditional formulation. The God in the heavens is necessarily the Demiurge or Mind of the World, Albinus' second God. To bring the Supreme God, as discussed in ch. 10, into a relationship of 'likeness' with Man would be to compromise his transcendence. This difficulty had not, it seems, occurred to the earlier Alexandrians, nor does Apuleius (*De Plat.* II 23) show any trace of such a refinement.

Chapter 28 ends with a formulation of the methods by which likeness to God may be attained which is worth repeating, as it is very much the same as that already presented by Philo (above, p. 152), and is thus plainly basic Middle Platonic doctrine, going back at least to the first century B.C.:

We may attain to the goal of becoming like unto God (a) by being in control of suitable natural faculties (*physis*), (b) by correct habituation and training and discipline (*askêsis*), and (c) most especially by the use of reason and teaching (*didaskalia*) and the transmission of doctrines, so as to transcend for the most part human concerns, and to be always in contact with intelligible realities.

We may note here the triad *physis—askêsis—didaskalia*, symbolized, for Philo, by the three figures of Abraham (*didaskalia*), Isaac (*physis*) and Jacob (*askêsis*), although Philo ranks *askêsis* after *didaskalia* (or *mathêsis*), giving it a slightly different significance ('practice of the doctrines learned', as against 'moral training preparatory to the reception of doctrine', as here. This formulation, as we have seen, was firmly established in scholastic Platonism by Philo's time.

He continues with another image much beloved of Philo, but also favoured by such writers as 'Heraclitus', author of *The Allegories of Homer* (ch. 3) and Theon of Smyrna (*Expos.* pp. 14, 17–16, 2 Hiller) that of the 'mysteries of philosophy'. Philo makes so much of this image that some scholars, such as E. R. Goodenough, have imagined that he was involved in, or acquainted with, Alexandrian mystery cults, but there is no need to suppose this. This is plainly just another Middle Platonic commonplace, into which Philo's rhetorical inventiveness infused a degree of life. Albinus here (182, 7ff.) makes the 'encyclic studies', music, arithmetic, astronomy, geometry (for the soul) and gymnastics (for the body), the preliminaries (*proteleia*) and 'introductory purifications' (*prokatharsia*) which prepare us for initiation into the Greater Mysteries.

(*iii*) *Virtue and the virtues.* In his discussion of virtue and the virtues, Albinus presents, in non-controversial terms, basic Middle Platonic doctrine, which itself draws much in terminology from both Aristotle and the Stoics. In ch. 29 Virtue is defined, in terms borrowed from Aristotle (*Pol.* 1323b13, *EE* 1218b37), as 'a perfect and supremely excellent condition (*diathesis*) of the soul, which renders a man orderly and harmonious and steadfast both in speaking and acting in relation both to himself and to others'. We then have a description of the four cardinal virtues, based on the doctrine of the *Republic*, but reflecting centuries of scholastic definition. (Other stages of this defining process may be observed in the Platonic *Definitions*, 411Dff.). The conclusion drawn from this doctrine, however, is expressed in Stoic terms, that the virtues are mutually interdependent (*antakolouthein*). In their developed, rational form, the virtues all involve 'right reason' (*orthos logos*); one cannot possess, for instance, rational courage without having also rational moderation, and so on. While the technical term *antakolouthia* is Stoic in origin, the doctrine itself, we may note, is to be found already in Plato's *Protagoras*, and Aristotle (*EN* 1144b32ff.)[1]

What one might call 'natural virtues', however, such as appear in children or animals, are not true virtues at all, and do not imply each other. The valour of the average soldier is not generally accompanied by temperance. For these Albinus employs both the Aristotelian term 'good natural endowments' (*euphyiai*, *EN* 1114b12) and the Stoic term 'progressions (towards virtue)' (*prokopai*). In ch. 30 he discusses first these, then the vices, and then the doctrine of Virtue as a mean, depending here again on the *Nicomachean Ethics*. Here we find him uttering what seems to be a common Middle Platonic doctrine, arising from a remark of Aristotle's (*EN* 1107a23), that the virtues, while being 'means', are also in a way 'summits' or 'extremes' (184, 12ff.):[2]

Although the virtues are extremes (*akrotētes*) by reason of being perfect, and are analogous to the straight line, in another way they might be seen as means (*mesotētes*), by reason of the fact that around all or at least most of them are to be seen two vices, one of excess, the other of deficiency.

[1] Though we may note in Diogenes Laertius' summary of Peripatetic doctrine that the virtues *mē antakolouthein* (v 30). This will reflect, presumably, the Peripatetic position in Albinus' day.

[2] cf. Plutarch, *Virt. Mor.* 444Dff., where the point that the virtues are both *akrotētes* and *mesotētes* is also made. Also Hippol. *Ref.* 1 19, 16, the virtues are 'extremes as regards honour, but means as regards their essence'.

He goes on to adopt the doctrine of 'moderation of the passions' (*metriopatheia*) as opposed to their extirpation (*apatheia*), thus setting himself at odds with Stoicism. Lack of passion Albinus regards as being just as much of a vice as excessive passion (184, 18ff.). Here he is in complete agreement with Plutarch and Taurus. What Atticus had to say on this question we do not know, but we may be excused, perhaps, for guessing that he took the Stoic line.

Albinus opposes also the extreme Stoic view that men must either be good or bad absolutely (the vast majority being, of course, bad). One cannot switch immediately from vice to virtue, he says (183, 28ff.), so that in fact most people are in a state (or process) of *prokopê*, '(moral) progress'. This was not a live issue at this time, since the Old Stoic paradox had been rejected long since by such thinkers as Panaetius and Posidonius, but in a basic handbook it is apparently a point still worth making.

Chapter 31 comprises a discussion of the Socratic paradox of the involuntariness of vice:

If someone turns himself towards vice, first of all it will not be as vice that he will be turning to it, but as to some good; and if someone comes to be in a state of vice, it can only be that he is deceived, in that he believes that he can derive from some lesser evil a greater good, and in this way he comes to vice without willing it.

The *Gorgias* is the chief influence here. Albinus is careful also to make the point that, although vice is in the strict intellectualist sense involuntary, yet punishment is in order, since ignorance and passion can be 'rubbed away' by remedial training. Otherwise one would be liable to the same charge as was brought against the Stoics in consequence of their theory of Fate, of having no reason to punish wrongdoing.

The mention of crime due to the passions leads to a chapter on the passions (ch. 32). Here the Old Stoic view that the passions are judgments or opinions, already abandoned long since by Posidonius, but perhaps not by more faithful Stoics, is dismissed, as failing to take account of an irrational part of the soul. This line was taken also by Plutarch in his essay *On Moral Virtue*.

As against the Stoic theory of four basic passions, Albinus asserts that there are really only two, Pleasure and Pain, here relying on various passages of Plato, but in particular *Philebus* 44Bff. To these Fear and Desire are only secondary. There follows a division of passions into 'wild' and 'tame', derived from *Rep.* IX 589B, which must have been popular in the first century B.C., since it turns up, for instance, in Philo *QG* II 57, in connexion with his distinction of the passions proper from the *eupatheiai* (above, p. 151). Albinus does not make use of that Stoic distinction here, but he distinguishes between natural degrees of the passions, and excessive, unmeasured degrees, which comes to the same thing. The natural condition for man, though, he describes, following *Philebus* 33A, as 'the mean between pain and pleasure, being the same as neither of them'. He thus rejects Aristotle's view of pleasure (presented in *EN* x 4–5) as the natural accompaniment of happiness, using, curiously, to describe it, a term, 'supervenient' (*epigennêmatikê*), which for Aristotle would not have been a negative description, but which for the Stoics, from whom the term is here borrowed, was.

After the discussion of Pleasure we find a chapter on Friendship (*philia*). This actually follows Aristotle's order of subjects in the *Nicomachean Ethics* (from the latter half of Book VII to Books VIII–IX), and is indeed thoroughly Aristotelian in influence, though at the same time containing nothing un-Platonic. The discussion of three kinds of love (noble (*asteia*), wicked (*phaulê*) and indifferent (*mesê*)) is based on *Laws* 837B–D, but employs Stoic terminology. Of the noble form of love it is possible to have a *technê*; it has *theorêmata*, to wit, how to recognize the worthy object of love, how to gain it, and how to behave with it.

(*iv*) *Politics.* There is little of interest here, except for a distinction which Albinus makes between the two types of state which Plato describes in his works, the non-hypothetical and the hypothetical. The former comprises all the states and constitutions dealt with in the *Republic*, the latter the ideal states of the *Laws* and of the *Eighth Letter*. The distinction presumably lies in the fact that the various schemes outlined in the *Republic* do not specify any material preconditions for their realization, whereas those of the *Laws* and of *Letter VIII* assume a new foundation in a certain place under certain definite conditions. Who first made this distinction is not clear (it does not figure in Apuleius), but it is hardly original to Albinus.

Chapter 34 ends with a definition of political virtue:

Political virtue is a virtue both theoretical and practical, which seeks to make a city good and happy and concordant and harmonious; it is concerned with giving commands (*epitaktikê*, *Polit.* 267A), and has subordinate to it the arts of war, generalship, and jurisprudence.

Banal certainly, but interesting as echoing closely in format Arius Didymus' equally banal definition of ethical virtue *ap*. Stob. II 145, 11ff.

The treatise ends with a comparison of the true philosopher with the sophist (189, 9ff.), based, naturally, on Plato's *Sophist*, and an apology to the reader for any failings in organization that may have appeared in the course of the work.

We may, I feel, accept Albinus' apology. Despite some annoying incoherences, the *Didaskalikos* is extremely valuable as a sketch of the state of school Platonism, of at least one tradition, in the mid-second century A.D. Even if much of it in fact goes back to Arius Didymus, we may still accept it as the substance of what was current doctrine in Albinus' own time. The *Theaetetus Commentary*, too, dull though it is in large part, gives us a glimpse in its turn of Middle Platonic methods of commentary, as well as contributing a few scholastic formulations to buttress the doctrine of the formal expository work.

(f) Albinus as a teacher

Of Albinus' activity as a teacher we can derive some notion from his brief work, *An Introduction (Eisagôgê) to the Dialogues of Plato*, the only work, indeed, unequivocally attached to his name, since the *Didaskalikos* is attributed unanimously in the manuscript tradition to 'Alkinoos'.

The *Eisagôgê* discusses, in six short chapters (comprising four and a half pages of the modern text), first the nature of the dialogue form in general (chs. 1–2), then the various types of Platonic dialogue (ch. 3), and lastly the order in which the dialogues should be read in order to provide a coherent course in Platonic philosophy. The whole is of a suitable length and format for an introductory lecture of about one hour. The fact that the text begins with an 'excerptor's *hoti*' might lead to the suspicion that this is merely a summary of Albinus by a later hand. Certainly the presentation is bald in the extreme, apart from a quotation at the outset of *Phaedrus* 237D (on the importance of settling clearly what one is talking about before starting to talk about it), but apart from the bothersome initial *hoti* there is nothing to indicate that this is an excerpt. Possibly it is a transcript of a student's notes, as is the case with some of the late Neoplatonist commentaries.

I wish to draw attention in particular here to the information that one can derive from this source as to the course of instruction in Plato practised by Albinus. He divides the dialogues (in ch. 3), along the lines laid down by Thrasyllus (above, p. 184), into dialogues of instruction and dialogues of inquiry. However, he simplifies Thrasyllus' elaborate diaeretic scheme drastically, to the extent that only from his list of the dialogues falling under each category does one realize that he is in fact following Thrasyllus' scheme.

It is worth dwelling awhile on Thrasyllus' arrangement of the dialogues, as it seems to have become the basic arrangement both in the second half of our period and thereafter for many centuries. Thrasyllus works out a Platonic diaeresis, as follows (*DL* III 49):

Of the Platonic dialogues there are two most general types, the dialogue of instruction (*hyphēgētikos*) and the dialogue of inquiry (*ʒētētikos*). The former is further divided into two types, the theoretical and the practical. And of these the theoretical is divided into the physical and the logical, and the practical into the ethical and the political. The dialogue of inquiry also has two main divisions, that which aims at training the mind (*gymnastikos*) and that which aims at victory in debate (*agōnistikos*). Again, the 'gymnastic' has two subdivisions, one which is analogous to midwifery (*maieutikos*), the other which tries out conclusions (*peirastikos*); and the 'agonistic' is also subdivided into a type which raises critical objections (*endeiktikos*), and one which overturns established positions (*anatreptikos*).

Albinus actually rejects Thrasyllus' order of the dialogues as a useful order for teaching. Thrasyllus' arrangement, by tetralogies, beginning with the *Euthyphro, Apology, Crito, Phaedo* (the order still preserved today) seems to follow, he says, a dramatic principle rather than a pedagogical one. Albinus prefers to begin with *Alcibiades I*, since it concerns knowledge of self, the first requisite for a would-be philosopher. Then one should turn to the *Phaedo*, which teaches the nature of the philosophic life, taking as a premise for this the immortality of the soul. Then the *Republic*, since it sketches a complete educational theory, and lastly the *Timaeus*, since it takes us through the whole range of things natural and divine, leading us to a clear view of divinity (*ta theia*). The *Parmenides*, we note, has not yet become anything more than a good exercise in logic. Thrasyllus had listed it among the 'logical' dialogues; Albinus moves it to the category of 'elenctic', a subdivision of the dialogues of inquiry, expressing thus a rather lower view of the amount of positive doctrine it contains. Only in certain Pythagorean circles, it seems, did anyone in our period see any 'higher' meaning in the hypotheses of the *Parmenides*.

In the final section (ch. 6) Albinus adds that before studying positive doctrine one should purge the mind of false notions and exercise the wits, by studying the dialogues of inquiry. What chronological order is to be observed in this is not made entirely clear, but we derive a picture of an articulated course of instruction in Plato which prefigures the elaborate order of Neoplatonic times, as set out, for instance, in the sixth-century *Anonymous Prolegomena to Platonic Philosophy*, ch. 26.

We get a glimpse, then, from this brief Introduction, of the nature of instruction in at least one Platonic school of the period. A course in Platonism is also intended to be a course in moral and spiritual development, beginning with knowledge of self, and ending with a complete course on physics and theology, based on the *Timaeus*. Thus the study of the dialogues of Plato is virtually coextensive with higher education in general.

C. APULEIUS OF MADAURA

I. LIFE AND WORKS

We must now turn to an examination of the other supposed pillar of the 'School of Gaius' the professional rhetorician and amateur philosopher, Lucius Apuleius. Apuleius was born in Madaura in North Africa in about A.D. 123, of respectable provincial family. He received the best rhetorical education available in Carthage, and then, in about A.D. 150, set out for Athens in search of more authentic Greek education, which would, inevitably, include philosophy.

Of Apuleius' period of study in Athens we receive some vague indications from his own statements in the *Florida*, an anthology of passages from his epideictic orations. At the end of *Flor.* 15, which concerns Pythagoras, and is useful evidence, indeed, for the state of the Pythagoras myth in his day, he adds (sect. 26):

Further, our own Plato, deviating no whit, or hardly at all, from this sect, is in large part a Pythagorean; and I myself, in order to be adopted by my masters into the Platonic family, had to learn, in the course of my academic exercises, both to speak up boldly when that was required, and, when silence was required, freely to keep silence.

Here he speaks as if he had a number of professors, and his report of 'Pythagorean' rules of behaviour is reminiscent of what Gellius reports Calvenus Taurus as at least wishing for in his pupils (*NA* 1 9, 8ff.). It is certainly chronologically possible that Apuleius took lectures from Taurus, but he seems to imply here a plurality of masters, and perhaps even an organized group of them. However, it is rash to press a rhetorical flourish like this too hard.

In *Flor.* 20, 4, he speaks of his studies at Athens as including poetry, geometry, music and dialectic, which are all, indeed, part of a philosophical training, but which suggests also that Apuleius was more interested in philosophy as part of general culture—the equipment of the complete rhetor—than in these disciplines as part of philosophy. At *Apol.* 36, he reveals a wide knowledge of the learned literature on fish—Aristotle, Theophrastus, Eudemus and Lycon—and he engaged in ichthyological researches while in Oea, thus incurring the suspicion of indulging in magical practices.

He pursued his studies in Athens for some years, in the course of which time he probably travelled a good deal around Greece—travels which would later serve as background for the *Metamorphoses*—and he certainly visited Samos (*Flor.* 15) and Phrygia (*De Mundo* 17). He was at this time initiated into many Mysteries, particularly those of Isis. That Book XI of the *Metamorphoses* is partly autobiographical is indicated by his admitted devotion to Isis at a later period (*Apol.* 55–6). He may then have returned home briefly, but we next meet him on his way to visit Alexandria, on a voyage which considerable disrupted his life. On stopping for a rest at Oea, near Tripoli in Libya, to visit a fellow-student of his from Athens, he took up with his friend's mother, who was widowed but still lusty, and not without resources, it seems. He married her, and the indignation of her relations was such that they prosecuted him for using magic to seduce her. This event occurred during the proconsulship of Claudius Maximus, which is datable to approximately A.D. 155–8. The prosecution failed (Apuleius' speech in his own defence is a most entertaining document), but he plainly had to leave town, taking his wife with him. Whether he ever reached Alexandria we do not know; he is found next, somewhat later (A.D. 161), back at Carthage, being held already in high honour as rhetorician, poet and Platonic philosopher.

We have no indication as to how long he lived after this. The fact that he uses in the *De Mundo*, chs. 13–14, a passage giving an account of the winds by Favorinus of Arles, a noted sophist of the previous generation, which is also relayed to us by Aulus Gellius (*NA* II 22) does not, unfortunately, help us very much with our chronology, although it does indicate that Apuleius knew of Gellius' work. Whether or not the traditional date (A.D. 169) for the publication of the *Attic*

Nights is correct, it is plain from Gellius' own words in his preface that he published the collection late in life, but had begun composing it already while studying in Athens. It has been thought that, if the *De Mundo* is genuine at all, it must be a relatively early work of Apuleius', a product of the years contiguous to his period of study in Athens, but the dedication to his son Faustinus would seem to preclude this.[1] It is also plain, from a comparison of Apuleius' and Gellius' accounts of Favorinus, that Apuleius is copying and summarizing Gellius, and not going back independently to Favorinus. Yet neither man mentions the other in any surviving work. They may even have been contemporaries in Athens, though Gellius would be somewhat senior, but, unless Apuleius lurks beneath some of the descriptions of nameless students rebuked by Taurus on various occasions in the *NA*, there is no sign of their acquaintance.

At any rate, Apuleius' use of Gellius in the *De Mundo* does not help us much with the problem of how long he lived, and for our purposes it is of little importance. His value as a philosophical source is dependent on when he was studying in Athens and whom he studied with, and that time we can locate with reasonable probability in the early 150s, a time at which the chief figure in Platonism at Athens was certainly Taurus. Whether or not some pupil of Gaius, or even Gaius himself, was also available at this time, we simply do not know, but there is no suggestion in the *NA* of there being any substantial rival to Taurus in Gellius' day. We must therefore consider with great care whether there is anything in Apuleius' account of Platonism which is incompatible with the (admittedly meagre) information that we have on Taurus, or which links him, more than any Platonist might be linked to any other, with the doctrines set out by Albinus.

Of Apuleius' works we are only concerned here with those that have to do with philosophy. He is most famous, of course, for a long novel, the *Metamorphoses* (Changes of Shape), better known, perhaps, as *The Golden Ass*. In this he is simply elaborating on an existing novel in Greek, by one Lucius of Patras, but his elaborations are of some interest. The story of Cupid and Psyche we will leave aside, but there is a detail at the beginning of the novel that requires comment here. The hero, in relating his ancestry, declares that his mother is of the family

---

[1] He had already, by the time of the delivery of the *Apologia* (c. A.D. 158), written a learned treatise on the species of fish and their habits (*Apol.* 38), which seems to have been largely an adaptation of the works of Aristotle and his pupils, with some observations by himself, so his adaptations of Aristotelian originals began early.

of Sextus of Chaeroneia, who was Plutarch's nephew, a Platonic philosopher in his own right, and a tutor of Marcus Aurelius. Why is Sextus introduced in this way? An obvious suggestion would be that he was one of Apuleius' teachers at Athens, and this is a sort of joking compliment to him. It is a completely isolated reference, of no importance for the rest of the story. The chronology is a little difficult, however. Sextus would have had to be a member of the imperial household already at the end of the 130s to be a tutor to Marcus, who was born in A.D. 121. We would have to suppose that he returned to Athens to teach in about 150 for a while, but there is nothing impossible about this, after all. This seems to me at least a rational explanation of this little bow in his direction by Apuleius, which otherwise appears unmotivated (there is no question, surely, of Apuleius himself being related in this way to Sextus).

To return to Apuleius' works, we have also, among the nonphilosophical ones, his speech in his own defence in the enticement case mentioned above (the *Apologia*), which contains a certain amount of autobiography; and a collection of extracts from his best epideictic orations delivered during his period of glory as a sophist at Carthage (the *Florida*). What concerns us particularly, however, are three works the subject-matter of which is philosophical, (1) an essay *On the Guardian Spirit of Socrates* (*De Deo Socratis*), (2) a basic survey of Platonic philosophy—or at least of Platonic physics and ethics—(*De Platone et eius Dogmate*), and (3) a rather free translation of the Pseudo-Aristotelian treatise *On the Cosmos* (*De Mundo*), in which we have seen Apuleius inserting a passage from Favorinus on winds. What induced him to undertake this translation is not clear; the work may have been read with attention in the Platonic circles in which he studied at Athens.

Of these works, the *De Deo Socratis* is plainly in Apuleius' 'epideictic' style, the style of the *Metamorphoses*, of the *Apologia*, and of the *Florida*, and its authorship has never been doubted; the genuineness of the other two works, however, has been called into question, certain significant stylistic differences being obvious between the *De Plat.* and *De Mundo* on the one hand and the main body of Apuleius' work on the other. It requires no elaborate investigation to discern that the comparatively bald and colourless style of the *De Plat.* differs markedly from the full-blown sophistic elaboration of the *De Deo*; the problem is to decide whether or not they could be by the same writer. The authority who has dealt with the question most thoroughly, the

Swedish scholar Redfors,[1] declines to pronounce the *De Plat.* and *De Mundo* spurious, and I think that he is wise. The style of Apuleius' other writings is not, after all, a natural style, but a most consciously artificial one. It is quite reasonable to suppose that Apuleius, being supremely alive to the overtones of different styles, chose when playing the philosopher seriously to preserve what was after all the normal dry, technical form of the Greek originals which he is certainly following. One would be tempted to declare the *De Plat.* an early work, and postulate a 'development' of Apuleius' style to its fully elaborated level, but Book II of the *De Plat.* opens (as does the *De Mundo*) with an address to his son Faustinus, presumably offspring of his union with Pudentilla (unless he was gravely deceiving that good lady), and if Faustinus is to be of an age to appreciate the contents, this demands a date not much earlier than A.D. 170.

One speaks of the dry, technical style of these works, but even within the *De Plat.* there are distinct variations of stylistic elaboration between Book I, which concerns Physics, a subject in which Apuleius is not vitally interested, and Book II, which concerns Ethics, a subject allowing development of themes dearer to his heart, such as true and false Rhetoric (II 8) or the Perfect Sage (II 20).

A further problem arises as regards another work found in the Apuleian corpus, the treatise *On Interpretation* (given in the mss. the Greek title *Peri Hermeneias*, in imitation, presumably, of Aristotle's treatise of that name, on which it is partially based). This is a brief survey, in fourteen chapters, of what is essentially Aristotelian logic (adopted, of course, as Platonic). The work has been declared by many authorities to be spurious, but on grounds which do not seem compelling. Linguistically it is certainly far from the style of the *Metamorphoses*, etc., but it is not distinguishable in aridity from the *De Platone*, and even starts out in its first chapter with a stylistic flourish worthy of the *Florida*.

It appears, however, to be an independently conceived work, not referring back to the *De Platone*, whereas Apuleius in Book I, ch. 4, declared his intention to treat of all three parts of philosophy in turn, taking logic, or the *pars rationalis*, third, and it is therefore argued that Apuleius never carried out his plan, and this work is an attempt to fill the gap by some later man. This argument has little force. Were this man a forger he would surely have striven to make his work sound like

---

[1] J. Redfors, *Echtheitskritische Untersuchung der apuleischen Schriften De Platone und De Mundo*, Lund 1960.

the missing third book. One would then have to suppose that this work was attached to the works of Apuleius by mistake. The alternative is that Apuleius carried out his original design piecemeal, composing separate works, which never held together more than loosely. Book II of the *De Plat.*, after all, does not refer back to Book I, and opens with a dedication to Faustinus, which Book I lacks. Surely if the work were a coherent whole, any such dedication would be proper at the beginning. Book I actually breaks off in the mss., so that we cannot be sure if there was any explicit reference forward at the end of it, but as it stands there is none. That Apuleius himself is quoted as an example in the *De Int.* is not necessarily the piece of impossibly bad taste that it has been declared to be. Good taste or bad, it is just the sort of touch one would expect of Apuleius.

In short, while certainty is impossible, there seems no serious reason not to regard the *Peri Hermeneias* as a work of Apuleius, and thus as a useful document of Middle Platonic logical theory. What we must always bear in mind is that Apuleius, despite his protestations, is not a philosopher, and his value as evidence is thus dependent upon how well he is relaying to us his source or sources.

2. PHILOSOPHY

What I propose to do here is to go through the *De Platone*, with a digression into the *De Deo Socratis* on the subject of daemons, considering at each point what relation the doctrine therein contained may have to what we otherwise know of contemporary Platonism, paying particularly close attention to the points both of contact and contrast with the parallel treatise of Albinus, since the chief purpose of this close comparison will be to test the validity of the long-held opinion that the two documents stem from a common immediate source, that source being, of course, the teaching of the Platonist Gaius.

The *De Plat.* begins with four chapters on the life of Plato, which are of no interest from a philosophical standpoint, but constitute valuable evidence for the state of the Plato myth in Apuleius' time. We may note, however, the insistence upon Plato's dependence on Pythagoras (ch. 3).

On the question of the order of the parts of philosophy, Apuleius is not of much help. In ch. 3 we find the three parts of philosophy listed in the order Physics–Logic–Ethics and in ch. 4 Ethics–Physics–Logic, but then Apuleius announces that he will discuss them in order, beginning with Physics and that is what he does. Book I of the *De Plat.* concerns the whole topic of Physics, from first principles all the way to health and disease, mainly depending, as one would expect, on the *Timaeus*; Book II covers the topic of Ethics, including Politics. Book III on Logic never saw the light as such, but the *Peri Hermeneias* fills the gap well enough.

(a) *Physics*

(*i*) *First principles*. Apuleius' exposition begins, then, with the subject which Albinus takes up next after Logic, that of first principles. Like Albinus, he postulates three, God, Matter and the Ideas, but, unlike Albinus, who begins with Matter, he begins (ch. 5) with God.

If we compare his much shorter account with that of Albinus in ch. 10 of the *Didaskalikos*, we find certain features in common, such as epithets of God, but at the same time the absence of many of the distinctive aspects of Albinus' account. God, in Apuleius' version, is, first, incorporeal. This obvious attribute is not given by Albinus in his initial list (164, 28ff.), but near the end of the chapter (166, 1), where it is the conclusion of a syllogism. Apuleius then goes on to describe God as 'one, unmeasurable (*aperimetros*), father and creator of all things (*Tim.* 28c), blessed (*beatus*), conferrer of blessedness (*beatificus*), excellent, lacking nothing (*nihil indigens=aprosdeês*), himself conferring everything'. Of these epithets, only 'good' and 'lacking nothing' answer to anything in *Did.* 10. Albinus calls his Supreme Being the First God, but he does not describe him as 'one' or 'The One'. The word *aperimetros*, which Apuleius gives in Greek, and which he thus seems to present as a technical term, occurs neither in Albinus nor anywhere else; *beatus* presumably translates *makarios*, but *beatificus* has no obvious equivalent in Greek, unless one were to propose *makaristês*. Apuleius appears to have coined the word himself. There is on the other hand in Apuleius no echo of most of the distinctive terms of *Did.* 10, such as the triad of terms ending in *-telês*, or *theiotês* and *ousiotês*. Even allowing for free adaptation by Apuleius of his source, this leaves a good deal that is mutually exclusive in the two treatises.

Apuleius continues his catalogue of epithets; God is 'heavenly (*caelestis=ouranios*), unspeakable, unnameable, invisible, unconquerable'. He ends the list with an inaccurate quotation in Greek of *Timaeus* 28c. None of these epithets except 'unspeakable' (=*arrhêtos*, 164, 29) occurs in Albinus. 'Heavenly' constitutes a particular difficulty. The supreme god of Platonism should be not 'heavenly' (*ouranios*), but supra-heavenly (*hyperouranios*), as indeed Apuleius has him further on (*ultramundanus*, 204 = *hyperkosmios*—a term, again, which is not found in extant Greek before the Neoplatonists). We must presume Apuleius to be using the epithet 'heavenly' loosely here.

There are brief descriptions of the supreme god also at *Apol.* 64, 7 and *De Deo* 3 which do not differ significantly from that given here, except that in the *Apology* passage God is described as *summus animi genitor*, 'supreme creator *of the Intellect*', answering to simple *genitor* in *De Plat.*, which leads Festugière (*Rév.* IV p. 105) plausibly to suggest inserting *animi* before *genitor* here. We may note Apuleius' use here of the passage on the Three Kings from Pseudo-Plat. *Ep.* II 312E.

What we find in this initial comparison is what we shall find all through our comparative study, that Apuleius and Albinus agree no more closely in their accounts than any two Platonists of the period might reasonably be expected to do, provided only that these two Platonists held that the world was not created in Time, and that they inclined in general to Peripateticism. In the discussion of God, there is nothing to indicate that the two authors are proceeding from the same immediate source, and much to suggest that they are not. The whole elaborate exposition undertaken by Albinus, with its developed negative theology, and its clearly articulated hierarchy of Being, is hardly reflected in Apuleius, except in a summary way at sect. 193, where a threefold distinction is made between the First God, Mind and Ideas, and Soul, which implies the placing of the *prôtos theos* above at least some form of *nous*.

We pass next to the subject of Matter, which Albinus had taken first. Apuleius makes all the obvious points, but here again, bearing in mind the inevitable similarities, his account could hardly be more different from that of Albinus. Both authors do indeed describe Matter as formless, quality-less and shapeless, but Albinus begins his description (162, 27) with a list of the Platonic epithets of Matter in *Timaeus* 50cff. 'mould, all-receiver, nurse, mother' and so on, whereas Apuleius begins (191) with the statement that Matter is uncreated and indestructible, a point not made by Albinus at all (though it turns up later in Calcidius' treatise on Matter, *In Tim.* ch. 306). His second point also, that Matter is unlimited (*infinita*), finds no echo in Albinus, though it again turns up in Calcidius (ch. 312). The only distinctive formulation common to both authors is the statement that Matter is 'neither corporeal nor incorporeal, but potentially corporeal' (Apuleius 192, Albinus 163, 6ff.), which does seem to point to some common source; and the source cannot be Arius, since he describes Matter rather as 'not a body, but corporeal in the sense of underlying all the qualities like a mould' (*Dox. Gr.* 448). To this formulation of Arius' has been added the Aristotelian concept of potentiality. But there are a hundred years and more between Arius and our authors during which this could have been done. The formula is found also in Hippolytus' account of Platonic philosophy (*Ref.* I 19, 3 = Diels, *Dox. Gr.* 567, 16), whatever be the source of that, and in Ocellus Lucanus, *De Univ. Nat.* 24, a Peripateticizing Neopythagorean treatise which at least antedates Philo.

In ch. 6 Apuleius turns to the Ideas, on the subject of which he does not match Albinus in elaboration at all, but confines himself to the most basic and obvious doctrine. No mention, above all, of the Ideas as thoughts of God (though there is no reason to think that Apuleius held that they were anything else), and nothing of the scholastic listing of the relations of the Ideas to other entities. They are, of course, simple, eternal and incorporeal. God takes from them the models of all things that are or will be. Only the comparison with impressions in wax is common to Apuleius and Albinus (ch. 12), but that is also found in Arius Didymus (*loc. cit.*).

Apuleius next makes a distinction between the two types of substance, intelligible and sensible, something that Albinus had done in ch. 4 when discussing the theory of knowledge. Apuleius, however, makes no mention of Albinus' distinction between primary and secondary intelligibles and sensibles. This passage corresponds in function to Albinus' ch. 11, which makes the distinction between immaterial and material, and forms a bridge to the discussion of the physical cosmos in chs. 12ff. Here Apuleius lists all the properties commonly applied to each type of substance, basing himself firmly on *Tim.* 37BC and *Phaedo* 65Aff. and 78Bff.   .

He now proceeds, in ch. 7, to the subject for which this distinction of substances was merely an introduction, namely the physical world, linking up here more closely with Albinus' exposition in ch. 12. Both authors now follow closely Plato's account in *Tim.* 52E–56D. Nevertheless, there are even here small but significant differences. Apuleius, like Calcidius (ch. 272), but unlike Albinus, gives Plato's comparison of the elements (*stoicheia*) of the universe to the letters (*stoicheia*) of the alphabet. On the other hand, Apuleius makes no mention at all of the controversial dodecahedron, the fifth geometrical figure of *Tim.* 55C, which Albinus seems inclined to equate with the aether (above, p. 286), but which more correct Platonism characterized simply as 'the universe in general'. Plutarch, as we have seen (p. 202), seems to vacillate between these two alternatives. As for Apuleius, we can see from the *De Deo* 137ff. that he did not accept the aether as a fifth element. He uses the word, but it means for him simply 'the purest type of fire'. He holds to a four-element universe. If in the *De Mundo* (291) we find aether recognized as a fifth element, that is simply because he is reflecting his source.

In ch. 8, Apuleius goes contrary to Albinus in turning back from the description of the elements in *Tim.* 52Eff. to the description of the cosmos as a whole in 31Aff., whereas Albinus (in chs. 12–13) goes forward, preserving Plato's order of topics. At the end of ch. 8, Apuleius reaches the question of the createdness of the world. Like Albinus, he rejects temporal creation, though he admits that Plato appears to proclaim it, but his choice of solution to the problem is significantly different from that of Albinus. Where Albinus chose Taurus' senses (3) and (4) of *genêtos* (above, p. 243), Apuleius chooses sense (1):

And this world he (*sc.* Plato) sometimes declares to be without beginning, but elsewhere to have an origin and to have been created. There is, he says, no beginning nor end to it, because it has always existed; but it appears 'created', *because its substance and nature are constituted from elements which have the characteristic of createdness.* For this reason it is tangible and visible, and in general accessible to the senses. But since God has provided the principle of its creation, for this reason it will always subsist with eternal permanence.

One could take one's pick, it seems, from among the senses of *genêtos,* and Apuleius' masters chose differently from Albinus.

(ii) Psychology: the soul in general; the World Soul. In ch. 9 Apuleius turns to the subject of the soul, and his discussion contains some interesting features. He begins with a description proper to the individual soul, taking his inspiration chiefly from *Phaedrus* 245Aff. The soul is incorporeal, imperishable, is prior to all created things, and therefore rules over them and is their source of motion. He then turns to the World Soul, and we find that in Apuleius this entity has taken on, in addition to the attributes of the World Soul of the *Timaeus,* the role also of the Young Gods in that dialogue:

But that celestial Soul, source of all other souls, Plato declares to be supremely good and wise, and endowed with generative power [if *virtute genetricem* can really mean this][1] and that it serves the will of the creator god and is at his disposal for all that he desires.

Albinus, it will be recalled, places the World Soul at the service of God (pp. 164, 36ff. and 169, 30ff.), but he makes a distinction between the Soul itself and the Soul's Mind, and for him the Soul is in need of rousing and organizing by God, seeming to have no intellectual principle of its own. Apuleius is here combining Mind and Soul to produce an entity much more like the World Soul of Atticus than that of Albinus. Admittedly the ontological relation between Soul and its Mind in Albinus is obscure (see above, p. 284), but they do seem to be distinguished to a greater degree by him than by Apuleius.

This World Soul Apuleius describes as the source (*fons*, Gk. *pêgê*) of all other souls, thus granting to it the role reserved in the *Timaeus* for the Demiurge, that of creator of individual souls. The term *pêgê* can be derived, it is true, from *Phaedrus* 245CD, but there the soul is described only as principle and source of *motion* to all things that are moved. Here we have a development on Plato, present also in Albinus, who when using this *Phaedrus* formulation in his ch. 25 (178, 13ff.), describes what is self-moved as 'principle of all motion and coming-to-be (*genesis*)', a significant addition to the original passage. On the other hand, Albinus also brings in the Young Gods in ch. 15, as obeying in all their actions the orders and example of their father, where they are being identified with daemons. If we are to attempt to reconcile these data, we must suppose the daemons to be subordinate to the World Soul, which is in its turn subordinate to the Father, but this relationship is nowhere stated.

Apuleius now goes on to refer to this soul as a mind, and to allude to its composition out of double and triple ratios, on the basis of *Tim.* 35A–36D. To refer to it thus as a *mens* is peculiar, and certainly emphasizes the fact that Apuleius is thinking of a *rational* World Soul. It is perhaps significant that he does not mention the splitting of the soul-stuff into two circles (*Tim.* 36D), whereas Albinus, in his parallel account (ch. 14) does.

Next, Apuleius returns (sect. 200) to the division that he has just

---

[1] Here *virtute* will have to translate the Greek *dynamei*, which Apuleius has elsewhere (ch. 5, 192) rendered *vi et ratione*, and which he may here be misunderstanding. Otherwise, if we keep the ablative, this must mean 'by its virtue or excellence', but this is hardly the meaning required.

made in ch. 6, 193, between intelligible and opinable (or sense-percep-tible) substance, in such a way as to suggest either absentmindedness or careless splicing of sources. The phraseology differs, but the doctrine is identical, except that the last sentence connects interestingly with a report that Proclus gives of Gaius and Albinus (*In Tim.* I 340, 25ff.)—that is, probably, Albinus quoting Gaius—*à propos Tim.* 29B, that Plato presents his doctrine in accordance with his subject-matter, in two modes, either scientifically (*epistêmonikôs*) or conjecturally (*eikotologikôs*). Apuleius says:

Hence, he says, there are two methods of interpretation; for the visible realm is grasped by fortuitous and impermanent conjecture, while that in-telligible realm has its existence proved by true, eternal and unchanging reason.

This is an interesting point of connexion, but not enough, I think, to bind Apuleius to the 'School of Gaius' with adamantine bonds. Proclus knows this, admittedly, as a distinctive formulation of Gaius, but it is nevertheless a very obvious remark, and no more copyright than, say, Taurus' listing of the meanings of *genêtos*. Indeed, the dis-tinction had been made in the previous century by Thrasyllus (*DL* III 52), and was doubtless not original to him either.

(*iii*) *Daemons*. In ch. 10, Apuleius turns to the subject of Time and its subdivisions, following *Tim.* 37Dff., and agreeing with Albinus, ch. 14. All this central part of the work, as I have said, answers in its order of topics to the *Didaskalikos*, indicating that this order is part of the handbook tradition. In ch. 11, Apuleius runs through the planets, then the elements, and then (204), answering to Albinus' ch. 15, turns to the daemons.

Here Apuleius understands *Timaeus* 40A a little better than Albinus, who seems to have understood Plato to say that there were 'gods' not only in the heavens, but in air and water as well, which he is certainly not saying. Apuleius sees the daemons as being the proper inhabitants of air only.

It is not in this work, however, that Apuleius gives his fullest account of daemons, but rather in the *De Deo Socratis*. There we find all the basic Middle Platonic doctrine on daemons set out in Apuleius' most florid rhetorical style. In ch. 6 of that work we have the doctrine that the world does not tolerate a gap, in this case between Man and God; there must be intermediaries, and these are the daemons. Again (ch. 8), all the other elements have their proper inhabitants—even fire, as Aristotle tells us; it is unreasonable that air alone should be devoid of them. Birds cannot be regarded as the proper inhabitants of air, being in fact earthy. This line of argument we have seen already in Philo (*Gig.* 6ff., above, p. 172). Philo does not there explicitly disqualify birds (he accepts them as inhabitants of air, indeed, in *Plant.* 12), but he makes it clear that he has in mind invisible souls, that is, daemons.

Apuleius next (chs. 9–12) adds a proof that daemons are formed of air (cf. *Epin.* 984C; Varro *ap.* Aug. *CD* VII 6; Philo, *Gig.* 8–9), albeit of the purest quality; otherwise they would rise into the aether! As regards their moral nature, they are subject to passions (ch. 13), can be roused to anger and pity, placated by gifts and prayers, and enraged by abuse. He sums up their nature in the following formula:

Daemons are beings of genus animate, of mind rational, of spirit passionate, of body aery, of duration eternal.[1]

The first three qualities, Apuleius points out, they have in common with ourselves, the fourth is peculiar to them, and the fifth they share with the gods. Of course, the first two qualities they share with the gods also, so that only their being subject to passions makes them akin to us.

Apuleius comes very close to Plutarch (*De Is.* 361B), and thus to Xenocrates (above, p. 32), when he describes the variety of worship in which these beings take pleasure:

Hence we may be confident, from the diverse forms of religious observance and the various types of sacrifice, that there are some among this number of divinities who like to be honoured by night or by day, openly or in secret, and with joyful or gloomy victims, ceremonies or rites, as for instance Egyptian divinities generally enjoy lamentations, while Greek ones usually prefer choral dances, and barbarian ones the noise of cymbals, drums or flutes.

This variety in rites Apuleius traces to the varieties of passion to which daemons are subject, without stating explicitly that any of them are positively evil. Nevertheless, his account here is plainly inspired by the Xenocratean tradition, whether through the intermediacy of Plu-

---

[1] cf. Calcidius *In Tim.* c. 135: 'The definition of a daemon will, then, be as follows: a daemon is a living being, rational, immortal, subject to passions, aetherial, having care for mortals.' The only substantive difference is the epithet 'aetherial', but Calc.'s aether is the aether of the *Epinomis*, not that of Aristotle. Calc. also recognizes daemons in the air.

tarch or another. Xenocrates' purpose was to argue that all the weird variety of religious observances was directed not at the Gods, but at satisfying the variously passionate natures of innumerable daemonic forces, and that is Apuleius' purpose here also.

In his account of the types of daemon, also, Apuleius agrees with Plutarch. He distinguishes three types (chs. 15–16):

(1) *The human soul itself* may be regarded as a daemon. In this connexion Apuleius refers to Xenocrates' etymology of *eudaimōn* (happy) as 'having a good daemon' (Fr. 81 Heinze)—a commonplace, admittedly, by this time, also used by Albinus (ch. 28, 182, 2). The idea of regarding a man's soul as his *daimōn* finds support in Plato *Tim.* 90C, but must be distinguished from the concept of guardian daemons, who come under Apuleius' third category.

(2) *Souls which have left their bodies.* There are two varieties of these, the good and the bad. Those who have graduated from the body with honours, so to speak, are entrusted with the care of definite parts of the earth, and even with individual households. Apuleius identifies these with the *lares*, perhaps in this following Varro, and gives such heroes as Amphiaraus, Mopsus and Osiris as examples.

Those who have died in sin, on the other hand, wander over the world in a sort of exile, causing what havoc they can. They can be used as punishment for wicked men, but should not cause alarm to the good. These he identifies with the *larvae*, or malicious ghosts (sect. 153).

These two types of disembodied soul correspond to those described by Plutarch in *Def. Or.* 416Dff. (Amphiaraus, indeed, is earlier used as an example, 412B.) Plainly there is not much difference in doctrine between Plutarch and whatever authority Apuleius is following, except perhaps on the question of inherently evil, permanently discarnate daemons, which Apuleius does not recognize.

(3) *Daemons who never enter bodies*, who are in fact the most exalted type of daemon (154). As examples Apuleius first mentions Eros (from *Symposium* 202E) and Hypnos (Sleep), who is not mentioned by Plato, but may be brought in here as presiding over dreams, which are one chief means by which the Gods communicate with men. What he is primarily concerned with, however, since it is with these that he proposes to link the daemon of Socrates, are the guardian daemons mentioned by Plato in the myths of the *Phaedo* (107Dff.) and *Republic*

X (617DE, 620DE), who accompany a man through life, know his in-most thoughts and most secret actions, and after death act as his advo-cate (or accuser) before the throne of judgment. The emphasis laid on the intimate knowledge of and care for the individual by his daemon is not found in Plato, but is found in Plutarch (*De Gen.* 593Dff., above, pp. 219f.), and in late Stoic writers, such as Seneca (*Ep.* 41, 2; 110, 1), Epictetus (1 14, 12ff.) and Marcus Aurelius (V 27). The distinction between this daemon and the rational soul or *nous* viewed as daemon is in danger of becoming obscured, but Apuleius definitely makes this guardian daemon a distinct, transcendent entity, while the nous-daemon is immanent in the individual.

We have here, then, in the *De Deo Socratis*, the most complete connected version of Middle Platonic demonology extant, distorted somewhat by Apuleius' highly-wrought epideictic style, but none the less extremely valuable for our purposes.

(*iv*) *Fate, Providence and Free Will.* We may now return to the *De Platone.* Apuleius turns next, in ch. 12, to one of the basic questions of Middle Platonism, that of Fate and Free Will, and here we uncover a fascinating nest of connected documents and their attendant problems. As we shall see directly, Apuleius' account, unlike Albinus', exhibits the distinctive features of the more elaborate account of Fate, Provi-dence and Free Will given by the author of the *De Fato* falsely ascribed to Plutarch, and by Calcidius, and reported more briefly by Nemesius of Emesa in his work *On the Nature of Man.* None of these documents is directly dependent on the others, yet they are so closely akin in terminology as to make it necessary that they derive from a common source. The possibility of this source being Gaius is more or less excluded, as I have said, by the fact that Albinus, his one attested pupil, shows no knowledge of its distinctive features. The indications point rather to Athenian scholasticism of the early second century A.D., but no plausible figure here suggests itself. For instance, there is unfortunately nothing which can connect these developments with Taurus. In Calcidius' case, as I shall argue later (p. 404), there may be the complication of the doctrine's being relayed to him through Numenius, but in that case Numenius was only adapting slightly the theology of his source to agree with his own.

Leaving the origin of this doctrine in obscurity, then, let us ex-amine its features, taking Pseudo-Plutarch (henceforth *PP*) as our foundation, and noting the agreements and divergences of the other documents where necessary. *PP* is simply recounting to his friend (or patron) Piso 'our doctrine on Fate, as clearly and concisely as I can' (568B), reminding him at the same time of 'the hesitation I have about writing'. He then launches into a highly organized summary of scholastic doctrine of which very little, if anything, is original to himself.

He first distinguishes two aspects of Fate (*heimarmenē*), fate as activity (*energeia*) and fate as substance (*ousia*) (568cff., cf. Calc. ch. 143, Nemes. ch. 38). For the former he produces a number of Platonic references (*Phaedrus* 248C, *Timaeus* 41E, *Rep.* x 617D), and derives from these three definitions: (1) 'A divine *logos* untransgressible because of inescapable causality'; (2) 'A law (*nomos*) in accord with the nature of the Universe (*akolouthos tē tou pantos physei*), according to which what comes to be takes place'; and (3) 'A divine law according to which future events are linked to past and present events.' There is much Stoic terminology in these definitions (cf. *SVF* II 917f., 1000), but they are being employed for an anti-Stoic purpose, a constant strategy of our author.

Calcidius (chs. 143–4) gives these same definitions, and Nemesius (*ibid.*) the first one only. Apuleius, however, makes no distinction between activity and substance, and gives two rather different definitions (205): (1) 'A divine *sententia* (translating *logos*?) which preserves the interests of him on whose behalf it assumed such a duty', and (2) 'A divine law, by which are accomplished the inescapable decisions and projects of God'. I take Apuleius' *inevitabiles* to correspond to *anapodrastos* of Definition (1) of *PP*. *Divina lex* is certainly *nomos theios* (*Def.* 3), and *divina sententia* is probably *logos theios* of *Def.* 1, but that is as near as Apuleius comes.

PP next turns to the substance of Fate (568Eff.). This he defines as 'the entire soul of the cosmos, apportioned in three divisions, the fixed portion (*moira*)'—i.e. that of the fixed stars—'the portion considered to wander'—that of the planets—'and the portion below the heavens, around the earth'. The word *moira*, here translated 'portion', may also be personified and used to refer to the three Fates, or Moirai, and it is these which the author now relates to each of his three divisions, Clotho to the highest, Atropos to the middle, and Lachesis to the lowest. The etymological explanation of Lachesis appended to this (*lachein*, 'to receive as one's portion') is interesting as providing some indication of a doctrine in *PP* of emanation within the universe. Lachesis 'receives the heavenly *energeiai* of her sisters, combines them together, and transmits them to the earthly regions under her command'. This triadic division of the cosmos may be traced back with probability to Xenocrates, as we saw in connexion with Plutarch (above, pp. 214f.), but more immediate authorities than that may be sought, and the most obvious one is Plutarch himself. Albinus, on the other hand, makes no use of the concept of a triadic division of the cosmos, so the evidence is against its being a characteristic of Gaius.

Calcidius, in a parallel passage, relates the three Moirai to the three divisions of the cosmos, but he differs from *PP* in associating Atropos with the fixed stars and Clotho with the sphere of the planets. This is a small detail, perhaps, but noteworthy nonetheless; it is not a casual slip, since Calcidius gives etymological reasons for placing Atropos and Clotho where he does. In fact it is Calcidius that is 'correct', agreeing as he does not only with Plato (reverse order, *Rep.* x 617C, 620DE) and Xenocrates (Fr. 5), but with Plutarch, who connects the Moirai with the divisions of the cosmos at *De Gen.* 591B, *De Fac.* 945C, and *QC* 745B. It looks rather as if it is *PP* who is unorthodox here, for whatever reason.

At any rate, after discussing the 'substance, quantity, quality and relations' of substantial fate, PP returns (568F) to the question of fate 'in activity'. He declares his intention of discussing a number of questions 'physical, ethical and logical' in connexion with it. Having discussed what it is (its substance), he now proposes to say what is its quality. This whole method of procedure emphasizes the scholastic nature of the work.

Fate, he says, though encompassing individual events that are infinite, cannot, being divine, be itself infinite. He then quotes *Tim.* 39D, a description of the Great Year, to support a theory of cyclic renewal, a version of the Stoic theory of *apokatastasis*, the periodic return of all things to their original position after cosmic destruction. It is because of its cyclic nature, then, that Fate can be considered finite, but we are committed here to the Stoic theory of an infinite series of worlds, as opposed to one eternal one.

This settles the quality of Fate in general. But what of that fate which presides over the life of the individual? Here the author introduces the doctrine of the hypothetical nature of Fate, and the analogy with the law of a state. We are back now with more traditional Middle Platonic doctrine, since, as we have seen (above, p. 295), Albinus is acquainted with this (Apuleius, on the other hand, makes no reference to it). The point of the comparison with law is that, like a law, Fate primarily prescribes what will happen in general—such-and-such will be the consequences of such-and-such an action—and only prescribes for individual instances incidentally. Its hypothetical nature has the same result. It says only 'If such-and-such is done, then . . .' The object of these formulations, as we have seen, is to leave some scope, within the overall sway of *heimarmenê*, for the free decisions of the individual soul. Fate becomes simply a general tendency for certain consequences to follow certain actions.

Having laid this down, at any rate, the author proceeds to the discussion of what he classifies as the 'relations (*ta pros ti*) of Fate in activity', and begins with what is in fact the most traditional part of his doctrine, the relation of Fate to those things which it 'encloses', but which do not 'conform to' it, to wit, the possible, the contingent, the voluntary, chance, and the spontaneous (570Eff.). All this is reflected, albeit in abbreviated form, in Albinus, ch. 26, as we have seen. It is, once again, not reflected in Apuleius.

Even in this traditional part, however, there is an element which is not only not found in Albinus but also absent from the parallel text of Calcidius (ch. 155). It is, however, found in Nemesius (ch. 34, p. 287 Matthaei), and so must be a distinctive elaboration of this school. This is an elaborate triadic distinction made between the various components of an action, the potent agent (*to dynamenon*), the potentiality or possibility (*dynamis*), and the possible action (*to dynaton*):

Of these three, then, possibility, the potent, and the possible, the potent, in its quality of substance (*ousia*), is prior as substrate to possibility, while possibility is prior in reality to the possible. It is plain, then, even from this statement, what the possible is; it might, however, be roughly defined in two ways: in a looser fashion as 'that whose nature it is to occur in conformity with possibility', while we might describe it more strictly by adding the clause 'when there is nothing outside it interfering with its occurrence.'

It is not clear how this distinction helps to establish the definitions of the possible, and of its subdivisions, the necessary and the contingent, which now follow in both *PP* and Nemesius. This may, indeed, explain why Calcidius (or his source) simply omitted it, as so much superfluous scholastic trumpery. Calcidius, as we shall see, considerably tones down also the doctrine of the three Providences, another elaborate flourish which does not succeed in resolving any substantive problems.

It is this doctrine, which comprises the second part of the discussion of the 'relations' of active Fate, that we must turn to next. It is entirely peculiar to this school, there being no trace of it in Albinus, whereas there are definite, though confused, traces of it in Apuleius. The distinctive feature here is the distinguishing of three Providences, recalling the triadic division of the substance of Fate at the beginning of the work.

Since Providence in general 'encloses' Fate, even as Fate 'encloses' the area of our free will, and yet in some fashion is co-ordinate with it, a system must be worked out which shows some Providence transcending Fate, and some on the same level as it. This doctrine deserves to be examined in some detail. He begins at 572F:

The highest, or primary, Providence is the intellection or will (*noêsis eite kai boulêsis*), beneficent to all things, of the primary God, and in conformity with it all things divine are primordially arranged throughout, each as is best and most excellent.

This will be, in effect, the Middle Platonic *logos*, organizing the intelligible realm and the celestial gods. As his authority for this, *PP* adduces *Timaeus* 29D–30A, the initial description of God's beneficent ordering of the universe. He continues:

Secondary Providence belongs to secondary gods, who move in heaven, and in conformity with it all mortal things come into being in orderly fashion, together with all that is requisite to the survival and preservation of the several genera.

Secondary Providence he sees described at *Tim.* 42DE, the passage which describes that part of creation which the Demiurge delegated to the Young Gods, namely the human soul, 'in order that He might not be chargeable for the future wickedness of which (men) would be severally guilty'. Since the Young Gods are in Middle Platonism generally identified with the planetary gods, this is a description of the planetary influences on souls. Our author declares this Providence to be 'begotten together with Fate' (574B). This, however is more or less meaningless, as he virtually admits a little further on (574C). In fact this secondary Providence would seem to be identical with Fate, and only our author's delight in triadic constructions keeps it separate.

Tertiary Providence is declared to be 'contained in' Fate. It is described as 'the providence and forethought which belongs to the daemons stationed in the terrestrial regions as watchers and overseers of human actions'. This he sees as being described also in *Tim.* 42DE, particularly by the phrase above-quoted. The planetary gods delegate a certain range of activities on earth to daemons. The only example quoted, strangely, is that of Socrates' daemon encouraging him to consort with Theages. The activities of these daemons are contained in Fate in the same way as are Chance and Free Will.

What, one might ask, does this triadic division of Providence and its connexion with Fate achieve? The primary Providence 'includes' Fate; the secondary 'is included together with it'; the tertiary 'is included by it'. I do not see, however, that we have come any nearer to a satisfactory answer to the Stoic challenge, interesting though this elaborate scheme may be in other respects. We are still left with the basic opposition of Fate and Providence, and our author has done no more than state the usual Middle Platonic position that God's Providence is superior to Fate, as is the highest element in the human soul, but that Fate rules all here below, including the lower element of the human soul. Our triadic division of Providence has really got us nowhere. It might be said of *PP*, I fear, that what is good in him is not original, and what is original is very little good.

We must now see how much of this doctrine is reflected in Apuleius. He begins as follows (*De Plat.* I 12):

The primary Providence is that of the supreme and most eminent of all the gods who has not only organised the heavenly gods, whom he has distributed throughout all the parts of the world for its protection and adornment, but has also created for the whole duration of time beings mortal by nature, superior in wisdom to the rest of terrestrial animals, for whom he has established laws, and then handed over to others the duty of organising and watching over their everyday existence.

These gods, then, having received charge of a secondary Providence, observe their duty so competently that everything, including those things which are visible to mortals in the heavens, preserve unaltered the order of their Father's dispensation.

So far so good. Apuleius gives an account of the two higher Providences, relying on the same passages of the *Timaeus* as did *PP*. The tertiary Providence he recognizes also, in fact, though he does not give it this title:

The daemons also, whom we may term *genii* and *lares*, he considers to be ministers of the gods and guardians and interpreters for men, if ever they want anything from the gods.

He adds this sentence almost as if he himself did not understand what relation it has to what precedes it, but it must be plain to us what

scheme he is following. He does not go on to relate these three Providences to Fate, but simply gives a brief summary of those things that
are 'not to be referred to the power of Fate'—i.e. Free Will and Chance.
He gives the impression here of conveying in a rather amateurish
way a doctrine the complexities of which he does not quite follow.
That he is acquainted with a form of the same doctrine as that which
we find developed in *PP*, Calcidius and Nemesius, however, there
can be no doubt.

(*v*) *Soul and body.* Apuleius next (ch. 13) expounds the doctrine of the
tripartite soul, in very much the same terms as Albinus used in chs. 17
and 23 of the *Didaskalikos*, though he makes no mention here of the
construction of the body and of its ensouling by the Young Gods, as
Albinus does at the beginning of ch. 17.

In chs. 14–18 he passes to a discussion of the senses, following now
the order appearing in *Did.* chs. 18–22, and depending very closely, as
does Albinus, on the *Timaeus*. He cannot be said, however, to be
following the same immediate source as Albinus. If we bear in mind
that any Platonist giving a survey of Platonic doctrine would cover
this part of the subject in more or less the same way, basing himself
closely on the *Timaeus*, then we must admit that Apuleius' account
could hardly be more remote than it is from that of Albinus.

A few points in particular may be noted. First, we find in Apuleius,
and not in Albinus, an explicit linking of the five senses to the elements
of the universe (209), sight with fire, hearing with air, taste with water,
touch with earth—and, lastly, smell with 'vapour or smoke'. In this
he follows precisely the scheme of Taurus (above, p. 244). Albinus
does, indeed, allude to the relevant passage of the *Timaeus* (66DE),
when discussing smell in ch. 19, but he does not make the identification
with the elements.

Then there is, at the end of ch. 14 (211), a praise of the philosophical
qualities of sight and hearing, taken from *Tim.* 47A–D. Albinus omits
this in his description of sight in ch. 18. On the other hand, we have
seen Plutarch dwelling on the virtues of sight in *De Sera* 550D (above,
p. 192). The comprehensive encomium of all the organs of sense that
Apuleius goes on to give, however, is not found elsewhere in Platonic
sources, though we can find it among the Stoics (e.g. Balbus in Cic.
ND II 57ff.).

In ch. 15 (214), Apuleius credits the liver with a part in the process
of digestion, something mentioned neither by Albinus nor by Plato

himself. On the other hand, he ignores the role of the liver in divination, which is stressed both by Plato (*Tim.* 72BC) and by Albinus (ch. 23). These are small details, perhaps, but they mount up.

Again, Albinus does not, it seems, care to mention in ch. 17 the organs and process of generation (*Tim.* 77CD, 91BC); Apuleius does so in sect. 215, actually altering Plato's account slightly. Just after this, in discussing the causes of disease (ch. 17, 215–16), he again 'improves on' Plato's account (*Tim.* 82A–86A) by distinguishing, not two, but three classes of substance in the body, to balance the three classes of disease. This further elaboration is derived—no doubt by Apuleius' source rather than by Apuleius himself—from Aristotle *On the Parts of Animals* (II 1, 646a12ff.), where three classes of substance in the body are distinguished. This piece of scholasticism is either unknown to Albinus or ignored by him (ch. 22)—not unreasonably, since it contributes nothing to the actual discussion of the origins of disease, as Plato's third class is not connected with the limbs (Aristotle's tertiary class) but with certain humours (84c). To assist in identifying a source for Apuleius in this, I will simply call to mind two facts about Taurus: first, we know that he rather prided himself on his medical knowledge (cf. *NA* XVII 10, where he sets a country doctor straight on the difference between veins and arteries); and second, we have seen that he took an interest in the scientific works of Aristotle (above, p. 238). We may note further that Apuleius, when delivering his *Apology* some years after his period of study at Athens, is concerned to show off his acquaintance with the scientific works of Aristotle (chs. 36–8), as well as those of his followers Theophrastus, Eudemus and Lycon. Incidentally, in the same work (chs. 49–50), he gives a fuller and clearer account of Plato's theory of the origins of disease, suggesting a more careful reading of the *Timaeus*.

Apuleius agrees with Albinus in ending his discussion of physiology with a renewed statement of the tripartition of the soul (ch. 18). In Apuleius' case, however, this restatement is rather more redundant than in that of Albinus, since he omitted at the beginning—what Albinus included—an account of the construction of the body and the lower soul by the Young Gods, and Apuleius, rather thoughtlessly, gives no indication that he has mentioned the tripartition of the soul before (Albinus, at the beginning of ch. 23, apologizes for seeming to repeat himself). It is very much like what we find in ch. 9 sect. 200, where Apuleius repeats what he had said in sect. 193 about intelligible and sensible natures without giving any indication that he had said this before. This is surely the activity of a man doggedly following a source work, and occasionally getting his lines crossed. This source work has many features in common with that which Albinus is following, but it is a cousin, in my view, rather than a twin brother.

(*b*) *Ethics*

(*i*) *First principles.* Apuleius now passes, in Book II of his work, to the subject of Ethics, covered by Albinus in chs. 27–34. He begins with a definition of the subject-matter of Ethics which, banal though it is, is to be found neither in Plato nor in Albinus: 'Knowledge of the means by which one may attain the happy life.' The influence behind this seems to be rather Aristotle's discussion in *EN* I 7, but it had been ground down into a commonplace long before Apuleius took it up.

He now proceeds to a classification of levels of good, as does Albinus in ch. 27. Goods in a primary sense he declares to be 'the supreme God and that intellect which Plato calls *nous*'. I think that we have to do here not with two metaphysical entities but rather with the supreme God, the Good of *Republic* VI (who may or may not be an intellect) and our own intellect, which cognizes him. Albinus is saying the same thing slightly differently when he speaks of our good lying 'in the knowledge and contemplation of the primal Good'. This involves two entities, a supreme object of knowledge and a faculty capable of entertaining such knowledge. Secondary goods are good only by participation in these.[1] These are, primarily, the four virtues, which Apuleius ranks in order of importance, basing this on the key text *Laws* I 631Bff., which he, like Albinus, is following at this juncture.

We now get, therefore, the distinction of 'divine' and 'human' goods, as we did in Albinus. The divine goods, the virtues, are absolutely good, for those who can attain them; the human goods, bodily excellences and external advantages, are within the grasp of anyone (though they depend on Chance), but are only *good* for those who also possess the virtues. All this doctrine stems from Plato's *Laws* (*loc. cit.* and III 697B), and is in accord with Albinus' account. At the end of ch. 2 (222), however, Apuleius makes an observation that finds no echo in Albinus:

Plato considers that he who is inspired by Nature towards following the Good has an affinity, not to himself alone, but to all men in addition; not to

---

[1] *Per praeceptionem* of the text must surely be emended to *per participationem*, as Moreschini proposes, to agree with Albinus' *metechein*, and with Plato *Phaedo* 100CD.

all to an equal degree, however, but primarily to his [immediate family], then to his nearest relations, and then to all those who are joined to him by friendship or acquaintance.

This is a reassertion of the Stoic principle of *oikeiôsis*, asserted by Antiochus, and rejected implicitly in the *Didaskalikos* (ch. 28)—and explicitly in the *Theaetetus Commentary* (7, 14ff.)—but accepted, we may note, by Taurus (*NA* XII 5, above, p. 241). The passage comes a little strangely into this discussion of the grades of good. It is as if a number of steps in the argument had been omitted. But there it is.

Next, in ch. 3 (222–3), Apuleius lays down the principle that man is born neither good nor evil, but having a nature which may incline either way. Seeds or virtue and of vice are sown in him at his birth, and it is the duty of education to foster the right ones, so that virtue and vice would come to coincide in the individual with pleasure and pain. The latter part of this section is plainly dependent upon *Laws* I 631DE, but in the first part the Budé editor, Beaujeu, claims to see a significant dualistic doctrine, implied in the inclusion of 'seeds' of evil as well as of good in man's initial makeup. Following Boyancé, he adduces the passage of Philo (*QE* I 23, quoted above, ch. III, p. 173) where there is mention of two powers entering every soul at birth, and alludes to Plutarch's dualistic tendencies. But he is surely making too much of this. The powers which Philo is talking about are supreme cosmic forces as well, whereas Apuleius here gives no sign of wishing to say more than that the human animal begins morally neutral, with the capacity to go either way. If Apuleius had serious dualistic tendencies, we would have heard about it in connexion with his cosmology.

He next (sect. 224) propounds the doctrine of the median nature, between the absolutely good and the absolutely bad, as the proper subject of ethical theory and instruction. This agrees with Albinus, ch. 30 (183, 14ff.), and is in fact a description of the *prokoptón*, the ordinary man who is improvable by instruction but who has not yet attained perfect virtue. Since strictly speaking, as we have seen, no one ever did attain this state, we are here talking about the human race in general. Besides median characters, we have a median state between virtue and vice. This, in its developed form, is a Peripatetic rather than a Platonic concept, at least so far as we can see. We have the testimony of Diogenes Laertius (VII 127) that the Peripatetics recognize a state between virtue and vice which they call *prokopê*. The more Platonic term for these median states is *euphyiai* (which is used, along with *prokopai*, by Albinus in ch. 30).

(*ii*) *Virtues and vices.* From this Apuleius goes on to a discussion of vice, in which connexion we find an interesting formulation which corresponds to nothing in Albinus, or indeed anywhere else in precisely this form. It is the Aristotelian doctrine of two vices to every virtue, one of excess, the other of deficiency, applied to the Platonic tripartite soul. The basic doctrine is found in Albinus, ch. 30, but not with this particular scholastic twist. Each of the three parts of the soul, says Apuleius (sect. 226)—or rather its virtue—is beset by its appropriate vice. His scheme is complicated at the outset, however, by his distinguishing of two virtues of the rational soul, practical virtue, or prudence (*phronêsis*), and theoretical virtue, or wisdom (*sophia*)—the distinction being based, of course, like the whole doctrine of the Mean, on Aristotle's doctrine in the *Ethics*. At any rate, *phronêsis*, we find, is confronted by *indocilitas*, which seems to translate *apaideusia*, 'unwillingness to learn'. This, we may note, was a prominent vice for Philo (e.g. *Ebr.* 12; *Fug.* 152; *Quod omn. prob.* 12), but it was also, after all, the state of the prisoners in the Cave of the *Republic* (VII 514A). This has two forms, *imperitia* (presumably translating *apeiria*) and *fatuitas* (probably *chaunotês*, cf. *Theaet.* 175B), this latter term meaning, presumably, 'an empty conceit of knowledge'. These should be two opposed extremes, but Apuleius now connects them with wisdom and prudence respectively. I suspect that here he has imperfectly understood his source. Both practical and theoretical wisdom, on this theory, should have corresponding vices of excess and deficiency. But the root of the problem, perhaps, is that theoretical wisdom should not have been brought into the discussion at all, as not being a mean between two extremes (cf. Plut. *Virt. Mor.* 444C). Albinus correctly omits it in ch. 30.

On the level of the spirited element, *thymos*, we have the vice of *audacia* (*thrasos* or *tolma*), which is divided into irascibility (*orgilotês*) and excessive placidity (*aorgêsia*); and on the level of passion, *epithymia*, we have sensuality (*akolasia*), which is divided into avarice (*aneleutheria*) and prodigality (*asôtia*)—I give in all cases the certain or near-certain Greek equivalents of Apuleius' Latin.

We can see what is being done here. A selection of the vices listed in Book II of Aristotle's *Nicomachean Ethics* is being fitted to the three parts of the Platonic soul. Of all this Albinus shows no knowledge. There is therefore no reason to attribute this to Gaius. The natural conclusion would be that Apuleius picked this up, as he picked up the doctrine on Fate and Providence, in the Athens of the 150s.

On the other hand, the next section (ch. 5), on Virtue, corresponds rather closely to Albinus' ch. 29, beginning with a definition of Virtue, not identical, indeed, but closely comparable: 'Virtue is an excellently and nobly structured condition of mind, which renders him in whom it is solidly implanted harmonious with himself, calm, constant, and in accord, not only in words but also in deeds, with both himself and others.' Immediately after this, however, there are divergences. Instead of going on directly to list the four virtues, Apuleius gives some further characteristics of Virtue as such. Virtue requires that the rational part of the soul is in command of the other two parts; it is uniform (*unimoda*, Gk. *monoeidês*, cf. Hipp. *Ref.* 19, 18) and self-sufficient (*perfecta*, Gk. *teleia*), as what is good by nature needs no external assistance; and it is coherent with itself. Here he is plainly relaying scholastic definitions, but they are different from those reported by Albinus—though, of course, drawing on the same remote doctrinal source. Apuleius does agree with Albinus in recognizing the *antakolouthia* of the virtues. Following on this (sect. 228), he repeats the doctrine of the virtues as means, adding that they are also *summitates* (*akrotêtês*), as do both Albinus, in ch. 30, and Plutarch, in *Virt. Mor.* 444D. This, then, is also basic doctrine.

In ch. 6, he turns, as does Albinus in ch. 30, to the distinction between perfect (*teleiai*) and incomplete (*ateleis*) virtues, and in this connexion produces an application of the triad *physis—ethos—logos* that we do not find elsewhere. Albinus, as we have seen, recognizes the triad, in the form *physis—askêsis—didaskalia*, in connexion with the attaining of the *telos* (ch. 28) but Apuleius uses it to distinguish between imperfect and perfect virtues, as follows:

Of virtues some are perfect, others imperfect. Imperfect are those which spring up in all men by the sole benefaction of nature (*physis*), or which are only transmitted by training (*ethos*), . . . and are learned under the guidance of reason (*logos*); those, then, which result from all these three factors we may term perfect.

I suspect a lacuna after 'training', as the dots indicate. The sentence is not quite coherent as it stands. We expect, I think, a contrast between virtues which result from either of the first two categories, and those, the perfect ones, which result from a combination of the first two with Reason, but none of the editors seem to share my suspicions. At any rate, there is here a clear enough contrast, based upon the distinction of *physis*, *ethos* and *logos*. The basis of this doctrine may be discerned, as we have seen, in the first chapter of Aristotle's *Eudemian Ethics*, and its various elements are to be found in Arius Didymus' account of Peripatetic ethics in Stobaeus (II 118, 5ff.; 131, 15ff.; 136, 16ff.), but not put together in quite this way. Between Arius and Apuleius someone with Peripatetic sympathies and scholastic tendencies has been at work.[1] Albinus knows nothing of this, simply distinguishing between *euphyiai* and *teleiai aretai* in terms of *antakolouthia* and invariability (though he does speak of *phronêsis* instilling *logos* into the two inferior parts of the soul by means of *ethos* and *askêsis*, 183, 36f.).

Apuleius follows this (228–9) by a survey of the four virtues, which is in agreement with Middle Platonic doctrine in general, but not particularly with Albinus. Apuleius persists in distinguishing, even when discussing ethics, between *sophia* and *phronêsis*. Where Albinus in ch. 29 simply gives a definition of *phronêsis*, Apuleius prefixes the traditional definition of *sophia* as 'the knowledge of things divine and human'. His definitions of Courage and Moderation do not answer to those of Albinus, though they come, naturally, to much the same thing; but when it comes to Justice, he leaves Albinus far behind.

Beginning with the basic Platonic account of Justice (cf. *Rep.* IV 433Aff.; 443DE) as 'the cause of each of the three parts accomplishing its function with reason and measure', he goes on to amplify this account variously. Justice, he says, is sometimes termed 'virtue in general' (Ar. *EN* V 3, 1130a9). It is also termed 'faithfulness' (*pistotês*, Plat. *Laws* I 630C—quoting Theognis). This, in so far as it internally benefits its possessor, is termed *benivolentia* (perh. tr. *eunoia*); in its outward aspect, as it concerns itself with the interests of others, it is termed Justice proper. This twofold division of 'general justice' into its internal and external, or absolute and relational, aspects, is a scholastic elaboration on Aristotle which, though inspired by the distinctions made in the *Republic*, is found nowhere else as such.

We pass next to 'particular justice', the fourth in the list of cardinal virtues. This he divides, following the *Euthyphro* (12E), into Justice in relation to the Gods, or Piety, and Justice in relation to Men, or Justice proper. This distinction we have seen made by Philo (above, p. 150), but Albinus pays no attention to it. The passage ends (230) with a description of the practical uses of Justice, leading to a defence of 'proportional equality' in the state—the better should have a greater share, the worse a lesser.

---

[1] The triad in this form appears also in Maximus of Tyre (Or. X 4) and Pseudo-Plutarch, *On the Education of Children* (ch. 4, 2A).

(*iii*) *Rhetoric*. From this he passes, in ch. 8, to a discussion of Rhetoric, a subject close to his heart. Here he exhibits the anxiety of many of the rhetors of the Second Sophistic who wished to be considered philosophers to turn the edge of Plato's attack on rhetoric away from themselves. Apuleius distinguishes two types of Rhetoric, one of which 'contemplates the Good', and is thus subordinated to Philosophy; the other is 'the science of flattery, hunting after semblances, a practice divorced from Reason'. Apuleius here uses a series of phrases from the *Phaedrus* and the *Gorgias*, culminating in a phrase, *alogos tribê*, which combines *Gorg.* 501A with *Phaedr.* 260E. Naturally, it is the nobler form of Rhetoric in which Apuleius is interested. In ch. 9 he shows how essential it is for good government and for teaching the virtues, which he ends the chapter by classifying once again. Albinus pays no attention to Rhetoric, except for a glancing reference in ch. 6.

(*iv*) *Absolute and relative goods*. In ch. 10, Apuleius makes a distinction between goods which we seek for themselves alone, such as Happiness, those which we seek only for the sake of something else, such as medical treatment, and others which we seek both for their own sake and for the sake of something else, such as foresight and the other virtues, which are both pleasing in themselves and lead to Happiness. This is an overlaying of Glaucon's distinguishing of three types of Good in *Rep.* II 357B–D, with Aristotle *EN* I 5, in the true spirit of Middle Platonic scholasticism. It is not, however, to be found in Albinus. Rather more peculiar, and found neither in Albinus nor in Plato, is a parallel triple distinction of classes of evil. There follows a distinction between absolute and relative goods, and absolute and relative evils, the former having its roots in *Laws* I 631BC, the latter being its logical corollary, but found nowhere else in Platonism.

In ch. 11, Apuleius resumes contact with Albinus (ch. 31), on the subject of the autonomy of virtue and the involuntariness of vice. They follow the same line, that no one could choose evil knowing it unreservedly to be evil, but Apuleius expands on this by adducing the parallel of no one wishing to be poor or ill as such, while Albinus is careful to make the point, not made by Apuleius, that although vice is technically involuntary, it should nevertheless be punished, punishment being, as it were, a medical remedy for the soul.

Apuleius then turns, in ch. 12, to a discussion of bodily and external goods, described as 'not good absolutely' (*non simpliciter bona*), picking up what he has already said in ch. 1 and again in ch. 10, in making the distinction between 'divine' and 'human' goods. Albinus does not accompany him in this (ch. 32), but turns instead to a discussion of the passions, not dealt with as such by Apuleius, though he deals with pleasure and pain as being relatively good and evil (238). They both, however, take the median state between pleasure and pain as the ideal, following *Philebus* 33A, although Albinus goes on to give a fuller exegesis of the *Philebus*, while Apuleius turns from this remark to the assertion that Virtue is the only Good.

(*v*) *Friendship and love.* They both then go on to discuss Friendship (*De Plat.* chs. 13–14; *Did.* ch. 33), but here again it is apparent that they are not so much following a common immediate source, as both drawing on the same basic Platonic tradition. Both authors define true friendship as that arising from mutual attraction and goodwill, arising out of similarity of disposition (*êthos*). But Apuleius then distinguishes love between members of a family as being in accordance with nature from love based on pleasure, which does violence to gentle feeling and does not admit of true reciprocity. He suddenly here takes all other love as that of the lover of the body, as condemned in the *Symposium* and *Phaedrus*. Albinus, on the other hand, dismisses parental love, along with political friendship and that existing among fellow club-members (*hetairikê*), as not invariably having the quality of reciprocity. Someone is out of line here, and it is probably Apuleius, to judge from the fact that his line of reasoning is the less coherent of the two. He does seem to be following some scheme, however, since he makes a distinction between friendship based on pleasure (bad) and friendship based on natural relationship (*necessitas*—good).

Both he and Albinus go on then to the distinction of three types of Love, the noble, the base and the median (cf. above, p. 303), and there they agree closely for a brief space, but Apuleius now goes on, perhaps on his own initiative, to contrast the love of the body, as bestial and diseased, with love of the soul, which is divine, leading up to a comparison of the third, median type of love with, in fact, the daemonic nature, since it partakes both of divine rationality and of earthly desire.

(*vi*) *The perfect sage.* What we may think of as the basic handbook would now turn from Ethics proper to Politics, but here Apuleius seems to launch out on his own, on a series of subjects which he could really get his teeth into. He discourses on the various types of evil man (ch. 15), culminating in a picture of the ultimate villain (ch. 16). All of this is based upon Books VIII and IX of the *Republic*, but given special treatment by Apuleius. This is followed by a discussion of punishments, based mainly on the *Gorgias* (chs. 17–18). There follows next a description, first, of the man of medium virtue (the *prokoptōn*) in ch. 19, and then of the Perfect Sage (chs. 20–2). Here Apuleius, carried away, perhaps, by rhetorical enthusiasm for his subject-matter, adopts distinctly Stoic attitudes. The Sage becomes perfect by a *sudden* transition; he comprehends both past and future, and becomes, so to speak, atemporal (*intemporalis*)—presumably by being united with the intelligible realm. He is totally self-sufficient. He is moved by no passion (248, 252). He looks upon death without fear, since—and here Platonism reasserts itself—he knows that the soul of the wise man is immortal, will return to the Gods, and, in reward for the excellence of its earthly life, will attain to the condition of a god (249). Now certainly Chrysippus and other Stoics claimed some immortality for the soul of the wise man, but the emphasis on the pre-existence of the soul and the personal existence of the Gods is Platonic.

In sect. 250 we find the Stoic 'paradox' that only the wise man is rich. In sect. 251 we learn that all wise men are friends of one another; in 252, that the wise man can never be sad. Albinus subscribes, as we have seen, to a number of characteristically Stoic ethical slogans, but there is nothing in the *Didaskalikos* to correspond to this barrage.

The encomium culminates in ch. 23 in a statement of the *telos* for the Sage, which is Likeness to God, which goal he will attain by the exercise of the virtues of Justice, Piety and Wisdom, involving the combining of the theoretical with the practical life. The Supreme God, after all, says Apuleius, does not simply meditate, but brings his desires to completion by the exercise of his providence. Albinus discussed the *telos* in ch. 28, giving the same trio of virtues by which it is to be attained, but the rest of his treatment, though it touches on some of the same motifs, is much more scholastic, including the triad of *physis*, *askêsis* and *didaskalia* (above, p. 300), not mentioned here by Apuleius.

(*vii*) *Politics*. Apuleius ends his work, as does Albinus, with a section on Plato's political theory (chs. 24–8). This is plainly traditional. Right away, however, there is a difference between the two authors. There is no trace in Apuleius of Albinus' scholastic division of Plato's constitutions into 'non-hypothetical' and 'hypothetical'. Instead we get a definition of the State, attributed to Plato, but corresponding to nothing in his works: 'A state is a community formed by a large number of men, in which some are rulers and others subordinate, joined to one another by concord and lending mutual aid and assistance, regulating their respective functions by the same laws, which must, however, be just. And this city, although enclosed within the same walls, will only be one if the minds of those inhabiting it are accustomed to desire and to reject the same things.' This may indeed be a summary of Plato's basic doctrine, but it is the product of later formulation, and contains none of Plato's distinctive innovations.

Apuleius deals first with the *Republic*, then with the *Laws*, which he describes as a more practical version of the ideal state. Then, in ch. 27, he declares that Plato's ideal was the Mixed Constitution, composed of monarchy, oligarchy and democracy, a doctrine going back to Aristotle (*Pol.* II 6), but not to Plato. It is a view, however, which accords well with the ideal of the Principate as conceived by Augustus, and was a comfortable view for a Platonist of the Empire to hold.

The work ends, abruptly, with a survey of four types of bad citizen, repeating the contents of ch. 15. Again, Apuleius seems to be imperfectly co-ordinating his sources. There being no formal ending to the work, we are at liberty to assume that it is unfinished, perhaps intended to be completed by a section on Logic.

(c) Logic

We may at this point briefly survey the contents of the work *On Logical Analysis* (*Peri Hermeneias*), since here also a contrast with Albinus makes itself evident. In ch. 6 of the *Didaskalikos*, Albinus, as we have seen, gives a brief account of Peripatetic logic, deriving this from a tradition which includes Theophrastus and Eudemus, and possibly also later writers such as Ariston of Alexandria. Apuleius' treatise arises from the same source, Theophrastus and Ariston both being referred to more than once (Theophrastus in chs. 11 and 13, Ariston in chs. 13 and 14). Disapproval is expressed at their innovations, however, which would seem to indicate a still later, and more 'conservative' source, probably Platonist, and possible nothing more august than Apuleius' lecture-notes from his studies at Athens, which he may simply be working up here, prefixing a rather flowery introduction and bringing his own name in as an illustrative example in ch. 4.

Apuleius gives a much fuller account of the categorical syllogism than does Albinus (though without relating the various figures to the Platonic dialogues), but he ignores the Theophrastean system of hypotheticals. On the other hand, in certain small but significant details, such as the order of the moods of the Third Figure (ch. 11), he follows Theophrastus as against Aristotle in placing Datisi before Disamis and Ferison before Bocardo, thus indicating his dependence rather upon later Peripatetic tradition than upon Aristotle himself.

The treatise constitutes an elementary introduction to Peripatetic logic, chs. 1–5 corresponding in subject-matter to chs. 1–7 of Aristotle's *De Interpretatione*, and chs. 6–14 to chs. 1–8 of the *Prior Analytics*, but this correspondence is not verbally close. Perhaps the most significant variation from Aristotle, among many small ones, is the fact that Apuleius presents the syllogisms as inferences (prefiguring the later, 'Classical' form of the syllogism), whereas Aristotle always presents them as implications. The change from the one system to the other must therefore have taken place in the Peripatetic School before Apuleius' time.

The Stoics come in for criticism on a number of questions—in ch. 3, for asserting that propositions with negatived predicates are still affirmative propositions; in ch. 7, for constructing 'superfluous', single-premised arguments that do not meet Aristotle's definition of a syllogism; and in ch. 12, for oversimplifying the results of negativing propositions. Apuleius makes no effort, however, to understand the principles of Stoic Logic, nor does he seem to realize the distinction between the Stoic logic of propositions and the Aristotelian logic of terms, though he does note (ch. 13) that the Stoics use numerals as variables where the Peripatetics use letters; like a good Peripatetic, he regards Stoic syllogisms as being merely imperfect Aristotelian syllogisms.

The *Peri Hermeneias*, then, like the rest of Apuleius' philosophical works, differs as much as it reasonably could (as between Platonists of essentially similar persuasion) from the parallel account given by Albinus.

3. CONCLUSION

This lengthy survey has been necessary in order to demonstrate that the thesis, first argued in detail by Th. Sinko, of the common origin of the treatises of Albinus and Apuleius in the teaching of Gaius, is open to grave objections. The analogies dwelt on by Sinko and others are not, for the most part, in dispute; there is a great deal that is common to both authors. What I have tried to emphasize, however, are the differences, which are not such as to be explained away as individual innovations by one author or the other. There are doubtless places where Apuleius, in particular, is either introducing confusion into his source or expatiating on a theme which interests him, but there are many other passages, as we have seen, where the two authors are plainly following different scholastic traditions. What is revealed, I think, is a considerable common stock of dogma, much of which can be traced back at least to the time of Arius Didymus, but much of which also had been elaborated by schoolmen in the hundred or so years since his time.

On to this stock has been grafted, by the more immediate teachers of Albinus and Apuleius respectively, a number of distinctive formulations. Albinus' master was Gaius—that we know. Apuleius' master or masters we do not know. I have suggested Taurus as one possibility, and Sextus of Chaeroneia as another, but I cannot claim to have much evidence to buttress either of these suggestions. Somewhere among the teachers of Apuleius, I suspect, lies the author of the distinctive doctrine on Fate and Providence that appears in the *De Fato* of Pseudo-Plutarch, in Calcidius and in Nemesius. His identity, however, remains mysterious.

In all this identification of sources we must bear in mind the obvious fact, all too often overlooked, that the chief vehicle for the transmission of Platonic doctrine during all this time is not so much a series of written and published treatises as the oral tradition of the schools, embodied, perhaps, in notes written up by either teacher or pupil (such as, for instance, Albinus' records of Gaius' lectures), but only rarely taking a public form even theoretically observable to us. To talk of the 'influence', then, of Antiochus, Posidonius, or Arius Didymus on the scholasticism of the mid-second century A.D. is grossly to oversimplify the situation. They are indeed there, as remote influences, but the chief influence upon a philosopher is that of his own teacher, and the works of Plato and Aristotle as seen through his eyes, and his chief influence in turn was *his* teacher, and so on. In any calculation of the influence of one written source available to us upon another, this fact of life must not be ignored.

D. GALEN

The physician Claudius Galenus (A.D. 129–*c*.200) merits a mention at the end of this chapter, although I do not propose to discuss him in detail, since he himself declares, as we have seen, that he took lectures from Albinus in Smyrna, as well as from another pupil of Gaius in Pergamum. Despite this valuable evidence, however, what exactly Galen learned from his mentors is not clear.

He was first and foremost a doctor, and he was also an independent-minded man who read primary sources for himself, and thus, though many of his works concern philosophical subjects, his doctrine is truly eclectic rather than based on any fixed school teaching. The philosophical topics which chiefly interested him were logic and psychology, in both cases because of their usefulness for medicine.

In logic he adopted essentially the same logical system as we have seen in Albinus and Apuleius—Aristotelian logic as augmented by Theophrastus,[1] with Stoic hypotheticals being accepted as a development of Theophrastean logic—but Galen, in his short work *An Introduction to Logic*, does not employ any of the distinctive terms used by Albinus, such as 'mixed' syllogisms, nor does he give the same illustrative examples (e.g. he gives Plato *Alc.* I 106Dff., as an example of the Second Indemonstrable, p. 38, 1ff. Kalbfleisch). In fact, he shows no sign of having read the *Didaskalikos*. He is hospitable to Stoic logic (chs. 7 and 14), dismissing as unimportant the vexed question as to which system is 'prior', or more basic (p. 17, 13–14). Yet he condemns Chrysippus' Third Indemonstrable in ch. 14 as an unwarranted addition to the original (Peripatetic) four. On the other hand, he adopts in ch. 18 Posidonius' theory of analogical syllogisms.

On the subject of psychology he wrote a good deal, his longest work being one in nine books, *On the Doctrine of Hippocrates and Plato*. Here he accepts the doctrine of the tripartite soul, and generally of the irrational soul, and criticizes Chrysippus' doctrine of the unitary soul and of the passions as merely mistaken judgments. In this connexion he gives high praise to Posidonius for having recognized the irrational soul.

Galen actually wrote a commentary on Plato's *Timaeus*, but what now survives is primarily concerned with things physiological rather

---

[1] Though he criticizes as superfluous in ch. 19 the Theophrastean innovation of 'prosleptic' syllogisms (p. 47, 18ff.).

than cosmogonical or metaphysical, and thus is of less interest in the present context than it might be.

I cannot claim to have gone through in any detail the voluminous works of Galen, and it is possible that this summary judgment on him does less than justice to his value for the history of Platonism, but it seems to me that it is precisely his virtues of independence of mind and attachment to autopsy and experiment that lessen his usefulness for our purpose. Certainly nothing emerges at first sight that contributes to our knowledge of the distinctive doctrines of the 'School of Gaius'.

E. CONCLUSION

It is not a happy task to set about trying to demolish one of the few apparently fixed points in the history of second-century Platonism, the assumption that there was a distinctive School of Gaius, the chief characteristic of which, as opposed to the Athenians, was 'eclecticism', and specifically hospitality to Peripateticism; but I hope that in the process some light may have been thrown on the true situation, to wit, that Middle Platonism is poised eternally between the two poles of Peripateticism and Stoicism, and takes a great deal, in matters both of terminology and of doctrine, from each of them, but may, for tactical reasons, launch an attack on either of them at any time. The idea that the 'Athenian School' preserves orthodoxy is just as erroneous as the idea that there is another 'school', the School of Gaius, that is eclectic. It arises as much as anything from the comparison of a tendentious tract by Atticus with a dry elementary handbook of Platonism by Albinus, and is a desperate attempt to hammer out fixed positions in a field where we have too little evidence at our disposal to make more than very tentative judgments.

My tentative judgment is that Albinus and Apuleius do not after all represent a definite sect within Platonism, but are simply both writing handbooks, at approximately the same time, based on approximately similar sources. Each shows too much that is distinctive for them to have had a common master. Only that which is in Albinus and not in Apuleius can reasonably be claimed for Gaius, and that turns out to be hardly worth claiming.

CHAPTER SEVEN

The Neopythagoreans

A. INTRODUCTORY

At various points in the preceding chapters, we have observed traces of the influence of Pythagoras, or of what was conceived to be his teaching, on the development of Platonism. Already in the Old Academy, with Speusippus and Xenocrates, there existed a lively interest in Pythagoreanism. Both Antiochus and Posidonius paid respect to Pythagoras, though neither could be said, on the evidence, to 'Pythagorize'. It is only with Eudorus that Pythagoreanism as a living force finds its way again into Platonism, prompted by influences that are obscure to us. Whatever these influences were, they are at work also, as we have seen, in Philo.

In the next century, Thrasyllus, Nero's court philosopher, shows strong Pythagorean tendencies (above, pp. 184f.), and a fascination with number symbolism, presumably of a Pythagorean nature, is a part of the intellectual background of the young Plutarch. But while a greater degree of Pythagorean influence than before now permeates orthodox Platonism, there are also on the fringes of Platonism, in the first and second centuries A.D., men who profess themselves to be Pythagoreans, and these men are in fact sufficiently closely linked with Platonism to require treatment in this work.

I will not deal here with that remarkable figure Apollonius of Tyana, interesting though he is, since he was much more of a prophet than a philosopher. Instead I will turn to the first figure known to us after Thrasyllus who professes philosophical Pythagoreanism, Moderatus of Gades, preceding this, however, with a brief survey of the accounts of Pythagorean doctrine given by Alexander Polyhistor and Sextus Empiricus.

B. THE PYTHAGOREANS OF ALEXANDER
POLYHISTOR AND SEXTUS EMPIRICUS

It seems desirable to set the doctrines of individual 'Pythagorizers', such as we shall be treating of in this chapter, against the reports of the Pythagorean doctrine of first principles which we find first in Alexander Polyhistor (*ap. DL* VIII 24-33) and then in Sextus Empiricus (*Adv. Phys.* II 248-84), in order to put them to some extent in perspective. Alexander we have met briefly in ch. 3 (p. 117). His source must be no later than the second century B.C., since he is writing in approximately 80 B.C. Sextus also is borrowing from sources well before his own time, and certainly shows no sure sign of acquaintance with the distinctive doctrines of Eudorus.

The doctrine set out in these documents is as follows. First Alexander:

The principle of all things is the Monad; from this Monad there comes into existence the Indefinite Dyad as matter for the Monad, which is cause (*aition*). From the Monad and the Indefinite Dyad arise the numbers; from numbers, points; from these, lines; from these, plane figures; from plane figures, solids; from solid figures there arise sensible bodies, the elements of which are four, fire, water, earth and air. These elements interchange and turn into one another completely and combine to produce a cosmos animate, intelligent, and spherical, with the earth at its centre, the earth itself too being spherical and inhabited round about.

Here there are two principles, but the Dyad is presented as somehow arising from the Monad, the process not being specified further. Sextus does not help much in the solution of this mystery, but at least provides more specific terminology (261ff.):

The Monad is the principle of existent things, by participation (*metochê*) in which each of the existent things is termed one; and this, when conceived in self-identity (*autotês*), is conceived as a monad, but when it is added to itself in virtue of otherness (*heterotês*) it creates the Indefinite Dyad, so-called because it is not itself any one of the numbered and definite dyads, but they are all conceived as dyads through their participation in it, even as they try to prove in the case of the Monad.

Use is here made, not only of the Platonic concept of 'participation', but also, more interestingly, of the Platonic categories of Absolute (*kath' hauto*) and Relative (*pros heteron*), which produce the terms *autotês* (not *tautotês*) and *heterotês* to represent two aspects of the Monad, the latter of which results in the Dyad. Here again we have the process of derivation of one principle from the other, though without any suggestion of a further supreme principle above both, such as we found in Eudorus.

Sextus goes on (263–9) to expound a 'Pythagorean' theory of categories, which is simply a development of the Old Academic, distinguishing things into Absolutes (*kata diaphoran*), Contraries (*kat' enantiôsin*) and Relatives (*pros ti*). Absolutes are what otherwise might be termed substances (e.g. man, horse, fire, water); contraries are such pairs as good/evil, in motion/at rest, life/death; relatives are such terms as right/left, above/below, double/half.[1] These latter complement each other, while in the case of contraries the presence of one involves the destruction of the other. This system of categories is distinctly reminiscent of the account of the Platonic categories given by Hermodorus (above, p. 8), and presumably represents an adaptation of this or some similar account by a Neopythagorean source.

The categories are linked to the Monad and the Dyad as follows (270–5): the One is the genus of all Absolutes (now termed also *kath' hauta*). Of Contraries the immediate genus is the Equal and the Unequal (a dyad, but not yet the Dyad), while of Relatives the immediate genus is Excess and Defect. These intermediate genera resolve themselves into the two supreme principles by Equality being ranked with the One, which is then ranked with the Monad, and Inequality being ranked with Excess and Defect, which in turn are then ranked with the Indefinite Dyad. The category of Contrary is thus seen to be a sort of 'bridge' category, drawing equally on Monad and Dyad. It may be noted that the virtues belong to the category of Opposite, and so, I would suggest, does Soul.

Having arrived at the supreme principles, our author next proceeds to the generation of Number (276–83). The numerical One springs from the Monad, the numerical Two from the 'doubling' influence which the Dyad exerts upon the Monad:

And in the same way the rest of the numbers were constructed from these, the One always imposing Limit, and the indefinite Dyad generating Two and extending the numbers to infinite multiplicity (*plêthos*). Hence they say

---

[1] This distinction between Contraries and Relatives is made by Aristotle in various places, e.g. *Cat.* 10, 11b24, *Topics* II 8, 114a13ff.; *Met.* x 3, 1024a23ff., but as part of a list of four types of Contrary, with no suggestion that they were categories.

that, of these principles, the Monad holds the position of efficient cause, and the Dyad that of the passive matter; and just as they have constructed the numbers composed of these, so also they have built up the cosmos and all things in the cosmos. (277)

There then follows the connexion of Point, Line, Plane and Solid with the first four numbers (278–80). This generation of Number is strangely reminiscent of the theory attacked by Aristotle in *Met.* XIII 7 (above, p. 4) as being put forward by the Old Academy, and once again I would suggest that an Old Academic source is being used here in the construction of 'Pythagorean' doctrine. The identification of the Monad as active Cause and the Dyad as passive Matter (agreeing with Alexander's document) serves to assimilate these principles also to the Stoic pair of basic principles.

Sextus makes a distinction in *282* between 'older' Pythagoreans who derived numbers from two principles, the Monad and the Dyad, and more recent ones who derive the generation of all things, numbers, figures and solid bodies, from the point alone, a more monistic doctrine. This could be a vague reference to the monism of Eudorus, as opposed to the dualistic tradition emanating from the Old Academy, but this is far from certain, as no reference is made to any supreme principle above the Monad and Dyad.

Whatever the origin of this passage in Sextus—and Thrasyllus comes to mind as one possibility—it constitutes a most valuable statement of basic Neopythagorean doctrine. It agrees with, and merely elaborates on, the document available to Alexander, and may indeed go directly back to the statements of 'Pythagorean' doctrine put out by Speusippus or Xenocrates. It is against the background of such basic doctrine that we may now proceed to examine the distinctive theories of some individual Pythagoreans.

C. MODERATUS OF GADES

I. LIFE AND WORKS

Of the details of Moderatus' life nothing is in fact known. His approximate period of activity is established by the fact that a pupil of his, one Lucius, is represented by Plutarch as being present at a party given for Plutarch in Rome by his friend Sextius Sulla, presumably in the 90s, as the party is given to celebrate Plutarch's return to Rome after a long absence (*QC* VIII 7–8). This Lucius is an Etruscan, and appears as a rather simpleminded Pythagorean 'of the strict observance'.[1] He abstains from meat, claims Pythagoras as an Etruscan born and bred,[2] and claims that only the Etruscans follow the Pythagorean *symbola* faithfully, implying acceptance of their literal sense. The rest of the company indulge in 'ethical' interpretations of various *symbola*, but Lucius remains silent, to the extent that some of the company think that he may be offended (728D). He is not, but simply feels that the true explanation of these things is shrouded in mystery.

It is dangerous, certainly, to extrapolate from a literary portrayal of a pupil to the beliefs of his master, but we can at least conclude, I think, that Moderatus adopted and taught the Pythagorean *bios*, or way of life, and not simply Pythagorean doctrines. It also seems likely, as one would expect in any case, that he taught at Rome for at least some portion of his career, which corresponds chronologically to that of Apollonius of Tyana.

Of his works we know only of one, entitled *Pythagorikai Scholai* (Lectures on Pythagoreanism) in either ten or eleven books (the mss. vary), quoted by Porphyry in his *Life of Pythagoras*, sects. 48–53, and perhaps used by him more extensively than we can know as his authority on Pythagorean doctrine. In this work, Porphyry says, Moderatus collected all the doctrine of the Pythagoreans, so that it must have been a fairly comprehensive work. From it comes also, we may presume, a passage preserved by Porphyry in Book II of his work *On Matter* (quoted by Simplicius, *In Phys.* p. 230, 34ff. Diels), which will be considered below. Iamblichus, in the *De Anima* (*ap.* Stob. *Anth.* I 364 Wachs.), gives a report of Moderatus' doctrine of the soul, from what work, however, is not specified. Two passages in Stobaeus (*Anth.* I p. 21 Wachs.) on Number, attributed to Moderatus, bear a suspiciously close resemblance to passages of Theon of Smyrna's *Expositio* (p. 18, 3ff. Hiller). Theon may be using Moderatus more or less verbatim, or Stobaeus may have mixed up his references. The

---

[1] There is a remote possibility that he is the Lucius who was Nicostratus' model in his hostile commentary on the *Categories* (above, p. 234), but apart from the name there is nothing to indicate this.

[2] This is a suggestion made nowhere else, though Aristoxenus (*ap.* DL VIII 1) declared that he was 'a Tyrrhenian from one of those islands which the Athenians held after clearing them of their Tyrrhenian inhabitants', and this could have led a patriotic Etruscan to lay claim to him. Diodorus Siculus x 3 ('Some say that he was a Tyrrhenian') is ambiguous, but may represent an intermediate stage in the rumour.

former alternative is quite likely, however, and may be accepted as a reasonable hypothesis.

2. PHILOSOPHY

(a) *First principles*

Moderatus was, as far as we can observe, an aggressive Pythagorean. He makes it clear that Plato and the Platonists are for him only followers of Pythagoras—followers, moreover, who seek to cover up the extent of their debt. At the end of the passage taken from him in Porphyry's *V. Pyth.* (53) we find the following (he has just explained that Pythagorean philosophy became extinct because of its difficult and enigmatic form, and because it was written in Doric):

And in addition Plato and Aristotle and Speusippus and Aristoxenus and Xenocrates appropriated for themselves what was fruitful with only minor touching up, while what was superficial or frivolous, and whatever could be put forward by way of refutation and mockery of the School by those who later were concerned to slander it, they collected and set apart as the distinctive teachings of the movement.

What were Moderatus' views on ethical questions we have no idea, but we may assume that they were austere. Just before he mentions Moderatus, Porphyry says (*V. Pyth.* 46) that the aim of Pythagoras' philosophy is 'to salvage and free our separable intellect from the snares and bonds' of bodily life. This purification of the *nous* is achieved by a step-by-step ascent to the vision of the 'immaterial essences which are its kin'. This very probably reflects Moderatus.

He is brought in explicitly just below (48) as the authority for taking mathematics and number-symbolism as a basic step in this philosophic ascent. Since, he says, the Pythagoreans could not give a clear description of the first principles in themselves because of their intrinsic ineffability, they resorted to the symbolism of numbers 'for the sake of clarity of exposition' (thus borrowing the formula used by Xenocrates to explain Plato's allegorizing in the *Timaeus*), as do geometers and grammarians:

Thus the principle of Unity and Sameness and Equality, and the cause of the *sympnoia* and *sympatheia* of the Universe and of the preservation of that which is always one and the same they call One, while the principle of Otherness and Inequality and of everything that is divisible and in the process of change and different at different times they termed the dual principle of Dyad; for such is the nature of Two even in the realm of particulars.

And so on for the other numbers, up to the Decad, which comprises all those which come before it; whence it is termed 'the receiver' (*dechas*)—an etymology found also in Philo (who attributes it to 'those who first gave names to things', *Dec.* 23), and no doubt set out in some such work as the Pythagorean *Hieros Logos* or 'Archytas' *On the Decad*, both of which spoke of the Decad as 'enclosing' all the other numbers.

Moderatus here appears to envisage an opposing pair of supreme principles, but there is another passage, that preserved by Simplicius, which has occasioned much dispute as to its true authorship, but which must, it seems to me, be attributed to Moderatus rather than Porphyry (although the identifications of the second and third 'Ones' sound like explanations by Porphyry). It seems to indicate that Moderatus' scheme was rather more elaborate:

It seems that this opinion concerning Matter was held first among Greeks by the Pythagoreans, and after them by Plato, as indeed Moderatus tells us. For he (*sc.* Plato), following the Pythagoreans, declares that the first One is above Being and all essence, while the second One—which is the 'truly existent' (*ontôs on*) and the object of intellection (*noêton*)—he says is the Forms; the third—which is the soul-realm (*psychikon*)—participates (*metechei*) in The One and the Forms, while the lowest nature which comes after it, that of the sense-realm, does not even participate, but receives order by reflection (*kat' emphasin*) from those others, Matter in the sense-realm being a shadow cast by Not-Being as it manifests itself primally in Quantity, and which is of a degree inferior even to that.

This last sentence is ill-expressed and consequently obscure, but the overall scheme presented here is clear enough, and most interesting. We seem to see here, not the supreme One presiding over a Dyad that we observed in Eudorus (and 'Archytas'), but rather three Ones, arranged to form what one might be excused for calling a system of hypostases. E. R. Dodds, in an article of fundamental importance,[1] argues that Moderatus' scheme here can best be explained as an interpretation of the first three Hypotheses of Plato's *Parmenides*, in a way that was previously thought to be exclusively Neoplatonic. The *Parmenides* can indeed be seen as an important influence on Neopythagorean transcendentalism, but the influence of the Second Platonic Letter (itself probably a Neopythagorean production) should not be ignored either.

[1] 'The *Parmenides* of Plato and the Origin of the Neoplatonic "One" ', *CQ* 22 (1928), pp. 129–42.

The First One is above Being, corresponding to the Good of the *Republic*. It is not formally described as being 'above *nous*', as is the first principle of 'Brotinus' or 'Archytas', but from the fact that the Second One is explicitly termed *noêton*, it is not unreasonable to assume that the first is to be taken as supranoetic.

The Second One is the realm of the Ideas, the Paradigm of the *Timaeus*, definitely here subordinated to the supreme entity. Whether we also term it the Logos is a matter of taste. Moderatus does not do so in this passage, but Porphyry in his subjoined interpretation speaks of a *heniaios logos* (unitary *logos*, or *logos* of the One?) which, 'wishing to produce from itself the generation of beings, by withdrawing itself (*kata sterêsin hautou*), left room for Quantity (*posotês*), depriving it of all its *logoi* and forms'. It is not clear whether Porphyry is here referring to Moderatus' First or Second One, but it seems to me better to take it as the latter. In this way, Moderatus' Second One will correspond both to Eudorus' Second One and to Numenius' Second God, to which we will come presently. The Second One will thus be described correctly as the *logos*, or active element, of the First.

It is at the level of the Second One that Matter comes into existence, in the form of *posotês*—'not', as Porphyry says, 'Quantity as a Form, but in the sense of privation, paralysis, dispersion and severance'. Here we can see the use being made of *poson* as a metaphysical concept, and the reason why Eudorus should have wished, like 'Archytas', to rank the category Quantity third, after Quality, in the list of Caregories. This *posotês* is the Indefinite Dyad under another title, and thus we have at the second level of Moderatus' universe an opposition between a Monad and a Dyad, just as we had in that of Eudorus. The First One is above this opposition, and takes no action such as 'withdrawing himself', or creating by imposing Forms on Quantity. That is the role of the demiurgic Second One.

The Soul is by Moderatus denominated a 'Third One', participating in the first two. This extension of the term 'One' to embrace the Soul is plausibly explained by Dodds as the result of interpreting the Third Hypothesis of the *Parmenides* to refer to Soul, an identification followed by later generations of Platonists. It does serve to emphasize that Moderatus envisaged a three-level hierarchy of Being—or even a four-level one, if we include Nature—each lower level being dependent in some way on those above it. The distinction between soul proper and Nature is one between a rational and irrational World

Soul, the latter being merely a 'reflection' (*emphasis*) of the former in the realm of Matter, not a true 'participant' in the higher realities. (This is a doctrine propounded later by Plotinus, in such a treatise as *Enn.* III 6, 'On the Impassivity of the Unembodied'.)

But it is Moderatus' doctrine of Matter, after all, that led Porphyry to refer to him when he did. Moderatus sees the matter of the sense-world as simply a shadow of the primal, intelligible Matter, which is the *posotēs* or Indefinite Dyad manifesting itself at the level of Nous. Matter is thus not to be found simply at the lowest level of the universe, but has an archetype at at least the second-highest level (as later for Plotinus, e.g. *Enn.* II 4). It is distressing that the sentence in which Porphyry reports Moderatus' views on this is so ill-constructed, but at least we can discern here a reference to 'Not-Being (*to mē on*) manifesting itself primally in Quantity'. This, though Moderatus would perhaps not admit it, is a development of the doctrine of Not-Being in the *Sophist*, and seems to provide evidence of a metaphysical interpretation of the dialogue.

The implications of this passage preserved by Porphyry, the authenticity and essential accuracy of which there is no serious reason to doubt, are considerable. First, we have evidence, in the Neopythagorean tradition, of a system of three hypostases, linked by 'participation', with a fourth entity, Nature, appearing as 'reflection' of the third. In addition we have the notion of 'Quantity' as an intelligible archetype of Matter. The First One is above Being and, by implication, above Intellect. All this seems to deprive Plotinus of the chief innovations in Platonism for which he is known, and scholars have in consequence been unwilling to accept this apparently isolated report. But two things must be noted in this connexion. First, Plotinus himself does not claim to be original in his doctrines (though he argues against certain Platonists who make the highest principle a Mind); and secondly, when Moderatus is viewed as part of a tradition extending from Eudorus and the pseudepigrapha through Nicomachus of Gerasa to Numenius, he is found not to be isolated.

(*b*) *The soul*

Apart from the characterization of the Soul as the 'Third One', which refers properly to the rational World Soul, some indications of Moderatus' doctrine as to the composition of the individual soul are preserved in Iamblichus' *De Anima*.

Iamblichus introduces Moderatus among those who would make the essence of the soul mathematical (*ap.* Stob. 1 364, Wachs.). Of these some see it as a Figure (*schêma*), others as Number:

And indeed some of the Pythagoreans define the Soul simply as that. Xenocrates defines it as a self-moved number; Moderatus the Pythagorean [also as Number], inasmuch as it comprises the ratios [reading *logous periechousêi*].

A little further down Moderatus is said to describe the soul as a harmony in the sense of 'that which renders symmetrical and agreeable those things which differ in any way'.

In this latter passage, Moderatus is plainly adopting loyally the doctrine of Philolaus as it is given in Plato's *Phaedo* (or perhaps, rather, in Philolaus' *On the Soul*), but the former passage shows that he took it—presumably as the number 4, the Pythagorean number for the Soul—as containing within itself all the harmonic ratios, the octave (2:1), the fifth (3:2) and the fourth (4:3). This would not preclude the immortality of the soul, in which Moderatus also believed (cf. Porph. *VP* 46 f.), since it only refers to the soul's activity in the body.

(c) *Number*

There are two passages preserved in Stobaeus (*Anth.* 1 p. 21 Wachs.) in which Moderatus gives a definition of the nature of Number. Of these a few extracts are worth recording, as they reflect to some extent —inevitably, for a Pythagorean—on his metaphysics:

Number is, to put it briefly, a system of monads, or a progression (*propodismos*) of multiplicity (*plêthos*) beginning from the monad, and a regression (*anapodismos*) ending in the monad.

This description, if we take it, as we surely may, to refer also to metaphysical realities, is a clear statement of the process of Progression and Return, which is such a feature, later, of Plotinus' philosophy, but which we will observe also present in Nicomachus.

The Monad is the limiting case of Quantity (*perainousa posotês*), that which is left behind when Multiplicity is diminished by the subtraction of each number in turn, and which thus takes on the characteristics of fixity (*monê*) and stability (*stasis*). For Quantity is not able to regress (*anapodizein*) farther than the Monad.[1]

---

[1] Adopting the emendation suggested by Wachsmuth. The mss. text is nonsensical.

This definition of the Monad is that attributed by Iamblichus (*In Nic.* p. 11 Pistelli) to the Old Pythagorean Thymaridas. The use of the active participle of *peraino* is peculiar, but this, I think, is what it must mean. Moderatus goes on to etymologize *monas* as being either from *menein* (to remain fixed) or from *monos* (alone), both traditional Pythagorean etymologies. It is pictured here as the limit beyond which Quantity cannot contract itself. Precisely what it envisaged here is not clear, but the Monad is certainly being described as the basic unit of number, which is in turn the system of division of limited Quantity, the original limiting having been performed by the One.

A second passage of Moderatus, immediately following in Stobaeus, makes a distinction between the Monad as first principle of numbers, and One as the first principle of things numbered (*arithmêta*). This latter One is obviously not The One itself, but an entity having body, or at least being inseparable from body, and thus infinitely divisible (p. 21, 19–20). (It seems to be this One that is being referred to by Syrianus, *In Met.* p. 151, 17ff. Kroll, a passage which has wrongly been taken (e.g. by Thesleff *PT* p. 47–8) as referring to the One above the Monad.)

3. CONCLUSION

We can see that, if the attribution and interpretation of these passages is correct, we have in the metaphysics of Moderatus, and perhaps in that of the Pythagorean movement even before his time, a great part of what has been conventionally taken to be the distinctive contribution of Plotinus. This has been pointed out in a number of articles by John Whittaker,[1] who has made a useful collection of references to a first principle above intellect and substance in the Neopythagorean tradition, as well as in Gnostic and Hermetic circles. Even if school Platonism maintained that the supreme principle was a *nous* of some sort, it is plain that there were other less 'respectable' traditions on which Plotinus (or perhaps, rather, his teacher Ammonius) could draw, which did not, and Dodds has shown that an interpretation of the *Parmenides* was a considerable influence in this regard.

---

[1] '*Epekeina nou kai ousias*', *Vigiliae Christianae* 23 (1969), pp. 91–104; 'Neopythagoreanism and Negative Theology', *Symbolae Osloenses* 44 (1969), pp. 109–25; 'Neopythagoreanism and the Transcendent Absolute', *ibid.* 48 (1973), pp. 77–86.

D. NICOMACHUS OF GERASA

I. LIFE AND WORKS

We know even less about Nicomachus than we do about Moderatus. We can fix his period only from references he makes (or does not make) in his works. On the one hand, he refers to Thrasyllus (*Harm.* I p. 24), which places him not earlier than the reign of Tiberius (A.D. 14–37); on the other hand, he fails to refer either to Theon of Smyrna (on mathematics) or Claudius Ptolemy (on music), which may tentatively be taken to imply that he was not familiar with their works, which should in turn imply that they were at least younger contemporaries. Neither of these writers, unfortunately, can himself be given secure dating, but both are taken as being active about the middle of the second century A.D. Further, Apuleius is recorded as having translated Nicomachus' *Introduction to Arithmetic* into Latin, which would tend to put Nicomachus into the first half of the century, and that will do well enough.

Of his works, we have the substance of four, two of which survive in full, and of two more of which we have considerable remains. First there is the *Introduction to Arithmetic*, a work embodying the basic Pythagorean-Platonic theory of mathematics, the popularity of which in later centuries was enormous. It became a basic school text, and commentaries on it were written by such eminent philosophers as Iamblichus, in the late third century, and John Philoponus in the sixth. Nicomachus composed also a basic handbook on music, the *Manual of Harmonics*, an introduction to the Pythagorean theory of Music. In both of these works certain basic philosophical principles are laid down which are useful for fixing Nicomachus' doctrinal position.

A third work is the *Theology of Arithmetic* (*Arithmetika Theologumena*), which gives a survey of Pythagorean numerology, or number symbolism, and in the process reveals much about the metaphysical scheme that Nicomachus is following.[1] We have an epitome of this work preserved by Photius, who, though hostile, gives an apparently accurate summary of the contents, and large sections are also found incorporated into a work of mysterious provenance, the *Theologumena Arithmetikēs*. This work is anonymous in the manuscripts, but was

[1] On this subject see the article of F. E. Robbins, 'The Tradition of Greek Arithmology', *Classical Philology* 16 (1921), pp. 97ff., where the relationships between the various sources are well set out.

attributed by early editors to Iamblichus, who is known to have written such a work. What we have, however, seems rather to be a later composition based on a work by Iamblichus, which itself incorporated extracts from works by Nicomachus and by Anatolius, Iamblichus' teacher. Indeed it is little more than a cento made up from these two sources. By a comparison, then, of the relevant portions of this work with Photius' epitome we can reconstruct a good deal of the original. It was in two books, the first culminating in a discussion of the Tetrad, the second in a discussion of the Decad.

Nicomachus also wrote a *Life of Pythagoras*, used extensively (though it is not clear how extensively) by both Porphyry (who gives partial acknowledgement of his debt) and Iamblichus (who does not) in their *Lives* of Pythagoras. The task of unravelling Nicomachus from Iamblichus, in particular, is not one which admits of any certain conclusions, and fortunately is not essential to our present purpose.

Nicomachus also mentions (*Intr. Ar.* II 6, 1) an *Introduction to Geometry* of his, to which he refers the reader, but it has not survived.

His works, then, constitute an introduction to Pythagorean 'science', together with an account of the Founder, a project repeated a hundred or so years later, on a somewhat more elaborate scale, by the Neoplatonist Iamblichus, who, however, in his ten-volume 'Pythagorean Sequence', is plainly heavily indebted, in respect of both method and contents, to Nicomachus.

We may note, in conclusion, that Nicomachus shows fairly extensive knowledge of Pythagorica, constituting a useful, if late testimony to their existence. In the *Intr. Ar.* he uses, besides Philolaus and Archytas, Androcydes (1 3, 3); in the *Man. Harm.* Philolaus again (ch. 9), on Harmony; while in the *Ar. Theol.* he refers to Androcydes, *On the Symbols*, and one Eubulides (*ap. Theol. Ar.* p. 52, 11–12), Aristaeus (p. 54, 9), and Prorus *On the Hebdomad* (p. 57, 15). He also had available to him writings of Zoroaster and Ostanes (56, 15). By the second century A.D., at least, there was plainly a fairly substantial corpus of Pythagorica on which to draw, above and beyond what we have seen attested for the first century B.C.

2. PHILOSOPHY

(a) First principles

Despite his 'Pythagorean' stance, Nicomachus' philosophy fits comfortably within the spectrum of contemporary Platonism. In the *Intr.*

Ar., he begins by making the basic Platonic distinction between the intelligible and sensible realms, in connexion with defining the proper object of philosophy (1 2, 1):

Those things, however, are immaterial, eternal, without end, and it is their nature to persist ever the same and unchanging, abiding in their own essential being, and each one of them is called real in the proper sense. But these things that are involved in birth and destruction, growth and diminution, all kinds of change and participation (*metousia*), are seen to vary continually, and while they are called real things homonymously with the former, in so far as they partake of them, they are of their own nature not really existent (*ouk ontôs onta*): for they do not abide for even the shortest moment in the same condition, but are always undergoing all sorts of changes.

He then quotes *Timaeus* 27D. The contents of the intelligible world are, of course, the Forms, but viewed, as one would expect of a 'Pythagorean', as mathematical entities.

Besides the dichotomy between intelligible and sensible, Nicomachus recognizes also the more Pythagorean distinction between Odd and Even, or Limit and Limitlessness (*ibid.* II 18, 4):

In this way, then, all numbers, and the objects in the cosmos which have been created in relation to them, are divided and classified and are seen to be opposed to one another, and well do the Ancients at the very beginning of their account of Nature make the first subdivision of their cosmogony on this principle. Thus Plato (*Tim.* 35A) mentions the distinction between the nature of the Same and the Other, and again, that between the essence which is indivisible and always the same, and that which is divided; and Philolaus says that existent things must all be either limitless or limited, or limited and limitless at the same time, by which it is generally agreed that he means that the cosmos is made up out of limited and limitless things at the same time, obviously after the image of number, for all number is composed from the Monad and the Dyad, even and odd, and these in truth display equality and inequality, Sameness and Otherness, the bounded and the boundless, the defined and the undefined.

All this is very elementary, but necessary to place Nicomachus in context. More interesting is his remark in 1 4, 2 that Arithmetic, which is the study of the primary forms, 'exists before all other sciences in the mind of the creating (*technitês*) god like some universal and exemplary plan (*logos . . . paradeigmatikos*), relying upon which as a design and archetypal example the Demiurge of the universe sets in order his creations in Matter and makes them attain to their proper ends' (cf. also 1 6, 1).

The Forms are thus set, as mathematical entities, in the mind of the Demiurge. What is not clear from this, or from anything in the *Intr. Ar.* is whether the Demiurge is for Nicomachus the highest God. For further enlightenment on that question we must turn to the remains of the *Ar. Theol.*, and specifically to the discussion of the Monad in that work.

God may be equated to the Monad, says Nicomachus (*ap. Theol. Ar.* p. 3, 1ff. De Falco), 'since He is seminally (*spermatikôs*) all things in Nature, even as it is all numbers, and inasmuch as it comprehends potentially (*dynamei*) things that appear actually as extreme opposites in absolutely every mode of opposition'. God is the principle of unity and knowledge of all things, the potentiality of all actualities. He is also, however (p. 4, 3ff.), a *nous* and a Demiurge. It looks very much as if Nicomachus makes no distinction between a supreme and a demiurgic God, such as seems to be the case with Moderatus.

There is considerable emphasis, though, on the *technikos logos* (p. 4, 6) or *spermatitês logos* (Photius), as the active principle which creates the world. The Monad also creates the Dyad, by a process of self-doubling (*diphorêtheisa*)—no mention in Nicomachus of 'withdrawal', as there was in Moderatus. The Monad is also described as 'Matter', not in the sense that it is the creator of the Dyad, which is Matter in the proper sense, and that it forms a base for the sum-total of the *logoi*. In this sense it is also given the titles of 'chaos' and *pandocheus*, 'all-receiver'. There is a dim suggestion here of the process of Procession from and Return to The One which is characteristic of Plotinus' philosophy, and of which we have other indications in Nicomachus, as we shall see directly.

As for the Dyad, if we could be sure that 'Iamblichus' was reporting Nicomachus unembellished at *Theol. Ar.* p. 9, 4ff., we could establish that, besides the title *tolma*, 'daring' which is attested for Nicomachus by Photius, he saw the Dyad as a 'distance-mark' (*kamptêr*) in the flow of existence from the Monad as starting-post back to the Monad as finishing-line, which certainly implies a theory of Procession and Return.[1] (This image, incidentally, is also used in connexion with the

---

[1] This image of starting post and distance mark is attested as a traditional Pythagorean one through its use by Philo (*Plant.* 76), though there the *kamptêr* is the myriad (10,000), not the dyad. The conclusion drawn, however, that God is 'the beginning and the end of all things', is the same.

Ennead, p. 78, 5, in a passage which is certainly Nicomachus.) This passage of the *Theol. Ar.* is an expansion of the bald list given by Photius, but it is not credited in the text to Nicomachus, and thus may be an elaboration of the compiler.

On the other hand, a scheme of cosmic procession and return, analogous to that adumbrated in the Pseudo-Plutarchan *De Fato* (above, pp. 324f.) is presented by Nicomachus in connexion with the Triad (p. 19, 5ff.):

And the Fates (*Moirai*) are stated in theology to be three, because the whole activity of the divine and human realms is governed by a process of emission (*proesis*), reception (*hypodochē*), and thirdly, recompense (*antapodosis*), the aetherial entities, so to speak, doing the sowing, the earthly ones, as it were, receiving the seed, and recompense being accomplished through the medium of those in the middle, assuming the role of an offspring between male and female.

Nicomachus here, it seems to me, is working with a triadic division of the universe not unlike that which emerges from Plutarch's myths. The fact that this scheme can be traced back to Xenocrates naturally does not preclude the possibility of its having worked its way into the Neopythagorean tradition. The Triad here seems to stand either for the class of daemons, or for the World Soul as situated in the Moon, performing its mediating role between Sun and Earth. The whole process is expressed in sexual terms, and this is reinforced by another epithet of the Triad given just below, to wit *gamos* ('marriage').

The scheme is, admittedly, not clearly represented in Photius' summary, but it is unequivocally attributed to Nicomachus in the *Theol. Ar.* Photius is, after all, being deliberately tendentious in his summary, only reporting the epithets bestowed on each number, with a minimum of explanation. Even so, he reports of the Triad that it 'has control over matters to do with Astronomy, and the nature and knowledge of the heavenly bodies, and holds them together and brings them to realization'. This could be a garbled summary of what Nicomachus is reported as saying in *Theol. Ar.* Photius also reports the epithet *gamos*.

The Triad may then be seen either as the Logos in the world, or as the World Soul in its rational aspect—in either case (and the distinction is only verbal) the force that holds the world together. At *Theol. Ar.* p. 17, 19ff., he describes it as follows: 'As the form (*eidos*) of the bringing-to-completion of the universe, and in very truth Number, the

Triad provides equality and, as it were, a removal of "more and less" from all things, giving definition and shape to Matter by means of the powers of all the qualities.'

This is a description of the Logos rather in its immanent aspect, as the structuring principle of the world; for a description of its transcendental aspect, as the active and outgoing element of the supreme God, we may turn to Nicomachus' exegesis of the Hebdomad (p. 57, 20ff.):

The reason for the reverend status of the number Seven is the following: the Providence of the God who made the world (*kosmopoios*) constructed all things by taking the starting-point and root of his creation from the first-born (*prôtogonos*) One, which goes forth as an impression and likeness of the highest Good (*to anôtatô kalon*).

The Hebdomad, he continues, must be taken as the primary instrument and 'limb' (*arthron*) of the creator God.

An awkward problem is here raised by the phrase 'first-born One'. This would imply a further principle above this One, if *prôtogonos* is to be taken literally (as it is taken, for instance, by Festugière, *Rév.* IV p. 23). Philo, certainly, used it in its literal sense as an epithet of the Logos. However, usage does permit it to be taken as simply 'primal', or even—though this is attested only from Pollux—'first-producing'. But then there is the question of the identity of the 'highest Good'. Is this identical with, or superior to, the 'first-born One'? It seems to me that once we begin the process of isolating entities here we find ourselves with even more than Festugière wants, to wit, (1) a Demiurge, (2) a first-born One, (3) a Highest Good. I would suggest that for Nicomachus the *kosmopoios theos* is supreme, and that both the One and the Good are simply aspects of him, the One being the originating principle of Idea-Numbers, the Good the model according to which all lower products are produced. But I must confess to considerable hesitation on this question. It would certainly be convenient to establish a distinction between Demiurge and Supreme God in Nicomachus, as is to be found in both Moderatus and Numenius; the evidence presented in connexion with the Monad, however, seems to be against it.

There is another good description of the *technikos nous* at the beginning of the exegesis of the Decad (p. 79, 5ff.), which is almost certainly Nicomachean. The *nous* uses 'the likenesses and similarities of Number' as his paradigm in the construction of the world and of all things in it. It is also referred to here as the *technités theos*. Such phrases, especially the latter, seem to imply an entity higher than this demi-urgic figure, with which it is being contrasted, but is this figure, per-haps, only the Logos of God? In fact, we must accept that there are two entities being distinguished in Nicomachus' system. The only question is whether they are being taken as a First and Second God, or rather as a Supreme God and his Logos. It is this latter distinction that I feel that Nicomachus is making.

What I see here, then, is not the more elaborate hierarchy of Moder-atus, and later of Numenius, but rather the more basic Platonic triad of principles, God, Matter and Form (the Ideas, or the Logos). The Logos is described as the 'offspring' (*engonos*) of the Monad and the Dyad (*Theol. Ar.* p. 19, 10), even as it was by Philo (e.g. *Fug.* 109, taking Sophia as the Dyad), and possibly as the 'first-born' (*ibid.* p. 58, 2), and it is given a mediating role, it seems, as well as a creative one. The most interesting aspect of Nicomachus' system, perhaps, is the indication of a process of Procession from and Return of all things to the Monad.

(b) *The soul and the world*

The rubric under which the Soul should be discussed is properly the Hexad, and here the *Theol. Ar.* gives no explicit section to Nicomachus, but by comparison with Photius we can identify Nicomachean mater-ial as being introduced at least from p. 45, 6. Here we learn that the soul, as the number Six, can be described as 'Form of Form', since it is its nature to mould the formlessness of Matter. It does this by imposing harmony upon opposites (45, 13ff.). This World Soul presumably receives forms from the Logos—thus earning its title 'Form of Form' —and projects them upon Matter as harmony and number. It will then be directly responsible for the imposition of the basic triangles on Matter, as described in the *Timaeus*. It is identified, significantly, with Lachesis (Photius), which is presumably to be etymologized as it was by Pseudo-Plutarch (*De Fato* 568E) as 'receiving as one's lot' influ-ences from above. Again, Six is given the title '*hekatêbeletis*' (lit. 'far-darting'), the feminine of an epithet of Apollo (*Theol. Ar.* 49, 11). This is etymologized as 'projection of Hekate', who for Nicomachus symbolizes the Triad. If the Triad is the Logos in the world, then the Hexad is its further projection, the World Soul; if we take the Triad as the rational World Soul, then the Hexad is the World Soul in its sub-rational but still ordering aspect. The Hexad is also termed *kosmos* (48, 18), by reason of its ordering and harmonizing power. In this connexion we may note evidence of Nicomachus' use of *gametria*, the calculation of the numerical values of words. *Kosmos*, he tells us, if you add it up, comes to 600, which demonstrates its hexadic quality.

We seem here to have two entities in the world, whether Logos and World Soul, or two aspects of the World Soul, one a projection of the other, not unlike the relation revealed in Moderatus' system. The Pythagoreans, whatever their claims, are working within a Platonic universe—heavily mathematicized, but none the less Platonic for that, after all.

(c) *The physical cosmos*

The physical cosmos is represented by the Tetrad, as it is only by the power of the Tetrad that things take on three-dimensional solidity. We have a long passage on the Tetrad in *Theol. Ar.* (pp. 20–9) which De Falco does not mark as Nicomachean (though the ms. E makes the attribution), but which, on the basis of many similarities of language and doctrine, may be claimed with reasonable certainty as his. Unfortunately, however, that does not put us in possession of much in the way of Nicomachus' physical theory, since the passage is more concerned with the praise of the number Four, but he does, as one would expect, believe in a four-element universe (p. 23, 19), with one quality assigned to each element, the whole held together by the harmonies represented by the Tetrad.

(d) *Ethics*

In the sphere of ethics, Nicomachus operates with the doctrine of Virtue as a mean between excess and deficiency. To this doctrine, whether or not it is Aristotelian in origin, Nicomachus gives a distinctly Pythagorean twist by associating it closely with mathematics. At *Intr. Ar.* 1 14, 2, he brings it into a discussion of perfect numbers, and *ibid.* 23, 4 he sums up his discussion of arithmetical relations by remarking that this investigation teaches us the primacy of the beautiful and definite and intelligible nature over its opposite, and how the former must order the latter, even as the rational part of the soul is properly designed to order the two irrational parts, *thymos* and *epithymia*, and to derive from this imposing of 'equality' or equilibrium (*episôsis*) the so-called ethical virtues, moderation, courage, gentleness, self-control, perseverance and the like. This doctrine is very close to that of Plutarch in the essay *On Moral Virtue* (above, p. 196), which is also an overlaying of Aristotelian doctrine with Pythagorean concepts.

In a passage of the *Theol. Ar.* on the Tetrad (p. 25, 7ff.), which, as I
have already indicated, can be claimed with fair certainty for Nicomachus, we have an interesting listing of the bodily and external
'virtues' corresponding to each of the four virtues proper, which
indicates that Nicomachus accepted the three kinds of good as all
contributing to the *telos*. Corresponding to Wisdom, we have 'excellence of the senses' (*euaisthêsia*) at the bodily level, and good fortune
at the external; corresponding to Moderation, health and good fame;
corresponding to Courage, strength and political power; and corresponding to Justice, beauty and friendship. None of this is new to us
except the strict schematization (though this can hardly be original to
Nicomachus), but, if it represents Nicomachus' true ethical position,
it once again shows him to be Peripatetic rather than Stoic in his
sympathies (he does, after all, refer to all three classes of good as
aretai), and thus again in substantial agreement with Plutarch.

(e) Providence and the problem of evil

Before leaving Nicomachus, there is an interesting passage preserved
verbatim in the *Theol. Ar.* (p. 42, 3ff.), which is worth quoting. It
concerns the problem of evil, and somehow arises out of the discussion
of the Pentad, at the beginning of Book II of Nicomachus' *Ar. Theol.*:

> When men suffer injustice, they are willing that the Gods should exist,
> but when they do injustice, they are not willing; and that is the reason they
> suffer injustice, that they may be willing to believe in the Gods. For if they
> did not believe in the Gods, they would not behave themselves. If then the
> cause of men's good behaviour is their belief in the Gods, and if they only
> believe in them when they are suffering injustice, and if injustice, though an
> evil, yet subserves the interests of Nature, and if what subserves the interests
> of Nature is the work of good beings, and Nature is good, and so is Provi-
> dence, then evils befall men according to Providence.

He then quotes Homer, *Iliad* VIII 69–74 (where Zeus weighs in the
balance the fates of the Trojans and the Achaeans) to support his
point. The couching of this piece of theodicy in the form of a Stoic
argument is further proof, if such were needed, that logic was by this
time very largely non-denominational.

3. CONCLUSION

Whether or not Nicomachus distinguished between a First Principle
and a Demiurge, he certainly envisages a hierarchy of Being of some

sort, distinguishing a Logos and two levels of World Soul, the upper one of which will be identical with the Logos in the world. He also appears to describe a process of Procession and Return from the highest to the lowest, describing the Monad in this connexion as a kind of 'Matter'. This seems to be a distinctive contribution of the Pythagorean strand in Middle Platonism. We have also observed Nicomachus' extensive use of Pythagorica, and his interest in the life-myth of Pythagoras. Naturally, also, he was an enthusiast for every variety of number symbolism, and indeed it is the interpreting of the variety of numerical and mythological identifications that Nicomachus, and other Pythagoreans, indulge in that makes the unravelling of their true doctrine a delicate task. This said, let us turn to the greatest figure among the Neopythagoreans, Numenius.

E. NUMENIUS OF APAMEA

1. LIFE AND WORKS

It is sad to relate that, in the case of this most fascinating figure in second-century philosophy, we know nothing more of his life than we do of that of Moderatus or Nicomachus. He is connected with the city of Apamea, a flourishing centre in the Orontes valley of northern Syria. That he was not only born there, but also taught there, is indicated by the fact that, a century or so after his death, Plotinus' follower Amelius, an ardent admirer of Numenius, went to live in Apamea just before Plotinus' death (Porph. *V. Plot.* 3), which there was little point in doing unless the city was associated in some substantive way with the philosopher. We need not imagine that Numenius remained all his life in Apamea, but what contact he may have had with philosophical circles in Alexandria or Athens is unknown to us. Johannes Lydus (*De Mens.* IV 80 = Fr. 57D) refers to him, mysteriously, as 'Numenius the Roman'. This may indicate a period of teaching at Rome, during which whatever work of Numenius' Lydus is using may have been written.

It is possible, however, that two striking images from his work *On the Unfaithfulness of the Academy to Plato* (Fr. 24D, 1. 71: Plato being torn apart like Pentheus, and Fr. 25, 1. 81: Arcesilaus putting forth *epochê* as a defence, as a cuttle-fish puts out ink) are being picked up by Atticus in his attack on Aristotle, which is, after all, a work of the same genre as this one of Numenius'. Admittedly Atticus uses each of the images somewhat differently—Plato is portrayed at Fr. 1, 14 Baudry as collecting the parts of philosophy together like the limbs of Pentheus, and Aristotle as behaving like a cuttle-fish in making a distinction between immortality of soul and immortality of mind in Fr. 7, 77— but since neither of these images are found in surviving literature before Numenius, the possibility arises that Atticus picked them up from this source. The fact that Atticus' pupil Harpocration was influenced by Numenius increases the possibility that Atticus knew of his work.

As regards Numenius' chronology, we have just been reminded that he influenced Harpocration, who was also a pupil of Atticus, and this would put his *floruit* at least back around A.D. 176. The consensus of scholarly opinion in fact fixes his *floruit* in and around A.D. 150, which would make him contemporary with Taurus and Albinus, and not much later than Nicomachus, and there is nothing to contradict this opinion. The earliest surviving author to mention him is Clement of Alexandria (*Strom.* 1 22). We have no very satisfactory *terminus post quem*, but Numenius is linked repeatedly in the doxographical tradition with one Cronius, described as his companion (*hetairos*) rather than as his pupil, and it is possible that it is this Cronius who is the recipient of Lucian's account of the death of Peregrinus, written in A.D. 165. This identification should not be dismissed out of hand. The Cronius addressed by Lucian had a particular interest in hearing of Peregrinus, who had operated most notoriously in Syria, and Lucian's mode of address to him marks him as of the Platonist persuasion. The identification would give us no more than a date, but it would at least give us that.

Numenius and Cronius are mentioned by Longinus (*ap. Porph. V. Plot.* 20) as constituting the culmination of a line of Pythagorean writers beginning with Thrasyllus and continuing with Moderatus, who 'fall far short of Plotinus in precision and fulness', which places him in a suitable context.

We may now consider his works. Here we are rather better informed, although we have nevertheless to subsist entirely on fragments. For these we are primarily indebted to Eusebius (in the *Praeparatio Evangelica*), with one large contribution from Calcidius, some references in Origen, and many notices in Neoplatonic sources, chiefly Proclus. It is even possible that Calcidius was indebted to Numenius, probably indirectly, for much of his commentary on the *Timaeus*, but that question will be discussed later.

The work of chief philosophical interest is a treatise, in at least six books, *On the Good*, being an enquiry into the nature of the First Principle, to wit, Being, or The Good, presented in the form of a dialogue between an informant, presumably to be taken as Numenius himself, and a stranger, who does very little in the extant fragments except ask for enlightenment and answer simple questions. It is dangerous, perhaps, to generalize on the basis of fragments, but what we have gives the impression much more of an Hermetic dialogue than of a Platonic one. Admittedly, the Stranger is not much more submissive than, say, Theaetetus in the *Sophist*, but the tone of the main speaker's pronouncements is much more hieratic than that of any Platonic main speaker—except, perhaps, Timaeus, and Timaeus is not, after all, indulging in dialogue. The main speaker in *On the Good* reminds one of nothing so much as of Hermes instructing Tat.

It is not, however, to the Hermetic Corpus that Numenius is commonly linked, but to another curious production of the second century A.D., the Chaldaean Oracles. These were produced, under circumstances totally unclear, by one Julianus, in the reign of Marcus Aurelius, and thus more or less contemporaneously with Numenius, and they in fact reflect, in elaborate poetic language (being written in pseudo-Homeric hexameters), a good deal of contemporary Platonic-Pythagorean doctrine.

One parallel in particular has aroused interest. In Book VI of Numenius' work (Fr. 17D; 26L), we find this:

Since Plato knew that among men the Demiurge is the only divinity known, whereas the Primal Intellect, which is called Being-in-Itself, is completely unknown to them, for this reason he spoke to them, as it were, as follows: 'O men, that Intellect which you imagine to be supreme is not so, but there is another Intellect prior to this one which is older and more divine.

In the *Oracles* (Fr. 7, Des Places) we have the following:

All things did the Father bring to completion, and handed them over to the Second Intellect, whom all you race of men call the First.

Both the subject-matter and the tone of these two passages are closely analogous, but it is not easy to say which is influencing the other. However, Numenius is attested as laying great emphasis in this work on the teachings of the Brahmans, Jews, Magi, and Egyptians (Fr. 1), and their agreement with the teachings of Plato and Pythagoras, so that he would be very receptive of a document such as the *Oracles*.

On the other hand, Julian, although claiming simply to be the mouth-piece of the ancient gods, is certainly influenced by some form of contemporary Platonism. Another conspicuous coincidence of doc-trine, in the matter of the double nature of the Demiurge, will be dis-cussed below (p. 394). Perhaps a third possibility should not be excluded, that both the *Oracles* and Numenius are influenced by the same currents of thought, Pythagorean, Gnostic and Hermetic, which constitute what one may term the 'underworld' of Platonism in this period.

Apart from the dialogue *On the Good*, we have evidence of a work *On the Indestructibility of the Soul* (Fr. 29), in at least two books. All we know of this, from a report in Origen, is that Numenius quoted sundry marvellous tales to prove his point. It is possible, however, that a series of notices in Proclus (= Frr. 39, 40) and Iamblichus' *De Anima* (= Frr. 41–3) also derive from this source. Another work, of very promising title, is that *On the Secret Doctrines of Plato*. Our only record of it, however (Fr. 23), is rather disappointing. It discusses Plato's use of the character Euthyphro to represent the popular religious attitudes of the Athenian People. This in itself is not very interesting, but it may be that in this work Numenius began the alle-gorical interpretation of the prefatory portions, and of the characters, of Plato's dialogues which is such a remarkable feature of Neoplatonic exegesis. We have no indication, however, as to how far he went in this direction. It is possible, for instance, that his exegesis of the battle between Atlantis and Athens recounted at *Timaeus* 23Dff., as a con-flict of more noble souls, followers of Athena, with others who are involved with generation, subjects of Poseidon, the overseer of generation (*ap.* Procl. *In Tim.* I 76, 30ff. Diehl = Fr. 37) is not from a *Timaeus Commentary*, for which there is no secure evidence, but from this work.

The exegesis of the myth of Er in the *Republic*, on the other hand, reports of which are given by Proclus in his *Commentaries on the Republic* (Fr. 35), does seem to have been a separate work, as Proclus expressly describes Numenius as a commentator on this myth (*In Remp.* II 96, 11ff. Kroll). I believe that Numenius' exegesis of the Cave of the Nymphs in *Odyssey* XIII, preserved by Porphyry in his work of that name (= Frr. 30–3) may come in fact from his commentary on the myth of the *Republic*, since in Fr. 35 the connexion between the two is made.

We have titles preserved of three other works, to which we can

attach no fragments, the *Epops*, or 'Hoopoe', a treatise *On Numbers*
and one *On Place* (or 'space', *topos*). Origen (*Contra Cels.* IV 51 = Fr.
1c) lists them all as being works in which, as in *On the Good*, Numenius
gives allegorical interpretations of the writings of Moses and the
Prophets. The title *Epops* probably involves a pun on *epopteia*, the
term for the mystical vision consequent upon initiation into mystery
cults, which suggests the revelation of secret doctrines. The treatise *On
Numbers* was no doubt an essay in Pythagorean numerology, much as
we have from the hand of Nicomachus. As for the work *On Place*, the
title suggests something rather sober and Aristotelian, but we have
Origen's word for it that it contained allegorizations of the Old
Testament, in what connexion one can only guess.

The long fragment from Calcidius' *Commentary on the Timaeus*
(chs. 295–9) concerns primarily Numenius' doctrine on Matter, and
could come from a treatise on that subject, but none such is attested.
There are a number of references to discussions by Numenius of the
nature of various gods—Sarapis (Fr. 53), Apollo (Fr. 54), Jahveh (Fr.
56), Hermes and Maia (Fr. 57) and Hephaestus (Fr. 58), which might
suggest a treatise *On the Gods*, but once again none is attested.

Last but not least, we have, preserved by Eusebius, lengthy passages
from a racy and entertaining polemic entitled *On the Divergence of the
Academics from Plato*, a survey of the sceptical New Academy from
Arcesilaus to Philo of Larisa (with, it must be added, a final broadside
directed against Antiochus for going over to Stoicism), alleging
personal motives of an unphilosophical nature for Arcesilaus' desertion of true Platonism. A most amusing tale is told of Lacydes'
problems with 'suspension of belief' (*epoché*) when faced with manifest
thievery on the part of his slaves, and Carneades is subjected to un-
flattering analysis. Numenius has no mercy on the Stoics either, and
dismisses Antiochus' claim to be reviving the Old Academy, which,
like Antiochus, he sees as extending from Speusippus to Polemon and
as remaining essentially faithful to Plato. Whether Numenius ended
his survey with Antiochus is not clear, but there, at any rate, Eusebius
stops quoting him. I would regard this as constituting fairly good
evidence that he did end there, and that in turn would be good evidence that in Numenius' mind the Platonic Academy as such ended
with Antiochus (and his immediate successors). This polemical tract is
most pleasant to have, even if its contents must be taken with more than
a grain of salt, as it shows quite another side to Numenius from that
exhibited in *On the Good*. He was also an accomplished polemicist,

utilizing even a fair number of distinctively Aristophanic words in the course of his narrative. It is not surprising that some scholars have felt that the story of Lacydes and his slaves must be taken from New Comedy. There is no need to assume this. It comes rather from the store of gossip-column Hellenistic historiography that is the source of so many stories in Diogenes Laertius, and we must not deprive Numenius of the credit of adding his own embroidery to it.

2. PHILOSOPHY

As in the case of the previous two thinkers, we have no pronouncement in the sphere of ethics preserved from Numenius, so that there is no occasion to devote a separate section to this topic. However, it is plain enough from this view of the world that his ethical position must have been ascetic. Man, as we shall see, is possessed, for Numenius, by two souls, a rational and an irrational. Descent into the body is an unqualified misfortune for the rational soul. Ethics must therefore be devoted to freeing the soul as far as possible from the body. It is probable that the ethical views of Plotinus, Porphyry and Iamblichus are much influenced by Numenius, but to extrapolate their views backwards onto him seems excessively conjectural. However, if one were to turn to such an essay as that of Plotinus *On the Virtues* (*Enn.* 1 2), with its advocacy of 'likeness to God', one would not, I think, be far from Numenius.

Logic, similarly, is a field which Numenius does not seem to have entered to any extent. Certainly we have no trace of his views. What has been preserved to a considerable extent is his metaphysics, and it is to that that we may now turn.

(a) First principles: the Father and the Demiurge

I will begin, not with a direct quotation from Numenius, but with an account of his doctrine given by Proclus (*In Tim.* 1 303, 27ff. = Fr. 21), since, unfriendly though it is, it sets out the basic scheme very succinctly:

Numenius proclaims three gods, calling the first 'Father', the second 'Creator' (*poiêtês*) and the third 'Creation' (*poiêma*); for the cosmos, according to him, is the third god. So, according to him, the Demiurge is double, being both the first god and the second, and the third god is the object of his demiurgic activity—it is better to use this terminology than to use the sort of dramatic bombast that he employs, naming them respectively Grandfather, Son and Grandson.

This is not an entirely accurate account, but it will do well enough as a starting-point. Let us observe at the outset two features. Numenius, like Moderatus, propounds a triad of Gods, encouraged to this, perhaps, in part at least, by the mysterious utterances of the *Second Platonic Epistle* (312E), which he himself declares to be the teaching of Socrates in his work *On the Divergence of the Academics from Plato* (Fr. 24, 1. 51): 'Related to the King of All are all things, and for his sake they are, and of all things fair he is the cause. And related to the Second are the second things; and related to the Third the third.' Whatever the author of this rigmarole meant by it, it exercised a considerable fascination in later times, particularly in Pythagorean circles. The triadic scheme becomes rather forced in the matter of the third God (or One), as we can see. This makes it all the more likely that those who adopted it were following some model, which they could adapt to their purposes only imperfectly.

The second feature of Numenius' scheme, one that he shares with all other Neopythagoreans (and with Albinus), is the distinction made between the Supreme God and the Demiurge. Even those Platonists who do not adopt a distinction between two gods, such as Philo, Plutarch or Atticus, make a strong distinction between God and his Logos, which amounts to very much the same thing. In the case of the Pythagoreans, however, the urge to make up a triad of hypostases favours an explicit distinction of gods.

Where Proclus is in error in this passage is in asserting that Numenius divides the demiurgic function between the first and second Gods. The surviving fragments present the situation differently. The Demiurge is indeed double, but he is divided, not between the first and second entities, but between the second and the third.

The distinction between the first and second Gods is made in a number of passages. We note in the Proclus passage that Numenius chooses for his own purposes to take the 'creator and father' of *Timaeus* 28C as referring to two different entities. In Fr. 11 we have the following:

The First God, existing in his own place, is simple and, consorting as he does with himself alone, can never be divisible. The Second and Third God, however, are in fact one; but in the process of coming into contact with Matter, which is the Dyad, He gives unity to it, but is Himself divided by it, since Matter has a character prone to desire and is in flux. So in virtue of not being in contact with the Intelligible (which would mean being turned in upon Himself), by reason of looking towards Matter and taking thought for it, He becomes unregarding (*aperioptos*) of Himself. And He seizes upon the sense realm and ministers to it and yet draws it up to His own character, as a result of this yearning towards Matter.

The First God, then, the Father, sits alone above all this activity, brooding on himself. He is the Good (Fr. 16) and One (Fr. 19). He is never in the surviving fragments called *the* One (though in Fr. 5 he acquires most of the characteristics of the One on the first hypothesis of the *Parmenides*). In Fr. 12 we are told that he does not create, and that he should be considered the father of the creator god. He is exempt from all activity, and is King. In Fr. 13 the relation of the First God to the Demiurge is compared to that of the owner of a farm, who is responsible for the initial sowing of the crops, to his workman, who cultivates the fields:

The former, as farmer, sows the seed of every soul into all the things which partake of it; while the lawgiver plants and distributes and transplants what has been sown from that source into each one of us.[1]

This notion would recall Nicomachus' description of the Monad as being seminally all things in Nature (above, p. 355), but it may also derive ultimately from *Timaeus* 41E, where, however, it is the Demiurge who is sowing the souls into the various 'organs of Time'.[2]

The First and Second Gods are contrasted also in Fr. 15:

Such are the lives, respectively, of the First and the Second God. Obviously the First God is at rest, while the Second, on the contrary, is in motion; the First is concerned with the intelligible realm, the Second with both the intelligible and the sensible. . . . In place of the motion inherent in the Second, I declare that the stability (*stasis*) inherent in the First is an innate motion, from which derives the order of the cosmos and its eternal permanence, and preservation is poured forth upon all things.

This revelation that the *stasis* of the First God is an innate motion is

---

[1] There is a nasty textual problem here. I read, with hesitation, *georgôn* for the *ge ôn* of the mss. Thillet suggests *gennôn*; Dodds (less felicitously than in his emendation of *epeita* in Fr. 16) *a* (=*prôtos*) *on*. I agree that Numenius is probably not using *ho ôn* here in the Philonic sense of He Who Is. The alternative is to take *sperma* (seed) as predicate of *ôn*, which would make the Father the seed of every soul.

[2] Some stimulus may have been provided for this image by the description of God as a 'planter' (*phytourgos*) of physical objects in *Rep.* x 597D. Philo, of course, makes much of this image.

recognized by Numenius himself as being paradoxical, as it is in conflict with the notion of the Unmoved Mover which dominates Middle Platonic theology, but he may have derived inspiration from a well-known passage of Plato's *Sophist* (248E), where motion, life, soul and knowledge are predicated of the 'Completely Existent'. This 'motionless motion' of the First God is the energy which produces the stability and order of everything else; for it to act at all on other things it must have motion in some sense. To this extent, perhaps, Proclus is justified in describing Numenius' First God as demiurgic.

In Fr. 16 we find an elaborate parallelism set up between the Demiurge and the First God, or the Good. The Demiurge is the god of Generation (*genesis*), while the Good is the first principle of Being. The Demiurge is the imitator (*mimêtês*) of the Good, and is himself good only by participation in the Good. All this is based on a combination of the doctrine of the *Timaeus* with that of the Good in *Republic* VI:

If the Demiurge of Generation is good, then in truth the Demiurge of Being will be the Good Itself, this being inherent in his essence. For the Second, being double, creates his own form and the cosmos as well, being a Demiurge, since the First[1] is wholly contemplative.

This insistence, repeated in Frr. 19 and 20, that the Demiurge is only good by participation in the Father, seems to imply at least a mild downgrading of this entity, in a rather Gnostic spirit. It is in Numenius with his negative view of the world, that one would expect to find the closest approximation to the Gnostic notion of a less-than-good, 'ignorant' Demiurge, who is responsible for the flawed creation in which we are imprisoned. Certainly, there are suggestions that the Demiurge creates as a result of a lust (*orexis*) for Matter (Fr. 11), by which he is 'split' (perhaps even rent asunder, in the manner of Dionysus or Osiris). In the heat of his enthusiasm for Matter, he becomes forgetful of himself. It would be going too far, however, to take Numenius' Demiurge as being in any sense an evil principle, despite the dangers of his position.

---

[1] I feel that Dodds' ingenious emendation of *epeita* into *epei ho a* (=*prôtos*) must be accepted. The whole structure, as well as the meaning, of the passage demands it. Certainly the Demiurge is partly *theorêtikos*, but the phrase here, 'then entirely contemplative', is bad Greek and doctrinally inconsistent. If it is taken to refer to some period of pure contemplation by the Demiurge on the model of the *Politicus* myth, then it is very cryptically and clumsily expressed. But see Dodds' discussion of this in *Les Sources de Plotin*, pp. 48–52. (Hadot's adducing of Seneca *Ep.* 9, 16 is interesting, but not, I think, compelling.)

Numenius' other main image, besides that of farmhand, to describe the Demiurge, is that of helmsman. We have this elaborate description in Fr. 18:

A helmsman, after all, sailing on the high seas, seated high above the tiller, directs the ship from his perch, and his eyes and his intellect are straining upwards to the aether, towards the heights of heaven, and his route comes down to him from above through the heavens, while he sails below on the sea; even so the Demiurge, binding Matter fast by harmony, so that it may not break loose or wander astray, himself takes his seat above it, as if above a ship upon the sea; and he directs the harmony, steering it with the Forms, and he looks, as upon the heavens, at the God above who attracts his eyes, and takes his critical faculty (*kritikon*) from this contemplation, while he derives his impulsive faculty (*hormêtikon*) from his desire (*orexis*).

We may note here, in passing, Numenius' use of the two terms *kritikon* and *hormêtikon* to describe faculties of the soul of the Demiurge, which recalls, though it does not reproduce exactly, Albinus' account of the faculties of divine souls (*Did.* 178, 32ff.). Again we have a reference to the Demiurge's *orexis*, presumably for Matter. He binds Matter together by *harmonia*—a colourless term, perhaps, but it occurs in an interesting way in the Hermetic *Poemandres* (ch. 14), as a term for the world order, and Numenius may be using it here with a consciousness of its Hermetic significance. The general image of the Demiurge contemplating a model is taken, of course, from the *Timaeus*.

The image of the Helmsman, however, also recalls the myth of the *Statesman* (esp. 272E). According to that, there are alternating world cycles of order and disorder, according to whether God has his hand on the tiller of the cosmos or has retired into his conning-tower, leaving the ship to drift where it may. In Fr. 12 there is a clear reference to this doctrine, though it is not clear to me how far it commits Numenius to a theory of cosmic cycles:

. . . the First God is inactive in respect of all works, and is King (*Rep.* x 597E; *Laws* x 904A), while the demiurgic God 'takes command in his progress through Heaven' [thus being equated with the Zeus of the *Phaedrus* myth]. And it is through him that our journey takes place also, when *nous* is sent down through the spheres[1] to all those who are ready to participate in it. When the God looks and directs himself towards each one of us, it then comes about that bodies live and flourish, since the God fosters them (read-

---

[1] *En diexodôi* thus taken, correctly, by Des Places. *Diexodos*, although it is used also of the orbits of the planets, means properly 'a going through and out'— in this case from the Demiurge, through the cosmos, to the individual.

ing *kêdeuontos*) with his rays (*akrobolismoi*); but when the God turns back into his conning-tower (*periôpê*), these things are extinguished, and *nous* lives in enjoyment of a happy life.

I have not translated *nous* here. It is not clear whose intellect is being referred to. I regard it in fact as being intentionally ambiguous, being both the intellect of the Demiurge, emanating from him as a separate entity, and the intellect in each one of us, or at least in all those of us who qualify to receive an intellect. This selective participation in intellect is reminiscent of the separable intellect which we met with in Plutarch, and even more of the *nous* of *Poemandres*, ch. 22, which is present only to the elect.

But what process is envisaged here? Are we to imagine a succession of cycles, during which the Demiurge alternately cares for and disregards his creation? Nothing else in the surviving fragments supports such a doctrine, although it is a legitimate doctrine for a Platonist to hold, and Numenius plainly has in mind here the *Statesman* myth, which would be the source of such a doctrine. The alternative is that it refers to shorter periods of time, or perhaps to alternating relationships between the Demiurge and individual intellects, there being times when the individual *nous* is cut off from the guidance of its creator, the cosmic *nous*. If this latter interpretation be accepted, then Numenius is taking the *Statesman* myth as an expression of two simultaneous tendencies within the Demiurge, the tension between which we have already observed.

Consideration of the Demiurge has led us away from the Father. To him we should now briefly return, before passing to an examination of Matter and the Soul. A vital question remains to be answered as regards the Father. Is he an Intellect, and if so, in what sense?

Although being described as the One and the Good, he is also called an Intellect (Fr. 16) and Primal Intellect, identical with Essential Being (*autoön*) (Fr. 17). On the other hand, in an exegesis of the noted passage *Tim.* 39E ('According, then, as Intellect perceives Forms existing in the Absolute Living Creature (*to ho esti ζôon*), such and so many as exist therein did he determine (*dienoêthê*) that this world should possess.'), Numenius equates the First God with the Absolute Living Creature, and declares that he intelligizes only by utilizing (*en proschrêsei*) the Second, which is Intellect proper. The Third God, he goes on to say (which, as we have seen, is only the lower aspect of the Second), is to be identified as the entity that does the 'determining' (*ho dianooumenos*), that is, who immediately presides over the creation of the physical cosmos.

The notion of *proschrêsis* is not easy to comprehend. It presumably means that the First God is only an active intellect in so far as he communes with the Second, even as the Second God, Numenius says, is only actively demiurgic in so far as he communes with the Third. In this latter case, though, the Third is only the lower aspect of the First, so the parallelism is not exact. Fr. 22, it must be said, is a testimony from Proclus, not a verbatim quotation, so that it is unsafe to rely too heavily on the details of its terminology. On balance, however, the First God is for Numenius a *nous* of some sort, so that we do not find in him the unequivocal placing of the supreme principle above *nous* that we find in Plotinus.

Finally, on the subject of the First God, it seems worth recording the account which Numenius gives of the ascent to it, as it incorporates another of his vivid images (Fr. 2):

We can acquire the notion of any material object from the comparison of similar objects and by the distinguishing characteristics of objects available to our sense; the Good, on the other hand, it is quite impossible to grasp on the basis of anything present to us or similar to it, but, like someone seated in a lookout post, who, straining his eyes, catches sight for one moment of one of those little fishing vessels, a one-man skiff all on its own, bobbing amid the waves, even so must one remove oneself far from the things of sense, and consort solitarily with the Good in its solitude, where there is neither man nor any other living thing, nor any body great or small, but some unspeakable and truly indescribable wondrous solitude, there where are the accustomed places, the haunts and pleasaunces of the Good, and it itself in peace, in benevolence, in its tranquillity, in its sovereignty, riding gently upon the surface of Being.

But if anyone who is devoted to things of sense imagines that the Good is wafting towards him, and flatters himself that he has encountered the Good, he is entirely in error. For, in truth, the attaining of it requires a method not easy, but rather divine; and the best thing is to neglect things of sense, and strive enthusiastically to master the mathematical sciences, contemplating numbers, and thus to develop by practice that science which teaches 'What is Being'.

This description of the mystical vision is a vivid poetical elaboration of the description of the intuitive comprehension of reality given by Plato in *Ep.* VII, 341C, and may itself have provided a stimulus to Plotinus' utterances on the subject (*Enn.* v. 5, 7; VI 7, 36). We are not yet, however, in the presence of the Plotinian One.

(b) Matter

Numenius' doctrine of Matter is set out most fully in a long passage of Calcidius' *Commentary on the Timaeus* (chs. 295–9 = Fr. 52). As a loyal Pythagorean, he attributes his doctrine to Pythagoras. Matter is identified with the Indefinite Dyad, and is eternal in its unorganized state, like the Evil Soul of Plutarch and Atticus, though generated in its organized state (by the Demiurge). Numenius actually criticizes (11. 15ff.) those Pythagoreans (like Moderatus, whom, however, he does not name) who think that 'that indefinite and immeasurable Dyad was produced by the Monad withdrawing from its own nature and departing into the form of the Dyad—an absurd situation, that that which was Monad should cease to be so, and that the Dyad which had no existence should come to subsist, and that thus Matter should come to be out of God, and out of unity immeasurable and limitless duality'.

Numenius thus takes a firmly dualist stand in an age-old controversy among Pythagoreans, as to whether there is one or two first principles, a Monad which produces a Dyad out of itself, or an eternally opposed pair of Monad and Dyad. Eudorus and Moderatus were of the former persuasion, as was the Pythagorean source available to Alexander Polyhistor (*DL* VIII 25); Numenius, in this agreeing with what we know of the Old Pythagoreans, takes the latter position.[1]

Numenius goes on (ll. 33ff.) to describe Matter as fluid[2] and without quality, but yet a positively evil force. He criticizes the Stoics for postulating Matter as 'indifferent, and of a median nature'. For Plato, he says, it is rather the compound of Form and Matter that has this quality, not Matter in itself. Like Plutarch, Numenius relies for his interpretation of Plato's doctrine on *Laws* x (ll. 65ff.).

The dualism exists in each of us as much as in the cosmos. Our lower, passionate soul derives from the evil, material Soul in the cosmos. I shall say more of that presently. Like Plutarch again (*Proc. An.* 1014B), Numenius points out that if the Demiurge in the *Timaeus* reduced Matter to order out of disorder, that implies a force outside the range of his Providence and pre-existing his ordering activity,

---

[1] We may note that the same opposition exists among the Gnostics, such sects as the Valentinians and Marcionites deriving Matter from God by a process of differentiation, the Manichaeans preserving the Persian position of two original opposed principles.

[2] He approves the allegorization of Odysseus in the *Odyssey* as man passing through successive generations, Matter being analogous to the sea and the waves (Fr. 33).

which is responsible for this disorderly motion. God is unable to overcome entirely this force, and can only keep it in check. It permeates everything in the cosmos (ll. 113ff.):

Finally, Numenius declares—and rightly so—that there cannot be found in the realm of generation any entity free from vice, neither in the creations of men, not in Nature, nor in the bodies of animals, nor yet in trees nor plants nor fruits, nor in the flow of air nor in the expanse of water, nor even in the heaven itself, since everywhere it mingles itself with Providence like the infection of an inferior nature.

Even the planetary gods, he seems to suggest (Fr. 50), have their potencies and activities mingled with Matter, though their essences remain unmixed. This importation of evil into the celestial realm is surely more Gnostic than Platonist, and did not commend itself to such successors as Plotinus or Porphyry, though it does seem to be accepted by Iamblichus (*In Tim.* Fr. 46 = Procl. *In Tim.* I 440, 16ff.).

In view of this marked dualism, it is remarkable that there is no report of Numenius' believing that the world had a beginning in time, a belief that is the corollary of the less extreme dualism of Plutarch and Atticus. It is hard to see how he could fail to hold this, but the fact remains that he is not reported as doing so (Plutarch and Atticus being the sole heretics mentioned in later sources), and there the matter must rest.

(c) World Soul and individual soul

It is into this malevolent, surging sea that the human soul is plunged, on its entry into the cosmos. But before discussing the fate of the individual soul, we must consider the role of the World Soul.

Plainly the World Soul, if such an entity can be distinguished in Numenius' philosophy, is closely implicated with the Demiurge. It may be seen as the Third God, misleadingly (I think) described by Proclus as 'creation' (*poiêma*), and better identified by him (Fr. 22) as '*nous* reasoning discursively', that is, projecting the Forms upon the physical world. The Third God, as we have seen, is only the lower aspect of the Second, the Demiurge as divided up by Matter as a result of his concern for it. There is a parallel here with the Soul and Body of Osiris as interpreted by Plutarch in the *Isis and Osiris* (above, p. 200). The Third God is thus not properly a World Soul, but an aspect of the Demiurge or Logos. The overlap in function between a rational World

Soul and an immanent Logos, however, is so complete that there is not room for both of them in a coherent metaphysical system, as I have had occasion to observe already in discussing Albinus and Apuleius (for Plutarch, too, Isis is only the World Soul in its subrational aspect). On the other hand, in Fr. 52 Numenius is led to talk of two opposed World Souls in connexion with his postulation of an evil World Soul. But here he is following Plato's doctrine in *Laws* x quite closely. In fact, the beneficent World Soul has the same function as the Third God.

The evil World Soul, however, is not simply the irrational aspect of the World Soul. It is more like Typhon or Ahriman than Isis, but yet it retains also the characteristics of the Receptacle of the *Timaeus*, which means that it serves as the 'mother' of mortal things, and even of the created gods of heaven (l. 101), and thus submits to the providential administration of the Demiurge to a greater extent than would such an entity as Typhon. To this extent Numenius remains more Platonic than Gnostic, in that he accepts that the 'evil' principle is subject to domination by the Good, albeit with certain irreducible recalcitrance.

The individual soul requires more detailed discussion. A good deal of the first book of the dialogue *On the Good* seems to have dealt, in rather tedious detail, with establishing its immaterial nature. In the course of this, Numenius produces all the traditional Platonic arguments (Frr. 2–4), which we need not go into here. What are worth considering, however, are questions which he turns to later, such as the soul's descent into body, its life in the body (including its relationship with the second soul, that which we acquire from the material cosmos), and its return to its supracosmic home.

In the course of his exegesis of the Cave of the Nymphs in the *Odyssey* and of the Myth of Er in the *Republic* (Frr. 30–5), Numenius describes the souls gathering in the Milky Way before descending through the planetary spheres to earthly bodies. The milk and honey which necromancers offer to the souls, he says, symbolize the lure of pleasure which has led them into the realm of generation. This idea of a fall of the soul prompted by yearning for the honey of bodily pleasures is analogous, for instance, to the image of the 'unmixed wine of Ignorance' with which mortal men are declared to be drunk at the opening of *Tractate* VII of the Hermetic Corpus. Proclus complains in his *Commentary on the Republic* (II 128, 26ff. = Fr. 35) that Numenius is combining Platonic doctrine with astrology and mystery cults in his theory of the soul's descent, and this presumably refers to his detailing of the steps by which the soul passes through the Zodiac and then down through the planetary spheres, picking up influences on the way, which, when compacted together, form its 'accreted soul' (*prosphyês psychê*). I borrow this term from the Basilidian Gnostics, because Numenius, although not using the adjective *prosphyês*, does use the verb *prosphyesthai* to describe the accretion of external influences upon the soul (*ap.* Iambl. *De An.* p. 375 Wachs. = Fr. 43). Numenius actually seems to call this simply the irrational soul (*alogos psychê* = Fr. 44), using a respectably Platonic term for what is a quite un-Platonic concept, that is to say, two separate (and warring) souls instead of two, or even three, parts or faculties of one. Admittedly Plato, as so often, gives an excuse for this, in his description of the construction of the soul in the *Timaeus*, where not only does he distinguish the two circles of the Same and the Other (35Aff.), but one might well conclude, and certain later Platonists did conclude, from the passage 41D–43A, that the Demiurge commissioned the Young Gods (in later interpretation, at least, the planetary gods) to fashion for the souls not only a body but also the passionate element in the soul. The vehicles (*ochêmata*) on which the Demiurge mounts the souls (41E) were later taken to be these passionate 'envelopes', and *ochêma* becomes a technical term for this.[1] *Phaedo* 113D and *Phaedr.* 247B were also appealed to in this connexion, though none of these passages would yield this interpretation to anyone who did not deliberately seek it there.

Laws 898Ef., although it is not in fact appealed to, does, as Dodds points out (*op. cit.*, p. 315), present something more like this theory in connexion with the problem of how the stars are guided by their souls. Plato refers also, just below (899A), to the soul 'riding in the chariot of the Sun', a more relevant use of the 'vehicle' image. Dodds suggests also Aristotle's doctrine of the *pneuma* which is the seat of the nutritive and sensitive soul and the physiological condition of *phantasia*, this being 'analogous to that element of which the stars are made' (*Gen. An.* 736b27ff.).

These sources certainly provided some stimulus to the development of the doctrine, which is simply an approach to the basic problem of the means of communication between body and the incorporeal, but there is a magical or astrological component in this theory as well. For

[1] E. R. Dodds, in *Proclus: The Elements of Theology*, Appendix II, pp. 313ff., gives a good account of the genesis of the doctrine.

Iamblichus (*De Myst.* VIII 6) this theory of two souls is distinctively Hermetic:

Man, as these (*sc.* Hermetic) writings assert, has two souls; and one derives from the primary intelligible, partaking also of the power of the Demiurge, while the other is contributed from the circuit of the heavenly bodies, into which there inserts itself the soul that sees God (*hê theoptikê psychê*).

Only the lower soul, he tells us, is properly subject to *heimarmenê*, or astral influences.

This would do equally well as a statement of Numenius' position. The descent of the soul into body and its dwelling there is for Numenius a total misfortune (Fr. 48). In this Gnostic attitude he is followed not only by his associate Cronius but, as we have seen, by Harpocration, the pupil of Atticus. This attitude more or less necessitates an ascetic, world-negating ethical theory, wherein 'following God' implies, not striving for harmony with the cosmos, but striving to cut off all ties with it. Numenius sees a constant struggle between the two opposed souls in man (Fr. 43), without any reconciliation such as that postulated by Plutarch and Atticus. Rather mysteriously, Numenius admits the irrational soul to some kind of immortality (Frr. 46c, 47), necessarily within the cosmos, and not a 'personal' immortality. It could presumably be used again for other incarnations, and meanwhile, perhaps, serve as a ghost. It obviously, on Numenius' theory, could not rise above the cosmos.

The rational soul, on the other hand, Numenius attached much more closely to the principles above it, from which it sprang, than later Neoplatonists, at least, were prepared to countenance. Iamblichus (= Frr. 41–2) criticizes him for distinguishing inadequately between the soul and the hypostases superior to it. Numenius' interest was obviously directed primarily towards asserting the soul's kinship with the supramundane, and qualifications such as those introduced by Iamblichus would have been of no concern to him.

He does seem to have believed, however, not only in reincarnation, as did every Platonist and Pythagorean, but in metempsychosis into animal bodies, if a soul became too burdened with evil (Fr. 49). This was admittedly the view prevalent among Middle Platonists (e.g. Albinus, *Did.* 178, 28f.), and followed also by Plotinus (e.g. *Enn.* III 4, 2; IV 3, 12), but it was rejected by Platonists from Porphyry on. What becomes of the higher soul in an animal body, or how it wins its way back to a human incarnation, is not made clear in our sources, but then nor is it in Plato's own theory.

(d) Daemons

We get a partial glimpse of Numenius' demonology from a passage of Proclus' *Commentary on the Timaeus* (I 76, 30ff. = Fr. 37), which concerns the interpretation of the battle between the Athenians and the Atlantians. Numenius, we learn, interpreted it allegorically, as portraying the (presumably permanent) conflict between 'more noble souls who are nurslings of Athena, and others who are agents of generation (*genesiourgoi*), who are in the service of the god who presides over generation (Poseidon)'. These are not described as daemons, but at least the latter category, the servants of Poseidon, sound very like material daemons, engaged in ensnaring souls into incarnation. It is intrinsically probable that Numenius believed in such daemons, but without further evidence that is all that can be said.

3. CONCLUSION

In Numenius we have a fascinating figure, about whom we know all too little, but who plainly combines in his doctrine various strands, Platonic and Neopythagorean, Hermetic and Gnostic, Zoroastrian and Jewish. In his person the 'underworld' of Platonic-influenced theorizing about which I shall speak briefly in the concluding chapter, attains some modicum of philosophic respectability. It is the Pythagorizing Platonism represented by Numenius that, through the mysterious Ammonius Saccas, exercises the most powerful influence upon Plotinus and later Platonism.

Whether Numenius knew Philo must remain less than clear, but he was certainly acquainted with the results of allegorical exegesis of the Pentateuch (Fr. 1), and if certain passages of Calcidius' *Commentary on the Timaeus* where 'Hebraei' are mentioned as giving such exegeses (e.g. chs. 250–6, on dreams; or ch. 219, on the composition of the soul) could be securely attributed to him, it would bring the connexion with Philo much closer.[1] But this suggestion is too speculative to be discussed in a work of this sort. Further, to take Numenius as a mediator

---

[1] See in this connexion the article of J. H. Waszink, 'Die sogenannte Fünfteilung der Träume bei Calcidius und ihre Quellen', *Mnemosyne* ser. III 9 (1940), pp. 65–85.

between Philo and Plotinus, as has been done by some, is to accord to Philo too much originality. Philo himself was, after all, as we have seen, greatly influenced by contemporary Platonism and Neopythagoreanism. It is only our imperfect vision that can make him seem an original contributor to Platonism.

Efforts to prove Numenius a Jew are surely also misguided. One did not have to be a Jew in the Syria of the second century A.D. to be acquainted with either Jewish or Christian writings. Numenius certainly accords to the God of the Jews high honour (Fr. 56), declaring him to be 'without communion with others (*akoinônêtos*), and Father of all the gods, who will not have it that anyone should share in his honour'—a fairly plain reference to the First Commandment—but this is a position that could be adopted by a friendly gentile philosopher with esoteric and syncretistic tendencies, such as Numenius certainly was.

As to his position within the Neopythagorean movement, we may observe first that these Pythagoreans do not seem to view themselves as a movement. None of them refers (at least in extant remains) to any of the others, approvingly or otherwise. They appear as individuals rather than as a school. Within the spectrum of Neopythagoreanism, Numenius appears, in opposition to his immediate predecessors, from Eudorus to Nicomachus, as a dualist, thus reverting to something more like the Old Pythagorean position. But even in Old Pythagoreanism the Dyad is really a passive principle, and subordinate to the Monad, so that Numenius' radical dualism must be seen as influenced by Persian ideas, even as was Plutarch's.

In an age which exhibits generally either dry scholasticism or overblown sophistic rhetoric, Numenius stands out as a man with something to say who knows how to say it. The extracts quoted by Eusebius from his work *On the Good* contain many passages of vivid imagery, and his 'history' of the New Academy shows a talent for mockery rivalling that of Lucian, that other island of wit in this sea of bores.

F. CRONIUS

Of Numenius' 'companion' Cronius we know even less than about Numenius himself, and he is plainly not of the same level of importance, but his name comes up among the authors read in Plotinus' circle (Porph. *V. Plot.* 14), so that he deserves a mention. It is possible, as I have said (above, p. 362), that he is to be identified with the Cronius who is the recipient of Lucian's sketch *The Death of Peregrinus*, written in A.D. 165. Lucian gives his friend the distinctively Platonic greeting *'eu prattein'*, but there is unfortunately nothing else in the essay that would serve to reinforce the identification. The name is not a common one, however.

Cronius' only named work is one *On Reincarnation* (mentioned by Nemesius of Emesa, *Nat. Hom.* p. 116, 3ff. Matthei), in which he apparently denied metempsychosis into animals, but he is quoted by Porphyry, along with Numenius, as an exegete of the Cave of the Nymphs, and by Proclus as commenting on at least the Nuptial Number (*In Remp.* II 22, 20ff. Kroll) and the Myth of Er (II 109, 7ff.) of the *Republic*. In the first passage he is referred to as refuting those (the Stoics) who assert that the cosmos is destructible by fire. Fire, he maintains, is not shown to be capable of destroying all other substances, and he adduces asbestos, or 'Carystian stone', as a proof of this. He is also quoted as declaring the ratio of man to woman to be as 10,000 to 7,500, these being the 'two harmonies' of 546c. In the second passage he is found asserting that Er really existed, and was the teacher of Zoroaster, of whom a (bogus) work was apparently extant, laying claim to Plato's myth. However, it is not clear whether he commented on the dialogue as a whole.

Apart from his efforts at allegory, all that is known of Cronius' doctrine is something of his theory of the soul, which agrees with that of Numenius. He is twice coupled with Numenius by Iamblichus in his *De Anima* (pp. 375, 12ff. and 380, 6ff. Wachs.), on the questions of the origin of evil in the soul (from Matter), and the entry of the soul into bodies (an unqualified misfortune). Plainly he follows Numenius' line, and probably presented his doctrine as an interpretation of that of Numenius. Certainly that is what he is doing in his exegesis of the Cave of the Nymphs. His relation to Numenius seems to be analogous to that of Albinus to Gaius, except that Numenius published a good deal himself, whereas Gaius did not.

G. AMMONIUS SACCAS

It is fitting to end this chapter, and with it the body of this book, with a survey of what we know of Ammonius Saccas, the teacher of Plotinus. Once again it must be said that we know almost nothing of him, and efforts to reconstruct the content of his teaching in any significant detail have repeatedly met with shipwreck.[1]

Let us begin with the testimony of Porphyry, in his *Life of Plotinus* (ch. 3):

At twenty-seven he (Plotinus) was caught by a passion for philosophy. He was directed to the most highly-reputed professors to be found at Alexandria; but he used to come home from their lectures saddened and discouraged. A friend to whom he opened his heart divined his temperamental craving and suggested Ammonius, whom he had not yet tried. Plotinus went, heard a lecture, and exclaimed to his comrade, 'This was the man I was looking for!' From that day he followed Ammonius continuously, and under his guidance made such progress in philosophy that he became eager to investigate that practised among the Persians and that perfected by the Indians.

What may we gather from this? First, I think, that Ammonius was not a member of the philosophical establishment. Porphyry (*ap.* Eus. *HE* VI 19, 7) says that he was born and brought up a Christian, but renounced that creed on coming into contact with philosophy. One did not come upon him in the normal academic round, but had to be put on to him, almost initiated into his circle. Secondly, extended study with Ammonius led at least one pupil to desire to know more of the wisdom of Persia and of India. There is much here, it seems to me, that is reminiscent of Numenius, and it is not unreasonable to suppose, from the fact that Numenius was a major influence upon Plotinus and his followers (as well as being highly respected by Origen the Christian, another pupil of Ammonius), that Ammonius served as the intermediary. Obviously, too, philosophy with Ammonius was a much more exciting activity than attending the lectures of the established professors. Porphyry (*V. Plot.* 14) talks of Plotinus' employing Ammonius' *nous* (technique?) in the exegesis of texts, by contrast with the normal method. This tells us something, but it is not quite clear what. At any rate, it looks as if, in the person of Ammonius, Plotinus came into contact with the 'Neopythagorean underground'.

We know of a number of other pupils of Ammonius, Herennius, Origen the Platonist, Origen the Christian (so these two are customarily distinguished by those who do not cling to the belief that they were the same person), and Longinus. The first two are attested by

[1] See for instance the article of H. Langerbeck, 'The Philosophy of Ammonius Saccas', *JHS* 77 (1957) and the comments thereon of Dodds in *Les Sources de Plotin*.

Porphyry in the passage above-mentioned, the third by Eusebius (*HE* VI 19), who is basing himself on Porphyry. If Eusebius has not got his lines crossed here—and there are many who believe that he has— Origen the Christian will have studied with Ammonius a good twenty years before Plotinus, in the first decade of the third century, whereas Plotinus studied with him from A.D. 231–42. Ammonius must then have been born not much later than 170, and is thus removed not far, if at all, from the lifetime of Numenius. About Longinus we learn a certain amount from his own testimony, quoted by Porphyry in ss. 19–20 of his *Life of Plotinus*. He may fairly rank as the last 'regular' Middle Platonist—a most civilized and learned man, but not an original philosopher of any significance.

What Ammonius taught his pupils it is not, unfortunately, possible to establish. The information presented by Nemesius of Emesa (*Nat. Hom.* ch. 2) that he believed in the immortality of the soul, is of very little interest; the only interesting thing is that he is here reported as adopting a Numenian argument (= Fr. 4b) in favour of immortality. Rather unexpectedly, in view of Plotinus' own attitude, he is attested by the Neoplatonist Hierocles (*ap.* Photius *Bibl.* 461A) as maintaining the agreement of Plato and Aristotle. This would put him at odds with the official Platonist school, at least if the influence of Atticus was still felt, and, it would seem with Numenius, who made a sharp distinction between Plato and Aristotle at least in his survey of the Academy (Fr. 24, 1. 68). But Hierocles is an unreliable witness. He may have confused Ammonius Saccas with a contemporary Peripatetic Ammonius (Longin, *ap.* Porph. *V. Plot.* 20). Plotinus, of course, is critical of Aristotle, but Porphyry re-establishes harmony between the two philosophers, although with Aristotle in a subordinate position.

Attempts have been made to abstract a common and distinctive body of doctrine from a comparison of Plotinus' *Enneads* and Origen's *De Principiis* (his most Platonist work). This was a good idea, but it does not in fact lead to the discovery of any distinctive doctrines. For one thing, Origen's God is still an Intellect, and rules the world through his Logos. In general, Origen's Platonism is based on Philo rather than any more recent influence. That the supreme principle remained for Ammonius an Intellect may also be indicated by the fact that Origen the Platonist composed a work entitled 'That the King is the Sole Creator' (Porph. *V.Plot.* ch. 3), which seems to imply that the supreme principle is active and demiurgic, and presumably a *nous* of some sort. The Plotinian concept of a supranoetic One cannot, therefore, plausibly be attributed to Ammonius, nor is there any evidence connecting him with the Plotinian system of hypostases, despite the various prefigurations of these theories that are dimly discernible in the Neopythagorean tradition.

On the whole it seems best to view Ammonius as little more than a charismatic purveyor of Numenian Neopythagoreanism (though they may have differed on the attitude to be taken up towards Aristotelianism). Whether Ammonius preserved Numenius' radical dualism is not clear, but as this is a tendency from which we see Plotinus progressively emancipating himself, it is probable that he did. The great respect that he generated in his pupils for the wisdom of the East is also in line with Numenius. The remarkable compact which three of his pupils, Plotinus, Origen and Herennius, made (and afterwards broke) not to divulge any of the doctrines which their master had revealed to them (Porph. *loc. cit.*) need be no more than a traditional Pythagorean attitude taken with unusual seriousness.

H. CONCLUSION

I have confined myself in this chapter to those identifiable characters within the Middle Platonic tradition who regarded themselves as Pythagoreans. I have not touched on the large mass of Pseudo-Pythagoric material (now collected in manageable format by Thesleff), much of which also springs from that tradition, although I have mentioned some of the more notable texts at the beginning of Chapter Three, in connexion with Eudorus. There is a good deal to be extracted from this body of material, but it would stretch the limits of this book beyond what is tolerable to embark on a study of it now.

What one may note in summary about the Neopythagorean tradition is its strong transcendental tendency, its emphasis on the mathematicization of reality, and its stress on the ineffability of God, even to the point of asserting his superiority to any qualities whatsoever, which might be taken to include intellectual activity. We see, in Moderatus at least, evidence of something like a system of hypostases or levels of Being, and, in both Moderatus and Nicomachus, a process of emanation. It is to the Pythagorean strand in Middle Platonism, it would seem, that the great renewer of Platonism, Plotinus, was most indebted.

CHAPTER EIGHT

Some Loose Ends

A. THE SPREAD OF PLATONIST INFLUENCE: THE 'PLATONIC UNDERWORLD'

Considerations of space have dictated that certain topics relevant to the field of Middle Platonism be touched upon only in summary form in this concluding chapter. In certain areas much basic research still remains to be done, and any account in a work like this would inevitably be superficial. One such large field is what one might term the 'underworld' of Platonism, in which category may be included such sub-philosophical phenomena as the Gnostic and Hermetic writings and the Chaldaean Oracles. This is still a murky area, with its own specialists and controversies, and despite its considerable relevance to the philosophy of such men as Numenius and even Plutarch, I have resolved to pass over it lightly. Until the Coptic Gnostic texts of the Nag Hammadi library are fully published and evaluated, for one thing, any survey of Gnosticism must remain incomplete. Much detailed work is necessary before acceptable conclusions can be reached about the type of Platonism that lies behind the elaborate metaphysical constructions of the Gnostics, Hermetics and Chaldaeans. I will content myself here with selecting one representative example from the Gnostic sects and the Hermetic corpus, and adding to that a brief survey of the doctrine of the *Oracles*.

I. VALENTINIAN GNOSTICISM

Valentinus, the founder of this school of Gnostics, was born in Egypt and educated in Alexandria. He taught in Rome between about A.D. 135 and 160. He is thus more or less a contemporary of Taurus, Albinus and Numenius. Valentinus had many pupils, all of whom, it seems, produced their own variants of his teaching, which makes a summary rather more difficult. It is, however, possible to isolate, behind the welter of details, a basic framework which can, I think, be seen to derive in part from certain forms of contemporary Platonism. I follow in this summary Irenaeus' account, which is generally agreed to be based on the doctrine of Valentinus' most distinguished follower, Ptolemaeus. This is to be found in Book I of Irenaeus' work *Against All Heresies*.

It is generally asserted that what chiefly distinguishes the Gnostic attitude from main-line Platonism is a conviction that this world is not only imperfect (a view with which all sides would concur), but the creation of an evil entity, and that we are total aliens in it. Plainly a radically world-negating philosophy must arise from this basic position. Within the Gnostic thought-world, however, Valentinus represents a relatively non-dualistic position. For him, the creation of the world results, not from the eternal confrontation between two archetypal powers, as it does for a thinker like Mani, but rather from a Fall occurring within the framework of a previously perfect system. The nature of this Fall is a mystery which every monistic system has to face, and Valentinus faces it manfully, as we shall see, spinning a myth which touches wonderfully on all the basic tensions that a creature is subject to in face of its creator.

We must note, before turning to details, the other salient characteristic of Gnostic systems, the riotous proliferation of entities and levels of being. Every action, every thought of the higher powers become hypostatized, and can sometimes even generate offspring itself. To anticipate slightly, when Sophia realizes that her ignorance concerning the Father is invincible, she is seized with grief, fear, bewilderment, shock and repentance. All these emotions become objectified and take on an existence of their own outside the universe (*plêrôma*) constituted by the Forefather and the Aeons, leading ultimately to the creation of the material world. Within the Pleroma, the ten aeons issuing from Logos and Zoe, and the twelve aeons issuing from Anthropos and Ecclesia, are all hypostatizations of mere abstractions, the male aeons being epithets such as 'ageless', 'motionless' or 'only-begotten', the female being abstract nouns such as 'Unity', 'Faith', 'Hope' and, last but not least, 'Wisdom' (*sophia*).

As for the basic framework of the system, it is, if anything, reminiscent of Pythagorean metaphysics. We have initially a monadic and a dyadic figure, the latter being subordinated to the former (in one variant of Valentinianism, indeed, the original Aeon is alone in his glory, and produces Nous and Aletheia without the aid of Ennoia

(Hippolytus, *Ref.* VI 29, 5ff.)). The name Ennoia, denoting as it does unuttered thought, is reminiscent of such figures as Philo's Sophia (in her capacity as mother of the Logos), or the Isis of the preface to Plutarch's *Isis and Osiris*. The monadic principle, the perfect, archetypal Aeon, is termed *proarchê* (fore-beginning), *propatôr* (forefather) and *bythos* (abyss). The female principle is called, besides *Ennoia*, also *charis* (grace) and *sigê* (silence). The Aeon puts forth a seed into Ennoia, and she produces Intellect (*nous*) and, as his consort, Truth (*alêtheia*). Nous receives the titles of 'only-begotten', 'Father' and 'First Principle of all things'.

We may note here a deliberate piece of oneupmanship on the part of the Gnostics. Their secondary, derived principle, Nous, is given the titles of the Platonic supreme god, 'Father' and 'first principle', while their own supreme principle is 'Forefather' and 'pre-first principle'. This is a motif apparent also in Chaldaean theology, and, as we saw in the last chapter, something of it rubbed off onto Numenius. At any rate, Nous is the only product of the Forefather that is granted knowledge of him, and in virtue of that knowledge he produces a further pair of principles, Logos and Zoe ('life'). In Logos we have another philosophic concept, familiar to us in particular (in this book) from Philo, but not much is made of it in the Valentinian system, except as a source of further aeons.

Passing over for our present purpose the further elaborations which make up the Pleroma, we come to the lastborn of the Aeons, the female principle Sophia. About her Fall something has been said just previously. It is a most interesting concept, representing as it does the striving of the religio-philosophic mind to account, not only for the imperfection of the physical world, but for its creation at all in any form. Plato himself was sufficiently dualistic to postulate a cause of imperfection, albeit a rather passive, negative one, external to God, on which God works as best he can. There is no question of imperfection or of a fall within the divine realm. Only in the case of the individual soul is there question (in the myth of the *Phaedrus*) of some fall from a previous perfection. But the postulation of the Indefinite Dyad introduces a cause of disequilibrium at the highest level, and it is the workings of this principle that are used to explain not only all that is imperfect, but all multiplicity and even existence. Speusippus, as we have seen, refused to characterize the Dyad as evil, which is a more logical attitude to take. For Valentinus, similarly, there is nothing evil about Ennoia. She is simply the condition for the generation of everything after the Forefather. Evil only arises at a much lower level, with the most junior of the aeons.

Sophia sins through her desire to know her origin, to comprehend the nature of the Forefather. She plunges recklessly into the abyss where he dwells, causing a disequilibrium in the Pleroma, and is only brought up short by the intervention of an entity previously not heard of, termed Horos ('boundary'—a variant, perhaps, of the Pythagorean *peras*, 'limit'). This entity seems to be an aspect of the Forefather generated by the imbalance within the Pleroma. It may be seen, in more philosophic terms, as the Logos in its regulating aspect, or, in Philo's system, the 'regal power' of God.

Sophia is restored to her place, but the result of her disruption remains, objectified as a 'formless entity', and causes pain to the other aeons. They cause a further aeon, Christos, to be produced, in order to deal with this formlessness. Christos, like Horos, is a logos-figure. He separates off the formless entity, and expels it from the Pleroma. It becomes the 'lower' Sophia, or Achamoth, a projection of the higher Sophia outside the intelligible world. It corresponds to the irrational World Soul of Middle Platonic metaphysics, an irrational entity which yet yearns for what is above it, and grieves because of its separation from the higher world. Its emotions, grief, fear, bewilderment and ignorance, all become hypostatized, and give rise to the four elements of the material world, while a fifth quality of Achamoth, its 'turning back' (*epistrophê*) to what is above it, produces Soul.

Out of this soul-substance, Achamoth produces a son, the Demiurge, and it is at this stage that we find in Valentinianism an explicit parody of the *Timaeus*, and through it of Platonic metaphysics in general, as well as an attack on Jehovah as portrayed in the Old Testament. The Valentinian Demiurge is not so much evil (as he is in certain other Gnostic traditions), as simply ignorant. He does not know the true nature of things; he cannot see the Forms, yet he thinks that he is the unique and supreme God. He organizes the material universe into seven heavens, over which, in the eighth sphere, he presides. This notion that our world is in the power of an evil, or at best ignorant, being is one that is characteristically Gnostic, but of which we have seen dim suggestions both in Philo and in Plutarch's teacher Ammonius, and even perhaps in Xenocrates' connexion of the sublunar realm with 'Titanic' deities and a 'lower Zeus'. It is plainly one explanation of the world's imperfection with which men like to torment themselves, and is after all only a personified development of Plato's notion of Necessity (*Anankê*) as irreducibly present in the material world.

The Demiurge tries to imitate the structure of the higher world in his creation of the material world, but fails systematically through ignorance. The parody of the *Timaeus* attains its sharpest manifestation, perhaps, in the description of the Demiurge's attempt to imitate Eternity (*Aiôn*) with the creation of Time (cf. *Tim.* 37cff.):

When the Demiurge further wanted to imitate the boundless, eternal, infinite and timeless nature of the upper Ogdoad, but could not express their immutable eternity, being as he was fruit of defect, he embodied their eternity in times, epochs, and great numbers of years, under the delusion that by the quantity of times he could represent their infinity. Thus truth escaped him and he followed the lie. Therefore his work shall pass away when the times are fulfilled. (Irenaeus, I 17, 2, trans. Jonas)

Under the administration of such a figure there would be no hope of upward movement, or 'salvation', for the individual soul. But in fact the Demiurge creates the instrument of his own defeat. In this connexion must be introduced the Gnostic doctrine, found also, as we have seen (above, pp. 211ff.) in Plutarch, of the threefold nature of man, not body and soul only, but body, soul and spirit (*pneuma*), which in Plutarch is given the more traditional title of *nous*. Each of these three elements arises from aspects of the experience of the lower Sophia— Matter, from her Passion; Soul, from her 'turning back'; and Spirit, from the light shed upon her by Christos, the *logos*-figure mentioned above. Spirit, therefore, is to some extent an element superior to Sophia and to the cosmos.

The Demiurge, for the completion of his realm, turned to the creation of man. He fashioned material bodies, and breathed souls into them. But he knew nothing of *pneuma*, and his mother was able to insert *pneuma* into his creations without his knowing. Her object in doing this is to initiate the process of salvation, whereby man may rise to attain union with the Pleroma. Ultimately, it is envisaged, all that is pneumatic in the material world will rise to reunion with the Pleroma, and the material world, the Demiurge included, will simply cease to exist.

The purpose of this very cursory sketch of at least one version of the Valentinian system has been to demonstrate the ways in which this school of Gnostics borrowed, and developed, certain basic Platonic-Pythagorean concepts, such as Monad, Dyad, Logos, World Soul and

Demiurge,[1] and to draw attention to certain other concepts, such as the Forefather—a 'super-supreme principle', as it were—the Fall of the Soul, the Demiurge as an imperfect, ignorant being, and the distinction of *pneuma* from *psychê*, which may have had an influence, in their turn, on contemporary Platonism. As to the precise steps by which such cross-fertilization may have taken place, I do not feel that it would be wise to comment further.

2. THE POEMANDRES

I wish to turn next to a brief survey of the doctrine of the first, and most famous, tractate of the *Corpus Hermeticum*, called the *Poemandres* after its chief figure, the Divine Intellect, who reveals the secrets of the universe to a pious, unnamed disciple.[2] The *Corpus Hermeticum* as a whole is of quite uncertain date. It is not in fact a coherent body of works, any more than Gnosticism is a coherent body of doctrine, so that the doctrine of the *Poemandres* cannot stand for Hermetic doctrine in general. But as a specimen of Hermeticism it will do well enough.

Poemandres describes himself at the outset as 'the *nous* of the Supreme Power (*authentia*)'. This may be simply a rendering of his Egyptian title (though the author probably does not know that), but it poses a problem none the less. The term *authentia* is remarkable in this context; it is elsewhere used to describe the majesty of the Roman Emperor, the supreme secular power, but never to describe the supreme power in the universe. The *authentia* might be taken here to be a supreme power above Nous, or simply as a characteristic of Nous. There is no clear mention of a principle superior to Poemandres himself elsewhere in the tractate, but that does not prove that none is postulated, simply that the author is unwilling to discuss it. Such a being would be analogous to the Forefather of the Valentinians.

---

[1] Hippolytus (*Ref.* VI 37, 5–6) declares that Valentinus actually derived inspiration from the Second Platonic Letter (312E) and its system of three Kings, but the connexion is not very clear in the surviving evidence.

[2] The name Poemandres is probably not derived from the Greek word *poimên*, 'shepherd', as is often supposed, but seems to be a rendering of the late Egyptian (Coptic) '*pe eime n Re*', 'the intellect of Ra'. Since this is not actually attested as an epithet of Thoth, and indeed is not of the form that such a title would take in real Egyptian (a word such as '*ib*,' 'heart', being used, rather than such an abstract concept as *eime*), one is tempted to suspect a back-formation into Egyptian from the Greek *noêsis theou*, or something such, which then returned to Greek, transliterated, as a proper name.

Poemandres first presents a vision which depicts a 'darkness' or 'wet substance' separating itself off from his essence, which is Light, and then a Logos leaping like a flame from the light into the darkness, causing the elements to separate themselves out from one another (sects. 4–5). This seems to owe something to the description of the Demiurge's working upon Matter in *Timaeus* 53Aff.

We find, therefore, a Nous and a Logos, the latter described, in terms analogous to those of Philo, as 'son of God' (sect. 6). A parallelism is now established between macrocosm and microcosm, in a passage unfortunately mangled, but which asserts that the faculties of sight and hearing (and presumably speech) in the individual correspond to, or rather are identical with, the *logos*, while the intellect of the individual is identical with the Father. The unity of these two, both in the individual and in the universe, is Life (*Zoê*). A kind of trinity emerges here, Life filling the role of the Holy Spirit (who, it must be remembered, is originally a female entity). No more is heard of Life in the tractate, but in sect. 8 we find mention of the Will (*boulêsis*) of God, 'who, taking to itself the *logos*, and looking upon the fair (intelligible) cosmos, made an imitation of it, creating a cosmos out of its own elements and productions, to wit, souls'. This entity sounds very much like the Sophia that we have met with in Philo—it is certainly of more exalted station than the Valentinian Sophia.

At this point entities begin to proliferate, though not by any means on the Gnostic scale. In sect. 9 we are told that the supreme Nous, Poemandres, generates another *nous demiourgos*, who is 'god of the Fire and the Pneuma', and who creates seven Administrators (the planetary Gods), 'who enclose the cosmos in their circles', and their administration is termed Fate (*Heimarmenê*). The Logos then (10) leaps upward from the downward-tending elements (earth, air, water?) towards this pure portion of Nature, and is united with the *nous demiourgos*, 'since he is of the same substance (*homoousios*)'. If they are indeed *homoousioi*, one might ask, then why do we need both of them? The answer may be that the Demiurge is fixed in his place (being to that extent analogous to a Gnostic Demiurge), while the Logos is free to move up and down the scale of being.

The Demiurge creates irrational animals in the various lower elements; meanwhile Nous the Father creates Man 'like unto himself, whom he loved as his own offspring; for he was beautiful, possessing as he did the image (*eikôn*) of the Father' (11). Again, this must remind us of Philo's description of the creation of archetypal Man (e.g.

Opif. 134, above, p. 176). Man is granted permission by the Father to enter the cosmos organized by his elder brother, the Demiurge, and he sets to work to create something himself, in emulation of the Demiurge. He is warmly received by the Administrators, each of whom bestows upon him the gift proper to his own nature. Man then breaks through the barrier of the upper world, and reveals himself and it to the lower (sublunar) Nature, which promptly falls in love with him. He sees his own image on the face of the waters of the lower world, and falls in love with that.

The result of this partly narcissistic love-affair is what one would expect. Out of the union of Man and Nature springs a twofold being, mortal man. By reason of his bodily nature he is subject to *heimarmenê*; from the life and light of the archetypal Man, on the other hand, he acquires soul and *nous*, and it is by virtue of this latter that he can win freedom from the cosmic order.

At this point we find a curious doctrine of a separate *nous*, of which we have seen intimations in Plutarch, particularly in the myth of the *De Facie* (above, p. 211). In sect. 22 of the tractate, the disciple asks Poemandres, 'Do not then all men possess *nous*?' Poemandres replies:

Restrain your tongue! I, as Nous, am present (only) to the holy and good and pure and charitable, to the pious, in a word, and my presence brings support to them, and they worship the Father with love, and give thanks to him with benedictions and hymns in due order with affection.

He goes on to say that as Nous he frees them from all bodily desires and affections, guarding them from the things of this world. To the wicked, on the other hand, he comes as an avenging spirit (*timôros daimôn*), 'applying to them the sharpness of fire', and stirring up their material desires and the tortures of the soul consequent upon them.

The same doctrine is found also in *Tractate* 10, called *The Key*, in sects. 19–21. Here the distinction is made between the pious soul, which acquires knowledge of God and thus becomes 'wholly *nous*', and the impious soul, which remains at the level of its own nature, and to which *nous* becomes, again, an avenging daemon.

Nous is in each of these passages a transcendent entity, helping the good and tormenting the evil, working in each case through the individual soul, of which it is also a part. It seems more likely that this concept of the *nous* as a faculty, or entity, operative only in a select few, is an alien concept working its influence on Plutarch, rather than a Platonist concept that is being reshaped by the Hermetics.

This has been at best a dip into the sea of Hermeticism, but it should suffice to demonstrate, once again, that certain basic entities of Platonic metaphysics have found their way into realms far removed from orthodox Platonism. Whether Poemandres is really the supreme being envisaged in this tractate is not clear. If he is, he is a Xeno-cratean-Aristotelian God rather than a Speusippean one,[1] but the nature of the *authentia* is left obscure. Below Poemandres, at any rate, we meet the familiar entities Demiurge and Logos (although it seems somewhat irregular to have both of them operating on more or less the same level, almost as rivals), and lower down again the irrational World Soul, or Physis, longing for impregnation from above. An-thropos, the archetypal Man, is borrowed rather from Philo than from orthodox Platonism (or from the tradition, if any, which Philo repre-sents), and there are many signs in the *Poemandres* that the author is familiar both with the Old Testament and with the allegorical inter-pretation of it. *Zoê*, or the Will of God, is an entity of ambiguous origin, but can be claimed as at least partly Platonic—the term 'life' in particular perhaps being inspired remotely by *Sophist* 248E. The separate *nous* is of more obscure provenance, though found in Plu-tarch.

The whole subject of Hermetic metaphysics requires further care-ful study. As for their ethics, it accords with that of such Pythagoreans as Numenius, and with that of more austere, 'Stoicizing' Platonism. The ideal is *apatheia*, freedom from all bodily concerns, and the directing of the *nous* to its noetic home. It is this ethical ideal which we find informing also our next subject for examination, the *Chaldaean Oracles*.

3. THE CHALDAEAN ORACLES

In contrast to the Hermetica, the chronology of whichi s quite obscure, we have a reasonably clear idea of the origins of the *Chaldaean Oracles*. They are attributed unanimously in later tradition to a certain Julian, surnamed 'the Theurgist' (to distinguish him from his father, Julian 'the Chaldaean'), a contemporary of the emperor Marcus Aurelius (A.D. 161–80). Julian himself, it is only fair to say, attributed the *Oracles* to the ancient gods of Chaldaea.

---

[1] Contrast the God of *CH* II 12–14, who is 'above *nous* and *pneuma* and light', as being their cause. Both types of supreme principle are to be found in the *Corpus Hermeticum*.

Julian served in the Roman Army in some capacity during Marcus' campaign against the Quadi, and claimed to have caused a miraculous rainstorm which saved the Roman camp in A.D. 173. This makes him an approximate contemporary of Numenius, a fact of some importance. It is not clear whether Julian or his father is to be credited with uttering the *Oracles*, and it is also not clear whether they were a conscious fraud, or, as E. R. Dodds acutely suggests (*The Greeks and the Irrational*, p. 284), delivered in the course of a series of mediumistic trances, but what is plain is that the Gods who spoke through Julian (*père* or *fils*) were influenced themselves to some extent by contemporary Platonism.

We have noted already (above, p. 363) some correspondences with Numenius, though in which direction the influence is going is uncertain. I will here confine myself, as in the case of the two previous investigations, to setting out the philosophical framework of the *Oracles*, disregarding as far as possible the mythological and poetical accretions.

It is plain, first of all, that, as in the case of Numenius, there is in the *Oracles* a distinction made between a higher and a lower God, both of whom appear to be regarded as intellects, although the Supreme God is usually termed simply 'Father'. In Fr. 7 Des Places, a passage which has been closely connected with Numenius, we find:

For all things did the Father bring to completion, and handed them over to the second Intellect, whom all you race of mortals calls the first.

This seems most naturally to imply that the Father is the *prôtos nous*. Like Numenius' First God, it is totally transcendent, and superior to any involvement in creation. It 'snatches itself away' (Fr. 3), not consorting even with its own Power (*dynamis*). It is not to be apprehended by any normal mental effort, but only as a result of transcendental meditation, by what is termed 'the flower of the mind' (Fr. 1). The Father is described also as 'the paternal abyss' (*bythos*, Fr. 18), a term reminiscent of Valentinian Gnosis. The 'God-nurtured Silence' is also mentioned (Fr. 16), but it is not clear how far this is being hypostasized.

The Power mentioned in Fr. 3 is distinguished in Fr. 4 from the Demiurgic, secondary *nous* as follows: 'The Power is with Him (*sc.* the Father), Intellect [proceeds] from Him.' We seem to have here once again a female entity intimately associated with the Supreme Principle, not unlike the Valentinian Ennoia, but whether the Dynamis has any role in generating the Nous is not clear from the fragments. The Neo-platonists discerned here a sort of Trinity, the Dynamis being a middle term between the unqualified essence of the Father and his actualiza-tion, the Demiurge.

As for the Demiurge, *nous* proper, he is represented as a Dyad, and here the connexion with Numenius is once again close. In Fr. 8 we find the following:

By this (*sc.* the Father) a Dyad sits; for it has two functions, both to com-prehend by intellect the intelligible realm, and to bring sense-perception to the (material) world.

Like Numenius' Second God, the Nous both contemplates its own realm, consisting of the Ideas generated by the Father (described in a long fragment, Fr. 37), and involves itself with the realm below it. It is described as 'the craftsman of the fiery (i.e. noetic) cosmos' (Frr. 5; 33), and it sends out, as does Poemandres, a fiery *logos* into the physical cosmos to organize it (e.g. Fr. 5).

Standing on the border between the intelligible and the sensible worlds, acting both as a barrier and as a link between them, we find an entity personified as Hecate, the goddess of the Underworld in tra-ditional Greek religion. She is described in the Oracles as a 'diaphragm' or 'membrane' (*hypeʒôkôs hymên*, Fr. 6), and appears to be the channel through which influences from above are shed upon the physical world. In Fr. 30 she is described as 'fount of founts, a womb containing all things'. She is regularly given the epithet 'life-producing (*ʒôogonos*, e.g. Fr. 32).

In Fr. 50 a complication is introduced, when Hecate is described as having 'her centre established in the midst of the Fathers'. If the 'Fathers' here are to be taken as the supreme Father and the Demi-urge, then Hecate becomes identical with the Dynamis. Either, I suggest, the 'Fathers' here referred to are the Demiurge and a pro-jection of himself within the cosmos of whom we have no other clear report, or else the 'centre' of Hecate is indeed to be taken as the Dynamis, and this would in fact not be impossible. The female prin-ciple in the universe can be seen, as I believe it was by Speusippus, as manifesting itself variously at every level of being, from the primor-dial Dyad through Soul down to Matter, and this may in fact be the case with Hecate. We have seen similar ambiguities manifesting them-selves, after all, in the cases of Philo's Sophia and Plutarch's Isis.

From Hecate is derived the World Soul (Fr. 51). In a sense, Hecate herself may be viewed as the transcendent World Soul, while the entity which springs 'from her right flank' (*ibid.*) can be taken as the Soul in its immanent aspect. It is described as ensouling 'light, fire, aether, *kosmoi*'—in other words, the heavenly spheres. Physis (Nature), which rules the sphere below the Moon, is presumably an emanation in its turn of this Soul.

At the bottom of the scale of being, as usual, we find Matter. It is described (Fr. 34) as 'springing from' the Demiurge (according to the evidence of Proclus), and ultimately from the Father (Fr. 35). Psellus, in his *Summary of Chaldaean Doctrine* (*Hypotypôsis*, sect. 27), gives it the epithet *patrogenês*, 'born of the Father'. In surviving fragments this is applied only to Hecate, but there is no reason to doubt Psellus' evidence. This would emphasize the radical monism of Chaldaean metaphysics, analogous to that which we discerned in Eudorus, who also derives Matter from the Supreme Principle.

The world is nevertheless emphatically a place from which to flee, as it is for the Hermetic and Gnostic writers, and for Numenius. 'You must hasten towards the light and towards the rays of the Father, whence your soul was sent to you, clothed in much *nous*', we are told in Fr. 115. One is urged repeatedly to avoid contamination by Matter: 'Do not befoul your *pneuma* nor deepen the plane (*epipedon*)' (Fr. 104) —the latter injunction being apparently an exhortation against developing three-dimensionality! 'Let the immortal depth of the soul be opened up! Strain upward with all the power of your eyes!' (Fr. 112). Ethical doctrine is thus based on the necessity for ascetic withdrawal from all material influences. The lower soul is subject to Nature and to Fate: 'Do not look upon Nature; that name is enmeshed with Fate!' (Fr. 102). 'Do not add to the portion of Fate!' (Fr. 103). Fr. 107 expatiates on this theme. This lower soul is described as the 'vehicle' (*ochêma*) which the rational soul sheds as it ascends through the planetary spheres to its true home beyond the cosmos.

The elaborate system of intermediate beings—daemons, angels and lesser gods—of the *Oracles* need not concern us, beyond noting their existence. They are an elaboration upon Platonism of the same type as the aeons and other hypostases of Gnosticism. The system of theurgy, centred upon Hecate, is another feature external to true Platonism, and thus need not detain us, important though it was to become for later Neoplatonism.

There is much, no doubt, in the *Oracles* that reflects Persian or popular magical influences, and the tone pervading them is hardly philosophical, but yet the basic metaphysical scheme may reasonably be seen as derived, in both substance and terminology, from some form of contemporary Platonism.

That is all that can be said in this work about what has been termed 'the underworld of Platonism'. It has been a rather superficial and selective survey, but it will, I hope, serve to indicate that the influence of the Platonic world-view penetrated very widely into the seething mass of sects and salvation-cults that sprang up within the Greco-Roman world in the first two centuries A.D.

All the systems that I have selected, the Valentinians, the *Poemandres*, and the *Oracles*, derive all existence, down even to Matter, from one Supreme Principle. They recognize also a distinction between this Supreme Principle and a Demiurge, the latter directly responsible for the creation of the world—though in Gnosticism proper the status of this entity is one of very doubtful honour. There is also recognized a pervasive female principle, responsible for multiplicity, differentiation, and the generation (and ultimate salvation or return) of all lower existence. The female principle tends to be split into two or three entities, arising at different levels. We have seen such a figure manifesting itself in this way within Platonism as well. The theory of the nature of the soul, its descent into matter, its strategy of escape, and its destiny after death, is also close to that of Platonism. In addition, there are such pervasive images as that of Light against Darkness, the inexhaustible Fount of Being, and the wings of the Soul, which, if not derived from Platonism, are certainly shared in common with it. Platonism, therefore, in its 'Middle' development, stands out as at least one important influence in the formation of these systems.

On one system of paramount importance Platonism had a most powerful influence, that of Christianity. The subject of Christian Platonism, however, in particular that of Clement and Origen, of the Alexandrian School of exegesis, would extend this book beyond reasonable limits. Clement, in fact, seems to derive much of his Platonism from Philo, though he must certainly have been influenced by contemporary trends. Origen is a figure of much greater interest, and deserves careful study. I can only hope that the clarification of the various trends in Platonism undertaken here will assist such a study.

B. SOME MISCELLANEOUS PLATONISTS

In the remainder of this chapter I propose to accord brief attention to those figures on the Middle Platonist scene who, because they fit into no obvious 'school' or trend, have not found a place in any of the previous chapters. These comprise, first, two 'popularizers', Theon of Smyrna and Maximus of Tyre, then the anti-Christian polemicist Celsus, then the *Timaeus*-commentator Calcidius (for whose essential Middle Platonism I shall try to argue), and lastly the summaries of Platonic doctrine given by Diogenes Laertius as an appendix to his *Life of Plato*, and by Hippolytus in Book I of the *Refutation of all Heresies*.

I. THEON OF SMYRNA

A statue found in Smyrna (IGR IV 1449), datable stylistically to the reign of Hadrian, which was set up by 'the priest Theon, for his father, Theon the Platonic philosopher', establishes Theon satisfactorily enough in the early decades of the second century. He is thus more or less contemporary with Nicomachus of Gerasa, with whose work he is in direct competition. Theon is noted for his one surviving treatise, *Mathematical Principles Useful for the Study of Plato* (abbrev. *Expos.*), a work which reveals him as an enthusiastic Platonist of Pythagorean tendency (inevitable, perhaps, in view of his subject-matter), but a dilettante rather than an expert in matters mathematical, musical and astronomical.

He makes, indeed, no claim to originality. Long passages are quoted verbatim and with acknowledgement from the Peripatetic commentator Adrastus of Aphrodisias (on mathematics and harmonics), and from Thrasyllus (on harmonics and astronomy), and the whole work is essentially a compilation from these two immediate sources—unless we include the mysterious Dercyllides, who is quoted on a number of occasions, as a source which Theon is using directly, rather than through Thrasyllus. We must be grateful, at any rate, to Theon for not making any serious attempt to cover his tracks.

Besides the *Expositio*, we also have a report, in an Arabic source, of a work of his on the correct order of reading the Platonic dialogues, in which he accepts Thrasyllus' arrangement by tetralogies. Thrasyllus is thus a major influence upon him. Whether or not he also made use of

Moderatus depends upon what value one gives to the attribution by Stobaeus to Moderatus of a short passage on Number, which is in fact identical with Theon, *Expos.* p. 18, 3ff. Hiller. Stobaeus may have confused his references (though he does not quote Theon elsewhere) or Theon may be copying Moderatus, or—more probably—both Theon and Moderatus are simply copying Thrasyllus.

Theon is not, at any rate, an original thinker. He is, however, useful as evidence for Middle Platonic theorizing on mathematics and astronomy. The book seems to have been intended to cover all the five subjects mentioned in *Republic* VII as essential components of education, arithmetic, harmonics, geometry, stereometry and astronomy, but the whole manuscript was split into two parts at some stage in the tradition, and the sections on geometry and stereometry were lost, leaving us with the first, second and fifth topics.

His introductory remarks are a salutary reminder to all Platonic scholars:

Everyone would agree that it is not possible to understand the mathematical material in Plato without being oneself practised in that discipline; and he himself seems to demonstrate in many places that such training is not useless nor without advantage in general. To come to a study of Plato's writings with training in the whole theory of geometry and music and astronomy is a blessed thing indeed for anyone lucky enough to possess it, and it is something by no means simple or easy to acquire, but which requires a good deal of hard work from childhood on.

He makes much use of Pythagorean material, possibly pseudo-epigraphic, though he quotes no one but Archytas, Hippasus and Philolaus. A passage on the all-pervasiveness of harmony (p. 12, 10–25), with its portrayal of God as harmonizer of all discords, and the threefold comparison of cosmos, city and household, found also in the *Pythagorica* (e.g. Eccelus, *On Justice*, p. 78, 6ff. Thesleff) and in Philo, *Prov.* II 15, is worth noting, as is the elaborate image of Platonic philosophy as an initiation into a mystery (pp. 14, 17—16, 2), an image dear to Philo's heart, as we have seen. Theon goes so far as to distinguish five stages in the initiation, purification, communication of the ritual, vision (*epopteia*), 'adornment with garlands' and, finally, 'the joy that comes from unity and converse with the gods', corresponding to the Platonic *homoiôsis theôi*. It is the most elaborate form of a conceit which we find also in the work of 'Heraclitus', *On the Allegories of Homer* (ch. 3), and Albinus, *Did.* 182, 7ff., and serves here as a dramatization of the claim of Platonism to be a religion in its own right.

The fact that both Nicomachus in Gerasa and Theon in Smyrna turned out handbooks of this sort at about the same time, and that they both survived into the Renaissance, together with such more general summaries of Platonism as those of Albinus and Apuleius, shows the great demand in the second century and later for such handy introductions. Theon doubtless wrote more advanced treatises—he alludes himself to his *Commentary on the Republic* in the course of his discussion of the myth of Er in the *Expositio* (p. 146, 4 Hiller)—but later demand decreed that this basic handbook was all that would survive, even as it declared in favour of Albinus' *Didaskalikos* over his commentaries.

2. MAXIMUS OF TYRE

Maximus of Tyre, like Apuleius, was a sophist rather than a philosopher, and a distinguished member of the Second Sophistic movement. Eusebius gives a *floruit* for him of A.D. 152, and he is said by the *Suda* to have spent some time in Rome during the reign of Commodus (A.D. 180–91). Certainly he visited Rome more than once, since the first six of his forty-one surviving epideictic discourses are described as having been delivered in Rome 'during his first stay'. No doubt he travelled all over the Graeco-Roman world, as did the other great sophists of his time, delivering both set and extemporaneous orations to large and appreciative audiences.

Maximus considers himself a philosopher, which for him means using all the resources of contemporary rhetoric to adorn traditional philosophic themes, very much as Apuleius was doing at the same time. Further, he is a Platonic philosopher, which means that he takes up a Platonic position on the questions with which he deals, and, like Apuleius, professes great reverence for the personality of Socrates, as well as for Plato and Pythagoras.

Although he is primarily concerned with the artistic embellishment of platitudes, Maximus contains much of interest for the general background of second-century Platonism. Particularly important are his *Oration* 11 Hobein (*Who is God according to Plato?*), which gives a useful survey of Middle Platonic formulations of the divine nature, complementing the accounts given by Albinus, Apuleius and Numenius, though showing no very strong affinity to any of them; *Orations*

8 and 9 (*On the Daemon of Socrates*) which present a comprehensive theory of daemons analogous to that of Apuleius in the *De Deo Socratis*: Orations 5 (*Whether one should Pray*) and 13 (*Whether, if Divination exists, there is Free Will*), discuss the knotty problem of providence and free will, and give what must be the basic Middle Platonic position, heavily influenced as it is by Stoicism, of which we have seen another good example in the *De Providentia* 1 of Philo, and of which we have a summary in ch. 26 of Albinus' *Didaskalikos*; and Oration 41 (*If God is Responsible for Good, then Whence comes Evil?*), which contains a good discussion of the problem of evil. Of all these, only in Orations 5 and 13, on the question of free will, does one get any sense that Maximus is giving very much of himself to the discussion, and even then nothing of much interest is revealed. All through the *Orations*, however, there can be found striking images and instances of scholastic terminology, which are useful evidence of what was common currency by way of Platonic philosophy in educated circles in the latter half of the second century.

Maximus' metaphysics are simple enough—God the Father and his Logos, which is his agent in the organizing of the universe, and a system of planetary gods and daemons—and it does not serve to connect him with any particular school or movement. Nor do his ethics place him firmly within either the Stoic or Peripatetic wing of Platonism. However, there is no question that he would repay rather closer study than I am prepared to give him in the present context.

3. CELSUS

We must not omit at least a mention, also, of the Platonist Celsus, who, probably in the 160s, composed a comprehensive polemic against the Christians, entitled the *True Account* (*Alêthês Logos*), of which we have a fairly complete summary preserved by Origen, in his polemic against Celsus composed some ninety years later. Celsus is the first Platonist, to our knowledge, to take official note of this upstart sect, and his work, even if not very important for its positive doctrine, is of great interest as an impassioned assertion, not only of the Platonist, but of the Hellenic view of God and the order of the universe—such matters as the immutability and impassivity of God and the regularity of Nature, principles against which Christianity offended grossly.

Celsus does not make a clear distinction between orthodox Christians and some of the wilder Gnostic sects, of whose antics he had heard rumours. He himself does not reveal any doctrinal tendencies which would place him in one 'school' or another among the Platonists. He shows the expected contempt for such a notion as the resurrection of the body (*ap.* Orig. *Contra Celsum* v 14), or the idea that God made man in his own image (vi 63), there being nothing that could resemble God. At vii 42, he gives a basic account of the Platonist view of the supreme God, which is incompatible with the notion of his involving himself too closely with Matter. He mentions in this conr exion three ways of attaining a conception of God, synthesis, analysis and analogy, which correspond approximately to the three ways distinguished by Albinus at *Did.* p. 165, 4ff. (above, pp. 284f.), though there is no indication that Celsus is following Albinus. Contact between man and God is effected, of course, through the agency of daemons (e.g. viii 28, 33, 35).

All this is very elementary, and thus not very useful to us, except as an indication of a sort of Platonist consensus, such as we observe also in Maximus. The *True Account* is a most interesting document, none the less; it is a sign that the Christians are coming to be of some weight in society, to such an extent as to merit the sort of polemic refutation which hitherto the schools had directed against each other. Celsus' work is of the same genre as Atticus' assault on the Peripatetics, or Plutarch's attacks on the Epicureans and the Stoics, and it serves very well to delineate the battle lines.

4. CALCIDIUS

There survives out of the ancient world only one commentary on a Platonic dialogue in Latin, that of Calcidius[1] on the *Timaeus*, and it presents great problems for the historian of Platonism. The only clue to Calcidius' time and place resides in his dedication of his work to one Osius, who has been taken, following the indications of a number of the manuscripts, to be none other than Bishop Osius of Corduba (A.D. 256–357), the spiritual adviser of Constantine and leading light of the Councils of Nicaea and Sardica. This identification has been challenged, notably by J. H. Waszink in his great edition of Calcidius, on two grounds. One is that, had Calcidius been thus connected with Bishop Osius, then Isidore of Seville (A.D. 560–636), who is most assiduous in mentioning all Spanish writers that he knows, could

---

[1] Ed. J. H. Waszink, *Timaeus a Calcidio translatus commentarioque instructus*, Plato Latinus, vol. iv London and Leiden 1962.

hardly have failed to mention him. As a counterweight, Waszink comes up with another Osius, an Imperial official attested at Milan in and around A.D. 395, though he offers this individual mainly to indicate that there were other Osii. This argument from silence cannot be taken as conclusive, however, and it involves dismissing as a mere fabrication the testimony of one family of manuscripts that Calcidius was an archdeacon in the service of Osius. All that the argument indicates is that Isidore was unaware of the existence of Calcidius' *Commentary*. A possible alternative explanation of this is that the work fell into obscurity for many centuries after it was written, only emerging in the late Middle Ages. It is, after all, a curiously ambiguous work for an orthodox Christian to write. Various small indications suggest that the author *is* a Christian, but it must be said that he wears his faith lightly. Even the one Christian author that he quotes, Origen, was distinctly out of favour by the latter half of the fourth century. It is almost incredible that anyone avowing himself a Christian could have written such a commentary on a pagan work much after A.D. 350. Even a man like Marius Victorinus makes it quite clear whose side he is on. With Calcidius, the argument still continues as to whether he was a Christian or not.

Waszink's second argument (*Intro.* pp. xiv–xv) is linguistic, and is not without weight. Calcidius' vocabulary is in many respects peculiar to himself, but a number of his distinctive words are attested first otherwise only in authors of the end of the fourth century and later, such as Jerome, Augustine, Ambrose, Macrobius, Boethius and Cassiodorus. It is hardly likely, argues Waszink, that a hack writer like Calcidius would be the innovator here. We may add to this that Augustine appears to know nothing of Calcidius' translation of the *Timaeus*, and still uses Cicero's version.

This argument has some force, but it is not absolutely compelling. Calcidius had to wrestle with the rendering of the technical terms of Middle Platonic scholasticism into Latin, and he rises to the occasion manfully. The coining of new items of jargon is after all not by any means the exclusive property of great minds, and our evidence is not, I think, so complete as to enable us to be certain when these words were coined. Certainly Calcidius writes late Latin, with all the turgidity and elaboration that that can imply, and on linguistic considerations alone would more comfortably be placed in the fifth rather than in the fourth century, but linguistic considerations are in this case, I feel, outweighed by considerations of content.

The chief conclusion that Waszink draws from all this is, it seems to me, unjustified by the evidence. Assuming Calcidius to date from at least the end of the fourth century, he concludes that he must have been influenced by Porphyry's *Commentary on the Timaeus*, and assembles an array of passages with a view to proving this. But to the unprejudiced eye there is nothing in Calcidius that requires us to postulate his acquaintance with any distinctively Neoplatonic doctrine, and much to suggest that he knew nothing of Porphyry's *Commentary*. Calcidius is by no means a mindless compiler, but he does not pretend to be doing more than rendering into Latin, with some explanatory comments and elaborations, a source work or works from which he departs very little. Waszink's theory demands that Calcidius pick and choose very selectively from Porphyry. For a start, Calcidius dismisses the introductory portion of the *Timaeus*— everything before 31C, in fact—as unworthy of comment, whereas Porphyry began commenting from the beginning, employing allegorical interpretation to deal with the introductory portions, including the Atlantis Myth. Nowhere does Calcidius show any knowledge of that technique of allegorical interpretation which is such a feature of Neoplatonic commentary. For example, at *Tim.* 38D, the discussion of the meaning of the 'contrary power' of Venus and Mercury, Calcidius shows no inkling of the elaborate, Chaldean-influenced exegesis of Porphyry (Procl. *In Tim.* III 64, 11ff.), but merely gives astronomical explanations.

To mention another detail, but the sort of detail which has great significance in the estimating of influences, there were two figures which were traditionally used to illustrate Plato's enumeration of the numbers of the soul at *Tim.* 35Bff., a lambda-shaped figure or a straight line. Calcidius (c. 32) employs a lambda-shaped figure; Porphyry (Procl. *In Tim.* II 171, 4ff.) favours the straight line, as did Severus before him (above, p. 264). It is plain here that Calcidius is following the Peripatetic commentator Adrastus (as is clear from many other indications), and owes nothing to Porphyry.

None of the alleged dependences on Porphyry, on the other hand, involve any compelling verbal or doctrinal similarity. In all cases they involve the dangerous assumption that the doctrine in question could not have been held by any Middle Platonist—Numenius, for example, to whom in any case Waszink admits Porphyry was much indebted. The passage in the discourse on Fate and Providence, where there is mention of a succession of divine entities (ch. 176), is a case in point:

In the first place all things that exist and the world itself are held together and ruled principally by the highest god (*summus deus*), who is the Supreme Good (*summum bonum*), beyond all substance and all nature, superior to all appraisal and understanding, after whom all things seek, whereas himself he possess full perfection and has no need of any fellowship.

This Supreme God is superior to a second principle 'which the Greeks call *nous*', which governs all other things but which itself derives goodness from the Supreme God, towards whom it is constantly turned. Third in this hierarchy comes 'that which is termed the "second mind", that is, the Soul of the World in its three divisions.'

This is certainly interesting, but is it necessarily Porphyrian? Looking at it against the background of Albinus' utterances in chapter 10 of the *Didaskalikos*, and of what we have seen of the doctrines of Numenius, what is there here that is new or unfamiliar? The supreme principle is above *nous* certainly, and 'above being' (using the famous phrase of *Republic* VI, 509B), but we have seen this latter term being used in the Neopythagorean tradition, by 'Brotinus' and by Moderatus (above, p. 347), although not by Numenius.[1] Numenius' supreme god manages to be above *nous*, while still being some sort of intellect himself; he is also 'The Good', while the demiurgic *nous* is only 'good'—essentially the doctrine which we find here. Calcidius' supreme god, we may note, is not described as The One or even as 'One'. I would prefer to try to fit Calcidius into the Middle Platonic spectrum. It has been noted above in Chapter Six (pp. 320ff.) that he is following here the doctrine on Fate of Pseudo-Plutarch and Apuleius, with certain modifications. Other indications, both in this portion of the work and in many others, point to a second source which Calcidius is interweaving with Adrastus, and that source is Numenian in influence. One hesitates to identify it with Numenius himself, both because there is no clear evidence that Numenius wrote a commentary on the *Timaeus*, and because Calcidius on a number of occasions mentions Numenius by name, a thing that one would not expect him to do if he were using Numenius directly (by contrast, he never mentions Adrastus, whom he is certainly using verbatim, even as he is plainly transcribing with minimal alterations his source on Fate).

The proportion of originality that all this leaves for Calcidius himself is small, but at the very least we must credit him with inserting references to Cicero (chs. 27; 266), Terence (ch. 184) and Vergil (chs.

---

[1] See on this J. Whittaker, '*Epekeina nou kai ousias*', *Vigiliae Christianae* 23 (1969), pp. 91–104.

66, and probably 353), and with a fair ability to render Greek verse into Latin, which he does on a number of occasions. The use of Origen (probably his lost *Commentary on Genesis*) in chs. 276–8, with the accompanying references to Acylas (Aquila), Symmachus, *Proverbs* and Philo (all, no doubt, taken from Origen) we may also credit to him rather than to his source, but we cannot be so certain about many of the other references to Scripture and to the doctrines of 'the Hebrews'. There is a fair possibility that in many cases he may be dependent on Numenius for his scriptural references, and if this were so, it would go far towards showing that Numenius had knowledge of Philo, since, as I have indicated in the last chapter (p. 378), these references to the *Hebraei* contain doctrines that appear Philonic. But the whole question is wrapped in uncertainties.

It is hardly suitable in the case of Calcidius to speak of a distinct philosophical position, since it is unclear how much of himself, if anything, he is putting into his commentary. I propose instead to survey, very briefly, the contents of the commentary, noting any doctrines or formulations that appear distinctive, or which would serve to link him to any school of thought in Middle Platonism. The commentary is arranged in sections, which he refers to himself as *tractatus* (c. 31, p. 80, 15 Wasz.), dealing with the text more or less continuously from *Tim.* 31c onwards. The introduction lists twenty-seven such sections, but only sixteen survive, ending with a section *On Matter*, which brings the commentary up to *Tim.* 53c. The text does not break off abruptly, and since the translation which accompanies the commentary breaks off at the same point, it is possible that Calcidius never completed his original design. The surviving work is divided into two books, the break being made at 39c3, the description of the Great Year. Book II begins with a section *On the Four Classes of Living Things*, commenting on 39e3ff. This division, we may note, bears no relation to the division into books followed by Proclus, who seems to be following ultimately that of Porphyry. We know, at least, that he is following Porphyry in ending his first book at 27B (*In Tim.* I 204, 24ff.), at a point at which Calcidius had not even begun. The *Commentary* is preceded by a dedicatory letter to Osius (beginning with a tag from Isocrates!), and then a translation of the *Timaeus* up to 53C, as I have mentioned.

After a short introduction, explaining the great difficulty of the *Timaeus* (chs. 1–7), in the course of which he dismisses the introductory portion as a simple narration of ancient history (p. 58, 26ff. Wasz.),

Calcidius begins his commentary with a section *On the Creation of the World* (chs. 8–25), being an exegesis of *Tim.* 31c3–32c8. This exegesis comprises, first, an exhaustive exposition of the theory of proportions, arithmetical, geometric and harmonic, illustrated by diagrams (chs. 8–19). A very similar exposition of astronomy from ch. 58 to ch. 91 can be seen to be a literal translation from the commentary of Adrastus (from the parallel text of Theon of Smyrna, who is avowedly using Adrastus), so that it is likely that chs. 8–19 derive from this source also. What is revealed to us is an insight into Calcidius' methods of compilation—the appropriation of large sections of a source work word for word, without acknowledgement.

That he is doing this in many places with Adrastus we know from the evidence of Theon. Adrastus' commentary seems to have been concerned, however, with matters mathematical and scientific, not with theology, and he was a Peripatetic, not a Platonist nor a Pythagorean, so that there are many parts of Calcidius' commentary that cannot reasonably be attributed to him. One such part, as we have seen, is the section on Fate, Providence and Freewill, where once again Calcidius is indulging in literal transcription of his source, as we can see from the parallel, though somewhat abbreviated text of Pseudo-Plutarch. This source exhibits tendencies that can be characterized as Numenian, but since Numenius is occasionally mentioned by name, I prefer, as I have said, not to identify this with Numenius himself. Let us call this second source simply *S*.

It is not always easy to discern where Adrastus ends and *S* begins, but in chs. 20–2 we can see a distinct change of tone and subject-matter from Adrastus. Here *S* states a problem arising out of the discussion of *analogia*, as to how Fire and Earth can be in any relation of proportion, one being essentially pyramidal, the other cubic. By way of solution, a theory of three qualities of each element is propounded which is not found elsewhere in extant Middle Platonic sources, though Proclus, later, is familiar with it (*In Tim.* II 39, 19ff.), as is Nemesius (*Nat. Hom.* 5, pp. 163–4 Matthaei). According to this theory, Fire is accorded the qualities of sharpness, rarity, and mobility, Earth those of bluntness, solidity and immobility. Thus the two intermediate elements, Air and Water, will act as ratios by appropriating respectively two qualities from the former and one from the latter, or one from the former and two from the latter. The whole scheme is a triumph of scholastic ingenuity. It is interesting to note that the only Middle Platonist, apart from Numenius himself, that Nemesius ever mentions by name is Numenius' friend Cronius. I hesitate to propose Cronius as Calcidius' second source, but I think that he may be borne in mind as a possible candidate.

In chs. 23–5 we turn to the question of the eternity of the world, in connexion with *Tim.* 28BC, and here we face the great problem, in what sense can the world be said to be 'created'? *S* first points out that Plato has been careful to detail all the factors in the world's creation, agent, material, model and purpose. Though the material is physical and subject to destruction, the agent is divine, and this is sufficient to confer immortality upon the product. All things, says *S*, are either works of God, or of Nature, or of Man imitating Nature (that is, Art). All works of Nature have a temporal origin; the works of God are eternal. The origin of a work of God is, then, not temporal but causal. That is to say, *S* adopts Taurus' meaning (4) of *genêtos*: 'dependent for its existence on a cause outside itself'. He thus rejects the doctrine of temporal creation.

The world is composed of all the material that there is (ch. 24), so that it cannot be destroyed by assault from without, nor by materials from within flowing away in any direction, since there is nowhere for them to flow to. Finally (ch. 25), the world is made in the image of an eternal exemplar, which it must thus imitate as closely as it can, by maintaining itself throughout all time.

I have gone into these details, from the early sections of the *Commentary*, merely to give a sample of the riches, in the way of Middle Platonic scholastic doctrine, which may be won from a careful study of this work. It is to be hoped that J. H. Waszink will complete his work of exegesis, of which the first part only has appeared.[1]

Of the rest of the work, most interesting, perhaps, are the sections on Providence and Fate, which we have already examined; the section on Daemons (chs. 129–36), ultimately dependent upon the *Epinomis*, but more immediately upon Numenius; and the long treatise on Matter (chs. 268–354), which brings at least the surviving portion of the commentary to a close. This reveals clear traces of Numenian doctrine, but the fact that Numenius is referred to by name on a number of occasions makes it the less likely, as I have said, that he is the immediate source. The doctrine that Matter is neither corporeal nor incorporeal, but rather potentially both (chs. 319–20) agrees with Albinus, Apuleius and Hippolytus (*Ref.* 1 19, 3), but this simply indicates that it is basic Middle Platonic doctrine.

[1] *Studien zum Timaioskommentar des Calcidius* I, Leiden 1964.

As we have seen, Calcidius' metaphysical scheme bears a strong resemblance to that of Numenius, with its hierarchy of three principles, the Good, Nous and a second *nous*, which is identified with the World Soul (ch. 176). Where he stands on questions of ethics or logic is not clear, since these subjects do not arise in the course of commenting upon the *Timaeus*. There is at any rate nothing that connects him with the Neoplatonist movement, and very little that identifies him as a Christian. He seems to be one of those intellectuals who, in those difficult times, managed to reconcile the new order of things with the old, finding shelter in the household of the Bishop of Corduba to pursue his Platonic studies, adopting enough of Christianity to satisfy that powerful cleric, while at the same time trying to interest him in some of the wonders of Platonism.

5. TWO SUMMARIES OF PLATONIC DOCTRINE

We may end our survey with a look at the summaries of Platonic doctrine given by Diogenes Laertius (III 67–109) and the Christian Hippolytus (*Refutation of All Heresies*, I 19).

(a) Diogenes Laertius

The evidence of Diogenes Laertius comes from the second and third of three appendices to his *Life of Plato* (the first being that account of his works by Thrasyllus to which we have already adverted (above, p. 305). The second appendix (sects. 67–80) sets out the doctrines of Plato in summary form, beginning with psychology (67–9), and going on to the rest of metaphysics and physics (69–77), drawing exclusively here on the *Timaeus*. We find then (78–80) a short account of ethics. For information on logic we have to wait until the end of the third appendix (108–9). The whole of this appendix (80–109), which simply lists a series of 'divisions' of entities ascribed to Plato, is said to derive from Aristotle, though no particular work of Aristotle's is mentioned, and the whole thing sounds much more like a later summary than anything that Aristotle would be responsible for.

Although Diogenes is writing probably in the early years of the third century A.D., his source for Platonic philosophy seems to be far older than this. It shows no sign of emanating from any particular school of Platonism, apart from exhibiting a mildly Peripatetic tendency in ethics, but merely states basic doctrine. Nevertheless, it is of some small value as background material. It begins as follows:

Plato held that the soul is immortal, and that by transmigration it puts on many bodies, and that it has an arithmetical first principle, whereas the body has a geometrical one; and he defined soul as 'the idea of the vital spirit (*pneuma*) omnidimensionally extended'.

This definition of the soul is a curious corruption of the mathematical definition of Speusippus, so curious that one suspects a corruption in the text, *pneumatos* wandering in from somewhere else. But perhaps Diogenes himself may take the credit for the muddle. Certainly for a materialist like Antiochus the Stoic definition '*pneuma enthermon*' would be perfectly acceptable, and this has rather mindlessly been combined with the mathematical model of the soul derived from the Old Academy. At any rate, the text goes on to give a description of the tripartite soul, drawing on various parts of the *Timaeus*.

Two basic principles are next distinguished, God and Matter (69), God being called Nous and Cause. It is not clear from Diogenes' account whether he holds that the universe was created in time, as he is following the *Timaeus* account closely and uncritically. Naturally, also, he holds to a four-element universe. The Ideas are introduced in sect. 76, as being impressed upon Matter. Their definition is a modified Xenocratean one: they are 'causes and principles of natural objects'. This is in accord with the basic Middle Platonic definition, as stated by Arius Didymus and by Albinus.

In the sphere of Ethics, the *telos* is 'likeness to God'. Virtue is first stated to be sufficient for Happiness, but this is immediately qualified by the assertion that it requires as instruments (*organa*) both bodily and external goods. Yet, we are told, the Sage can achieve happiness even without these. Such vacillation in fact represents well enough the spectrum of possible Platonist positions. A belief in Providence and in daemons is also proclaimed. Finally, to complete the synthesis of definitions, the Good is stated to be that which is in accord and in agreement with Nature.

There is no mention here of logical questions, but the 'Aristotelian' section ends with the following statement:

Of existing things, some are termed absolute (*kath' hauta*) and others relative (*pros ti*). Those termed absolute are such as require no other term to complete their sense, such as 'man', 'horse', and all ther animals. . . . To those which are called relative belong those which req ire something else o complete the sense, as for instance 'greater than', 'less than', 'faster than', 'better than', and so on.

This is a simplified form of the division attributed to Plato by Hermodorus (above, p. 8). The authority of Aristotle is adduced for attributing it to Plato here, which would be of some interest if we could trust Diogenes. At any rate, there is no attempt being made here to father Aristotelian logic on Plato. The Old Academic pair of categories is still recognized as Platonic by Diogenes' source.

(b) *Hippolytus*

Rather more interesting than the account given by Diogenes is that found in the work of the Christian apologist Hippolytus, *The Refutation of All Heresies* (*Ref.*), written at some time in the early decades of the third century in Rome, when Hippolytus was anti-pope (or pope, depending on whose side one was on) in rivalry to Calixtus. His purpose in writing was to show that all Christian heresies derived from one or other of the pagan philosophical sects, whose tenets the heresiarchs had incorporated into their doctrine. Whatever about the theory, we are grateful for his summaries, cursory though they are, of the various philosophies. His summary of Platonism is of particular interest, as it coincides at a number of points with Albinus and Apuleius, while adding certain formulations of its own, and thus provides further evidence of what we may call 'the basic handbook'—post-Arius Didymus vintage. The summary is contained in *Ref.* 1 19 (given also by Diels in *Doxographi Graeci* pp. 567–70).

Hippolytus begins with the three first principles, God, Matter and Archetype (*paradeigma*). God is the 'creator' (*poiêtês*) and organizer of this universe, and exercises *pronoia* over it. Matter is that which underlies everything, which we call 'the receiving agent' and 'nurse' (*Tim.* 52D). From the ordering of this entity spring the four elements, from which all the other composite entities (*synkrimata*, a Stoic term) in turn arise. The Paradigm is the thought (*dianoia*) of God, 'which Plato also calls *idea*, as being a kind of image on which God can concentrate in his soul when constructing the universe.'

The Ideas, then, are thoughts of God, as we should expect. The mention of God's 'soul' is thoroughly peculiar, but may be a contribution of Hippolytus' own.

God is incorporeal, formless (*aneideos*), and cognizable only by the wise. The term *aneideos* is, again, most peculiar in this connexion, being elsewhere (e.g. Philo, *Conf.* 85; Albinus, *Did.* p. 163, 5) always an epithet of Matter, never, even among the Neoplatonists, of God.

Again, Hippolytus may be simply being rather cavalier about his apportioning of epithets here.

Matter is now described as 'potentially body, but never actually so', a Peripateticizing formulation that we have found also in Albinus (p. 163, 6–7) and Apuleius (*De Plat.* 1 5, 192), but not in Arius Didymus, a circumstance which, while not tying Hippolytus' source to the 'school of Gaius', serves, it seems to me, to give it a *terminus post quem*.

Matter, he continues, is coeval (*synchronos*) with God, and thus the world is uncreated (*agenêtos*), since Plato says that it is constructed from Matter. From its being uncreated it follows that it is indestructible. Only in so far as it is a body, composed of many qualities and forms, can it be said to be 'created' and 'destructible'. Hippolytus' source thus plunges into one of the chief controversies of Middle Platonism, the true meaning of *genêtos*, and comes down on the side of the majority (though employing the provocative term *agenêtos*). In the process, however, he contributes a further interpretation of *genêtos* to the four given by Taurus (above, p. 243):

Some of the Platonists mixed both concepts (*sc.* createdness and eternity), using the following example: even as a wagon can be said to survive as indestructible by having each of its parts renewed in turn, so that even if each individual part suffer destruction, it itself as a whole remains unimpaired; even so the cosmos is constantly experiencing destruction in its parts, but yet remains eternally because the parts that are removed are restored and replaced with equal parts (19, 5).

This 'wagon' image is related to Taurus' third sense of 'created' i.e 'always in process of generation', but it introduces a different notion, that of periodic renewal of parts, rather than of the constant flux of change. It in fact ties in most interestingly with a passage of Plutarch, *Theseus* 23, where Plutarch introduces a 'footnote' about the *Theoris*, the sacred ship which carried in historical times the yearly Athenian delegation to Delos (cf. *Phaedo* 58Aff.):

The ship on which Theseus sailed with the youths and returned in safety, the thirty-oared galley, was preserved by the Athenians down to the time of Demetrius of Phaleron (regent of Athens, 317–307 B.C.). They took away the old timbers from time to time, and put new and sound ones in their places, so that the vessel became a standing illustration for the philosophers in the much-debated 'Augmentation Argument' (*auxomenos logos*), some declaring that it remained the same, others that it was not the same vessel.

The *auxomenos logos*, of which we have no other ancient evidence,

presumably was originally a puzzle concerning identity, possibly propounded by Sceptics (it need not necessarily, after all, predate the
demise of the *Theoris*). Hippolytus' source is here reporting its use as
an argument for the eternity of the world, which is an interesting
development. The *Theoris* as an *exemplum* has given way to a humble
wagon.

On the nature of God and the Soul (19, 6–11), Hippolytus is being
eristic and thus of little interest. He juxtaposes *Laws* IV 715E, *Tim.*
41A, *Phaedrus* 246E and *Tim.* 40E to try to show that Plato believes
both in one God and in many, and created ones at that. On the Soul,
he juxtaposes *Phaedrus* 245C and *Tim.* 41D to indicate that the soul is
both immortal, and composite and mortal. He pretends that such
contradictory views are held by different sets of Platonists, a manifest
travesty. He next credits Plato with belief in both good and evil
daemons (19, 9), and reports, more credibly, uncertainty among
Platonists on the question of reincarnation (the term *metensômatosis*,
incidentally, receives its first surviving mention here, 19, 12). Some
believe that souls re-enter bodies at fixed intervals and acquire stations
in life in accordance with their previous performance. Others argue,
basing themselves on the heavenly ride described in *Phaedrus* 246Eff.,
that souls are assigned a fixed place in the universe after death, good
or bad, and remain there. This latter seems less a Platonist than a
Christian belief, and how it is derived from the *Phaedrus* myth escapes
me.

Hippolytus turns next to ethics, beginning with a division of
Opposites into (a) those which have no means between them (*amesa*)
and (b) those which have (*emmesa*).[1] As examples of *amesa* he gives
waking and sleeping; of *emmesa*, goods and evils. As an example of
means, he mentions grey, between black and white. This rather obvious
distinction is not found in surviving sources before Alexander of
Aphrodisias, in the 2nd century A.D., so that once again Hippolytus is a
valuable source. His point in bringing in this distinction here seems to
be that good and evil, being *emmesa*, have a mean between them,
constituted by bodily and external 'goods', which are thus not properly
goods, but rather *mesa*, since they may be used for good or ill. In this

---

[1] Hippolytus actually gives a threefold division of 'things' (*pragmata*) into
amesa, *emmesa* and *mesa* ('means'). That this is a garbled form of the true schol-
astic division is shown by Simplicius' references to it in his *Commentary on the
De Caelo* (pp. 332, 1ff.; 340, 19ff.; 721, 25ff.). It was a subject of dispute in later
Platonism, it seems, whether there were *amesa* opposites at all. Also Alexander,
In Metaph. 257, 32; 644, 7, 9.

rather Stoic attitude he is in agreement with Albinus and Apuleius, though expressing himself somewhat differently. From now on, indeed, the order of topics, as well as the doctrine, agrees very well with both the *Didaskalikos* and the *De Platone*, showing that we are here close to the format of the 'basic handbook'.

The four virtues, we learn, are 'in respect of value, extremes (*akrotêtes*), but as regards their essence means (*mesotêtes*)', agreeing with *Did.* 184, 12ff. On either side of them they have attendant vices of excess and defect. Hippolytus lists all eight of these, which Albinus does not bother to do, while Apuleius, as we have seen (p. 330), combines the doctrine in a peculiar way with the Platonic three divisions of the soul.

Happiness, of course, consists in becoming like unto God (sect. 17), and this results when one becomes holy and just, with the accompaniment of wisdom (*phronêsis*). This pair of basic virtues, Holiness and Justice, are found in Apuleius (*De Plat.* II 7), but not in Albinus. The virtues are mutually entailed (*antakolouthein*), and are described as uniform (*monoeidês*)—this epithet answering to Apuleius' *unimoda* (II 5: 227), but to nothing in Albinus.

There is such a thing as Fate (sect. 19), but not everything is 'in accordance with it'. There is room for Free Will. Hippolytus then quotes two basic tags, *Phaedrus* 248C ('This is the ordinance of Adrasteia ...') and *Rep.* X 617E ('The responsibility is his who chooses; God is not responsible'). The first is quoted by the *De Fato* (568B, 570A), the second by Maximus of Tyre (*Or.* 41, 5) and Calcidius (ch. 154), but neither in fact by Albinus or Apuleius. We may note also that Hippolytus puts the discussion of Fate into the middle of his survey of Ethics, whereas in our other two sources it precedes this topic, being taken as a physical question.

Hippolytus resumes the order of the *Didaskalikos* with a remark on the involuntariness of vice (sect. 20), which corresponds rather closely to Albinus' ch. 31. He quotes in this connexion *Clitophon* 407D (wrongly attributing it to the *Republic*), and then raises the question as to how one can reasonably exact punishment for vice if it is involuntary. His answer is the same as that given by Albinus, that punishment should be administered as a cure, vice being a disease, and it should be welcomed as such.

Finally (sect. 23), he deals with the nature of Evil, denying that it is from God, or that it has any true existence. It arises merely by opposition to and as a byproduct (*kata parakolouthêsin*) of the Good. This latter phrase is a Stoic formulation in origin (cf. Gellius *NA* VII 1, 8), but plainly by this stage long since received into Platonism (Philo, *Prov.* II 82, seems already to recognize it). The problem of evil is not discussed as such by Albinus or Apuleius, but we have an oration on the subject by Maximus of Tyre (*Or.* 41), which takes the same line as that adumbrated here.

To conclude, Hippolytus' evidence (or that of his source), brief and sketchy as it is, nevertheless reveals a number of interesting formulations of doctrine of which we have no other evidence, and helps to round out our idea of what constituted the basic course in Platonism (at least in respect of Physics and Ethics) in the second century A.D.

C. CONCLUSION

With this pair of summary accounts of Platonic doctrine we close our survey of this period in Platonism. This final chapter has, I fear, been little more than a succession of loose ends, subjects and figures that could not properly be ignored in a survey of the period, but to do justice to which would have the book quite intolerably long. The purpose of this book, after all, has been to establish the main lines which Platonism followed during the period from Antiochus to Plotinus. I have tried to distinguish the main schools of thought and issues addressed, paying particular attention to the ramified growth of technical vocabulary and scholastic formulations which form the background out of which Plotinus and later Platonism could develop.

Despite my efforts to treat the figures of this period as philosophers in their own right and not simply as precursors of Neoplatonism, the fact remains that this period is important not for any great thinkers that it produced, but rather as a period in which certain basic philosophical issues were formulated, and approaches to their solution developed, which would come to brilliant fruition in the speculations of Plotinus. We must not forget that it was primarily the works of such men as Severus, Gaius, Numenius, Cronius, and Atticus (together with the Peripatetics Adrastus, Aspasius and Alexander of Aphrodisias) that Plotinus used as starting-points for his speculations. Plato is seen by him primarily through the eyes of these men (which is not, of course, to say that he did not know Plato's works intimately at first hand). To confront Plotinus with Plato directly, therefore, is to do violence to the historical process. To bring Posidonius or Philo into the picture as direct precursors is even more inappropriate. Likewise, such Stoic influences as have been discerned in Plotinus must be seen as mediated through centuries of Platonist scholasticism.

The claim, then, that I make for these men is a modest one. Like those humble sea-creatures whose concerted action slowly builds a coral reef, the philosophers of this period each contributed some detail to the formation of what was to become perhaps the greatest philosophical edifice of all time, that Platonism which, gathering to itself much of Aristotelianism and Stoicism, was to dominate the Late Antique world and the Middle Ages, and continue as a vital force through the Renaissance to the present day.[1]

[1] For a good summary of that movement, see ch. 6 of R. T. Wallis' *Neoplatonism*, in the present series.

Bibliography

THIS bibliography is not intended to be comprehensive, and is confined as far as possible to books, articles being cited only where no books on the subject in question exist. I have had to give many references to French and German works, since virtually nothing has been written in English on this period of Platonism.

I. GENERAL

The only useful summary of this period in English is contained in *The Cambridge History of Later Greek and Early Mediaeval Philosophy*, ed. A. H. Armstrong (Cambridge 1967), Parts I ('Greek Philosophy from Plato to Plotinus', by Philip Merlan) and II ('Philo and the Beginnings of Christian Thought', by Henry Chadwick), but Merlan's survey is distinctly sketchy. There is a useful collection of texts in C. J. De Vogel, *Greek Philosophy*, vol. III, 2nd ed. Leiden, 1964. In German there is vol. III: 2 of Eduard Zeller's *Philosophie der Griechen*, and Karl Praechter's revision of Überweg, *Die Philosophie des Altertums* (13th ed., Basel 1953).

Other works of general interest are: P. Merlan, *From Platonism to Neoplatonism*, 2nd ed., The Hague, 1960 (in fact dealing with a series of points of detail); W. Theiler, *Die Vorbereitung des Neuplatonismus*, Berlin, 1930 (again concentrating on details, but full of enlightenment); H. J. Krämer, *Der Ursprung des Geistmetaphysik*, Amsterdam, 1964; *Entretiens Hardt* III: 'Recherches sur la tradition platonicienne', Vandoeuvres-Genève, 1957; *Entretiens Hardt* V: 'Les sources de Plotin', Vandoeuvres-Genève, 1960.

2. THE OLD ACADEMY

A useful collection of passages relating to Plato's 'unwritten doctrines' is to be found as an appendix to Konrad Gaiser's *Platons Ungeschriebene Lehre*, Stuttgart 1963. The book itself, however, is very speculative, and to be recommended only with reservations. There is a useful collection of essays in *Das Problem der Ungeschriebenen Lehre*

Platons, ed. Jürgen Wippern, Darmstadt 1972. The fragments of Speusippus are collected by P. Lang, *De Speusippi Academici Scriptis*, Bonn 1911 (repr. Frankfurt 1964), and those of Xenocrates by R. Heinze, *Xenokrates*, Leipzig 1892 (repr. Hildesheim 1965). A sceptical view of the possibility of recovering Plato's unwritten doctrines from the existing evidence is provided by Harold Cherniss in *The Riddle of the Early Academy*, Berkeley 1945, and in *Aristotle's Criticism of Platu and the Academy*, Baltimore 1944. A new study of the Old Academy is badly needed.

3. ANTIOCHUS AND POSIDONIUS

Texts of the relevant works of Cicero are readily available in the Loeb Classical Library series: *De Finibus*, by H. Rackham; *De Natura Deorum* and *Academica*, by H. Rackham; *De Re Publica* and *De Legibus*, by Clinton W. Keyes; *Tusculan Disputations*, by J. E. King; *De Fato*, by H. Rackham. On Antiochus there are studies by A. Lüder, *Die philosophische Persönlichkeit des Antiochos von Askalon*, Göttingen 1940; H. Strache, *Der Eklektizismus des Antiochos von Askalon*, Berlin 1921; and Georg Luck, *Der Akademiker Antiochos*, Bern and Stuttgart 1953 (with collection of fragments). On Posidonius there is Karl Reinhardt's *RE* article, now separately printed as *Poseidonios von Apamea*, Stuttgart 1954; G. Pfligersdorffer, *Studien zu Poseidonios*, Vienna 1959; M. Laffranque, *Poseidonios d'Apamée*, Paris 1964; A. D. Nock, 'Posidonius', *Journal of Hellenic Studies*, 49 (1959), pp. 1–16; and now L. Edelstein and I. G. Kidd, *Posidonius: Vol. I, The Fragments*, Cambridge 1972 (*Vol. II: Commentary* is still awaited at this writing, and may be expected to contain a most comprehensive and judicious account of Posidonius' philosophical position and influence.) On Cicero, R. Hirzel, *Untersuchungen zu Ciceros philosophischen Schriften*, Leipzig 1877–83, is still useful; Wilhelm Süss, *Cicero: Eine Einführung in seine philosophischen Schriften*, Wiesbaden 1966, gives a good account of Cicero's works, but is of little use on sources.

4. EUDORUS AND PHILO

On Eudorus there are only articles: H. Dörrie, 'Der Platoniker Eudoros von Alexandria', *Hermes* 79 (1944); W. Theiler, 'Philo von Alexandria und der Beginn des kaiserzeitlichen Platonismus', in

Parusia, Festschrift für J. Hirschberger, Frankfurt 1965 (repr. in *Untersuchungen zur antiken Literatur*, 1970); P. Boyancé, 'Études philoniennes', *Révue des études grecs*, 76 (1963)—both these latter articles concerning Eudorus as well as Philo.

On Philo we are better served, though much that has been written is misleading or irrelevant for our present purpose. The standard edition is that of Cohn and Wendland, 7 vols. Berlin 1896–1915. Also Loeb edition by Whitaker and Colson, with two supplementary volumes containing translation of texts preserved only in Armenian, by Ralph Marcus. There is a French edition, by various hands, with useful introductions, translation, and some notes, issued by the University of Lyons, 1961–75. Some basic works on Philo are: E. R. Goodenough, *Introduction to Philo Judaeus*, 2nd ed., Oxford 1962; *The Politics of Philo Judaeus*, Yale 1938 (with a comprehensive bibliography); Émile Bréhier, *Les Idées philosophiques et religieuses de Philon d'Alexandrie*, 3rd ed. Paris 1950 (an excellent survey of Philo's doctrines, with copious references); T. H. Billings, *The Platonism of Philo Judaeus*, Chicago 1919, is a Chicago Ph.D. thesis, done under Paul Shorey, and is mainly useful for lists of Platonic parallels; H. A. Wolfson, *Philo*, 2 vols. Harvard 1947, while exhibiting very wide learning, gives, I feel, a most misleading view of Philo's relation to contemporary Greek philosophy. H. Chadwick's chapter in the *Cambridge History* (see above, sect. 1) gives a sound, clear account. The Philo symposium held at Lyons in 1966, *Philon d'Alexandrie*, Paris 1967, contains also much that is useful. A short sketch of philosophical activity in Alexandria is given in P. M. Frazer, *Ptolemaic Alexandria*, Oxford 1972, pp. 480–94.

5. PLUTARCH

The best text of the *Moralia* as a whole is the Teubner edition of Hubert, Pohlenz and others, Leipzig 1952–. There is a complete edition, in 15 volumes, in the Loeb series, though the standards of the volumes vary, vols. 6–15, with which we are mainly concerned, being fortunately much superior to the first five. Not much that is useful has been written on Plutarch's philosophical position. A good general survey is given by K. Ziegler in his *RE* article 'Plutarchos' (in vol. 21:1). R. M. Jones, *The Platonism of Plutarch*, Menasha, Wisc. 1916, is of some value, but oversimplifies the situation. It is a Ph.D. thesis, done under Paul Shorey, like the monograph of Billings on Philo.

Other useful works include: Guy Soury, *La Démonologie de Plutarque*, Paris 1942; P. Thevenaz, *L'Âme du monde, le devenir, et la matière chez Plutarque*, Paris 1938 (including a trans. of the first part of the *Proc. An.*); D. Babut, *Plutarque et le Sto cisme*, Paris 1969. D. A. Russell's *Plutarch* in the present series gives an excellent view of Plutarch the whole man.

6. THE ATHENIAN SCHOOL

Very little has been written on the figures comprised in this chapter. On Taurus, K. Praechter's *RE* article 'Tauros'; on Nicostratus, Praechter's article 'Nikostratos der Platoniker', *Hermes* 57 (1922); on Atticus, a collection of fragments with introduction in the Budé series by J. Baudry, Paris 1931. Some discussion also in Hal Koch's *Pronoia und Paideusis* (pp. 163–304), Berlin and Leipzig 1932.

7. ALBINUS, APULEIUS, GALEN

Texts of Albinus' *Eisagôgê* and *Didaskalikos* in vol. 6 of C. F. Hermann's edition of Plato, Leipzig 1921–36; Budé ed. by P. Louis, Paris 1945. (A new text of the *Didaskalikos* is to be expected from J. Whittaker in the near future.) For Apuleius' philosophical works there is the Teubner ed. of P. Thomas, Leipzig 1908, and now a Budé ed. by J. Beaujeu, Paris 1973. The work that laid the foundation of the 'School of Gaius' hypothesis was T. Sinko, *De Apulei et Albini doctrinae Platonicae adumbratione*, Krakow 1905. This line was followed by R. E. Witt, *Albinus and the History of Middle Platonism* (Cambridge 1937, repr. Hakkert 1971), and by all writers on the subject since. Witt also tries to connect Albinus directly with Antiochus. A defence of Albinus' coherence as a thinker is undertaken by J. H. Loenen, 'Albinus' Metaphysics: An Attempt at Rehabilitation', *Mnemosyne*, series 4, vols. 9 and 10. The *Anonymous Theaetetus Commentary* is edited by Diels and Schubart, *Berliner Klassikertexte* II, Berlin 1905. There is no study, so far as I know, of Galen's philosophical position. Works in the complete edition of C. G. Kühn, *Claudii Galeni Opera Omnia*, Leipzig (Teubner), 1821–33. *De Placitis Hippocratis et Platonis*, ed. I. Müller, Leipzig 1874. *Institutio Logica*, ed. C. Kalbfleisch, Leipzig (Teubner) 1896.

8. THE NEOPYTHAGOREANS

An excellent study of early Pythagoreanism and the evidence for it in W. Burkert, *Weisheit und Wissenschaft*, Nuremburg 1962 (trans. as *Lore and Science in Ancient Pythagoreanism*, by E. L. Minar, Harvard 1972). Pseudo-Pythagorica collected by Holger Thesleff, *The Pythagorean Texts of the Hellenistic Period*, Abo, 1965. There is a good edition of Ocellus Lucanus by R. Harder, Berlin 1926.

On Moderatus, an important article is E. R. Dodds, 'The Parmenides of Plato and the Origin of the Neoplatonic "One"', *Classical Quarterly*, 22 (1928). Nicomachus, *Introductio Arithmetica* is edited by R. Hoche, Leipzig (Teubner), 1866, and there is a translation, with mathematical commentary, by D'Ooge, Robbins and Karpinski, *Nicomachus of Gerasa, Introduction to Mathematics*, Ann Arbor 1938. Edition of *Manuale Harmonicum*, by C. Jan, *Musici Scriptores Graeci*, Leipzig 1895. The *Theologumena Arithmeticae* is edited by V. De Falco, Leipzig (Teubner), 1922. Editions of Numenius are: E. A. Leemans, Brussels 1937, and É. des Places, Paris (Budé), 1973. I have used Des Places' numeration of the fragments. On Ammonius, there is a good discussion by E. R. Dodds in *Entretiens Hardt* v ('Les Sources de Plotin'), see above, sect. 1; also H. Dörrie in *Hermes* 83, 1955.

9. MISCELLANEOUS

For a survey of Gnosticism in English, see Hans Jonas, *The Gnostic Religion*, Boston 1958. A useful collection of the texts in translation now in W. Foerster, *Gnosis: A Selection of Gnostic Texts*, 2 vols. Oxford 1974. For the *Hermetica*, there is the Budé ed. of Nock and Festugière, 4 vols. 3rd ed. Paris 1972; and A. J. Festugière, *La Révélation d' Hermes Trismégiste*, 4 vols., Paris 1944–54. The edition of Scott is most unreliable. For the *Chaldaean Oracles*, there is the Budé ed. of E. Des Places, *Oracles Chaldaiques*, Paris 1971. Hans Lewy, *Chaldaean Oracles and Theurgy*, Cairo 1956, is still fundamental.

On Christian Platonism, which I have not covered in this book, I would recommend: S. Lilla, *Clement of Alexandria: A Study in Christian Platonism and Gnosticism*, Oxford 1971; J. Daniélou, *Origène*, Paris 1948 (Eng. trans. 1955); Hal Koch, *Pronoia und Paideusis: Studien über Origenes und sein Verhältnis zum Platonismus*, Leipzig 1932; C.

Andresen, *Logos und Nomos*, Berlin 1955; H. Chadwick, *Early Christian Thought and the Classical Tradition*, Oxford 1966; and his contributions to the *Cambridge History*, chs. 10 and 11 (see sect. 1 above). Eng. trans. of Origen, *De Principiis* by G. W. Butterworth, Harper Torchbooks, 1966; of *Contra Celsum* by H. Chadwick, Cambridge 1953.

Theon of Smyrna, *Expositio Rerum Mathematicarum ad legendum Platonem utilium*, is edited by E. Hiller, Leipzig (Teubner) 1878. The *Orations* of Maximus of Tyre are edited by H. Hobein, *Maximus Tyrius: Philosophumena*, Leipzig (Teubner) 1910. Useful discussion by Guy Soury, *Aperçus de philosophie réligieuse chez Maxime de Tyre*, Paris 1942. Celsus is edited by O. Glöckner, Bonn 1924. Calcidius *In Timaeum* is edited by J. H. Waszink, *Plato Latinus* vol. IV (of Warburg Inst. series), London and Leiden 1962. Monographs by J. H. Waszink, *Studien zum Timaioskommentar des Calcidius I* (*Philosophia Antiqua* series, vol. XII), Leiden 1964; J. C. M. van Winden, *Calcidius on Matter: His Doctrine and Sources* (*Phil. Ant.* vol. IX), Leiden 1965; J. den Boeft, *Calcidius on Fate: His Doctrine and Sources* (*Phil. Ant.* vol. XVIII), Leiden 1970. (Van Winden and den Boeft are pupils of Waszink, and did their studies as theses under his direction.) Diogenes Laertius' *Life of Plato* is most readily available in the Loeb edition (vol. I). Hippolytus' summary of Platonic doctrine is most conveniently to be found in Diels, *Doxographi Graeci*, pp. 567–70.

Afterword, 1996

1. It is now very nearly twenty years since the first publication of this book, and in that interval a great deal of useful work has taken place in the field of Middle Platonism, some of it leading me to abandon or modify positions that I had taken up here, so that I am glad to have the opportunity to put out a new impression of the work.

I will begin by surveying the most important general contributions that have been made since 1977 to our understanding of the Middle Platonic period, and then proceed through my individual chapters, detailing the issues on which I feel my views require modification.

The first question to which I would call attention is the further refinement of the concept of what constitutes Middle Platonism. In this book, I presented it as both a chronological period (extending, roughly, from Antiochus' re-establishment of the 'Academy' in Athens after the 'liberation' of the city by Sulla in 88 B.C. to the establishment of Plotinus' school in Rome in the mid-third century A.D.), and a movement held together by certain ideological principles (broadly, a return to dogmatism, consisting of a synthesis of Old Academic doctrine with much of Aristotelianism and Stoicism, to which came to be added, after Antiochus, a strand of Pythagorean transcendentalism). This latter position has been challenged and modified in various ways in the intervening period.

First of all, in a review of the book in *Nous* for 1980 (pp. 291-5), along with a number of pertinent particular criticisms which I shall address, the distinguished American scholar Phillip De Lacy complained that I was too restrictive in my view of the nature of Middle Platonism, in that I disregarded the persistence of the tradition of the sceptical Academy in such thinkers as Cicero and Galen, and even in Plutarch. Other scholars since have pursued this line of argument, such as Harold Tarrant in his important study of the so-called 'Fourth Academy' of Philo of Larissa.[1]

---

[1] *Scepticism or Platonism? The Philosophy of the Fourth Academy*, CUP, 1985.

Specifically, De Lacy and others make the point that the Platonists of the period between Antiochus and Plotinus did not see themselves as constituting a coherent movement, nor did they view Antiochus as in any sense their spiritual father. Opinion continued to be divided on the important question of whether the sceptical New Academy constituted an integral part of the Platonic heritage, or a deviation, such a figure as Plutarch maintaining the essential unity of the Platonic tradition, while the Neopythagorean Numenius directs a satirical attack on the New Academy for betraying the traditions of Platonism (not even sparing Antiochus of Ascalon from his strictures, it must be said).

Now it must be admitted that being a 'middle' anything is a rather troublesome state. If one declares oneself, or is identified as, a 'neo-X' (a neo-Thomist, say, or a neo-Kantian, a neo-Marxist, or a neo-Freudian), one knows more or less where one stands. One is basically remaining true to the basic insights of the revered figure in question, while reserving the right to reinterpret them in the light of more recent developments. But who ever claimed to be a *middle-X*? No one can, I think, conceive of himself as such a creature. It is not, therefore, I think, to be expected that 'Middle Platonists' should ever have seen themselves as such.[2]

That said, however, the term remains, I think, valid and useful, with proper reservations. Certainly, the Middle Platonists did not think of themselves as a movement, nor did they revere Antiochus as their founder; and they quarrelled fairly vigorously among themselves. Nevertheless, from the point of view of the modern historian of philosophy, they do seem to constitute a period in the history of Platonism which it is useful to demarcate.

2. I will deal first with the major works of synthesis that have appeared in the field in the last twenty years, together with a number of important relevant projects or series.

First I must repair an omission. At the time of writing, I had failed

---

[2] Nor, of course, did the Neoplatonists see themselves as 'Neoplatonists', but they did come to see Plotinus as having made a new beginning, in the sense of reviving a true understanding of the depths of Platonic wisdom, after a long period of darkness, covering the New Academic and 'Middle Platonic' periods. For a good statement of this view, see the preface to Proclus' *Platonic Theology*.

to note the existence of a considerable work of Italian scholarship, *I dossografi di etica*, by Michelangelo Giusta.[3] This seeks to prove, on the basis of a systematic study of the surviving ethical doxographies contained in the works of Cicero, Arius Didymus (in Stobaeus), Apuleius, Alcinous and Diogenes Laertius, which exhibit certain regularities in the treatment of topics, that they go back to a common source, and that that source is the account of the subject-matter of ethics composed by Eudorus of Alexandria in the late first century B.C., relayed to us by Arius Didymus (cf. pp. 122-6). While one may salute the scholarship exhibited in the book, the basic thesis seems wildly optimistic. Apuleius and Alcinous, at least, have much in common, indicating a common *proximate* source, but the similarities are less striking between the other sources concerned, and Eudorus' own scheme is quite distinctive, with its special category of *hormê* inserted between *theoria and praxis*. If there is a common source, and there may be, it is not likely to be Eudorus, though it may possibly be Arius Didymus. However, Giusta's assemblage of data remains useful.

Next we should note a major study of the institutional background to Platonism, from the Old Academy to the end of antiquity, *Antiochus and the Late Academy*, by John Glucker.[4] This confirms, with a wealth of corroborative detail, the thesis which I (who was indebted in this to the work of John Lynch – see Bibliography) propound here, that, from Antiochus on until at least the end of the second century A.D. (when the holders of the official chair of Platonism established in Athens by Marcus Aurelius may progressively have reconstituted themselves into an 'Academy', such as we do find in Athens in the following centuries), there was no official centre of Platonism that could serve as a watchdog for 'orthodoxy', and that the transmission of philosophical doctrine was very much a matter of individual teachers and small groups practising a sort of self-identification. Glucker discusses most usefully what it means to be a philosophical *hairesis*, and how the terms 'Platonikos' and 'Academikos' come to be used, as well as a great many other interesting questions, such as the break between Philo and

---

[3] 2 vols., Torino, 1964, 1967.
[4] (Hypomnemata, Heft. 56), Vandenhoeck & Ruprecht: Göttingen, 1978.

Antiochus, and the precise stance of Plutarch towards the sceptical Academy. It is unfortunate that his book was not available to me.

Another work that I just missed benefiting from was the first volume of Matthias Baltes' major study, *Die Weltenstehung des Platonischen Timaios nach den antiken Interpreten*,[5] in which he deals with the various exegeses of Plato's description of the creation of the world in the *Timaeus* from the Old Academy down to Syrianus (Proclus is reserved for Vol. II), taking in Speusippus and Xenocrates, and all the Middle Platonists and Neopythagoreans, most notably Plutarch and Atticus, Taurus, Albinus (Alcinous), and Apuleius.

Another most useful study, directed towards the central question of the nature of the soul, is that of Werner Deuse, *Untersuchungen zur mittelplatonischen und neuplatonischen Seelenlehre*.[6] Only the first half of the study is relevant to our period, but there he deals with the doctrines on the soul of Plutarch, Atticus, Numenius, Albinus (Alcinous), and other minor figures (including Galen), bringing out, in particular, more clearly than I did, the essentially *irrational* nature of the soul in Plutarch's theory, and showing that certain distinctions in doctrine can be made between him and Atticus (see below).

Important also for the understanding of our period of philosophy is the work of Pier-Luigi Donini, *Le scuole, l'anima, l'impero: la filosofia antica da Antioco a Plotino*,[7] which deals with Stoicism and Aristotelianism as well as Platonism, but devotes many pages (73-159) to such interesting questions as the status and doctrines of Antiochus and the contribution of Eudorus and Alexandrian Platonism. He is particularly concerned with the interaction of Platonism and Aristotelianism in this period. Donini is very sound (that is, he agrees with me) on the question of the unsuitability of 'eclecticism' as a category to apply to the Platonism of this period.[8] He takes me to task at one point (p. 149, n. 7) for on the one hand denying Antiochus the role of 'founder' of Middle Platonism on the ground

[5] Teil I (Philosophia Antiqua XXX), Brill: Leiden, 1976.
[6] Franz Steiner Verlag: Wiesbaden, 1983.
[7] Rosenberg & Sellier: Torino, 1982.
[8] He has also contributed an excellent overview of the history of the term 'eclecticism' in Dillon and Long (edd.), *The Question of 'Eclecticism': Studies in Later Greek Philosophy*, Berkeley/Los Angeles, 1988, pp. 15-33.

of his excessive Stoicism, and then declaring that the Platonism of Eudorus (and of Philo of Alexandria) is more Stoic in its formulations than that of Antiochus. However, what concerns me in Antiochus is the apparent Stoic materialism in his metaphysics (see further below), whereas what I am noting in Alexandrian Platonism is its Stoicizing stance in *ethics* (and to some extent in logic), while maintaining its properly Platonist transcendentalism. He also complains of the excessive space devoted to Philo, since I do not claim that he is properly part of the Platonist school. But my justification for that is simply the excellent evidence that I deem him to provide for contemporary trends in Platonism (again, see further below).

Another major study relevant to the field is that of Stephen Gersh, *Middle Platonism and Neoplatonism: The Latin Tradition*,[9] in which he devotes chapters to Cicero, Seneca (as a source), Aulus Gellius, Apuleius, the *Asclepius*, and Calcidius (whom he follows Waszink in treating as influenced by Porphyry, and thus 'Neoplatonist' – a position which I dispute). While I am not sure how meaningfully one can talk about a 'Latin tradition' in Middle Platonism, this does not greatly take away from the considerable value of the book. One substantial question, on which dispute will continue, is that as to how much of a philosopher Cicero really was, or aspired to be, and thus how freely one can recover from his pages the doctrines of Antiochus of Ascalon. I am rather minimalist on the subject of Cicero the Philosopher, and am not inclined to recant (despite taking on board some of the cautions expressed by Jonathan Barnes – on which see below, à propos Antiochus); Gersh, by the very nature of his project, is inclined to maximize his originality (as has always been the tendency in particular among French scholars, such as Pierre Boyancé). I do not dispute that Cicero had sincerely held philosophical views, but I persist in regarding him primarily as a well-informed and intelligent philosophical journalist.

Also important, as providing a different (though rather speculative) view of the development of Platonism in this era, and specifically of the fate and influence of Philo of Larisa's philosophical position (the so-called 'Fourth Academy') in later times, is the monograph of Harold Tarrant, *Scepticism or Platonism? The Philosophy of the Fourth Academy*.[10] This concerns primarily a topic which

[9] 2 vols., University of Notre Dame, 1986.
[10] See above, n. 1.

is outside my purview, but it relates to the subject of the present book in two chief ways: first, on the question of the relations between Philo and Antiochus and his predecessors (primarily Philo, but also Carneades), on which I have no dispute with Tarrant, and find him most enlightening; but secondly, in that he fastens on the *Anonymous Theaetetus Commentary*, and wishes to claim it for a 'Fourth-Academic' work, probably (though he is understandably tentative about this) composed by Eudorus of Alexandria, who would therefore not be the Pythagoreanizing dogmatist that I have presented him as being, but in some sense a Philonian Academic. I will return to this question at the appropriate place.

We may turn now to a number of communal enterprises, or works of synthesis, which have relevance to the field. First of all, there is the mighty, and well-nigh interminable, series of volumes of the *Aufstieg und Niedergang der römischen Welt* (*ANRW*), edited by W. Haase and H. Temporini, Volume 36 of Part II of which, being devoted to the philosophy of the Principate, contains many articles bearing on Middle Platonism, some of them of considerable importance.[11] Volume 36 is itself sub-divided into seven large volumes, published at regular intervals since 1987, all of which contain relevant material, though most of this is concentrated in the first two. I will mention individual articles at relevant junctures, but I may mention here the very useful bibliographical survey of Luc Deitz in 36:1.[12] It extends, necessarily, only to 1986, but it is admirably complete for its period. A problem of the *ANRW* is the rather spotty and random nature of many of the contributions, but there are many also that are definitive. From this same volume, we may also note two survey articles, J.-M. André on 'Les écoles philosophiques aux deux premières siècles de l'Empire' (5-77), and John Whittaker's 'Platonic Philosophy in the Early Centuries of the Empire', 81-123 (which, however, concentrates mainly on one of his favourite subjects, the philosopher Alcinous and his *Didaskalikos*). As for André, he seems more *au fait* with Stoicism than with Platonism. He still speaks vaguely of an 'Academy' pursuing its activities (p. 19), and of a 'School of Gaius', of whom a member is 'the enigmatic

---

[11] De Gruyter: Berlin, 1987-.
[12] 'Bibliographie du platonisme impérial antérieur à Plotin: 1926-1986', pp. 124-82.

Albinus/Alkinoos' (p. 59). Neither of these concepts is, I would have thought, any longer respectable.[13]

Another great enterprise is that which Heinrich Dörrie had planned for many years, and which on his death in 1983 he bequeathed to his successor in Münster, Matthias Baltes, *Der Platonismus in der Antike*.[14] This is an effort, first to identify the essential features of Platonism in its historical perspective, and then to assemble a complete set of testimonia to the various doctrines of Platonism, arranged by theme rather than author. Dörrie did not believe in the originality of the majority of the personalities with whom I am concerned in this book. Indeed, I am taken to task in the introduction to Volume I (p. 47) for adopting the misguided procedure of trying to isolate and develop the individual contributions of particular Platonist philosophers, instead of recognising that these men are just faithful schoolmen, and that it is impossible to attribute distinctive doctrines to them. Instead, one should concentrate on issues and *dogmata*.

I must say that I am unrepentant. I do not see Platonism as a monolithic phenomenon, but rather as a (fairly distinctive) spectrum of beliefs, within the ambit of which individual thinkers could, and did, take up quite a variety of positions. Certainly we do not know as much about men like Eudorus or Atticus or Severus as we would like, but it still seems to me to be worth trying to bring what I see as a centuries-long creative dialectical process to some sort of life.

However, that is not to say that enormous value is not to be derived from the mass of material that Dörrie has assembled, and that Baltes is currently bringing into order and adorning with excellent commentaries. There are to be eight volumes in all, of which three have appeared so far (August 1995), with a fourth on the way. The text is divided into 'Bausteine', groups of texts on a given theme, of which about 300 are ultimately projected, and of which 100 have appeared in the three volumes so far published. So far the actual doctrines have hardly been broached, the first three volumes being largely concerned with the overall nature of Platonism, its structure, and its reputation in society. Even in Volume 3, we are still con-

[13] No doubt Gaius had a school, and Albinus was his pupil, but there is no evidence that either Alcinous or Apuleius was a member of it.

[14] Frommann-Holzboog: Stuttgart/Bad Cannstatt, Vol. 1, 1987; Vol. 2, 1990; Vol. 3, 1993; Vol. 4, 1996 (projected).

cerned with the forms which publication took (commentaries, treatises, dialogues, and so on). Only in Volume 4 will we really get down to doctrines. But ultimately *Der Platonismus in der Antike* will constitute a vast encyclopedia of ancient Platonism.

One should perhaps note at this stage also the mighty work of Paul Moraux, *Der Aristotelismus bei den Griechen*,[15] in the second volume of which he includes useful studies of various Middle Platonists who related in some way or other to Peripateticism, either by adopting its doctrines or formulations, or by criticising it, such as Albinus (Alcinous), the Anonymous Theaetetus Commentator, and Pseudo-Plutarch *De Fato* (friendly), and Eudorus, Lucius and Nicostratus, and Atticus (hostile). Moraux offers no specific criticisms of my positions, and I in turn find little to quarrel with in his. What little there may be will be adverted to at the appropriate place.

A number of more general works have appeared recently which make good use of the new level of interest in, and understanding of, the Middle Platonic period. As an example I would cite John Peter Kenney's *Mystical Monotheism: A Study in Ancient Platonic Theology*,[16] which in its first two sections devotes an enlightening discussion to the theologies of Plutarch, Alcinous and Numenius, expanding on what is said here. Another useful work is *Knowledge of God in the Graeco-Roman World*,[17] containing articles by Matthias Baltes on the theology of Xenocrates, David Runia on Philo, and Pier-Luigi Donini on Albinus (Alcinous) – and myself on Origen.

3. But now to turn to specifics: in Chapter One, on the Old Academy, I find myself in retrospect rather embarrassingly dogmatic on the question of the 'unwritten doctrines' of Plato. However, I was reacting then, as I still would now, against the prevailing Anglo-American tendency, of which the most extreme recent representative was Harold Cherniss, to look no further than the dialogues in trying to form a judgement as to the full range of Plato's philosophical speculations. Such an attitude, it seems to me, is a counsel of despair. It is certainly unsettling to have to admit that there was a dimension of Plato's teaching that was not committed to

---

[15] De Gruyter: Berlin/New York, Vol. I, 1973; Vol. II, 1984.
[16] Brown Univ. Press; Hanover/London, 1991.
[17] edd. R. van den Broek, T. Baarda, and J. Mansfeld, Brill: Leiden, 1988.

writing, because he did not *wish* it to be committed to writing, but the alternative is to make two assumptions, one unjustified, the other improbable. The first is that we actually know what role the dialogues were intended by Plato to play in the intellectual life of the school; the other is that when Plato was not writing dialogues, he and all other members of the school stood around like cigar-store Indians, saying nothing to each other whatever.

Surely we must accept that in fact a great deal of speculation went on in the Academy that did not find its way into any dialogue, or is represented therein only allusively (as, for example, the theory of first principles in the *Philebus*). What should be done is to divest the notion of 'unwritten doctrines' from any overtones of esotericism (though doubtless Plato was not in favour of publicizing his speculations to all and sundry), and regard them simply as 'work in progress'. Such a book as that of Kenneth Sayre, *Plato's Late Ontology*,[18] which has appeared since I wrote, seems to me to treat the topic very well.

As for the chief figures of the Old Academy, some useful work has been done since 1977. Of particular note is the magisterial edition of the 'fragments' of Speusippus by Leonardo Tarán, which appeared in 1981.[19] This provides a very full discussion of Speusippus' metaphysics, epistemology, logic, and ethics, together with an exegesis of all the ancient testimonies. Tarán, however, maintains a sceptical attitude (pp. 86–107) to the controversial passage (ch. 4) of Iamblichus' *De Communi Mathematica Scientia*, on which I, following Philip Merlan, would place much store in reconstructing Speusippus' metaphysics, but I am unrepentant. I have answered his arguments, I hope adequately, in an article in *Phronesis*.[20] Tarán sees a series of irreconcilable contradictions between what we think we know of Speusippus' doctrines from Aristotle and what we have in *DCMS* IV. It seems to me that the contradictions are by no means irreconcilable, and that in at least two instances (his interpretations of *Met.* N. 1091a29–b3 and 1092a1–17), Tarán is in error. However,

---

[18] Princeton Univ. Press, 1983. See especially ch. 2. See also his very sensible critique of the position of H.-J. Krämer in *Ancient Philosophy* XIII (1993), 167–84.

[19] *Speusippus of Athens: A Critical Study with a Collection of the Related Texts and Commentary*, by Leonardo Tarán (Philosophia Antiqua series, Vol. XXXIX). Brill: Leiden.

[20] 'Speusippus in Iamblichus', *Phronesis* XXIX (1984), 325–32.

even if I am right, Tarán has, with this book, much enriched our knowledge of Speusippus. As a collection of fragments, he supersedes Lang.

Also useful in relation to both Speusippus and Eudoxus (with whom I do not deal) is a short monograph (or bigraph?) by R.M. Dancy, *Two Studies in the Early Academy*,[21] the second of which is entitled 'Ancient non-Beings: Speusippus and Others'.[22] Dancy, I am glad to say, broadly accepts my treatment of *DCMS* IV (of which he helpfully prints a text and annotated translation as an appendix to his work), and gives the sort of in-depth treatment to Speusippus' metaphysics that it deserves.

Another scholar who deserves respectful mention in connection with the Old Academy is the Italian Margherita Isnardi Parente, who has been very active in this area since the early seventies. In 1980 she produced a collection of the fragments of Speusippus,[23] which has been rather overshadowed, in the English-speaking world, by that of Tarán (who is not very kind to it), but in 1981 she produced a collection of the fragments of Xenocrates and (as a small appendix) Hermodorus,[24] with translations and notes, which must now be regarded as the definitive edition, superseding that of Heinze. I am glad to say that she gives me no reason to change my view of Xenocrates. Mention should also be made of her *Studi sull' Accademia platonica antica*, of 1979, bringing together three essays, on Ideas and Principles, Soul and Cosmos, and *Theoria* and *Praxis* respectively, which, while going more deeply than I could into such knotty questions as the relations between ideas and numbers in Speusippus and Xenocrates, and the significance of their respective definitions of the soul, does not require me to revise radically my account of them. She is also, as the editor of the section on the Old Academy in the updated Italian edition of Zeller's history of Greek philosophy,[25] author of the nearest thing to an extended study of the Old Academy, such as is, in my view, still badly needed.

---

[21] State University of New York Press: Albany, 1991.

[22] This previously appeared in *Ancient Philosophy* 9 (1989), 207-43.

[23] *Speusippo: Frammenti*, Bibliopolis: Napoli.

[24] *Senocrate – Ermodoro: Frammenti*, Bibliopolis: Napoli.

[25] E. Zeller – R. Mondolfo, *La filosofia dei Greci nel suo sviluppo storico*, II 3, *Platone e l'Accademia antica*, a cura di M. Isnardi Parente, Firenze, 1974. See also her updating of her views in a set of lectures published as *L'eredità di Platone nell' Accademia antica*, Guerini e assoc.: Milano, 1989.

On Xenocrates, I have myself pursued further[26] the interpretation of a vexed doxographic fragment (Fr. 15 Heinze = 213 Isnardi Parente), which purports to give an account of Xenocrates' first principles (cf. p. 26 of the text). I am not now so sure as I was then that a lacuna is the answer. The confusion may be worse than that. But it still seems to me that the dyad in Xenocrates' system cannot be identified with the world soul, if only because, in his interpreta- tion of the creation of the soul in the *Timaeus*, the soul is composed of monad and dyad.

On Polemon and the more minor Academics, not much that is new has been contributed in the intervening years. However, con- temporaneously with this book there appeared a collection of the 'fragments' of Polemon (all testimonia, in fact), by Marcello Gi- gante,[27] with a short introduction, but no notes, which is a pity. My inclination, following Kurt von Fritz in his *RE* article (and Antio- chus himself), to see Polemon as the key figure in Antiochus' synthesis of Platonism and Aristotelianism has been challenged by Jonathan Barnes (in the essay to be discussed just below, p. 78, n. 97), on the grounds that we know little enough about Polemon. All that Barnes is doing here, though, is reminding us of the sad fact, true of so many of the thinkers dealt with in this book, that we are dealing with hints and scraps of evidence. If one is not inclined to make the most of these, then one should probably leave the field alone.[28]

Lastly, we may welcome the edition by Tiziano Dorandi of Philodemus' *History of the Academic School*,[29] a most useful updating of the so-called *Index Herculanensis*, previously only available in

---

[26] 'Xenocrates' Metaphysics: Fr. 1 5 (Heinze) Re-examined', *Ancient Philosophy* 5 (1986), 47-52. See also the essay of Baltes mentioned above, 'Zur Theologie des Xenokrates', in *Knowledge of God in the Graeco-Roman World* (see n. 17 above).

[27] *Polemonis Academici Fragmenta*, coll. M. Gigante, Napoli, 1977.

[28] A quotation from Jonathan Barnes (see note 30) is apposite here, though it refers to Antiochus rather than to Polemon: 'Any attempt to reconstruct Antio- chus' thought requires fantasy and imagination. But fantasy must be responsible to the evidence, and imagination must acknowledge one sobering fact: we do not know much about Antiochus.' This states excellently the problem facing anyone who deals with the great majority of the figures presented in this book.

[29] *Filodemo, Storia dei Filosofi: Platone e l'Academia*, ed. T. Dorandi. Bibliopolis: Napoli, 1991.

Mekler's 1902 edition, with greatly improved readings of the papyri, translation and commentary.

4. We may turn now to Antiochus, the subject of my second chapter. Here, apart from the insights provided by Glucker and Tarrant in their books discussed above, the main contribution has come from a most penetrating and witty study by Jonathan Barnes,[30] in which he takes me to task on various points. He begins by waxing rather satirical on the elevation of Antiochus to the status of 'a very great man indeed'. This may be a fair dig at Willy Theiler (whose honorific treatment of Antiochus in *Die Vorbereitung des Neuplatonismus* did certainly influence me), but I don't feel that it is quite fair to my presentation of him. However, let me clarify my position further. I regard Antiochus, not as a great philosopher, nor even as the 'founder' of Middle Platonism, but as a figure of considerable interest and importance in the development of Platonism, and specifically in the return to dogmatism which took place in the first century B.C. In fact, when Barnes has duly cut Antiochus and his supporters down to size, he freely concedes to him all that I would concede to him, so that I do not regard us as being in serious dispute.

Certainly Antiochus cannot be regarded as more than a precursor of the Middle Platonic synthesis, for the good reason that he is far too much of a Stoic. He was led into this position by his preoccupation with the central issue of *katalêpsis*, or 'certainty', which led to his break with his master Philo. However, it seems to me that he undoubtedly started various productive lines of enquiry, which led in the next generation to a return to transcendentalism in the person of Eudorus.[31]

One issue of some importance on which we are in dispute[32] is that

---

[30] 'Antiochus of Ascalon' in *Philosophia Togata: Essays on Philosophy and Roman Society*, edd. M. Griffin and J. Barnes, Clarendon Press: Oxford, 1989, 51-96. There has also been a new collection of the fragments by H.J. Mette, 'Philon von Larisa und Antiochos von Ascalon', *Lustrum* 28/9 (1986/7), 9-63.

[31] I do not, by the way, claim Eudorus as a direct pupil of Antiochus, as did Georg Luck, in *Der Akademiker Antiochus*, p. 27 (for which he is duly reprimanded by Barnes, p. 52), but have proposed some such figure as the unfortunate Dion, who settled in Alexandria, as a plausible intermediary (cf. p. 115).

[32] On many points I would concede to Barnes. I was certainly too open-handed in claiming Ciceronian texts as Antiochian. I agree that uncertainty attends all

of Antiochus' attitude to the Platonic Theory of Forms. In 'Appendix E' to his essay ('Antiochus and Plato's Forms') he considers the view of Theiler, followed by myself and Donini,[33] that Antiochus is responsible for 'the reintroduction of the Theory of Forms into serious philosophy'. This he finds highly improbable, in view particularly of the fact that Antiochus, after giving a brief account at *Acad.* 30 of the Platonic theory, remarks just below, at *Acad.* 33, that Aristotle 'was the first to undermine it (*primus ... labefactavit*)'.[34] But Aristotle is an honoured member of Antiochus' canon of true philosophers, so that he must be right in this undermining. Thus runs the argument; and there is something in it. I therefore suggested that Antiochus saw the forms in terms of Stoicism, and rather rashly suggested that 'he identified them with [Stoic] "cognitive perceptions" ' — that is, *kataléptikai phantasiai* — and for this I am properly taken to task. What I really meant to say was that Antiochus may have adopted what one might term a 'Kantian' interpretation of the forms, seeing them as inherent in the structure of the human mind, but also as present in the cosmic mind, that is the mind of God, in his Stoicising system. They would thus be nearer to Stoic 'preconceptions' (*prolépseis*). The point of contact with *kataléptikai phantasiai*

---

except the basic expositions of Antiochian doctrine at *Acad.* 14-42 and *Fin.* V 9-74, though I think that we can range much further than that, with due caution. In general, we must ask, I think, what other sources Cicero had for his accounts of dogmatic Platonism. Certainly, he read Plato himself, and *could* have gone back for himself to the works of Speusippus and Xenocrates. But did he? I think not, when he had a guide nearer to hand. The real question, surely, is whether a coherent philosophical position emerges from the various passages which could have been held by someone of Antiochus' known views. If it does, I do not think that we need to look further. However, I agree with him (and with De Lacy in his review) that it is rash to claim the *Topica* for Antiochus (though all I say [p. 103] is that 'it employs a logical scheme which accords very well with what we should expect of Antiochus', which I think I would stand over). The case is similar to the *De Fato*. *Tusculan Disputations* I, however, does continue to bother me (cf. pp. 96-101). I don't think that it coheres very well with Antiochus' Stoicism, and one should probably leave it aside.

[33] *Le scuole*, p. 95, n. 4.

[34] I discuss this passage at pp. 92-3, and in the course of that note what seems to me a tone of mild irony ('*quas mirifice Plato erat amplexatus*') in Antiochus' description of the enthusiasm of Plato for the forms, which I suggest might indicate a feeling that the theory at least needed modification.

is simply that Varro-Antiochus declares at *Acad.* 30-2 that the criterion of truth resides in the mind, because it is in touch with 'that which is eternally simple and uniform and true to its own quality',[35] which is what Platonists call Idea; whereas for the Stoics, as we learn from Diogenes Laertius 7.54 (= *SVF* 2.105) and elsewhere, the criterion of truth is the *kataléptiké phantasia*. Since we learn in the same passage that Chrysippus in Book I of his *Peri Logou* declared the criterion to be *prolépsis*,[36] that brings us a step closer to what I mean. I will rephrase, therefore, my claim, but not retract it. I am also not inclined to retract my adoption of Theiler's proposal to ascribe to Antiochus the famous text on beauty in Cicero's *Orator*, 8ff., since it fits what should be his position very well. I agree with Barnes, certainly, that the adoption of an unreconstructed version of Plato's Theory of Forms need not have been regarded as essential to being a Platonist. One did, however, I think, have to face up to it, and attempt to bring it into line with more modern, 'scientific' (i.e. Stoic) thinking, and that is what Antiochus is doing.

On the question of Posidonius, we may just note the appearance of Ian Kidd's great commentary on the fragments, in two volumes,[37] which has added greatly to our appreciation of that thinker, but has not caused me to change my estimate of his importance. Particularly useful comments may be found on Fr. 5 (on first principles), Frs. 100-1 (on God), Fr. 103 (on Fate being 'third from Zeus'), Fr. 141 (on the definition of soul), and of course Frs. 150-69 – the passages from Galen on Posidonius' ethics and psychology. On the interesting question of whether Posidonius declared the first principles (God and Matter) to be 'bodies' (*somata*) or 'incorporeal' (*asomatous*), I am inclined to the latter, mainly because of noting the strange ways in which the term 'incorporeal' is used by a man like Philo, to describe the heavenly bodies (e.g. *Conf.* 1 76-7), but one cannot be sure. On the problem of Fate being third from Zeus, Kidd gives a good survey of the various suggestions, and settles, cautiously, for

---

[35] Using the language of *Phaedo* 78CD.

[36] He has just been reported as having in Book 2 of his *Physics* declared the criterion as *kataléptiké phantasia*, whereas here he is actually credited with saying that it is 'sense-perception and preconception', and is accused by Diogenes of falling into contradiction, which he need not in fact be seen as doing.

[37] *Posidonius, Vol. II: the Commentary*, 2 vols. CUP, 1988.

the solution of M. Dragona-Monachou, in an article that I should
have noticed,[38] which adduces a passage from Cicero's *De Divinatione* (= Fr. 107), and explains it simply as a presentational or
explanatory sequence, with no hierarchy implied. I would accept
this.

5. We turn next to Eudorus and Philo of Alexandria. On
Eudorus, first of all, we have now a collection of fragments by C.
Mazzarelli, with commentary in Italian, published rather inconven-
iently in two numbers of the *Rivista di filosofia neoscolastica*.[39] To
produce these as a separate monograph would be a considerable
service. There also appeared in the same journal, in the same year as
my book, an article by G. Calvetti on Eudorus, 'Eudoro di Alessandria: medioplatonismo e neopythagorismo nel I secolo a. C.',[40]
which is a useful discussion of the evidence. The main contribution,
however, has been from Paul Moraux, in a chapter which he
devotes to Eudorus in pp. 509-27 of Vol. II of *Der Aristotelismus bei
den Griechen*.[41] He does not, I am glad to say, contradict my view of
Eudorus, but he adds certain interesting observations. One is that,
unlike Antiochus, Eudorus is plainly directly concerned with the
exegesis of the text of both Plato and Aristotle (the latter – that is to
say, the esoteric works – was after all probably not available to
Antiochus). This develops a view of Heinrich Dörrie's[42] that Antiochus, like his predecessors in the New Academy, did not concern
himself directly with the dialogues of Plato, whereas Eudorus and
later Platonists did (and in particular with the *Timaeus*), and this
constitutes a new beginning in Platonism. I am not so sure that
Antiochus was not concerned with the exegesis of at least such
dialogues as the *Timaeus* and the *Phaedo* (indeed the fact that Cicero

---

[38] 'Posidonius' "Hierarchy" between God, Fate and Nature', *Philosophia* 4
(1974), 286-301.
[39] 'Raccolta e interpretazione delle testimonianze e dei frammenti del mediopla-
tonico Eudoro di Alessandria. Parte prima: Testo e traduzione delle testimonianze
e dei frammenti sicuri', *RFNsc.* 77 (1985), 197-205; Parte seconda: Testo e traduzione delle testimonianze non sicure', *ibid.*, 535-55.
[40] *RFNsc.* 69 (1977), 3-19.
[41] See above, n. 15.
[42] Expressed, for instance, in his essay 'Von Platon zum Platonismus: Ein Bruch
in der Überlieferung und seine Überwindung', in *Rheinische-Westfälische Akademie
der Wissenschaften*, Vorträge G211, Westdeutscher Verlag: Opladen, 1976.

makes some effort to translate both of them might indicate the contrary), but I agree that it is only in the generation of Eudorus that the tradition of formal commentary on both Plato and Aristotle seems to begin, and that is of some significance.

Moraux has useful discussions, in particular, of Eudorus' role in Achilles' *Commentary on Aratus*,[43] and on his criticisms of Aristotle's *Categories*, with which latter he is particularly concerned. He is good, particularly, on Eudorus' criticisms of the category of Quality, to which I should have given more attention.

On the matter of Eudorus' ethics: first, I should, I now think, have made more of a fuss about Eudorus' highlighting of 'impulse' (*hormê*). This does seem to betoken a notable degree of interest in what in modern philosophy would be termed 'intentionality' and 'action theory', and perhaps deserves to be celebrated as such (though Eudorus' concerns were primarily ethical, not in the philosophy of mind). We are given by Seneca, in *Letter* 89, 14 (which I noted, but did not dwell on, p. 122) a brief rationale for putting *hormê* between *theoria* and *praxis*, which may well be Eudoran (we know of no one else who adopted this tripartition), and is worth quoting: 'The first requirement is that you make a judgement of the value of each thing (or situation); the second, that you adopt an impulse (*impetus*) towards the object or objects that is orderly and temperate; the third, that your action be coherent with your impulse, in order that in all these situations you should be in accord with yourself. If any of these steps be deficient, it disturbs the others.' No doubt there is much of Seneca in the formulation of this, but the basic theory is that of his source.

Secondly, though, I should not, perhaps, have been so cavalier (though I think that I was correct) in assuming that the sections that follow on Arius' description of Eudorus' division of ethics also derive from Eudorus. My reasoning was, as I say (p. 116), that Arius describes Eudorus as proceeding in his exposition *problêmatikôs*, 'by means of (setting out) *problêmata*', and then he himself sets out a series of *problêmata*. A.A. Long has pointed out to me, however, that

---

[43] I am encouraged by Moraux's treatment to resist the criticisms of De Lacy (in the review mentioned at the outset) that I am attributing too much to Eudorus both of Achilles and of Plutarch in the *Proc. An.* We must simply agree to differ. It is a question of some delicacy to decide when an ancient author is using someone as a primary source without admitting it. One must look for small hints, inadvertent or otherwise, and that is what I would persist in doing.

Arius does say, at the beginning of this section (p. 45, 6-10 Wachs.), that, in embarking upon the *problêmata*, he will proceed 'according to the arrangement which seems best to me'. This does certainly betoken a certain measure of editorial tailoring, but it is not, I would maintain, a claim of authorship. Nevertheless, I should have acknowledged it. Eudoran authorship has to be regarded as less than certain.

In the case of Philo, we turn to a field that is far larger, and one which has been far more actively tilled. There has, indeed, been something of an explosion in Philo studies since 1977, and a certain amount of it has involved criticism of my treatment of him. The main figures have been Valentin Nikiprowetsky,[44] David Runia,[45] David Winston,[46] Roberto Radice,[47] and Richard Goulet.[48] It cannot be said that any degree of consensus has emerged on Philo's place in the history of Greek philosophy, but the problems have at least been more clearly set out.[49]

First, a word on the relation postulated in this book between Philo and Eudorus, and the general rationale of including him in the book at all. Despite my cautionary remarks, I have been repeatedly

[44] His main work being *Le commentaire de l'écriture chez Philon d'Alexandrie*, Leiden, 1977.

[45] Author of a massive work of great importance, *Philo of Alexandria and the Timaeus of Plato*, Leiden, 1986, and many articles. He is also founder and editor, since 1989, of the *Studia Philonica Annual*, a basic tool of research in the field. With Roberto Radice (see below), he has also produced *Philo of Alexandria, An Annotated Bibliography, 1937-1986*, Leiden, 1988, another most useful resource.

[46] Author of *Philo of Alexandria: The Contemplative Life, The Giants, and Selections*, New York/Toronto, 1981, *Logos and Mystical Theology in Philo of Alexandria*, Cincinnati, 1985, and many articles. He and I have cooperated in a commentary on Philo's *De Gigantibus and Quod Deus sit Immutabilis, Two Treatises of Philo of Alexandria* (Brown Judaic Studies 25), Chico, 1983, which involved Nikiprowetsky as well. Winston is at work on a major book on Philo.

[47] Author, with Giovanni Reale and Clara Kraus Reggiani, of a translation, with introduction and commentary, of the *De Opificio Mundi* and the *Allegories of the Laws, Filone di Alessandria, La filosofia mosaica*, Milan, 1987; of *Platonismo e creazionismo in Filone di Alessandria*, Milan, 1989; and, with David Runia, of the above-mentioned Bibliography.

[48] Author of *La philosophie de Moïse: essai de reconstitution d'un commentaire philosophique préphilonienne du Pentateuch*, Paris, 1987.

[49] Apart from the books mentioned here, one should mention the *ANRW* volume devoted to Philo, II 21:1, Berlin: De Gruyter, 1984, including articles by Peder Borgen, on Philo research since World War II, Burton Mack, on 'Philo Judaeus and Exegetical Traditions in Alexandria' (pursuing what is to my mind a

accused (or worse, commended), for presenting Philo as a pupil of Eudorus, and as a Middle Platonist. Let me make it clear once again that I wish to make neither claim. There is no evidence that Philo had ever heard of Eudorus (though I regard it as very probable that he did). All I would claim is that Philo shows the influence of a brand of Platonism that is in many ways close to that of Eudorus, and that he constitutes good evidence for prevailing trends in contemporary Platonism. That is why he is included in this book – not as a Platonist in his own right. Philo's precise philosophical position is a most interesting question, on which I have had a certain amount to say myself over the years, but it is not properly my concern here. I am concerned with the Platonist school tradition, to which he is peripheral – as is a Christian philosopher such as Clement or Origen (to whom, unfortunately, I was not able to devote any space, much though they deserve it).

However, that said, it is still relevant, I think, to comment on two tendencies which have manifested themselves in Philonic studies in recent years, which have some impact on the evaluation of him as a source for Platonism.[50] The first is that represented by Roberto Radice, who, particularly in *Platonismo e creazionismo*, in connection with claiming that Philo maintains a doctrine of *creatio ex nihilo*, wants to argue for his being the originator of the doctrine of the Ideas as thoughts of God, and thus a major contributor to later Platonist doctrine. As for the notion that Philo maintains *creatio ex nihilo*, it seems to me that this has been adequately refuted by David Winston (see below, n. 51). The second part of Radice's thesis

---

misguided search for Philonic predecessors, cf. my remarks on Goulet below), Abraham Terian (who has made many valuable contributions to our understanding of the works of Philo preserved in Armenian) on 'A Critical Introduction to Philo's Dialogues', and David Winston on 'Philo's Ethical Theory'. I leave aside in the present context the remarkable hermeneutical excesses of Jacques Cazeaux (*La trame et la chaîne*, 2 vols., Leiden, 1983, 1989), who also has an article in this volume, as they have little bearing on Philo's Platonism.

As regards texts, not much has happened since 1977, except for the completion of the Lyons series of texts with the appearance of editions of the *Questions and Answers on Genesis and Exodus*, Vol. 33 (the Greek fragments), ed. F. Petit, Paris 1978, and Vols. 34A & B (trans. of the Armenian text, with Aucher's Latin facing), ed. C. Mercier, Paris, 1979, 1984.

[50] I have no criticisms of David Runia or David Winston in this connection, which is why I do not dwell on them further, despite their important contributions to Philo scholarship.

seems to me wildly improbable, and involves him, among other
things, in having to sweep aside the evidence of Varro (cf. p. 95, n.
1 above), and in assuming that such men as Seneca and Alcinous
were appreciative readers of Philo.

Another odd notion (though pursued with prodigous learning) is
that propounded by the French scholar Richard Goulet, in *La
philosophie de Moïse*, namely that Philo himself is only the heir to a
rich tradition of Alexandrian Jewish allegorical exegesis, which he is
relaying to us as an epigonus, only occasionally contributing an
interpretation of his own. This is a line of investigation pursued also
by Burton Mack, and I find it quite unprofitable. No doubt there
were rabbis in Alexandria who indulged in 'ethical' interpretations
of the Bible, and Philo was acquainted with them, and we know of
a few persons like Aristobulus and Pseudo-Aristeas, who indulge in
tentative and non-systematic 'physical' allegorizations in the generations before Philo, making some use of Stoic theory, but there is no
independent evidence, outside the works of Philo himself, of any
person or group of persons who were engaged in anything like his
own vast and systematic enterprise, nor is it necessary to postulate
any such persons. All Goulet is able to show, on occasion, is that
Philo develops his exegeses of various passages in interesting ways,
and that he claims on occasion to be refuting allegorizing predecessors, whom I prefer to maintain he is very largely inventing, in order
to keep up with the (Greek) Joneses. Philo is a determined practi-
tioner of oneupmanship when it comes to competing with Greek
learning, and he is quite capable, I believe, of creating his own
predecessors. I don't feel that Goulet's position (unlike that of
Radice) can be absolutely refuted; all I would claim is that my
explanation of the phenomena is far less troublesome than his.
However, from the perspective of contemporary Platonism, this
question is not actually of great importance. It concerns only the
originality of Philo as an exegete.

An issue of some importance, however, and of continuing controversy, which relates to Radice's speculations, is whether Philo
does or does not propound a doctrine of *creatio ex nihilo*. My position
continues to be (and in this I am supported by David Winston, at
least[51]) that, despite his very creationist language, especially in the *De*

---

[51] Cf. e.g. his section on this subject in the introduction to his *Philo of Alexandria:
The Contemplative Life*, pp. 7-21, where the evidence is well set out.

Providentia, Philo's primary concern is only to establish the *logical* dependency of the world on God, and his authorship of it. Since both Moses and Plato are prepared to talk in temporal terms about the creation, he feels at liberty to do so as well, but he is too deeply imbued with Greek philosophy to be able to tolerate such a concept as temporal creation *out of nothing.* At most, he envisages God as creating the world, both the intelligible and the sensible, *out of himself.* But it must be admitted that this controversy is on-going among Philo scholars.

Another question on which there has been some fruitful on-going discussion is that of Philo's dualism, and his possible relationship with contemporary Gnosticism, or proto-Gnosticism. Birger Pearson's survey article in the *ANRW* Philo volume[52] is useful, but since, by his own admission, it was completed in 1976, though the volume was only published in 1984, he was unable to address the particular passages to which I draw attention, such as *QG* IV 8 (pp. 168-9 above).[53] His unsurprising conclusion is that Philo is not a Gnostic, with which I entirely agree. The interesting question, though, is how far he constitutes evidence for the dissemination of proto-Gnostic or Iranian religious ideas, and this remains unsettled.

On one aspect of Philo's 'dualism' I would concede a point to Valentin Nikiprowetsky who, in an article in 1980, 'Sur une lecture démonologique de Philon d'Alexandrie, *De gigantibus* 6-18',[54] argues convincingly that the apparent 'evil angels or daemons' described there are simply souls that have fallen into human bodies. However, there remains the problematic passage *QE* I 23, where it seems to me that evil angels are envisaged, though under the ultimate control of God (see p. 173 above).

Philonic studies, then, continue to be an actively volcanic area, and no consensus has been reached on the nature of his relationship to the Platonist tradition.

---

[52] 'Philo and Gnosticism', II 21: 1, 295-342.

[53] I would now add the distinction of three classes of men in *Gig.* 60-1, which could be seen to correspond to the Gnostic distinction between 'sarkics', 'psychics', and 'pneumatics', on which I have discoursed in 'The Theory of Three Classes of Men in Plotinus and in Philo', in *Scholars, Savants and Their Texts: Essays in Honor of Arthur Hyman,* ed. R. Link-Salinger, New York, 1989, 69-76 (incl. in *The Golden Chain*).

[54] In *Hommage à G. Vajda,* edd. G. Nahon & C. Touati, Louvain, 43-71.

6. On the subject of Plutarch, on the other hand, though there has been much activity over the last twenty years (much of it under the auspices of the International Plutarch Society and its local off-shoots, notably the Italian branch, which has been most prolific), I have not seen anything which would cause me substantially to modify my view of him. Useful items that have appeared since I wrote include F.E. Brenk, *In Mist Apparelled: Religious Themes in Plutarch's Moralia and Lives*,[55] which includes an extended discussion of Philo's views on daemons, with the conclusions of which I am largely in agreement; ch. 6 (pp. 257-80) of John Glucker's *Antiochus and the Late Academy*,[56] in which he discusses Plutarch's relation to the Academy and the Academic tradition; Yvonne Vernière's study, *Symboles et Mythes dans la Pensée de Plutarque*,[57] which provides a good discussion of the three great myths of the *De Facie*, the *De Genio*, and the *De Sera*, though without causing me to change my views; ch. 2 of Werner Deuse's *Untersuchungen*,[58] where he provides a better articulated account than I do of Plutarch's doctrine of the soul (as *essentially* irrational); and Christian Froidefond's survey article in *ANRW* II 36 (pp. 184-233), in which, among other things, he pleases me by emphasising the central importance of the metaphysics of the *De Iside et Osiride* (of which he subsequently produced the Budé text) and in particular its *logos*-doctrine, which I had been criticised in reviews for emphasising[59] (I remain unrepentant).

Since Thrasyllus is mentioned at the beginning of ch. 4 (pp. 184-5), I should mention here the most stimulating study of him by Harold Tarrant, *Thrasyllan Platonism*,[60] in which he enters first into an exhaustive study of the history of the arranging of Plato's dialogues, à propos of Thrasyllus' activities as an editor, and then looks at evidence for his epistemology and in particular for his *logos*-

---

[55] Brill: Leiden, 1977. He has also contributed a useful *ANRW* article in II 36: 1, 'An Imperial Heritage: The Religious Spirit of Plutarch of Chaeroneia', pp. 248-349.

[56] See above, n. 4.

[57] Paris, 1977.

[58] See above, n. 6.

[59] Notably by Harold Tarrant, in *Prudentia*, X (1978), 111. Tarrant, we may note, has himself since produced interesting evidence for a developed *logos*-doctrine in the Middle Platonist Thrasyllus (see below).

[60] Cornell Univ. Press: Ithaca/London, 1993.

doctrine. All this I find most useful and persuasive; not so persuasive, however, his attempts to pin on Thrasyllus a series of interpolations into the dialogues and forgeries of Letters, notably *Letter 2*. Nonetheless, this is a most useful book (it also includes a collection of Thrasyllan testimonia).

7. I have seen nothing significant appearing in respect of most of the figures dealt with in ch. 5, Nicostratus, Taurus, Harpocration and Severus, such as would cause a change of mind. There has, however, been some work done on Atticus. The new Budé edition of his fragments by Édouard Des Places[61] appeared just too late for me to make use of it. Des Places provides a useful summary of Atticus' philosophical position in his introduction, and of his relation to Plutarch, Taurus and Numenius, and adds a number of testimonia from Proclus and others which Baudry had ignored.

More important, however, for the further elucidation of Atticus' doctrine is an article by Matthias Baltes, 'Zur Philosophie des Platonikers Attikos',[62] in which he throws light on a number of points left unresolved by me, notably the relationship of the Demiurge (who is for Atticus the supreme God) to the forms (or the Paradigm), and relation of the forms in turn to the soul, as well as various points about the formation of the human soul.

On the first question, Atticus is not necessarily concerned, as I had suggested (pp. 255-6), about preserving the 'transcendent simplicity' of his primal God. He is more concerned, as Baltes suggests, to maintain the objective existence of the forms *along with* their status as thoughts of God; hence his insistence on their independent subsistence (a position he bequeaths to Longinus in the next century).

Secondly, I agree with Baltes that the 'essence of soul' in which the forms are said by Syrianus to subsist as 'universal reason-principles' (*hoi katholou logoi*, Fr. 40 Des Places) cannot be, as I suggest (p. 256), the world soul, but must rather be the demiurgic soul, or divine soul (*theia psychê*), which Atticus also identifies as the 'undivided essence' of *Timaeus* 35A, out of which (along with the 'essence divided about bodies', which he identifies as the irrational disorderly soul) the world soul is formed.

---

[61] *Atticus: Fragments*, Paris, 1977.

[62] In *Platonismus und Christentum: Festschrift für Heinrich Dörrie*, edd. H.-D. Blume & F. Mann, Münster, 1983, 38-57.

A third point on which I stand corrected is the question as to what part of the soul it is to which Atticus denies immortality (cf. p. 256 above). This is not so much the irrational *soul*, which is one of the basic components out of which human souls are formed, but rather what he terms 'irrational life' (*alogos zôê*, Fr. 15 Des Places), the life principle which comes into existence when the embryo is ensouled, and which may be identified with the 'pneumatic vehicle', which dissolves on death.

Two other interesting details of Atticus' doctrine which had escaped me are drawn attention to by Baltes. First, he attempted a response to the obvious objection that can be raised to the concept of temporal creation: 'Why did God decide to create the world just when he did, and not earlier or later?' by suggesting that he waited till the condition of matter was somehow *right* – a pretty desperate proposal, but better than nothing, perhaps.[63] The other is that Atticus (like Plotinus after him, cf. *Enn.* IV 8, 4, 35f.) assumes that Plato is postulating two mixing-bowls at *Tim.* 41D, one for the world soul, the other for individual souls, since Plato does after all speak there of the Demiurge turning back to the 'former' mixing-bowl (*epi ton proteron kratêra*), as if there were a 'latter' one as well.[64] It is not actually easy to see what the point might be of postulating two mixing-bowls, but it must have something to do with setting up a greater degree of differentiation between world soul and individual souls. At any rate, it is an interesting example of Atticus' pedantic attention to the text, on which Proclus remarks (cf. p. 257 above).

This article, then, is a most useful contribution to our understanding of Atticus. Most helpful also is ch. 3 of Werner Deuse's *Untersuchungen*,[65] dealing with Atticus' doctrine on the soul, which appeared more or less simultaneously with Baltes' article. Deuse shows (partly by adducing the evidence of Galen's *Compendium of the Timaeus*, which he shows to be influenced by Atticus) how Atticus has developed Plutarch's position on various points in a

---

[63] This occurs in a passage of Proclus, *In Tim.* (I 394, 17ff.), which is missed by Des Places, as it is not explicitly tied to Atticus, but correctly identified as belonging to him by Baltes.

[64] Presumably what the Greek actually means is 'the mixing-bowl *which he had previously used*', but it is interesting how the scholastic mind can indulge in creative misinterpretation.

[65] See above, n. 6.

scholastic direction (though not necessarily for the better). For instance, where Plutarch refers (at *Plat. Quaest.* 1007C) to the pre-cosmic state as 'an as it were formless raw material of time', Atticus talks unequivocally of pre-cosmic time (Fr. 31 Des Places), incoherent though this concept may be. Again, where Plutarch sees the world soul (and individual souls) in the *Timaeus* as being formed from *Nous* and the irrational soul, Atticus (as mentioned above) identifies the 'undivided essence' of *Tim.* 35A as 'divine soul' (Fr. 35 Des Places). The distinction here is not a great one, since this soul is for Atticus the soul of the Demiurge, but it is significant enough, as it means that Atticus is distinguishing an aspect of the Demiurge (his supreme god) which is *soul*, and thus a principle of motion, which intellect proper should not be.

As Deuse points out, such distinctions in doctrine are systematically obscured by the bald doxographic linkage of 'Plutarch and Atticus'. It is worth looking more closely at the scraps of evidence we have, if we want to appreciate properly the on-going development of Middle Platonist scholasticism.

These, then, are very useful contributions. From the essay of Claudio Moreschini in *ANRW* II 36: 1 (1987), 477-91, 'Attico: una figura singolare del medioplatonismo', on the other hand, I did not derive any great value. He makes use of Baltes and Donini,[66] but he does not seem acquainted either with my work or with that of Deuse, and he fails to address the most interesting aspects of Atticus, though his treatment of him is sound enough. He persists, however, in regarding him as a marginal figure in Middle Platonism, which seems to me most implausible.

8. As regards the subject of the next chapter, 'The School of Gaius', the major alteration I would make concerns the changing back of the name of the author of the *Didaskalikos* from Albinus to Alcinous. The force of the arguments of Giusta[67] and, latterly, Whittaker[68] has finally got through to me. Freudenthal's proposal (cf. p. 268 above) was ingenious, but goes against the palaeographical probabilities. Since I was no great supporter of the 'School of

[66] See above, n. 7.

[67] In '*Albinou Epitome o Alkinoou Didaskalikos?*', *Atti della Accademia delle Scienze di Torino, Classe di scienze morali, storiche e filologiche* 95 (1960/1), 167-94.

[68] In a series of articles, but ultimately in the introduction to his Budé edition of Alcinous, *Alcinoos, Enseignement des doctrines de Platon*, Paris, 1990, pp. vii-xiii.

Gaius' theory anyway, this change of name was no great wrench. More important is the great deepening of our undertanding of the contents of, and the range of influences on, Alcinous' work resulting from Whittaker's excellent Budé edition, on which I have already drawn for my own translation and commentary on the *Didaskalikos*. However, I am glad to say that I find nothing in my account of Alcinous' doctrine here that is incorrect, so far as it goes. The precise nature of his metaphysical scheme in ch. 10 still remains somewhat obscure to me, I am sorry to say.

On the one remaining work of Albinus, the *Introduction to Plato's Dialogues*, I should mention the useful edition of this, with commentary, by Olaf Nüsser, *Albins Prolog und die Dialogtheorie des Platonismus*,[69] which contains an excellent discussion of the question of the ordering of Plato's dialogues in general. Useful also in this regard is the work of Harold Tarrant mentioned above in connection with Thrasyllus,[70] and the recent study of Jaap Mansfeld, *Prolegomena: Questions to be Settled before the Study of an Author, or a Text*,[71] ch. 2 of which is devoted to Thrasyllus, Albinus and Diogenes Laertius.

Intertwined in my account with Albinus/Alcinous is the problem of the *Anonymous Theaetetus Commentary* and its author (cf. pp. 270-1 above). I was inclined to identify this person with Albinus, mainly on grounds of doctrinal affinities, while recognising the problem of his misquotation of *Meno* 98A, which goes against Albinus' correct rendering of it in the *Introduction*. Since then, Harold Tarrant, in the work mentioned above, *Scepticism or Platonism?*,[72] has attempted to roll back the time of composition of the commentary to the first century B.C., and connect it with Eudorus. I would have no strong objection to this (Eudorus does, after all, seem to have written a commentary on the *Timaeus*, as did the author of the *Theaetetus Commentary*), if it were not tied in with trying to make Eudorus an adherent of the Fourth Academy, which

---

[69] Teubner: Stuttgart, 1991.

[70] Cf. above, n. 56.

[71] Brill: Leiden, 1994. Mansfeld, it should be said, has done a great deal to elucidate the ramifications of the doxographic tradition in later Greek philosophy, in a host of articles (mostly collected in *Studies in Later Greek Philosophy and Gnosticism*, Variorum: London, 1989, and *Studies in the Historiography of Greek Philosophy*, Van Gorcum: Assen, 1990), and in his massive *Heresiography in Context: Hippolytus' Elenchus as a Source for Greek Philosophy*, Brill: Leiden, 1992.

[72] Above, n. 1.

seems to me most implausible. However, Jaap Mansfeld has dealt a
blow to this identification by acutely pointing out[73] that the author
does not adopt Eudorus' switching of the categories of Quantity and
Quality. More significant will be the translation and commentary by
David Sedley in the Clarendon Later Ancient Philosophy series
(soon to appear), of which we have an advance version in Italian in
the form of his edition of the work in the *Corpus dei papiri filosofici
greci e latini* III.[74] There he gives good reasons against identifying the
author with any known Platonist, while broadly accepting a second
century A.D. date. He also does greater justice than I did to the
various virtues of the work. I regret having spoken of the Anon. so
harshly at the time ('in general maintains a level of stupefying
banality' – a phrase frequently quoted against me since!). He does
not really deserve that. I was being youthfully intolerant.

On Apuleius much useful work has been done by Claudio
Moreschini,[75] but he still operates with the thesis of the existence of
a School of Gaius, and is thus not inclined to notice the divergences
between Apuleius and Alcinous. There is a curiously uninformative
article by B.L. Hijsmans in *ANRW* II 36:1 (1987).[76] He seems more
interested in style than in philosophic content, and shows a curious
disposition to accept the translation of the Hermetic *Asclepius* as a
genuine work of Apuleius, which goes against all stylistic probability, and would not in any case tell us much about Apuleius' own
views. On the other hand, the edition of the *Peri Hermeneias* (which
I am still prepared to accept as genuine) by David Londey and
Carmen Johanson,[77] is a most useful contribution, giving a most
competent account of the logical background to the work.

On Galen, whom I rather neglected,[78] there has been a useful
collection of papers edited by Vivian Nutton, *Galen, Problems and
Prospects*,[79] including 'On Galen's Epistemology', by Michael Frede,

---

[73] 'Two Attributions', *CQ* 41 (1991), 541-4.
[74] Olschki: Firenze, 1995, 227-562.
[75] His articles, which had escaped my notice at the time, are collected in *Apuleio
e il Platonismo*, Olschki: Firenze, 1978.
[76] 'Apuleius, Philosophus Platonicus', pp. 395-475.
[77] *The Logic of Apuleius*, Brill: Leiden, 1987.
[78] I should have noted an article by Phillip De Lacy, 'Galen's Platonism', *AJP* 93
(1972), 27-39. He takes me to task, reasonably, for neglecting Galen (and by
implication him) in his review of this book.
[79] Wellcome Institute: London, 1981.

'Galien comme philosophe: la philosophie de la nature', by Paul Moraux, and F. Kudlein on 'Galen's Religious Belief'. His great work *On the Doctrines of Hippocrates and Plato* has received an excellent edition (with English translation) by Phillip De Lacy,[80] though without any notes that would elucidate his philosophical position. Back in 1977, R.B. Edlow produced an edition, with translation and commentary, of his work *On Fallacies*,[81] which gives a good account of Galen's philosophy of language. In the introduction to his translation of Galen's *On the Therapeutic Method*, Books I and II, for the Clarendon Later Ancient Philosophy series, R.J. Hankinson has a good discussion of Galen's philosophical position. Galen probably deserves a chapter to himself in a book on Middle Platonism, and I am sorry that I was not in a position to give him the attention he merits.

9. We come now to the Neopythagoreans. On Moderatus and Nicomachus I have found nothing of significance, but on Numenius there has been an important article by Michael Frede in *ANRW* II 36:2 (1034-75), containing sections on his ontology, his theology, and his psychology. On just a few points he takes issue with me. One concerns the troublesome question of the relation between Numenius' 'second' and 'third' gods, that is to say the Demiurge and the world soul. Fr. 11 Des Places, quoted by me on p. 367, really says, as Frede acutely points out, not that the second and third gods *are* one, but that 'the second-and-third god *is* one'. I grant this gladly, as it in fact reinforces what I wish to maintain about the relation of the Demiurge to the world soul (cf. pp. 374-5), that really they are only aspects of the same entity, the 'splitting' within it being caused by its inclination towards matter.

Again, on the question of Numenius' doctrine of an 'evil' or material soul subsisting in us side by side with a 'heavenly' soul (cf. Frs. 43-4), he takes me to task (p. 1073) for identifying this with the irrational faculties picked up in the descent of the soul through the planetary spheres to incarnation (cf. p. 376). Frede's objection is that there are 'rational' elements attached to the 'evil' soul as well. It is in fact more like what St Paul talks of (e.g. Rom. 7:23; 8:7-8) as 'the law of sin which dwells in my members' and wars against the Spirit,

---

[80] Akademie-Verlag: Berlin, 2 vols. 1980-1.
[81] *Galen on Language and Ambiguity*, Brill: Leiden.

a source of psychic energy which is not so much irrational as downright perverse. This is a most interesting insight, and I am persuaded by it. It makes better sense of Porphyry's insistence in Fr. 44 that Numenius' postulation of two souls is *not* just a contrast between a rational and an irrational part of the soul. It also gives extra point to an interesting chapter of Origen's *De Principiis* (III 4), which he devotes to a discussion of the postulate that we have within us not just a Platonic tripartite or bipartite soul, but *two souls*. His immediate targets here seem to be Gnostics of some sort (since they quote scripture – notably Paul – to their purpose), but Origen also knew Numenius perfectly well, and may well have him in mind too. We might ask whence Numenius himself derived this rather un-Hellenic concept. Is he influencing the Gnostics, or are they influencing him?

At any rate, Frede's exposition adds greatly to our understanding of Numenius. I also derived value from John Peter Kenny's shorter discussion in *Mystical Monotheism*,[82] ch. 2, on 'Numenius and the Degrees of Divinity', though without feeling the need to change my views on any issue. I am still, by the way, unconvinced by John Whittaker's defence[83] of the reading *ho ge ôn* (the Biblical/Philonic 'He who Is') in Fr. 13 (cf. p. 368 above), despite my belief in Numenius' openness to Jewish influences (and even in his acquaintance with Philo's works). The syntax continues to bother me, even though I would not fight to the death for my own emendation *geôrgôn*. If *ôn* is to be retained, I would prefer to take it with *sperma*.

Lastly, on the shadowy figure of Ammonius Saccas, I can commend the most useful summary of the evidence and of previous discussion by F.M. Schroeder in *ANRW* 36:1 (1987), 493-526, with ample bibliography. He does not add anything to what I have said (pp. 380-3), but that can not be hoped for, I think.[84]

---

[82] Cf. above n. 16.

[83] 'Numenius and Alcinous on the First Principle', *Phoenix* 32 (1978), 144-6.

[84] It is a pity, by the way, that he still has to take up so much space refuting the absurd notion, still clung to by some patristic scholars, that the two Origens, Platonist and Christian, are one and the same. It is a little odd, perhaps, that they were both connected with Ammonius Saccas, but I think the proper answer to the puzzle is that, if one were to consult the Alexandria phone-book for the year 220 or so, one would find about two and a half columns of Origens (and about the same number of Ammoniuses).

10. On the subject of my final chapter, a certain amount has been done on various aspects of the 'underworld' that is worthy of note (though I am not, of course, claiming to present more than a sample of Gnostic, Hermetic or Chaldaean lore). The Gnostics have received great publicity in the last twenty years, though the full publication of the Nag Hammadi documents has really only confused the issue from the point of view of estimating Platonist influences.[85] It really looks, when one contemplates the originals, as if the Church Fathers were reading a certain amount of Platonism into their sources. At any rate, one may mention, first of all, the most useful general work by Kurt Rudolph;[86] but also the two volumes resulting from a major conference on Gnosticism at Yale in 1978, one devoted to Valentinian, the other to Sethian Gnosticism,[87] which included all the major scholars in the field, and contains many papers concerning the relationship of Gnosticism to Greek philosophy. There was also a conference on Neoplatonism and Gnosticism, under the auspices of the International Society for Neoplatonic Studies, in Oklahoma in 1980 which resulted (eventually) in a most useful volume,[88] containing a good deal that is relevant to Middle Platonism. I took part in both these events, and learned a good deal, but nothing that causes me to alter the fairly elementary remarks made here (pp. 384-9).

As regards Hermeticism, one may mention the excellent study by Garth Fowden, *The Egyptian Hermes*,[89] which tries to identify the *Sitz im Leben* of the authors of the Hermetic tractates, though Fowden, as an historian, is not particularly concerned with the philosophical aspects of the tractates. Also, we have now in English a reliable translation, with introduction and notes, of the corpus by Brian Copenhaver.[90] The only slight inconvenience is that he did not include the fragments in Stobaeus, which often contain philo-

---

[85] The documents first appeared in generally accessible form in *The Nag Hammadi Library in English*, ed. J.M. Robinson, Harper & Row: New York/San Francisco, 1977. Definitive editions of the individual tractates have since been appearing at regular intervals from Brill in Leiden.

[86] *Gnosis: The Nature and History of Gnosticism*, Engl. trans. by R. McL. Wilson, New York, 1983 (German original, Leipzig, 1977).

[87] *The Rediscovery of Gnosticism*, ed. B. Layton, 2 vols. Brill: Leiden, 1980-1.

[88] *Neoplatonism and Gnosticism*, edd. R.T. Wallis & J. Bregman, Albany, 1992.

[89] *The Egyptian Hermes: A Historical Approach to the Late Pagan Mind*, CUP, 1986.

[90] *Hermetica: The Greek Corpus Hermeticum and the Latin Asclepius in New English Translation*, CUP, 1992.

sophically interesting material, but they are readily enough available in the Nock-Festugière Budé edition (the notes of which, I must say, remain indispensable for the whole corpus).

As regards the Chaldaean Oracles, there has been a most helpful republication, with much additional material, as well as corrections and indices, of Hans Lewy's rather rare book (originally published in Cairo in 1956), *Chaldaean Oracles and Theurgy*,[91] by Michel Tardieu,[92] with an appendix by Pierre Hadot surveying recent work. Somewhat more recently, there has been a useful survey article by Edouard Des Places, the Budé editor of the *Oracles*, in *ANRW*.[93] I may also draw attention here to the excellent monograph of Sarah Iles Johnson, *Hekate Soteira*,[94] in which she devotes one chapter to the cosmic soul in Middle Platonism, and another to 'Hekate and the Chaldaean Cosmic Soul', together with an appendix on the evidence for equating Hekate to the world soul. She does not, however, any more than I do, venture to solve definitively the relation between the world soul and the *dynamis* of the Father (cf. p. 394).

On the figures dealt with in the latter part of the chapter, only on Calcidius has anything of significance been written in the interval, in the form of a chapter by Stephen Gersh in his large work *Middle Platonism and Neoplatonism: The Latin Tradition*.[95] He gives a very sound analysis of the contents, but is inclined to side with Waszink, as against me, on the question of Calcidius' dependence on Porphyry. He draws attention to two points of doctrine in particular, both of which I should have dealt with: (1) the fact that Calcidius (in ch. 198), like Porphyry (ap. Aug. *CD* X 30, 1-10 = *De Regressu Animae*, Fr. 300 Smith – but probably repeated in his *Timaeus Commentary*), claims that Plato's doctrine of transmigration teaches, not the reincarnation of a human soul in the body of an animal as punishment for vice, but only its reincarnation in the body of a more bestial man; and (2) that he maintains (in ch. 301), like Porphyry (*in*

---

[91] Paris, 1978.

[92] Tardieu, I should mention, also contributes an excellent paper to *The Redis-covery of Gnosticism I* (see above, n. 84) on 'La gnose valentinienne et les oracles chaldaïques', pp. 194-237.

[93] 'Les oracles chaldaïques', *ANRW* II 36:4 (1984), 2299-2335.

[94] Scholars Press: Atlanta, 1990.

[95] Cf. above, n. 9. In Vol. II, pp. 421-92.

Tim. Frs. 47-9 Sodano, from John Philoponus) that Plato's teaching about the disorderly motion in the Receptacle does not signify that matter itself is subject to instability, but only the bodies arising from the initial imposition of form.

Of these, the first is more telling than the second, but even this is not, I think, conclusive, since there is in fact one Middle Platonist known who denied metempsychosis into animals, and that is none other than Numenius' 'companion', Cronius (cf. p. 308), whom I have actually tentatively proposed (p. 407) as Calcidius' source for at least the Numenian parts of his commentary. As for the second detail, I can only say that I see nothing in it that a Middle Platonist could not have maintained. If John Philoponus credits it to Porphyry, that is because that is where he found it, and Porphyry himself does not attribute it to a predecessor. I realise that this does not absolutely disprove Calcidius' acquaintance with Porphyry's commentary, but it seems to me to render the hypothesis unnecessary. However, the question of Calcidius' technical language remains troublesome, and I have to admit that Calcidius is a problem figure, who would repay further study.

That seems to me to cover the most significant additions to our knowledge or resources for the study of Middle Platonism since the first publication of this book. As in the case of the first edition, where I was urged by Colin Haycraft (to whose blessed memory I would like to dedicate this new impression) to keep footnotes to a minimum, I have not aspired to absolute comprehensiveness in my bibliographical survey, but I trust that I have overlooked nothing of great significance. The basic thrust of the book seems to have survived twenty years of scholarly scrutiny well enough, and I hope that, thus updated, it may survive a while longer.

I. General Index

This index is necessarily selective. I have tried to include all significant allusions to all important figures or concepts, though normally without duplicating information derivable from the table of contents. I give Greek versions of technical terms, but with cross-references to the English equivalent, unless no ready equivalent exists.

II. Index of Platonic Passages

Note: I have included all references in the text to specific passages of the dialogues, even where a later author is not explicitly quoting Plato, in order to give the fullest picture of the influence of the various Platonic passages on later Platonism.

III. Modern Authorities Quoted